Accession no.
36210377

KU-300-508

throughout
noted 19/05/17

Years of Expansion British History, 1815–1914

Editor:

MICHAEL SCOTT-BAUMANN

Contributors

PAULA BARTLEY, MICHAEL SCOTT-BAUMANN,
CLIVE BEHAGG, MIKE BYRNE,
DAVID COOPER, MICHAEL LYNCH
AND EDWARD TOWNLEY

LIS - LIBRARY

Date	Fund
19/05/17	Xi-Shr

Order No.
0 28l5382

University of Chester

Hodder & Stoughton

A MEMBER OF THE HODDER HEADLINE GROUP

～ ACKNOWLEDGEMENTS ～

The front cover illustration shows *House of Commons* 1833 by George Hayter, reproduced by courtesy of the National Gallery.

The Publishers would like to thank the following for permission to reproduce the following material in this book:

Brill Academic Publishers Inc., for an extract from *Chartism: A New Organization of the People* by William Lovett & John Collins (1969) used on page 82; Chrysalis (B. T. Batsford Ltd.), for an extract from *Chartism* by John Towers Ward (1974) used on page 126; Gregg Revivals, for an extract from *The Chartist Movement* by Mark Hovell (1994) used on pages 132–3; Harper Collins (Fontana), for an extract from *How Tory Governments Fall: The Tory Party in Power since 1783* by Norman Gash (1996) used on page 20; Merlin Press Ltd, for an extract from *A History of the Chartist Movement* by R. G. Gammage (1976) used on page 77; Oxford University Press, for an extract from *Alton Locke: Tailor & Poet* by Charles Kingsley, used on page 123; Oxford University Press, for an extract from *British History 1815–1906* by Norman McCord (1991) used on page 45; Pearson Education Ltd (Longman), for an extract from *Before the Welfare State* by Ursula Henriques (1979) used on page 72; Pearson Education Ltd (Longman), for an extract from *The Forging of the Modern State: Early Industrial Britain* by Eric J. Evans (1983) used on pages 50–1; Random House Inc., New York (Vintage Books), for an extract from *The Making of the English Working Class* by Edward Thompson (1996) used on page 45; Routledge (I.T.P.S.), for an extract from *The Great Reform Act of 1832* by Eric J. Evans (1993) used on page 60; Simon Publications, for an extract from *War Memoirs of David Lloyd George* by David Lloyd George (2001) used on page 344; Taylor & Francis Inc., for an extract from *The Story of the Dockers Strike* by H. Llewellyn Smith & Vaughan Nash (1984) used on pages 376–7.

The Publishers would like to thank the following for permission to reproduce the following copyright illustrations in this book:

Aerofilms Limited page 4; © Bettmann/Corbis page 223; British Library Reproductions © British Library Westminster Gazette 6/10/1903 page 316; British Museum page 400: © Corbis page 181; Hulton Archive pages 193, 300, 313, 410; © Hulton Deutsch Collection/Corbis pages 101, 111, 275, 286, 363, 384, 408, 453; Hulton Getty pages 113, 278, 388; Illustrated London News pages 136, 177, 222, 369, 406; Imperial War Museum, London page 432; Mary Evans Picture Library pages 1, 11, 36, 393; Mines Report page 78; National Library of Ireland page 290; National Museum of Labour History, Manchester page 367; National Portrait Gallery, London pages 214, 245; Public Record Office Image Library (Reference: FO 93/14/44) page 348; Punch Publications pages 71, 73, 122, 159, 169, 203, 207, 232, 251, 255, 371, 416, 422 (above); Radio Times Hulton Picture Library page 268; The Royal Collection © HM Queen Elizabeth II page 145; University of London Library page 78 (below).

Every effort has been made to trace and acknowledge ownership of copyright. The publishers will be glad to make suitable arrangements with any copyright holders whom it has not been possible to contact.

Orders: please contact Bookpoint Ltd, 130 Milton Park, Abingdon, Oxon OX14 4SB. Telephone: (44) 01235 827720. Fax: (44) 01235 400454. Lines are open from 9.00–6.00, Monday to Saturday, with a 24 hours message answering service. Email address: orders@bookpoint.co.uk

British Library Cataloguing in Publication Data
A catalogue record for this title is available from the British Library

ISBN 0 340 790814

First published 2002
Impression number   10 9 8 7 6 5 4 3 2 1
Year   2007   2006   2005   2004   2003   2002

Copyright © 2002 Paula Bartley, Michael Scott-Baumann, Clive Behagg, Mike Byrne, David Cooper, Michael Lynch and Edward Townley

All rights reserved. This work is copyright. Permission is given for copies to be made of pages provided they are used exclusively within the institution for which this work has been purchased. For reproduction for any other purpose, permission must first be obtained in writing from the publishers.

Produced and typeset by Gray Publishing, Tunbridge Wells, Kent
Printed in Great Britain for Hodder & Stoughton Educational, a division of Hodder Headline Plc, 338 Euston Road, London NW1 3BH by J.W. Arrowsmith Ltd, Bristol.

Contents

⤳ LIST OF TABLES ⤳

∽ LIST OF MAPS ∽

∽ LIST OF DIAGRAMS ∽

∽ LIST OF ILLUSTRATIONS ∽

∽ LIST OF PROFILES ∽

∽ LIST OF ANALYSES ∽

Preface: How to use this book

An increasing number of AS and A level students are embarking on the study of nineteenth-century British history. There are numerous topic books but very few textbooks, especially ones that are geared to the AS and A2 exams. This book meets that need. At its core is the explanatory narrative, informed by recent historical scholarship and made accessible by experienced A Level practitioners. But it is more than a textbook: it is also a workbook, with a rich variety of exercises, piloted with sixth formers, which are intended both for class use and for self study.

The book contains advice for students on the study of sources, both primary and secondary, on note-making, on structured writing and on building up answers to essay questions. The chapters are tailored to meet the needs of students following the AS and A2 modules contained in the exam specifications with the final chapter taking a synoptic, whole-century, look at some of the main themes.

KEY ISSUES

Key issues are indicated in the margins. They pose questions which reflect the issues highlighted by the AS and A level exam specifications. Writing short answers to the questions would be an effective way of taking structured notes.

DOCUMENTS

Throughout the book, short documentary extracts, as well as photographs, statistics and cartoons, are incorporated into the body of the text. They form an important part of the narrative and **your** answers to the questions that follow will provide some of the facts or interpretations essential to a full understanding.

BIBLIOGRAPHIES

At the end of every chapter are suggestions for further reading. These are divided into:

- **Articles** from journals like *Modern History Review* and *New Perspectives*, both of which are produced for sixth formers
- **Books for AS/A level students** like those in the Access to History series (Hodder & Stoughton) and Lancaster Pamphlets (Routledge) as well as other textbooks, some of which are written for both A level and undergraduate students
- **Further Reading** which includes books for more advanced reading and also for wider or more specialist reading which will be useful for course-

work and individual research. All of the books recommended are likely to be available in libraries and bookshops. Brief comments are also made on the content of the books listed and on how each might be used.

INTERNET RESOURCES

Internet resources are identified at the end of some chapters (e.g. Chapter 6 on Peel). Even limited use of a search engine to call up references to a Prime Minister or an issue like Chartism will produce many, many sites. These are likely to be of varying quality and often the author has to be taken on trust. Some, however, such as the 'Peel Web' are very good. The Peel Web has been designed for A level students and has some very good time-lines, explanatory narrative and documentary extracts on Parliamentary Reform, Chartism, the 'Condition of England Question' as well as on other issues, like Repeal of the Corn Laws, which were so central to Peel's political career.

STRUCTURED AND ESSAY QUESTIONS

There are a number of structured and essay questions at the end of each chapter. They are intended to test understanding of the main issues outlined in the chapter. They can also be used to stimulate class debate and to guide note-making. The **structured questions** are similar to those set in AS Level papers and the **essay questions** are similar to those set at A2 Level.

EXERCISES

Each chapter, apart from the introductory one, contains one or more exercises. Some of these give guidance on answering **structured writing questions** set at AS level. Others introduce you to the different types of A2 level **essay question** and suggest how to address them. They provide guidance on how to plan and build up an answer and they invite you to exercise your essay-writing skills in answering a wide variety of questions.

The **documentary exercises** usually consist of three, four or five sources and several questions. They require you to analyse and compare the sources and thus to engage in historical debate on one or more of the chapter's central themes. Some of these exercises are aimed at AS level students and consist, mainly, of primary sources. Others are aimed primarily at A2 level students and present you with contrasting historical interpretations so that you are confronted with more of the challenges and problems of the practising historian. Some of these documentary exercises contain advice and guidance on how to interpret, analyse and evaluate the sources while others are in the form of exam-type questions and indicate the suggested number of marks for each question.

There are some exercises in role-playing, mostly based on primary sources, and in the analysis of photographs, cartoons and statistics. There are also suggestions for pursuing particular lines of historical enquiry through coursework.

Introduction: Britain in 1815

INTRODUCTION

Today we all live in a rapidly changing society. Whereas 30 years ago there were no computers in our classrooms, today we take them for granted. In a few years time, every student may well have his or her own laptop at school or college. We all expect change; it is commonplace.

In 1815, most of Britain looked very much as it had done for hundreds of years previously. There were vast areas of mountain and forest, while much of the rest was divided into fields enclosed by hedges, fences and ditches in what was the most cultivated land in Europe. Most people lived in small villages and worked on the land. Agriculture was by far the biggest source of employment. The country was sparsely populated: there were only 13 million people (a mere half million of

PICTURE 1 *This was the main form of travel, apart from walking, in 1815. It took several days to go from Edinburgh to London. By 1914, the journey took less than eight hours by rail.*

them in Wales and 1.5 million in Scotland) and only three cities had populations of more than 100 000.

By 1914, when World War I broke out, all this had changed. The population had more than trebled and Britain had become a highly industrialised nation. There were 42 million people (including 2.5 million in Wales and 4.5 million in Scotland) and there were over 40 towns or cities with populations of more than 100 000.

This chapter will outline some of the major features of these 'years of expansion' and then examine the economic and political structure of Britain in 1815 in more detail.

1 ⌁ A CENTURY OF EXPANSION

In 1815, most Britons earned their living by working on farms. By 1914, most worked in factories and workshops and lived in the towns and cities. These were now linked by a railway network which had reduced the travelling time from Edinburgh to London to less than eight hours. A huge industrial working class had developed. This workforce was largely literate: by 1914, all children were sent to school and most men (although no women) became voters at 21. Politics had been transformed from the pastime of the landowners to something recognisably similar to the business it is today. Furthermore, there had been a huge increase in the role of government. (For instance, education and public health, in which the state had played no part in 1815, were major governmental responsibilities by 1914.) The three main political parties of today had emerged by 1914 – the Conservatives, the Liberals and the Labour Party. MPs from middle-class backgrounds outnumbered those from the aristocracy and the first working-class man had entered Parliament.

This process of change and expansion did not take place without strain and stress. The rise in population led to the growth of a society that threatened to burst apart at the seams. Trying to prevent this happening occupied the energies of nearly every government in the nineteenth century; time and again crises were overcome by stitching together political alliances and by hurrying through social and political reforms. In this way the fabric of society was kept intact.

It is the purpose of this book to identify and analyse all these and many other developments. But, first, it is necessary to look more closely at what Britain was actually like in 1815.

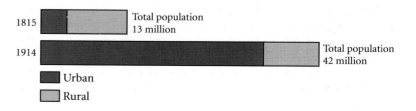

DIAGRAM 1   *Population in England, Wales and Scotland*

2 ⌁ THE INDUSTRIAL REVOLUTION

Some of the preceding paragraphs might lead you to believe that economy and society were more or less static in 1815 and that change was to come only *after* that date. In reality, Britain in 1815 was already undergoing major structural changes. Compared to today's changes, they may seem less dramatic. Certainly they were taking place more gradually but they were, nevertheless, of fundamental importance because they were transforming the very way people lived and worked.

Central to these revolutionary changes were new developments in technology. For instance, instead of relying almost solely on muscle power, more and more workshops, factories, mills and mines were using water power, or even steam power. There were still, it is true, far more handloom weavers producing woollen and cotton cloth than there were factory workers. However, the most advanced factories and mills were now being built on the coalfields so that they could employ steam-driven machinery to produce cloth, to pump water out of coal-mines and to provide the blast for iron-producing furnaces. William Cobbett, who travelled thousands of miles round Britain on horseback, wrote:

> All the way along from Leeds to Sheffield it is coal and iron, and iron and coal. It was dark before we reached Sheffield; so that we saw the iron furnaces in all the horrible splendour of their everlasting blaze. Nothing can be conceived more grand or more terrific than the yellow waves of fire that incessantly issue from the top of these furnaces ... .

The installation of large, heavy and expensive machinery led to the growth of factories employing not just 10 or 20, but hundreds of workers. Housing for these workers was built alongside the factories so that large new towns grew up. These areas were densely populated and polluted, with foul-smelling air and blackened buildings. In the 1830s, Sheffield was described as 'poisoned in its own excrement'.

The new factories and towns in the north of England, the Midlands, South Wales and the Scottish Lowlands depended on a ready supply of coal. They also needed cheap labour. This was only made possible by the rise in population which had been taking place since the mid-eighteenth century and by the improvements in agriculture and transport which enabled more and more urban workers to rely on a regular supply of cheap, plentiful food from the countryside. These population changes, the increased productivity of agriculture, the technological developments in the coal, iron and textile industries and the improved transport provided by the canals, together constituted what historians have since come to call the Industrial Revolution.

PICTURE 2   *Oldham, an industrial town in Lancashire, at the beginning of the twentieth century*

> **Q**
>
> *What key features of the Industrial Revolution are shown in this photograph?*

3 ～ THE POLITICAL STRUCTURE

In 1815, as we have seen, Britain was undergoing sweeping economic and social changes. Yet the political structure remained largely unchanged. At the very top of this structure was the Crown. In 1815, George III was on the throne. He had been King since 1760 but he was increasingly ill; amongst other symptoms, he had been found talking to trees at Windsor and, in 1811, he had been declared unfit to govern. His eldest son, George, became Prince Regent (and later King, in 1820, when his father died). The Prince Regent, for his part, was too lazy or incompetent to take much interest in government and politics so that the government of the country continued to be left more and more to the king's ministers.

The king could still appoint and dismiss a Prime Minister and he could also insist on having a say in the appointment of other ministers. However, the monarch had to take account of the wishes of Parliament if he was to influence their policies and get them to agree to the taxes without which his government could not operate. Thus, if a parliamentary leader had a large body of support in the House of Commons, the king was usually obliged to make him Prime Minister. That person, in 1815, was Lord Liverpool. He had already been Prime Minister for three years, and the Prince Regent relied very heavily on Liverpool and his Cabinet ministers to control Parliament and govern the land.

Both Government and Parliament were dominated by the landowning classes. Britain was largely governed by a few thousand landowning families who, between them, owned more than half the agricultural land. Generation after generation inherited the land and, with it, the wide-ranging power and influence which they had wielded for hundreds of years. The most important of these landowning families were members of the **aristocracy**. Their ancestors had been made nobles (with titles like Lord, Duke or Earl) by earlier Kings (and Queens) and they had thus become members of the House of Lords.

The landowning aristocracy assumed their right to supremacy to be natural. Their status was hereditary so that the right to a seat in the House of Lords was passed on to succeeding generations. Their central power base was the House of Lords but they had huge influence over the House of Commons as well. This was because nearly half of the Members of Parliament (MPs) owed their seats to peers (as members of the House of Lords were known) and many were related to them. The landed classes held the highest positions in the Church, the armed services, the judiciary and the civil service. They also ruled the countryside and dominated local government.

The main responsibilities of the State, or central government, were limited to defence, the control of trade (through taxes and customs duties) and the supervision of law and order. (The Government was not expected to provide schools and hospitals as it does today.) It was *local* government which most affected people in the nineteenth century. Here, as at Westminster, it was the landowning classes who predominated. At the top of local society was the Lord-Lieutenant of the county who was usually the biggest landowner. He was the king's representative in the county and he reported back to the central government in London. Under him were the **magistrates** or **Justices of the Peace (JPs)**. These were the men who bore the brunt of the governing of Britain.

The JPs had the major responsibility for preserving peace and for preventing crime and disorder in an age when there was no professional police force. They were appointed by a Royal Commission (as they are today), usually on the recommendation of the Lord-Lieutenant, and were mostly landowners. About a quarter were clergy of the Church of England. JPs were unpaid and untrained. As men of property (they were often the biggest employers in a locality) they possessed considerable status while their role as JPs brought them added power and influence. They had the authority to arrest, fine and imprison people for minor offences and to recommend trial by a higher court for major offences. They also saw to the upkeep of roads and bridges and were responsible for prisons and the care of the poor. Many people were dependent on the landowning JPs, as their tenants or hired labourers, so great respect was paid to them. If, however, they proved unable to deal with local disorder, they could call out the yeomanry, a mounted volunteer force which, like the JPs, was unpaid and consisted largely of men of property. In the case of a major disturbance, and there were

aristocracy The nobles, or peers, who inherited titles granted to their ancestors by previous monarchs. They sat in the House of Lords

magistrates, also known as **Justices of the Peace (JPs)**, had the main responsibility for maintaining law and order in the localities

Q

Make a list of the ways in which the landowning classes dominated British political life.

many in the years after 1815, the central government could be asked to send in troops to restore order.

4 ↜ BRITAIN IN 1815: A POST-WAR SOCIETY

In 1815, Britain was a society under strain. The most obvious reason for this was the population explosion. (In the decade from 1810 to 1820 the population rose faster than in any decade before or since.) The twin processes of industrialisation and **urbanisation** also contributed. For instance, many handloom weavers and other skilled craftsmen feared that they would be thrown out of work by the increasing use of machines in the new factories. Coming on top of these developments, and making the strain even greater, was post-war depression.

With the defeat of the French under Napoleon at the Battle of Waterloo in 1815, Britain emerged from the longest war (1793–1815) in which she had been engaged since the fifteenth century. She was now established as the greatest of the Great Powers. She had the largest navy, the biggest share of the world's trade and the most developed industry, while London was the biggest city and the financial capital of the world. However, the war was also the costliest in Britain's history and the country emerged with a vastly increased National Debt of £861 million and an unprecedentedly high tax burden, much of which fell on those sections of society which were least able to pay. Furthermore, several industries which had depended on government contracts during the war would now be forced to cut back: the textile industry and the iron and armaments industries, which had supplied uniforms and weapons, had to reduce their workforce, thus leading to increased unemployment. The demobilisation of hundreds of thousands of soldiers and sailors, with no pension or any other kind of government aid, increased the extent of the hardship. If there was a bad harvest and bread prices rose (and the average price of wheat was higher at this time than at any other time in the nineteenth century), millions faced the prospect of great hunger, if not starvation.

'Distress', as contemporaries called it, undoubtedly contributed to the growth of working-class unrest in the period after 1815. The government reacted to such unrest and, in particular, to demands from the working classes for a voice in Parliament, with great alarm and fear. They remembered from their youth hearing about the overthrow of the monarchy and of the ruling classes in the French Revolution. This period of popular agitation, and the government's response to it, is the subject of the next chapter.

---

urbanisation The growth of towns and cities

KEY ISSUE

What reasons are given for describing Britain as a 'society under strain' in 1815?

---

5 ↜ BIBLIOGRAPHY

There are a number of books that cover the whole, or most, of the period from 1815 to 1914.

BOOKS FOR AS/A LEVEL STUDENTS

M. Lynch *Nineteenth-Century British History, 1800–1914*, Hodder & Stoughton, 1999. Chapter 1 is a useful, straightforward survey of the British economy – population, industrialisation, trade, shipping and finance – over the whole century.

E. Evans *The complete A–Z of Nineteenth and Twentieth Century British History*, Hodder & Stoughton, 1998, is an excellent reference book.

Stephen Lee *Aspects of British Political History, 1815–1914*, Routledge, 1994) is a collection of essays on the main political developments.

FURTHER READING

E. Evans *The Forging of the Modern State 1783–1870*, Longman, 1983, covers over half of the century.

N. McCord *British History 1815–1906*, Oxford University Press, 1991, covers nearly all of the period. These are both aimed at the undergraduate reader but are accessible to many Advanced Level students.

A. Briggs *The Age of Improvement 1787–1867*, Longman, 1959, is a little dated, but marvellously perceptive.

N. Gash *Aristocracy and People, Britain 1815–1865*, Edward Arnold, 1979, is demanding, but expert and sophisticated.

F. M. L. Thompson *The Rise of Respectable Society – A Social History of Victorian Britain 1830–1900*, Fontana, 1988, is a good, wide-ranging, general survey from an economic and social perspective.

2

The Age of Lord Liverpool, 1812–27

The period of Tory Government, from 1812 to 1830, saw changes of great significance in Britain. The strain of the wars with France, which lasted from 1793 to 1815, had encouraged a demand for what was called 'economical' reform. The main feature of this was an attack upon inefficiency and corruption, such as the buying and selling of government offices. Prominent among those making the attack were the middle classes who had become wealthy during the rapid industrialisation process that had begun in Britain around the middle of the eighteenth century. At the end of the war in 1815, there was high expectation that the Government would begin to concede these demands. However, the poor economic situation in post-war Britain did not give the Government the freedom to introduce major reforms. Indeed, so grim were conditions that much of the period is a story of social unrest; those who were worst affected by poverty and hunger protested violently against their suffering.

Economic conditions did improve in the 1820s which allowed the Government to introduce reform. Textbooks traditionally divide the Tory post-war period of office into two main sections: 1815–22 and 1822–7. This is because 1822 is regarded as marking a break between the 'repressive' and the 'liberal' years of Tory Government. Although these two labels are a little misleading, and the break in 1822 was by no means complete, the date still provides a useful reference point. Before 1822, the Government was largely concerned with controlling unrest; after that date, better economic circumstances allowed it to consider reform.

1822 is also a significant date in British foreign policy. It marked the year when George Canning became Foreign Secretary on the death of his predecessor, Lord Castlereagh. Because the two men were very different in character, it was customary to regard their foreign policies as being very different. But, what historians now stress is how similar Castelreagh and Canning were in making the protection of British interests the chief aim in their approach to international questions.

Although it is appropriate to think of the House of Commons as being dominated in this period by two major parties, **the Whigs** and **the Tories**, it would be unhistorical to regard these as representing two fundamentally opposed political and social groups. What impresses us now is how alike the members of both parties were in outlook and social background. Even the new middle class, who made their money from industry, tended to use their profits to buy land so that they became almost indistinguishable in their life-style from the established landed class.

Whigs and Tories

These were the two largest political parties in Parliament at the beginning of the nineteenth century. They had originally developed out of the struggle between King and Parliament in the seventeenth century. In general terms, the Tories were those who believed in the combined authority of monarch, Anglican Church and Parliament to rule the nation. The Whigs were those who believed that Parliament was the major authority and were suspicious of the monarch and the Church having too much power. A further distinction is that the Tories tended to be more resistant to change and slower to accept new ideas than were the Whigs. However, the differences between the parties at this stage of history should not be overstated.

Q

How clear were the distinctions between Tories and Whigs in the period 1815–30?

1 ✐ LORD LIVERPOOL'S POST-WAR GOVERNMENT, 1815–22

The Tory Government during these years was led by Robert Banks Jenkinson, Second Earl of Liverpool. The Tory Party of his day was not the organised and disciplined affair that it later became. In the early nineteenth century, allegiance to party was seldom clear-cut or fixed, so there was no guarantee that a government could rely on support in a vote in the Commons or the Lords. Government simply did not have the means of forcing Parliament to accept unpopular proposals. It was through 'management' (influence and persuasion) that the Government got its way, rather than by trying to impose its will on parliament. Above all, what enabled government to operate was that most members of parliament were in broad agreement on most important issues. There was also a prevailing understanding that it was the primary duty of parliament to support the King and his ministers so that effective government could be maintained. The idea of an official opposition, eager to bring down the Government and replace it, did not establish itself until later in the century.

Lord Liverpool's Government was in a difficult position in 1815. In the words of Norman Gash, the modern expert on this period, the effect of the war had been 'to create expectations while removing the means of satisfying them'. Not only were there demands for 'economical' reform, but there was a general anticipation that peace would bring a return to cheap food and goods, the ending of taxation, and a general increase in prosperity. But since Britain went into post-war **recession**,

recession The war had created a demand for industrial goods; this sharply declined with the coming of peace. Workers were either laid off or had their wages reduced. Their plight was worsened by job competition from the demobilised troops who returned looking for work. Low wages and unemployment were also experienced by agricultural workers.

KEY ISSUE

Why, and with what effects, were the Corn Laws passed in 1815?

See page 63 on Adam Smith

the Government was able to deliver none of these. The severe decline in trade after 1815 brought lower wages and unemployment rather than the expected prosperity.

A *The Corn Laws, 1815*

A striking example of Liverpool's inability to go against the wishes of Parliament occurred with the passing of the Corn laws immediately after the war. As a supporter of the economic ideas of Adam Smith, Liverpool would have preferred to pursue a free-trade policy after 1815. But the landed class, which dominated Parliament, believed that protection was the best means of maintaining the profits it had made during the war. It obliged the Government to accept the **Corn laws**.

Corn laws, 1815

The wartime blockades which had prevented food supplies coming easily into the country had meant prosperity for British farmers. But, with the end of the war, home-grown food had again to compete with foreign produce which was often cheaper than its British counterpart. In an attempt to retain the farmers' profits, the new Laws imposed a set of import duties on foreign grain. These effectively prohibited the import of grain until the domestic variety had reached 80 shillings for a quarter bushel (equivalent today to £4 for nine dry litres).

---

indirect taxation
Unlike direct taxation, which is a levy on an individual's income, indirect taxation is a tax on goods which takes no account of the buyer's ability to pay. This form of tax hit the poorer classes particularly hard since they had to spend a far higher proportion of their income on taxed goods. This is known as 'regressive taxation'.

A direct consequence of the Corn Laws was an increase in the price of bread, the staple diet of the working classes, at a time when wages were falling. In addition, the working classes bore the brunt of the Government's taxation policy. Britain had incurred massive debts as a result of its heavy borrowings during the French wars. To meet the costs of government and pay its debts, post-war Britain needed an income of £20 million. Yet its revenue income amounted to only £12 million. The answer appeared to be to increase taxation. However, in 1816, Parliament rejected the Government's proposal to renew income tax, which had been a temporary wartime measure. This meant that if taxation was still to be raised to meet the deficit it would have to be **indirect taxation**, levied on basic goods. Among these were tea, sugar, tobacco, beer and candles, which at this time, along with bread, were the basic items of consumption of ordinary people. So now, a raft of increases on essential goods had been added to the already inflated price of bread. It was hard not to conclude that the poor were being taxed for the benefit of the rich.

That is precisely what the labouring classes *did* conclude. Many became convinced that Government and Parliament did not care about the economic difficulties confronting the workers. Until Parliament was reformed by allowing working-class representation, their miseries would

PICTURE 3 *'The Blessings of Peace or the Curse of the Corn Bill' a cartoon by the celebrated satirical cartoonist, Cruikshank, 1815*

continue. A powerful voice that articulated such views was that of the radical agitator, William Cobbett. As a journalist, who sold his writings widely and cheaply among the workers, he savaged the corrupt political system that was prepared to let the labourers and their families starve while the privileged classes grew richer. He saw the selfishness and irresponsibility of the wealthy most clearly expressed in the regressive taxation system. In his influential journal, *Political Register*, he asked what was the root cause of the workers' woes:

It is the *enormous amount of taxes*, which the government compels us to pay for the support of its army, its placemen, its pensioners etc. and for the payment of the interest of its debt. That this is the *real* cause has been a thousand times proved; and it is now so acknowledged by the creatures of the government themselves. The tax gatherers do not, indeed, come to you and demand money of you: but, there are few articles which you use, in the purchase of which you do not pay *a tax*.

William Cobbett, Political Register, *2 November 1816*

Q

What, according to the cartoonist, are the views on the issue of importing foreign corn of (i) the French traders, (ii) the English landlords, and (iii) the English worker?

Q

1. *Put into your own words the main points made by Cobbett.*
2. *What type of tax is he condemning?*

Cobbett's arguments found a responsive ear among the lower classes suffering from the economic depression. The degree of social unrest and the frequency with which direct challenges to authority occurred in the post war years were clear signs of the exceptional bitterness and frustration of both urban workers and landed labourers.

B *Major disturbances, 1815–22*

LUDDISM

KEY ISSUE

Why was social unrest so widespread in Britain after 1815?

This movement, which had begun in the textile industry around 1811, was essentially the reaction of dispossessed handloom weavers to the rapid decline in their fortunes. At one time their skills had been in high demand and brought them wealth that had made them princes among craftsmen. But the introduction of mechanical looms had rapidly made their skills obsolete. In their frustration, groups of them took to smashing the machines that had displaced them and destroying stocks of finished cotton. Since many of the weavers came from Nottinghamshire, their tactics acquired the name Luddism, a reference to the mythical King Ludd of Sherwood Forest, a sort of latter day Robin Hood figure. Between 1811 and 1817, groups of Luddites attacked knitting frames in a number of cotton mills in Nottinghamshire, Cheshire, and Lancashire. Luddism entered the language as a word meaning blind resistance to technological change.

THE SPA FIELDS RIOTS, 1816

These incidents from 1816 to 1819 are developed, in the context of the popular radical movements, in pages 40–41 of Chapter 3

London had seen a series of organised protests against the Corn laws. These reached their most serious in 1816, when a mass meeting, gathered in Spa Fields on the outskirts of the city, got out hand; demonstrators looted a number of properties, including a gunsmith's, and were only dispersed when the Lord Mayor called out the troops.

THE DERBYSHIRE RISING, 1817

This affair is an interesting example of the Government's use of **agents provocateurs**. One of the most notorious agents, known simply as Oliver, infiltrated a number of radical groups and exposed the ringleaders to the authorities. His greatest success came with his contribution to the failure of the rising of the unemployed workers in Derbyshire. Led by Jeremiah Brandreth, the jobless textile workers of the region attempted to join up with protesters in neighbouring counties in a broad movement. Their most ambitious, and, as it proved, most ill-advised, venture was an attack upon Nottingham Castle, which they hoped to capture and hold. Forewarned by Oliver, troops were waiting for the attackers who were easily overpowered. Brandreth was tried and subsequently hanged; his leading supporters in the abortive attack were transported or imprisoned.

agents provocateurs
In an effort to limit disorder the Government resorted to sending agents into areas of potential trouble. By deliberately inciting unrest, the agents were able to identify likely agitators and have them arrested

PETERLOO, 1819

Henry 'Orator' Hunt, a leading radical and an associate of William Cobbett, was the principal speaker at a mass meeting at St. Peter's Fields in Manchester, which had been called to demand parliamentary reform. It was intended to be a peaceful demonstration, but the size of the crowd frightened the local magistrates into ordering a cavalry detachment to disperse it. The riders went into the crowd with drawn sabres. In the confusion and panic that ensued, 11 people, including two women and a child, were killed and around 400 were injured. The Government's immediate reaction was to introduce the Six Acts. Opponents of the Government christened the event 'Peterloo', an ironic play of words on Waterloo, the celebrated British victory in 1815.

See page 14 for details of the Six Acts

THE CATO STREET CONSPIRACY, 1820

Government fears that the unrest had a more dangerous side to it than simply protest against economic conditions were reinforced by a desperate assassination plot unmasked in 1820. A group of extremists, led by Arthur Thistlewood, had devised a wild plan which involved blowing up all the members of Liverpool's Cabinet and then seizing London. Rumours of the plan reached the Government who sent a force to arrest the plotters at their headquarters in Cato Street. A fight broke out, in the course of which Thistlewood killed one of the agents trying to arrest him. The death sentence that was subsequently passed on Thistlewood has its own particular historical interest in that he was the last person to be executed in Britain by beheading.

THE QUEEN CAROLINE AFFAIR, 1821

A notable disturbance, whose origins were not economic, occurred at the time of the coronation of George IV. Before he became King in 1820, George, as Prince Regent, had led a scandalous private life which involved bigamy, fathering illegitimate children and wife-desertion. The wife in question was Princess Caroline whom he had first tried to dump in 1806. However, Caroline proved unwilling to go quietly. In the intervening years, she gathered a sizeable number of supporters including the Whig peer, Lord Brougham. She was determined to become Queen when the Prince Regent acceded to the throne. In an attempt to prevent this, he threatened that he would not back the Government when he became King if it did not take formal steps to dismiss Caroline's claims. Liverpool's Cabinet bowed before the threat and introduced a Bill which deprived Caroline of her marital and royal status. Despite this, Caroline with considerable popular support behind her, turned up at the Coronation and tried to force her way into Westminster Abbey. Pro-Caroline and anti-Caroline factions clashed violently in the streets around the Abbey. The Life Guards eventually restored order, but not before two demonstrators had been killed. Fortunately for the new King and the Government, Caroline's death a month later effectively ended the scandal.

C *The Government's handling of the disturbances*

The social disturbance which Liverpool's Government faced after 1815 was sporadic but widespread and highly troublesome. The methods which the authorities used to contain it earned the Government the bitter condemnation of many contemporaries and created an image of an uncaring administration that made no attempt to understand the underlying causes of the distress, but simply resorted to repression and punishment. It was an image that stuck; until relatively recently few books had a good word to say about Liverpool's record between 1815 and 1822. However, of late, historians have begun to show greater sympathy towards the Tories in this period and to question whether the term 'repressive' to describe their policies is entirely appropriate. Before examining the pros and cons of the argument we need to list the ways the Tories responded to the disturbances of the time.

KEY ISSUE

What methods did Liverpool's Government adopt to contain the unrest?

- Following the anti-Corn Law riots in London in 1815, special constables were enrolled to assist the troops in preventing disorder.
- In the wake of Spa Fields riots in 1816, a system of 'agents provocateurs' was introduced by the Home Secretary, Lord Sidmouth.
- *Habeas corpus*, the law which required that a person could not be arrested and held unless he was formally charged with an offence, was suspended in 1817. This empowered the authorities to arrest potential troublemakers merely on suspicion, without having to prove guilt or intent.
- In 1817, a Seditious Meetings Act forbade public gatherings of more than 50 people, unless permission had been granted by a magistrate (or JP).
- 'The Six Acts' were rushed through in 1819 in the aftermath of Peterloo:
  - a ban was placed on public meetings called to draft protests and petitions
  - magistrates were empowered to confiscate arms
  - magistrates were authorised to confiscate seditious literature
  - the stamp duty on newspapers and pamphlets was increased, with the aim of making radical writings, such as Cobbett's, prohibitively expensive for workers and labourers
  - the prosecution was given greater powers in treason trials
  - the training of private armies was prohibited.

HISTORIANS' DEBATE

How repressive were the Tories between 1815 and 1822?

An effective way of tackling this question is to treat the issue as if the Tories were on trial in court. This allows the historical argument to be put in terms of the case for the prosecution and the case for the defence.

The case for the prosecution

In a sonnet of 1819, Shelley, the poet and political radical, described Liverpool's Government as: 'Rulers who neither see, nor feel, nor know'.

This condemnation was repeated a century and a half later by another radical, the social historian, E. P. Thompson, who charged Liverpool's Government with thinking only in terms of repression and making no attempt to tackle the root problems that had caused the unrest. The accusation obviously has weight. Although the Corn Laws and the increased indirect taxation were measures forced on the Government by Parliament, Liverpool and his Cabinet were still basically responsible for their operation thereafter. There was little evidence that the Government ever made the relief of the burdens borne by the poorer classes a priority.

One of Thompson's many creative contributions to the study of the past was that he tried to examine events from the point of view what he called 'the losers'. As a socialist, he was fascinated by such groups as the Luddites and the radical agitators who, although they lost the battle in their own time, developed political and economic ideas that later generations would come to admire and accept. In the 1960s and 1970s revisionist historians picked up on Thompson's ideas that history had always been written by the winners and began to look at history from the 'bottom up' rather than the traditional 'top down'. Prompted by Thompson's desire to rescue history's losers from what he had called 'the enormous condescension of posterity', the revisionists showed great sympathy for working-class movements. It was understandable, therefore, that when they examined the early nineteenth century they should have been very critical of Liverpool's Government (the winners) in suppressing the labouring class (the losers).

The case for the defence
A contemporary of E. P. Thompson's, the political historian, George Kitson Clark, suggested that, before passing judgement on an apparently repressive regime, the student should take into account the scale of the dangers it was facing. This approach appealed to scholars who wanted to achieve balance by stressing the historical context in which Liverpool's Government operated. Norman Gash (see Bibliography, page 30) pointed out that after 1815 'there was a widespread conviction among the governing classes that something like a national conspiracy existed to subvert the constitution'. It is a generally accepted principle in all societies that the prime function of government is to maintain law and order. However, in Liverpool's day, the resources for doing this were very limited. When faced by the threat of disorder the local magistrates, whose task it was to keep the peace, were very restricted in their options. There were as yet no police forces; the authorities had to rely on the army. But, at this time, Britain did not have a regular army on permanent stand-by. Calling out the troops took time. The troops used at Peterloo were largely drawn from the Manchester Yeomanry, which was a volunteer cavalry force. Few other parts of Britain had even an irregular force of this kind on which they could call.

Q

Does the Tory Government of 1815–22 deserve the harsh criticism it has customarily received?

Since disorder was difficult to control, the obvious policy was for the Government to prevent its occurring in the first place. This was the logic behind the Tories' firm measures. The suspension of *habeas corpus* and the use of *agents provocateurs* were essentially preventative not punitive measures, and were intended as temporary adjustments to meet an emergency, not permanent changes in the law. Even the Six Acts, which have attracted particular scorn from critics of Liverpool's Government, do not now appear unnecessarily restrictive. Indeed, two of the Acts, the ban on keeping arms and the proscription of private armies, could be said to be entirely reasonable measures for a government to introduce. Moreover, given that the Government had a deep-rooted fear that social disorder could easily descend into mob rule, the treatment of those arrested during the disturbances was not particularly vindictive. Norman Gash suggests that, judged by the European standards of its day, Tory policy was remarkably lenient. As he puts it, in a deliberate understatement, 'it was not exactly a reign of terror'.

Another point emphasised by those who urge that the period be seen in context is that the Government simply lacked the means for dealing effectively on a national scale with problems such as hunger, poverty and unemployment. To have tackled the underlying causes of distress would have required organisations that did not exist in 1815 and would take more than a century to develop. Furthermore, the prevailing view was that government should intervene as little as possible in economic affairs. To criticise Liverpool's Government for failing to find solutions to the social ills of the day is, therefore, both unrealistic and unhistorical.

2 ⌐ LORD LIVERPOOL'S LIBERAL TORY GOVERNMENT, 1822–7

The term 'Liberal Tories' suggests that in this period the Government became more progressive and willing to contemplate reform. This is broadly true; the pace and range of reform did increase, a development usually ascribed to the fact that a number of new men entered the Cabinet. However, the extent of the Cabinet changes should not be exaggerated. Liverpool, after all, remained Prime Minister, and two of the most prominent reformers after 1822, Robinson and Huskisson, had been in the Cabinet since 1814. What principally enabled the Liberal Tories to consider reform was an improvement in the economy. The severity of the post-war depression began to ease considerably in the 1820s. A major contribution to this was a run of exceptionally good weather and plentiful harvests in the years 1820–4. This reduced social tension and made it possible to lift the political repression. Such developments encouraged the new ministers to introduce policies that had been discussed as early as 1819 but which circumstances had made impractical.

> **KEY ISSUE**
>
> *Why, and in what ways, did the pace of reform quicken after 1822?*

William Huskisson	Secretary of the Board of Trade
Robert Peel	Home Secretary
Frederick Robinson (Viscount Goderich)	Chancellor of the Exchequer
George Canning	Foreign Secretary

TABLE 1
The leading Liberal Tories after 1822

A *The major reforms of the Liberal Tories*

FINANCIAL AND ECONOMIC REFORMS

Robinson and Huskisson co-operated in a free-trade programme, begun in 1822, that sought to rationalise the complex and unwieldy 'Book of Rates' by which levies and duties were calculated. In line with the request of British traders and manufacturers, duties on a whole range of items, including cotton, linen and glass were reduced, while the general duty on manufactured goods was slashed from 50 to 20 per cent. The Corn Laws remained, but were modified in 1823 by substituting a sliding-scale for the previous fixed rate: as British wheat rose in price, the duty on foreign wheat was reduced. These significant moves away from protection were complemented in 1823 by the Reciprocity of Duties Act; this repealed the Navigation Laws and allowed foreign ships to carry goods into British ports.

LEGAL REFORMS

Robert Peel, the son of a highly successful Lancashire cotton manufacturer, had shown his progressive attitude by introducing a factory reform Bill in 1819, which had restricted the working hours of children in textile mills. As Home Secretary after 1822, he presided over a wide-ranging review of the English penal code. This resulted, in 1824, in the removal of many antiquated laws and punishments; the death penalty was lifted from over 100 offences. Accompanying the changes in the law were measures to make conditions in prisons more humane. It was also in 1824 that the Combination Acts of 1799 and 1800, which had made trade unions illegal, were repealed. This was the initiative of Francis Place, a private member, but Peel's support was of considerable value in getting the proposed repeal through the Commons. Although the freedom of the unions were restricted a year later in an Amending Act, their legal right to exist remained. A measure for which Peel is perhaps best remembered in the popular imagination was the foundation in 1829 of the Metropolitan Police, an unarmed civilian force intended to be the defender of the public rather than its oppressor.

The improved economic conditions and the Government's reforming policies had combined by the mid-1820s to bring considerable benefits to the people at large. Taxation had been lowered, inflation had dropped, unemployment had lessened, and manufacturing and trade had reached unprecedented levels of success. Having weathered the difficult post-war years of economic depression and social unrest, Liverpool's Government was now presiding over a time of peace and prosperity. But

---

KEY ISSUE

Why, despite their successes, did the Tories become divided in the late 1820s?

appearances were deceptive. The Tory Government was beset by problems. Interestingly, these came not from outside, but from within the party itself, a fact which was brought out in the following letter from Palmerston. Viscount Palmerston was later to switch parties and become a Whig leader and Prime Minister, but at this time he was a Tory MP and Secretary for War. His description, therefore, provides a valuable insider's view of the difficulties confronting the Liberal Tories:

Q

1. *What does Palmerston mean by 'the stupid old Tory party'?*
2. *How valuable is this letter as an insight into the problems that faced the Tory Government in the late 1820s?*

From a letter by Viscount Palmerston to William Temple, 17 July 1826

The Government are as strong as any Government can wish to be, as far as regards those who sit facing them; but in truth the real opposition of the present day sit behind the Treasury Bench [i.e. the Government's own supporters]; and it is by the stupid old Tory party, who bawl out the memory and praises of Pitt while they are opposing all the measures and principles which he held most important; it is by these that the progress of the Government in every improvement which they are attempting is thwarted and impeded. On the Catholic [Emancipation] question; on the principles of commerce; on the corn laws; on the settlement of the currency; on the laws regulating trade; on colonial slavery; on all these questions, and everything like them, the Government find support from the Whigs and resistance from their self-denominated friends.

Palmerston's words highlight the dilemma in which the Tory party found itself in this period. It was a problem of identity. By tradition, the Tories were committed to maintaining the existing political and social system. When, therefore, the Liberal Tories introduced what they saw as necessary reforms, the traditionally minded members, those referred to by Palmerston as the 'the stupid old Tory party', accused them of betraying party principles. A notable feature of Palmerston's letter was that he put **Catholic Emancipation** at the top of the list of

Catholic Emancipation

In 1800, the Act of Union had formally ended Irish independence. William Pitt, the Tory Prime Minister, hoped to persuade the Irish to accept the Union by promising to introduce Catholic Emancipation – the extension to the Catholic population of full political and civil rights. However, despite Pitt's personal commitment, other influential members of the Cabinet joined the King in refusing to honour the promise of Emancipation. The failure to gain their rights left the Irish Catholics angry and resentful.

issues dividing the Tories. This was one of the demanding questions that was unresolved at the time of Liverpool's retirement in 1827. His successor George, Canning, was very conscious of the problems he had inherited.

B *Catholic Emancipation*

In 1827, Canning wrote an illuminating letter:

1. The Catholic question is to remain an open question, upon which each member of the Cabinet is at perfect liberty to exercise his own judgement.

2. The inconvenience of having one open question in the Cabinet, makes it the more necessary to agree that there should be no other. All the existing members of the Cabinet are united in opposing the question of Parliamentary Reform, and could not acquiesce in its being brought forward or supported by any member of the Cabinet.

3. The present members of the Cabinet are also united in opposition to the repeal of the Test Act.

From a letter of George Canning to Lord Lansdowne, 23 April 1827

Canning was well aware why 'high' (i.e. traditional) Tories opposed religious and parliamentary reform. They regarded Church and Parliament as guarantees of their social and political status. That is why they were determined to preserve the Anglican Church as the official state religion. Since the **Test and Corporation Acts**, passed in the seventeenth century, it had been necessary for people to be professed Anglicans (members of the Church of England) if they wished to hold public office. If equal rights were now to be granted to Catholics or **Nonconformists**, the established political and social order would be undermined.

When Canning died in August 1827, only six months after succeeding Liverpool, the issues which he had identified had already begun to destroy Tory unity. Whig pressure began to mount, so much so that when the Duke of Wellington became Prime Minister in 1828, he decided not to oppose the Bill, introduced by the Whigs in the Commons, for the repeal of the Test and Corporation Acts. Superficially, the repeal appeared to be of little significance since the laws it removed had not been applied for generations. However, the measure raised a demanding question. If the civil rights of Nonconformists were now legally recognised, why should the same liberties be denied to Catholics? The repeal of the Test and Corporation Acts thus gave weight to the argument for Catholic Emancipation which was being fervently pressed in Ireland. By the late 1820s, the Catholic demand was unstoppable.

Test and Corporation Acts, 1661 and 1673 These were measures that debarred those who were not members of the Anglican Church from holding public office, in local or central government.

Nonconformists (Dissenters) This was the broad term for members of Protestant denominations, such as Methodists, Baptists, and Congregationalists, who did not accept the authority of the Established Anglican Church.

In 1828, Daniel O'Connell, the champion of Emancipation, won a resounding victory in the County Clare election. Technically, as a Catholic, O'Connell was not legally entitled to enter Westminster as an MP. However, things were so tense in Ireland following his election that Wellington feared civil war there if O'Connell were barred. The Prime Minister and Robert Peel convinced their reluctant Cabinet colleagues that Emancipation would have to be granted; public order, if not principle, demanded it. The Relief (Emancipation) Bill which Peel then introduced was fiercely contested in both the Commons and the Lords, but was eventually passed in June 1829. In an act of vengeance, the embittered high Tories joined with the Whigs in 1830 in defeating the Government in the Commons. Wellington resigned, thus ending half a century of Tory rule.

The struggle over Emancipation and the fall of the Tories marked the end of the system that Liverpool had successfully operated. Between 1812 and 1827 he had managed, often with great difficulty, to hold the balance between those who wanted to preserve an unchanging constitution and those who believed in the necessity of reform. His greatest problems had come not from outside the party but from within. In the three years after his retirement those internal problems weakened the Tories to the point where the balance that he had achieved finally broke down. A precise summary has been by provided by Norman Gash:

> **1.** *The extract speaks of Liverpool's achievements during his 15 years. List what you regard as Liverpool's main successes in that time.*
> **2.** *Identify the 'forces of change' to which Gash refers.*

… what is surprising is not how little but how much Lord Liverpool's ministry had been able to achieve in its fifteen years of office. But by 1827–30 its divisions had become too open, its resources too restricted, and its political aims too limited to provide an adequate political channel for the forces of change in British and Irish society.

Norman Gash, '1812–30' in Anthony Seldon (Ed.) How Tory Governments Fall: The Tory Party in Power since 1783, Fontana, 1996, p. 99

3 ⌐ FOREIGN POLICY, 1815–27

During Lord Liverpool's premiership, British foreign policy was conducted successively by Lord Castlereagh and George Canning. The two men differed sharply in character and style and had such a strong dislike of each other that on one occasion they fought a duel. Yet in their approach to foreign affairs their principal aims converged. These aims can be identified as:

KEY ISSUE

Did British foreign policy in this period ever have any other motive than the protection of British interests?

- the preservation of the balance of power in Europe
- the detachment of Britain from military action in Europe unless circumstances made it unavoidable
- the protection of Britain's international commercial interests.

A *Castlereagh as Foreign Secretary, 1812–22*

Castlereagh has been called the 'father' of the Congress System, a reference to the seminal role he played in the development of European diplomatic co-operation in the post-war years. He had laid the groundwork for this during the last phase of the allied struggle against Napoleon. Castlereagh had become Foreign Secretary in 1812, and had made it his main task to form an effective anti-French coalition between Britain, Russia and Prussia. The success of his efforts came in the spring of 1815 when coalition forces took Paris and forced Napoleon into exile on the Isle of Elba. Barely had the allies begun to celebrate their victory, when Napoleon escaped and threatened the peace of Europe once more. Castlereagh was again foremost in renewing the alliance which led to the final defeat of Napoleon at Waterloo in June 1815. There was little doubt that, when the allies gathered at the Congress of Vienna to draw up a peace settlement, Castlereagh's recent record made him a dominant figure.

There was an important sense in which the Vienna Treaty left a legacy of bitterness. The principles of nationalism and representative government were largely ignored in the settlement. It became the object of nationalists in Poland, Italy, Germany, Belgium and Norway to break the control of the Governments they had been placed under in 1815. Although Britain's gains at the time seemed scattered and unimportant, the growth of the British empire later in the nineteenth century would show that these had been vital acquisitions.

Castlereagh's specific objectives in Europe were limited to producing a peace which would be lasting and which would keep France in check.

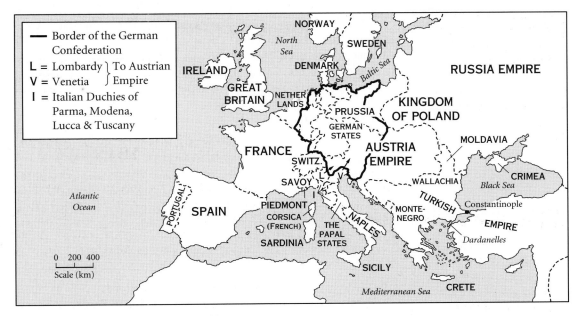

MAP 1   *Europe in 1815 after the Congress of Vienna*

The major terms of the Congress of Vienna, 1815

- The French Bourbon monarchy was restored with Louis XVIII as King.
- The map of Europe was redrawn based on the principle of legitimacy – the right of hereditary monarchies to continue to rule.
- The continental allies, Prussia, Russia, and Austria, rewarded themselves by taking large areas of neighbouring territory. Castlereagh tolerated this because he judged that it would help keep a European balance of power. If Prussia expanded into northern Germany while Austria moved into Italy, this would compensate for any Russian territorial moves westward into Poland.
- Holland became an independent state and was enlarged by union with Belgium. This was largely at Castlereagh's insistence; he believed that a strong Holland would be both a block on French expansion and a guarantee of stability in the Low Countries, a trading area of vital concern to the British.
- Britain gained the Cape, Malta, the Ionian Islands, Ceylon, Tobago, St Lucia, Mauritius and Heligoland.

KEY ISSUE

In what ways did the Holy Alliance and the Quadruple Alliance differ?

To achieve this, he proposed to his wartime allies that they should be prepared to meet regularly in formal congresses so that they could discuss any issues which seemed likely to threaten European peace. It was this proposal that underlay Castlereagh's idea of the 'Quadruple Alliance', made up of Austria, Prussia, Russia and Britain. However, from the beginning, Castlereagh's scheme was in competition with an alternative concept of European co-operation – the Holy Alliance. The following two documents provide an insight into the difference in character and intention between the two systems.

To facilitate and to secure the execution of the present Treaty [of Vienna], and to consolidate the connections which at the present moment so closely unite the four Sovereigns for the happiness of the World, the High Contracting Parties [Austria, Great Britain, Prussia and Russia] have agreed to renew their meetings at fixed periods, either under the immediate auspices of the Sovereigns themselves, or by their respective Ministers, for the purpose of consulting upon their common interests, and for the consideration of the measures which at each of these periods shall be considered the most salutary for the repose and prosperity of Nations, and for the maintenance of the Peace of Europe.

Article VI of the Quadruple Alliance, 20 November 1815

Conformable to the words of the Holy Scriptures, which command all men to consider each other as brethren, the Three contracting Monarchs [Alexander I of Russia, Francis I of Austria and Frederick William III of Prussia] will remain united by the bonds of a true and indissoluble fraternity, and considering each other as fellow countrymen, they will, on all occasions and in all places, lend each other aid and assistance; and, regarding themselves towards their subjects and armies as fathers of families, they will lead them, in the same spirit of fraternity with which they are animated, to protect Religion, Peace, and Justice.

Article 1 of the Holy Alliance, 26 September 1815

Q

1. *How far does your reading of the Sources and your own knowledge lead you to support the view that 'the Holy Alliance was simply the Quadruple Alliance with religion added on'?*
2. *In what ways may these Sources be used to explain why a Congress system developed after 1815 and why it eventually failed?*

The Holy Alliance was the brainchild of the Russian Tsar, Alexander I, who was determined after 1815 to extinguish the last traces in Europe of the disruptive ideas of equality and liberty that that had inspired the French Revolution. He called on the crowned heads of Russia, Austria and Prussia to join in a re-assertion of the God-given and absolute right of monarchs to rule their people. They should be ready to combine whenever a challenge to their absolutism arose in the form of movements for constitutional or political freedom.

Castlereagh was unmoved by the religious conviction that inspired the Holy Alliance, which he dismissed as 'a piece of sublime mysticism and nonsense'. His saw his own Quadruple Alliance as a realistic and practical arrangement for controlling France and upholding the Vienna settlement. For Russia, Austria and Prussia, the Holy Alliance confirmed their right not only to suppress opposition within their own countries, but collectively to do the same in other member states. It was here that Castlereagh parted company with his former allies. He declined to commit Britain to the Holy Alliance and refused to accept that its members were entitled to assume a general right to interfere in the domestic affairs of Europe. There was clearly a conflict of attitude between the two alliance systems, which raised doubts that genuine co-operation between Britain and the European powers would last.

The Congresses

AIX-LA-CHAPELLE (AACHEN), 1818
Castlereagh persuaded the other powers to admit France to the Quadruple Alliance, thus making it a Quintuple Alliance.

TROPPAU, 1820 (TRANSFERRED TO LAIBACH, 1821)
Castlereagh declined to attend; instead, he sent an observer to convey the message that Britain would intervene on the continent only in case of a rising against the restored French monarchy.

VERONA, 1822
Called to discuss the problem of revolutions in the Spanish colonies and in Greece. Castlereagh again refused to attend personally. It was while the Congress was in session that Castlereagh committed suicide and Canning succeeded him as Foreign Secretary.

ST PETERSBURG, 1825
Britain did not attend what proved to be the last of the congresses. It produced little of note.

The doubts proved well founded. Of the Congresses convened in the decade after 1815, it was only the first one, at Aix-la-Chapelle, that Britain considered to be of value, since it produced the agreement to extend the Quadruple Alliance to include France. Thereafter, Britain made little attempt to hide its disdain for a congress system that merely served to further the interests of the Holy Alliance. The evidence supported British scepticism. After 1818 there were a number of anti-government risings in Europe organised by **constitutionalists** and **liberals**. Spain, Portugal, Naples and Piedmont (in Italy), were the main areas affected. Hoping to achieve a united response to crush these threats, Alexander I called a congress at Troppau in 1820. Since Britain and France chose not to attend, Troppau was a gathering solely of Holy Alliance members, who were thus unchallenged in adopting a repressive policy against the liberal movements. The strength of the Holy Alliance's reaction was evident in the notorious Protocol, issued at the end of the Congress.

constitutionalists and **liberals** These terms were applied to those groups who challenged the absolutist regimes and pressed for the adoption of a constitution which would allow the people a say in choosing the government

Q
1. Identify 'the Allied Powers', referred to in the opening sentence.
2. Using the Source and your own knowledge, explain the term 'beneficial action'.

The Allied Powers agree to refuse recognition to changes brought about by illegal methods. When States where such changes have been made, cause, by their proximity, other countries to fear immediate danger, and when the Allied Powers can exercise effective and beneficial action towards them, they will employ, in order to bring them back to the bosom of the Alliance, first friendly representation, secondly measures of coercion, if the employment of such coercion is indispensable.

The Troppau Protocol, October 1820

In effect, what the Protocol asserted was the right of the Holy Alliance to suppress political movements in Europe of which it did not approve. Castlereagh had already rejected the claims in the Protocol. In May 1820, he had anticipated the outcome of the Troppau Congress with a public State Paper in which he set out Britain's attitude towards the liberal movements in Europe. He acknowledged the disruption that was occurring in countries trying to reshape their constitutions 'upon the **Representative Principle**', but did not accept that the disturbances were a reason for interference from outside.

> There can be no doubt of the general Danger which menaces the stability of all existing Governments from the Principles which are afloat, and from the circumstances that so many States of Europe are now employed in the difficult task of casting anew their Governments upon the Representative Principle; but the notion of limiting or regulating such Experiments, either by foreign Council or by foreign force, would be as dangerous to avow as it would be impossible to execute.
>
> In this Alliance as in all other human Arrangements, nothing is more likely to impair or even destroy its real utility, than any attempt to push its duties and obligations beyond the Sphere which its original Conception and understood Principles will warrant: It was an union for the Reconquest and liberation of the Continent of Europe from the Military Dominion of France. It never was, however, intended as an Union for the Superintendence of the Internal Affairs of other States.
>
> Our Allies should in fairness understand that we are a power that must take our principle of action from those maxims, which a system of government strongly popular and national in its character, has irresistibly imposed upon us. We shall be found in our place when actual danger menaces the System of Europe, but this Country cannot, and will not, act upon abstract and speculative Principles of Precaution.

From Viscount Castlereagh's State Paper, 5 May 1820

Representative Principle This is the notion that the people, rather than having authority imposed upon them, are entitled to be represented in government. It is usually held that the best way of securing this is by an electoral system which enables the people to vote governments in or out of office

Q

1. *What does Castlereagh mean by 'the Representative Principle'?*
2. *In what ways does this extract illustrate the incompatibility between the Quadruple Alliance and the Holy Alliance?*

Castlereagh had never intended the Congress system to be a means of regulating the internal affairs of other nations. The purpose of the Quadruple Alliance, which he had created, was to defeat Napoleon and thereafter to prevent French military recovery. Castlereagh was not a supporter of the liberal ideas that were causing such concern to the absolutist regimes in Europe, but neither was he prepared to assist those regimes in crushing liberal movements in the name of what he called 'abstract Principles of Precaution'. France had been the enemy. But once France had been brought into the Quadruple Alliance in 1818 on British terms, Britain's essential objective of containing the French had been accomplished. Apart from its traditional wish to keep the Low Countries safe for commerce, Britain had no territorial interest in Europe. For the sake of its own security, Castlereagh's Britain wanted the continental balance of power to be preserved but, that consideration aside, there was no other reason for direct involvement in European politics.

Castlereagh took his own life in 1822. With the possible exception of the Prime Minister, Foreign Secretaries worked harder than any other members of the Cabinet. They were the ministers who routinely remained at their desks throughout the long parliamentary recesses. This daily grind proved highly stressful. It is thought that over-work deepened the depression from which he constantly suffered and drove him to suicide.

B *Canning as Foreign Secretary, 1822–7*

KEY ISSUE

How far did Canning diverge from his predecessor's policies?

George Canning's flair and extrovert style made him appear very dissimilar to the stolid and introspective Castlereagh whom he replaced in 1822. Many contemporaries, aware how different the new Foreign Minister was from his predecessor as an individual, expected there to be a major change in policy also. But this did not happen. It was the difference in manner rather than any real divergence of policy that provided the contrast. Castlereagh had treated diplomacy as a private, closed activity in which the public played no part. Canning, on the other hand, loved an audience and took every opportunity to speak publicly about his policies. Yet one of Canning's first acts was to publish Castlereagh's State Paper, which he then adopted as the basis of his own policy. He also approved the instructions which Castlereagh had drafted for the Verona Congress shortly before his death. This continuity set the pattern which Canning followed over the next five years. 1822 had not marked a major break in the conduct of Britain's foreign affairs.

Where there was a detectable difference was in the political circumstances in which the two men operated. Both Castlereagh and Canning had combined the office of Foreign Minister with that of Leader of the House of Commons. The latter post was critically important whenever the Prime Minister of the day happened to be in the House of Lords, as was the case with Lord Liverpool. Between 1815 and 1820, Castlereagh, as the Prime Minister's spokesman in the Commons, had had to deal with a series of domestic crises caused by the economic depression and the social unrest that accompanied it. Defending the government at a very difficult time domestically, while also representing Britain in foreign affairs, created a huge burden for Castlereagh. Even when attending the Vienna Congress in 1815, he was being urged by Liverpool to return home as soon as possible to reassert Government authority over an unruly House of Commons. Canning, in contrast, faced no such extreme pressures in the calmer domestic waters of the 1820s.

It was also the case that foreign affairs in Canning's time had a much clearer aspect. The task of reconstructing Europe had been achieved and the Congress system, as far as Britain was concerned, had ceased to function. The idea that Castlereagh had operated policy by means of the Congress system which Canning then chose to reject, has long been dismissed. Canning had no need to detach Britain from the Congress system; Castlereagh had already done that. The modern view among scholars is that Canning continued the line of approach laid down by

Castlereagh. Changes were minor and were matters of emphasis. Canning tended to be more sympathetic towards liberal movements in Europe; provided Britain's interests were not at risk, he was prepared to give such movements diplomatic backing and, on occasion, military support.

THE SPANISH RISING, 1822–3

Canning's immediate task was to deal with the situation created by the Holy Alliance's determination to intervene in Spain to restore absolute monarchy and destroy the liberal constitution set up there following a revolution in 1812. Adopting Castlereagh's plan precisely, Canning instructed his representative, the Duke of Wellington, to refuse to give Britain's agreement to the proposal that France directly assist the deposed Spanish monarchy and that the other powers give their 'moral support'. When a French army did enter Spain, Canning encouraged the constitutionalists to continue their resistance. They did so, but could not prevent the restoration of the Spanish King in 1823.

How did Canning react to the Spanish question?

THE SPANISH COLONIES, 1823–4

Canning's defeat over Spain came because he was not willing to interfere with military force. However, over the issue of the Spanish colonies in South America, which had declared their independence from Spain, Canning took a much stronger stance. He made it clear that Britain was prepared to resist with force any attempt to reimpose Spain's control over her former colonies. The difference of commitment is explained by economic motives. In the few years of the colonies' independence, their trade with Britain had become 15 times greater. Manifestly, it would not serve British commercial interests for the colonies to be returned to Spanish authority. In the face of Britain's resolve over this, France and Russia, which had been preparing to send forces to support Spain, backed off and the colonies were left to themselves.

Why did Canning take a stronger line over the Spanish colonies?

An historic aspect of this issue was the involvement of the USA. Many Americans were keen that their young country, which in the 1820s was still barely 50 years old, should assert itself internationally. In 1823 President Monroe gave formal expression to this mood by issuing what became known as **the Monroe Doctrine**. In this he warned the European powers that the new spirit of national independence in the Americas meant that the Europeans must abandon their claims to territory and dominance there. Canning was disappointed by Monroe's move. Having had talks with the President over the Spanish colonies, he had hoped that there would be a joint Anglo-American declaration. Nevertheless, he suppressed his hurt and announced that Britain, in the spirit of the Doctrine, would now extend diplomatic recognition to the Latin-American republics of Mexico, Buenos Aires (Argentina) and Colombia. This, he declared, marked the dawn of a new era in international relations. In a memorable turn of phrase Canning told the House of Commons, 'I have called the New World into existence to redress the balance of the old'.

The Monroe Doctrine, 1823

President Monroe declared that any encroachment by an outside power on the liberties of the newly independent republics in central or southern America would be viewed by the USA as 'the manifestation of an unfriendly disposition to the United States'. This was intended to convey to the world that the USA was now to be regarded as the armed protector of all the peoples of the Americas.

PORTUGAL, 1823–6

With the tide of events apparently running against the absolutists, Canning felt able to take a much tougher line over Portugal than he had previously over Spain. In Portugal, Prince Michael, supported by reactionary monarchists, was trying to overthrow his liberal father, King John. Canning gave the King his backing and sent a British fleet to Lisbon in 1824 to protect him. After lengthy political wrangling between the rival Portuguese factions had failed to produce a clear result, Canning made an even stronger show of force by dispatching 5000 British ground troops to Portugal in 1827. The outcome of such pressure was that the Portuguese agreed to the succession of John's grand-daughter, Maria, and adopted a liberal constitution for the country.

Q *How did Canning approach the Portuguese question?*

THE GREEK WAR OF INDEPENDENCE, 1821–30

In 1821, the Greeks had begun a sustained national revolt against domination by Turkey. Canning's natural inclinations made him a supporter of the Greeks in their struggle against Turkish control. He belonged to an educated class that had been brought up on Greek history and had been trained to view Ancient Greece as the pinnacle of civilisation. But Canning was not free to follow his inclinations. He was confronted by a dilemma which consistently worried the makers of British foreign policy throughout the nineteenth century. The problem was this: to support Greece might further weaken the tottering Turkish Empire and thus encourage Russian expansion into areas of British interest. This, for Britain, was the heart of the Eastern Question. When, in 1825, the Russians moved their forces into southern Greece to save the population from being massacred by Turkish forces, Britain's worst fears seemed about to be realised.

Q *Why did the Greek struggle against the Turks present Britain with a dilemma?*

To save the situation, Canning attempted to achieve a compromise. He put forward a scheme by which the Greeks would stay nominally under Turkish authority but would, in practice, be granted all the rights and liberties of self-government. A Franco-British-Russian treaty based on Canning's proposal was signed in London in July 1827. The agreement required the Turks and Greeks to observe an armistice. An allied fleet was sent to the waters off southern Greece to keep the peace. However, in a confused sequence of events, fighting broke out between the

See page 320 for further explanation of the Eastern Question allied ships and the Turkish fleet in Navarino Bay. This resulted in the total destruction of the Turkish vessels and effectively won the war for the Greeks.

Canning, however, did not live to see the outcome since he died a few months before the Navarino battle. Wellington, who succeeded him as Prime Minister, was faced by a rush of events which involved a further outbreak of war between Russia and Turkey, with the Turks again being defeated. Wellington judged that, in such a situation, to continue with the odd notion of a semi-independent Greece would simply invite Russia to interfere continually. He decided it was best that Greece be granted the status of a fully independent state. This was accepted internationally at the London conference of 1830 which recognised Greece as a sovereign nation.

One of Canning's last recorded statements, made shortly before died, referred to the international situation. He remarked, 'Things are getting back to a wholesome state again – every nation for itself and God for us all'. He was being deliberately ironic, but his observation provides an apt commentary on the period 1815–30. The congress system had failed to establish itself as a mechanism for controlling international relations; national self-interest remained the motivating force in foreign affairs.

4 ↪ BIBLIOGRAPHY

ARTICLES

G. Goodlad 'Liberal and "High" Tories in the Age of Lord Liverpool', *History Review*, November 1995.

Eric Evans 'The Premiership of Lord Liverpool' *History Review*, April 1990.

John Plowright 'Lord Liverpool and "Repression" in Regency England'. *History Review*, September 1997.

BOOKS FOR AS/A LEVEL STUDENTS

Vyvyen Brendon *The Age of Reform, 1820–50*, Hodder & Stoughton, 1994.

John Plowright *Regency England: the Age of Lord Liverpool*, Lancaster Pamphlets, 1996. These are both excellent short studies for the beginner.

Eric Evans *Britain before the Reform Act: Politics and Society 1815–1832*, Longman, 1989, examines the politics of the age of Lord Liverpool.

W. D. Rubinstein *Britain's Century A Political and Social History 1815–1905*, Arnold, 1998, contains very helpful chapters on party politics before 1830.

FURTHER READING

E. P. Thompson *The Making of the English Working Class*, Penguin, 1968, is a long book but all students should dip into this controversial and highly influential study, which presents the case for the 'losing' side in the Liverpool years.

J. Dinwiddy *Radicalism and Reform in Britain 1780–1850*, Hambledon,

1992, and J. Cookson, *Lord Liverpool's Administration 1815–1822*, Scottish Academic Press, 1983, offer more measured if less dramatic accounts of developments in this period.

Anthony Seldon (Ed.) *How Tory Governments Fall: The Tory Party in Power since 1783*, Fontana, 1996, contains a very readable and up-to-date treatment of the 1815–30 period.

George Kitson Clark *The Making of Victorian England*, Methuen, 1962, remains a key analysis which has inspired many other writers on the period.

Norman Gash *Lord Liverpool*, Weidenfeld, 1984, an important biography by an outstanding modern scholar, helps repair the relative neglect suffered by its subject.

5 ∽ STRUCTURED AND ESSAY QUESTIONS

The following questions relate to the separate sections in this chapter. The questions are closely linked to the Key Issues that are there to guide you through the material you are reading. So, in preparing your answers, do look back to the relevant Key Issues. They will point you towards the information and ideas that you need.

A *Structured questions for AS level*
1. (a) Why did the Corn Laws arouse such intense opposition outside Parliament?
   (b) 'Rulers who neither see, nor feel, nor know.' How fitting do you find this as a description of Lord Liverpool's Government between 1815 and 1822?
2. (a) What were the most important reforms introduced by the Liberal Tories between 1822 and 1827?
   (b) 'It was not a change of attitude but a change in circumstances that enabled the Liberal Tories to introduce reform after 1822.' To what extent is this an acceptable explanation?
3. (a) What were the main aims in foreign policy of: (i) Castlereagh, and (ii) Canning?
   (b) How far do you agree with the view that the foreign policies pursued by Castlereagh and Canning differed in detail but not in principle?

B *Essay Questions for A2*
1. To what extent was the Tory Government responsible for the social unrest that occurred in the period 1815–21?
2. Why did the Catholic Emancipation question prove so politically damaging to the Tories in the late 1820s?
3. Examine the view that 'what is surprising is not how little but how much Lord Liverpool's ministry achieved in its 15 years of office'.
4. Why, by the time of his death in 1822, had Castlereagh lost faith in the Congress system?

5. 'British foreign policy under both Castlereagh and Canning had no other motive than the protection of British interests.' How acceptable do you find this claim?

You will note that all the questions in the B section require judgement and opinion on your part. Factual knowledge on its own is not enough. Taking Question 1 as an example, the vital aspect to appreciate is that the questioner assumes that you are informed about the unrest of the period and the response to it of Liverpool's Government. What is needed from you is a reasoned assessment of the Government's responsibility for the troubles. In preparing your answer, you should, of course list the main facts. That will provide the basis on which to build your argument. Then, to help put the question in perspective, set yourself a list of supplementary questions. The following should be useful. Did the Government start the troubles or simply respond to them? That is to say, did the Government's economic policies (or lack of them) create the conditions from which the unrest grew? Even if the Government did not start the unrest, did its policies make the problem worse? Did the Government show too little understanding of the needs of ordinary people? Were its policies too repressive? What alternative courses of action, if any, could it have taken? Did the Government exaggerate the scale of the dangers which the country faced? The views of historians, such as E. P. Thompson and Norman Gash, would be worth quoting in this context. Notice that you are being asked, 'to what extent?' This provides an opportunity for you to show some subtlety. You should aim to provide a balanced answer by setting the scale and seriousness of the troubles against the range of options open to the Government.

3

The Government and the People: The Movement for Parliamentary Reform, 1815–32

INTRODUCTION

The period 1815–50 saw the appearance of a series of mass-based political protest movements. These were supported by an active press and drew together a large number of followers through a rich variety of political organisations. Undoubtedly, the most spectacular expressions of the strength of feeling were the many mass meetings held throughout this period, often consisting of tens of thousands of people, at which Parliament was called upon to reform itself into a more democratic body. Within a few years of the end of the Napoleonic Wars a loosely defined political programme had begun to emerge, which successive movements made their own. Among the many changes in the political system that were called for by these movements were:

● that all men over the age of 21 should have the vote (universal manhood suffrage)
● that there should be a shorter time between parliaments (to increase the number of elections)
● that voting should become a private matter by means of the secret ballot (to ensure that working people could vote without interference from their employers or landlords)
● that particular forms of taxation, particularly the hated Corn Laws of 1815, should be reduced.

Added together, these measures represented a demand for a dramatic change in the way the country was governed. Because of the scale of the support and the critical nature of the programme that emerged, this is often referred to as a period of popular **radicalism**. This public debate about how the country should be run, would continue throughout the nineteenth century, and it will be traced in subsequent chapters via the Chartist movement (Chapter 5), the creation of a mass electorate (Chapter 8) and the emergence of the Labour Party (Chapter 12).

In the years 1815–32 we can see both the origins of popular radicalism and its apparent success in 1832 when, what is often known as, the 'Great Reform Act' was passed. This significantly changed the structure

radicalism the belief in the need for radical, or fundamental, reform

of the electorate but it was far from being a 'great' Act for the thousands of working people who had campaigned for reform in these years. For them, the Reform Act of 1832 was a huge disappointment and a spur to further reform activity.

In this chapter we will explore the radical movements of these years and the response to them of the governments of the day. In particular we will concentrate on two significant sub-periods, 1815–20 and 1830–2, when the call for political change was intense and the social order appeared to be threatened. The growing participation of working people in politics will form the main focus of the chapter.

But first we must turn to the structure of politics at the start of the period and the arguments that were marshalled at the time both for and against the unreformed system.

1 ⌐ 'OLD CORRUPTION': THE UNREFORMED PARLIAMENTARY SYSTEM

British government revolved around the monarch, the House of Lords, and the House of Commons. The House of Commons controlled finances, although the monarch and the Lords possessed the right to reject (veto) legislation introduced by the Lower House. As the centre-piece of the system, the Commons drew its authority from its elected status. British government, therefore, was focused on a body, the Commons, which saw itself as representative of the nation as a whole. Yet just how representative of the people of the United Kingdom was the House of Commons before 1832?

> **KEY ISSUES**
>
> *What was the British electoral system like before 1832?*

A *Representation*

After 1800, there were 658 Members of Parliament sitting in the Commons. The English MPs made up well over three-quarters of this number. Four of these members represented the universities of Oxford and Cambridge. The rest of the English members came from two types of **constituencies**, the counties and the Parliamentary boroughs. The size of the electorate in each of these constituencies varied greatly as did the nature of the voting qualification (franchise). In the English counties, which were responsible for electing a total of 82 MPs, the vote was held by individuals owning freehold land to the value of 40 shillings (£2). This franchise dated from 1430 and the changing value of money from that time meant that most county electorates were large. They varied from Rutland with 800 voters to Yorkshire with a massive 23 000 electors.

The Parliamentary boroughs were mostly towns which had been granted the right to elect MPs at some time, often in the distant past. These were numerically the most significant of all constituencies since they accounted for 403 of the total MPs in the House of Commons. In

> **constituencies** The units into which the country was divided for elections. In England, each county constituency and most borough constituencies returned two MPs

the boroughs the franchise varied widely and was often of antique origin. For example, in the 'scot and lot' boroughs, the franchise was held by any man who paid the poor rates. Here the electorate was often numerous; for example the borough of Westminster had 10 000 voters. Yet 24 of these boroughs had less than 600 voters, the most extreme case being Gatton in Surrey. This consisted of only six houses, the owner of which was free to nominate two MPs. In the burgage boroughs, the vote was held by virtue of ownership of particular pieces of land and none of the 35 constituencies in this category possessed more than 300 electors. In fact, Old Sarum in Wiltshire possessed no voters at all. In this case, whoever owned the piece of land, which the radical journalist William Cobbett referred to as the 'Accursed Hill', also nominated two MPs. In Dunwich, a freeman borough in Suffolk, few of the 30 men who qualified to vote by virtue of their status as freemen of the borough, actually lived in the constituency. One could hardly blame them because most of Dunwich had long since disappeared under the North Sea as a result of coastal erosion.

The main features of Parliamentary representation might be summarised as follows:

- most MPs in the House of Commons were elected by the English boroughs
- over half of these boroughs had less than 600 electors and the majority were located in the south of the country
- the large towns of the Midlands and the north like Manchester, Leeds and Birmingham, which grew from the mid-eighteenth century as a result of industrialisation, were often unrepresented except by their county members.

B *Corruption*

There was also widespread concern at the apparent corruption of the electoral procedure and this was most marked in the constituencies with small electorates. In the absence of a secret ballot, voters were, it was argued, open to bribery and intimidation. Tenants might vote for their landlord's choice of candidate to curry favour or to escape eviction. Others simply sold their vote to the highest bidder. Seats were also marketable commodities and were bought and sold openly. In boroughs with small electorates the process of controlling elections was easiest and these were termed '**pocket boroughs**', or '**rotten boroughs**'. In 1827 one authority estimated that 276 seats were owned by individuals who were effectively in a position to appoint the MP. Ownership of a borough was highly prized. It showed social status, and possibly material rewards in the form of government positions or pensions, for the owner and his dependants. Involvement in politics was expensive and, it was felt, becoming more so as time went on. The 'rotten borough' of Gatton, for example, changed hands for the last time in 1830 for £180 000.

pocket boroughs were in the control, hence the pocket, of a particular patron, usually a large landowner

rotten boroughs had few or no constituents yet returned at least one MP to Parliament

Have historians represented the old system fairly?

The unreformed system was not, it has often been argued, a system of active voters, voting for the person and party which they felt would best govern the country. Rather, this was an electorate that could be manipulated, cajoled and purchased. But this common interpretation of the pre-reform electorate has been robustly challenged by Frank O'Gorman in a detailed study of the electoral history of the period before 1832, *Voters, Patrons and Parties* (1989). The unreformed system has, he argues, been misunderstood by modern historians applying their contemporary perspectives. In charting the growth of a mass electorate in the nineteenth and twentieth centuries, historians demonised, to the point of distortion, the unreformed system by which it had been preceded.

O'Gorman draws our attention to the high level of activity that surrounded elections in the eighteenth and early nineteenth centuries. Although set in a national context, general elections were an expression of the nature of local authority. Through them, local elites attempted to maintain their position within the community, by securing the election of the members of their choice. Nevertheless, in order to do, this they had to secure the support of local interests, as represented by the electorate. Elections also often involved the active participation of non-electors, who expressed their views through public meetings and rituals. Elections were not just token gestures or excuses for excessive indulgence as they are often portrayed: elections were a serious business in the unreformed system. Whilst voters were open to persuasion, elections were not closed affairs whose outcomes were foregone conclusions. Rather, voters saw themselves as exercising a high degree of independent choice. From this point of view, the electoral system may be seen to have contributed significantly to the acknowledged stability of eighteenth and early nineteenth century Britain.

O'Gorman's work is helpful in a number of ways. Above all, it reminds us that in order to judge the unreformed system we have to appreciate the way it worked at the time. Clearly, by 1832, many voices were being raised against the old system. Nevertheless, O'Gorman's work helps us to understand the difficulties of changing a system that had always fulfilled an important role in establishing and maintaining the **status quo**. He helps us to see that in criticising the old system, contemporaries (and historians after them) have played up its worst aspects and overlooked its stabilising role in a pre-industrial society. By 1830, however, society had changed and this needed to be reflected in the political system.

ANALYSIS

KEY ISSUE

In what ways were different social groups represented, or not, by the unreformed electoral system?

status quo the existing situation

PICTURE 4   *A view of the unreformed system:* The Election at Eatenswill, *an illustration from* The Pickwick Papers *by Charles Dickens, 1836*

Q

1. *To which aspects of unreformed elections does the print draw attention?*
2. *Why did the Victorians stress the excesses of the old system when they looked back?*
3. *How might this have influenced the views of historians?*

C   *Contemporary views of the political system*

For many at the time, the best argument in favour of the existing system was that it appeared to have worked well for generations. In 1790, the respected Whig statesman, Edmund Burke, expressed his opposition to the democratic forces associated with the French Revolution, which had occurred the previous year. His *Reflections on the Revolution in France*, was effectively a defence of the existing British system. For him, Parliament was a representative body: a point that he made as follows:

KEY ISSUE

How did people at the time justify the system to themselves?

We know that the British House of Commons, without shutting its doors to any merit in any class, is ... filled with everything illustrious in rank, in descent, in hereditary and in acquired opulence, in cultivated talents, in military, civil, naval, and politic distinction that the country can afford.

He argued that the system had withstood the test of time, and that it worked, performing an important stabilising function at both a national and a local level. Government, it was argued, should represent, not numbers of population, as we should expect, but rather the significant 'interest groups' in the nation, such as Land, the City of London, the Church (of England), the Universities and the ancient towns that had been given their own local government in medieval times (corporate towns). If these interest groups were represented at Westminster then, the argument ran, the nation was represented. Most importantly, the rich would represent the poor. Very few among the wealthy disputed this definition of representative government. However, after 1815, it was being increasingly recognised that industrialisation had created a *new* interest group in the form of the industrial middle class. Without a sizeable reform of the system, this interest group would remain effectively excluded from the political system. It is important to note that when reform did come, in 1832, it was designed to rectify this problem and not to remodel the system on fundamentally different principles.

The period from 1815 to 1820 saw the origins and growth of popular radicalism, which drew its support from the working community. This was based on a very different analysis of politics and representative government. Far from arguing that the existing system needed only to be extended to include the interests of the new industrial elite in the large towns, popular radicals recommended far-reaching change. Their arguments had been perhaps most effectively made by Thomas Paine in his book *The Rights of Man* (1791). This was published to counter Burke's earlier defence of the system. Drawing on personal experience of both the American and French Revolutions, Paine argued that the corruption of the British Parliamentary system lay in its failure to represent 'the people' in any direct sense. He claimed that, while most of the country was crippled by high levels of taxation, the small minority who controlled politics lived off the proceeds of taxation. This state of affairs was perpetuated by the restriction of the right to vote to a small section of the population. The vote, he argued, was a 'natural right', to which every man was entitled and which had been taken away at some point in the past. If this right was restored it would lead to the regaining of other important freedoms. Among these were the freedoms of expression, assembly, conscience and equality before the law.

Paine's book was said to have sold 200 000 copies by 1793. The Government, recognising its subversive nature (particularly in the light of revolutionary events in France), declared it to be illegal. This act of censorship only served to strengthen Paine's points about the loss of

Q

1. What does Burke mean by the phrase 'without shutting its doors to any merit in any class'?
2. Which groups are left out of Burke's list and why?

KEY ISSUE

What was the radicals' vision of an alternative political system?

The Rights of Woman?

Paine argued his case in terms of men only. It fell to another writer, Mary Wollstonecraft, to point out in her book, *A Vindication of the Rights of Woman* (1792), that if there really were 'natural rights' then women were also entitled to exercise them. This claim attracted little attention in this period.

Q

How do the views of Burke and Paine differ on who should be represented?

fundamental freedoms, and this increased the book's popularity. At the heart of Paine's argument was the notion that ordinary people were entitled to participate in national politics.

KEY ISSUE

Why were so many ordinary people involved in political protest in this period?

2 ⌐ THE GROWTH OF POPULAR RADICALISM, 1815–20

A *The effect of the war*

During the war with France (1793–1815) the governments of the day succeeded in restricting the radical supporters of Paine's views to small, isolated, groups in centres like Manchester, London, Norwich, Sheffield and Birmingham. This changed with the end of the war in 1815. British industry had grown in response to a wartime economy. This often meant the introduction of machinery, or the employment of less skilled workers, perhaps child workers. This re-organisation to meet increased demand caused resentment among the workforce and the **Combination Acts**, which were meant to make unions of workers illegal, were often unable to prevent strikes and wage demands. In Lancashire and Yorkshire, in the years 1811–13, working men destroyed the new machines being introduced into the textile industries. In Nottinghamshire, in the same years, stocking weavers who agreed to work for employers at lower than trade society prices were attacked. The self-styled 'Luddites', in these areas, claimed to be following the orders of

Combination Acts
A series of Acts passed in 1799 to prevent the growth of revolutionary movements. The Acts made it illegal for two or more workers to combine in order to agitate for higher wages or better working conditions. In effect, they made trade union activity illegal. The Acts were repealed in 1824.

HISTORIANS' DEBATE

Popular radicalism

It is the involvement of large numbers of working people in these developments that is the main source of discussion and speculation among historians. Some historians share the view of many contemporaries, that mass participation in radical politics was largely the result of hunger, initially induced by the end of the wars and subsequently worsened by the instability of the new industrial economy as it grew. This notion of 'hunger politics' is, however, contested by others who point to a fundamental shift in outlook on the part of the working community in these years and relate this to the wider changes associated with the Industrial Revolution. In particular, Edward Thompson, in his book *The Making of the English Working Class* (1963), has argued that the period from 1780–1832 saw the conversion of the highly fragmented 'labouring poor' into a far more coherent and unified 'working class'. Thompson argued that the role of the post-war period was central to the creation of a new kind of social formation; a class with a common experience of economic change and a shared position on radical politics.

the mythical leader General Ned Ludd, but their actions were not co-ordinated by any one leader. Rather, these outbreaks reflected a fairly widespread concern that industrialisation was damaging the way of life of well-established working communities. The Luddites were suppressed by military intervention and the declaration, in 1812, that machine smashing was a capital offence. In 1813, 16 Yorkshire Luddites were executed for attacks on factories and the murder of an employer.

The end of the war with France in 1815 ushered in a period of economic depression. As government contracts for uniforms and armaments fell off, so the demand for textiles and for coal and iron dropped. As troops were demobilised so the cost of **poor relief** rose dramatically. The labouring population found itself underemployed. Parliament, consisting largely of landowners, passed the Corn Laws of 1815 prohibiting the importation of foreign corn until home-grown corn reached the price of 80 shillings (£4) per quarter. This was intended to ensure that the price of corn remained high, and therefore landowners' profits and rents remained high. It had the effect of raising the cost of a loaf of bread. Increasing numbers of working people found themselves dependent upon parish relief for the basic necessities of life.

poor relief aid for the poor, distributed by the parishes

HAMPDEN CLUBS 1812–17

The immediate post-war years also saw a growth of political radicalism which was inspired by the writings of Thomas Paine. Often the lead was taken by 'gentlemen reformers', members of the upper class who, unlike most of their social equals, accepted the need for a really extensive Parliamentary reform. For example, John Cartwright established the **Hampden Club** in London in 1812, to agitate for what was called a 'general suffrage' (the right to vote). Cartwright was a landed gentleman from Lincolnshire. His political writings, from the 1770s onwards, expressed the view that manhood suffrage and other rights had been guaranteed under a Saxon constitution and had been lost at the time of the Norman conquest in 1066. The London Hampden Club never attracted the 'respectable' support he had hoped for; most members of his own class still feared a re-enactment of the French Revolution on British soil. Nevertheless, the idea was taken up enthusiastically outside London. Over the next few years Hampden clubs were set up by working people in towns and villages in the industrial areas of Lancashire, the Midlands, and Yorkshire. They were open to any man able to pay a penny a week subscription, this money being devoted to the publication of pamphlets and broadsheets supporting a programme which included universal suffrage, annual parliaments and the abolition of the Corn Laws.

Hampden Club
This was named after John Hampden, the seventeenth-century Parliamentarian and supporter of Oliver Cromwell against Charles I

SPA-FIELDS MEETINGS 1816

In November and December 1816 Henry Hunt held three large public meetings in Spa-Fields, London, calling upon Parliament to introduce universal manhood **suffrage** and extensive Parliamentary reform. Hunt, the son of a Wiltshire farmer, was the leading radical of his day

suffrage the right to vote

and a good example of a new breed of radical politician, the platform orator. Hunt, more than any other radical, popularised the large-scale, open-air, public meeting as a strategy for expressing the strength of radical opinion. The intention behind such meetings was to exercise the right to petition Parliament to request that it address their concerns. But, at the second of the Spa-Fields meetings, a part of the crowd rioted. The following January the unpopular Prince Regent was mobbed while returning from the opening of Parliament and the window of his coach was smashed. Lord Liverpool's Tory administration, fearful of the development of the Hampden clubs in the provinces, used these two incidents to introduce repressive legislation, which became known as the 'Gagging Acts'. *Habeas corpus*, under which an arrested person has to be charged within 24 hours or be released, was suspended for four months, thus allowing arrest and imprisonment on suspicion only, and restrictions on public meetings were extended.

MARCH OF THE BLANKETEERS 1817

This did little to discourage the growth of radical organisations. The parliamentary session of 1817 saw the submission of nearly 700 petitions for reform, from localities throughout the country, as part of a national campaign organised by Sir Francis Burdett. A gentleman reformer, Burdett was a Leicestershire landowner who had been in France from 1790 to 1793 and witnessed the French Revolution at first hand. As MP for Westminster, he led the small group of members who supported the cause of radical reform in Parliament. The 1817 campaign demonstrated the strength of support in the country as a whole. In March 1817, a group of Lancashire weavers set out to march to London to present their petition personally, intending to hold meetings along the way and to draw in numbers for a tumultuous entry to the capital. This was the 'March of the Blanketeers', so-called because each man carried only a blanket and provisions for the journey. Fearing the implications of even an unarmed march on London, the Government ordered the arrest of the leaders and the marchers were turned back.

PENTRIDGE (OR DERBYSHIRE) UPRISING 1817

As the radical movement gathered strength, it built itself around peaceful and constitutional strategies, though there were those among the radicals who advocated the more direct methods of confrontation and revolution. The Government's repressive legislation in 1817 drove the movement underground and increased the fear of a violent uprising. In order to counteract this, the Home Office employed an *agent provocateur*, a spy code-named 'Oliver', to travel through the country and to make contact with radical groups. He was to pretend to be planning exactly the rebellion which the Government feared and in this way draw local activists into the open. This resulted in the tragedy of the 'Pentridge Uprising'. On the night of 9 June 1817 (the date Oliver had set for his 'uprising') 200–300 armed men set out from the remote weaving village of Pentridge in Derbyshire, intent on taking Nottingham, as agreed with Oliver. In the process a local farmer was killed and the would-be rebels were easily rounded-up. The trial and subsequent execution of the leaders exposed details of the Government's involvement and this led to a public outcry. The last words on the scaffold of William Turner, one of the rebels, were 'This is the work of the Government and Oliver'.

PETERLOO 1819

Despite the repressive measures of Liverpool's Government, the movement for reform grew, particularly in the industrial districts. In August 1819, Hunt called a meeting in St. Peter's Fields, Manchester. Estimates of the numbers involved varied enormously, but somewhere between 50 000 and 200 000 people from the towns and villages throughout Lancashire marched to the meeting. In the event the meeting was broken up by the Manchester Yeomanry, attempting to arrest Hunt, under orders from the magistrates. The Yeomanry was a volunteer cavalry force drawn from the Manchester middle class, mostly businessmen and shopkeepers. Their inexperience in dealing with large crowds, as well as their resentment at the nature of the meeting, showed as they panicked and began cutting at the crowd with their sabres. In the ensuing confusion 11 members of the crowd were killed and over 400 were injured in what swiftly became known as the 'Peterloo Massacre' (an ironic reference to the Battle of Waterloo in 1815). The reformers protested that the presence of small children at the meeting showed its peaceful intent. The Home Secretary, Lord Sidmouth, praised the magistrates for what he called their 'prompt, decisive and efficient measures for the preservation of public tranquility.' As a result the public outcry that followed was directed as much at the Government as it was at the Manchester authorities.

There is some speculation among historians as to whether this should be seen as a premeditated attack or simply a piece of policing which got out of hand as a result of the inexperience of local officials. There is no doubt, however, that the telling and re-telling of the story of the 'Peterloo Massacre' did much to popularise the radical cause, providing a clear-cut example that Government at local and national level did not represent the interests of the 'people'. It also enabled the Government to depict the radicals as violent Revolutionaries. George Cruikshank's cartoon (Picture 5) used the Cap of Liberty (the hat worn by French revolutionaries) as well as some frankly sexual symbolism to suggest that radicalism was an evil force despoiling the purity of the British constitution (as depicted by Britannia) under the guise of peaceful reform.

THE SIX ACTS 1819 AND
THE CATO STREET CONSPIRACY 1820

In the event, it was Liverpool's Government that took the initiative by passing what were known as the Six Acts. These Acts:

- suppressed the popular movement by restricting public meetings
- tightened the definition of seditious libel (to restrict what radical papers could publish about the Government)

PICTURE 5   Death or Liberty *by George Cruikshank, December 1819*

> **Q**
> *What imagery does Cruikshank use to depict radicalism as a threat?*

● increased the tax on newspapers (to hit the working-class readership of radical journals)
● extended the right to enter and search private premises.

Successful prosecutions of radicals increased dramatically, in both London and the provinces. This broke up the reform organisation, whilst an improvement in trade, in the early 1820s, eroded popular support for the cause. The arrest and execution, in 1820, of Arthur Thistlewood and his three collaborators for their part in the desperate 'Cato Street Conspiracy', which plotted to kill the members of the Cabinet, marks the end of this period of agitation.

As far as the reformers were concerned the popular movement had, by 1820, gained a political programme and also a taste of firm opposition from a determined government. It was the vulnerability of the movement to repression that was the great lesson of the 1815–20 period. 'Oliver' and 'Peterloo' made subsequent movements, like Chartism, fear a direct attack by the State. Although the post-war movement had attracted its share of gentleman-reformers, such as Cartwright and Burdett, its strength lay in the support of artisans (craftsmen) and other workers in the towns and villages of the industrial districts. The new middle class took little part in the campaign, fearing the breakdown of law and order, and failing to share the radicals' enthusiasm for votes for the property-less. The ease with which Liverpool's Government contained the campaign also emphasised the fact that a popular movement would always be vulnerable to repression unless it could muster the support of the wealthy. Having learned this lesson the hard way, the radicals endeavoured, during the Reform Bill campaign of 1830–2 to maintain a good working alliance with the middle class supporters of the Bill.

ANALYSIS

Why did the Radicals not resort to physical force?

In his biography of Henry Hunt, *Orator Hunt* (1985), John Belchem argues that the radicals failed to capitalise on Peterloo, largely because the leadership were so committed to legal strategies and refused to contemplate the use of force. His view is that the reformers demonstrated a 'debilitating obsession with legitimacy.' By this, he means that the commitment of the radicals to peaceful protest undermined their effectiveness. This highlights an important point about the radical tradition as it emerged in these years. In the main, the popular movement for radical reform of Parliament utilised peaceful means to achieve its aim: for example, the mass demonstration of public support, the press, the petition to Parliament, and the public defence in open court when accused. These strategies were all inherited by the Chartists (see Chapter 5) and a number of historians would agree with Belchem's point that this provided a fatal weakness for the movement. Alternatively, of course, we should recognise that the British army was strong, battle-tested and loyal. The Chartist leader, Feargus O'Connor, was later to warn constantly against armed opposition for the simple reason that a citizen army would not succeed against such a trained force. In addition, any resort to force enabled the Government to depict the radicals as French revolutionaries, as shown in the Cruikshank print from 1819 (Picture 5).

HISTORIANS' DEBATE

Was the growth of political protest from 1815–20 simply the product of hunger?

Before the last decade of the eighteenth century it is difficult to see any great involvement in radical politics by the labouring poor. The most common form of protest was the food riot, which was a swift and direct way of making feelings known to the authorities. So, where did the crowds come from to fill St Peter's Field in August 1819? How did the radical journalist William Cobbett manage to find a huge readership for his *Political Register* from such unpromising material? We may identify two main ways of interpreting the growth of popular radicalism. These are presented in the table below. At the heart of the controversy lies the issue of what the labouring poor were really capable of: was working-class support for political reform simply an instinctive reaction to hunger and despair or was it a reasoned response?

Political protest was primarily a response to hunger	**Political protest was primarily the response of an educated and increasingly cohesive 'working class'**
The war was followed by a trade depression and hunger. This made working people inclined to accept the arguments of the radical leaders.	In the period from 1780–1832 the non-political 'labouring poor' became the radical 'working class'.
It is indisputable that this, and all subsequent mass-based political movements, took place during times of hunger. The reform Bill agitation 1830–2 and the main periods of Chartist strength, 1838–9, 1842 and 1848 all coincided with economic distress. The historian, W.W. Rostow, has demonstrated this by means of a 'social tension chart' by which he is able to correlate closely the development of protest movements and the high price of bread.	At exactly the moment when the economic changes of the Industrial Revolution were having their maximum effect, the political ideas of the French Revolution became available.
Behind this approach to the popular reform movement lies a view of the labouring poor which stresses its lack of formal education and also its regional fragmentation. For a popular movement to be really cohesive it would have had to unite, within a national identity, groups of people whose loyalties and vision went no further than their locality and their trade.	Combined with the repressive actions of the wartime and post-war governments, this created a common experience for working people which enabled them to empathise with one another despite the regional or trade variations in their daily lives. The labouring poor had adopted a political outlook; that is to say, the radical movements which first emerged in 1815–20 were a deeply-felt expression of the way the working class now saw the world.
The repeated failure of popular radical initiatives to achieve universal manhood suffrage and other aims, can be seen to reinforce the point that working people did not form a unified block of public opinion that any government felt it had to recognise.	The view that working people were incapable of understanding political debate underestimates their capabilities. The extent of the readership of the radical press suggests a higher level of literacy within the working community than is sometimes recognised.
	Hunger was a particularly good political educator; a political system which cannot ensure the necessities of life for its workforce advertises itself as the object of reform. The result of the twin experiences of social change and political repression brought into being an articulate and politically active working class.

LIBRARY UNIVERSITY OF CHESTER

Norman McCord argues in his book *British History 1815–1906* (Oxford, 1991) that:

> In a society in which farm labourers and domestic servants provided the largest elements among the workers, in which many workers lived in small, locally oriented communities, in which many workers worked long hours for low wages, and in which communications and the level of literacy were still limited, there was not much in the way of promising material for class conflict on a broad scale.

Edward Thompson argues in his book, *The Making of the English Working Class* (1963) that:

> In the period between 1780 and 1832 most English working people came to feel an identity of interests as between themselves and as against their rulers and employers.

He attempts to free the working class of the time from what he calls 'the enormous **condescension** of posterity'.

Liberal historians, tend to stress the points of mutual agreement between social groups as being the really important moments in any historical period.

From historians with this point of view, the feeling is that Thompson has overstated the potential for independent action as a cohesive class by a fragmented workforce.

Left-wing or Marxist historians, focus on class conflict, seeing the most significant historical moments as those points of conflict between working people and their rulers where both sides acted in united ways.

For historians with this point of view, liberal history takes a very condescending view of the working class.

condescension To take a superior and patronising attitude

3 ～ THE REFORM BILL CAMPAIGN

A *Political changes 1820–30*

Lord Liverpool, who was Prime Minister from 1812 until 1827 (he died in 1828), remained implacably opposed to any radical reform of Parliament despite the extensive post-war popular movement. He did accept, however, that the growing middle class, and the changing economic basis of the country, would have to be recognised. The notion of 'Liberal Toryism' is sometimes applied to the Government in the years after 1822 while the period before is generally seen as a different, reactionary, phase of the administration. In fact, Liverpool saw these two approaches as being closely related. To maintain aristocratic control, in the face of change, he sought to uphold law and order, by containing working-class discontent, and to placate the growing industrial middle-class interest in a way that fell short of Parliamentary reform.

Q

1. *What does McCord mean by 'class conflict'? Why does he see so little material for class conflict at this time?*
2. *How does Thompson show that he opposes McCord's view?*

CRISIS IN THE TORY PARTY

Despite the beneficial effect of 'Liberal Toryism' upon trade in the 1820s, the issue of Parliamentary reform would not go away. In 1823, an Irish barrister, named Daniel O'Connell, formed the Catholic Association, in Ireland, to campaign for the right of Roman Catholics to enter Parliament (see page 268). Then a trade depression, from 1827, revived middle-class demands to be represented in government by men of their own class. Liverpool's death seemed to open up the possibility

KEY ISSUE

Why did the movement for Parliamentary reform re-emerge in the late 1820s?

of change. Nevertheless, attempts to use private members' bills to disenfranchise the 'rotten boroughs' of Penryn and East Retford, and transfer their seats to Manchester and Birmingham, failed. Clearly, the time had come for a more general measure that the Government would sponsor and the House of Commons would support, and this point was increasingly accepted across the country. One notable exception to this feeling was the Duke of Wellington, who became Prime Minister in 1828 following very brief periods in that office by George Canning and Viscount Goderich. In 1828 the Test and Corporations Acts were repealed, thus lifting the restrictions on Nonconformists entering Parliament. This was followed by a protracted, and for the Tories, damaging battle over Roman Catholic emancipation. Backed by the Catholic Association, O'Connell was elected MP for County Clare in Ireland in 1828, directly challenging the law which debarred Roman Catholics from Parliament. Such was the intensity of the agitation that, fearing civil war, Wellington's Government reluctantly supported emancipation, which was achieved in 1829. (The divisions which this led to in the Tory party are discussed further in Chapter 2.)

The issue of Catholic emancipation put the Tory party under considerable internal stress. Yet the pressure was building for a further reform, to adjust the franchise to recognise formally the industrial and commercial interest. This was further than Wellington was prepared to take his party and he was forced to resign in November 1830.

B *The Whig Reform Bill*

The Whigs, in opposition almost continuously since 1784, saw their chance to seize and retain power. Under the leadership of Earl Grey they formed a government and introduced a Reform Bill. This planned to redistribute parliamentary seats from a number of rotten boroughs to new industrial districts and, at the same time, introduce a uniform £10 householder franchise in all boroughs. By this, men who owned a house rated at the value of £10 a year would be able to vote. Grey was a wealthy landowner who, unlike Wellington, understood how widespread the call for reform had become. But there was a good deal of opposition from the Commons and Grey's first bill passed its second reading, in March 1831, by only one vote (it was then defeated in the Committee stage). Following this, Grey persuaded the king to dissolve Parliament so he might seek support from the country in a general election. The Whigs were re-elected, on a reform platform, by a large majority of over 130 seats.

Grey took this as a **mandate** to re-introduce reform and a second Reform Bill passed through the Commons in July 1831. Yet it is worth bearing in mind that, however revolutionary and threatening the Whigs' proposals were seen to be amongst the landed classes, Grey had no wish to change the *status quo*. He wanted to use what was really a rather limited reform to reinforce the system rather than to change it fundamentally. Above all, the working-class voter was to be excluded. As Grey assured the House of Lords in November 1832, 'there is no one

KEY ISSUE

What were the Whigs' motives in introducing the Reform Bill?

mandate the authority, given by the electorate, to do something

more decided against annual parliaments, universal suffrage, and vote by ballot, than I am. My object is not to favour, but to put an end to such hopes'.

C *The campaign in the country*

Outside Parliament, agitation for reform focused on the figure of Thomas Attwood, a Birmingham banker whose family fortune had been made in the Midlands iron trade. He had taken no part in the post-war reform movement since he was deeply opposed to universal suffrage. However, Attwood attracted the support of men of his own class when he argued that the economy would continue to be unstable while the new industrial middle class was excluded from government.

THE BIRMINGHAM POLITICAL UNION

Attwood, and many others who shared his views, were inspired by the success of the Catholic Association in extracting emancipation from Wellington's Government by the use of popular pressure. O'Connell's success certainly stressed the potential of a mass-based movement. In 1830 Attwood formed the Birmingham Political Union (BPU) and modelled it closely on O'Connell's organisation. Attwood's objective was a political union in which a middle-class leadership and a working-class rank and file would be bound together by a common objective. The problem with Parliament, he now argued, was the absence of men who were active in the world of commerce and industry (in fact, men like Attwood!). He stressed the common interests of employers and employees who he saw as making up a single 'productive' class. As he said:

See page 269, in Chapter 9, on the Catholic Association

> The interests of masters and men are, in fact, one. If the masters flourish, the men flourish with them; and if the masters suffer difficulties their difficulties must shortly affect the workmen in three-fold degree.

Attwood argued that the worker would be represented by his employer because their interests were supposedly similar. It was not always a convincing argument. After all, if the economic interests of the two groups were so close how does one explain the growth of so much aggressive trade unionism in this period? It is also important to note that Attwood's argument was very different from the Painite position (on the need for universal manhood suffrage) that most of the BPU's working-class membership supported. For Attwood, universal suffrage was not necessary. Given the common interests of employers and employees, in that both stood to gain if industry flourished, the needs of the labouring population would be fully catered for by the election of employers to Parliament. This approach was also enshrined in the structure of the BPU, whose central Political Council consisted entirely of middle-class men. As Attwood put it: 'Who would ever think of sending even a disciplined army into the field without officers?'.

Despite this heavily qualified commitment to democracy on the part of its founder, the BPU was enormously popular and it attracted extensive working-class support. Its outdoor meetings, at which Attwood was a regular and favourite speaker, frequently drew audiences of 50 000–100 000 people. Similar political unions were established in towns throughout the country, most significantly the Northern Political Union in Newcastle and, in London, the National Political Union. The latter was organised by Francis Place, a tailor who had been active in the earlier period of radicalism and who now accepted the need to work with, in his words, men of 'money and influence'. These political unions now backed the Whig reform bill. Yet, given the far wider objectives of the earlier period of radicalism, why was there now so much support for the comparatively limited Whig proposal and for a reform organisation that was self-consciously elitist in structure?

THE GROWTH OF POLITICAL UNIONS

In fact, the earlier radical programme had not been forgotten. Throughout the Reform Bill campaign it was advocated by the London-based National Union of the Working Classes, formed in 1831. This organisation never attracted mass support but, with its radical programme and its network of branches throughout the country, it was an influential forerunner of Chartism. Through the medium of its illegal but very popular newspaper, the *Poor Man's Guardian*, the NUWC expressed distrust for the Bill and its middle-class advocates, particularly Attwood. Yet, taken as a whole, working people do seem to have given the Bill their genuine support. This partly reflected a belief that its enactment would be the initial step towards full democracy. This was certainly not in the minds of the men who framed the Bill. They sought the minimum adjustment necessary to retain the *status quo*. But, at this stage, gradual reform still seemed a viable way forward. After all, the earlier movement, with its wider programme, had failed. The lessons of 1815–20 had been learned, and the advantages of lining up behind men of wealth were recognised within the working community. As Bronterre O'Brien, editor of the *Poor Man's Guardian* (and later a prominent Chartist), said of the Bill

KEY ISSUE

Why was there working-class support for such a moderate reform measure?

with all its faults we are willing to accept it as an instalment or part payment of the debt of right due to us.

For their part, Attwood and his supporters recognised that the greater the numbers behind the political unions, the more they could claim to represent 'the people' with all the authority that this suggested. This point was made constantly through 1831 and 1832 by means of a large number of public meetings calling upon Parliament to accept the

Q

1. What does O'Brien mean by the phrase 'the debt of right due to us?'
2. Why did gradual reform look like a winning strategy at this point?

Bill. The House of Commons seems to have been influenced by this pressure. Here the opposition to the Bill was fragmented anyway. Robert Peel, who led the Tories in the Commons, certainly opposed the bill as being too far-reaching but he also rejected the traditional Tory-ism of the die-hard Ultra-Tories who would consider no reform at all. Peel did not accept that the unreformed system was as exclusive as its critics suggested: his own father had been a textile manufacturer who had entered Parliament by purchasing a seat. But he did accept that the system was now discredited and needed its worst excesses removed to restore public confidence in government. Tory disunity in the Commons was to prove crucial to the Bill's eventual success. The House of Lords, where Wellington was the main Tory influence, was a different matter. Made up largely of the landed aristocracy, it was less aware of, or concerned about, the agitation centred on the large towns and industrial districts. The Bill was passed in the Commons in September 1831, but was rejected by the Lords in October.

TIMELINE
The passage of the Reform Bill

Nov 1830	Earl Grey becomes Prime Minister of a Whig Government
March 1831	First Reform Bill introduced; defeated in committee stage in House of Commons
April 1831	Whigs win General Election with large majority
July 1831	A second Reform Bill introduced
Oct 1831	Second Reform Bill rejected by House of Lords. Rioting in Bristol, Nottingham and Derby
March 1832	Third Reform Bill passed in House of Commons
May 1832	Grey asks King to appoint new Whig peers to secure passage of bill in Lords. King refuses; Grey resigns; Wellington fails to form a government; Grey is recalled
June 1832	Third Reform Act passed

D *The 'Days of May' 1832*

The rejection gave rise to extensive rioting in Nottingham, Derby and Bristol which had to be suppressed by troops. In November 1831, the BPU announced its intention to put itself on a military footing. This was immediately declared illegal by Royal Proclamation and the plan was dropped, but Attwood had made his point. A revised Bill, with a slightly more restrictive franchise, was now introduced. This was passed in the Commons in March 1832, but it was widely feared that the Lords would reject it when they debated it in May 1832. The Cabinet demanded that the king, William IV, create new peers to ensure the bill's passage in the Upper House. When he refused, Grey resigned. It was now expected that the king would appoint Wellington as Prime Minister and that he, in turn, would order the arrest of the leading reformers.

> **KEY ISSUE**
>
> *How important was popular support for reform in the passing of the Reform Bill?*

> William IV had succeeded his brother, George IV, in 1830

On 11 May 1832, representatives of the BPU and other political unions met Francis Place in London to discuss their possible response to such moves. According to Place, they considered a run on the banks, under the slogan 'To defeat the Duke go for gold!' (i.e. that those holding paper money should demand its gold equivalent from the banks, thus provoking a cash crisis), non-payment of taxes, and a plan of armed resistance. The days that followed were particularly tense. At a rally in Birmingham Attwood told an audience of around 200 000 people:

> I would rather die than see the great Bill of reform rejected or mutilated ... I see that you are all of one mind on the subject. Answer me then, had you not all rather die than live the slaves of the boroughmongers? (All! All!)

This notion of a resort to force if necessary was part of the heroic image that Attwood created for himself as a platform orator and this kind of oratory was very popular. Wellington found himself in a dilemma. Even he accepted that some form of Reform Bill would have to be passed. The Tory leader in the Commons, however, was Peel and he was unwilling to steer such a Bill through as he realised that this would split the Party, perhaps permanently (as had nearly happened with Catholic Emancipation). In the event, the Commons voted to support Grey's outgoing ministry, Wellington recognised that he could not form a government that could be viable in the Commons, and the king agreed to the creation of new peers. This proved to be unnecessary: under threat, the Lords gave in and passed the Bill which then became law in June.

HISTORIANS' DEBATE

How close did Britain come to a revolution during the Reform Bill campaign?

E. P. Thompson claims that 'Britain was within an ace of revolution' and he identifies the autumn of 1831 with the riots that followed the Lords' rejection, and the 'Days of May' 1832, as the potentially revolutionary moments. It may be, of course, that Thompson's political perspective as a Marxist historian leads him to overstate the existence of revolutionary situations in this period. But most historians would agree that autumn 1831 and May 1832 are the critical moments to be examined. Eric Evans, in his book *The Forging of the Modern State* (1983), accepts Francis Place's account of the drawing-up of a plan of resistance in May 1832, but adds

'whether Place and his co-adjutors had any intention of bringing it into effect is a matter of doubt. Certainly, a revolution led by Francis Place would have been an incongruous phenomenon.'

Joseph Hamburger, in his book *James Mill and the Art of Revolution* (1963), claims that the middle-class reformers were engaged in an elaborate form of bluff. They played up the extent of their national support and exaggerated its violent potential, in order to force the Bill through a reluctant Parliament. There never was a real threat of revolution; 'The professional reformer like the public relations man', claims Hamburger, 'dealt in images.' Others have argued that the heroic stand of figures such as Attwood became part of the folklore of the radical tradition and their actions became exaggerated in the re-telling. It could also be said that the major factor influencing Wellington to stand down in May 1832 was the vote in the House of Commons and not the pressure of the popular movement.

As both government and reformers alike were aware, the popular movement always carried with it the threat of a violent confrontation with the authorities. This had been the case in 1815–20 and, from this experience, working-class reformers knew what to expect from an anti-reform Tory Government of the sort that Wellington might have formed in May 1832. Far from massaging images and manipulating figures of attendance at their meetings, as Hamburger claims, the middle-class leaders of the campaign were '**riding the tiger**' of working-class agitation. As we have seen, the working community possessed by this time a tradition of political activity and also a programme of reform far more radical than that envisaged by men like Place and Attwood. The crucial problem for the middle-class radicals was not the creation of false images to frighten the Government, but rather retaining the leadership of a mass-based movement and directing it towards a moderate reform of Parliament. Also, it is arguable that Wellington ignored popular pressure in reaching his decision to stand down and that this made the situation more revolutionary in nature rather than less. It was precisely Wellington's lack of awareness of public feeling that would have made him a dangerous man as Prime Minister.

This is not to deny that bluff figured somewhere in the reformers' calculations. Attwood frequently referred to, what he called, the tactics of 'wholesome terror' whereby the peaceful process of petitioning Parliament was backed by the rhetoric of violent language. An example of this, from May 1832, was cited earlier. Such oratory was designed to have its impact not only upon the audience, but also upon those in authority. There had been another revolution in France in 1830, and memories of the post-war radical movement were still fresh. Certainly, when the BPU published its plan to arm in November 1831, the king wrote to Wellington that he feared a revolutionary intent on the Union's part. Nevertheless, we should remember that this was primarily a peaceful movement to petition Parliament in support of a limited reform measure (however radical it might look to the Ultra-Tories) which had the sponsorship of

---

Q

Was revolution in May 1832:

(**a**) *intended by the reformers*
(**b**) *a massive bluff by the popular leaders?*
(**c**) *a likely, if unintended, outcome of Wellington's actions had he been made Prime Minister?*

---

riding the tiger An Indian proverb warns he who would ride the tiger: it is an exhilirating experience until the rider dismounts – at which point the tiger will eat him!

the Government of the day and had already been accepted by the Commons.

Any revolutionary threat came not from the conscious intent of the reformers, but from the circumstances of the moment, and these were, in many ways, beyond their control. Above all, this was the only time in British history when the working class and the middle class were firmly united in an extra-Parliamentary campaign for political reform. This had not been the case in the post-war period and it would not be so in Chartism. By May 1832, the movement included a broad social spectrum. Support ranged from wealthy industrialists, professionals and merchants, who simply sought an adjustment to allow the urban interest into the political system via a restricted property franchise, right through to the labouring poor who saw the Bill as the first step towards full citizenship. The wealth of an excluded middle class, backed by the numerical strength of an excluded working class, united behind the slogan 'The Bill, the whole Bill and nothing but the Bill!'. Facing them was the House of Lords led by a man who had announced, when Prime Minister in 1830, that in his view the political system needed no reform of any kind.

If Wellington had become Prime Minister in May 1832 and moved against the reformers, it is difficult to see how bloodshed would have been avoided. The riots of 1831 had given some idea of what a Lords' rejection might trigger. In April 1832, in the run-up to the debate in the House of Lords, the *Poor Man's Guardian* published a guide to street fighting which included, among other things, detailed instructions on the construction of home-made pikes and how they might be employed against troops to maximum advantage. Thus, revolution was more likely to be sparked off by an unwise act by Wellington, had he become Prime Minister in May 1832, than by the conscious intent of reformers like Attwood and Place.

4 ᔖ THE REFORM ACT AND ITS SIGNIFICANCE

The main terms of the 1832 Reform Act

- Fifty-six borough constituencies were disenfranchised and lost both MPs.
- Thirty boroughs lost one of their MPs.
- Over 140 seats were thus released for re-distribution and these were mostly assigned to the industrial towns with some increase in some of the larger county constituencies.
- 19 new parliamentary boroughs created, each with one MP, and 22 new boroughs with two MPs each.
- Five new seats were given to Ireland; eight to Scotland; four to Wales.
- In the boroughs the older franchises were replaced by the £10 householder franchise (all male residents whose houses were valued, for the purposes of levying rates, at £10 a year or over were given the vote).
- In 1831, 11% of adult males in England and Wales could vote; in 1833 this was 18%.

KEY ISSUE

What changes to the political system did the Reform Act make?

KEY ISSUES

How big an impact did the 1832 Act have on politics?
Why did it disappoint so many of its supporters?

The opposition of the House of Lords converted the Reform Act into a heroic measure, an image which it could scarcely have sustained on its own merits. Its passing did little to dismantle the old system since it accepted the principle that the franchise should be based on the ownership of property. The new electoral system was actually more restrictive than it may appear to us. In England and Wales one man in every five now had the vote, in Scotland one man in eight, and in Ireland one man in twenty. In Birmingham, for example, some 4000 men were entitled to vote in the newly created borough from a total population of around 144 000.

In the years to come the majority of MPs continued to come from landed backgrounds. This was not surprising: there was no salary for MPs and most middle-class men could not abandon their jobs. Nor did elections become less boisterous. Voting remained open and it has been calculated that the cost of electioneering did not fall before the Ballot Act of 1872. Most elections continued to be uncontested (for example, there were no contests in three-fifths of constituencies in the 1847 elections). Women were still excluded.

The basis of the political system had not been changed. The new House of Commons, elected in 1832, looked very much like the old institution and acted in very familiar ways. But the urban middle class had been admitted to political life and their presence would be felt increasingly over the coming decades. This was really all that most middle-class reformers had wished to achieve; a recognition of the new middle-class 'interest' within a stable system built upon the defence of property. Some, like Attwood, had expected a swift change in the way the country was run, to favour the 'men of productive capital'. Elected MP for Birmingham in the reformed Parliament, he made no secret of his disappointment. He told a meeting only a year after the passing of the Act, 'My friends I have been grievously deceived. Almost on the first day of the session I discovered this . . . '.

For their part, the landed aristocracy had succeeded in preventing a lasting alliance between middle-class and working-class reformers by drawing the middle-class 'interest' into the existing political system with a moderate reform. For the Whig leaders, the Act was a conservative measure designed to forestall more radical change. Nevertheless, in looking back, we can see a precedent had been set: Parliament had shown that it could reform itself and thus paved the way for further political, social and economic reform.

For working people, however, there was only disappointment. The 'reforming Whigs' were, after all, a party of traditional landowners. The actions of the reformed Parliament, particularly the passing of the Poor Law Amendment Act and the Whigs' attack on trade unions in 1834, left working-class radicals in no doubt that the Act had not, in fact, been passed as a 'first instalment' of a wider reform of the system. The Reform Act left a legacy of bitterness, such that working-class joy at its passing did not last long. This sense of betrayal took working-class reformers back to their earlier, and more radical, political programme and this was now expressed in Chartism. Despite this, the Reform Bill campaign became the model which all subsequent popular movements attempted to emulate. The combination of massive public meetings, good publicity through an active press, and the use of constitutional arguments backed by 'wholesome terror' would all be characteristics of Chartism.

5 ⌐ BIBLIOGRAPHY

ARTICLES

M. Cole and D. Hartley '1832: An Unseen Advance for Democracy?', *Modern History Review*, November 1997 and February 1998. The first article examines the pre-1832 electoral system and the second assesses the merits and failings of the 1832 Act.

R. E. Foster 'Reflections on the Unreformed Electoral System', *Modern History Review*, September 2000.

BOOKS FOR AS/A LEVEL STUDENTS

C. Behagg *Labour and Reform: Working-Class Movements 1815–1914*, Chapter 2, Access to History series, Hodder & Stoughton, 2000.

J. R. Dinwiddy *From Luddism to the Great Reform Act*, Blackwell, 1986. This Historical Association pamphlet provides detail on, and insight into, a range of popular movements in the period.

E. Evans *The Great Reform Act of 1832*, Lancaster Pamphlet, Routledge, 1983, is an accessible account of the passing of the 1832 Act.

R. Pearce and R. Stearn *Government and Reform: Britain, 1815–1918*, Chapters 2 and 3, Access to History series, Hodder & Stoughton, 1994.

FURTHER READING

C. Behagg *Politics and Production in the Early Nineteenth Century*, Routledge, 1990, the author's study of class relations in Birmingham provides a local study of the themes of the chapter you have just read. Chapter 4 ('Riding the Tiger') deals with popular radicalism 1815–32.

J. Belchem's *Orator Hunt*, Oxford University Press, 1985, is an overview of Hunt's role in the popular radical movement and provides a detailed insight into the importance of the 'mass-platform' in the period 1815–20. The same author's *Popular Radicalism in Nineteenth Century Britain*, Macmillan, 1996, provides an overview of radicalism in the period in Chapters 2–5.

M. Brock's *The Great Reform Act*, Hutchinson, 1973, is perhaps the best detailed study of the passing of the Reform Act. The author matches events in Parliament with the growth of the popular movement to provide a good blend of 'high politics' and 'history from below'.

E. P. Thompson's *The Making of the English Working Class*, Pelican, 1968, is a central text for any analysis of the period under discussion. It is a very long book which will reward detailed study; but a good sense of the argument presented will be derived from the Preface (not to be missed under any circumstances) followed by Chapters 4, 6, 8, 10, 15 and 16.

6 ↝ STRUCTURED AND ESSAY QUESTIONS

A *Structured questions for AS Level*

1. (a) What methods were adopted by political radicals from 1815 to 1820 in order to achieve their aims?
    (b) To what extent was hunger the cause of popular radicalism?
2. (a) What was wrong with the electoral system before 1832?
    (b) Why did the Whigs introduce a Reform Bill in 1831?
3. (a) What were the main terms of the Reform Act?
    (b) To what extent does it deserve to be described as 'Great'?

STUDENT ADVICE

1. To answer Question 2(a) above, you will need to explain why the political system was so unsatisfactory to so many different social groups. It is a good idea to identify specific groups (the aristocracy, new middle class, working people) and explore their different positions. Do not be afraid to quote particular individuals. To answer Question 2(b), you will need to divide your answer into the long-term social reasons – by developing the points you made in response to part (a) of the question – such as the need to preserve social stability, the growth of new classes and interest groups, etc.

and the short-term reasons that relate to the Whigs' own political position after 1827.

Question 3(a) asks for a summary of the Act's main provisions; you should concentrate on what you think are the most significant ones. Part (b) asks for an overall opinion from you as to whether the measure often referred to as 'The Great Reform Act' deserves this name. Ask yourself how the Act would have been seen at the time by the different social groups. How extensive were the changes? Why were so many disappointed by the measure? Which groups benefited and who was left out?

B *Essay Questions for A2*
1. 'The Radicals failed to achieve their objectives in the period from 1815 to 1820 because they refused to adopt the use of physical force'. To what extent is this true?
2. How close did Britain come to a revolution in the reform crisis of 1831–2?
3. The Reform Act was essentially a conservative measure designed to stave off further parliamentary reform. Do you agree?

ESSAY PLANNING

Take the second question:

How close did Britain come to a revolution in the reform crisis of 1831–2?

(i) Read again the historical debate on pp. 50–2. To answer this question, you will need to assess carefully the evidence of a revolutionary situation, always bearing in mind one indisputable historical fact: that a revolution did not take place. It is equally certain, however, that contemporaries did not have the benefit of hindsight and it is helpful to our understanding to speculate on how the situation looked at the time. It might be useful to define first what is meant by the term 'revolution'; a good dictionary will help here.

(ii) Once you have this straight in your head, you may begin the weighing of the evidence. Begin by simply listing your thoughts under two appropriate headings, perhaps as follows:

Crisis of 1831–2

threat of revolution	elements of political stability

(iii) You should not forget the historiographical element (the way different historians have interpreted the movement) in a question of this sort, since it is asking you to interpret the events. Frankly, nobody knows for certain how close revolution was, so it will be useful to identify alternative ways in which historians have analysed the situation.

(iv) Also, you must recognise the importance of chronology in any history essay. Here, you are asked to make a judgement on 1832 but it is perfectly legitimate to widen the chronological scope, to take in the build-up to 1832 or even the earlier period of radicalism, *as long as you are relating earlier events to the year in question.* After each paragraph ask yourself the question 'How does the information I have given in this paragraph help the reader to understand 1832?'.

(v) Do not be afraid to use case studies. For example, having established the main arguments and evidence for stability/revolution, look closely at the crisis of the 'Days of May'. Your answer should include detail on how this crisis unfolded, using this as a case study to demonstrate your points.

(vi) Finally, one pitfall to avoid: you must not leave the reader in doubt as to your view. It is easy, in undertaking a listing exercise such as suggested above, to conclude that there is much evidence on both sides and so you cannot make a judgement; or that, since learned historians clearly disagree on the subject, who are you to say one way or the other? Historical analysis is about reaching conclusions that are, ultimately, a matter of opinion and interpretation. In writing this essay you are a historian and you must have an opinion and one which you can justify by taking the reader through the evidence. So, build-up your courage, look at your lists of evidence, and offer the reader a clear and reasoned viewpoint!

Role play – contemporary views of Parliamentary reform

This may be carried out as an individual exercise, or in three small groups (one group representing the views of the aristocracy, one the middle class and one the working class):

(i) How might the aristocracy have justified their dominance of government in the period before 1832?

(ii) What was the case for the franchise being extended to the middle class?

(iii) What was the case for the vote being extended to the working class?

7 ⌐ DOCUMENTARY EXERCISES

AS LEVEL EXERCISE ON THE RADICALS AND REFORM

Study the following primary sources and then answer the questions which follow.

See Picture 5 on page 42.

SOURCE A
George Cruikshank, Death or
Liberty, *December 1819*

SOURCE B
*Speech by Henry Hunt at
Manchester, April 1831*

When Sir Robert Peel charged them [the Whig ministers]: with going to make a democratical House of Commons … they said 'No, we are going to keep the power out of the hands of the rabble' ….Their policy … was to get one million of the middle classes, the little shopkeepers and those people, to join the higher classes, in order to raise the yeomanry corps and keep up standing armies, and thus unite together to keep their hands still in the pockets of the seven millions.

SOURCE C
Letter from William Carpenter,
Poor Man's Guardian,
3 December 1831

The Bill *admits* the necessity of Reform on *general theoretical* principles, and as a concession to *popular opinion.* This once recognised leads necessarily to every desired change in the government. The Bill concedes, *to some extent* the right of representation on the basis of *population*; and this concession once made, in however trifling a degree, *must* be carried forward to its *full extent.*

SOURCE D
*Poor Man's Guardian,
24 September 1831*

It is clear *we* GAIN nothing by it; but it is said that these middle men, whom this measure admits into a share of the legislature, will be more inclined to hear our appeal for justice, and will return a majority favourable to it: think it not; – why already – before even they have gained their own admittance – do they not shut the doors of Parliament against you? for will they *tolerate our mention* of 'Universal Suffrage' etc? … – do they not plainly tell you, even when they solicit your 'sweet voices' to swell *their own cry* for *their own* reform, – do they not plainly tell you that they like not *universal suffrage?* – do they not scout the very mention of equality? – and is not 'property', which you have not, the very pivot on which all their thoughts and wishes turn?

(Sources C and D give two different views of the Bill from the pages of the same radical newspaper. Carpenter was a leading exponent of universal suffrage, here arguing that the Bill could change the principles upon which politics operated.)

So join your hands with Attwood boys,
Unto his wish comply,
He says he'll set the nation free
Or he will nobly die.

SOURCE E
Popular ballad, May 1832

1. *What can you learn from source A about why radical reformers were criticised in the period? (4 marks)*
2. *Using Sources B and C and a reading of pages 38–43, explain the principles upon which the radical reformers felt the political system should be based. (5 marks)*
3. *Compare Source C with Source D and explain why large numbers of the working class supported the Reform Bill campaign and why they were disappointed with the result. (9 marks)*
4. *Using Sources A and E, and your wider reading, explain how threatening the reform campaigns of 1815–32 would have been seen at the time. (12 marks)*

Total 30 marks

A2 EXERCISE ON THE NATURE OF THE REFORM ACT

Every argument, sir, which would induce me to oppose universal suffrage, induces me to support this measure which is now before us. I oppose universal suffrage because I think it would produce a destructive revolution ... I support this measure because I am sure that it is now our best security against a revolution ... I support this measure as a measure of reform; but I support it still more as a measure of conservation.

SOURCE A
Speech by the Whig Thomas Macaulay in the House of Commons, 2 July 1831

SOURCE B
Sir James Graham (writing in 1851) recalling the instructions given by the Cabinet to a committee of four (of whom he was one), appointed to draft the Reform Bill in January 1831

to prepare: the outline of a measure ... large enough to satisfy public opinion and to afford sure ground of resistance to further innovation, yet so based on property, and on existing franchises and territorial divisions, as to run no risk of overthrowing the existing form of government.

SOURCE C
Eric Evans The Great Reform
Act of 1832 *(1983)*

The Reform Act was not a piece of timeless constitution-making, the product of a full and dispassionate consideration of the nation's needs. It was a compromise stitched together during a crisis. It dissatisfied a substantial majority of those who had most strenuously urged the need for parliamentary reform. Yet from the government's point of view, it served its major purpose: it removed the immediate threat to the security of the state.

1. *Using Sources A and B, explain why the Whigs felt it necessary to introduce a reform bill. (6 marks)*

2. *Using Source B and your own knowledge, explain how the Whigs planned to retain the essence of the old system whilst introducing a measure of reform. (7 marks)*

3. *Study Source C and use your own knowledge. To what extent was the Act a 'compromise stitched together during a crisis'? (12 marks)*

Total 25 marks

The 'Condition of England Question', 1815–50

INTRODUCTION

The way a nation deals with the social and economic problems that confront it provides a powerful insight into its underlying ideas and beliefs. This chapter is devoted to an examination of **the Condition of England question** and how Britain tried to tackle the social issues that it faced as the world's first industrial society.

In the generation after 1815, Britain's economy was in a state of severe depression. The Napoleonic wars had created a demand for industrial goods; this sharply declined with the coming of peace. Workers were either laid off or had their wages reduced. Their plight was worsened by job competition from the demobilised troops who returned looking for work. Low wages and unemployment were also experienced by agricultural workers. The wartime blockades, which had prevented imports coming easily into the country, had created a boom time for British food producers. But British farmers after 1815 had again to compete with foreign produce which was often cheaper than its British counterpart. This resulted in an agricultural depression.

Initially, governments were slow to take action. This was largely because, although the State had undertaken reforms in many areas, it had yet to concern itself with the improvement of social conditions. Until the 1830s, there was little effort by the authorities to deal with the causes of economic hardship and suffering. They restricted themselves to suppress-

> **The Condition of England question** was the term used by contemporaries to refer to the economic distress experienced by the workers and the social unrest to which this gave rise.

See Chapter 2, pages 9–16

Protection

In 1815, Parliament, which was dominated by the farming interest, passed the Corn Laws. These were an attempt to protect the British farmers from being undersold by cheaper grain from Europe. The Corn Laws placed a high tariff on foreign corn thus making it unprofitable to import. However, in practice, the Corn Laws did not lead to prosperity for the farmers. Chronic low wages meant that the workers simply did not have enough money to buy bread at the inflated prices. The grim result was bread shortage and hunger for the working classes without any real financial gains for the farmers. Nonetheless, for 30 years after 1815, the landed classes clung on to protection in the belief that it would prevent cheaper foreign food from being imported and so preserve the profits on their own produce.

TIMELINE

Financial reforms

1822   Many tariffs and
restrictions on
imports were
removed

1823   The Corn Laws were
modified by
substituting a sliding-
scale for the previous
fixed rate. As wheat
prices rose, the duty
on foreign wheat was
reduced

1823   The Reciprocity of
Duties Act allowed
foreign ships to carry
goods into British
ports

Q

*Why did
Parliament turn its
attention to social
reform after 1830?*

Q

*What were the
major social problems of
the day?*

ing the outbreaks of disorder which the suffering frequently produced. They were prepared to act over economic matters, but this was largely with the aim of preserving the status quo by a policy of **protection**. It is true that a number of significant financial reforms were introduced in the 1820s, but the basic causes of social distress were given little attention.

Having largely ignored the causes of social distress between 1815 and 1830, Parliament did begin to introduce legislation to deal with a range of related problems. This was prompted by growing evidence of the seriousness of the social ills in the nation and by the willingness of the Whigs, who were in office for most of the 1830s, to consider reform. The principal areas in which reforms were attempted were poverty, public health, local government, factory conditions, education, and law and order. This thrust towards reform was part cause, part effect, of a widespread debate about social conditions in Britain. The influential political writer, Thomas Carlyle, was a major contributor to the discussion. He drew attention to the potential threat to society by describing the 'ominous' attitude of the working classes and asking:

What means this bitter discontent of the working classes? Whence comes it, whither goes it? Above all, at what price, on what terms will it probably consent to depart from us and die into rest?

Thomas Carlyle, Chartism, *1839*

Like many of his contemporaries, Carlyle was concerned at the problems created by the social and economic changes that had been taking place since the middle years of the eighteenth century. Industrialisation, and particularly the rapid growth of towns, had produced the problems that required intervention. These were not new; poverty, crime, and disease long pre-dated the eighteenth-century. But what industrialisation had done was to swell and intensify these problems. In pre-industrial society, where the population was small and where people knew each other, it had been possible to maintain stability and order and to deal fairly effectively with poverty at a local level. However it was much harder to do these things in an industrial society. A rapidly expanding and mobile population living in large urban areas placed impossible demands on the existing systems for relieving poverty and improving conditions.

1 ⌐ RESPONSES TO SOCIAL PROBLEMS

The reasons why Government and Parliament undertook social reform in the middle years of the nineteenth century and why such reform met resistance are best understood by examining the prevailing ideas and theories that influenced the law makers and legislators of the day.

A *Laissez-faire*

As was noted with regard to the Corn Laws (see page 61), government policy on economic matters tended traditionally to be restrictive rather than expansive. But, with the growth in commerce that accompanied Britain's rapid industrial expansion, powerful new ideas began to challenge the old notions. An outstandingly influential thinker was the Scottish economist, Adam Smith. He argued in his celebrated book, *The Wealth of Nations* (1776), that the economy should be allowed to operate without government control. Individuals should be left to follow what they judged as their own best interests; this would result in a flourishing economy which would be of benefit to all. As he put it: 'It is not from the benevolence of the butcher, the brewer, or the baker, that we expect our dinner but from their regard for their own interest'.

Smith insisted, above all, that the contract between employer and employee should be free from government interference. When an employer and a worker negotiated over wages, each tried to obtain the best for himself. The level of wages that was finally agreed between them was determined by a number of factors. These might include the skill that the worker could offer, the amount of labour available to the employer, the profit derived from the employer's business, and the demand from buyers for the goods that were produced. For governments to intervene in this relationship, by setting levels of wages or conditions of employment was, in Smith's words, 'as impertinent as it is oppressive'.

This interpretation is now referred to as the free-market analysis of the way a society should operate. It was essentially optimistic. Smith believed that contractual freedom between individuals would create an economy that would provide full employment, high profits and good wages. This was because the interests of employers and employees were fundamentally the same; both stood to gain from a sound economy. Smith's views were highly influential throughout the nineteenth century, but they did not go unchallenged in his own time or later. During the second half of the century, the German revolutionary, Karl Marx, attacked the concept of economic individualism. He asserted that, far from creating social harmony, unrestricted individualism would lead to dominance by the stronger over the weaker. Workers would be exploited by grasping employers who, in order to maximise profits, would pay only minimum wages. The result would be class war between capitalist bosses and deprived workers.

laissez-faire is a French term, best translated as 'leave alone' or 'do not interfere'

KEY ISSUE

Why did Adam Smith consider the right of free contract to be so important?

Nevertheless, Smith's theory of economic freedom, sometimes referred to as 'laissez-faire', gained extensive support in Britain. It was widely accepted that individuals should be free to dispose of their property as they saw fit. This deep-rooted commitment to individualism helps to explain the fierce objections that were often expressed towards government taxes and local rates. Such impositions were an affront to free market economics. Taxes took away an individual's power to sell his goods or his labour as he chose. This was a restriction of the economic freedom that Smith regarded as vital to the efficient operation of the market system. Such reasoning produced firm resistance to the extension of central and local government activity in social and economic affairs.

Individualism, however, raised obvious ethical questions. What if the interests of the individual were at odds with the public good? What if the individual, in pursuing what he saw as his own 'best interests', engaged in anti-social activity, such as slum building or the exploitation of groups unable to defend themselves? Furthermore, if strong individuals or groups were able to prevent increases in taxes or rates, would this not thwart the Government in its attempts to improve social conditions? The fundamental issue was how to reconcile individual freedom with governmental authority. One striking answer was offered in the early nineteenth century by Utilitarianism, a social theory most closely associated with the philosopher Jeremy Bentham.

KEY ISSUE

In what respects did Bentham's ideas correspond with, or differ from, those of Adam Smith?

B *Benthamism and Utilitarianism*

The preserved remains of Jeremy Bentham (1748–1832) can still be seen in a glass case at University College London, the institution which was founded as a centre for the study of his ideas. He accepted Adam Smith's concept of individualism and the free market as the keys to economic growth. However, Bentham also considered that there were occasions when government intervention was necessary. He recognised, for example, that the State was needed to provide security for its people. Laws had to be maintained so that individuals would be free to pursue their own interests.

Bentham also held that there were practical considerations that could not be ignored. However much the economy flourished, there would always be the **'indigent poor'** who would need to be provided for in some way. Individuals would also have to be protected against accidents or epidemics by public health and safety regulations. The centre-piece of Bentham's thinking was **Utilitarianism**.

Bentham's utilitarian principle recognised that there would be individuals whose criminal or irresponsible behaviour would threaten the happiness of society at large. Clearly such individuals could not be left to follow their own interests. They would have to be coerced by the State for the good of the majority. But Bentham also recognised that, while government intervention was justifiable in particular circumstances, there was always a danger it might go too far and encroach on

'indigent poor' The term described those unfortunate workers who, though willing to work, could not find paid employment or whose wages were too low to meet their basic needs

---

Utilitarianism

Utilitarianism was a set of ideas founded on the belief that human beings act out of self-interest in accordance with the pleasure–pain principle. That is to say, they are motivated by the desire to seek pleasure and to avoid pain. It follows, therefore, that to be successful a social policy has to offer either reward or punishment. If people know that a certain course of action will make them suffer they will avoid it, but if they judge it will bring them advantages they will pursue it. Consequently, social reform, to be at its most effective or 'utilitarian', should be based on the pleasure–pain concept. In this way, by satisfying the majority, it will achieve 'the greatest happiness of the greatest number'.

---

the economic freedom of the majority. To prevent this, he proposed a series of tests against which government action should be measured:

(i) Rule and exception

As a rule, the State should not intervene. It should do so only in exceptional cases. This notion of 'rule and exception' was widely accepted throughout the nineteenth century and is one reason why social legislation was so patchy in its nature – it invariably aimed to deal with a problem by a minimum of intervention.

(ii) Investigation and analysis

In order to establish whether and how the State should intervene, any action should be preceded by a thorough investigation of the problem. Legislation should follow analysis. Again, this point was broadly accepted and it became standard procedure to investigate issues prior to legislation by means of either a Select Committee of the House of Commons or the House of Lords or by a Royal Commission. It was in this context that the Registration Act of 1837 (which required the recording of births, deaths and marriages) proved so significant since it provided the means of gathering vital data and statistics.

(iii) Centralised authority

If the necessary reforms taken by the Government were to work, they would have to be accompanied by an efficient system of administration and inspection. Bentham argued that administration, to be efficient, should be centralised since dispersed authority made it much harder to maintain standards. Yet the centralisation of power aroused great controversy in the nineteenth century. Traditionally, the landed classes had controlled their own areas; rates were levied locally, and magistrates were locally appointed. Any move towards centralisation was likely to be opposed in the localities as an attack upon local independence.

KEY ISSUE

What were the religious impulses behind reform?

C *Evangelicalism and humanitarianism*

Evangelicalism

Evangelicalism was not a separate religious denomination; rather it was a movement to bring enthusiasm and commitment back to the Church. It became popular from around the middle years of the eighteenth century, and was particularly associated with the Nonconformist sects that grew up in this period, most notably the Methodist movement led by John Wesley. Wesley felt that the Church must re-generate itself and make contact with the people of the industrial areas, who had been left godless and without moral guidance. He developed a form of service which emphasised the active participation of the congregation. Many Evangelicals were also humanitarians.

If Utilitarianism was one of the two strongest influences creating a reforming atmosphere in this period, **Evangelicalism** was the other. The roots of this movement lay in the religious revival which had accompanied the Industrial Revolution. Many industrialists sought a set of beliefs that would explain their successful enterprises and justify their new wealth. They found this in Evangelicalism, a very active form of religion which stressed the importance of hard work and sobriety. But the appeal of this movement was not restricted to the successful and the wealthy. The labouring poor also looked to religion for comfort. The harshness of their lives was made bearable by their involvement in a faith which emphasised the virtue of charity and good works.

For Evangelicals, religion was not simply a matter of formal worship. It was an all-embracing affair which shaped the whole of their lives. All the actions that they took as individuals were seen and judged by God. They were duty-bound, therefore, to avoid sin and embrace virtue. A sure way to do this was by performing good works to help their fellow men. Such attitudes are part of the explanation of why Evangelicals were prominent in the ranks of those pressing for the reform of the grim living and working conditions that were the lot of so many people in Britain.

By 1850, half the people who attended religious services belonged to Evangelical Nonconformist sects such as the Methodists. But Evangelicalism was not restricted to the Nonconformists; there were also Evangelicals in the Church of England who wanted religion to be a living force among the people. Evangelicals were especially influential in the movement for social reform. They argued that social issues were also moral issues and, therefore, more a matter for the individual rather than the State. Each person must make his own decision to reform and lead a better life. It was not the State's task to prevent the individual from being confronted with the choice between sin and salvation. The role of the State was to protect the vulnerable and to create the appropriate moral environment within which individuals would be encouraged to make the 'right' moral choice. It was in defence of the vulnerable that a significant off-shoot of Evangelicalism developed – **humanitarianism**.

Humanitarianism
Humanitarianism was not a formally organised movement but an attitude of mind, which stood in marked contrast to Utilitarianism. It judged things not by their usefulness but by their impact on human beings. It took its inspiration from Christ's teaching that charity was the greatest of the virtues and held that true Christianity was a religion of compassion, best expressed in the relief of suffering. Humanitarians, such as William Wilberforce and Lord Shaftesbury, were inspirational in the campaigns against negro slavery and child labour.

2 ⌇ DEALING WITH POVERTY: THE POOR LAW AMENDMENT ACT, 1834

The existing Poor Law, which dated back to the seventeenth century, had established a system by which each of the 15 000 local parishes in England and Wales was responsible for dealing with poverty in its own area. At the heart of the system was the belief that the poor should work hard. Vagrants who would not work were punished severely. Yet it was recognised that if individuals could not work, through no fault of their own, they were entitled to relief from the parish. This was mostly given in the form of money or food (known as out-relief), although 'poor-houses' were built to house the sick and the aged who were known as the impotent poor. The cost of such relief was met from a 'poor-rate' levied on the wealthier members of the parish. A scheme, which was tried in many counties in southern England, was the Speenhamland System (so-called after the parish in Berkshire which first adopted the scheme in 1795). Under this, the wages of the poor were supplemented by the parish once they fell below a certain level. The level varied from parish to parish, but was usually calculated by the size of the labourer's family and the cost of bread in the area.

Cost of a gallon loaf (4 kilos)	Labourer's wage subsidised up to	Allowance for his wife	Allowance for each child
Is	3s per week	Is 6d per week	Is 6d per week
Is Id	3s 3d per week	Is 7d per week	Is 7d per week
Is 2d	3s 6d per week	Is 8d per week	Is 8d per week
Is 3d	3s 9d per week	Is 9d per week	Is 9d per week

TABLE 2
The Speenhamland System

There were 12 pence (d) to the shilling (s) and 20 shillings to the £. One shilling was equivalent to 5p today.

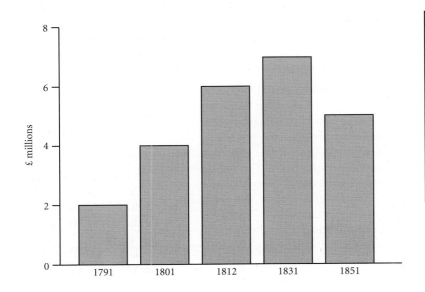

DIAGRAM 2
Cost of the Poor Rate in England

Q

Using Diagram 2, showing the rise in the cost of the poor rate, and Table 2, showing the increased payments under the Speenhamland system, explain why rate payers would have been eager to see a major reform of the existing Poor Law.

The **'Swing' riots**, 1830–1, were violent protests, in a number of southern counties, against the unemployment and hunger caused by bad harvests. The riots, which involved machine smashing and burning of hay-barns, took their name from the threatening letters, signed 'Captain Swing', that were sent to land-owners

The cost of trying to cope with poverty continued to climb. As Diagram 2 shows, in the 40 years after 1791, the poor rate increased by three-and-a-half times. Yet despite the increasing amounts spent on supporting the poor, the **'Swing' riots** of 1830–1 suggested that the rural poor were no longer convinced that they were being protected: it was in the agricultural districts of southern and eastern England, where the poor rates had increased most markedly, that the worst disturbances occurred. By the 1830s it had become all too clear that the existing Poor Law was no longer fulfilling its original purpose. Something had to be done.

The task of creating a relief system attuned to the industrial age fell to the Royal Commission on the Poor Laws established in 1832. Among its 26 members were two particularly significant individuals: the Benthamite, Edwin Chadwick, and the economist, Nassau Senior. In order to identify the weakness in the Poor Law, the Commissioners visited nearly 3000 parishes, and studied the returns to questionnaires sent to another 1000 parishes. The investigations confirmed that the existing system, far from relieving poverty, was actually increasing it. By supplementing wages, the parishes were encouraging a reliance upon relief rather than leading the poor to seek work.

The Report of the Royal Commission, which ran to eight thick volumes, ranks as one of the most important social documents of the nineteenth century. Its analysis of poverty combined both economic and moral judgements. One of its fundamental convictions was that Britain as an industrial nation required a productive and responsible workforce. The encouragement given by the Poor Law to able-bodied workers to live off parish relief undermined the 'habits of industry' among the labouring classes. Employers were able to lower wages because they knew that the parish would make them up to subsistence level. The availability of artificially cheap labour in certain areas interfered with the operation of the free market. As the report put it 'a Macclesfield manufacturer may find himself undersold in consequence of the maladministration of the poor laws in Essex'. By subsidising labour, the parish overseers were distorting the workings of the market.

In order to bring down the poor rates and oblige the able-bodied pauper to take up work, the Commission advised that a programme be introduced based on the following three principles.

KEY ISSUE

Why was the old Poor Law regarded as inadequate?

KEY ISSUE

What were the Commission's main proposals?

- **The 'workhouse test'**. Outdoor relief was to be abolished and poor relief was to be available only within efficiently run workhouses. The measure of an individual's real need of assistance would be demonstrated by his willingness to enter a workhouse.
- **'Less eligibility'**. It was argued that conditions in the workhouses should be 'less eligible' (i.e. less desirable) than the worst conditions endured outside the workhouse by workers in employment. Thus, nobody would opt for the workhouse if there was the chance of employment outside.
- **Centralisation**. The administration of poor relief would have to be uniform or, it was argued, paupers would simply congregate in parishes where relief was given on a lenient basis. Such uniformity could only be achieved by a centralised system.

A *The Poor Law Amendment Act, 1834*

This measure turned the Commission's recommendations into practice:

- a Poor Law Commission was established, based in London, and with Chadwick as its Secretary
- parishes were to be grouped together in Poor Law Unions, each with its own workhouse and a set of locally-elected Guardians of the Poor
- 12 Assistant Commissioners were to be appointed to co-ordinate the application of the law in the regions.

This degree of centralisation was unprecedented in any area of administration and was largely due to Edwin Chadwick's presence on the Commission. Chadwick believed that good order was the basis of civilisation, and that good order was best achieved by centralised uniform administration, since this avoided the inefficiencies that came with variation. The new system was to be operated by the Commissioners through a series of directives issued from their London headquarters. This would reduce local initiative and produce a standardised approach to the provision of relief. Although the Amendment Act had not specifically referred to the workhouse test and the 'less eligibility' notion, it was on these principles that the new Poor Law Unions based their treatment of poverty.

Working people immediately came to detest the new Act. Its central concept of poverty being the fault of the poor was seen as degrading. In the workhouses which operated under the new Poor Law, less eligibility was achieved by a variety of repellent strategies. The sexes were separated, families were parted, inmates wore prison-style uniforms, and were put to repetitive and often pointless labour. Food was frugal and coarse and had to be eaten in silence. Mothers of illegitimate children were often singled out for special treatment; they might, for example, be segregated at meal times or in the compulsory chapel services. The old Poor Law had forced unmarried fathers to support their children, but the new law implied that illegitimacy was the fault of the mother.

The Commission's assumption that people had chosen to be poor because they knew that they could rely on parish charity was based on a myth. The historian, Mark Blaug, has shown that no more than 18 English rural parishes regularly operated a system of topping up wages; the Commission had exaggerated the system's extent and impact. The truth was that poverty resulted from economic factors over which the poor had little control. When the trade cycle dipped, depression invariably followed producing large numbers of unemployed. Moreover, it soon became evident that such numbers were too great to be contained in the new workhouses. This was why the practice of giving outdoor relief continued throughout the nineteenth century. Research has indicated that it was often far less expensive than taking the paupers into the workhouse.

> **KEY ISSUE**
>
> *Why was the new Poor Law hated by the labouring classes?*

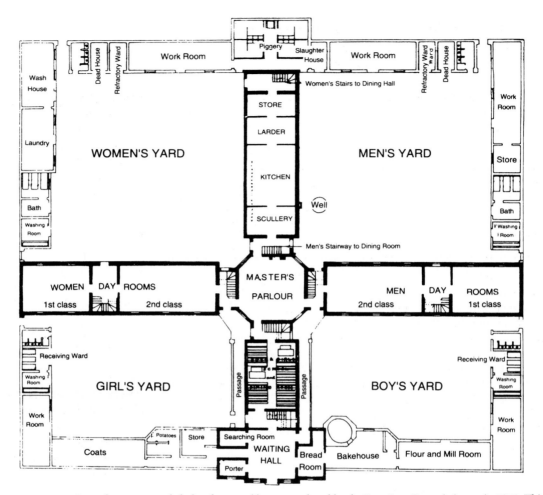

PICTURE 6   *Part of a recommended plan for a workhouse, produced by the Poor Law Commissioners in 1870. This is the ground floor of a two-level building, which was intended to accommodate 300 inmates.*

1. *What do you find the most striking features of the plan?*
2. *In what ways does the plan illustrate the intention of the Poor Law Commissioners to apply the 'less eligibility' principle to the workhouse?*

The new workhouses became the focus for widespread concern and anger. A serious scandal arose over the Andover Workhouse where, in 1845, hungry paupers, set to work on bone crushing, were said to have gnawed the rancid gristle left on the bones. A Select Committee found that the food levels at the Andover workhouse were below those set by the Commissioners, and blamed the Guardians for mismanagement. But it also recognised that the Guardians had simply been following the directions from the Poor Law Commissioners. Chadwick, in particular, was criticised for his inflexible approach. In 1847, the Poor Law Commission was replaced by a Poor Law Board under a President, who was also to be a government minister and therefore accountable to Parliament. This led to the dismissal of the widely disliked Chadwick. However, the historian, Ursula Henriques, concludes that 'there is no indication that this direct ministerial responsibility made any substantial difference to the conduct of the Victorian Poor Law'.

3 ∽ DEALING WITH DISEASE AND SQUALOR – THE PUBLIC HEALTH ACT, 1848

As the accompanying table shows, a huge and rapid growth in the population of Britain's cities occurred during the first half of the nineteenth century.

	1811	*1821*	*1831*	*1841*	*1851*
Birmingham	83 000	102 000	144 000	183 000	233 000
Glasgow	101 000	147 000	202 000	275 000	345 000
Leeds	63 000	84 000	123 000	152 000	172 000
Liverpool	104 000	138 000	202 000	286 000	376 000
Manchester	89 000	126 000	182 000	235 000	303 000
Sheffield	53 000	65 000	92 000	111 000	135 000

KEY ISSUE

Why had public health problems become so alarming to contemporaries?

TABLE 3
Populations of the major cities

This took place almost entirely without planning. In the words of a contemporary sanitary reformer, Sir John Simon, the towns had expanded 'with scarcely more reference to the legitimate necessities of life than if they had clustered there by crystallisation.' As a consequence, the towns grew up overcrowded and unhealthy; they lacked the systems of sewerage, refuse disposal and fresh water provision that are now regarded as fundamental to health. Death rates increased dramatically in the first half of the century, with a majority of deaths in the large towns being from infectious diseases. In a large city like Manchester, well over half the children born in this period did not survive to the age of five. Serious outbreaks of **cholera** in Britain in 1831–2, 1848–9 and 1853 made still plainer the need for the efficient cleansing of towns.

cholera is a highly infectious disease of the stomach, carried by polluted water, and causing violent vomiting and uncontrollable diarrhoea. The acute dehydration which this produced frequently proved fatal. In 1853, recorded cholera deaths numbered 53 293

PICTURE 7
Punch *cartoon 'A drop of London water'*

To some extent the problem was one of medical ignorance. For example, it was not until 1848 that cholera was recognised as a waterborne, rather than an airborne, disease. But even with the gathering of scientific knowledge, death rates did not drop until the last quarter of the century. Ignorance alone does not explain the difficulties which contemporaries had in improving public health. The other explanations have been neatly summarised by the historian Ursula Henriques:

Q

1. *According to Henriques, what were the main obstacles to achieving health improvements in the towns?*
2. *What do you think Henriques means by the phrase 'the collapse of communal responsibility' in the above passage?*

> Apathy, the flight of the wealthy from the town centres, the collapse of communal responsibility and communal administration, rather than knowledge, were responsible for the spreading squalor. Overcrowding, filth and disease stole upon the nation like a thief in the night.
>
> *Ursula Henriques,* Before the Welfare State, *1979*

In a number of the large towns, Improvement Boards, sometimes called Street Commissioners, were established to tackle local problems. Between 1800 and 1845, nearly 400 local improvement acts were passed by Parliament but their impact on the urban problem was limited since they tended to focus only on those areas where the wealthier people lived. Public health reform invariably required a good deal of money to be spent; sewerage and water systems were large and expensive projects. But ratepayers were reluctant to provide general improvements which everyone enjoyed but only they paid for:

From a ratepayer's letter to The Leeds Intelligencer, *23 October 1836*

> Shall the town obtain money by a tax upon a few and appropriate it for the benefit of the many – and that tax interminable without those few who find the money having any direct control over its expenditure or any possible means of having it repaid?

There was also considerable tension between the sanitary reformers and the agencies responsible for carrying out the reforms. Edwin Chadwick expressed his exasperation over this:

Q

1. *In what ways does the letter to the Leeds newspaper illustrate the type of obstruction met by supporters of social reform?*
2. *What are the grounds for Chadwick's complaints about the Commissioners?*

> Frequently interested parties are seated at the Boards of Guardians who are ready to stop anything which many lead to expenditure for the proper repair of the dwellings of the labouring classes. Where measures of drainage are proposed and the works carried out by Commissioners of Sewers are found to be defective, a cry is raised: nothing must be done for fear of offending the Commissioners. When additional supplies of water are called for one cry raised is 'Oh the interest of the companies is too powerful to be touched.'

From a letter by Edwin Chadwick to Lord Ashley, also known as Lord Shaftesbury, April 1844

PICTURE 8 *This* Punch *cartoon of 1849 carries the caption,* The City Narcissus, or, the Alderman Enamoured of his Dirty Appearance *(Narcissus was a character in Greek mythology who fell in love with his own reflection. An alderman is a local government official)*

Chadwick was very anxious to stress the link between poverty and disease. It was as a result of his pressure that the Civil Registration Act of 1837, which made the formal recording of births, deaths and marriages compulsory, contained an amendment requiring the cause of death to be entered. Chadwick believed that such national data would provide a basis for tackling what he considered to be preventable disease. In 1842 his *Report on the Sanitary Conditions of the Labouring Population of Great Britain* was published. This remarkable survey of conditions in the urban areas concluded that the main causes of disease were bad drainage, poor ventilation, and an impure water supply. One particularly pressing need was to find ways of removing the piles of rotting matter which disfigured the towns and harboured the germs that spread infection. Chadwick advocated the creation of a network of sewers built to the design of a London engineer, John Roe. The pipes of these sewers would be small, egg-shaped in cross-section, and made of strong glazed earthenware. Houses could be drained and streets cleaned using the same set of sewers stretching like a system of arteries under-

Q

What features of the attitude of local governments towards public-health reform is the cartoonist ridiculing?

neath the streets. Chadwick also attacked the previous attempts to deal with the problem (by such organisations as the London Commissioners of Sewers) as inefficient and, above all, expensive. True to his Benthamite convictions, Chadwick recommended the creation of a strong central authority, on the model of the Poor Law Commission, to deal with the problem nationwide.

As a result of Chadwick's *Report* of 1842, Peel's Government established the Royal Commission on the Health of Towns, under R. A. Slaney, a Liberal MP. Slaney shared the view of such Evangelicals as Lord Shaftesbury that conditions in the industrial cities were a morally corrupting influence on society. He saw the benefits of industrialisation, but feared that, unless reforms were introduced, social conflict would follow. A great supporter of the new Poor Law, he wanted public administration rationalised so that it both aided the economy and drew the classes together. This approach gained wide support through the Health of Towns Association, formed in 1844, of which Shaftesbury was a leading member. Sanitary reform presented an opportunity, in his words, 'to Christianise' the working population.

The report of the Commission on the Health of Towns confirmed Chadwick's earlier findings on the chaotic nature of the existing organisations for dealing with public health. Nevertheless, there was considerable opposition to the Bill, sponsored in Parliament in 1848 by Lord Morpeth, to establish a central Board of Health. Strong challenges came from MPs representing urban areas, who were concerned that central government would encroach upon the independence of the localities. There was also resistance from county MPs who feared that the rural areas would be obliged to raise their rates to pay for health reform in the towns. From the start, the public health movement found itself opposed by a coalition of ratepayers and local authorities.

The reformers fought back by stressing the economic case for sanitary reform. They claimed that a healthy workforce would be more productive than a sick one; it would more regularly employed and so have less need of poor relief. Slaney made this point strongly in Parliament.

> **KEY ISSUE**
>
> *On what grounds were health reforms opposed?*

> **Q**
>
> *What did Slaney claim would be the economic and social benefits of public health reform?*

> Instead of causing additional expense, it would effect a considerable saving — it would be a measure of economy. It would diminish the poor rates, and it would diminish crime, inasmuch as it would remove many of the causes of crime.
>
> *From a speech by R. F. Slaney in the House of Commons, 1848*

> **The Public Health Act, 1848**
>
> ● Established a General Board of Health, with three members responsible to Parliament. These were, initially, Morpeth, Chadwick and Shaftesbury.

- The Board was empowered to establish local boards of health following a petition from at least one-tenth of the local ratepayers or when the annual death rate exceeded the high figure of 23 per 1000 of the population.
- The local Boards were given wide powers over public health concerns, including sewerage, drainage and water supply, road building and the sanitation of new houses. They could buy up property in areas that needed to be cleared and could provide amenities like parks, public conveniences, and cemeteries.

The Act represented a major shift towards intervention by central government in an area previously considered outside its authority. Yet historians have been anxious to point out that the Act was permissive, not compulsory. It did not oblige the councils to introduce public health schemes; it only granted them the power to do so if they wished. Once the local boards had been established, the General Board of Health could not force them to undertake any course of action. Its role was simply to advise and provide information, through a number of inspectors. Not all local authorities chose to use these services.

By 1853, 182 towns had established local boards of health. Of these, 71 had plans for sewage and water supply systems but only 13 had put their plans into effect. In both Leeds and Birmingham, for example, the dominance of a group of shopkeepers and small businessmen on the town council, who were keen to minimise local expenditure, prevented any substantial local reform that might raise local rates. The 1848 Public Health Act had excluded London from its provisions since the capital had its own sanitary authority – the Metropolitan Commission of Sewers, established in 1848. Chadwick was determined that the power of the Metropolitan Commission should be absorbed under the authority of the General Board. Much of the General Board's time and energy was spent in attempting, unsuccessfully, to bring this about in the face of stiff opposition from the Anti-Centralisation Union. In 1858 a measure was passed in Parliament, which enabled local authorities to establish their own sanitary bodies free from central control.

This constant in-fighting over how the 1848 Public Health Act was to be implemented demonstrates two especially notable points about social reform in this period:

- The opposition that reformers faced suggests that public health reform was not simply a matter of using current knowledge to solve a particular problem. Indeed, by the 1850s, scientific developments had solved most of the physical and technical problems in sanitary engineering. The limitations on reform were not scientific but political.
- There were strong forces working against reform, the most powerful being cost-conscious local authorities who were anxious to retain their local independence in the face of what they saw as growing centralisation. Even *The Lancet*, the journal of the medical profession, celebrated the disbanding of the Central Board of Health, and saw it

KEY ISSUE

How effective was the Act?

Q

What does the controversy over the Act reveal about the wider issue of social reform?

as a rejection of the idea of centralised administration. 'The truth is', the journal said in 1858, 'we do not like paternal governments'.

Yet, for all the resistance it met, the Public Health Act of 1848 proved a landmark piece of legislation. It created the base on which all subsequent reforms were structured in the nineteenth century. As the historian Oliver MacDonagh puts it: 'The supreme irony was that the public health act of 1848 failed at precisely the moment when the essential correctness of its main principles was being established.' Although reluctance to introduce health reforms continued throughout the century, the mounting evidence of both the need for, and the benefits of, reform made it increasingly difficult for councils to justify their resistance.

TIMELINE
Major public health reforms after 1848

1868   the Torrens Act empowered local authorities to knock down insanitary dwellings

1871   Local Government Board created with authority to oversee health policies of local councils

1875   Artisans Dwelling Act permitted councils to replace slums with new housing

1875   Public Health Act – the first compulsory measure. It required councils to appoint a Medical Officer of Health and to provide fresh water, sewerage and public lavatories

Death rates remained high for most of the nineteenth century but, as the accompanying table shows, by the century's end a significant decline had occurred in deaths from infectious diseases.

Q

How far does the data suggest that public health reform had had a beneficial impact by 1900?

Deaths from various causes	1850	1900
Infectious and contagious diseases	32%	10%
Respiratory diseases	17%	17%
Heart failure	9%	20%
Infant mortality	25%	24%
Cancer	4%	5%
Accidents	3%	3%
Other	10%	21%

TABLE 4 *Causes of deaths in 1850 and 1900*

4 ⌁ IMPROVING WORKING CONDITIONS: THE FACTORY ACTS, 1833–50

KEY ISSUE

Why was there a strong demand for factory reform in this period?

Since the development of industry in the eighteenth century, factories, with their often-appalling working conditions, had attracted the attention of reformers. There had been attempts, in the factory acts in 1802 and 1819, to restrict the working hours of children in the cotton mills, but these had been of only limited effect. By the 1830s the evidence of the brutal exploitation of child labour had become too powerful to ignore, and a movement developed for the reform of factory conditions. In south-east Lancashire and the West Riding of Yorkshire, factory workers formed Short Time Committees to agitate for a ten-hour day for all workers, both children and adults.

Although the campaign concentrated on the issue of child labour, the objection to the factory system had broader aspects. Many working people entered the factory reluctantly. At home they had been able to work at their own pace. Factory hours were long, monotonous and imposed by the employer. Historical balance is needed here. The exploitation of workers did not begin with industrialisation. Labourers on the land had suffered throughout the ages. At its best, factory life offered regular hours and pay. That is why examples of labourers going eagerly from the land into the factories are not uncommon. However, at its worst, and it was the worst that the reformers concentrated on, factory life intensified the suffering of the workers.

Factory reform attracted a range of support from across the social spectrum. Richard Oastler, the manager of a large landed estate outside Huddersfield, argued that the exploitation of small children in the factories was the unacceptable face of industrialisation. The paternalism that had previously created a harmony between the landlord and the labourer had been replaced by a relationship in which an employer's obligation towards his employees began and ended with the payment of a wage. It was what Karl Marx later defined as the 'cash nexus'. A major inspiration in the Chartist movement was the hatred the workers felt for the new poor law; its callousness proved to them that their needs were no longer understood by those in authority.

The operative [worker] looked upon the new enactment, as the breaking of the last link in the chain of sympathy. Huge, prison-like workhouses had risen serving to remind the poor of their coming doom. With scanty wages, in many instances insufficient to support life in a tolerable state of comfort, there was nothing before them but misery in the present, and the Bastille [an infamous and hated prison in pre-Revolutionary Paris] in the future, in which they were to be immured when the rich oppressor no longer required their services.

R. G. Gammage, A History of the Chartist Movement, *1854*

Q

1. *What do you understand by the reference to 'the breaking of the last link in the chain of sympathy'?*
2. *How does this extract help us to understand the hatred felt by the labouring classes towards the new poor law?*

Some sympathetic factory owners, like John Fielden, a cotton manufacturer and MP for Oldham, argued that the intense competition between employers meant that they would never be persuaded to operate a system of voluntary regulation. Their desire for profits would undermine any sympathy they had for the workers. Therefore, if factory conditions were to be improved even to a minimum standard, it required the intervention of the State.

PICTURE 9 *Drawings depicting children at work in the mines, reproduced in the Parliamentary Commission's Report on Employment of Children in Mines, 1842. The top picture shows two young boys, the bottom picture a young girl. In the days before dependable photography, such drawings were the only way of providing visual evidence of conditions in the mines to those who had not visited them. Parliament came to put great reliance on the illustrations. Many MPs were disturbed by what they saw; others claimed the pictures gave a false impression of working conditions.*

Q

1. *From what you have read in this chapter, suggest the likely reaction to these illustrations of child labour by*
(i) Evangelicals and
(ii) MPs.
2. *How reliable were such drawings as evidence of conditions in the mines?*

In 1832 a Select Committee, chaired by the MP Michael Sadler, took evidence from the factory districts and recommended a Bill to limit the work of all textile factory workers to ten hours per day. This recommendation was rejected as being too intrusive into private enterprise. Instead, in 1833, a Royal Commission was appointed to investigate the matter, under the chairmanship of Edwin Chadwick. This resulted in the 1833 Factory Act, the first of five major pieces of legislation in the period down to 1850:

● **The Factory Act of 1833**, often referred to as Althorp's Act, was a direct result of this inquiry and it proved to be a great disappointment to the Short Time Committees.
  – The Act prohibited the employment of children under the age of 9.
  – Children from nine to 12 to work a maximum of 12 hours a day and no more than 48 hours a week.
  – Young persons from 13 to 18 restricted to a maximum of 12 hours a day and 69 hours a week.
  – Children from 9 to 11 to be given 2 hours of schooling a day.

- **1842 Mines and Collieries Act**. This followed a Royal Commission into mining conditions.
  - Prohibited women, girls, and also boys under ten from working below ground.
  - Appointed inspectors to oversee conditions in the mines.
- **1844 Factory Act**, known as Graham's Act.
  - Children under 8 not permitted to work.
  - Women were restricted to 12 hours work per day.
  - Children under 13 were reduced to a maximum of 3.5 hours work per day and their schooling was increased to 3 hours.
- **1847 Factory Act**, known as the Ten Hours Act
  - Restricted the hours of labour for women and young persons to 10 hours per day.
- **1850 Factory Act**, specified the hours of the work of those covered by the 1847 Act
  - They were to work only between 6 am and 6 pm, with an hour's break for meals, and not after 2 pm on a Saturday.

These measures demonstrate many of the influences at work that were identified earlier. In accordance with Benthamite principles, each Act followed an extensive parliamentary investigation into the 'problem', either by Royal Commission or Select Committee. Similarly, each piece of legislation involved the appointment of an inspectorate to ensure that the Acts were obeyed. Yet the appearance was more impressive than the reality. The Select Committees and Royal Commissions generally found what they set out to find, and the inspectors were so few in number (four for the whole United Kingdom under the 1833 Act) that the laws were easily avoided. Despite this, however, the notions of investigation and inspection had become, by 1850, an enduring feature of social reform legislation.

The legislation was very much a product of the age. The Benthamite notion of 'rule and exception' was clearly applied. Normally, the State should not interfere in the contractual relationship between workers and employers; exceptionally it might have to. The exceptions were defined as those groups unable to agree on a contract of employment since they were not free agents; in practice, this meant children and (from 1842) women. It had been the hope of Oastler and the working people who agitated through the Short Time Committees, that the restriction of children's hours would also limit that of the adults they worked alongside. But employers got round this by using children in relays. Adult male labour remained unprotected by legislation until the end of the century. It was argued that adult men were free contracting agents: in a free market economy it was vital that the State allow individuals to pursue what they regarded as their own best interests.

The Evangelical influence is also evident in this legislation in that factory reform was intended as moral reform. Factories and mines were seen as places where the morals of the young were likely to be corrupted; hence, the linking of reform with education. In 1842, the Mine Commissioners

> **KEY ISSUE**
>
> *How effective were the Factory Acts?*

> **Q**
>
> *In what ways did these measures reflect the influence of Benthamism?*

Q

In what ways did these measures reflect the influence of Evangelicalism?

were dismayed to find that women worked underground, stripped to the waist, cutting coal alongside the men. They considered this to be a dangerous sexual temptation and a moral affront; the legislation of 1842 and 1844, which protected women at work, was as much about defining 'acceptable' moral standards as it was about improving working conditions.

The Factory Acts have traditionally been regarded as a victory for humanitarian values and there is no doubt that the sincerity and conviction of men like Sadler and Shaftesbury did much to persuade others of the need to protect the innocent and the vulnerable. But it is worth remembering how limited these five Acts were when set against the larger industrial picture. The legislation applied only to textile factories and mines. It did not extend to factories in other industries until 1867, when a factory was defined as a place where 50 or more people were employed. Smaller places were not covered until the Factory and Workshop Act of 1878. This meant that for the greater part of the nineteenth century most workers laboured in conditions that were not regulated by law.

5 ～ EDUCATING THE YOUNG: REFORMS IN EDUCATION

The promotion of education became a major reforming interest of the Victorians. It was natural in a society with a strong belief in individual freedom that it should place a great emphasis on education. It was held that an educated population would make the right moral choices. By the middle years of the century, middle-class observers saw education as an answer to the problems of poverty, disease, crime and disorder. However, while the education of the young was regarded as a high ideal, the means of achieving it simply did not exist. It is true that the upper classes were able to send their sons to public schools, but, outside Scotland, where most villages had their own school, there was no formal education available to the mass of the population in Britain in 1830.

For those who believed in a rapid expansion of education, the obvious answer was simply to build more schools. But such a solution was not practically possible. The few schools that did exist and on which any expansion would be based were provided by Christian groups who were in bitter conflict with each other. The established Anglican Church had created the National Society for the Education of the Poor in Accordance with the Principles of the Established Church (known for short as the National Society). As indicated by its full title, the essential purpose of the National Society was religious. It had been formed to battle with the Nonconformist churches in a war to gain converts. As for the Nonconformists, they had already founded a number of voluntary schools, that is, schools paid for by voluntary contributions. Any proposal for expanding education would come up against the problem of the competition between Anglicans and Nonconformists. The opposed viewpoints of the two denominations are well illustrated in the following extracts:

KEY ISSUE

Why were there strong demands for a national system of education in this period?

The [Anglican] Church has no more claim for exclusive pecuniary [financial] aid from the State or for any pecuniary aid at all, than is possessed by any other of those many corporations with which our country abounds. To call upon Parliament to vote any money for the exclusive support of the Church of England is to call upon Parliament to do what is unjust. The taxes are collected from persons of all religions and cannot be fairly expended for the exclusive maintenance of one.

The Nonconformist argument (from a letter of W. F. Hook, a Leeds clergyman, to the Anglican Bishop of St. David's, 1846)

The late Report on the state of education in our great towns had showed that the Church had done nearly everything there. It had established good schools, and carried them on quietly and unostentatiously for years. If anybody desired to know which religious body was the most earnest in the cause of education, let him consult any one of the Reports of the Committee of Council, and he would see how Churchmen had laboured, what large sums they had expended, and how many schools they had maintained.

The Anglican argument (from a speech by Robert Montagu, the Conservative spokesman on Education, in the House of Commons, 1870)

Q

1. *What do you understand to be W. F. Hook's main objections to State aid being paid for the upkeep of Anglican schools?*
2. *On what grounds does Robert Montagu justify the record of the Anglican Church in regard to education?*

Given the very basic nature of the schooling available and the religious rivalry of the age, educational advance was necessarily slow and halting. Yet, despite these difficulties, there was by the middle of the nineteenth century a broad acceptance that education was so important that it had to be organised on a national basis. In 1844, Lord Shaftesbury's Ragged School Union was set up with the aim of providing basic education for the children of the city slums, thus saving them from sliding into crime and anti-social behaviour. Such voluntary initiatives were supported by government funds distributed by the Committee of the Privy Council on Education. The first government grant for education had been made in 1833 when £20 000 had been allocated. By 1860, the figure had risen to £1 270 000. The grants were linked to a system of school inspection. The findings of the Newcastle Commission, established in 1858 to investigate the education of the poorer classes, led to the introduction of what was called 'The Revised Code'. By this, school grants were linked to attendance levels and examination results.

Thus, by the 1860s, a system of schooling of sorts was in existence. The truth was the industrial age demanded it. Despite the disputes between Anglicans and Nonconformists and the clash between the

1833	£20 000
1840	£170 000
1850	£370 000
1860	£1 270 000
1870	£1 620 000

TABLE 5
Government grants for education

voluntary principle and State funding, there were irresistible economic arguments for the provision of a system of elementary education that would equip all children with the ability to read and to count. Factories could not be fully productive unless the workers were capable of reading notices and written instructions, and making simple mathematical calculations. Equally interesting the Chartists saw education as major means of advancing the economic interests of the workers. However, they were unwilling to accept a national education system if it was controlled by government:

Q

Explain in your own words why the writers objected to 'placing the education of our children in the hands of any government'.

There is evil to be apprehended from placing the education of our children in the hands of any government. It becomes one of the most important duties of the working and middle classes to establish a just and liberal system of education, lest the power of educating their own children be taken from them by the arbitrary act of a corrupt and exclusive government.

William Lovett and John Collins, Chartism, *1840*

TIMELINE

Key stages in the development of the educational system

By 1800	public schools and grammar schools existed, but only for the children of the wealthy
By 1811	The National Society (Anglican) and the British and Foreign Society (Nonconformist) had begun to compete with each other in setting up elementary schools
1833	First annual government grant (£20 000) for education, divided between the two societies
1839	Cabinet Committee appointed to monitor spending of the education grant (which had increased to £900 000 by 1858)
1844	Lord Shaftesbury's Ragged School Union set up to provide basic education for the children of the city slums
1858	Newcastle Commission reported on inadequate provision of education in Britain
1862	The Education Department of the Privy Council which produced a Revised Code recommending 'payment by results' as a way of improving school standards
1869	Birmingham Education League, led by the radical Liberal Joseph Chamberlain, pressed for the introduction of a national system of state education
1870	Forster's Education Act took the first steps towards creating a national system of elementary education (see page 217)

See page 217 on Gladstone's educational reforms

There was also a growing conviction among the governing classes that the extension of the vote to increasing numbers of the working classes meant that it was important to raise their educational level. Robert Lowe, a Liberal politician, said memorably at the time of the passing of the second Reform in 1867 that it was now 'absolutely necessary to compel our new masters to learn their letters'. It was such thinking that, three years later, led Gladstone's Liberal Government to attempt to resolve the religious conflict and create a workable national system of education.

6 ➴ REFORMING THE LOCALITIES: THE MUNICIPAL CORPORATIONS ACT, 1835

The Municipal Corporations Act was described by a contemporary as 'a postscript to the Reform Act'. The reform of Parliament in 1832 had granted the vote to the middle classes (see page 53). The Act of 1835 gave this same group the franchise in local elections, which, in effect, left them in control of the large towns

KEY ISSUE
What were the chief effects of the Municipal Corporations Act?

- the Act abolished 178 boroughs with 'closed' or corrupt local corporations and replaced them with elected borough corporations (town councils) elected by all the male ratepayers in the area
- the elected councillors would then elect their own aldermen (higher officials to hold office for six years) and mayor
- the councils were entitled to raise loans and receive grants from the central government
- the councils were to form watch committees to organise local police forces
- large towns without corporations could apply for incorporation.

Over the next 20 years, 22 new town councils were established under this legislation, the first being Manchester and Birmingham in 1838. This created a system of elected town councils throughout the country, but the municipal franchise was as narrow as that for parliamentary elections and effectively excluded the working class in the towns. What it did create was a system of local government that was reasonably sensitive to the wishes of local ratepayers. However, as was noted earlier (page 75), these were not always willing to play an active role in the field of reform. The voters and officials of the new system were the new middle class, believers in the free market and careful in their spending of ratepayers' money. The only reform which the new local authorities were obliged to undertake under the 1835 legislation was the establishment of a Watch Committee to supervise the policing of the area. Other than this, town councils tended to find arguments against schemes that involved large-scale expenditure.

  The development of local councils raised the issue of the balance of power between local and central government. Where did the authority of each begin and end? This was a particularly important question in regard to the mounting problem of law and order. Crime rates were on the increase. The numbers of individuals committed to trial for serious offences had risen from 4 605 in 1805 to 24 303 in 1845. Even allowing for the increasing size of population, this was an alarming growth in

Q

Why was the question of policing in the localities such a contentious one?

crime. Edwin Chadwick saw the solution in the form of a national police force that would be centrally controlled by the Home Office. The Metropolitan Police, established in 1829, seemed to be the first step towards this national force, but the move was ferociously resisted in the localities. A centralised police force was seen as the equivalent of a standing army imposed on local people. Thomas Attwood, a radical, voiced a commonly held view when he described a national police force as 'a species of tyranny'. The result of this strong local resistance was that the new police forces which were created in the nineteenth century were all organised on a county, rather than a national, basis although they were ultimately responsible to the Home Secretary.

7 ⌢ CONCLUSION – 'RIOTS, RATES AND ROTTING MATTER'

This chapter has identified the following as the most influential motives behind social reform in the early nineteenth century:

- Evangelicalism and Humanitarianism
- economic individualism
- Utilitarianism and the desire for efficiency
- the need to maintain a productive workforce
- the fear of social disorder and instability.

These considerations produced a debate that focused on the question of how to achieve a balance between central and local government. Intimately tied to the debate was the issue of the cost of reform and who should pay for it. Such issues occasioned great argument between opposed interests, which explains the uneven pattern of reform. It is always worth bearing in mind that the 'Condition of England Question' was primarily a concern of the middle and upper classes of the day. For the working classes, as the story of Chartism demonstrates, the ills of industrial society and their remedy were easily understandable. For them, Britain had an undemocratic political system; once this was genuinely reformed by extending the vote to working men, a better society would follow.

But for the majority of the social reformers of the early nineteenth century there was no such single or simple solution. That is why the motives behind reform and the methods of achieving it varied so considerably. Yet one conclusion does present itself: the driving impulse behind reform was not idealism but fear. There was a conviction that united all the reformers whatever their differences in attitude: if the 'Condition of England Question' was not dealt with, the result would be the moral and physical degradation of Britain's urban areas, violent disorder among the working classes and uncontrollable social disruption.

TIMELINE

Summary of major social reforms, 1832–50

1833	Factory Act (Althorp's Act) – restricted the working hours of children and women in textile mills and mines
1833	Slavery abolished in British colonies
1834	Poor Law Amendment Act – restructured the system for relieving poverty
1835	Municipal Corporations Act – reformed local government
1835	Prisons Act – overhauled the corrupt prison system
1837	Civil Registration and Marriages Acts – made it compulsory to record details of births, deaths and marriages
1839	County Police Act – established police forces in country areas
1842	Mines and Collieries Act – prohibited females and child under 10 from working below ground
1844	Factory Act (Ashley's) – limited the working hours of females, and males under 18
1847	Factory Act (Ten Hours Act) – established the 10 hour (maximum) working day for females and young males
1848	Public Health Act – took the first major steps towards ending the insanitary conditions in urban areas
1850	Factory Act – gave factory inspectors greater powers

8 ⌁ BIBLIOGRAPHY

ARTICLES

J. Garrard 'The New Poor Law', *New Perspectives*, March 1997.

Phil Chapple 'The Victorian Slaughter of the Innocents', *History Review*, March 2000.

Clive Emsley 'Crime in Victorian England', *History Review*, March 1998.

BOOKS FOR AS/A LEVEL STUDENTS

Vyvyen Brendon *The Age of Reform, 1820–50*, Hodder & Stoughton, 1994, is a documentary study that deals very helpfully with all the major themes in this chapter.

Joe Finn *Chartists and Chartism*, Hodder & Stoughton, 1992, is a similar style of book that has many useful things to say on the economic and social background of the period.

Peter Murray *Poverty and Welfare*, Access to History series, Hodder & Stoughton, 1999, deals with the reform of the Poor Law.

Andrina Stiles *Religion, Society and Reform 1800–1914*, Access to History series, Hodder & Stoughton, 1995, offers insights into such themes as Evangelicalism and educational reform.

Gillian Sutherland *Elementary Education in the Nineteenth Century*, Historical Association, 1971, is an excellent brief account of educational reform.

Eric Midwinter *Victorian Social Reform*, Longman, 1982, and R. C. Birch, *The Shaping of the Welfare State*, Longman, 1976, are documentary studies which contain illuminating commentaries.

FURTHER READING

Ursula Henriques *Before the Welfare State*, Longman, 1979, provides an excellent coverage of the competing demands of central and local government.

O. MacDonagh *Early Victorian Government 1830–1870*, Weidenfeld and Nicolson, 1977, covers much the same ground as Henriques and argues that reform occurred because conditions had become intolerable.

A. J. Taylor *Laissez-faire and State Intervention in the Nineteenth Century*, Macmillan, 1972, summarises the debate that has taken place between historians over this issue.

Derek Fraser *The Evolution of the British Welfare State*, Macmillan, 1978 is, arguably, the most authoritative study of the social reforms and the influences behind them. Another established modern classic is J. F. C. Harrison, *Early Victorian Britain*, Fontana, 1988.

A. Wohl *Endangered Lives, Public Health in Victorian Britain*, Dent, 1990, concentrates on the disputes over public health issues.

Short studies which are renowned for the quality of their analysis are: Roderick Floud *The People and the British Economy 1830–1914*, OUP, 1998, and A. Digby, *The Poor Law in Nineteenth-Century England and Wales*, Historical Association, 1982.

Students who are interested in knowing more about the lives and characters of the reformers will enjoy dipping into the following: J. R. Dinwiddy, *Bentham*, Oxford University Press, 1989; S. E. Finer, *The Life and Times of Edwin Chadwick*, Methuen, 1952, and Georgina Battiscombe, *Shaftesbury*, Purnell, 1974.

9 ∽ STRUCTURED AND ESSAY QUESTIONS

A *Structured questions for AS Level*

The following questions relate to the separate sections in this chapter. The questions are closely linked to the Key Issues and margin questions that are there to guide you through the material you are reading. So, in preparing your answers, do look back to the relevant Key Issues and Q boxes. They will point you to the information and ideas that you need. You will notice that some questions are straightforward in that they ask you to *describe*, while others are more demanding in that they ask you to *explain*. The number of marks allocated to each question reflects this difference. In the first case you have simply to use your *knowledge* to answer the question; in the second case you have to use your *judgement*. Put simply, it is the difference between being asked *what* happened and being asked *why* it happened.

No matter what type of question you are attempting, it is always worth your drawing up lists of key facts and points. If you find that the question is of the straightforward descriptive type, then a well-ordered and shaped list will provide the answer. If, however, you are being asked for an explanation or a judgement, then your list will provide the backing evidence that you then use in developing your argument.

1. (a) What major social problems had developed in Britain by the 1830s? (30)
   (b) In what ways did Utilitarianism differ from Humanitarianism in its approach to social problems? (60)
2. (a) What conditions and circumstances led Parliament to amend the Poor Law in 1834? (30)
   (b) In what ways did the Poor Law Amendment Act of 1834 attempt to deal with the problem of poverty? (60)
3. (a) Describe the main symptoms of cholera and explain why outbreaks of this disease were so frequent in Britain in the first half of the nineteenth century. (30)
   (b) What were the main obstacles to the improvement of public health in the 1830s and 1840s? (60)
4. (a) Describe the chief ways in which Parliament tried, between 1833 and 1850, to improve conditions for Britain's factory workers. (30)
   (b) Why did reformers meet strong opposition in their attempts improve working conditions in the factories in this period? (60)
5. (a) What social and economic developments had occurred by the 1830s to make education an important issue in Britain? (30)
   (b) Describe the contribution of (i) the Anglican Church, and (ii) the Nonconformist Churches to the provision of education in Britain in the first half of the nineteenth century. (60)
6. (a) What were the main terms of the Municipal Corporations Act of 1835? (30)
   (b) Explain why the reform of local government was not always welcomed in the localities. (60)

B *Essays for A2*
1. Which set of ideas had the greater influence on the social reformers of the 1830s and 1840s – Utilitarianism or Humanitarianism? Give reasons for your choice. (60)
2. How far do you agree with the view that the Poor Law Amendment Act of 1834 dealt with the symptoms of poverty rather than its causes? (60)
3. How important a role was played by Edwin Chadwick in the provision of public health in Britain in the nineteenth century? (60)
4. 'The factory reforms of the years 1833 to 1850 did not actually improve working conditions; they only pointed the way forward.' How accurate do you consider this statement to be? (60)
5. 'Whatever contribution the Anglican and Nonconformist Churches made to the cause of education was undermined by the results of the rivalry between them.' How far do you find this an acceptable assessment? (60)
6. How appropriate do you think it is to describe the Municipal Corporations Act of 1835 as 'a postscript to the Reform Act'? (60)

10 ⌐ DOCUMENTARY QUESTION ON THE POOR LAW

Read the following Sources on the effects of the New Poor Law. Then tackle the questions that follow. You are advised to spend approximately half your time answering Question 4.

SOURCE A
A report from an auditor is quoted in support of the New Poor Law

Here was upwards of £1000 left in the hands of the ratepayers, to meet the demands of labourers willing to earn it. Ratepayers who had been opposed to the Union, had now substantial proofs in their own pockets of its advantages, and the labourers began to think it was high time 'to look out'. Employment was now sought after. The farmers answered the demand without taking advantage of circumstances to reduce the wages, and the gratitude of the workmen was shown by their civility and industry.

SOURCE B *A new Assistant Poor Law Commissioner, who had personally witnessed the Ampthill Riots of 1835, answers questions put to him by a Parliamentary Select Committee (Minutes of evidence before the Select Committee on the Poor Law Amendment, Parliamentary Papers, 1837–8)*

When was the riot?
At the formation of the Poor Law Union in 1835.

What was the origin of the riot?
The origin was the change of the allowance system from money to bread, but the general feeling against the introduction of the law was another cause, the men being worried at being shut up in the work-house, and they stated to me most distinctly that all they wanted was work.

Have you heard that there is any improvement in cultivation arising from the greater employment of labourers?
I believe there is no doubt at all of that.

Do you perceive any difference between the employer and the employed?
There can be no doubt whatever. Four years back the employed were always sulky, and now they are civil and polite.

SOURCE C *The New Poor Law Commission defends the Amendment Act in an 1840 report to Parliament (Parliamentary Papers, 1840)*

Recall the state of England before the Poor Law Amendment Act. The amount of poor rates had become oppressive so as to threaten the abandonment of the land. The Speenhamland System had enabled the predominant interest in each locality to force their weaker neigh-bours to contribute to a common fund from which they did not derive an equal benefit, and had converted the state of the labourer to that of slavery. The consequences were the agrarian disturbances and fires of 1830 and 1831. Now the causes of evil have been extin-guished. Systematic relief of able-bodied men in aid of wages only exists in a few Poor law Unions which do not yet possess an efficient workhouse.

Had there been no Poor Law, Chartism would never have been heard of, nor Birmingham have been heated with fire or fury nor Newport run red. Rural Police and increased taxation are the Act's necessary assistants on the Government's side, and hayrick-firing and the manufacturing of weapons its accompaniments on the side of the governed.

SOURCE D
G. R. W. Baxter, a writer who hated the New Poor Law, describes its harmful consequences (from G. R. W. Baxter, The Book of the Bastilles, *1841)*

1. *Study Source C. Using Source C and your own knowledge, explain what the 'Speenhamland System' was. (10)*
2. *Study Source A. How valuable would you judge Source A to be as evidence of the effects the New Poor Law? (25)*
3. *Study Sources B and D. In what respects do Sources B and D coincide in their judgement of the effects of the New Poor Law? (25)*
4. *Study all the sources. Using* all *these sources and* your own knowledge, *say to what extent you accept the view that 'the 1834 Act effectively encouraged self-reliance amongst the poor but did not address their real needs'. (60)*   ***Total 120 marks***

Advice for students: Points to consider in answering the questions:
A critical first point to note is that you are advised 'to spend about half your time answering Question 4'. Since this particular question carries 60 marks, twice as many as any other single question, it is advice you ignore at your peril. Even when you are not directly advised how long to spend on a question, the mark allocation will always provide the clue. It is waste of precious time and space to write long answers to questions which carry a low number of marks.

● **Question 1.** The danger of over-writing applies to this question. You may well know a great deal about the 'Speenhamland System' but you are not being asked to write an essay; make you answer brief and to the point. Notice that you are asked to use the source and your own knowledge. If you ignore one of these instructions you are unlikely to gain more than half marks at most. You will note that the extract is from an official report by the Poor Law Commission, which obviously took a poor view of the 'Speenhamland System'. After all, it was to get rid of such schemes that the Poor Law was amended in 1834. Although the extract describes the harmful results of Speenhamland system, it does not tell you how the scheme actually operated. That is where you should draw on your own knowledge to explain how it had operated and what it had been meant to achieve.

● **Question 2.** This is a very different type of question from the preceding one. It is not asking you to explain the meaning of the source but to make a judgement about its value. Of course, to do this you need to understand what is being said in the extract. The auditor writes glowingly of the effect of the new Poor Law in Uckfield. In his view, it has saved money for the ratepayers, encouraged the labourers to seek work, and has met with the co-operation of the farmers who have maintained wages and thus earned the goodwill of the workmen. How valuable is all this? These are some thoughts you might consider. An auditor deals with facts and figures, so this makes his findings important. He has studied the matter first-hand, so this gives him the chance to be realistic in his judgement. On the other hand, he has obviously been employed by the Poor Law Union to make his report. Is he likely to say anything that is not favourable towards the new system? In addition, even though his report may be honest and accurate, it is based on a study of only one particular union. Does this make Source A of limited value? Does the picture presented here need to be compared and contrasted with reports from other unions before its value can be finally assessed?

Question 3. This is a comparative question asking you to estimate the level of agreement between two sources. As always, read them carefully to make sure you understand what each is saying. In Source D it is clear that Baxter is totally convinced that the new Poor Law has been a disastrous failure. For him, it has stimulated, not lessened, the causes of unrest. Adey is more circumspect. He sees a connection between the Poor Law and the rioting but considers that this was caused initially by the workers' understandable but unnecessary fears and their failure to grasp the merits of the new system. Once they had begun to appreciate these, they became contented and docile. So Source D and Source B agree that the Poor Law was the reason for the violent reaction in the localities, but Source B goes further in its explanation of why there was violence and why it later subsided. Is that how you read the two sources? Do not be afraid to challenge or qualify what has just been said. These 'points to consider' are meant as much to stimulate your thinking as to provide you with a definitive answer.

Question 4. The high number of marks indicates how important it is that you spend the greater part of your time on this question. Note that it asks you to use two key resources – all the sources and your own knowledge – and to address two key aspects of a proposition – that the 1834 Act encouraged self-reliance amongst the poor but failed to recognise their real needs. A good first step in preparing your response would be to run through the sources to note where and whether the evidence in them supports or challenges the proposition. What is there in the extracts that relates to the encouragement of self-reliance or the failure to address real needs? With that material at your disposal you can then check it against your own knowledge and understanding of the effects of new Poor Law. It would help your case to define what you understand 'real needs' to have been. You can then apply your reading of the sources and your own knowledge to that definition. Also note that the question asks you to what extent you agree with the view. This is an open invitation to you to accept or reject, or only partially accept, the main proposition. You are entitled, for example, to agree with one part of it, that it failed to recognise the real needs of the poor, and disagree with the other part, that it encouraged self-reliance. The choice and decision are yours. The only proviso is that you always back your verdict by referring to the evidence in the sources and your own knowledge.

5 The Chartist Experience

Chartism was a movement for Parliamentary reform which ran from 1838 to 1858. During the first ten years of its existence it involved hundreds of thousands of working people, in districts throughout the country. The Chartists' main concern was with agitating for Parliament to accept the 'People's Charter' with its celebrated 'six points', which were mostly drawn from the earlier period of radical discontent in 1815–20.

THE SIX POINTS

- **universal manhood suffrage** – that all men over the age of 21 be allowed to vote
- **vote by secret ballot** – so that votes could be cast without fear of pressure from landlords or employers
- **annual Parliaments** – general elections to take place every year instead of every seven years
- **equal electoral districts** – constituencies should contain roughly equal numbers of electors
- **abolition of the property qualification for MPs** – at that time a Member of Parliament had to own a certain amount of property
- **payment for members of Parliament** – MPs received no salary so an MP had to be a man of independent means or else be sponsored by a patron or party.

Implementation of the first two of these points, it was anticipated, would create a mass-based democracy where voting would be free of the 'influence' which was such a central part of the existing system. The idea behind annual parliaments was that those elected should be regularly accountable to the electors. The last three points all signalled a determination on the part of the Chartists to create working-class participation in politics at all levels, not simply as voters but also as members of the House of Commons and of the Government. Thus, Chartism contained within it a vision of a political system that was radically different from that which currently existed under the the Reform Act of 1832. It is hardly surprising, therefore, that when the Chartists made their demands for change, in the form of a petition to Parliament submitted on three separate occasions (in 1839, 1842 and 1848), they failed to persuade the House of Commons to accept the six points.

This failure is at the root of a good deal of the controversy that has always surrounded the movement. There are two main interpretations of Chartism and these may be summarised as follows.

Chartism as 'hunger politics'	Chartism as a serious political movement
Chartism was largely fuelled by hunger amongst a working class that was not yet ready for citizenship. Many historians have argued, as did hostile contemporaries, that the working class in 1839 was not yet 'ready' for full citizenship since its members were uneducated and, by implication, politically immature. They argue that Chartism was a fragmented movement fired by the hunger of economic depression and prone to irrational outbursts of violence. Essentially it was the politics of hunger on a massive scale. Seen in this light, its failure seems to confirm the premature nature of the Chartist claims; that they wanted the vote before they were able to use it responsibly. **Chartism failed because it wanted too much too soon**.	**Chartism was a rational, politically-motivated, movement**. It reflected a politically-aware working community and grew out of a tradition of political activity. Reasons for its failure must be sought outside the movement, in the attitudes of the Government and the middle class of the day. To put this another way, Chartism did not fail because the working community was not yet 'ready' for the vote, but rather because they were all *too* 'ready' in the sense that their aspiration to run the country generated real alarm in the ranks of the ruling classes. **Chartism failed because it represented an alternative vision of politics that was unacceptable to those in power**.

As we will see when we return to the issue of interpretation in Section 6 on page 124, historians tend to be polarised over their explanations of Chartism and its failure to achieve its aims. In order to understand this polarity it is important to reconstruct the movement as it was seen and experienced by the Chartists themselves, as well as taking account of how it looked to others at the time.

1 ✏ THE CAUSES OF CHARTISM: THE 'UMBRELLA MOVEMENT'

Chartism has been described by the historian, Dorothy Thompson, as an 'umbrella movement' which gathered under its shelter a series of smaller movements that had emerged in the 1830s. To understand this evocative image it is important to identify the way that Chartism drew upon the experience of the 1830s (Diagram 3).

> **KEY ISSUE**
>
> *Why did Chartism emerge in the late 1830s?*

A *Actions of the reformed parliament*

The Reform Act of 1832 won extensive support from working people and its passing was greeted with acclaim. However, the sense of excitement was short-lived. For all the changes, the reformed House of Commons looked remarkably like the unreformed House and acted in depressingly familiar ways. Most of the achievements of the 'reforming Whigs' over the next few years were seen to confirm the suspicion that the working community could expect little from the new arrangement, and any suggestion that the Reform Act was simply the first step towards a more democratic society was swiftly dispelled.

The years following 1832 seemed to confirm this point. The reforms of the Whig ministries of the 1830s may have broken important new

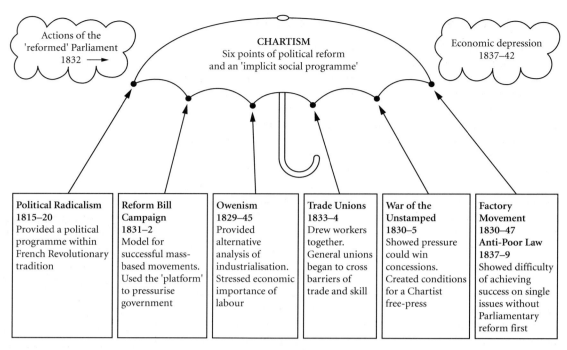

DIAGRAM 3 *Chartism as an 'Umbrella Movement'*

ground in terms of the role of government, but to the labouring population they appeared as an attack on a way of life.

● The **Factory Act of 1833** was a huge disappointment to the working-class factory reformers who campaigned for legal restrictions on the number of hours worked by adults in the textile mills of Lancashire and Yorkshire. In restricting only child labour, the Act indicated to adult workers that only political reform would produce a government that would pass legislation to protect their working conditions.

● The **Poor Law Amendment Act of 1834** was seen to withdraw the 'right' of the poor to outdoor relief.

● The **Municipal Corporations Act of 1835** was seen by the working community as simply the extension of a restricted national franchise to the localities. The Reform Act ensured that working people could not participate in national government. This new Act, with the narrow franchise by which town councils would now be elected, ensured that they were similarly excluded from local government.

● The **police forces** established by town councils after 1835, were seen as an intrusive element by the working community; they were felt to be modelled on the hated Metropolitan Police Force established in1829; in the towns of Lancashire the police forces established in the 1830s were referred to by local workers as the 'plague of blue locusts'.

Chapter 4 deals with these reforms

B *The war of the unstamped, 1831–5*

Even as the Reform Bill was inching its way to becoming an Act of Parliament, an illegal newspaper press was beginning to emerge which was critical of the proposed measure. The restriction to the freedom of the press established by the 'Six Acts' in 1819 (see page 14) was still in operation in 1830. This meant that any publication appearing at less than 26-day intervals and containing news had to bear a government stamp and be sold at the huge cost of 7d (3p). By 1831, as part of the growing interest in politics connected with the Reform Bill campaign, various radicals and organisations were beginning to test the effectiveness of the laws. In 1831 Henry Hetherington published his *Poor Man's Guardian* as an outright challenge to authority. Published at only a penny per weekly copy it bore the explicit heading: *Published contrary to 'law' to try the power of 'might' against 'right'*. This paper claimed that the newspaper stamp was a tax on knowledge and carried the significant motto '*Knowledge is power*'.

KEY ISSUE

How did the campaign for freedom of the press, from 1831 to 1835, influence the development of Chartism?

Hetherington's paper was enormously successful and managed to achieve a nationwide sale of 15 000 copies a week despite being London-based. Many other radical papers followed the *Guardian*'s lead and the Government responded by prosecuting publishers and retailers of the unstamped press. Hetherington himself suffered imprisonment twice although this did not interrupt the weekly publication of the *Guardian* from secret locations. In London alone, 740 vendors of the unstamped press were brought to trial between 1831 and 1836. Eventually the Whig Government of Lord Melbourne gave in and, in 1836, lowered the tax to a point where newspapers could be sold at 4d (1.5p).

This was a significant victory since it secured a legal status and a lower price for subsequent Chartist publications. In fact, appearing as a stamped newspaper the Chartist paper, the *Northern Star*, published from 1837 onwards, was even entitled to the benefit of free delivery by the Post Office! Perhaps more importantly, success in the war of the unstamped seemed to suggest that governments of the day did sometimes yield to the pressure that could be applied by a determined and well-organised campaign. Radicals drew as much encouragement as was possible from this isolated success.

C *The attack on trade unions, 1834*

Disappointment with the fruits of the Reform Act also led working people back to the familiar organisation of the trade union as a way of improving their position. With the repeal of the Combination Acts in 1824, it was no longer illegal for workers to band together in order to gain better conditions for themselves. By 1824 it had become a common belief in government that the Combination Acts made the control of trade unions more difficult for the authorities by pushing union organisation underground and encouraging a tradition of secrecy. With the repeal of the Combination Acts workplace organisations flourished in most trades.

This kind of activity was also encouraged by the improvement in trade between 1833 and 1835 and the accompanying demand for labour. There were a number of small-scale strikes throughout the country in 1833 and 1834. More alarmingly for the Government, in the wake of the Reform Act, a relatively new kind of trade organisation began to emerge in the form of general unions. These attempted to break away from the traditional forms of combination, based on one trade in one locality. The general unions aimed to unite workers from a number of trades in a cohesive and permanent form of organisation. The way had been shown by the leader of the Manchester cotton spinners, John Doherty, who formed the National Association for the Protection of Labour (NAPL) in 1829. This ran until 1832, had its own newspaper, *The Voice of the People*, and accumulated between 60 000 and 80 000 members in its short life.

Similarly, the Grand National Consolidated Trades Union (GNCTU) was launched in February 1834. This aimed to be a national organisation of all workers in all trades and it was organised by followers of Robert Owen. The GNCTU probably never attracted a membership of more than 16 000. It did, however, draw fire from the Whig Government, which was alarmed at the trend which the GNCTU seemed to represent. When six farm labourers from Tolpuddle, in Dorset, were prosecuted, in March 1834, for swearing illegal oaths on being initiated into a union, many saw the trial as a signal that the Government would not tolerate this growing form of organisation. The sentencing of the 'Tolpuddle Martyrs' to seven years transportation shocked the working community; the maximum sentence under the Combination Act had been six months of hard labour. The GNCTU took up the cause of the Dorset men and called a protest rally of 35 000 people in London, but the Whigs would not reverse their position. Trade unionism, hit by this harsh judgement and by the depression in trade in 1836, began to decline in support. With the failure of general unionism, it became clear that an alternative strategy was necessary.

D *The anti-poor law campaign, 1837–38*

Probably the radical campaign that most influenced the structure and shape of the Chartist movement was the agitation against the New Poor Law in the Midlands, Wales and the North, from 1837. The new Poor Law had been passed with the conditions of the rural south of England in mind. At first it applied only to these areas, but from 1837 it was extended to the rest of England and Wales. Yet the high levels of unemployment, which were particularly acute in the Yorkshire woollen industry, demonstrated the inadequacy of the New Poor Law with its refusal to see poverty as anything other than a self-inflicted wound.

The North of England saw the emergence of a highly organised protest movement and angry crowds. West Yorkshire and south-east Lancashire had been the focus of agitation for factory reform from 1830 onwards with the formation of the Short Time Committees in the factory districts. These now simply changed their names to Anti-Poor

---

Robert Owen

A wealthy factory owner who led a series of movements from the 1820s to the late 1840s. He established co-operative communities where property was held in common, co-operative shops where profits were shared and labour exchanges using their own currency. None of these schemes were a success, but he was widely supported by working-class people including a number, like William Lovett, who went on to become Chartists.

See pages 67–70 for details of the new Poor Law

Law Associations and directed their attentions to any attempt to apply the new law. Radicals, like Oastler and the Revd J. R. Stephens, saw workhouses for poor relief as a rejection by the ratepayers of their responsibilities to the poor. Stephens was a preacher who had been expelled from the Methodists for his involvement in politics. He now ran an independent chapel in Ashton-under-Lyne in Lancashire, and applied evangelical 'hellfire and damnation' oratory to the actions of the Poor Law Commissioners.

The anti-Poor Law campaign also introduced Feargus O'Connor to the Yorkshire audience that would be the basis of his personal support during the next decade. The son of a wealthy Irish family, O'Connor was trained in law and was MP for County Cork from 1832 to 1835. In 1837 he moved to Leeds and started the *Northern Star* as an anti-Poor Law paper. Support for the agitation was extensive and resulted in a Parliamentary motion, put by the radical MP John Fielden in February 1838, to repeal the New Poor Law. The failure of this motion by a huge margin, 309 votes to 17, provided a powerful impetus for a political movement with a much wider programme. The lesson seemed to be that before individual motions could be successful there would first have to be a complete overhaul of the system of representation. Significantly, 14 of the 20 northern delegates to the first Chartist Convention had been active in the anti-Poor Law campaign.

KEY ISSUE

In what ways was the Anti-Poor Law campaign important in the development of Chartism?

FEARGUS O'CONNOR (1794–1855)

O'Connor was undoubtedly the leading figure of the Chartist movement. He was born into a wealthy Protestant land-owning family in County Cork. Both his father and his uncle had been involved in the revolutionary struggles for an independent Ireland in the 1790s. Both men had been leaders of the illegal organisation, the United Irishmen, and both suffered terms of imprisonment as a result. Feargus was trained in law and became a Barrister. He was elected as a MP for County Cork in the reformed Parliament of 1832. As a supporter of Daniel O'Connell, who had forced through Roman Catholic emancipation in 1829, he swiftly came into contact with radical groups in London such as the National Union of the Working Classes. However, he broke with O'Connell, who wished to support the Whig Government, in 1835. O'Connor held his seat in the general election of 1835, but lost it when local Tories revealed that he lacked the necessary £600 freehold property qualification. In November 1837 he established the *Northern Star* in Leeds, initially as an anti-Poor Law newspaper. This paper was to gain a huge readership nationally over the next few years. The people of the West Riding of Yorkshire, with its developing woollen industry, became the basis of his popular support. He took a leading role in the growing Chartist agitation in 1838. Elected a dele-

PROFILE

PICTURE 10
Feargus O'Connor

gate to the Chartist Convention in 1839, he was imprisoned for 18 months in 1840 for seditious libel. He continued to write regularly for the *Northern Star* during his imprisonment and, on his release, he became a fierce critic of any attempt to divert the movement from its major concern with the vote. This was the basis of his renowned dispute with Lovett. O'Connor was elected as MP for Nottingham in 1842 and was, from 1843 onwards, absorbed with the Land Plan. This proved to be phenomenally popular, far exceeding even O'Connor's expectations. But it was made the subject of a Parliamentary investigation in 1848. Although this cleared him of any personal corruption, the pressure of work and worry connected with the Land Plan eventually led to a breakdown in his health. Declining into insanity after 1852, he died in an asylum. Sixty thousand people lined the streets to pay their respects at his funeral. O'Connor was probably the best-loved of all the radical leaders of his day. He is also the most maligned by generations of historians who have blamed him for the failure of Chartism.

E *The case of the Glasgow spinners*

Any political movement aiming at mass support needs clear-cut issues to build its case around. What Chartism needed in its early stages were issues that related directly to the everyday experience of the working man and woman and which could readily be related to his or her own situation. The application of the New Poor Law had provided just such an issue, with the Government clearly playing the part of the villain of the piece. Another was provided by the case of the Glasgow Spinners.

The county of Lanarkshire, with its focus on the town of Glasgow, was the centre of the Scottish cotton trade. Like its counterpart south of the border it was hit by the depression of the late 1830s. The local employers reacted to this situation by reducing wages and announcing the introduction of larger spinning mules which would require a workforce that was less skilled and therefore cheaper. In response the Spinners' Association, which had emerged during the growth of trade unions in the years after the Reform Act, brought 800 men out on strike in April 1837. The employers decided to fight it out and introduced strike-breaking labour from other areas. One of these strike breakers was shot dead in July 1837. Without any evidence as to their involvement in this or any other violent incidents, the committee of the Cotton Spinners' Association was arrested and five of them were put on trial for murder and conspiracy to intimidate and molest. Within the wider working-class public, there was a good deal of sympathy for the spinners. It all seemed depressingly familiar, the more so since the 'Tolpuddle Martyrs', to whose case it was widely compared, had arrived back from Australia, following a Royal pardon, in June 1837, to much public acclaim. It appeared that the attack on trade union rights was being initiated again. As regular chapelgoers the Spinners' leaders made unconvincing thugs. The jury found the charge of murder 'not proven' but the five men were, nevertheless, sentenced to seven years' transportation for conspiring to use 'intimidation, molestation and threats'. The judge's summing-up gives a good insight into the fear of trade unions on the part of the authorities at this time. This was, he claimed:

> a conspiracy, ... by force and violence, to rob the one class of their rights to employ labourers at such prices as the latter were willing to receive, and to rob the other classes of their rights to dispose of their labour, at such prices as may be agreeable to themselves.

The *Northern Star* took a different view, defending the record of the Spinners' leaders and featuring a print of the five convicted men in January 1838. The incident provided a focus for the emergent Chartist movement, to the extent that it was a meeting in Glasgow, in May 1838, that saw the launching of the Chartist movement.

1. *What are the objections to the Spinners' Association contained in the Judge's summing-up above?*
2. *What are the 'rights' of employers and labourers referred to by the Judge in the statement?*
3. *How might the Spinner's Association have viewed the exercise of these 'rights'?*
4. *Why would the Chartists be keen to champion the cause of the Glasgow spinners?*

Summary: Origins of Chartism

In summarising this section it may be useful to return to the image of Chartism as an 'umbrella movement' (see page 94) which drew together a whole series of grievances and expressed them through the demand for the 'People's Charter'. Each of the movements, identified in the chapter so far, contributed to the nature of Chartism. They did this in three ways.

1 They demonstrated the distance between the classes. The reformed Parliament acted in ways that seemed to injure specifically working-class interests. At the same time the

TIMELINE

Whig reforms and the origins of Chartism

1833	Factory Act
	Formation of GNCTU
1834	New Poor Law
	Tolpuddle Case
1835	Municipal Corporations Act
1836	Taxes on newspapers lowered
1837	New Poor Law applied to the Midlands and North. *Northern Star* established in Leeds by Feargus O'Connor. Case of the five Glasgow cotton spinners.

trade union movement created a sense of the economic importance of labour; the popular union slogan was that 'Labour is the source of all wealth'. The Chartists subsequently adopted this slogan.

2 Issues like the abolition of the New Poor Law, legal recognition for trade unions, the Ten Hours Act and the freedom of the press are sometimes referred to as part of the 'implicit Social Programme' of Chartism; these measures were among those that Chartists hoped a reformed Parliament would pass.

3 The experience of each of these movements influenced the organisation of the Chartist movement. Much of the Chartists' strategy, for example, was based on the Reform Bill campaign with its mass meetings and often violent language. More than this, however, the radical movements of the 1830s created a body of individuals with much experience of campaigning and this was to be vital to the development of the movement. The Chartists drew upon a rich radical tradition.

2 ᔑ CHARTISM: A NATIONAL POLITICAL MOVEMENT

See page 92 for a list of The Six Points

KEY ISSUE

To what extent was Chartism a national movement?

The 'People's Charter', containing the six points of political reform was first published in May 1838 by the London Working Men's Association (LWMA) which had been formed two years earlier. In the same month the Charter was enshrined in a national petition to Parliament. Signatures to the petition were collected locally by representatives who were elected at mass meetings during the second half of 1838. The representatives met at a National Convention in London in February 1839 which drew the signatures together ready for delivery of the petition to Parliament in June 1839. The Convention also discussed strategy and acted as an organisational centre for the movement as a whole.

The notion that Chartism was a working-class movement suggests that there was a body of ideas that was shared by working people throughout the country. In other words it was not simply that many different communities experienced, say, the effects of trade depressions, or that they endured the same New Poor Law, or the same downward pressure on wages. Chartism grew because the communities in the different localities *interpreted* their experience in a similar way. This was more likely to happen in the Chartist period than at any previous time. The Industrial Revolution brought an improvement in communications. This reduced the apparent distances between areas and it was not only commodities that were transported but also ideas and news. This created the context within which a national movement could develop. Of course, the dispersal of Chartist support throughout the different localities always posed the problem of fragmentation. Nevertheless, Chartism was always more than a collection of local initiatives. Chartism can be seen to have emerged as a national movement by examining its organisation and ideology. These are detailed on the next page.

WILLIAM LOVETT (1800–77)

William Lovett was born in Newlyn, Cornwall. His father, the captain of a small coasting vessel, died before he was born and Lovett was brought up by his mother, a strict Methodist. As a boy he was apprenticed to a rope-maker, but this was a dying trade. In 1821 he went to London to look for work and obtained employment as a cabinet-maker. He had learned to read and write as a child and now attended classes at the London Mechanics Institute (a night school for working men). Here he made contact with a number of leading radicals and became a convert to the principle of co-operation. He was appointed secretary of the British Association for the Promotion of Co-operative Knowledge. In the early 1830s he was a leading figure in the creation of a 'Victims Fund' to assist people imprisoned for selling the *Poor Man's Guardian*. In 1831 he and a group of radical friends formed the National Union of the Working Classes which argued the case for universal manhood suffrage at a time when most radicals were fighting for the very limited suffrage promised by the Reform Act. This was succeeded by the London Working Men's Association in 1836, one of the originating bodies behind Chartism. In February 1837, with Lovett's guidance, the LWMA produced the 'People's Charter' with the 'Six Points' of parliamentary reform. Originally intended as the basis of a petition to Parliament, to be presented by a radical MP, this became the central programme of a nationwide campaign. Combining with the ferment in the north created by the Anti-Poor Law campaign, and with the re-formed Birmingham Political Union, the Chartist movement emerged. Lovett was chosen as Secretary to the Chartist Convention which met in February 1839. He attended all sixty-seven meetings of the Convention held up to the time of his arrest. He was arrested in July 1839 for publishing a statement, on behalf of the Convention, condemning the Metropolitan Police for breaking up a meeting in Birmingham. He conducted his own defence, and was imprisoned for 12 months. In prison he and John Collins wrote *Chartism: A New Organisation of the People* and he was greeted as a hero on his release. But his National Association for Promoting the Political and Social Improvements of the People was never a success. His quarrel with O'Connor is often seen as a central cause of Chartist failure. This split in the movement is discussed in more detail on page 117.

PICTURE 11
William Lovett, who drew up the People's Charter

A *The Charter*

The People's Charter was drawn up by William Lovett, the Secretary of the London Working Men's Association. It was intended that the Charter, drawn up with the assistance of a number of radical MPs, would form the basis of an Act of Parliament. This was not anything unusual in itself; in 1829 Lovett had assisted radical MPs to draw up a Friendly Societies Act which was subsequently passed by Parliament. Nor, by 1838, was there anything new, or unexpected, in the six points of the Charter. Each had formed part of radical demands since 1815. Collectively, the Six Points embodied the view that individuals had a right to participate in politics and that they should not be excluded from citizenship because they did not own property. The Chartist points were really only a re-statement of the radical programme which had inspired the followers of Hunt and Cobbett in the post-war years. It was now revived in the wake of a Reform Act which had clearly failed to deliver basic political 'rights' to working men.

The Charter was adopted enthusiastically in the Midlands and the North. In these areas the Anti-Poor Law movement had attracted much popular support, a good deal of it inspired by Feargus O'Connor's Leeds-based newspaper, the *Northern Star*. The *Star* endorsed the new movement and encouraged its readership to support the campaign for the Charter.

B *The National Petition*

KEY ISSUE

Why was a National Petition adopted?

See page 47 for Birmingham Political Union

The idea of incorporating the Charter into a massive National Petition to Parliament came from Birmingham. In April 1837, Thomas Attwood had reformed the Birmingham Political Union, largely to encourage local support for the establishment of a new town council. On the crucial issue of universal suffrage Attwood retained his doubts and, throughout 1837, the BPU advocated household suffrage. By this, all houseowners would be given the right to vote, rather than only those who owned houses worth £10 or above, as specified in the 1832 Act. Although this would have created a larger electorate, the franchise would still have been based on property ownership and so would have excluded large numbers of working men. As a result, working people did not join the reformed BPU in the numbers that Attwood had anticipated. Working-class reformers were no longer prepared to wait for gradual reform to deliver the vote; it was now male universal suffrage or nothing. Attwood recognised this change and, in January 1838, he reluctantly adopted the wider franchise as part of the BPU's programme. 'I am now a thorough convert to universal suffrage', he announced, 'and if ever I uttered a word against it I now altogether retract it.' To demonstrate its newfound conviction, the BPU floated the idea of a national petition for universal suffrage. Clearly, Attwood's intention was to place himself at the head of a nationwide agitation as he had in 1831–2.

Again, there was popular support for the idea of a national petition, and for Attwood's agreement to the scheme. Attwood had been a member of the reformed House of Commons since 1832. His support for universal suffrage represented a clear condemnation of the settlement of 1832 by a respectable public figure who retained enormous popularity for having defied Wellington and the King during the 'Days of May' in May 1832. The Chartist petition was launched at a mass meeting in Glasgow, called to support the imprisoned Spinners at the end of May 1838. Here the representatives of the LWMA, the BPU Northern activists like O'Connor came together to discuss the way forward. In front of an audience of 150 000, amid attacks on the New Poor Law and support for trade union rights, the idea was floated of the National Petition that would incorporate the six points of the People's Charter.

There was nothing new about petitioning for political reform. Such petitions were an accepted part of radical strategy and were perfectly constitutional in their nature. What made this move very different to anything that had gone before was the widely accepted belief that this would be the 'last petition'. This would be a demonstration of popular feeling that would be so strong that no government could ignore it and still claim that it represented 'the people'. This left open the question of what would happen if the petition was rejected. Nevertheless, it was widely accepted in 1838 that this was to be a last push for change by constitutional means.

C *The Chartist Convention*

The Glasgow meeting of May 1838 also launched the Convention which would meet in London and consist of Chartist delegates, elected at public meetings throughout the country. The delegates would carry the signatures to the petition from their areas and also represent their local 'constituency' in the Convention's discussions. The similarity between the Convention and the House of Commons was deliberate. British radicals had long toyed with the idea of establishing a national convention, along the lines of that adopted by the revolutionaries during the French Revolution, and always with the intention that such a body would carry symbolic significance. The Convention would be elected by a form of universal suffrage (in this case, hands raised at public meetings), and so it would represent 'the people' in a way that the House of Commons, elected under the restricted franchise of 1832, could never do. The Convention would meet in London and be a shining alternative to the corrupt Parliament; a kind of 'anti-Parliament', or what many Chartists called the 'real Parliament'. The submission of the petition to the Parliament by the anti-parliament would be an enormously symbolic moment. As O'Connor put it:

> **KEY ISSUE**
>
> *Why did the Chartists form themselves into a convention?*

let them attend to the number of 300 000 or 400 000 with a petition on their shoulders to the door of the House of Commons and let them tell the House of Commons that the constituency of England were waiting in the Palace Yard for an answer.

> **Q**
>
> *What does O'Connor mean by the phrase 'the constituency of England'?*

As a group, the Convention was initially less representative of the movement as a whole than it might have been. One contemporary observer estimated that the delegates included 24 working men and 29 from other classes. There are a number of reasons for this. The movements that had preceded Chartism had encouraged some alignment of middle-class and working-class radicals. This had occurred most spectacularly in the Reform Bill agitation. The campaigns against the Factory Act and against the New Poor Law had also created alliances that crossed class barriers. These alliances carried over into the initial phases of Chartism. But also, we should not underestimate the difficulties confronting working men who aspired to be Chartist delegates. Their families had to be supported, and victimisation from employers often followed. Sympathetic 'gentleman reformers' or tradesmen had more independence to act and were often seen to be natural representatives in this respect. 'Gentleman reformers' like O'Connor were seen to operate in the traditions established by Henry Hunt and John Cartwright in the 1815–20 period. Besides which, the acid test of a delegate's commitment to the cause was his support for the Charter itself.

D *Local Associations*

In June 1838, O'Connor launched the Great Northern Union. This was based in Leeds but it had branches throughout the north of England. It was O'Connor's intention to re-direct the radical energies in these areas from the Poor Law issue into the wider movement for political rights. By February 1839 the GNU had 62 000 members. Also in June, the Northern Political Union was started in Newcastle. Branches of the London Working Men's Association were established in South Wales. Chartism proved to be hugely popular in the Welsh valleys and, by 1839, it has been estimated that there were 25 000 enrolled or committed Chartists in South Wales. By the end of 1838 there were 76 Chartist associations established in Scotland.

TIMELINE

Chartism: early events

1837	(April)	Attwood re-forms the Birmingham Political Union (BPU) committed to household suffrage; not attractive to working people.
1838	(Jan)	Attwood commits the BPU to Universal suffrage; working people now join in large numbers
	(May)	People's Charter published. Mass meeting in Glasgow to support the Glasgow Spinners and float the idea of a National Petition
	(June)	O'Connor establishes the Great Northern Union
	(Aug–Oct)	Mass meetings to elect delegates to the Chartist Convention held throughout the country, including huge rallies in Birmingham, Manchester, Leeds and Newcastle.

Throughout England, Scotland and Wales, locally based associations were set up to campaign for a common objective. Chartism was formed by the coming together of local organisations and this was a significant element in the nature of the movement. Nevertheless, there was always a certain amount of tension between a national and a local organisation, with the tendency towards fragmentation as an ever-present problem. This was exacerbated by communication difficulties between areas and also by the poverty of most Chartists, which made the task of full-time agitation difficult.

E *The Mass Meeting*

Despite these problems, it was clear from the start that Chartism drew on a rich vein of mass support and thus expressed the frustrations and aspirations of the wider working community. This was shown in the mass meetings to elect delegates to the Convention and to collect signatures for the petition. For example, at a meeting in Birmingham, in August 1838, 200 000 people saw Attwood and O'Connor share the same platform and declare for the same programme. In September, John Fielden chaired a meeting just outside Manchester at which even the unsympathetic *Times* estimated the attendance at 300 000. In October, 250 000 turned out for a similar occasion at Peep Green in the West Riding of Yorkshire. One of the speakers at the September meeting was Robert Lowery, a tailor by trade and a Chartist delegate from Newcastle. In his autobiography he remembers; 'One dense mass of faces beaming with earnestness – as far as you could distinguish faces – then beyond still an enormous crowd.' (In assessing the significance of the large numbers at these meetings it is worth bearing in mind that a Wembley Cup Final crowd used to contain about 90 000 people.) One can only guess at the uplifting experience of attending such a meeting. Certainly for Lowery, the Manchester meeting was an almost religious experience; 'There is something in the appearances of such multitudes … something which for the moment seems to realise the truths of the ancient saying – "The voice of the people is as the voice of God".'

Meetings like this took their form from the experience of the Reform Bill campaign and the same use was made of the 'language of menace' carefully encased within a broadly constitutional approach. Attwood led the way here and this is significant since he later claimed to have left the movement early because of the violence of its leaders' speeches. At the August 1838 meeting he raised the issue of violence himself by saying, 'No blood shall be shed by us; but if our enemies shed blood – if they attack the people – they must take the consequences upon their own heads.' This was by now the tried and tested formula of a mass movement, committed to a constitutional strategy, but utilising threatening language to make its points. There was a widespread belief within the movement that the Government might well intervene violently and that, if this occurred, the Chartists had a constitutional right to defend themselves. The strategies of 'physical force' and 'moral force' were not seen at this stage to be alternatives

KEY ISSUE

What was the relationship between 'physical force' and 'moral force' in Chartist strategy?

between which the Chartists would have to choose. Rather, both were interwoven into a fundamentally constitutional strategy based on petitioning, with the Convention representing the legitimacy of the Chartists' claim to speak for 'the people'. One of the commonest Chartist slogans was 'Peacefully if we can, forcefully if we must'. Perhaps the concept of 'defensive violence' is summed up best by the slogan carried on banners to meetings by the Newcastle Chartists (referring to Napoleon's destruction of the Russian capital in 1812); 'If they Peterloo us we'll Moscow them'.

At the same meeting that Attwood made his statement on the use of 'defensive violence', O'Connor identified the importance of the constitutional approach and the possibility of a violent confrontation (his speech is taken from a local newspaper and is reported in the third person):

Q

1. *Using your knowledge of popular movements since 1815, why do you think the Chartists felt they could expect a violent reaction from the Government?*
2. *What does O'Connor mean by the term 'the moral power of the nation'?*
3. *What is the position of both Attwood and O'Connor on the use of physical force by the Chartists?*

He was there representing the wishes and feelings of 300 000 of determined minds and stalwart arms. There was not a man among them who was not satisfied to trust the moral power of the nation, … They were ready to do this, rather than rush into any maddening conflict. They might be sure that the man who was marshalling physical force, would be the first to desert it when it was resorted to. [Cheers] The moral power was that principle of the human mind which taught man how to reason, and when to bear, and when to forbear. But he was not to be understood to imply that he was content to live a slave. No! … But when the moral force was expended, and the mind drawn out at last, then, as Mr Attwood had said, if wrong should come from any party, cursed be that virtuous man who refused to repel force by force.

The 53 delegates elected at these and many other meetings came together as the General Convention of the Industrious Classes, in London in February 1839. This group met regularly, discussed strategy and sent agitators throughout the country to increase support and to collect signatures for the petition. By June the massive petition with its 1 280 000 signatures was ready for presentation. It was rejected by the House of Commons by 235 votes to 46.

F *The Chartist Press*

The Chartist press did more than any other single agency to create a common set of ideas within Chartism. The *Northern Star* was the most popular of the many Chartist newspapers and, at the height of its popularity in 1839, it sold 50 000 copies a week. But it was only one of scores of newspapers that served the Chartist communities. Thomas Cooper ran four, at different times, in the Leicester region alone. In Glasgow, *The Chartist Circular* appeared; *Mcdouall's Chartist and Republican Journal*, served the Manchester area, whilst *Udgorn Cymru* (*The Trumpet of Wales*) was published in South Wales and Henry Vincent's *Western Vindicator* served the West Country. Each of these, and numerous others, established their own working-class readership.

G *Chartist Support*

Chartism drew the body of its support from what were called at the time 'the manufacturing districts'. This contemporary term should not be interpreted to mean 'the large towns'. Rather it refers to the, often relatively small, industrial communities which characterised Britain in the early stages of the Industrial Revolution. Asa Briggs suggested, in his book, *Chartist Studies* (1959), that Chartism recruited better in the older, decaying trades of the increasingly outmoded domestic system rather than among the newer factory workers. Research carried out since his book was published, however, has suggested that it was the size of the community that was more important than the type of industry carried out. Dorothy Thompson (*The Chartists*, 1984) argues that Chartism flourished most extensively in industrial areas 'in which the actual communities were small enough to sustain a unity of purpose, in which communication was easy and in which the authority of church and state was weak.' These might be centres of factory production, mining, the domestic system, or workshop industries. Chartist support came from the home-based handloom weavers, and the factory-based textile workers of south-east Lancashire and Lanarkshire (cotton), and the West Riding of Yorkshire (wool). It also drew in the framework knitters of the East Midlands (Nottinghamshire, Derbyshire and Leicestershire), and the metal workers of Birmingham and the Black Country. In nearly all of these, the typical work unit was the small workshop. Chartism was strong among coalminers and iron workers in areas like South Wales and the north-east of England, the pottery workers of Staffordshire and among the more traditional trades like tailoring, building and shoemaking. What was important, in generating and sustaining Chartist membership locally, was the shared experience of early industrialisation.

These tightly-knit communities bred a fiercely independent workforce. Early industrial workers expected to exercise a good deal of control over their own working environment. This was partly because British industrialisation began in the domestic system where workers worked in their own homes and determined their own work-pace. There is evidence of the persistence of these attitudes, with workers carrying them into the early factories. For example, there were no formally agreed holidays at this time, but the community would observe particular days as holidays. Employers were expected to fit in with these arrangements and they could expect trouble from their workforce if they did not. In most areas it was common to take Monday as a day of rest. This was known as the observance of 'Saint Monday'. For this reason the Chartists held many of their mass meetings on a Monday.

Many of these communities had undergone a religious revival in the early nineteenth century and there appears to be a link between Chartism and evangelical Nonconformity. Many of the Chartists belonged to

KEY ISSUE

Who were the Chartists?

See page 66 on Evangelicalism

the Methodists, Baptists or other Nonconformist sects. This was also a culture which carried a commitment to self-education. Britain's was a fairly literate workforce, with the skills of reading and writing passed down through the generations. As Richard Cobden explained to a Select Committee in 1838, 'the operatives living so much together, and generally having families, there is generally one in the family or connection who can write'. Often the educational role of the family was reinforced by the use of the Sunday school. Certainly, many working people were highly literate in these years before a formal system of education was introduced. One Leicester stockinger's recollections of his workplace provide a fairly typical example of the way politics had entered the mainstream of working-class culture by this period. 'After tea' he remembers, 'a short article would be read from the *Northern Star*, and this would form the subject matter for consideration and chat during the remainder of the day'. Throughout the Chartist period working men defended themselves in court, delivered speeches at mass rallies and penned articles and reports for the many Chartist newspapers that held the movement together.

Women were also far more active in Chartism than was recognised by the early historians of the movement. The Chartists themselves adopted a rather ambivalent approach to women's political activity. The Charter specified universal *manhood* suffrage and women were never part of the national leadership of the movement. The Chartist imagery, even that used by the women themselves, also appears to have accepted the notion of the woman's place being in the home. Nevertheless, his-

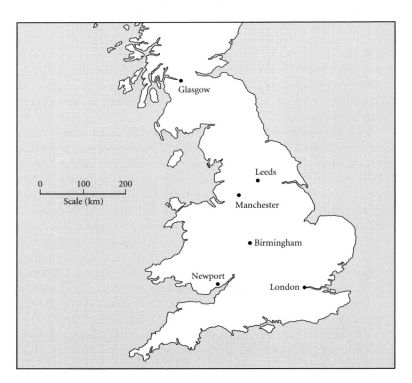

MAP 2 *Chartism: a national movement. The Charter was drawn up in London, the Petition originated in Birmingham, the Convention was launched in Glasgow and met in London, later Birmingham. The* Northern Star *was published in Leeds*

torical research has shown that Chartist women adopted a role of pushing for reform on behalf of their menfolk by adopting 'the pose of radical wife and motherhood'. Women's involvement came at a time when politics was not seen as an appropriate sphere for women. Their extensive participation in Chartism therefore represented a rejection, by working-class women, of the dominant definition of 'proper' feminine behaviour. We know of the existence of over 100 female radical associations formed to agitate for the Charter. The involvement of women in the areas where Chartism was strong shows that the movement was to be the expression of integrated communities.

See J. Schwarzkopf *'Women in the Chartist Movement'* (1991) in Bibliography on page 129

H *A common political tradition*

In using their six-point political programme, the Chartists were echoing earlier movements and drawing on a rich radical tradition that served to unite the movement. They also shared the views put forward by Thomas Paine in *The Rights of Man*. He had argued that the vote was a right which no government could legitimately withhold. This and other freedoms were the rights of the 'free born Englishman' which had been confiscated at some point in the past. Thus the Chartists embraced a sense of the past, with historical precedent frequently quoted to back their case. The very term 'People's Charter' was designed to evoke the image of Magna Carta, seen as a medieval protection against tyranny. The continued refusal to admit the working class to the franchise was seen as a continuing conspiracy by those who held power. Bronterre O'Brien, writing on the 'Rotten House of Commons' in *McDouall's Chartist and Republican Journal* in 1841, put it as follows:

See page 37 for more on Thomas Paine

What have we gained by the increase in the constituency made by the Reform Bill? – I answer worse than nothing. We have merely augmented the number of our enemies . . . The men who made the Reform Bill were not fools; neither were the middle classes for whom it was made. – the Whigs saw, and the middle classes saw, that the effect of the Bill would be to unite all property against all poverty.

Q

What do you think O'Brien meant by 'the effect of the Bill would be to unite all property against all poverty'?

Was Chartism a political or an economic movement?

ANALYSIS

Mass-based political movements often coincided with a downturn in trade. (Britain had become more dependent on foreign markets – for instance, for sales of its textiles. This meant that if there were poor harvests in Europe, food prices were higher and, therefore, people had less money left over to buy British goods). An economic depression accompanied such downturns in trade. Cobbett's famous words, 'I defy you to agitate a fellow with a full stomach',

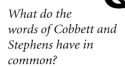

What do the words of Cobbett and Stephens have in common?

have echoed through much of the historical interpretation of the Chartist movement. Similarly, the view of the Revd J. R. Stephens, that Chartism was essentially a 'knife and fork' question, has also found a place in traditional accounts.

It is indisputable that the periods of maximum support for Chartism (1838–9, 1842 and 1848) were also years of hunger. However, economic explanations are sometimes used by historians, as they were by contemporaries, to discredit the movement's serious political intent, arguing that when people are hungry and angry they become riotous and do irrational things. But if we accept that Chartism was a rational movement, with a clear political programme built around a legal, constitutional strategy of petitioning, then the 'hunger politics' explanation is unhelpful by itself. What we need to understand is why the hungry and distressed in this period chose to express their feelings through a constitutional demand for the vote. We need to note that:

- The periods 1838–9, 1842 and 1848 were times when the existing economic and political structure was seen most clearly not to be working: it was difficult to avoid the view that a system that could provide neither regular employment nor a sufficient wage was ripe for reform.
- Economic depression undoubtedly affected the structure and running of industrial enterprises. In order to maintain profits in the face of declining prices, manufacturers often tried to produce more goods for less cost by re-organising work. Depression might provide the employer with the opportunity and the justification to introduce new machinery or to increase cheap child or female labour at the expense of skilled men. Workers felt strongly about these issues.
- A period of depression put particular strains on the small-scale producers since they operated with the narrowest of profit margins at all times, and consequently they were the first to go under. As a result, the periodic dips in the trade cycle encouraged the concentration of industrial concerns into the hands of a smaller number of people. For example, in Nottingham's hosiery trade it had been common at one time for the working family to own its own stocking frame, working in its own home. As time went by, however, ownership of the looms was increasingly concentrated in the hands of a few individuals who then rented them to their workforce, taking their own profit. In 1831 there had been 1382 owners of looms in the town, but by 1836 there were only 837. This means that, in this period, 500 owners of one, two and three looms had fallen back into the ranks of the labourers. One firm now owned 5000 frames. The take-over of small looms, with its associated loss of independence for stocking weavers, was easier to achieve in times of hardship when working people were forced to accept the changes.

● Historian Eric Hobsbawm has pointed out that when unemployment was high, trade unions were always weak (strikes were of little use if those on strike could be replaced easily): so working people turned to political solutions in these periods. He describes this as the 'pendulum effect'; in good times workers organised in trade unions, in bad times they organised in large political movements, swinging between these forms of agitation depending on which would be the most effective for the economic moment.

So, the relationship between economic depression and radical movements is complex. Besides creating the obvious problems of unemployment and hunger, depression tended to speed up the structural changes in manufacturing industry. This meant that at periods of distress, when they were most vulnerable, working people found their lives changed in important ways which they could not control. Chartism was certainly fuelled by unemployment, but the fact that this resulted in a call for the vote was a reflection of the working community's wish to control their own lives in the face of far-reaching industrial change. This desire to control change was acutely felt at times of depression when those changes came more rapidly. Historians who suggest that Chartism was composed of the hungry and the uneducated misunderstand the complexity of working-class culture in the period. Nevertheless, Chartism can be seen as both an economic and a political movement, in the sense that it was composed of political activists who wanted to use politics to resolve a number of economic and social issues.

Q

1. *List the ways in which Chartism was a political movement.*
2. *To what extent do you think it was a political movement?*

3 ⌐ 1839: REJECTION AND REACTION

Tension had grown in the months leading up to June 1839 when the Charter was to be submitted to Parliament. The arrest of the Revd J. R. Stephens for the violence of his speeches in November 1838 had merely increased working-class support for the Chartists by creating a martyr. Throughout the country working people contributed to the Stephens defence fund. In April 1839 the use of the Metropolitan Police at Llanidloes in Wales sparked off three days of rioting in the town which had to be suppressed by the army. In May 1839 the Convention moved to Birmingham to be closer to its basis of popular support as it readied itself for the submission of the Charter.

With this build-up of tension, middle-class support for the Chartists had begun to melt away. By May 1839, 14 of the Convention delegates, all middle-class men, had resigned. They generally cited the issue of violent language used in the speeches of O'Connor, Oastler and Stephens as their reasons for going. In June, when Attwood presented the petition to the House of Commons, his support for the movement was obviously wavering. Despite his own use of the 'language of menace' as recently as the previous August, he now found it necessary to state that he 'washed his hands of any idea, of any appeal to physical force'.

A *Riots in the Bull Ring, Birmingham, July 1839*

On 4 July 1839 rioting broke out in Birmingham, when the Mayor used the hated Metropolitan police to break up a peaceful Chartist meeting in the Bull Ring (a market place). This was particularly unfortunate since the Mayor had been an early supporter of Chartism, being one of the middle-class delegates to the Convention who had resigned the previous March. Birmingham now had a town council, the first since the passing of the 1835 Municipal Corporations Act. Many of the middle-class members of the Birmingham Political Union had been elected to it. With more interest in local than national affairs, their enthusiasm for the People's Charter evaporated. They now saw Chartism, not as an issue of principle, but as a question of public order. The fact that during the Reform Bill campaign the town's middle class had encouraged political meetings in the Bull Ring was also forgotten in the desire to demonstrate their new found authority. The fortnight of rioting that followed 4 July was exacerbated by news of the rejection of the petition. William Lovett, as Secretary to the Convention, issued a placard condemning the actions of the town council:

> That this Convention is of opinion that a wanton, flagrant and unjust outrage has been made upon the people of Birmingham by a blood-thirsty and unconstitutional force from London, acting under the authority of men who, when out of office, sanctioned and took part in the meetings of the people; and now, when they share in the public plunder, seek to keep the people in social slavery and political degradation.

For this, Lovett was arrested and sentenced to a year in prison. Lovett is often seen as the chief advocate of what is termed 'moral force', that is, strategies of persuasion as opposed to 'physical force'. Yet here he defends the actions of the Birmingham crowd in fighting the police.

B *The Newport Rising, November 1839*

The Convention broke up in disarray in September 1839. An attempt in August to call a general strike, (the 'grand national holiday' or the 'Sacred Month' as it was variously called) had failed. There remained a good deal of support for continuing with the agitation but the failure of petitioning had thrown the movement into a state of confusion as to the way forward. The delegates returned to their areas and the movement lost its central direction. From this fragmentation, the Newport Rising emerged as a local initiative.

Q

1. *Why did Lovett consider the Metropolitan Police to be 'an unconstitutional force'?*
2. *What does Lovett mean by the phrase, 'now when they share in the public plunder'?*
3. *Using the words of the placard as evidence, what is Lovett's position on the use of violence?*

KEY ISSUE

Was the Newport Rising an attempt to overthrow the Government by armed force or a demonstration that went wrong?

PICTURE 12   *Chartists at the Westgate Hotel, Newport 1839*

On the night of 3–4 November 1839 nearly 10 000 men marched from the darkness of the hills surrounding Newport in South Wales. Mostly coalminers and iron-workers from the valleys, they were armed with pikes and firearms and marched in close military formation, each detachment directed by a 'captain'. Led by local Chartist leaders John Frost, Zephaniah Williams and William Jones, the advance column clashed with troops firing from the Westgate Hotel in the town square. The Chartists fled, leaving between 20 and 30 of their number dead. At their trial Frost, Williams and Jones were convicted of high treason and sentenced to death for attempting to overthrow the state by force of arms. The Whig Government, however, had learned the importance of not creating martyrs for the cause, and swiftly commuted the sentences to transportation for life.

The Newport Rising continues to puzzle historians as much as it did contemporaries. We may see it, as many did at the time, as the violent confrontation that had always seemed likely. The prosecution alleged at the subsequent trial that Newport was to have been the first blow of a nationwide uprising that was nipped in the bud by the swift response of the authorities. On the other hand, the accused , defending a plea of not guilty, argued that they had simply planned a huge and spectacular demonstration of Chartist strength as a protest against the recent arrest

Q

What were the intentions of the local leadership and of the rank and file Chartists in marching on Newport?

of the local leader, Henry Vincent. Frost and the others were simply the victims of over-reaction on the part of the local garrison.

David Williams, writing his biography of Frost a century later in 1939, accepted this argument and concluded that Newport had really been a 'monster demonstration'. This view was strongly contested by David Jones in his 1985 book, *The Last Rising*. He locates the events in their local context and sees the rising as an expression of small mine- and iron-working communities tightly bound together by Nonconformity, radical politics and a tradition of violence. The organisation of the rising was very different from most Chartist activities by virtue of its almost total secrecy. As Jones puts it; 'there was none of the defiant openness and publicity which characterised the wider movement'. Nor did the participants seem to have felt that they were simply part of a 'demonstration'. One Chartist, a 17-year-old cabinet-maker by the name of George Shell, wrote to his parents before setting off, 'I shall this night be engaged in a struggle for freedom and should it please God to spare my life I shall see you soon; but if not, grieve not for me for I shall fall in a noble cause.' Whilst the rising was not part of a nationwide plot, the plan was to take Newport as an inspiration to Chartist groups elsewhere to do the same. The capture of the town would have been followed by a forced march to Monmouth to release Henry Vincent and other Chartist prisoners from the town's goal.

The Newport Rising gave the Government the reason it had been seeking to move firmly against the Chartists. As a result, nearly 500 people were sent to prison for Chartist-related activity between 1839 and 1841. The first phase of the movement was over.

See the Bibliography on page 129

TIMELINE

1839	Feb	Chartist Convention meets in London
	April	Llanidloes riots in mid-Wales
	May	Chartist Convention reconvenes in Birmingham
	July	First Chartist Petition (presented in June by Attwood) is rejected Bull Ring Riots, Birmingham; Lovett arrested
	Aug	Attempt at a general strike, 'the Sacred Month' fails to gain support
	Sept	Chartist Convention dissolves itself
	Nov	Newport Rising

4 ⌐ REORGANISATION, 1840–7

A *The National Charter Association (NCA) and the second petition, 1840–2*

KEY ISSUE

Why did new strategies appear after 1839 and to what extent were they divisive?

The Chartist leadership remained remarkably resilient in the face of its setbacks. Plans were immediately laid for reconstructing the movement and gathering signatures for a second petition. Most Chartists accepted that a stronger central organisation was needed to hold together the local initiatives. Encouraged by a series of articles in the *Northern Star*, written by O'Connor from his prison cell in York, the National Charter Association (NCA) was established in Manchester in July 1840. This was to exist for a decade as the most important of the Chartist organisations. By the summer of 1842 it boasted a national membership of 50 000.

The experience of the first phase of the Chartist movement led many to reconsider the strategy of simply petitioning for the Charter. Some now argued that the working community needed to demonstrate its readiness for universal suffrage. Whilst in prison Lovett and his fellow-prisoner John Collins, a tool setter from Birmingham, devised a national system of education for the working community. Their scheme included schools for each age group, libraries, community halls, adult education, and teacher training colleges. This represented a remarkable vision of educational provision which was to be financed by weekly contributions of a penny from everybody who had signed the petition. Lovett and Collins argued that a formally educated working class could not long be denied the vote. Henry Vincent emerged from prison certain that the demonstration of overtly respectable behaviour would calm middle-class fears and secure the franchise. He, along with Robert Lowery, encouraged the establishment of teetotal Chartist associations in which working people would take the pledge to abstain from alcohol. Arthur O'Neill, a Nonconformist minister from Glasgow, established a Chartist Church in Birmingham in 1841, arguing that a formal commitment to Christianity by the movement might gain the vote.

These 'new moves', as they were called, aimed to achieve the vote by explicitly 'moral force' strategies. A public demonstration of respectability by the working class would nullify the major argument against enfranchisement. None of these initiatives ever gained the level of support achieved by the NCA under O'Connor's leadership. O'Connor attacked the 'new moves' but not because he rejected education, sobriety or Christianity. His concern, and that of the NCA, was simply that these strategies were a distraction from the main task of achieving the Charter through the strategy of partitioning.

Supporters of these moves also accepted the reason most frequently given for the Charter's rejection; that the working class were not yet 'ready' for the vote. The NCA argued that, if the vote was a right, as had always been argued by the Chartists, then individuals should not have to qualify for it. Nobody would argue, for example, that one should have to sign the pledge before being entitled to enjoy, say freedom of conscience, or equality before the law. The NCA felt the same point applied to the 'moral force' schemes for achieving the vote. The debate between the various groups within Chartism on the issue of strategy was often bitter. Many historians argue that these divisions were disastrous for the future of a movement that was already fragmented by the geographical spread of its support. 'The quarrel thus begun,' remarked Mark Hovell in *The Chartist Movement* (1917), 'was never healed, and exercised a baneful effect upon the Chartist agitation'.

The NCA organised the collection of three million signatures for the second petition. This was presented to Parliament by a new Convention in May 1842. Assisted again by an economic depression, 1842 was probably the year of Chartism's greatest strength in terms of mass support. This made no difference to the prospects of the National Petition, which was rejected by a Commons vote of 287 to 46.

B *Middle-class initiatives*

KEY ISSUE

Why was there so little successful co-operation between middle and working classes?

See page 155 on the Anti-Corn Law League

In the period of reorganisation that followed Newport, the Chartists were wooed by a number of middle-class organisations who wished to draw working people away from the Chartist leadership. However, the Chartists, with remarkable unanimity, consistently refused to align with middle-class radical groups unless it was on their own terms. Whilst accepting that the support of the middle class would strengthen their case, acceptance of the Charter remained the acid-test of any middle-class movement's sincerity. The Anti-Corn Law League, established in 1839, consistently failed to attract working-class support in any numbers although it established Operative Associations. For the Chartists, the League was a distraction from the task of agitating for the Charter, although the abolition of the Corn Laws remained an important element in the Chartists' 'implicit social programme'. Richard Cobden, leader of the League, wanted working-class support as 'something in our rear to frighten the aristocracy.' The League was happy to have working men as members but would not allow them onto their executive committee. The Chartists were not interested in such a subordinate role.

Nevertheless, the Free Traders tried twice more to draw in Chartist support by establishing rival political organisations based specifically on the idea of an alliance between the classes. The Leeds Reform Association, launched in 1841 by leading members of the League, advocated household suffrage. The hope was that, following the failure of the petition, and the disaster of Newport, a gradualist programme of step-by-step reform might now be more appealing. Its founding meeting was boycotted by most Chartists, and those who attended did so only to insist that the Charter was accepted as the Association's programme. O'Connor dubbed it the 'Fox and Goose Club', suggesting that for the working class to join a political association run by the middle class was rather like inviting geese to join a club run by foxes. The Complete Suffrage Union (CSU) fared little better. Launched early in 1842, to distract workers from the re-vamped Chartist movement, the CSU was started by Joseph Sturge, a corn merchant from Birmingham and a keen member of the Anti-Corn Law League. Sturge was prepared to accept all six points of the Charter but refused to accept the name 'People's Charter' for the CSU's programme. A number of Chartist delegates attended the CSU's conferences in April and December 1842, since the movement remained keen to widen support. In the December conference Lovett moved a resolution, seconded by O'Connor, that the Charter be accepted in name. These two Chartists, who disagreed over so many issues of strategy, were happy to ally on this issue. When the motion was passed by the Conference, packed by Chartists, Sturge and his middle-class supporters left and the CSU was effectively dead.

Middle-class organisations aspiring to lead mass movements now found themselves dealing with a working class which had its own reasonably coherent view of the political and economic world. It was the fact that characters like Attwood, Sturge, and Cobden did not share this view that proved the main stumbling block to co-operation between the classes in radical political movements in this period. In this sense, the Chartist experience served to reinforce existing class differences.

Lovett and O'Connor: 'physical-force' and 'moral force'

Historians have frequently portrayed the disagreements between O'Connor and Lovett as a conflict between 'physical force' tactics and those of 'moral force'. In fact, this is not an analysis that can be sustained. Because 'new movers' like Lovett (Education Chartism), O'Neill (Church Chartism) and Vincent (Teetotal Chartism) adopted overtly 'moral force' strategies, it is sometimes assumed that the rest of the Chartists were committed to 'physical force' strategies. The Chartists themselves used these two terms, 'physical force' and 'moral force', and it has been assumed that they represented opposing strategies that were always mutually exclusive. Historians have often felt that, after the rejection of the first petition in 1839, the mass of Chartists made a mistake in following O'Connor and the NCA, rather than going down the path of moral reform. This is partly because the first real historians of the movement, writing in the early twentieth century, were members of the early Labour Party which was itself committed to gradual change from within rather than any form of confrontation (see Chapter 14). Thus Mark Hovell, a Labour Party supporter, writing before World War I, was much taken by Lovett's education scheme. In Hovell's influential history of the movement, O'Connor emerges as the villain of the piece, luring working people away from the strategy which might have given the movement success. As he put it; 'It was ... a division between Lovett and a man whose methods of agitation included ... hero-worship, clap-trap speeches, mass demonstrations leading to physical force ideas and even more reckless oratory.' In Hovell's work, O'Connor represented 'physical force' and Lovett represented 'moral force' Chartism. Subsequent historians tended to follow Hovell's lead, particularly in the condemnation of O'Connor's leadership.

This interpretation is reinforced by the fact that by May 1839, before the Charter was presented, 14 of the middle-class delegates had resigned from the Convention (to be replaced by working men) and the public support of Attwood (never a delegate) was clearly wavering. Resigning delegates complained of the violent speeches from some of the leaders, yet the use of violent rhetoric was by now a well-established tradition within radical move-ments. As we have seen, Attwood could hardly complain about the 'language of menace' since he peppered his own speeches with references to defensive violence. The rising tensions of the early months of 1839 may have frightened the middle-class delegates. Alternatively, it may have been their experience of the Chartist Convention that persuaded them to leave the movement. This confronted them with a group of politically-active working men preparing themselves for political power. This was always the dilemma of universal suffrage for the middle class. It was all very well for the Chartists to argue that 'labour is the source of all wealth', but if a society was based on this assumption where would this leave the employers? To put this another way, to what extent was the Chartist concern for trade union rights compatible with the desire of industrialists to run their businesses as they saw fit? If the vote were given to the propertyless, how would they act towards the propertied?

Attwood's view was always that working-class interests could be represented by the election of men of 'productive capital', mid-dle-class men like himself. Universal suffrage would bring this about, with the working class voting deferentially (respectfully) for employers who understood the needs of their workers. Later, looking back on his short flirtation with universal suffrage, he re-iterated his view that the middle class were the natural leaders. 'There is no instance in history in which political movements have been successful without leaders and in almost every instance those leaders were men of wealth and influence.' The working-class delegates to the Chartist Convention saw things rather dif-ferently. Referring to the role of the middle class within the movement, one of them asked, 'Did they think they were going to lead the working class by the nose any longer?'.

In the movement as a whole the issue of violence was never as divisive as historians have sometimes suggested. Most Chartists accepted and promoted the right to arm in one's own defence, and to respond if attacked. William Lovett was the apostle of 'moral force' methods, yet even he was prepared to go to prison in 1839 for the right to exercise defensive violence, as we saw earlier. In the tradition of Attwood, platform orators used the 'language of menace' as they had in 1832 and, in the context of meetings of many thousands, this was intended to have an intimidatory effect. But most Chartist demonstrations were peaceful. On the rare occasions when Chartist violence did occur it was generally in the form of riots where the crowd and the authorities confronted each other in the well-established fashion of the food riot. The 'Plug Disturbances' detailed in the next section provide an exam-ple of this. Yet, as Dorothy Thompson points out, Chartism expe-rienced comparatively little of this 'folk violence'. Throughout the period thousands came together at meetings, both large and small, without involving any great disruption to public order.

When Chartism was relaunched as a mass movement with a new petition in 1842, most Chartists chose to follow O'Connor's lead rather than Lovett's. His biographer, James Epstein argues that this was not because he misled them with his stunning speeches. Rather, O'Connor represented the kind of position that was closest to their own. Petitioning Parliament with massive public support and the hint of menace still seemed the best and quickest way to achieve the Charter and this was the strategy to which the NCA, O'Connor and most Chartists were committed.

Unlike many of the movements that preceded it, Chartism was not a secret organisation; it conducted its business openly and peacefully. In fact, O'Connor and 42 other Chartists were acquitted of seditious conspiracy at Lancaster Assizes in 1843 on the grounds that everything he had done had been publicly proclaimed and open. Like most Chartist leaders, O'Connor had been unaware of what was being planned in Newport and alarmed at its outcome. In this sense, Newport was exceptional. Here, a plot was laid to seize power by force of arms. Small groups of Chartists throughout the country were drawn to this approach. In the wake of Newport there was the arrest of armed Chartists in January 1840, in Sheffield, Dewsbury, Bradford and Bethnal Green (East London). But revolution was always a minority interest within the movement. O'Connor had long advised against such a strategy on purely pragmatic grounds. As the *Northern Star* put it in April 1839, 'the odds are fearful against those who are not trained to arms.' Tragically, Newport confirmed this view. The dispute between Lovett and O'Connor was real enough, but it was not focussed on whether or not to overthrow the Government by force of arms since both men opposed this strategy. It was partly a clash of personality (Lovett the introvert, O'Connor the extrovert) between two men from different social backgrounds. At its heart, however, was disagreement over whether the constitutional strategy of petitioning would ever produce the desired result.

Q

(a) *Why did the early historians of Chartism paint Lovett as the hero and O'Connor as the villain?*
(b) *What arguments can be identified to challenge this view?*
(c) *What evidence is there to support the view that O'Connor was not a 'physical force' leader?*

C *The 'plug' disturbances 1842*

In August 1842, a series of large-scale strikes broke out in the Midlands, Lancashire, Yorkshire, and Lanarkshire. In these, the workers used the traditional method of calling a strike; they went from factory to factory inviting the workers to join and to draw the plugs from the boilers, so closing their works. In this way work was stopped in 19 Lancashire towns, where the strikes were led predominantly by powerloom weavers. Yorkshire followed this example, with factories in 29 towns brought to a standstill. There were many clashes between the strikers and the authorities. Historians are divided on whether or not these were 'Chartist' strikes or more general trade union unrest. Studies of Lancashire and Staffordshire, however, suggest that the men and women involved in the strikes had also been involved in Chartism, and the strikers frequently argued at their meetings that their objective was to gain the Charter. It would seem that the strikes were led by local Chartist activists, rather than being a centrally orchestrated strategy on the part of the national leadership, many of whom were surprised by the events.

Another round-up of Chartists followed the strikes. If anything, Peel's Tory Government was firmer in their dealings with the Chartists than the Whigs had been in 1839. By the end of 1842 around 1500 people had been brought to court for Chartist-related offences. Chartism went into decline. By 1844 the *Northern Star* was failing to reach its break-even point of 4000 sales per week.

D *The Land Plan, 1845–8*

KEY ISSUE

What was the Chartist Land Plan and why was it so popular?

Chartism never regained the mass support it had enjoyed in 1839 and 1842. Nevertheless, its fortunes, which by 1844 seemed to be in terminal decline, were revived considerably by the Land Plan. This was a scheme that O'Connor had been contemplating for some time: the creation of rural communities of Chartists. (This was to be different from the Owenite communities where the land was held in common.) The Chartist Land Company, established in 1845, aimed to create a group of free-holders, each cultivating a patch of land which they owned. Chartists were invited to buy shares in the company, as members of local branches of the Land Company. The scheme was phenomenally successful in attracting support. By 1848, 100 000 people were registered subscribers, hopeful that their names would be drawn by lot and their families settled in a Chartist community. Five such communities were established, each with its own impressive facilities of schools, parks and public baths. This was O'Connor at his most visionary, and it is clear from the strength of the response over this issue that he made contact with the aspirations of the world's first industrial working class, to an extraordinary extent. A hunger to return to the land was clearly latent and O'Connor drew this out. The Land Plan would provide an alternative to waged employment and, by absorbing surplus labour, reduce unemployment and raise wages throughout the economy.

Yet the scheme was not a success. Even O'Connor, with his boundless optimism, was unprepared for the high level of support and the Land Company's administration was chaotic. More importantly, the Government was openly hostile. In 1848 it investigated the affairs of the Company in the hope that it would uncover enough scandal to disgrace O'Connor. In the event, O'Connor was found to have acted with integrity; in fact, the Company owed him £23 000 which he never recovered. Nevertheless, the Company was wound up by Act of Parliament. The reason given was that places in the community were drawn by lot and that this element of chance meant that the Company was not a friendly society as it had claimed. Without the protection of the legislation covering friendly societies, the company was technically an illegal body. There seems little doubt that worry and strain caused by running the Company, with his honesty questioned in public, contributed significantly to O'Connor's subsequent decline into insanity and his early death in 1855.

5 ✍ THE THIRD PETITION: 1848 AND THE FEAR OF REVOLUTION

The popularity of the Land Plan meant that Chartism was flourishing again by 1848. A number of Chartist candidates had stood in the general election of 1847, in which a Whig Government, under Lord John Russell, had been returned to office. In an electrifying campaign, O'Connor was elected for Nottingham. Inspired by this and a revolution in France, a Chartist Convention met in London in April 1848 to organise the delivery of a third petition to Parliament. This was to follow a mass meeting, on 10 April, at Kennington Common in London.

> **KEY ISSUE**
>
> *Were the Government right to fear a Chartist revolution in 1848?*

Chartism's last appearance as a mass movement was acted out against a backdrop of events on the mainland of Europe and in Ireland. European developments had always been important to British radicals. The French Revolution of 1789 figured prominently in the imagery of the Chartist movement, though the Chartists were always careful to divorce themselves from the violence of the Terror. The Cap of Liberty was frequently worn by Chartists or used to adorn their placards. From 1847 Frederick Engels, a joint author, with Karl Marx, of the *Communist Manifesto*, was the Paris correspondent of the *Northern Star*. When, in February 1848, he sent word of a revolution in Paris the news was greeted enthusiastically. The National Charter Association sent a three-man delegation with a congratulatory address to be delivered to the new provisional government in Paris.

Radicalism in Ireland had been fairly subdued since the boisterous days of the the Catholic Association (see Chapter 9) but the failure of the potato crop in 1845 and the subsequent famine in Ireland only added to the Government's fear of a direct response. A placard put out by the Chartist Convention on 5 April 1848 began; 'Irishmen resident in London, on the part of the democrats in England we extend to you the warm hand of fraternization; your principles are ours, and our principles are yours'.

The authorities found themselves confronted with the prospect of a simultaneous revival of both Chartism and Irish nationalism, in the broader context of turmoil throughout many European capitals. This goes some way to explaining the Government's response to the intended meeting on 10 April. Besides the 7122 regular troops and 4000 policemen available in London in April 1848, Russell's Government authorised the enrollment of 85 000 special constables, mostly men from the middle class. The meeting planned for 10 April was declared illegal and the Queen was evacuated to the Isle of Wight.

In the event the meeting on 10 April, which went ahead despite the ban, passed off without major incident. Around 20 000 people met on Kennington Common in London and set off, in an orderly procession, to present the petition to Parliament. The procession was stopped before it reached Westminster. After calming speeches from O'Connor and Jones, a small group proceeded with the petition to the House of Commons. A parliamentary committee swiftly declared that, of the five and a half million signatures on the petition, less than two million were genuine. In the light of this, the Commons decided not to receive the petition formally.

So great was the relief that the scenes of revolution which Berlin, Vienna, and Paris had witnessed in 1848, were not to be re-enacted on the streets of London, that the Government's anxiety, which had led to such a massive response by the authorities, swiftly turned to contempt.

In the rush to condemn the Chartist Convention as a farce, it was forgotten that even Parliament accepted that the Petition contained over one-and-a-half million genuine signatures. Despite the rejection of two previous petitions, Chartism could still muster a huge body of support. Also, rumours of the death of Chartism on 10 April were grossly overstated. The Chartists themselves tended to see 10 April as a moral victory or, in their words, a 'triumph'. Despite the Government's

PICTURE 13
'A Physical Force Chartist Arming for the Fight',
Punch, *1848*

apparent determination to provoke a confrontation, the petition had been delivered without bloodshed. The movement continued to grow in many areas until well into the summer of 1848 when nearly 300 Chartists were arrested following riots in Bradford, Manchester and Liverpool. After this the movement went into a slow decline that lasted ten years. Although it never again attracted the kind of support that had characterised 1839, 1842 and 1848, Chartist Conventions continued to meet until 1858.

Yet the myth that Chartism died of shame on the day it was revealed that 'Mr Punch' and 'Queen Victoria' had signed the petition, has proved hard to dispel. This is partly because it reflects the way many contemporaries wanted to see Chartism; as a misguided attempt by the hungry and uneducated to achieve a political citizenship for which they could surely have no real use or understanding. There is much of this feeling of superiority in the cartoon that appeared in *Punch* after the Kennington Common meeting (Picture 13).

Similarly, when Charles Kingsley, the novelist and Anglican clergyman, depicted Chartism in his novel *Alton Locke* (1850), he used the meeting on 10 April as a way of depicting the folly of the movement. His leading character, a tailor, gives Kingsley's account of the event and the role of the Chartist leadership:

> The meeting which was to have been counted by hundreds of thousands, numbered hardly its tens of thousands; and of them a frightful proportion of those very rascal classes, against whom we ourselves had offered to be sworn in as special constables. O'Connor's courage failed him after all. He contrived to be called away by some problematical superintendent of police.... while the monster petition crawled ludicrously away in a hack-cab, to be dragged to the floor of the House of Commons amidst roars of laughter ...

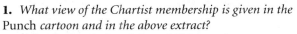

Q

1. *What view of the Chartist membership is given in the* Punch *cartoon and in the above extract?*
2. *What is Kingsley's opinion of O'Connor?*
3. *How fair in their analysis of the Chartists do you consider these sources to be?*
4. *What do these two sources tell us about the relationship between the middle class and the working class at this time?*

TIMELINE

1840	National Charter Association established Trials of Chartist leaders, including O'Connor
1841	'New moves' Chartist Church, Chartist Teetotal Association and Lovett's National Association (for educational reform) established; middle class reformers establish the Leeds Reform Association.
1842	(April) Chartist Convention meets in London Second Chartist Petition rejected by Parliament Complete Suffrage Union established (conferences held April and December). (August) 'Plug' disturbances.
1845	Chartist Land Company established
1846	Repeal of The Corn Laws
1847	O'Connor elected as MP for Nottingham 10 Hours Act passed
1848	Chartist Convention sends a delegation to Paris to congratulate the provisional Government, following the revolution of that year. Land Company declared illegal (April) Third Chartist petition presented following Kennington Common meeting.

6 ⌐ INTERPRETING THE FAILURE OF CHARTISM

KEY ISSUE

*Why did Chartism fail
to achieve its
immediate objectives?*

There is little doubt that, despite mobilising large numbers of people, Chartism must be judged an overall failure. Five of the six points of political reform were not brought about until well into the next century (one, annual parliaments, has never been accepted) and it is difficult to attribute their acceptance then, in any direct way, to the Chartist movement. The 'implicit social programme' remained similarly elusive: the hated Poor Law was a feature of British life until the abolition of the workhouse system in 1929; trade unions faced a constant battle for legal status, and working men did not enter Parliament in any numbers until the advent of the Labour Party. Sooner or later all historians of Chartism find themselves facing the central question, 'Why did Chartism fail?'.

Six years after Kennington Common, R. G. Gammage, a working man from Northampton who had been a local Chartist leader, reflected bitterly on a movement which, he felt, had failed through poor leadership. His *History of the Chartist Movement*, first published in 1854, blamed O'Connor. Other ex-Chartists shared Gammage's disappointment that the high hopes of the movement had come to nothing, but challenged his interpretation of its cause. The Cheltenham Chartist, W. E. Adams, criticised Gammage for concentrating too much on the 'personal squabbles of the leaders' and thereby missing, what he called the 'inspiring light of the movement.' He also expressed the hope that, 'Someday ... a work worthy of the movement will be taken in hand by a competent historian.' These contemporary views are a reminder that our explanation of why Chartism failed depends very much on how we see the movement. *Punch*, Kingsley, and Gammage present us with a movement that was fragmented by disagreement and poorly led. Yet Adams' abiding memory of his experience is of the extraordinary motivation that made millions become Chartists.

Modern-day analysis of the reasons for failure tends to fall into one of the two camps identified above: those who see the Chartists as architects of their own doom and those who choose to concentrate more on the 'inspiring light' of the movement. The distinction is really between those who blame Chartism's failure on its internal divisions and those who relate its failure to the hostile nature of the Government's response.

**HISTORIANS'
DEBATE**

'Hunger politics': Feargus O'Connor as the pantomime villain

Undoubtedly, the simplest way to explain both the rise and the demise of Chartism is to see it as a form of 'hunger politics': the reaction to hunger by an illiterate working class, misled by disaffected members of other classes. When times improved, Chartism disappeared. Certainly middle-class observers at the time feared the motivation behind Chartism from this point of view. The philosopher Thomas Carlyle, writing in 1839, described it as 'bitter discontent grown fierce and mad'. From this perspective, it is easy to sympathise with the accompanying argument that the working class were not yet 'ready' to exercise the vote. Their political immaturity, the argument goes, was best expressed in their wiliingness to follow 'mob-orators' like O'Connor. In this way the analysis of the leadership also reflects a very critical view of the 'rank and file' of the movement. It is always worth remembering this point: that any commentary on the leaders also involves a judgement on the 'rank and file' who followed them.

Yet the closer we get to the Chartists themselves the less this interpretation seems to fit. As we have seen, Chartism was a predominantly peaceful, constitutional movement. The image of an irrational and uneducated following, ill-equipped to exercise the responsibilities of citizenship, does not accord well with what we know of the Chartists' own commitment to self-improvement and education. Chartism clearly drew strong support from people suffering severe economic hardship. But thinking of the movement as a 'hungry mob' tells us more about the fears of many contemporary observers than about the experience of the Chartists themselves. Speaking in the Parliamentary debate on the Chartist petition in 1842, the Whig politician T. B. Macaulay argued that 'universal suffrage is utterly incompatible with the very existence of civilisation.' His words echoed those of Edmund Burke who had warned in 1790 of the threat from the 'swinish multitude'. The Chartists, on the other hand, saw universal suffrage in terms of protecting a civilised society. The Scottish newspaper, the *Chartist Circular*, argued that universal suffrage 'is the only security against bad laws, and for good government'. Of course the Chartists often translated their demand for the vote as a right into more obvious images. For example, a speaker at one Chartist meeting said that, after the Charter had been accepted, there would be 'plenty of roast beef, plum pudding and strong beer by working three hours a day'. Such statements were often delivered 'tongue in cheek' to elicit an ironic response from the audience and cannot be taken as evidence of political immaturity.

Hunger was then, as it remains today, a good political educator. Whenever an economic and political system proves incapable of feeding its population, it inevitably runs into opposition. But hunger has generally been equated with irrational behaviour where it has figured in the analysis of Chartism. This has provided a compelling explanation of Chartist failure with a convenient scapegoat in the shape of Feargus O'Connor, the most revered of the radical leaders and the most consistently maligned by historians. Mark Hovell, in his book *The Chartist Movement* (1917), refers to him as a 'blustering, egotistical, blarneying, managing, but intellectually and morally very unreliable Irishman'. Behind this, of course, lies a criticism of the thousands of working men and women who followed O'Connor: Hovell refers to their 'dog-like devotion'.

Echoing this position, J. T. Ward, in *Chartism* (1974), finds that:

> The most impressive and moving aspect of Chartist history was that, despite all its charlatans [impostors], cowards and crooks, the movement retained the devoted loyalty of so many working men.

This image is extended through the language used to describe working people, who are seen individually as honest simpletons but collectively as a threatening mob. For Ward, they are 'humble folk looking to the weekly spelling out of the *Star*' and also, 'The ragged hordes who swept over the Pennines to close Yorkshire mills in 1842'. The tragedy of Chartism, from this sort of perspective, is that O'Connor was allowed to advocate an empty 'physical force' strategy, at the expense of the moderate and conciliatory 'moral force' tactics advocated by men like William Lovett. Middle-class support, which might have been forthcoming, was frightened off by what Asa Briggs refers to as O'Connor's 'oratorical fireworks'.

Chartism defeated by the State: O'Connor as the hero

The 'hunger politics' analysis above assumes a particular view of the Chartist leadership, particularly O'Connor who appears in some accounts as almost a pantomime villain to be hissed at by historians. But a very different view of O'Connor has emerged over the last 20 years. James Epstein, in his biography of O'Connor, presents him as an energetic and capable leader. Behind this analysis of the leader lies a more positive interpretation of the Chartist rank and file. Chartism is seen as the product of a politically aware working community threatened by the changes of the Industrial Revolution. O'Connor was accepted as a leader because he recognised this; as Epstein puts it:

> It was O'Connor's insistence upon the need to construct and maintain an independent working class movement which won him the support of working-class radicals.

The Chartists wanted political change to take place on their terms and it was this, and not O'Connor's so called 'oratorical fireworks', that frightened many observers. The Whig and Tory Governments feared what they saw as a genuinely revolutionary movement. Furthermore, as Dorothy Thompson stresses, far from being a fragmented movement, the Chartists were able to conjure up a degree of cohesion that was truly remarkable. She describes Chartism as 'the response of a literate and sophisticated working class'.

Following in the tradition established by E. P. Thompson, these historians have turned the 'hunger politics' view on its head. Here we are back to Adams' 'inspiring light'. Given its circumstances, perhaps Chartism was a pretty impressive movement, so the argument goes. It

See the Bibliography on page 129

mobilised hundreds of thousands and demonstrated the existence of a working class able to think and act for itself. The 'threat' of Chartism was not that of the 'mob' driven to despair but rather that of a group challenging for power. This challenge was met by firm action from a political establishment that was, since 1832, reinforced by its alliance with the new wealth of the middle class. What we can be certain of, is that the Whig and Tory Governments who rejected the petitions in 1839, 1842 and 1848, feared the consequences of accepting the Charter far more than the dangers involved in turning it down.

In this interpretation, Chartist failure was a reflection of the strength of its adversaries, rather than its own inherent weakness. The resolute stance to each petition was born of a confidence in the political settlement of 1832. The army remained loyal and the police force was extended in these years. Chartism as a problem of 'law and order' was less threatening than the prospect of accepting the Charter. Chartism as a movement was very efficiently suppressed, and the Chartists' own commitment to peaceful methods undoubtedly assisted the task of the authorities. Also, it is clear that with the repeal of the Corn Laws in 1846 and the passing of the long-awaited Ten Hours Act in 1848, it became more difficult to assert that only a 'root and branch' change in the political system could bring about improvement. The Governments of the day seemed to be signalling their willingness to alleviate the lot of working people through reforming laws and thus to take the sting out of Chartism. Certainly, with the end of Chartism, working people turned their attention to the achievement of less ambitious, but more obviously attainable, objectives.

A *Movement before its time?*

In 1982, the historian Gareth Stedman-Jones, argued that Chartism failed because it looked backwards. It looked back to the ideas of men like Tom Paine who saw the aristocracy, rather than the new class of factory and mill owners, as the villains. Therefore, the Chartists saw the main focus of their attack being a Government that was dominated by the aristocracy rather than the new class of capitalists. Thus when the state began to introduce real and tangible reforms like the repeal of the Corn Laws (1846) or the Ten Hours Act (1847), it became more difficult for the Chartists to continue to argue that the Government was totally corrupt and unwilling to change. Looked at this way, Chartism failed because changing circumstances made its argument less relevant to the situation in which working people found themselves.

KEY ISSUE

Was Chartism the last movement of eighteenth-century radicalism rather than the first modern protest movement ?

Nevertheless, there is a well-established tradition of interpreting Chartism as a movement *before* its time. This view sees Chartism as coming too soon to claim to represent a coherent working class; the regions were too diverse and the workforce too divided within itself. In fact, many historians, rejecting E. P. Thompson's view, don't see anything like a united or coherent working class emerging until the more heavily-industrialised, urban Britain of the early twentieth century.

In rejecting this interpretation, recent historians have turned their attention to the lasting achievements of the movement which they see in the continued demand for political and social reform into the early twentieth century. Miles Taylor (1999) suggests, 'The Charter should not be seen as the last shot in the radical attack on 'old corruption', but as the opening sally in the long campaign to clean up electoral procedure and extend the franchise…'. In the same vein, Eric Evans (1999) has suggested that we stop asking why Chartism failed and recognise the contribution made by the movement to what followed. As he puts it, 'Detailed research on later movements designed to assert the rights and improve the conditions of working people shows how firmly embedded the Chartist tradition became, whether in education, temperance reform, trade unionism, socialism or even the early development of Labour politics in the 1880s and 1890s'.

7 ⌐ BIBLIOGRAPHY

ARTICLES

Clive Behagg 'Taking Chartism Seriously', *Modern History Review*, April 1994.

Eric Evans 'Chartism Revisited', *History Review*, March 1999.

Miles Taylor 'Putting the Politics Back into Chartism' *Modern History Review*, April 1999.

BOOKS FOR AS/A LEVEL STUDENTS

R. Brown, *Chartism*, Cambridge University Press, 1998.

H. Browne *Chartism*, Access to History series, Hodder & Stoughton, 1999.

Joe Finn *Chartism and The Chartists*, Hodder & Stoughton, 1992, is a good source for documentary material on the movement.

Edward Royle, *Chartism*, Longman, 1996.

FURTHER READING

Asa Briggs (Ed.) *Chartist Studies*, Macmillan, 1959. Briggs' volume made the case for the regional study of Chartism and this collection includes studies of the movement in a number of localities. Also included are some good essays dealing with 'national' aspects of the movement (see especially F. C. Mather on the Government and the Chartists and Lucy Brown on relations with the Anti-Corn Law League).

J. Epstein *The Lion of Freedom*, Croom Helm, 1982. This book offers a much-needed revision of the orthodox view of O'Connor, and sees him as the leader chosen by a politically conscious working class.

J. Epstein and D. Thompson (Eds) *The Chartist Experience*, Macmillan, 1982. This collection of essays picks up the regional approach established by Briggs, but pursues a particular theme in each area. See especially R. Sykes, on Chartism and trade unions in the north-west. Also contains Stedman-Jones' controversial essay 'The language of Chartism'.

D. Jones *The Last Rising*, Clarendon Press, 1985, is a sympathetic and thorough account of the Newport rising.

J. Saville *1848*, Cambridge University Press, 1987. This is a systematic treatment of one important year in the life of Chartism. Saville explores the relationship between 'high' politics and the popular movement and challenges the myth that grew up about the meeting of 10 April, 1848.

J. Schwarzkopf *Women in the Chartist Movement*, Macmillan, 1991, charts the extensive role which women played in the movement.

D. Thompson *The Chartists*, Temple Smith, 1984. If you were only ever going to read one book on Chartism this ought to be the one. Dorothy Thompson's book explores the role of particular groups within the movement, particularly in terms of their values and beliefs.

J. T. Ward *Chartism*, Batsford, 1973. This book provides a narrative account of Chartism. It is sceptical about the claim that the movement's supporters were a politically conscious working class and depicts a movement betrayed by inept leaders and fragmented strategy.

8 ∽ STRUCTURED AND ESSAY QUESTIONS

A *Structured questions for AS Level*

1. Why did Chartism emerge in 1838? (10 marks)
2. To what extent were government fears of Chartist violence justified? (15 marks)
3. How far are we right to see Chartism as simply 'hunger politics'? (25 marks).

Question 1 asks you to focus on the factors surrounding the emergence of Chartism; here you need to explore the contribution of radical movements leading up to 1838 and those short-term factors that relate more specifically to 1838 itself. In Question 2 you are asked to explore the potential for Chartist violence; look back over the chapter for sections on the Bull Ring riots, Newport, the 'language of menace' and the 1848 Kennington Common meeting. In Question 3 your view of the movement as a whole is required. Here you are making a judgement on the awareness and organisational capabilities of those involved in the movement.

Beware, particularly, of the apparently easy answer. The hypothesis that Chartism rose with economic decline and failed when the economy recovered will appear to relieve you of the burden of a detailed knowledge of the movement. But it does not! You will still need to explain, for example, why a 'hungry' working class read 60 000 copies of the *Northern Star* each week in 1839, why so many chose to express their hunger through politics, and so on. Hunger may provide the chronology of the movement but it does not explain why it took the form that it did.

B *Essay Questions for A2*

Before embarking on essay questions on Chartism you should ask a question yourself: why do examiners love posing questions about Chartism? Movements that fail rarely draw such fulsome attention, and herein lies the paradox that makes all questions on Chartism so open to differing interpretation (and thus irresistible to examiners). Chartism was a *mass* movement, with *huge* support, which failed to achieve *any* of its objectives in its own time. Many of the questions you are likely to be asked on Chartism will require you to explore the relationship between mass support and abject failure.

Here are some typical examples of the sort of question that you might be asked on Chartism:

1. 'Its failure stemmed from inept leadership'. Discuss this verdict on the Chartist movement.
2. 'Chartism was a good deal more than a movement for social reform'. Discuss.
3. How much working-class solidarity was shown between 1838 and 1848?
4. To what extent did support for Chartism reflect the fluctuations in the British economy in the 1830s and 1840s?
5. With what justification have historians identified the growth of working-class consciousness between 1815 and 1850?
6. Did Chartism fail because lower-class unrest was basically a 'knife and fork' question?
7. Was Chartism primarily an economic or a political movement?

The focus of these questions varies; some of them place the nature of the movement in the foreground, some of them concentrate on the movement's failure, and others ask you to use Chartism as an exemplar of developments across a wider time-span. Yet all of them deal in some way with the *motivation* behind Chartism, e.g. some are more explicit than others on the contentious issue of how far Chartism embodied a cohesive, working-class political consciousness. To answer any of these questions you need not only to be able to give a considered overview of the movement but also to support this by reference to the specific events and personalities involved.

C *Exercise*

Re-read Section 1. Construct a list of the laws that might have been passed, or repealed, by a Parliament elected on the basis of the Charter.

For each item on your list you should explain any evidence from your study of the movement, and its precursors, that supports its inclusion. In doing this remember the image of Chartism as an 'umbrella movement' carrying with it an 'implicit social programme'.

9 ⌐ DOCUMENTARY EXERCISE – FOR AND AGAINST THE CHARTER

I believe that universal suffrage would be fatal to all purposes for which governments exist, and for which aristocracies and all other things exist, and that it is utterly incompatible with the very existence of civilisation. I conceive that civilisation rests on the security of property ...

... I believe that nothing is more natural than that the feelings of the people should be such as they are described to be. Even we, ourselves, with all our advantages of education, when we are tried by the temporary pressure of circumstances, are too ready to catch at everything which may hold out the hope of relief ... and I cannot but see, that a man having a wife at home to whom he is attached, growing thinner every day, children whose wants become every day more pressing, whose mind is principally employed in mechanical toil, may have been driven to entertain such views as are here expressed, partly from his own position, and partly from the culpable neglect of the government in omitting to supply him with the means and the power of forming a better judgement. Let us grant that education would remedy these things, shall we not wait until it has done so, before we agree to such a motion as this ...

SOURCE A *This extract is from a speech delivered in the House of Commons, 3 May 1842, by T. B. Macaulay, Whig MP for Edinburgh, on the motion that the House accept the Charter*

Do you think it [universal suffrage] essential to obtain and secure good government? I do for the following reasons: – First, because the possession of the franchise is the only difference between a freeman and the Russian serf, who is sold with the land and the cattle ... It is the only security against bad laws and for good government which otherwise depends upon the caprice and fears of the master class who make the laws; and while the exclusive few have a profitable interest in bad laws, there will be no barrier to tyranny and corruption ...

Why do you prefer Annual Parliaments to Septennial, as at present? Because we should be enabled, by this means, to get rid of a bad servant at the end of one year, instead of being fixed with him for seven as at present.

SOURCE B *These extracts are from an article which appeared in January 1841 in* The Chartist Circular *in which each of the six points is considered in turn. This article adopted a popular format in Chartist journalism, that of a dialogue between two parties, one a sceptic and the other a convinced Chartist. They begin with the issue of universal manhood suffrage*

But would a man be able, in one year, to obtain an insight into the forms of Parliament, and would it be prudent to dismiss a man as soon as he became useful? This is begging the question; we should not dismiss an honest and capable man, and the sooner a dishonest or incapable one is dismissed the better.

… But would you send men to Parliament not worth a shilling? I doubt whether a man without a shilling would be elected; but the present property qualification is a farce; if a man has money or interest enough to get into Parliament he can purchase a sham qualification for £100. But why should not a poor man, if he has ability sufficient, and the majority of the electors have confidence in him, be elected? If none but rich men are sent to Parliament, the feelings of the poor cannot be fairly represented.

1. *What are the arguments against accepting the Charter, as put by Macaulay?*
2. *What are the arguments in favour of accepting the Charter, as put by the Chartist Circular?*
3. *What does Macaulay mean by 'civilisation rests on the security of property?'*
4. *Can you think of any reasons why the Chartist Circular chose to present its case in the form of a conversation between two parties?*
5. *What view of the working community comes through from each of these extracts?*
6. *What light do these documents cast on the failure of Chartism?*
7. *Using these documents as a basis for the exercise, write out a defence for each of the six points of the Charter.*

10 ⌐ DOCUMENTARY EXERCISE ON THE NATURE OF CHARTISM

Study Sources A–D and answer the questions which follow.

The Manchester Union proclaimed its abhorrence of violent language and physical force, but its first great demonstration on Kersal Moor, on September 24, was graced by the presence of Stephens, O'Connor, and others who were advocates of violent courses. This demonstration was one of the most remarkable of all Chartist meetings. The *Leeds Times* thought there were a quarter of a million people present, which is scarcely credible. There was an immense array of speakers, representing all parts of the Chartist world. The dominant note was struck by Stephens, who declared that the Charter was not a political question but a knife and fork question: not a matter of ballot-boxes but of bread and butter. This tone sounded throughout all the subsequent babble about arming or not arming, about natural rights and legal rights, which filled up the debates of the Convention. For Chartism was in these manufacturing areas a cry of distress, the shout of men, women and children drowning in deep waters, rather that the reasoned logical creed of Lovett, or the fanatical money-mongering theories of Attwood. Impatience, engendered by fireless grates and breakfastless tables, was the driving force of much northern Chartism.

SOURCE A *From Mark Hovell* The Chartist Movement *published in 1917*

One of O'Connor's greatest strengths was the attention which he paid to local Chartism and his constant efforts to bring a national perspective to local working-class agitation. Furthermore, the task of revising the traditional view of O'Connor is integrally linked to the task of asserting the independence, intelligence and agency of Chartism's rank and file. The consistent failure of historians to deal with O'Connor as a serious political leader, the assertion that he lacked principles and was willing to place his individual designs above the interests of the movement are not merely unfair to O'Connor but involve an implicit judgement upon the hundreds of thousands of working people who supported him. Chartism's rank and file did not blindly follow O'Connor; their support was founded upon astute political judgement stemming from their own political experience.

SOURCE B *From James Epstein* The Lion of Freedom *published in 1975.*

Why is it that, in the midst of plenty, we are in such a condition? Why is it that those who are willing to work, that those who have produced everything in society, without whom the factories would not have been built, the machinery made, the railroads constructed, the canals cut, who build and man the ships, who fight the battles, make the hats, shoes and coats, and till the land – cannot get enough to quell the ravings of hunger?

SOURCE C *Letter from the women Chartists of Manchester, in the columns of the* Northern Star *in January 1842*

After breakfast I went to the committee-room, where I found F. O'Connor and a number of delegates from the different towns in the district, as well as representatives from the local committees. The programme of speakers and resolutions was arranged with a view to adopt the charter and to petition Parliament for it. The meeting was to

SOURCE D *Extract from Robert Lowery's autobiography published in 1856, recalling a Chartist rally in 1838*

take place on Kersal Moor, outside the town. Local and district processions soon began to fill the streets and we joined them. Although I had often seen 1 000 000 at a meeting in Newcastle I never had a clear conception of a multitude until that day. The day was exceedingly fine, and there were processions from Rochdale and Oldham and the chief places for fourteen miles or upwards round about Manchester; I should think there were hundreds of bands of music. I could not conceive where the people came from, for at every open space or corner there would be thousands standing, besides the crowd passing. When we got out of the streets it was an exciting sight to see the processions arriving on the Moor from different places, with their flags flying and the music of the bands swelling in the air, ever and anon overtopped by a loud cheer which ran along the different lines. On ascending the hustings a still more exciting sight awaited us. *The Times* estimated the meeting at about 300 000. One dense mass of faces beaming with earnestness – as far as you could distinguish faces – then beyond still an immense crowd, but with indistinct countenances.

Q

1. *From Source C and your own knowledge, what can you learn about the part played by women in the Chartist movement?* (**5 marks**)
2. *How useful is Source B as evidence of the importance of O'Connor's role in the Chartist movement?* (**6 marks**)
3. *How far do Sources A and D explain the extent of support for Chartism?* (**7 marks**)
4. *Use the sources and your own knowledge to explain how far you would agree that 'Impatience, engendered by breakfastless tables and fireless grates, was the driving force' of much of the Chartist movement.* (**12 marks**)

Total 30 marks

Peel and the Conservative Party, 1829–46

6

INTRODUCTION

Whig governments dominated politics in the 1830s. Tory fortunes were at a low ebb in the early years of the decade but had recovered dramatically by the election of 1841 when they won a majority of seats in the House of Commons and formed a government, under Sir Robert Peel, which lasted until 1846.

THE TORY RECOVERY AFTER 1832

This topic has aroused intense historical debate. Understanding it involves some study of the many things that went wrong for the party after the death of their great Prime Minister, Lord Liverpool, in 1827. Tory problems arose from the deep divisions in the Party over Catholic Emancipation in 1829 and the subsequent election defeat in 1830. From 1830 to 1832 the party was embroiled in frustrating and eventually fruitless opposition to the Whig Government's reform of the parliamentary system which almost all Tories saw as potentially disastrous for themselves and for the country. Peel was at his least effective in these years. The reasons for the recovery in party fortunes after 1832, including Peel's role in it and the adoption of the new name of Conservative Party, are the basis of one of the most interesting debates among historians studying nineteenth-century politics. Controversy has centred on whether it was Peel's work in modernising the party, making it acceptable to the enlarged post-1832 electorate, or whether it was the normal swing of party fortunes from the depths of the early 1830s that allowed what was a *largely unchanged* party to resume its natural role of government. In short, did a new Conservative Party emerge in these years from the ashes of Lord Liverpool's Tory Party or was it essentially the same party revived?

PEEL AS PRIME MINISTER 1841–6

This ministry followed a brief period as prime minister in 1834 and so is referred to as his second administration. Peel's style as Prime Minister has attracted much attention both for his tremendous capacity for work and for his aloofness from party members. The Government's reform record, especially its financial and economic measures, was hugely successful but the growing disillusion among its supporters has recently attracted more attention from historians. This is because the dramatic events surrounding the final collapse of the Government, which was brought about by Peel's decision to repeal the Corn Laws, have overshadowed its earlier achievements.

The two main issues of this chapter are:

● How do you explain the Tory party's recovery from 1832 to 1841?
● Why did Peel's Government fall, and the party split so irretrievably, in 1846?

Most topics relating to Peel's career after 1830 can be grouped around these two issues although a separate assessment of the success of Peel's second ministry in domestic policy is also important.

PROFILE

SIR ROBERT PEEL (1788–1850)

Peel's family fortune came from the Lancashire cotton industry though, by the time of his birth, his father had acquired a large landed estate at Tamworth in Staffordshire. Peel was educated at Harrow public school and Oxford University in preparation for a political career. Only an occasionally evident Lancashire accent remained to remind him and political audiences of his more humble origins. At Oxford he excelled academically and at the age of 21, in 1809, his father's money bought him a Commons seat for the Irish pocket borough of Cashel. In 1817 he became an MP for Oxford University and on his father's death in 1830 for the 'family seat' at Tamworth, in each case being spared the anxieties involved in fighting fiercely contested elections. By 1810 he was holding minor office as Under-Secretary for War and the Colonies under Lord Liverpool. For the remainder of his political life he was always close to or at the centre of power, rarely out of government except during the Whig-dominated 1830s. His major offices were:

● **Chief Secretary for Ireland**, 1812–18 where he supported the 'Protestant ascendancy' and reformed the police.
● **Home Secretary**, 1822–7, 1828–30 where he promoted prison and penal reforms and, controversially and against his earlier convictions, helped Wellington carry Catholic Emancipation in 1829.
● **Leader of the Tory/Conservative Party**, 1834–46.
● **Prime Minister**, 1834–5, 1841–6.

He was a masterly Commons debater and worked prodigiously hard at the business of government in an era when this was growing rapidly, so that he was perhaps the last prime minister to try to keep an eye on, or exert influence upon, most branches of government business. In the wider world he did not make friends quickly or mix easily with acquaintances though he came to inspire the warmest affection from most of his close government colleagues. Gladstone, himself active at the top of politics until the 1890s, thought him the greatest man he had ever met. His stilted manner and inability to reach out to win the commitment of his supporters made him, in government, an isolated figure and never more so than in times of

PICTURE 14
Portrait of Peel by Linnell

political crisis. The abrupt end to his political career might well owe as much to his failure to reach out to Conservative backbenchers as it did to the gravity of the political dilemma he found himself in. Some historians, notably Gash, have seen Peel as a pragmatic politician who calmly sought practical solutions to the pressing political problems of his time – a government man, above all an efficient administrator who, believing in the overriding importance of public order, could see no greater priority than that effective government should be protected and promoted, at times at great cost to himself and to his party. More recent writers have challenged this view and stress Peel's emotional commitment to free trade as a means to economic growth, based on a deep Christian conviction that the state had a duty to provide a just society in which the weak, the disadvantaged and the poor had opportunities to provide for themselves and to live godly lives. His passionate support for the free trade cause, together with his own personal inability easily to win his party's support for it, led in 1846 to his abrupt fall from the highest political office to political obscurity and the scorn of the majority of his party. Only after his death in 1850, the result of a fall from a horse, was his reputation restored amid surprisingly fervent expressions of public grief.

See Bibliography on page 171

1 ᔕ PEEL'S CAREER TO 1832

A *His early political career*

Peel, born in 1788, was the son of a Lancashire manufacturer and yet, by 1829, he had held important posts, at the highest level, in Lord Liverpool's pre-reform, aristocratic-based, governments. Peel entered Parliament at the height of the wars against Napoleonic France when vivid memories of the horrors of the French Revolution were still alive and Britain itself was being transformed by rapid population growth and by industrialisation of its economy. Peel's concerns about the importance of maintaining the authority of the Government of the state, so as to preserve public order, date from his early years in politics.

Almost immediately Peel was given a series of junior ministerial appointments, and then rapidly promoted to be Chief Secretary for Ireland from 1812 to 1818. In this post he was responsible for creating Ireland's first professional police force. In 1819 he was chairman of the Currency Committee that worked to restore Britain's currency to the gold standard. This gave Peel an expertise in financial matters which came to full fruition during his 1841–6 ministry. His association after 1822 with William Huskisson, Liverpool's chief financial minister, extended his grasp of commercial affairs. From 1822 to 1827 Peel was Home Secretary in Liverpool's Government and was responsible for introducing both the legal and prison reforms which are discussed in

1812–18	Chief Secretary for Ireland
1819	Chairman Currency Committee
1822–7	Home Secretary
1828–30	Home Secretary

TABLE 6 *Peel's posts to 1830*

See page 17 on Peel's reforms as Home Secretary

Chapter 2. In these years he revealed a growing mastery of administration and an astonishing capacity for sustained hard work so that, by 1827, he had made himself a key figure in the complicated political manoeuvres, which were to follow the end of the Liverpool ministry. In 1828 Peel refused to serve in Canning's short-lived Government because he was a leading opponent of Catholic Emancipation, which Canning was known to favour. In 1828 he was again appointed Home Secretary, this time by Wellington, another committed opponent of any political concessions to Catholics. In 1829 he transformed the prospects for law and order in London when he founded the Metropolitan Police Force. (Police officers are still sometimes referred to as 'Bobbies' after Sir Robert Peel.)

By 1829 Peel had been in government for almost all his parliamentary career. He had shown himself to be strongly committed to the effective government of the country yet also willing to remedy abuses and make suitable administrative reforms. However he remained firmly opposed to any change in the constitution lest it lead to anarchy. In all these respects he typified the approach adopted by Lord Liverpool in the period from 1822 to 1827.

B *Catholic Emancipation 1829*

Since the sixteenth century, Roman Catholics had been prevented from becoming MPs or holding important public offices. In the nineteenth century most Britons were deeply suspicious of, and prejudiced against, Catholics. Yet the vast majority of Irish people were Catholic and were still forced to pay for the upkeep of the **Anglican Church in Ireland**.

The resentment that the Irish felt came to a head with the Act of Union in 1800. This Act abolished the Irish Parliament in Dublin and stated that 100 Irish MPs would attend the House of Commons in London. However, since the seventeenth century, every MP had been required to take an oath renouncing certain beliefs central to Catholic doctrine before he could take his seat in Parliament. This was intended to safeguard the country's Protestant constitution as secured in the so-called Revolution Settlement of 1689. Irish Catholic grievances over the issue reached a climax with the 1828 election to the Commons of the Catholic leader, Daniel O'Connell.

The political difficulties to which Irish grievances gave rise are central to an understanding of Peel's later career and it is this aspect that is examined here.

In 1828 the Duke of Wellington, as Prime minister, decided that public order in Ireland would only be maintained if the goodwill of leading Catholics was secured by political concessions allowing them to be elected to the Westminster Parliament that governed them. Such concessions would have to be fought for against fierce Protestant prejudices in Parliament and in the rest of Britain. Peel himself had, from 1817, been the most effective speaker defending the privileged political position of the Anglican Church in Ireland as essential to the political stability of the United Kingdom but, as Irish Catholic agitation reached a dangerous

KEY ISSUE

Why did Peel change his mind on Catholic Emancipation and how did this affect his later career?

The Anglican Church in Ireland was a branch of the Church of England established by Henry VIII in the 1530s. The Church of England is sometimes therefore referred to as the Established Church

For O'Connell and Ireland see Chapter 9, pages 267–70

level in the late 1820s, he had privately begun to doubt whether the protestant monopoly of political power could be sustained. His public position had however been all too clearly spelled out and had attracted great support from hard-line (Ultra) members of the Tory Party. Since Wellington sat in the House of Lords he made it clear that Peel alone would be able to persuade the Commons to agree to removal of the disabilities on Catholics. This put Peel in an impossible situation.

If Catholic Emancipation did not come soon then there was a possibility of serious disorder, even outright rebellion, in Ireland. If Wellington's Government introduced such a measure and it was defeated in Parliament then, in the absence of any obvious successor, a period of dangerous political confusion would certainly ensue at Westminster. In these circumstances Peel, who had already shown his commitment to maintaining the Government's authority, could not ignore Wellington's pleas. The Catholic Emancipation Bill was actually introduced into the Commons by Peel himself and it was *his* support for it, allied to his parliamentary tactical skill, which ensured that Wellington's bill became law.

Peel paid a heavy price for his loyalty and his sense of duty. The Ultra Protestant sections of the Tory Party rounded on him as having betrayed not only the Anglican Church in Ireland but also the very basis of the Protestant constitution of the United Kingdom. Great numbers of his own party, nearly all of whom were members of the Church of England, talked in terms of Peel having betrayed the constitution and felt that he could never be fully trusted again. Emancipation had been pushed through the unreformed Parliament by an anxious Government using the full weight of its influence to secure the support of the Commons and the Lords. Their actions flew in the face of vast public anti-Catholic prejudice. Influential sections of the Tory Party never forgave Peel for his public-spirited 'betrayal' of the Protestant constitution and, in 1846, this became a significant element in the defeat of his Government.

C *The Tory Party and the 1832 Reform Act*

It had been a central principle of Lord Liverpool's Tory policy in the 1820s that, whilst specific abuses might be put right by particular measures, no major reform of the British constitution was either desirable or necessary. With memories of the way in which, in revolutionary France, reform had swiftly degenerated into anarchy, many Tories held that general reform of the constitutional arrangements for governing the country would be dangerous in arousing unreasonable expectations and lead to ever more extreme changes. No credible politician, Tory or Whig, wanted democracy; a term with overtones of anarchy.

The Tory split over Catholic Emancipation led to their losing many seats in the 1830 General Election. The new Whig Government, which emerged under Lord Grey, was committed to some measure of parliamentary reform if only to end the inbuilt bias of the unreformed system towards the Tories. The full account of their efforts and their

For a full account of the 1832 Reform of Parliament see pages 46–54

consequences can be found in Chapter 3 and here it is only Peel's reactions to his opponents' reform proposals that are considered.

D *Peel's opposition to the Reform Bill*

The first draft of the Whig reform proposals outraged Peel by their extremism and, throughout the ensuing struggle to pass the Reform Bill, Peel did what he could to oppose the Whig measure. He never gave way to the total despair of some in the Tory Party but still feared that Parliament was being bulldozed into carrying an extreme reform measure through fear of excitable public opinion in support of the measure. The Whigs were, he felt, arousing revolutionary forces that they might well not be able to control. The overthrow of the French Bourbon Monarchy in 1830, with echoes of the 1790s French Revolution, encouraged his alarm to such an extent that he took steps to fortify his country residence against possible attack by an armed mob. Peel also realised that any measure of reform would probably lead to demands for further reforms, setting a precedent that would be difficult to ignore. In this he was more perceptive than Whigs like Russell who claimed that the 1832 Reform Act could be 'a final measure' of parliamentary reform.

KEY ISSUE

Why was Peel so totally opposed to the Whig reform proposals?

Peel also realised that reform of the Commons would alter its relations with both the House of Lords and with the Monarchy. At the very least an elected Commons, having to bear in mind the opinions of the electors, would be much more difficult for any government to control. Peel was aware that he had managed to push Catholic Emancipation through the Commons, despite widespread public hatred of Catholicism, because the Commons was unreformed and so protected from the full weight of public opinion. The MPs for rotten and pocket boroughs were precisely those most open to pressure from any government anxious to push through controversial measures. The Crown, almost invariably supporting the Government of the day, was of course the largest 'controller' of pocket boroughs.

From 1830 to 1832 Peel was pushed onto the defensive over the question of parliamentary reform. There is little evidence that he appreciated the Whig strategy, of carrying a modest reform in order to prevent a more radical one and so, crucially, conceding the vote to most of the 'respectable' middle class, many of whom were property owners, in order to separate them from those with more extreme political demands and indeed from the working class generally.

In his opposition to passing any measure of constitutional reform he remained a true supporter of the traditions of Lord Liverpool. When forming a judgement on Peel's general reputation as a reformer these limitations need to be remembered: in the greatest reform crisis of his time in Parliament he failed to see the true issues at stake and remained tied to the outmoded principles absorbed in his early career under the shadow of the French Revolution. The consequences of passing the 1832 Reform Act were on the whole advantageous to the continuing aristocratic exercise of power and effective over the next 35 years in promoting political stability. It seems remarkable that, at the time of the Act's passage through Parliament, Peel never seemed to grasp this possibility but persisted throughout in strongly criticising the Whig reform proposals.

In May 1832, at the height of the crisis over the passing of the Reform Bill, his behaviour placed him in a difficult position. William IV had refused to promise Grey, his Prime Minister, that he would create enough Whig peers to carry the Government's Reform Bill through the Tory-dominated House of Lords if it became necessary. Grey resigned and, in this extreme crisis, the king turned to the Tories to form a Government. Wellington thought that with Peel's help a Tory Government could be set up which could carry out a suitably modest reform, capable of pacifying excitable public opinion and at the same time thwarting the Whig proposals.

At this extreme crisis Peel refused to back Wellington's plan, and so dashed William IV's hopes. His reasons were personal and arose from his previous year's strenuous opposition to the Whig reform. He believed that, if he now joined a government that introduced even a very limited measure of reform, as Wellington certainly considered essential, then he would once again, as with Catholic Emancipation, be labelled a traitor. He refused to face this prospect. The central principle of Peel's political life has been described as placing national needs before party advantage. Whatever may be the case in other crises, such as the earlier Catholic Emancipation crisis or later in the 1846 Corn Law crisis, it can be argued that Peel's conduct in May 1832 placed personal reputation above duty to both party and to monarch. This conduct, at the precise moment when the reform crisis could well have exploded into bloody confrontation, infuriated Wellington and it was some years before cordial relations between the two men were restored. It is worth noting this often-neglected episode when making an overall assessment of Peel.

The lessons Peel learned in the difficult years 1829–32 certainly affected his conduct of politics during his second ministry, most importantly:

- he became sensitive to the difficulties involved in keeping Catholic Ireland tranquil
- his conviction that in these years the state had been close to violent disruption convinced him that future governments must ensure that revolutionary situations were prevented by timely reforms. Politics had to be kept out of the hands of the mob at all costs.

> **KEY ISSUE**
>
> *Did Peel in 1832 place his personal reputation above his duty to both his Party and his Monarch?*

2 ∽ THE RECOVERY IN CONSERVATIVE FORTUNES, 1832–41

A *The low point, 1832*

In the aftermath of the passing of the 1832 Parliamentary Reform Act, the Tory Party in the House of Commons was a disheartened and fear-

TIMELINE

Major Whig reforms
of the 1830s

1832	Parliamentary reform
1833	First Education grant Factory Act Abolition of Slavery
1834	Poor Law Amendment Act
1835	Town government reform (Municipal Reform Act)

ful minority grouping. Leading Whigs spoke of the end of the Tory Party. The Whig Government, backed at first by large majorities in the Commons, went on to carry out a series of major reforms that led historians to label the 1830s as a decade of reform.

And yet, after the 1841 election, Peel was able to form a government backed by a substantial majority of MPs. The number of Tory MPs in the Commons after each of the four general Elections of the period indicates the scale of the Party's electoral recovery:

Date	Whigs	Tories/Conservatives
December 1832	473	185
January 1835	379	279
August 1837	344	314
July 1841	291	367

TABLE 7   *General election results 1832–41: number of MPs*

KEY ISSUE

How did the end of the reform crisis affect the fortunes of both the Tories and the Whigs?

The Tories weak position in 1832 was a result of their mishandling of the issue of parliamentary reform. Their die-hard opposition had seemed a less and less appropriate response to the growing pressure and agitation in the country. By May 1832 even Wellington, but apparently not Peel, had come to realise this. The scale of the Tory humiliation did, however, hide the fact that they still represented important interests in society with most landowners, many in the professions and many of the wealthy seeing the Tory Party as their natural home. The Church of England, and often the monarchy, could also be relied on to use their considerable influence in support of the Tories. Once parliamentary reform was out of the way the Tory leadership had the opportunity to bring back many of their disaffected followers by accepting the Act's provisions.

The Whigs, on the other hand, had benefited greatly, not least in terms of party unity, by the focus on the reform question. After 1832 that issue was at an end and differences of opinion among the Whigs over a wide range of other issues were likely to create divisions among those who had been united over parliamentary reform. Whig divisions appeared quite soon when Russell proposed a scheme to take away some of the accumulated wealth of the (Anglican) Church of Ireland which would be used for practical and desperately needed improvements in education and for building hospitals. Russell was the most radical of the Whigs and his proposals outraged other prominent members of his party. This confiscation of Church property was seen as robbery by prominent Anglican Whigs such as Lord Stanley and Sir James Graham. The former was a member of a family owning vast estates in Lancashire and with great political influence there and the latter had been a member of the small committee that had drawn up the Whig parliamentary reform proposals. For these men, the attack on the rights of property was aggravated by what seemed to be an attack on the position and privileges of the Anglican Church and, unable to work any longer with the more radical Russell, they left the Whigs and within months had moved over to join Peel and the Tories, a remarkable boost to the struggling party.

B *Peel as Prime Minister, 1834–5*

The elderly Whig Prime Minister, Grey, already exhausted by the rigours of the fight for parliamentary reform, felt unable to cope with these deep divisions in his party and, in 1834, resigned. The equally elderly Whig peer, Melbourne, succeeded him as Prime Minister. Within a few months, however, William IV, long-troubled by the political agitations of the time and increasingly disenchanted by the quarrelsome Whigs, required him to resign and appointed Wellington as a provisional one-man government until Peel could return from abroad and form a government. This was the last occasion on which a British monarch was to interfere so directly and forcefully in the business of forming governments. Peel's ministry in any case survived for only five months. In the general election held in January 1835, the Tories regained almost 100 of the seats lost in 1832 but still had 100 fewer seats than the Whigs. They were unable to govern in the face of the overwhelming Whig majority in the Commons and, after defeats in six votes in six weeks, Peel resigned in April 1835.

The royal intervention had however a decisive effect on Peel's career and considerable influence on future Conservative prospects. Appointment as Prime Minister ensured Peel's leadership of his party, which had been by no means certain after the Catholic and Reform Bill controversies. The brief experience of government, even a minority one, meant the restoration of normal political life and put an end to Whig assumptions that the Tories were finished. Peel's Government attempted modest reforms in colonial administration and took an important step, in the formation of the Ecclesiastical Commission, to re-organise the finances and administration of the Church of England. It is important to remember that Church affairs and religious issues loomed much larger in nineteenth century political life than they did in the twentieth century. Peel's constructive record here, when contrasted with the Whig assaults on the Church in Ireland and the subsequent Whig defections, did much to establish the Tory Party as the best hope of the Church of England. This ensured the often unthinking, but still influential, support of the Church for the Party.

THE TAMWORTH MANIFESTO

The January 1835 election is now best remembered for Peel's issuing (in December 1834) his Tamworth Manifesto, so called because, like many similar election pamphlets, it was addressed to the electors of his own constituency of Tamworth. On this occasion, and after approval by Peel's cabinet, the document was immediately given national attention by being released to the press. The 'manifesto, as Peel himself referred to it though the word *manifesto* does not appear within it, was his response to the new political world that followed the 1832 Reform Act.

> **KEY ISSUE**
>
> *Why was Peel's brief period as Prime Minister, in 1834–5, so important for him?*

> See Table 6 on page 142

> **Tory/Conservative –**
> **Tory** had its origins in the seventeenth century. **Conservative** came into common use at the time of the Tamworth Manifesto when Peel, though pledged to reform proven abuses, promised supporters that he would also seek to *conserve* the nation's institutions. From 1835 the Tory party can be referred to as the Conservative Party (although, confusingly, *Tory* continued to be used)

KEY ISSUE

How did the Tamworth Manifesto widen the electoral appeal of the Conservative Party?

It was intended to secure the Conservative Party's place in the new politics. Its form was slightly unusual in the stress placed on general political principles. It remains an important document in the history of electioneering and, more particularly, in the history of the Conservative Party. It acted as a warning to reactionaries in his own party that he would not lead the party down their path and, at the same time, its moderation could appeal to earlier supporters of reform who were now disenchanted by the extremist policies of the Whig Government over Ireland and in Church matters.

Read the following extract from the Tamworth Manifesto and then answer the questions that follow, consulting other sections of this chapter when necessary.

> But the Reform Bill, it is said, constitutes a new era, and it is the duty of a Minister to declare explicitly – first, whether he will maintain the Bill itself, and secondly, whether he will act upon the spirit in which it was conceived. With respect to the Reform Bill itself, I will repeat now the declaration which I made when I entered the House of Commons as a Member of the Reformed Parliament, that I consider the Reform Bill a final and irrevocable settlement of a great Constitutional question – a settlement which no friend to the peace and welfare of this country would attempt to disturb, either by direct or insidious means.
>
> Then, as to the spirit of the Reform Bill, and the willingness to adopt and enforce it as a rule of government; if, by adopting the spirit of the Reform Bill, it be meant that we are to live in a perpetual vortex of agitation; that public men can only support themselves in public estimation by adopting every popular impression of the day, – by promising the instant redress of anything which anybody may call an abuse, if this be the spirit of the Reform Bill, I will not undertake to adopt it. But if the spirit of the Reform Bill implies merely a careful review of institutions, civil and ecclesiastical, undertaken in a friendly temper, combining, with the firm maintenance of established rights, the correction of proved abuses and the redress of real grievances – in that case, I can for myself and colleagues undertake to act in such a spirit and with such intentions. Our object will be – the maintenance of peace ... the support of public credit – the enforcement of strict economy – and the just and impartial consideration of what is due to all interests – agricultural, manufacturing, and commercial.

Extract from the Tamworth Manifesto

1. (a) *Why should it be 'said' that 'the Reform Bill constitutes a new era'?*

(b) *How consistent is Peel's claim that 'I consider the Reform Bill a final and irrevocable settlement of a great constitutional question' with the fears he expressed during the passage of the Bill?*

(c) *How might Peel hope that his views on the Reform Bill, as expressed in the first few lines of this extract, be helpful to the fortunes of the Tory party?*
2. (a) *Explain in your own words what image of the Tory/ Conservative Party Peel, in the second paragraph of this extract, was trying to create.*
    (b) *How might this image help the party in future elections? Who might it attract?*

CONSERVATIVE RECOVERY AND THE BEDCHAMBER CRISIS

The 'manifesto', the work of Peel's Government and the results of the 1835 election created a framework for day to day politics which produced further Conservative electoral gains in the 1837 election and a sweeping election victory in 1841. Melbourne's Whig Government gradually lost reforming momentum and the tensions between its radical and its aristocratic wings remained unresolved.

Melbourne himself proved to be uninterested in promoting major new legislation and became content simply to see the Government survive. At the end of the 1830s the Whig Government, facing a more confident opposition, was also plagued with financial difficulties and seemed incapable of bringing its annual budget deficits under control. This Whig 'loss of direction' greatly helped the recovery in Conservative fortunes and in 1839 Melbourne resigned.

Peel agreed to form a Conservative Government but first asked that the new, young Queen, Victoria, replace certain of the ladies of her court whose husbands were well-known Whigs. When Victoria refused to do this, Peel in turn declined to take office arguing that the Queen clearly had no confidence in his proposed Government. Melbourne and the Whigs then returned to government. The episode has been labelled 'The Bedchamber Crisis' and described as 'an absurd business'. It rested on a personality clash between Victoria and the reserved and cautious Peel. It seems evident that Peel did not wish to lead another minority government or he would either have been more conciliatory to the young queen or more forceful in pressing his case. Fortunately relations between Victoria and Peel improved greatly after her marriage to Prince Albert in 1840.

KEY ISSUE

How important is the Whig decline in the late 1830s in explaining the Conservative revival?

PICTURE 15
A sketch of herself by the future Queen Victoria in 1835. She became Queen in 1837

Why did the Conservatives win the 1841 election so convincingly?

ANALYSIS

1. Conservative strengths

The Conservative victory in 1841 was built on the revival in their electoral fortunes in 1835 and 1837. The reasons for it have produced one of the most interesting, and easily followed, debates among historians studying nineteenth-century politics. Most of those involved in the debate would agree that:

● a starting point of any explanation lies in the fact that Tory fortunes in 1832 were not as meagre as triumphalist Whigs argued at the time
● the Tories still controlled the unreformed House of Lords and, in William IV, had a sympathetic monarch to assist them
● they represented real and important interests in the country
● the 1832 election had followed Tory divisions over Catholic Emancipation and their misguided total opposition to parliamentary reform. With these two issues out of the way, they could expect some revival in their support in the country at large
● the Whigs then antagonised many moderate men with what were seen as their extreme policies in religious and Irish matters.

2. Peel's achievement as party leader in the 1830s

Peel's role is central to the debate on the reasons for the outcome in 1841. His parliamentary tactics during his years in opposition were clever. He carefully avoided outright opposition to Whig reform measures, supporting the Poor Law Amendment Act and even the attack on the Tory, dominated, but essentially corrupt, Town Corporations which formed the basis of the Municipal Reform Act. He shrewdly portrayed the Whigs as too extremist and their government as dependent on Catholic Irish and radical support, sentiments likely to arouse the sympathies of those Tories who had only abandoned their party in the frenzy of the parliamentary reform crisis.

In the Tamworth Manifesto Peel then sought to present the Tory Party as one that would introduce reforms to deal with proven abuses but one that would also resist unnecessary attacks on the nation's institutions. This has been seen as a shrewd move to appeal to those, almost entirely of the property-owning and respectable middle class, who had been enfranchised in1832.

The Manifesto, in this explanation at least, helped Peel to create a cautiously reforming Conservative Party out of the outdated reactionary Tory Party of 1831–2 and his success in developing this message was the main reason for the triumph he enjoyed in 1841. The Government that Peel formed in 1841 then went on to put Tamworth's principles into practice in a series of great financial and commercial reforms. The sheer scale of government activity after 1841 far out-weighed anything attempted by previous 'Tory' governments. The old Tory Party now renamed 'Conservative', had entered a new era and its creator was Robert Peel. This view, that a new Conservative Party emerged in these years, arguably makes Peel the founder of modern conservatism. It has not convinced all historians. Their version of what happened is best considered after the achievements of Peel's 1841–6 ministry have been examined.

See Section 6 of this chapter, pages 165–70, for a challenging, different explanation of the Conservative revival

3 ⁓ PEEL'S SECOND MINISTRY, 1841–6

A *Peel and his ministerial team*

PEEL AS LEADER

Peel dominated his Cabinet, often regarded as one of the strongest of the nineteenth century, and was the driving force behind his Government's policies. His brilliant disciple and pupil, Gladstone, rated him 'the best man of business who was ever Prime Minister' and certainly the scale of government activity increased greatly during this ministry. His range and his capacity for hard work were astonishing. Finance was Peel's area of special expertise and he personally introduced the two great budgets of 1842 and 1845. He also made sure he was well enough informed to be able to intervene decisively in practically every other area of government, from Factory Reform to Foreign Policy. Peel enjoyed a commanding overview of his Government's responsibilities and activities that has never been equalled before or since.

Not surprisingly, he sometimes overstretched himself. But his Cabinet colleagues rarely found his promptings and guidance intrusive. Rather, the combination of Peel's rigour in formulating policy and his own readiness to take on board their advice won their loyalty and profound respect. Some, particularly the young Gladstone, became almost literally his disciples, seeing it as their life's mission to carry on their master's work.

Such a style of government has its weaknesses, however. The sheer professionalism and expertise of Peel and his Cabinet colleagues bred an arrogant, impatient, even contemptuous attitude towards the Tory backbenchers – especially when the latter presumed to criticise the Government. Peel gave vent to these feelings in a letter to his wife late in 1845:

> **KEY ISSUE**
>
> *Why was Peel's style of government likely to upset Conservative backbenchers?*

how can those who spend their time in hunting and shooting and eating and drinking know what were the motives of those who are responsible for the public security, who have access to the best information, and who have no other object under heaven but to provide against danger, and consult the general interests of all classes?

Peel was, doubtless, better informed than his backbenchers. But his judgement was not infallible. And worse, as he himself admitted, he could not or would not lower himself to flatter the vanity of the party rank and file with soft words or conciliatory gestures. As early as 1843, a leading backbencher feared that:

Peel has committed great and grievous mistakes in omitting to call his friends frequently together to state his desires and rouse their zeal. A few minutes and a few words would have sufficed: energy and fellow-

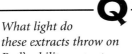

What light do these extracts throw on Peel's ability as party leader?

ship would have been infused: men would have felt they were companions in arms; they now have the sentiment of being followers in a drill.'

PEEL'S CABINET

By themselves, Peel's aloofness and intellectual arrogance would not have been seriously damaging to the coherence of the Conservative Party. What made these flaws fatal was the failure of other Cabinet members to compensate for them. Here, the very different fortunes of Lord Stanley and Sir James Graham are instructive.

These two former Whigs were Peel's most significant recruits to the Conservatives' ranks in the 1830s, and both seemed destined to play a key role in the ministry. Stanley was Peel's Secretary for War and Colonies. He loved hunting, horseracing and shooting as well as any Tory squire, and would have been the natural channel of raw Tory sentiment to the Cabinet. But he found himself progressively excluded from Peel's inner circle, and ultimately became one of the leaders of the old-style Tories against Peel. Instead, it was Graham, the ministry's Home Secretary, who became Peel's right-hand man. He fully shared Peel's high ideals of public service, and almost matched his breath-taking industry. But unfortunately, he was even more high-handed and tactless than the Prime Minister and, accordingly, was intensely disliked even before the ministry began – in the eyes of its backbenchers – its wholesale betrayal of Tory principles. These flaws in Peel's personality, combined with severe failures of man-management, aggravated by the vigorous assertion of the principle that the Cabinet always knew best, go some way towards explaining why, within five years of coming into power, Peel's ministry – one of the ablest of the century – was to find itself first repudiated, and then destroyed, by its own party. These weaknesses need to form a part of any assessment of Peel's overall political achievement.

B *1842: A law and order crisis*

KEY ISSUE

How effectively did Peel's Government react to the prospect of public disorder?

In August 1842, against a background of high unemployment and wage-cuts, the new government faced a major outbreak of public disorder across the north of England. There were Chartist demonstrations, spontaneous strikes and industrial sabotage.

Peel and the Home Secretary, Graham, were convinced that they were facing an organised revolutionary conspiracy aimed at overthrowing the state. In this crisis they acted with energy and determination, monitoring the situation via regular reports from the troubled areas and using the newly developed railway system to despatch troops who could back up the hard-pressed local authorities. A planned Chartist demonstration in London was prevented by the Metropolitan Police and troops in the North fired on protestors, some of whom were killed. Peel again fortified his Tamworth home against armed attack. Graham urged army leaders to 'act with vigour and without parley' against the strikers.

For more on the Chartists see Chapter 5

The Government had clearly misread the nature of the crisis, which was largely spontaneous and had been brought about by the bad economic conditions of the 'worst year of the century'. Peel, wrongly believing that middle-class agitators from the Anti-Corn Law League had fomented the disturbances for their own subversive political ends, had over-reacted. By September the crisis was over without the feared attack on the state or property materialising. The strikers returned to work, the Chartists dispersed. No doubt the Government's determination played some part in this but a good harvest and signs of economic recovery also played their part. Most importantly, there had been no conspiracy but only the actions of men driven to desperation by their plight.

The Government, however, persisted in its repressive policies: scores of strike leaders were imprisoned or transported to Australia. Graham sought to prevent future troubles by further developing the network of borough and county police forces. Government agents worked long and hard to gather information that would implicate Chartist and Anti-Corn Law League leaders in a treasonable conspiracy and lead to a state trial. This plan had to be dropped when no hard evidence could be found. In fact, none existed.

The events of 1842 do much to illustrate the authoritarian streak in Peelite Conservatism. The Government's heavy-handed response to the wave of strikes points up the exaggerated fear of revolution which always coloured Peel's perception of popular political movements. He was, however, more than merely a reactionary Tory in his response to the threat of disorder and was able to see that more troops and harsher laws were not the real long-term answer.

Instead, he believed that the Government should do what it could to address the root causes of disorder by counteracting the twin evils of unemployment and poverty. He believed this could only be done by stimulating the economy and his efforts to bring this about, by removing man-made brakes on economic growth, now became a moral issue. Freeing trade, not for its own sake but in order to achieve social and political ends, became central to his economic policy.

> Peel saw economic recovery as the key to long-term political stability

C *Peelite economic policies*

FINANCE: THE 1842 BUDGET

> **KEY ISSUE**
>
> *What made Peel's 1842 budget such an important success?*

The catastrophe of 1845–6 would not have been predicted by anybody witnessing the triumph of Peel's first budget in 1842. When he came to power Peel faced grave **fiscal** problems. He inherited an annual deficit, which amounted to the vast total (by nineteenth-century standards) of £7.5 million and which had defeated successive Whig attempts to reduce it. The atmosphere of crisis at Westminster was worsened by the deep depression into which the economy as a whole was plunging and by the associated resurgence of Chartism and the rise of the Anti-Corn Law League. Events seemed to be slipping out of the control of the governing class.

> **fiscal** relating to public finances

In this context, Peel's dramatic introduction in the 1842 budget of an 'income tax' – only ever raised before in times of war – had an all-important psychological impact. Kept secret until the budget speech itself, the very boldness of the proposal matched the mood of national emergency. Peel 'took the House [of Commons] by storm', a contemporary noted. Here at last, many felt, was a leader of vision and political courage, equal to the gravity of the country's needs. Perhaps the secret of Peel's success was the sense of moral urgency which he communicated. He explained that the income tax, levied at the rate of 7d (3p) in the pound on those with annual incomes of over £150, would call for a special sacrifice on the part of the wealthier members of society. Every alternative means of raising government revenue entailed taxing those articles of consumption on which the poor depended. How much better, Peel insisted, that the rich should bear this extra burden at a time of national distress.

The introduction of income tax was more than a psychological masterstroke, however. The revenue it was expected to generate would gradually clear the accumulated deficit. It would also give Peel room for manoeuvre in lowering **tariffs**.

The corn duties had already been modestly reduced in the 1820s. Import duties on raw materials, manufactured goods and (to the annoyance of Peel's agricultural backbenchers) barley, meat and live cattle, could now be cut too. Peel was convinced that tariff reduction was the key to economic recovery and social stability.

> **tariffs** duties on trade, usually on imports to the country

Domestic industrial production would be stimulated (e.g. through making raw cotton cheaper to import). The working classes' standard of living would be improved too, with duties on selected food imports cut. As Peel explained, it was one of his great objectives to 'make this country a cheap country for living'. In the long run, it was even possible that the reduced rates of duty might lead to an *increase* in the Government's revenues from tariffs – for cheaper goods should encourage extra consumption, and so the Government's net revenue from tariffs would actually go up. In 1842 he cut duties on 769 of the 1046 articles on which they were levied and, within three years, thanks to increased consumption, the reduced duties brought in almost as much revenue as before. The national economic recovery which began in 1843 and an astonishing £4 million surplus in government finances in 1844, fully justified Peel's policy and contrasted remarkably with the dreadful financial situation he had inherited. He had shown political boldness and a farsighted social vision. The 1842 Budget was one of the greatest triumphs of his career.

> *Peel as financial innovator*
> His 1842 budget marked the first time that government financial policy had been used as a remedy for poverty and to avert distress

FACTORY LAW

These bold financial and commercial schemes attracted opposition and Peel hesitated to add to this by introducing measures on factory law, which would be unpopular with manufacturers. As a result, despite a build-up of pressure outside government for such legislation, the results were very meagre. Peel caused particular offence by blocking a radical amendment to the Government's 1844 Factory Act, which would have given some protection on working hours to women and adolescents in the textile industry. Peel went so far as to threaten to resign unless the Commons reversed their vote in favour of this amendment, which had been introduced by the leading humanitarian Lord Ashley (later better known as the Earl of Shaftesbury). Further restriction of working hours had to wait beyond the fall of the Peel Government and, despite an 1842 Act on child labour in mines, Peel's administration has a very limited record of humanitarian reform. This episode had also soured his relations with many of his own backbenchers.

THE BANK CHARTER ACT 1844

Another financial triumph occurred in 1844 with the passing of the Bank Charter Act. This aimed to give some stability to the banking system after public confidence had been shaken by a series of bank crises in the late 1830s. To contemporaries it appeared to bring a new stability to banking and Peel's reputation as the greatest expert of his day on banking matters has only recently been challenged by modern historians like Boyd Hilton (see Bibliography).

FINANCE: THE 1845 BUDGET

In 1845 Peel continued to pursue his strategy of encouraging economic growth by reducing or eliminating tariffs on imports. The Sugar Duties Bill was intended to provide a modest reduction in the duties paid on sugar imports. Those who supported free trade were dissatisfied with the scale of the reductions. A more serious problem for Peel was that many important Conservative backbenchers, anxious to protect both the British shipping industry and the prosperity of the sugar plantation owners in the British colonies in the West Indies, wanted to see sugar imports from these colonies protected by high tariffs against sugar imported from elsewhere. The two opposing groups came together to support a cleverly-worded amendment to the Bill and succeeded in defeating it, thanks to the 62 Conservative backbenchers who voted against their own government. As with the setback over factory legislation, Peel again threatened to resign if the original terms of the Sugar Bill were not restored and again he got his way. His ungracious behaviour in 'victory' over his own supporters produced such great anger among them so that even the usually admiring Gladstone felt Peel had made a serious mistake. A year later he and his party were to pay dearly for this misjudgement.

> *Terms of the Bank Charter Act*
> - Limited the power of the Bank of England to issue notes to 14 million pounds unless they were backed by gold reserves held by the bank
> - Restricted other banks to the number of notes they already had in circulation
> - Prohibited newly-established banks from issuing notes

Why did Conservative backbenchers come to dislike and distrust Peel?

ANALYSIS

Serious economic issues underlay the increasingly bitter divisions within the Conservative Party. On the questions of factory reform and sugar duties alike, Peel would have claimed that his policies were intellectually correct and his expectation of unquestioning party obedience was politically proper. Intellectually, Peel believed that any government intervention in the free workings of the economy was likely to be for the worse:

● The relevance of this to factory legislation was clear. Experts warned Peel that the imposition of a ten-hour working day would cripple the cotton manufacturers' profitability. Bankruptcies, mass unemployment with all its miseries would be the consequences. With national economic recovery only just under way in 1844, and cotton production accounting for 80 per cent of British exports, Peel was in no hurry to turn the clock back to the desperate days of 1842.

● The case with regard to sugar duties was similar: economic theory and recent practical experience had made the virtues of freer trade self-evident to Peel. The privileges accorded to the West Indies interest made the price of sugar – a major factor in the budget of working families – artificially high. Peel remained determined to make Britain 'a cheap country to live [in]': excessive sugar tariffs simply could not be justified.

But economic common sense, at least as Peel saw it, was not the only consideration that determined the Prime Minister's hard line over these questions. Peel believed that his backbenchers needed teaching a constitutional lesson. They had to learn that it was the job of the government to direct, and of the party to follow. The Cabinet alone had the necessary expertise and information to formulate policy. If backbenchers did not accept its decision in good faith, 'the Queen's Government' could not be carried on. By twice rudely bringing his backbenchers face to face with the prospect of his resignation, Peel hoped to drive home to them the dangerous constitutional implications of their actions, and thus restore discipline.

Unfortunately for Peel and the cohesion of the Conservative Party, many of his backbenchers saw the issues in a different light. By 1844, the overall direction of the Government's economic policies was causing much concern: the course being charted seemed to lead away from protectionism and inevitably towards free trade. This was the very opposite of the policy which the Tories had been elected to pursue in 1841. The appalling thought was dawning on some Tories that Peel might be ready to abandon the Corn Laws themselves! After all, the man who had abandoned the Irish Protestants in 1829 was capable of anything.

Neither were Peel's backbenchers convinced by his increasingly self-interested constitutional arguments about the duty of the Party to follow the Executive (i.e. the Government). To them, the Conservative Party existed to defend distinct interests in the nation, of which 'the land' was the greatest of all. Yet Peel seemed more eager to please the Tories' enemies, like the middle-class mill owners, than to satisfy his supporters.

Finally, there was Peel's style. Conservative backbenchers (MPs not holding ministerial posts) were invariably men of wealth and standing and their pride and sense of dignity had been repeatedly affronted by Peel's dictatorial attitude. No less than Peel, they lived by principles of honour and personal consistency. They were *gentlemen* and should not be made to reverse their votes or betray their constituents even at the command of a Prime Minister. Their judgement, loyalties and feelings deserved respect and understanding. But Peel showed them neither. The worst of the problem was that Peel seemed to have little appreciation of the depth of offence he was causing.

4 ↝ PEEL AND IRELAND

A *Coercion and conciliation*

coercion to force into, to compel (obedience)

Early in Peel's ministry he faced the prospect of serious disorder in Ireland where Daniel O'Connell, the great Irish Nationalist leader, mounted a movement for the repeal of the Act of Union and had organised a series of mass meetings, each attended by crowds of up to half a million. The extent of anti-British feeling and the plans to set up a separate Irish Parliament in Dublin required a prompt response from the British Government. Peel was at his best in this crisis. In 1843 he made clear that he would use armed force to defend the Union, banned the next proposed 'monster meeting' and had O'Connell arrested, tried and imprisoned for sedition. O'Connell, fearing the inevitable blood-shed of armed rebellion, agreed to the meeting being called off. On appeal he was released from prison but his reputation among Irish nationalists never recovered and the movement for repeal of the Union fell into disarray. Peel's tough-minded stand in the face of a most serious political crisis had saved the day. He now had the opportunity to bring calm to Ireland and to restore Irish confidence in rule from London.

For affairs in Ireland see Chapter 9

Peel explained to his Home Secretary, Graham, a few days after O'Connell's arrest that, 'mere force, however necessary the application of it, will do nothing as a permanent remedy for the social evils of [Ireland]'. Accordingly, he put in train a series of measures designed to bring long-term peace and stability to Ireland. This package of measures constituted a brave and farsighted departure in the policy of British governments towards Ireland. It is one of the tragedies of Peel's career, however, that their actual impact on the Irish problem was, in fact, minimal, while their impact on British politics was disastrous.

In 1845, an Irish Colleges Bill set up three colleges in Ireland, which would be free from the control of any Church. They were intended to promote an educated Irish Catholic elite who would be capable, admittedly in the long term, of forming a new Irish middle class bringing both prosperity and political calm to the country.

However, the keystone of Peel's ambitious conciliation plans was his wish to raise the status of the Irish Catholic clergy by improving the facilities at the Catholic seminary (or training college) at Maynooth, where most Irish priests were trained. He was convinced that a better, less radical, class of trainee-priests would be attracted and that whilst at Maynooth, they would learn to be grateful to the British Government. In short, the next generation of Irish Catholic priests, so powerful in their parishes, would become defenders of the Union rather than recruiters for Irish nationalism.

Catholic Emancipation, which, in 1829, had made it possible for Catholics to become MPs, had made it essential that the British state win over the loyalty of the Catholic majority in Ireland. The key to this, Peel believed, was establishing a good working relationship between the British Government and the Irish Catholic Church. It was widely acknowledged that Catholic priests had played a central part in mobilising the mass movements that had pressed with such force for Emancipation in the 1820s and for the Repeal of the Union in the early 1840s. Therefore, central to Peel's policy for conciliating Ireland, was his determination to win the priests away from Irish nationalism and, if possible, to convert the Irish Catholic hierarchy into supporters of British rule in Ireland.

Peel's bold and imaginative plans for Ireland failed. They were already faltering before the whole course of Irish history was transformed by the onset of the 1845–46 Potato Famine. His attempted conciliation of the Catholic Church soon broke down when the bishops were alerted to the 'godless nature' of the proposed new colleges while the new generation of priests were to prove just as radical as, and no more keen on the virtues of the Union with Britain than, their predecessors.

For Potato Famine see pages 159–60 and Chapter 9, pages 271–2

B   *The impact of Peel's Irish policies on British politics*

The positive impact of Peel's policies in Ireland was negligible: by contrast, their negative impact in Britain itself was tremendous. The keystone of Peel's Irish policy, Maynooth, was the problem. British Protestants, both inside and outside the established Anglican Church, united to attack Peel's proposal to increase the state funding of the Catholic seminary with an intensity that staggered Peel. *The Times* led the way, accusing Peel of 'forcing [Romanism] on the nation', denouncing Maynooth as 'a name and a thing above all odious and suspicious to England'. Over a million and a quarter signatures were collected in a petition urging him to change his policy. In the House of Commons itself, Peel had to rely on Whig support to get the Maynooth Bill through. Maynooth provoked the worst Tory rebellion against Peel so far, with the party dividing 149 votes against, 148 for. It became law in April 1845, but its passage left the Tory party shattered.

How can we explain the popular fury outside Parliament, and the bitter antagonisms within? Catholicism was widely despised and loathed in

KEY ISSUE

Why did the proposed increase in the Maynooth grant anger so many Conservative MPs?

Victorian England. It was believed to be alien, superstitious and backward looking. *Irish* Catholicism was still worse: it was the engine of disloyalty and rebellion, as the career of O'Connell proved. The Irish themselves were widely regarded as racially inferior, naturally violent and brutishly ignorant. Yet Peel was proposing to increase state support for Maynooth College, the very centre of Irish Catholic subversion!

Peel's backbenchers found this very hard to swallow. As many had asserted during the 1841 election, one of the main functions of the Tory Party was to uphold the privileges of the Anglican religion and keep Catholics in their place. Peel had recently shown himself a poor friend of Anglican causes: in the 1844 Factory Act he had abandoned plans to guarantee the Church of England the major responsibility for the education of factory children and he had recently refused a government subsidy to a church-building programme for the rapidly expanding industrial towns of the Midlands and the north of England. But when it came to doling out taxpayers' money for the training of Catholic priests in Ireland, Peel seemed only too happy to oblige! For many Conservative backbenchers, this was one betrayal too many.

Contrast these Conservative feelings about Peel with the boxed analysis of his success in modernising the Party on pages 145–6. Then see pages 165–70 for further analysis of his record as party leader

Peel regarded such sentiments with withering contempt. He stuck to his great principle that it was the duty of the Queen's minister, regardless of party pledges or connections, to do what he believed was in the best interests of the nation. To Peel, the Maynooth Bill was the centrepiece of his Government's Irish policy through which he hoped to bring lasting peace to Ireland and to put the Union on a new and much firmer foundation. With such a prize at stake, he believed the prejudices and pledges of his backbenchers could be discounted, and their cries of treachery ignored.

By May 1845, the feelings of mutual distrust and dislike between Peel and his backbenchers had bitten deep. Writing to a friend, he made a list of his ministry's achievements: industrial recovery was underway, Chartism had been defeated, the working classes were better off, and the nation's finances restored to a good order. 'But', he concluded with exasperated irony, 'we have reduced protection to agriculture, and tried to lay the foundations of peace in Ireland, and these are offences for which nothing can atone'. Quite simply, he no longer cared about whether his party held together. The Home Secretary, Graham, was even more fatalistic, not merely expecting but actually hoping that the 'country gentlemen' would 'give us the death blow'.

This mood – embattled, exhausted, but stubborn and self-righteous – was now to characterise the Conservative leaders until the very end. It is the frame of mind in which people who see themselves as heroes seek to do great deeds and make great sacrifices. It was the frame of mind in which Peel and Graham approached the Corn Laws.

5 ⮌ THE ANTI-CORN LAW LEAGUE

The Corn Laws dated back to the seventeenth century but the most important of them was the Corn Law of 1815. It prohibited the import of wheat until the price of British wheat reached the very high figure of 80 shillings (£4) per quarter (28 lb or about 13 kg). In 1828 the prohibition ended and was replaced by a sliding scale of duty on foreign wheat imports: the lower the price of British wheat, the higher the duty on foreign imports. Peel's 1842 budget altering the sliding scale had the effect of further reducing the charges on foreign wheat.

The 1815 Corn Law had always been controversial. Its defenders saw it as an essential protection for the landed interest (farmers and landowners) which was the best guardian of political stability. Radicals saw it as an obnoxious piece of class legislation protecting the interests of farmers and great landowners by artificially raising the price of bread for town dwellers in general and the working-class in particular. In the late 1830s the Anti-Corn Law League took up the case against the Corn Laws.

The Anti-Corn Law League became a legend in Victorian politics. It was founded in Manchester in 1838 and only eight years later it had apparently pressurised a Conservative Government into a complete reversal on one of its central policy commitments: **agricultural protectionism**.

The League's success was taken as proof of the irresistible power of rational argument when backed by the properly organised will of the nation, and every successive nineteenth-century Radical pressure group regarded it as their model and inspiration. But on closer examination, the success of the Anti-Corn Law League is surprisingly open to doubt.

The League's greatest advantage was the basic intellectual power of the free trade argument. From Adam Smith onwards, political economists argued that '*laissez-faire*' policies, opening markets to free competition and thus driving prices down, served the interests of the consumer best. A flexible and industrious producer, too, had much to gain in a dynamic and expanding economy. These were the lessons learnt in turn by Huskisson, Peel and Gladstone. So compelling was the argument that, even without the League, the Corn Laws – which protected the British farmer from foreign competition by imposing a prohibitive tariff on corn imports – were probably doomed.

The Anti-Corn Law League, led by Richard Cobden and John Bright, turned the intellectual case for Repeal into a passionate and brilliantly organised middle-class crusade to put pressure on Parliament. The main reason for the League's growth was the widespread support it enjoyed amongst northern manufacturers. They identified the Corn Laws as the root cause of the economic depression which was having such a devastating impact on the cotton industry at the time. There were two main strands to their analysis.

● First, by keeping corn imports from the European continent out, the Corn Laws indirectly crippled Britain's potential export markets – for foreign landowners and their labourers, deprived of *their* most attractive export market, were too poor to buy British manufactured goods.

KEY ISSUE

How important was the Anti-Corn Law League in securing repeal of the Corn Laws?

---

agricultural protectionism
pursuing economic policies to protect British farming from foreign competition

● Secondly, the Corn Laws were blamed for keeping the price of bread artificially high. Bread was the basic foodstuff for working-class families. If its cost fell, such families would have more money to spend on manufactured goods themselves – or alternatively, factory owners would be able to cut wages without forcing their workers towards starvation.

In either case, self-interest clearly played a major role in explaining the manufacturing classes' support for the League: their increasingly large donations to its funds were, in effect, a good business investment.

A *The League's campaign*

THE AIMS OF THE LEAGUE

The appeal of the League went beyond material calculation. The cry for 'cheap bread' gave the League the appearance of a campaign for social justice. Religious groups like the Nonconformists felt that the crusade against the Corn Laws was sanctioned by God himself. The most idealistic saw in universal free trade the prospect of establishing the reign of peace between nations, arguing that the free exchange of goods would draw the peoples of Europe ever closer together in shared prosperity and understanding. Such sentiments help to explain the righteous passion with which committed Leaguers pursued their cause.

The League's activists, however, were also pursuing an underlying political agenda. The Corn Laws were a godsend to those Radicals who had been consciously searching for an issue around which to mobilise popular support for their continuing assault on the landed aristocracy. 'Never yet,' a Radical exulted, 'had the people a fairer battleground than on the question of the Corn Laws'.

But, however alarming the League's growth was to the defenders of the landed interest, a close analysis of its fortunes would have made it difficult to forecast its ultimate success. All the optimism and resourcefulness of Richard Cobden, its most prominent leader, cannot disguise the fact that, until 1844 at least, it mostly stumbled from failure to failure. Its numerous shifts of strategy reveal Cobden's genius for improvisation, but they just as surely indicate the number of dead-ends down which the League travelled, however energetically. Indeed it is far from clear that the League was near to attaining its goal right until the very end.

For the sake of simplicity, the various stages of the League's campaign have been tabulated on page 158.

Before we can judge how important was the immediate political threat posed by the League in 1845–6 in driving Peel towards Repeal, we need to consider:

● what part the Irish potato blight played in forcing through Repeal
● Peel's own views, already arrived at without the help of the League, of what needed to be done for the good of the country and indeed in the best interests of the 'landed aristocracy' itself

> **KEY ISSUE**
>
> *In what ways did the Repeal issue become a moral crusade?*

> **KEY ISSUE**
>
> *How important was the League's contribution in bringing about Repeal?*

TABLE 8

The Anti-Corn Law League Campaign

Stage	Year	Main tactic	Success?
1	1838 onwards	Propaganda – spread by pamphlets, lecture tours and the League's own newspaper. Main target areas were northern industrial towns and southern agricultural districts The power of the League's argument was by itself expected to force the abolition of the Corn Laws	Very limited impact – League nearly bankrupt in 1839. Chartists convinced many workers that the League was a front for wage-cutting factory owners. In rural areas - farmers and farm labourers resented the intrusion of League activists and distrusted their arguments
2	1841	A shift to direct involvement in party politics. Cobden convinced the other League leaders of a need to win a majority in Parliament to ensure Repeal. A committed free trader was to be selected to fight every by-election. Only gradually did Cobden accept that the League must concentrate on the most winnable seats	Cobden, only narrowly defeated in Walsall by-election, shows League can battle effectively and he is later elected MP for Stockport. But General Election was a crushing victory for Toryism – and protectionism. Even in promising-looking industrial seats like Bradford, Free Trade candidates did badly
3	1842	Lack of political progress and economic recession meant desperate remedies considered (tax strike/co-operation with Chartists? Close factories to create mass unemployment and force government to repeal?)	None of these 'plans' got far. Chartists distrusted the predominantly middle-class League. Illegality of tax strike and the obvious revolutionary dangers with the factory closures enabled Cobden to block both proposals
4	1843	League argument increasingly accepted but its strategy remained uncertain. Cobden considered success would come from concentrating on the southern agricultural districts.	Impressive fund raising efforts but no significant electoral progress. Cobden's latest campaign in agricultural areas had little success. Very limited by-election success
5	1844	Cobden decided to concentrate on getting League supporters on constituency electoral rolls and also to secure the disqualification of known supporters of protection	League morale and activity high but number of seats winnable by these tactics, (using the voter registration clauses of the 1832 Reform Act in this way for the first time) looked to be limited
6	1845	Change in electoral tactics. Cobden realised that by buying property in county seats valued at 40s (£2) supporters could buy parliamentary election votes. League propaganda and legal machinery concentrated on purchasing enough votes now in key constituencies to buy control of them	Tremendous successes in South Lancashire and West Riding of Yorkshire by-elections. Cobden was convinced that this was the key to victory but modern calculations suggest that no more than 30 seats were vulnerable to such tactics. If so the League was a longway from building up a major presence in the Commons. Arguably the successes may have increased Peel's anxiety that to fight a general election on food taxation would be disastrous for his Government

FAILURE OF THE LEAGUE'S WIDER POLITICAL AIMS

Of one thing we can be certain already. In its *wider* political objectives, the League failed. Britain was to remain for the rest of the century a country which was ruled by the landed aristocracy and its friends. Until World War I men of commerce and industry were a rare sight in any Cabinet, Conservative or Liberal. Not the least reason for this is that few industrialists shared Cobden's confidence or class-consciousness, instead preferring local pre-eminence – and making more money – to the distractions and uncertainties of a political career on the national stage. With the Repeal of the Corn Laws, the most clearly partisan and objectionable element of aristocratic domination of the state had been overthrown. But the bastion of aristocratic power seemed to have remained perfectly intact – as Peel, of course, had intended it should.

THE IRISH FAMINE

Peel was a politician of courage and vision, but even he must have felt daunted by the scale of the disaster that began to overtake Ireland late in 1845. In mid-October he learnt that a mystery disease, which had

Q

Where do Mr Punch's sympathies lie in the repeal debate?

PICTURE 16

The new satirical magazine, Punch, *notes the onward march of Free Trade*

already ruined mainland Europe's potato crop, had finally reached Ireland. This 'Potato Blight' seemed certain to have a quite catastrophic effect there, because the potato was the staple diet of the bulk of the Irish peasantry. So it proved: between 1845 and 1851 Ireland lost over two-and-a-quarter million people through disease and starvation or emigration.

Whether the British Government could have done much to alleviate the tragedy over these years may be doubted. It is, however, clear that the centrepiece of Peel's supposed cure for the famine – the Repeal of the Corn Laws – did little to alleviate the appalling suffering and was to have a far greater impact on the history of mainland Britain than it was ever to have on the history of Ireland.

B *Peel's motives for Repeal*

COPING WITH THE IRISH FAMINE

KEY ISSUE

Was there no alternative to Repeal?

At the onset of the crisis, Peel made a clear and apparently compelling connection between the impending disaster in Ireland and the need for the Corn Laws to be repealed. 'The remedy [for the failure of the potato crop],' he insisted, 'is the total and absolute repeal for ever of all duties on all articles of subsistence'. It would be intolerable, he insisted, to allow the Corn Laws to obstruct the passage of foodstuffs through Ireland's ports when a whole nation was facing starvation.

But for once, Peel's cabinet colleagues were not convinced by Peel's logic. It does indeed seem faulty:

● first, as they pointed out, it was quite within the British Government's powers to suspend the Corn Laws in Ireland *temporarily*. Indeed, this course had clear advantages: suspension could be speedily effected, while full Repeal would require the recall of Parliament. Repeal would also bitterly divide the Conservative Party.
● secondly, the sceptics knew that the earlier failure of the European potato crop meant that practically every alternative continental supply of food had been used up: there were no stockpiles of grain waiting to be imported into Ireland, and anyway the Irish peasantry were too impoverished to afford what reserves there were.

To put the matter with brutal simplicity, Peel's proposal to repeal the Corn Laws would not save the life of a single Irishman or Irishwoman.

It is hard to avoid the conclusion that Peel was using Ireland's impending catastrophe as an excuse, or cover, for the implementation of a policy upon which he had already decided for completely separate reasons. His contemporaries suspected as much, and the element of dishonesty they detected in his presentation of the case for Repeal added to their sense of outrage at being 'sold'.

PEEL'S ECONOMIC MOTIVES

We cannot be certain as to when Peel first came to regard the Repeal of the Corn Laws as desirable. Dr Hilton (see Bibliography) has suggested that Peel's work with Huskisson, on the revision of the Corn Laws between 1825 and 1828, may have been decisive in persuading him of the ultimate desirability of Repeal. After that time he certainly made no clear-cut defence of 'protectionism'. Peel was biding his time, and keeping his options open.

However, Peel felt those options diminishing rapidly once in power, for the Corn Laws became progressively less and less defensible. Britain's economic recovery after 1842 was interpreted by Peel and others as incontestable proof of the merits of free trade. Therefore, to Peel's intellectual conviction that free trade was best, was added the evidence of experience that it was a cure for social distress. This lesson was put into practice with supreme confidence in the 1845 budget, in which over 400 remaining important duties were abolished. But this only left the Corn Laws even more exposed as unjustifiable. As one well-informed insider noted in his diary, in August 1845, 'everybody expects that he means to go on, and in the end to knock the Corn Laws on the head … but nobody knows how or when he will do [it]'.

KEY ISSUE

When and why did Peel become convinced that the Corn Laws had to be Repealed?

PEEL'S SOCIAL AND POLITICAL MOTIVES

Economic pressures alone, however, cannot explain the urgency and determination with which Peel was to drive Repeal through, regardless of the cost to himself or to his party. The answer lies in Peel's growing fears for the long-term well-being of British society. Peel had thought deeply about the course of Britain's social development since the Industrial Revolution, and was more confident than most other right-wing politicians about the capacity of the old landed order to survive in the new Britain. But, by 1845, Peel had become convinced that Britain was heading for a double disaster, each indirectly brought about by industrialisation, which could only be averted by the Repeal of the Corn Laws.

- **The first potential disaster was demographic**. Britain's inability to feed its rapidly expanding population by its own agricultural resources had been an underlying anxiety for governments since the late 1810s. Between then and 1841, Britain's population had grown by almost 50 per cent. In one of his earliest skirmishes over agricultural protection in 1842, Peel had explained to the Commons that 'I have a deep impression, a firm conviction, that population is increasing more rapidly than the supply of provision in this country … '. The Irish famine itself, and the associated revelations of how easily the whole European food supply network could be overstretched, served to confirm Peel in his free trade convictions. Only by opening Britain's ports permanently to foreign corn would increased continental production be stimulated, and entirely new sources of supply be opened up.
- **The second potential disaster was political**. Here, the Anti-Corn Law League was the problem. It seems unlikely that Peel's main anxiety was about the League's *immediate* electoral prospects. But Peel *was* appalled by the wider political impact which the League

was having, and its potential to do still greater damage to the stability of British society. To Peel, the League was a revolutionary conspiracy. He knew that the fundamental objectives of its leaders were the break-up of the 'territorial constitution' and the overthrow of aristocratic rule. The Corn Laws – or, as League propaganda styled them, the 'Bread Tax' – were a potent symbol of the unacceptable face of aristocratic power around which anti-aristocratic feeling could be whipped up in the next election. Therefore, by repealing the Corn Laws, Peel would in his own words, 'remove the contest entirely from the dangerous ground upon which it has got – that of a war between the manufacturers, the hungry and the poor against the landed proprietors [and] the aristocracy, which can only end in the ruin of the latter'.

Peel, with a general election imminent, was determined to defuse the class struggle which Cobden and his friends in the Anti-Corn Law League were waging. At a stroke, Repeal would destroy the platform on which the Radicals were mounting their agitation, and would give the lie to the Chartists' old claim that a Parliament dominated by the landed classes was by definition incapable of legislating in the interest of the nation as a whole. Above all, Repeal would be done when and how Peel and Parliament chose. It would not be conceded by a defeated aristocracy desperate to appease the clamour of the mob. Thus, the Government's authority would be maintained.

This was the real case for Repeal but months of agonised and acrimonious debate would be required before Peel could persuade even his Cabinet colleagues that they had no choice but to press for it, and before Parliament could be persuaded to pass it. The majority of his own party members were not to be persuaded at all.

The chronology of events in those last tense months before Repeal deserves close study and is tabulated on page 163.

C *The opposition to repeal*

KEY ISSUE

Why was the Tory reaction to Peel's Repeal proposals so furious?

For Protectionists, the Corn Laws were a constitutional as well as an economic issue

By the end of 1845, Peel was well used to expressions of dissent and dissatisfaction on his backbenches. But the savagery of the rebellion provoked by his proposal to repeal the Corn Laws caught him by surprise. By late 1845, Peel's backbenchers had had enough of being bullied and duped. His behaviour over the Factory Act and the Sugar Duties had been offensive, and the reversal over Maynooth was obnoxious – but Repeal was intolerable. The Tory Party believed it stood for two great principles, in whose cause it had fought and won the 1841 general election: the defence of the Anglican Church and of the landed interest. Peel had had the arrogance to abandon both within the course of one year.

To rank-and-file Tories, the Corn Laws were not just a package of tariffs protecting agriculture: they symbolised aristocratic, landed predominance in British society, and were at the heart of what made the nation great.

TIMELINE

The chronology of repeal 1845–6

15 October 1845	Peel wrote to the Lord Lieutenant of Ireland, stating that the 'remedy' for the potato blight is the Repeal of the Corn Laws.
1 November	Peel opened a Cabinet debate with a memorandum suggesting Repeal as a possible response to the likely Irish famine. Protracted and difficult discussions followed; apart from Graham, the Cabinet was unconvinced.
22 November	Lord John Russell, Leader of the Whigs, announced his conversion to the total Repeal of the Corn Laws.
Late November	Peel gradually won over a majority in the Cabinet for Repeal. The secret import of maize from America was arranged.
5 December	Lord Stanley and Lord Buccleuch still refused to accept Peel's case for Repeal. Convinced that only a unified Cabinet could carry the measure, Peel resigned. Russell tried to form a pro-Repeal Whig ministry.
20 December	After difficult negotiations with leading Whigs, it became clear that Russell was unable to form a ministry. Peel saw this as a moment of destiny. He became the 'Queen's Minister' again, determined to press on with Repeal regardless of the cost. In fact, only Stanley refused to join the reconstituted Cabinet.
22 January 1846	Peel introduced a Bill to Repeal the Corn Laws into the Commons. Bitter debates followed, in which Lord George Bentinck and Benjamin Disraeli led the assault on Peel from the Conservatives' own back benches.
15 May	Peel had a majority of 98 in favour of Repeal in the final vote in the Commons. But Whig support was essential in this outcome: 241 Conservatives voted against Repeal – only 112 for.
June	The House of Lords, heavily influenced by the Duke of Wellington, voted for Repeal.
26 June	The hard core of irreconcilable Tory protectionists joined forces with Whigs, Radicals and Irish MPs to vote against an Irish Coercion Bill in order to demonstrate their opposition to Peel. The Government was defeated and Peel resigned the following day. Russell became the new Prime Minister.

A leading Tory journalist explained the deeper significance of the Corn Laws to a friend in 1843:

> I look farther, much, than the mere questions of prices of corn and rates of wages ... [what is at stake] is the existence of a landed gentry, which has made England what she has been and is, without which no representative government can last; without which there can be no steady mean (middle way) between democracy and despotism ... [the Repeal of the Corn Laws] would mean the overthrow of the existing social and political system of our country.

Q *What does this quotation tell us about the nature of the issues raised by Corn Law repeal?*

Yet only three years after this was written, the cotton-barons of Manchester had triumphed over the good Old England of squire and parson – and the enemy had been aided and abetted by Peel!

The depth of the anger which Peel faced in early 1846 was terrible: but this cannot explain how the backbenchers' revolt was transformed into a permanent break in the party. To understand this, we must turn our focus to the English counties. By 1845, the Tory heartlands of the shires were in revolt. The farmers had long been anxious at the free trade tendencies of Peel's policies, and in 1844 they had founded the Central Agricultural Protection Society to defend their interests. As Peel became more unreliable in defence of the Corn Laws, the 'Anti-League', as the Protectionists' organisation soon became known, grew more militant. County MPs who were reluctant to join the attack on Peel were told to present themselves for re-election by their constituents. They were invariably 'de-selected'. Convinced Protectionist MPs, on the other hand, became bolder in their assault. Thus, the Anti-League's organisation, tenacity and its concentrated bitterness first helped to inspire the Tory backbench revolt, then to sustain it, and finally to ensure that, after Repeal was passed, the party would depose Peel and turn him and his followers into political outcasts.

The parliamentary leaders of the Protectionists played a vital role in determining the depth of these divisions. In some of the most savage debates the Commons has ever seen, Peel was mercilessly harried and hunted down. Lord George Bentinck and Benjamin Disraeli were his two most venomous foes. In Bentinck, son of a Duke and a fanatical racehorse owner, the fury of rural England found its ideal mouthpiece – relentless, utterly convinced that right and honour was on the protectionists' side and furious in the face of Peel's contemptible treachery. And in Disraeli, the Tory backbenchers discovered a parliamentary genius whose brilliant sarcasms could wound, torment and humiliate Peel in a way they had not thought possible.

For more on Disraeli's role see Chapter 7, pages 196–7

The Protectionists would not call off their assault until Peel was crippled. Repeal itself could not be stopped: the Whigs in the Commons and the Lords mostly favoured it and would join the Conservative frontbenchers to give the bill a majority. But Peel himself could be stopped. After repeal was carried, in June 1846, 69 of the most embittered Conservative backbenchers joined forces with Whigs, Radicals and Irish Catholics to defeat the Irish Coercion Bill and overthrow Peel's ministry. As they had hoped, his resignation ended Peel's career as a political leader. Four years later, he died after a riding accident. To some he was a sort of martyr – to others, the foulest of villains. But what the Protectionists could not have guessed, in their blind passion, was that the split that they were helping to bring about in the Conservative Party was to keep it out of effective power for the best part of 30 years.

THE CASE FOR THE PROTECTIONISTS

Historically, the Protectionists have received 'a bad press' for their actions in 1846. Bentinck is sometimes presented as little less than insane in the violence of his attacks on Peel, while Disraeli, notoriously, was supposedly driven by personal hatred against Peel. The Protectionists as a whole are damned for bad economics and bad politics: the

Repeal of the Corn Laws opened the door to three decades of unparalleled economic growth and social stability, while they condemned themselves and their party to almost 30 years of impotence and opposition.

It is, however, possible to construct an analysis of the crisis and its consequences that is distinctly more favourable to the Protectionists.

The Protectionist case

- Peel was widely regarded to have made – following Catholic Emancipation, for the second time in his career – a complete U-turn on the most important and bitterly disputed question of the day. However much Peel might argue that he had only acted in the service of the national interest, Conservatives who had supported him in the 1841 election, believing they were supporting protection, regarded him as a traitor and an outcast.
- If Peel was over-optimistic about the capacity of British agriculture to respond to world competition, he may have been too pessimistic about the threat posed to the aristocratic order by the Anti-Corn Law League. Wellington, for one, detected an element of 'panic' in Peel's behaviour in 1845–6. Perhaps Peel's experiences between 1829 and 1832 – when Parliament had come terribly near to losing control of events – had made Peel oversensitive to the threat of popular pressure, and too anxious to defuse crises with concessions that were in fact premature and overgenerous.
- Peel seemed to ignore the constraints which the Great Reform Act placed on the Government's freedom of manoeuvre. In fact, as Disraeli realised, the backing of 'party' would now be required if Prime Ministers were to enjoy stable parliamentary majorities. Peel had seen that the 1832 Reform Act would make it more difficult for the Government to get its own way in the Commons but he had spent too long as an 'executive man', immersed in the problems of government under the old system, to find tolerable – or perhaps even to understand – the new rules of the game.

6 ⌁ THE VERDICT ON PEEL

A *Peel as leader of the Conservative Party*

THE CONSERVATIVE REVIVAL OF 1832–41

The argument that, between 1834 and 1841 a new Conservative Party was founded by Peel, is considered in Section 2. In 1845–6, however,

See Section 2 of this chapter, pages 145–6

Class debate
One-half of the class to argue, as if in Parliament in February 1846, in support of Peel's case for Corn Law Repeal and the other half to support the Protectionist case.

many Conservative MPs refused to follow Peel's Corn Law Repeal strategy. They proved unwilling to abandon the traditional landed interests of the Party in favour of the interests of wider, industrial, urban and working-class, or indeed national interests. This suggests that, despite the Tamworth Manifesto and all Peel's other reforming tendencies, the new Conservative Party was not all that different from the old Tory Party. The 1841 election was perhaps not won on the basis of the support of the electors newly enfranchised in 1832 so much as because the Party's traditional supporters returned to their old Tory loyalties. In 1846 the Conservative backbenchers who had been elected in 1841 remained loyal to their traditional roots. This of course has serious implications for Peel's claims as founder of a new Conservative Party and these issues are considered further in the historiographical section below.

B *A poor party manager?*

By presenting a balanced account of the issues at stake when Peel and the Protectionists clashed, it becomes possible to identify some of Peel's political blind spots more clearly:

- he failed to appreciate the strength of the protectionists' case, the intensity with which they were committed to it, or the true consequences of his course of action. The most immediate of these was the destruction of the Tory Party
- he was warned by Cabinet colleagues that Repeal would smash the Tories and thus leave Britain at the mercy of extreme Whigs and Radicals. It was lucky for the old aristocracy that, instead, they ended up facing the cautious Whig leader, Lord Palmerston
- in 1845–6, Peel gave every impression that he could not care less about the fate of the Conservative Party. Peel has some claim to be one of the worst party managers ever to lead the Tories.

HISTORIANS' DEBATE

Peel and the historians

Not surprisingly, Peel's place in the Conservative tradition remains a matter of controversy.

- **Lord Blake,** in his well-known history of the Conservative Party (see Bibliography page 171) denies Peel a place in the 'Hall of Fame': after all, the split for which Blake believes Peel was mostly responsible, crippled the Conservatives as a political force for almost three decades.
- **Norman Gash** has a very different emphasis. According to him '[Peel's] place as the founder of modern Conservatism is unchallengeable ... His central achievement was to refashion the principles of Toryism for a new age'. Gash continues: 'only on the basis

of [Peel's] principles could a party of the right in the conditions of Victorian political life obtain and retain power'.

For long Professor Gash's views tended to dominate Peel scholarship. But, as long ago as 1979, this 'orthodoxy' came under increasing attack. The most radical challenge to Gash's interpretation of Peel has come from Dr Hilton (*see Bibliography*).

Hilton's arguments are complex and difficult, and only two elements can be noted here:

● First, Hilton provided a totally fresh interpretation of Peel's way of thinking. Whereas Gash finds Peel to be a great pragmatist, always learning from experience, and a master of politics as 'the art of the possible', Hilton sees Peel's whole approach as dogmatic and divisive – and underpinned less by rational calculation than Christian commitment. Peel's faith in the free market was in part the product of highly intellectual theorising, in part sprung from his conviction that *laissez-faire* capitalism was God's means of punishing the thriftless and vicious, who did not deserve to be *protected* by the state from the consequences of their actions.
● Secondly, and in direct contrast to Gash, Hilton insists that 'Peel was not the founder of the Conservative Party, but the progenitor [father] of Gladstonian Liberalism.' This claim may appear to be perverse, but in fact it makes a lot of sense.

C *Gladstone and Disraeli's debt to Peel*

GLADSTONE

Gladstone always revered Peel as his greatest political teacher:

● from Peel, he learnt how fiscal policy – the delicate interplay of free trade, tariffs and income tax – could be used to strengthen economic prosperity and social harmony
● Gladstone's attitude towards the power and function of the Government owed much to Peel too. Gladstone, like Peel, was supremely confident that there was no political problem that a courageous and expert government could not resolve
● also like Peel, Gladstone was single-minded in his determination that the Government should not be made the servant of any class or selfish party interest
● above all, he derived from Peel an urgent sense of the need, in Hilton's words, to 'persuade the toiling masses that there was a moral energy at the centre of the state which was not indifferent to their fears and aspirations'.

Peel himself saw this as his central responsibility. In one of his final defences of the Repeal of the Corn Laws, he said:

> **KEY ISSUE**
>
> *Did Peel contribute more to the future of the Liberal Party than he did to that of the Conservatives?*

Q

What does this extract tell us about Peel's view of the purpose of politics?

My earnest wish has been, during my tenure of power, to impress the people of the country with a belief that the legislature (Parliament) was animated with a sincere desire to frame its legislation upon the principles of equity and justice. I have a strong belief that the greatest object which we or any other government can contemplate should be to elevate the social condition of that class of the people with whom we are brought into no direct relationship by the exercise of the elective franchise.

DISRAELI

There can be little doubt that Peel was a great and farsighted conservative – but a conservative with a small 'c'. It is much less easy, however, to assess his contribution to the Conservative Party, and its ideology and practice, in the later nineteenth century. A list of the most prominent characteristics of Peelism would probably include:

- great technical expertise in the arts of government
- a taste for big bills and finding bold solutions to major problems
- and a distrust and loathing of the dynamics of popular politics.

One would have to look very hard to find much trace of any of these in Disraeli's political practice. And although the Disraelian Conservative Party did begin to attract to its banner the middle-class manufacturers and men of commerce to whom Peel had tried to appeal, this was rather because of the excesses they began to see in Gladstonian Liberalism than because Disraeli was pursuing Peelite policies. Only as a free trader did Disraeli become a Peelite, but as everyone else was a free trader in mid-Victorian Britain, it was not a policy with which Disraeli was going to win many votes, or carve out a distinctively Conservative identity.

It is, indeed, hard not to conclude, as Hilton first proposed, that Gladstone has a stronger claim to the Peelite mantle than any Conservative.

D *Peel's reputation as a great statesman*

KEY ISSUE

To what extent has Peel's reputation as a great statesman been exaggerated?

Just as Gash's claims for Peel as the founding father of modern Conservatism have been under attack, so are his claims for the achievements of Peel's statesmanship. Gash argued that it was Peel above all others who guided Britain out of the social and political turmoil of the 1830s and 1840s towards an era of stability and prosperity in the 1850s and 1860s. For most – although not all of his career – Peel did live up to his ideal of statesmanship: a commitment to serve the interests of the nation with courage and foresight, ignoring all temptations to satisfy personal advantage, and if necessary, ignoring the claims of party.

Peel's achievement is, however, open to challenge:

● how far it was his tax and tariff reforms that brought about Britain's economic recovery, is open to doubt. Some economic historians believe that the cycle of boom and slump, which characterised the early nineteenth-century economy, went on regardless of government policy
● Peel certainly overreacted to the threat posed by the Chartists and the 'general strike' of 1842
● he may well have overreacted to the threat posed by the Anti-Corn Law League too.

Late in 1848, having retired from the political front rank, Peel reflected on the question of why the British state had survived the revolutionary upheavals of that year so much better than had the continental monarchies. He concluded, with an element of self-congratulation, that the main reason was because the Repeal of the Corn Laws had demonstrated to the British working classes that an aristocratic parliament could respond to their needs, even at the cost of sacrificing its own material interests. The British State was just and was seen to be just.

But Peel should perhaps also have asked himself what the Great Reform Act had contributed to the survival of the established order. The

KEY ISSUE

Did the Whigs contribute more to Victorian stability than Peel?

PICTURE 17 Punch's 'Monument to Peel' published in 1850, the year in which Peel died

Q

1. *Explain the nature of* Punch's *tribute to Peel.*
2. *Who, among Peel's contemporaries (a) would agree with* Punch *and (b) strongly reject the tribute by* Punch?

middle classes, who in their tens of thousands offered their services as special constables to face the Chartists in 1848, had not been impressed enough by the principles of Tamworth Conservatism to back Peel in any great numbers in 1841. But Grey's bold extension of the franchise – the scale of which had outraged and amazed Peel – had successfully recruited enough of the forces of 'property and respectability' to the side of the aristocracy to see the British state and its 'territorial constitution' through the crisis of the 1840s. There was no *one* architect of the prosperity and stability of mid-Victorian Britain. Peel achieved much, particularly in economic matters, but perhaps the Whigs achieved more? It was they who had had to fight for parliamentary reform – and indeed, it was they who provided most of the votes by which the Repeal of the Corn Laws was finally carried.

7 ⌐ BIBLIOGRAPHY

ARTICLES

All of the articles in this section should be within the scope of AS and A2 students. None are of great length and all will give you valuable and relatively painless practice in reading academic history.

D. Eastwood 'Peel and the Tory Party Reconsidered', *History Today*, March 1992.

W. Hinde 'The Corn Laws', *Modern History Review*, 1998: an article on the repeal debate and its outcome.

N. Gash 'Sir Robert Peel and the Conservative Party', *Modern History Review*, February 1990, and 'Peel and Ireland', *Modern History Review*, April 1992. These two very useful articles by the scholar whose work dominates this topic area are the most accessible way into his views on Peel.

T. A. Jenkins 'Peel helped to form the modern Conservative party but followed policies which alienated many of his supporters', *New Perspective*, March 2000.

D. Watts 'Peel's Sense of National Needs Laid Conservative Foundations but Unresolved Tensions Split the Party', *New Perspective*, 1999.

BOOKS FOR AS/A LEVEL STUDENTS

When working towards examinations it is best to have specific tasks in mind before you start reading books of even modest length. Then you can use the contents pages and the index to get where you want to be quickly.

P. Adelman *Peel and the Conservative Party 1830–50*, Longman Seminar Studies, 1989, easily understood and providing a rich array of documents but perhaps A2 rather than AS level

E. J. Evans *Sir Robert Peel: Statesmanship, Power and Party*, Routledge, Lancaster Pamphlet, 1991, an excellent synthesis of views on Peel.

T. A. Jenkins *Sir Robert Peel*, Macmillan, 1999, aimed at A-level students and first year university students, very good on Peel's 1841–6 ministry

D. Watts *Tories, Conservatives and Unionists 1815–1914*, Access to History series, Hodder & Stoughton, 2002, Chapter 4 will repay study by any serious AS or A level student

FURTHER READING

Articles

Scholarly historical articles can be daunting. Cut your teeth on A-level articles first. Then, at A2 level, do try to obtain (consult a librarian) and read at least parts of a few more academic pieces. These can have two great merits:

● they are often by people who are in the process of revising accepted historical ideas
● the article format compels the author to put ideas across quite briefly and directly.

Tip: read the first and last paragraphs (or pages) of the article to see if it seems useful for your purposes. If it does, then skim the body of the article for further ideas and only read systematically if it seems of outstanding importance for your purpose. Do not panic if it is above your head: this is a common feeling – just move on to something else.

Articles that, in the past, have caused accepted views of Peel to be challenged and revised include:

B. Hilton 'Peel: A Reappraisal', *The Historical Journal*, 1979 which is certainly not for the faint-hearted but essential for a full understanding of the author's views on the Liberal Party's debt to Peel.
I. Newbould 'Sir Robert Peel and the Conservative Party, 1832–1841: A Study in Failure?', *English Historical Review*, 1983: an article that opened up a new debate in interpreting the reasons for the Conservative victory in the 1841 election.

In their time, these articles caused serious academic historians to rethink their views so they are worth at least a brief visit by the ambitious A2 student. You will then have been on the frontiers of historical interpretation.

Books

Probably for dipping into on key events and at A2 rather than AS level.

R. Blake *The Conservative Party from Peel to Major*, Fontana, 1996, where Chapters 1 and 2 contain a lucid account of the problems Peel faced followed by a series of challenging insights into what he achieved.
B. Coleman *Conservatism and the Conservative Party in Nineteenth-century Britain*, Edward Arnold, 1988.
N. Gash *Peel*, The one-volume biography, Longman 1976.
R. Stewart *Party and Politics 1830–52*, Macmillan, 1989, a direct and readable account in Chapters 5 and 6.

Internet resources

Even limited use of one of the major search engines to call up references to 'Peel + Prime Minister' will produce literally thousands of sites, unfortunately of very varying quality and relevance. However, the 'Peel Web' is very useful and is particularly designed for A level students. www.adw03.dial.pipex.com/peel/peelhome.htm is the home page but you could simply type in 'Robert Peel' and then go to the 'Peel Web'.

8 ⌐ STRUCTURED AND ESSAY QUESTIONS

STUDENT ADVICE: ORGANISING YOUR WORK ON PEEL

Any study of Peel and the Conservative Party will involve much reading. At the end of several weeks of study you will have accumulated a great mass of information that will need organising. There is little virtue in this unless your knowledge is then geared to the assessment tasks, which will confront you at the end of the unit of study. You should first note that the examination boards providing study units on Peel have decided that your performance in these units will be largely tested by essay or other forms of extended writing. Your study of this topic should be organised with this in mind.

You will be well advised from the start to study and revise in terms of historical problems and organise your historical knowledge in terms of the essay tasks you will eventually face. This approach will make you

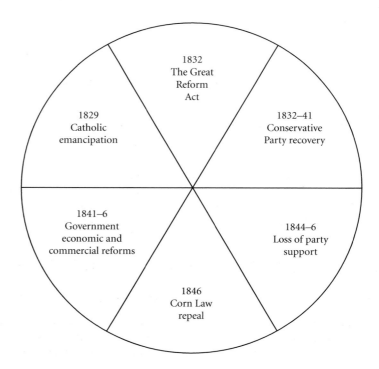

DIAGRAM 4
Peel: examination revision topics 1829–46

think about the history you are studying rather than encourage you to accumulate vast amounts of historical information for its own sake. This critical approach will give the best basis for selecting, interpreting and answering the essay questions you will then have to answer. The 'Key issues', set in the chapter margin, are there to help you to identify appropriate historical problems.

This is not the most useful topic on which to practise skills in document analysis

A *Structured Questions for AS Level*

This section consists of questions or points that might be used for class discussions (or for practice in producing brief written answers) but, most importantly, it will form the basis for expanding on this chapter and testing your understanding of it. It will also be particularly useful for AS students wishing to practise writing structured essays.

1. What was Peel's role in the crisis over Catholic Emancipation and parliamentary reform? How did these events help shape his later career?
2. How can we explain the Conservative electoral recovery between 1832 and 1841?
3. What financial problems did Peel face in 1841–2 and why was his 1842 Budget such a success?
4. What problems were posed by political disorder in mainland Britain in Peel's second ministry, and how did he cope with them?
5. Why did relationships between Peel and his backbenchers deteriorate in 1844?
6. Why did the Anti-Corn Law League want to repeal the Corn Laws, and how did they set about trying to achieve their objective?
7. Why did Peel want to Repeal the Corn Laws?
8. Why did the 1846 Repeal of the Corn Laws split the Conservative Party?

B *Essays for A2*

1. 'A great statesman but a poor party leader'. Discuss this evaluation of Peel.
2. 'A Conservative is a Tory who has learned to live with the Industrial Revolution'. Discuss with reference to Peel's career.
3. 'The root of Peel's difficulties lies in his attempt to govern through a reformed Parliament according to pre-reform rules'. Discuss.
4. Why, twice in Peel's career, did he find himself having to make a complete U-turn on the most important political issues of the day?
5. Why did Peel become the most hated man in British politics?
6. 'Peel's achievements have been exaggerated'. Discuss.

The information and explanation in this chapter will provide the basis for a good answer to any of these essay questions

9 ⤳ ESSAYS: INTERPRETING QUESTIONS

Some ideas to help you on your way with the essays in Section 8B:

● **Question 1** has a clear assertion which you have to discuss. Think about the claim that has been made. Often a quick way into this type of question is to think about what you would like to challenge in the assertion. Here two claims are made about Peel. You might be happy to agree that he was a poor party leader but wish to challenge the claim that he was a great statesman. The essay then falls naturally into two parts. The second part might open with what you think are the qualities of a great statesman but do this very briefly and get back quickly to your verdict on Peel

● **Question 2** has a clever play on words and you will need to have clear definitions of Tory and Conservative in mind before answering. Even something simple like 'a Tory was one who resisted all change whereas a Conservative was prepared to adapt to inevitable change and remedy proven abuses'. Peel's Tamworth Manifesto could be used here. You may want to start by explaining how the Industrial Revolution had changed the country and how politicians had to choose whether to resist (ignore?) these changes or try to control and influence them.

● **Question 3** calls out for you to explain what is meant by pre-reform rules. It almost relates to the pre-1832 governments being able to command the support of MPs from the rotten boroughs, which largely disappeared in 1832. Now governments would have to work harder and listen more closely in order to keep the loyalty of MPs who were more answerable to their constituents. Peel did not do this very well. The 1832 Act strengthened the role of political parties but arguably Peel was not prepared to accept this.

● **Question 4** involves correct identification of Catholic Emancipation and Corn Law Repeal as the two occasions. The essay should then fall easily into two more or less equal parts. A good answer would then conclude by relating the two occasions to each other and perhaps show how the first (Emancipation) did much to help create the second (Repeal).

● **Question 5** covers the same ground as Question 4 but requires different treatment. You could take Emancipation and Repeal in turn and explain who was infuriated by what Peel did in each case. The charge is the same – that he betrayed people who were entitled to expect that he would support their interests. You could then briefly add that Peel, rightly or wrongly, felt each time that he had no alternative to acting as he did. You do not need to describe what each crisis was about, just get on with answering the question

● **Question 6** is perhaps best answered by briefly indicating in the opening paragraph what Peel's main 'achievements' were; creating the Conservative Party and establishing the basis for mid-Victorian prosperity are large enough claims. You will then need more detail to explore their validity and the easiest approach might well be to knock them down. A more sophisticated approach to this question would be to identify the historians who have exaggerated Peel's achievement (Gash?) and then point to the later historians who have questioned and challenged it. You may then be entitled to claim that, although this assertion may once have been true, recent historical writing has largely undermined it. Avoid this approach if you are not totally confident about the historiography involved.

Whigs, Liberals and Conservatives, 1846–68

7

INTRODUCTION

POLITICAL FLUIDITY

The 1846 drama of Corn Law Repeal heralded a new era in political life. The next 22 years, opening with the defeat of Peel's Conservative Government in 1846, have frequently been seen as a period of fluidity in parliamentary politics. The nine different governments formed in those years suggest that there is some justice in this claim and yet Russell's first Whig Government survived from 1846 to 1852 and Palmerston's Whig–Liberal Government from 1859 to 1865.

The apparent fluidity at Westminster was in fact caused by the short-lived nature of the four Conservative Governments. In 1846 the Conservatives were divided between a group of around one hundred who had continued to support Peel in the Corn Law crisis and the bulk of the party who had voted against him on the repeal issue. The Peelites represented the leaders of the old Conservative Party, too few in number to command power on their own. Peel refused to give the group any political lead. Lacking direction and despite their numbers gradually dwindling, they were, for a time, a source of political instability. Their one-time Conservative colleagues, though numerically stronger, could not form a majority party and, because of their outright rejection of free trade in corn, were in grave danger of becoming a marginal agrarian party committed only to the protection of landed and farming interests. In an increasingly industrial and urban world this could well have doomed them to early political extinction.

Dates	Party	Prime Minister
1846–52	Whig	Russell
1852	Cons	Derby
1852–5	Peelite/Whig	Aberdeen
1855–8	Whig	Palmerston
1858–9	Cons	Derby
1859–65	Whig/Lib	Palmerston
1865–6	Whig/Lib	Russell
1866–8	Cons	Derby
1868	Cons	Disraeli

TABLE 9 *Governments, 1846–68*

THE POLITICAL PARTIES

The main party political issues of the period which have interested historians are:

- the emergence of the Liberal Party: involving the fate of the Peelites from 1846 to 1859 and the continuing importance of the Whigs within the Liberal party
- the role of William Gladstone as Liberal leader, both in Parliament and in the country at large.
- the factors that promoted the rise of the Liberals and the principles on which Gladstonian Liberalism was based.
- the survival and eventual recovery, in difficult circumstances, of the Conservative Party led by Lord Derby and Disraeli.

PARLIAMENTARY REFORM

This again became a major issue towards the end of the period when political debate and much political manoeuvring largely centred on the attempts, by both major parties, to bring about a second reform in the electoral system, following the 1832 Act

- a Liberal attempt in 1866 failed
- that by the Conservatives, succeeding in 1867, brought about the Second Reform Act.

The process of reform and the terms of the Act have both been the subject of much controversy among historians.

THE 1868 GENERAL ELECTION

This resulted in a great Liberal victory, which saw Gladstone become Prime Minister. It marked a clear boundary to this period of government 'fluidity' and heralded in a period of 17 years of political stability dominated by party-based governments, much as in the period from 1830 to 1846.

1 ᗡ WHIGS AND PEELITES

A *The Whigs*

KEY ISSUE

Why did the Whigs remain so important politically?

The Whigs had governed the country from 1830 to 1841 and, until the 1890s, provided the core of the Liberal party. The typical Whig was a wealthy aristocratic landowner who could trace his family line, and political allegiance, well back into the eighteenth century, or even beyond. The two most prominent Whigs in this period were Lords Palmerston and Russell.

The Whigs believed that they were born with a right to rule and, even after Gladstone became Liberal leader in the 1860s, they could expect to fill half or more of the seats in Cabinet. The Whigs believed that it was because they combined a love of order with political sensitivity and imagination that the country had been spared a bloody revolution, not least in 1831–2. Certainly in the period from 1846 to 1868, with the Conservative Party in eclipse, a Whig presence was an essential element in government stability.

From the 1860s the continued importance of the Whigs rested on their willingness to work with Gladstone. They respected Gladstone's superb administrative skills, demonstrated at the Board of Trade in Peel's earlier government and as Chancellor of the Exchequer during the 1850s and 1860s. In the 1860s they also became aware that his growing mastery of public speaking and the press gave their party access to sources of political support that they were incapable of mobilising themselves. Despite his appearing radical on some issues they sensed that at heart he respected tradition and the role of the aristocracy, and for a long time trusted his judgement. The more perceptive Whig leaders saw that Gladstone's influence over Radicals and Nonconformists was the best hope of containing the threat to property and the Establishment that these outsiders seemed to pose. In the 1860s other Whigs became suspicious of his popular reputation and his radical lurches that seemed as rash as they were unpredictable. Despite such friction this unlikely alliance at the heart of Liberal Government survived for more than 20 years before Gladstone/Whig differences generated the party split of 1886. The dangers and tensions were, however, there from the start.

B *The fate of the Peelites*

Corn Law Repeal and the immediate end of Peel's Government in 1846 left Robert Peel, and those eminent but few Conservatives who had remained loyal to him, in a quandary. Peel himself withdrew from active politics, confining himself to giving general advice to those who had followed him into the political wilderness. Even Gladstone, his greatest admirer, felt that he should have given more of a lead. Peel, however, did no more than ensure that general support for Russell's Whig Government would prevent any Conservative attempt to restore the Corn Laws. He made no move either to organise his followers, to negotiate their return to the Conservative fold or to do a formal deal with the Whigs. His sudden death in 1850 scarcely added to their dilemma.

With party loyalties in a state of flux, inevitably estimates of Peelite numbers have varied. One contemporary estimate of their number in 1847 gave them 117 of the 640 members of the Commons, another in the same year suggested only 85–90: too few to provide a government on their own but too many, and too able, to be ignored by the other party groupings. Their numbers dwindled over time as some died and others chose to leave the Commons. During the 1850s they manoeuvred from position to position. From 1852 to 1855 Lord Aberdeen, Foreign-Secretary under Peel, headed a coalition Peelite–Whig Government which, but for the military disasters of the Crimean War which destroyed it, might have led directly to a more permanent arrangement

PICTURE 18
Lord Palmerston: a leading Whig and Foreign Secretary (1830–4, 1835–41, 1846–51). A great rival of Russell, he was Prime Minister 1855–8 and 1859–65; in this post he was an obstacle to further parliamentary reform measures. He sat in the Commons for 58 successive years and he was a government minister for 48 of those years.

KEY ISSUE

Why, after 1846, were Peel's followers in the political wilderness?

between the partners. Eventually the few Peelites who remained, and notably Gladstone among them, moved towards the Whigs and, in so doing, helped to create the Liberal Party. There was nothing inevitable about this for, even as late as 1858, Gladstone seriously considered an invitation to join Lord Derby's Conservative Government. It was probably intense dislike of Disraeli, the leading Conservative in the Commons, rather than any issue of principle over free trade, which prevented Gladstone returning to his political roots, for by this time the official Conservatives had quietly abandoned any intention of restoring the Corn Laws.

C *A historic decision 1859?*

Historians differ over the importance of the Willis Rooms meeting in 1859 in creating the Liberal Party

See Bibliography, page 209, for book titles

In 1859 at an apparently historic meeting between Peelites, Whigs and some radical politicians, the participants agreed to form an anti-Conservative alliance in order to defeat Derby's Government. Some historians have seen the agreements reached at this meeting, in the Willis Rooms in London, as the key moment in the foundation of the parliamentary Liberal Party. Historians like Matthew see Gladstone's role as central in bringing this accord about. Winstanley, however, sees Gladstone's role as much less significant and emphasises the negative, anti-Conservative nature of the meeting rather than its central importance in the emergence of the Liberal Party. Gladstone didn't in fact attend the so-called 'historic' meeting. In fact, at this stage he actually voted with the Conservative Government in the crucial debate that turned them out of office. Later in 1859, however, Gladstone overcame his strong dislike of Palmerston in order to become Palmerston's Chancellor in the Whig Government. The Peelites had for some years been a declining force and Gladstone's decision marked their end. Of the other leading Peelites, Aberdeen never held public office after 1855. He died in 1860. Sir James Graham left politics in 1855 and died in 1861. Gladstone, on the other hand, had only just embarked on the most remarkable political career of the nineteenth century.

2 ↪ LIBERAL FOUNDATIONS

The first stage in the history of the Liberal Party falls into the years from 1859, with the Whig-Gladstone anti-Conservative alliance, to the Party's great victory in the 1868 election. It grew from being a convenient anti-Conservative coalition to become the dominant force in British politics through to 1886. It was able to do this because it came to represent important new interests in a country undergoing vast economic and social changes. These favourable circumstances included:

● the existence of a growing, middle-class electorate, enfranchised in 1832 and which had been made both prosperous and increasingly self-confident by the Industrial Revolution

- the creation in 1832 of a significant number of large urban constituencies, relatively free of electoral corruption, where the new middle-class voters could act free of pressure from the landed and aristocratic interests in the state. In such constituencies, there could be genuine political debate and political ideas and principles became important
- the emergence of closely-knit, well-organised and rapidly expanding Protestant religious groups outside the Church of England. These dissenters, or Nonconformists, resented the many privileges of the Established Church and sought to remove them through political action. Nonconformist grievances at this time centred on their having to pay compulsory Church Rates for the upkeep and development of Anglican churches, a practice ended only in 1868. They also feared Anglican domination of elementary education
- Nonconformist self-confidence was greatly boosted by the 1851 Religious Census which showed that as many people attended the Nonconformist churches – mainly Methodists, Baptists and Congregationalists – as attended the services of the Church of England. The Nonconformist churches in many towns supported the new Liberal Party as the best means of opposing the claims and privileges of the Church of England. The more the Conservatives claimed to be the defenders of those privileges, the more they confirmed Nonconformist allegiance to the Liberal Party. The Nonconformist contribution within Parliament was however very limited; they had, for example, only 32 out of 656 MPs in 1852. Nonconformity was, however, important *outside* Parliament in delivering the urban constituency votes that became the bedrock of the Liberal Party. By harnessing the Party to a range of moral causes the Nonconformists also influenced, for good and ill, its future character as a party of reform and, all too frequently, of moral outrage
- the growth of town newspapers in the middle years of the century created a platform on which political debate could flourish. The Liberals were the chief beneficiaries of this development
- a developing skilled working class, still usually without the vote, looked to the Liberals as the likely party of franchise and social reform. This extra-parliamentary presence was skilfully harnessed to Liberal causes by the oratory of Bright and Gladstone, which was in turn frequently reported at length in the new provincial newspapers.

THE EARLY GLADSTONE

PROFILE

William Ewart Gladstone (1809–1898) came from a very wealthy Liverpool commercial family with close links to the Liberal Tories, Huskisson and Canning. He was educated at Eton and Oxford so that he could then follow a political career but briefly thought of becoming an Anglican priest. In fact, the interests of the Church of England were to remain important to him throughout his career. He entered the Commons immediately after the passing of the 1832

| **KEY ISSUE** |

How important was religious belief in shaping Gladstone's political life and actions?

Reform Act thanks to the patronage of the Tory Duke of Newcastle who still controlled the small constituency of Newark.

Gladstone's career spanned a period of unprecedented change: when he was summoned to fight the election in Newark (in Nottinghamshire) he was staying in Torquay, in Devon, and the journey took him three days, by stage coaches. By the time he became Prime Minister in 1868 there were over 13000 miles of railway track. Gladstone's career needs to be seen against this background of dramatic growth in population, urbanisation, manufacturing, trade and empire. By enabling him to travel long distances quickly, the railway certainly made possible his emergence as the first truly national politician.

Gladstone's maiden speech of 1832 was made in opposing the measure to abolish slavery in the British Empire for his father was in fact the most important of the owners of West Indian slave plantations. (In making historical judgements we need to remember that the nineteenth century was one of immense changes in moral and social values to which indeed Gladstone made a significant contribution.) Gladstone held minor office in Peel's brief government in 1834, a happy result of there being so few Tories elected to Parliament immediately following the 1832 Reform Act. After 1841, as President of the Board of Trade in Peel's second government, he was involved in the major financial and taxation reforms, an excellent training for the future Chancellor of the Exchequer.

The unparalleled prosperity and self-confidence of Britain in the 1850s and 1860s suggested that industrialisation and urbanisation had a benign as well as a threatening political face. Gladstone and the Liberal Party were the most obvious political beneficiaries of this transformation. His years as Chancellor of the Exchequer (1852–5 and 1859–66) firmly established his position in the front rank at Westminster, while the Whigs and Liberals – with whom Gladstone finally joined up in 1859 – were rarely out of office in these decades.

This first Liberal era culminated in Gladstone's own great first ministry (1868–74). By this time, he had established himself as a powerful public speaker and, in so doing, had created a political power base outside Westminster, in the rapidly expanding towns of the industrial North.

Gladstone was no mere spectator of the great political and social changes that transformed Victorian England. But the exact nature of his contributions remains a matter of intense debate. In any judgement of his career two interrelated questions loom large:

- How is Gladstone's transformation from reactionary Toryism in the 1830s to his later, deliberately radical, Liberalism to be explained?
- What was the place of principle, as opposed to ambition, in his career?

TIMELINE

Gladstone to 1874

1832	became an MP
1834	minor post in Peel's ministry
1841–6	at the Board of Trade
1852–5	Chancellor of the Exchequer
1859–66	Chancellor of the Exchequer
1868–74	Prime Minister

PICTURE 19 *Gladstone*

3 ∽ GLADSTONE: FROM TORY TO LIBERAL, 1832–59

A *The 1830s: Gladstone – Tory and Anglican origins*

The early Gladstone was something of a prig and on most issues a political reactionary; for example, his book *The State in its Relations with the Church*, was an elaborate assertion of the privileged position of the Church of England as the only Church that the state should recognise. It was so extreme that on one occasion Peel crossed the road to avoid having to speak about it to its author. Gladstone's views changed after 1841 when, as a member of Peel's Government he came to see that, in an age when Nonconformist Churches flourished and most Irish people remained staunchly Roman Catholic, his earlier ideas were impracticable. By the 1850s and 1860s he was conveniently willing to advance his career by forging links with both British Nonconformists and Irish Catholics.

Although Gladstone's views on the role of religion changed, he never lost the intense Christian faith given to him by his mother. In most important personal respects he remained true to his early beliefs. Practically speaking, he worked hard to defend the integrity and extend the influence of the Church of England. More fundamentally, he held to his conviction that the state had a duty to choose between right and wrong, and that society might yet be inspired by Christian zeal and purpose. These beliefs were to shape the practice and objectives of his statesmanship to end of his days. Underpinning all of this was his personal faith. Here, an intense and ever-present sense of sin was balanced with a conviction that it was within our powers to discern God's purposes for us, and that we should throw ourselves into the battle against evil and injustice. He was to bring the same passion and zeal – and, in his opponents' eyes, fanaticism – to his political crusades of the 1870s and 1880s, as he had brought to his ultra-Tory defence of the Establishment in the 1830s.

B *The 1840s: Peel's legacy to Gladstone*

It was not Gladstone's passionate religious convictions that first brought him to Peel's attention. What impressed Peel about Gladstone was his obvious political and administrative ability and, at the age of 26, he was given office as Under-Secretary for War and the Colonies in Peel's first brief ministry of 1834. When Peel returned to power in 1841, Gladstone served at the Board of Trade and was promoted to Cabinet rank in 1843. But his career suffered a major set-back in 1845, when he startled his contemporaries by resigning over the Maynooth question. Only reluctantly did he agree with the Government's decision to increase its grant to the Irish Catholic Seminary at Maynooth. It was justified as part of Peel's strategy to detach moderate Catholics from nationalist extremists. But the Maynooth grant was in clear opposition to the rigid principles which Gladstone had spelled out seven years earlier in his book on Church and State, and Gladstone believed that personal honour and public consistency required his resignation. He then confused most MPs, including Peel, by voting *for* the grant increase.

The experience of working in Peel's great administration had a profound impact on Gladstone's future political career. At a time when government was far busier than it had ever been, he made his name as an immensely able and industrious minister. As Peel's Home Secretary had remarked, 'Gladstone could do in four hours what it took any other man sixteen hours to do, and he worked sixteen hours a day'. Furthermore, the business of government helped to give Gladstone's political life a new meaning and purpose. Ministerial responsibilities themselves

For details on the Maynooth grant issue see Chapter 6, page 154

proved to be a joy, not a burden. He found great intellectual pleasure in mastering the details of a political issue, a pleasure enhanced by his sense that his work was a form of service to the state, and thus worthy in God's eye.

FOR GLADSTONE FREE TRADE WAS A MORAL ISSUE

Gladstone still saw his goals as Christian ones. The steady reduction or abolition of the tariffs on hundreds of articles may seem a dry and dreary administrative task. For Gladstone, however, the progress towards Free Trade had a moral and Christian content. At the most general level, the creation and preservation of wealth – which Free Trade would facilitate – was a Christian duty. More specifically, as the state's interference in the workings of the economy decreased, so greater responsibility would be thrown on the individual. Free trade would be an instrument doing God's work, rewarding the virtuous and thrifty, and punishing the vicious and spendthrift.

KEY ISSUE

Why, for Gladstone, did good government, backed by sound finance, become a moral issue?

Above all, Free Trade was welcome to Gladstone as a means of securing social harmony and justice. The Repeal of the Corn Laws was intended to show worker, industrialist and landowner alike that the state served no vested interest, but rather the whole community. Its achievement was as much a crusade for Gladstone as it was for Peel. This model of the right use of government power, soothing away agitation and doing what was right, regardless of the political cost to those in office, was to remain with Gladstone throughout his career in politics.

The immediate price that Gladstone paid in 1846 for his support of Peel was the loss of his protectionist patron, the Duke of Newcastle. But the academics and clergymen who elected Oxford University's very own two MPs came to his rescue. Between 1847 and 1865, Gladstone sat for this most prestigious and most Anglican of all constituencies.

These years also saw:

● his transition from Peelite Conservative to radical Liberal
● his acceptance as leader of the Liberals
● his discovery that he had a political power base among the general public
● his great success in government as Chancellor of the Exchequer (1852–5 and 1859–66)
● his emergence as one of the most dominant mid-Victorian political figures both at Westminster and in the country at large.

C *Gladstone as Chancellor, 1852–5*

As a loyal Peelite, Gladstone had followed his leader into political exile in 1846. Both his administrative skills and his ability as a speaker in the Commons remained widely admired, never more so than in 1852 when his lengthy attack destroyed the basis of Disraeli's Conservative budget.

In the confused politics of the 1850s, Whig and Conservative Prime Ministers alike attempted to recruit Gladstone to their ranks, believing that his support would greatly increase their Governments' stability. Lord Aberdeen's coalition (1852–5) made the first successful bid and Gladstone became Chancellor in December 1852 and, in 1853, produced one of the century's most celebrated budgets. His speech in parliament, lasting four-and-three-quarter hours, guaranteed his reputation as a financier and as a parliamentary speaker. To us, in the early twenty-first century, such a long speech seems unthinkable. But contemporaries were full of praise. As Lord Aberdeen wrote:

> The display of power was wonderful; it was agreed in all quarters that there had been nothing like the speech for many years, and that under the impression of his commanding eloquence the reception of the budget had been most favourable.

GLADSTONE'S 1853 BUDGET

The principles of Gladstone's budget were essentially Peelite. *Laissez-faire* and **retrenchment** were its keywords. The state should interfere with the nation's economic life as little as possible, and cut its own spending to a minimum. In practice, this meant the reduction or abolition of tariffs, the elimination of bureaucratic waste, and keeping a tight rein on defence expenditure.

retrenchment
money-saving,
cost-cutting

The scope of Gladstone's budget was impressive:

- income tax, despite its unpopularity, was maintained at 7d (3p)
- the threshold above which it was to be paid was lowered from £150 to £100
- almost 300 duties on goods were lowered or abolished
- Gladstone aimed at final abolition of income tax in 1860, anticipating that extra revenue to compensate for this would be generated by continued economic growth and the increasing consumption of 'luxuries' like beer and tobacco on which duties still fell.

> ## KEY ISSUE
>
> *Why was the 1853 Budget so important to Gladstone's career?*

The contributions made to the Exchequer by direct and indirect taxation were carefully balanced in the budget in order to reflect the respective abilities of the propertied classes and the workingman to pay. If government was seen to be even-handed, spreading the burden of taxation fairly between rich and poor, then class harmony would be promoted and the state's authority more readily accepted, even amongst those who had no vote. Here, as elsewhere, Gladstone was following Peel. Gladstone indeed relished the role of Chancellor, and helped to make Budget Day into a great piece of political theatre. His contemporaries believed that the 1853 budget had displayed a combination of precision, professionalism and far-sightedness to rival Peel himself. It confirmed his pre-eminence, both in financial matters and as a parliamentary speaker.

GLADSTONE AND THE CRIMEAN WAR 1854–6

However, Gladstone was never the easiest of colleagues. The Crimean War which, he believed, could have been avoided, wrecked his plans for retrenchment and made him struggle to balance the books. His ill-temper was aggravated by the threat of a Committee of Inquiry into the Government's mismanagement of the war, and he resigned in 1855. The Crimean War destroyed Aberdeen's Government and Gladstone handling of war finances left much to be desired. He was perhaps fortunate that his reputation as a wartime financier did not come under closer scrutiny.

See page 323–6 on the Crimean War

D *Gladstone's progress towards the Liberals*

Gladstone was out of government for four years, eventually returning as a Liberal Chancellor of the Exchequer in 1859. But there was nothing inevitable about Gladstone ultimately throwing his weight behind the Liberal cause. On three occasions in the 1850s, Lord Derby, the Conservative Party leader, tried to tempt him back to his Tory roots. But each time, though with some reluctance, Gladstone turned him down.

ANALYSIS

The 1850s: Gladstone's political options

GLADSTONE AND THE CONSERVATIVES IN THE 1850S

- Gladstone could not stomach the prospect of working with Disraeli. They were not merely rivals for pre-eminence: they came to loathe each other. Gladstone believed Disraeli's immorality and opportunism threatened to corrupt British politics. He never forgave Disraeli for the latter's savage attacks on Peel in 1846. Disraeli, in turn, regarded Gladstone as an insufferable and self-deceiving prig.
- Gladstone was highly ambitious, and was desperate to be in government. But the Tories practically never *were* in government. They lost every general election between 1841 and 1874! Purely for the sake of his own career, there was only one choice for Gladstone: the Liberals.
- Gladstone was also supremely conscious of his energies and abilities, which were going to waste while he was out of office (as he was for most of the 1850s). He shared with Peelite friends, and Radicals, an anxiety that vital British institutions – the ancient Universities, the Civil Service, and the Army – needed shaking out of their privileged complacency. The British performance in the Crimean War (1854–6) certainly gave no cause for confidence. Only a party with a stable parlia-

KEY ISSUE

Why did Gladstone eventually join the Liberals rather than re-join the Conservatives?

mentary majority and a broad popular mandate would be strong enough to take on the opposing vested interests. The 'Liberal Party' seemed capable of doing the job. By contrast, the Tories lacked both the power and the will to carry out vital reforms.

GLADSTONE AND THE LIBERALS

In three vital policy areas, Gladstone was nearer to the Liberal way of thinking than he was to the Conservatives.

- **First, religious policy.** In the 1840s, Gladstone had to abandon his early hopes that a revitalised Church of England might come to dominate the religious life of the whole nation. Instead, he was learning to live with, and make the most of, religious pluralism. British Liberalism, which combined a core of tolerant Anglicanism with distinctive Nonconformist influences, was ideally constituted to help Gladstone get the best out of all the strands of British Christianity. It was certainly more spiritually vital than mid-century Toryism.
- **Second, economic policy.** The 1853 budget had established Gladstone's reputation as Peel's political heir. Gladstone felt that the Tories could not match the Liberals in their commitment to the principles of Free Trade and prudent finance – a suspicion that Disraeli's shifty and abortive Budget of 1852 had confirmed. The Liberals clearly offered the best platform for the defence – and extension – of the principles of Peelite finance.
- **Third, foreign policy.** Gladstone took a great interest in Italian culture and politics. Until 1860, Italy was split up into a dozen states. They were mostly backward and almost all dependent – directly or indirectly – on Austrian military force to keep Italian nationalist and liberal forces down. Gladstone deplored this situation, and gave his full support to the cause of moderate Italian nationalism. Whigs, especially Palmerston, and Radicals felt the same: but the Tories seemed either lukewarm or opposed to Italian unification.

1859, GLADSTONE JOINS PALMERSTON

In April 1859, fighting broke out in northern Italy. Two months later leading Peelites, Radicals and Whigs, at a meeting in the Willis Rooms, expressed their solidarity with the Italian nationalists, and agreed to co-ordinate their efforts to bring down Derby's minority government. Many historians have regarded this meeting as marking the foundation of the Liberal Party. It is significant that Gladstone did not attend and, although the meeting led to the downfall of the Conservative Government, Gladstone actually voted *with* the Government.

It was later in 1859 that Gladstone accepted Palmerston's offer to become Chancellor of the Exchequer, despite strong reservations about

See page 178

Palmerston's personal reputation and his style of conducting foreign policy. Gladstone's personal decision, to enter Palmerston's government, thus uniting the Whigs with the last important Peelite, rather than the earlier Willis Rooms meeting, may be *the* significant moment in the emergence of the Liberal Party. Dislike of Disraeli, dissatisfaction with being out of power, the temptation of again being Chancellor may all have been compelling reasons for his momentous decision. With the years passing – he was now 50 – Gladstone wanted office. He was, in any event, increasingly aware of the power of public opinion and had to recognise Palmerston's immense reputation with the general public. His decision meant that the years of uncertainty were over and generally historians have identified 1859, if not the Willis Rooms meeting in particular, and the partnership of the leading Peelite with the Whigs, as the moment when the British Liberal Party was conceived. In 1859, however, Gladstone himself was probably advancing his own career rather than working to create a new political party.

CHANCELLOR, 1859–66

Gladstone was to be Palmerston's Chancellor for six years. His budgets of the 1860s continued the themes of *laissez-faire* and retrenchment proclaimed in his 1853 budget. Already by 1860, import duties had been abolished on all but 15 articles. Income tax was raised to 10d (4p) – but only as an emergency measure, to cover the financial mismanagement and military extravagance that Gladstone claimed had characterised government while he was out of office! To sweeten this pill, Gladstone promised its progressive reduction – which he was to achieve (income tax was at 6d by 1865). But for all his forecasts, its abolition was to prove elusive: little wars and war-scares just seemed to keep on happening.

There were some new features in the 1860 budget, like the abolition of the duties on paper, which had wide-ranging political consequences in allowing a considerable development of national and provincial newspapers. Also important was a treaty with France (1860) for mutual tariff reduction. Richard Cobden, one-time leader of the Anti-Corn Law League, negotiated this under Gladstone's guidance, at a time of great international tension between the two countries. Many, including Palmerston, believed war a distinct possibility. To Gladstone, the impetus the treaty would give to trade was less important than the prospect that greater trade would 'bind the two countries together by interest and affection'. Again, there was a moral dimension to Gladstone's economic policies.

Palmerston, however, did not share Gladstone's internationalism, or his hopes that the threat from France was to be so easily or cheaply defused. Accordingly, to his Chancellor's dismay, Palmerston decided to press on with a programme of naval construction and fortification that seemed set to wreck the prospects of tax reduction. The debate in Cabinet was intense and recurrent. Despite repeated threats of resignation, the ironclad ships were built. Gladstone retreated – and stayed in office.

> ## KEY ISSUE
>
> *Was Gladstone the 'creator' of mid-Victorian prosperity or simply fortunate to be Chancellor at a time of remarkable prosperity?*

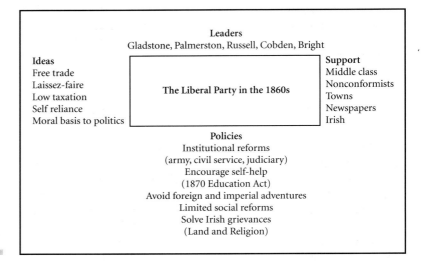

DIAGRAM 5

The Liberal Party in the 1860s

What had Gladstone achieved as Chancellor in the 1850s and 1860s? It can be argued that:

- he had made the Liberals the party of Free Trade, and low-taxing, low-spending government, as well as supremely competent administration
- he had strengthened his own reputation for technical expertise and gained the admiration of the political elite
- his tax cuts left more money in ordinary people's pockets. He was becoming a popular hero.

But on closer inspection, the scale of Gladstone's achievements can be questioned:

- the passion and drama with which Gladstone presented his budgets was remarkable but their contents were less so.
- Gladstone was the inheritor rather than the creator of a tradition of public finance. In the history of *laissez-faire* economics, Peel has greater claims to fame for his political courage. Has too much been claimed for the effect of Free Trade anyway? Economic historians now dispute how far it contributed to Britain's economic recovery in the 1840s and 1850s. The natural cycle of slump and boom may well have progressed without Peel's encouragement. Even if Peel can claim to be one of the architects of mid-Victorian prosperity, Gladstone as Chancellor cannot.
- it was his good fortune to be responsible for administering the Government's finances for much of the boom of the 1850s and 1860s. Then, a dynamic economy guaranteed the Chancellor his surpluses: he had the pleasant task of deciding how to give them away. Gladstone was a superb administrator, with a remarkable vision of the

social and moral implications of his policies. His work as Chancellor elevated him to the threshold of party leadership. But we must not forget that he was also lucky enough to be in the right place at the right time.

E *Gladstone's growing popularity: 'The People's William'*

With his second spell as Chancellor (1859–66), Gladstone's place near the top of British politics was secure, but until now he had been a strangely isolated figure. All acknowledged his great talents. But many – Whigs as well as Tories – found his arrogance and self-righteousness intolerable. He was also highly unpredictable. Salisbury, the future Conservative Prime Minister, wrote that 'no psychologist that has ever existed' could fathom his motives. Less kindly, Clarendon (later Gladstone's Foreign Secretary!) put the rumour about that a leading medical authority had claimed that Gladstone was so imbalanced that he would die insane.

KEY ISSUE

Why was Gladstone's growing popular reputation so important to him and yet so controversial?

The explosive growth of popular support for Gladstone in the 1860s made the suspicions and resentments of rivals largely irrelevant for the progress of his career. He became 'The People's William', building up an extraordinary personal relationship with large sections of the British middle and working classes. This was in surprising contrast to the course of his earlier political career, first as the Duke of Newcastle's man at Newark and then as MP for Oxford University with its entirely graduate electorate and its tradition that parliamentary candidates did not canvass for votes.

A feature of the 1850s had been the rise of a skilled working-class, with its new model trade unions. From the early 1860s, Gladstone was in contact with their representatives, and was invariably impressed by their sense of 'responsibility' – for example, by their thrifty desire to make use of his new Post Office Savings Bank, established in 1861. Equally important, this 'labour aristocracy' believed they had an ally in Gladstone.

His newly found popular reputation combined with his administrative abilities, made Gladstone the likeliest successor to the Liberal leadership in the 1860s. He now saw a virtuous force for change in the people at large who flocked to his meetings. This was to be more than a means to personal advancement: it was to provide a moral dimension to his political life. Gladstone believed that the morality of the crowd could be tapped and channelled, to reinvigorate and energise government and give it the strength to tackle problems that, since the fall of Peel, it had mostly seemed too feeble to face. This idea of the moral energy of the masses driving the state on the right moral path replaced Gladstone's earlier and impractical vision of the Church of England as the conscience of the nation. In part, the working men who thronged to see him were simply flattered by his presence: Gladstone was one of the very first nineteenth-century politicians to condescend to address the people at all. But what made Gladstone unique on these public occasions was his moral grandeur. The people sensed Gladstone's passionate commitment to justice, and he flattered their growing sense of personal independence and moral integrity by inviting them to share the trials of his fight for what was right.

Gladstone was beginning to earn something of the reputation of a Radical. The abolition of paper duties, finally forced through by Gladstone in 1861, was important here. These 'taxes on knowledge' had long been resented by radicals, for they tended to put the price of newspapers beyond the reach of the working classes and allowed *The Times* to dominate the formation of public opinion. The fact that the House of Lords at first resisted Gladstone's plans only added to his reputation as an opponent of privilege.

The popular press proved eager to repay Gladstone for ending the near-monopoly of *The Times*. They gave his speeches and public tours generous and approving coverage. With the circulation of the *Daily Telegraph* – then a Liberal paper – leaping to 150 000 in 1861 (more than twice that of *The Times*), Gladstone could afford to lose the latter's support. Particularly important was the role of the rapidly expanding radical provincial newspapers like the *Leeds Mercury* and the *Newcastle Chronicle*. These were to become the essential means of communication between Gladstone and his new audience, and were also to prove powerful local opinion formers in their own right.

WAS GLADSTONE TOO RADICAL FOR THE WHIGS?

By now, Gladstone's colleagues were becoming alarmed. Whigs prided themselves on their responsiveness to the genuine grievances of the people, but they had no time for **demagogues** and viewed popular excitement with the greatest suspicion. Cynics were likely to see Gladstone's 'moral grandeur' as career-serving hypocrisy. To some, it seemed as though Gladstone was set on becoming the mob's pet. In the 1860s the question of further reform of the parliamentary system was again being raised, inside and outside Parliament. The Whigs' worst fears about Gladstone were confirmed in 1864 when he made the following startling declaration:

> every man who is not presumably incapacitated by some consideration of personal unfitness or of political danger is morally entitled to come within the pale of the Constitution.

For a moment, Gladstone had sounded like an advocate of manhood suffrage and, in the uproar that followed, it was easy to miss the significance of what might be the severe limitations to his proposed extension of the franchise. Palmerston, for one, was furious. He expressly denied that 'every sane and not disqualified man [had] a moral right to vote'. After all, as he had earlier quipped, it was scum that always came to the

---

KEY ISSUE

Why, in the 1860s did some Whigs come to distrust Gladstone?

demagogue a political agitator appealing to popular wishes or prejudices

Q

1. *What do you think is meant by 'the pale of the Constitution'?*
2. *Why might some men be excluded from voting?*

top in democracies. Gladstone was reprimanded: his speech had been fit for a radical agitator, not a member of the Queen's Cabinet.

Only Palmerston's death in 1865 ended this battle of wills. Lord John Russell took over as the Liberal leader, with Gladstone as his deputy. 'Little Johnnie', who had been one of the Whigs' heroes in the crisis surrounding the 1832 Reform Act, hoped to end his career with a matching triumph, and gave Gladstone the job of devising a new measure for parliamentary reform. Gladstone introduced a Reform Bill in 1866 and, if he had managed to get it passed into law, then his career as the People's William would have been fully realised. However, it was far less radical than a quick reading of his 1864 speech might have suggested it would be. Nevertheless some right-wing Whigs, bewildered and resentful at Gladstone's radicalism and unpredictability, helped to defeat his Bill and split the Liberals. A year later, in 1867, it was Disraeli's extraordinary political manoeuvrings that secured a (surprisingly radical) instalment of parliamentary reform.

4 ⌐ DISRAELI AND THE CONSERVATIVES, 1846–68

A *The Conservatives in the aftermath of Corn Law Repeal*

In 1846, Peel had no intention of undermining the world which the Tories held dear. But he believed it was in the national interest, and the interest of the aristocracy itself, for the traditional order to be defended with greater flexibility and imagination. Stubborn and undiluted resistance to change would be self-defeating. In particular, Peel believed it was time the Government recognised the vital contribution which industry was making to the life of the nation. By 1846, he had concluded that the Corn Laws – which gave special protection to agriculture – could no longer be justified. With Whig help, Peel repealed them in 1846.

His backbenchers felt utterly betrayed. Repeal broke every promise they had made to their rural constituents, and seemed to threaten farmers with economic ruin. In some of the most bitter debates ever heard in Parliament – in which Benjamin Disraeli emerged as the unlikely champion of the protectionists – the Conservative Party was split in two. Peel's own backbenchers overthrew his leadership, and the most embittered helped to vote him out of office. They then reconstituted their party along protectionist lines.

The consequences of this were catastrophic for the Conservatives. For, in destroying Peel, they condemned themselves to almost three decades in the political wilderness.

> **KEY ISSUE**
>
> *Why did Corn Law Repeal have such a devastating effect on the Conservative Party?*

For details on Corn Law repeal see Chapter 6, pages 155–65

There were various reasons for this:

- practically all the men of administrative talent – the 'brains' of the party – followed Peel. Voters knew that there was not enough ability and experience left in the party for a competent Cabinet to be formed out of its leading members
- by expelling Peel, they had reduced themselves to a narrowly agrarian party, incapable of speaking for the wider nation. Although the land had been at the core of the old party, wealthy financiers and merchants, as well as a few great industrialists, like Peel's own father, had supported the Tories in the past. But they would not give their votes to a mere rump of 'agricultural fanatics'
- the Conservatives appeared to be resentful and backward-looking reactionaries. The Whigs, the Liberals and their Peelite friends were optimistic and positive-thinking by comparison: in a word, they stood for progress. And the fact was that the Whigs matched the mood of mid-century Britain so much better.

The 1850s and 1860s were the great 'years of expansion'. Free trade worked: the British economy dominated the world as no other had done before, or has done since. The fruit of this prosperity was unparalleled social harmony, and a confidence about the prospects of future progress which is hard for us even to imagine. It must have been all the more striking to Victorians, coming after the despair of the late 1830s and early 1840s, when at some awful moments Britain had seemed on the verge of social disintegration. Having jettisoned Peel, the Tories apparently had nothing to say of relevance to a Britain newly at peace with itself. The Tory backbenchers' gut instinct had been that industrial society was not viable, and they had turned their back on the world created by Manchester. But Manchester represented the future – and it worked.

The Conservatives would have to find means of coming to terms with the new Britain; otherwise they faced a future simply as a rump party representing nothing but the declining agrarian interest. It was not until 1874 that a Conservative Government, with a working Commons majority, was elected. During those frustrating years Disraeli, the man who bore the single greatest responsibility for splitting the party, emerged against all the odds to become its leader and, in 1874, Prime Minister commanding a substantial majority in the Commons.

PROFILE

AN UNLIKELY LEADER: BENJAMIN DISRAELI (1804–77)

The Conservative Party has never had a less likely leader than Disraeli. He was a Jew by birth in an age when anti-Semitism was far more widespread and 'respectable' than it is today, and when Conservative backbenchers were overwhelmingly Anglican and fiercely committed to the defence of the privileges of the Church of England. His background was literary rather than landed: his father was a celebrated author and 'man of letters'. He was poorly educated, at a string of obscure private schools, and so totally lacked the contacts immediately available to Gladstone.

Disraeli was not only the great outsider of Victorian politics: he was its great latecomer. He had turned 40 years of age before he won any recognition as a significant figure in the House of Commons. But Disraeli was not easily put off. Lord Blake, in his great biography (see Bibliography on page 209) has characterised the young Disraeli as a man of 'immense ambition consumed with an almost insolent determination to make his mark'. He was convinced of his own genius and desperately wanted the rest of the world to acknowledge it. Quite where or how he was to do this seemed almost irrelevant.

Instead, Disraeli managed to convince most of those in respectable society that he was a scoundrel, shamelessly ambitious and utterly untrustworthy. For 15 years, until his marriage in 1839 to a wealthy widow 12 years his senior, he lived recklessly. He got involved in the promotion of shady South American mining companies and in the launching of a new daily newspaper – both of which landed him chronically in debt. After suffering a nervous breakdown, he went on a 16-month tour of the Mediterranean and experienced an intriguing variety of sexual and narcotic delights, of the sort that would keep one of today's tabloid newspapers busy with exposés for months. His flamboyant style, brilliant conversation and spectacular appearance (one outfit featured 'green velvet trousers, silver buckles, lace at his wrists, and his hair in ringlets') created a sensation – not always agreeable – wherever he went. His love life, too – which included a passionate and public affair with the wife of a baronet – further increased his notoriety.

In the early 1830s, however, a more definite interest in politics began to emerge and, in 1837, with the help of a good deal of bribery, he was elected MP for Maidstone. The Commons was now to provide Disraeli with a new stage on which to make the sensation he craved. But Disraeli's first years in the Commons were neither happy nor successful. His maiden speech was nothing short of a disaster. His dandified appearance, flamboyant manner and flowery language provoked sections of the House to shout him down. He soon learnt that this new stage required a new style, and he began to acquire the virtues of dullness and sobriety.

His ambition remained, however. No sooner had Peel become Prime Minister in 1841 than Disraeli was writing to him begging for office. Peel had many more urgent or deserving calls on his patronage, and no government post was found. Had Disraeli enjoyed greater fortune, his attitude towards Peel over the next few years would almost certainly have been very different.

Q

Why did Disraeli fail to make a real mark in politics before 1846?

AUTHOR OF 'VIVIAN GREY'

PICTURE 20
Sketch of Disraeli

KEY ISSUE

What did Disraeli's books, and his links to 'Young England', contribute to the future of Conservatism?

paternalism looking after the welfare and ordering the lives of the people as a father would for his family

B 'Young England' and the Origins of Disraelian Conservatism

As an outsider entering Parliament, Disraeli had to find some ways of making his mark. A group of young aristocratic Conservative MPs, calling themselves Young England, soon fell under his spell. Young England was as much a dining club as a parliamentary group. Its members delighted in each other's wit and humour. It had no political programme but it believed in resurrecting a style of aristocratic **paternalism** quite different from Peel's cold and unsentimental brand of Conservatism, which seemed obsessed with theories of political economy at the expense of any feeling for community or tradition.

In the 1840s, Young England's aristocratic members were in part the audience, in part the inspiration, for Disraeli's ideas about the true nature of Toryism. According to Disraeli, England's history was largely the story of the battle between a selfish group of Whigs, on the one hand, and the Tory aristocracy of England, supported by and representing the English people as a whole, on the other. Disraeli insisted that the Whigs were a great threat to the freedoms and traditions of Englishmen. To Disraeli, the widely hated new Poor Law and the local government 'reforms' of the mid-1830s were examples of this. The Whigs were conspiring with Radicals to strip the traditional English rulers – the aristocracy and gentry – of their proper influence and power. The ordinary people of England would thus be left at the mercy of a harsh, unfeeling, centralising state. Just as bad was the Whigs' attack on the Anglican Church in Ireland. The parliamentary alliance struck up between the Whigs and Irish Catholics in 1835 enabled Disraeli to portray them as the un-English party ready to sacrifice other people's privileges and property to stay in power. Disraeli's strategy here – however unfair – clearly anticipates his later attacks on Gladstone's Liberal Party, which Disraeli portrayed as a 'front' for the operations of subversive Radicals, dependent for its hold on power on Irish and Nonconformist votes.

TORY DEMOCRACY

All this cleared the ground for a major redefinition of what the Tory Party stood for: it was 'the national party ... the really democratic party of England'. Here is the origin of the concept most closely associated with Disraelian Conservatism: Tory Democracy.

Disraeli did not, of course, mean that the Tories should be the instruments for transferring power to the working classes. But he was implying that the Tories were the natural leaders of the people and that the party should trust the people's instinctive patriotism and conservatism. Such ideas would have seemed startling and novel to Disraeli's audience in the 1830s. To most Tories then, standing up to the threat posed by 'democracy' was the only strategy that made political sense. But Disraeli seemed to be suggesting that the best way to defeat the Whigs was to outflank them by seeking an alliance with the people against the Whig elite.

Disraeli was soon developing these ideas, and communicating them to a wider audience. In the 1840s, he produced his celebrated trilogy of Young England novels: *Coningsby* (1844), *Sybil* (1845), and *Tancred* (1847). Together they constitute an analysis of the 'Condition of England' in the troubled 1840s, and a vision of how English society might be refashioned along more harmonious lines.

Class conflict and the chances for survival of the aristocratic order were Disraeli's great themes. Some Tories believed that Chartism had simply to be crushed, and that industrial capitalism threatened social stability and the political power of the landed classes. Disraeli was neither as negative nor as pessimistic. It was true that England had become, in his words, 'two nations, ignorant of each others' habits, thoughts and feelings: THE RICH AND THE POOR'.

But Disraeli believed he had identified the remedies for social disintegration:

- First, a more charismatic style of political leadership was required, to guide the people and convince them that those in power understood their needs and problems.
- Secondly, at the local level, he demanded a more paternalistic approach from the wealthy to the poor: factory owners had just as big a responsibility to their workers as landed aristocrats had towards their 'peasants'.

Through the provision of schools, churches and better housing, class conflict would be dissolved and radical agitation destroyed. Thus would a true spirit of community be restored, in the parish and in the nation.

The political significance of Disraeli's novels

Robert Blake

Disraeli's great biographer believes that the novels have little political importance. Their essential function was to amuse and entertain. In no way do the novels constitute a basis for practical politics. As far as Disraeli did have a political purpose, so Blake believes, it was to condemn Peel for his supposed failings. This was merely a personal vendetta which Disraeli had been pursuing since Peel had turned down his bids for a post in the Government.

John Vincent,

John Vincent, however, has argued that there is much more to the novels than this. They may not contain a blueprint for the social legislation of Disraeli's ministry of 30 years later but they permanently shaped his political outlook. We will find, in the 1870s, a concern for

HISTORIANS' DEBATE

See Bibliography on page 209 for titles of these authors' books

the rights of labour and the living and working conditions of the poor. We will find, in Disraeli's style of leadership, an attempt to capture the public imagination with a calculated flamboyance and theatricality. Not least, we will find that Disraeli still believed that the statesman's greatest function was to create a spirit of community, so that English society could live in harmony with itself, and be spared the aggressive individualism of Liberals, the class-bitterness of Radicals, and the self-righteous separatism of Nonconformity. Thus, society would recover its true nature as one large, extended, happy family. In this analysis, the Young England novels remain the single most important source for the myths and imagery which constituted later Disraelian Conservatism.

C *Disraeli* vs *Peel 1844–6*

KEY ISSUE

Why was Disraeli's attack on Peel so important for both his party and himself?

See pages 151–3 for more on the tension between Peel and his party

In terms of practical politics in the 1840s, the impact of Young England as a parliamentary faction was very limited. But through Disraeli's novels their ideas had a wider impact on the Victorian public. Key phrases and arguments passed into the currency of political debate, where they had a more lasting impact than any politician's 'sound-bite' does today. Disraeli was beginning to perform one of the functions of the statesman in the age of the popular press: he was, through his writings, helping to shape the public mind. But, unlike Gladstone, he made no attempt to *speak* to public audiences.

By 1844 Disraeli's own career began its upturn in the Commons. Tory backbenchers were becoming infuriated by Peel's arrogance and dictatorial ways. Twice that year he had demanded that they reverse their votes and thereby undo defeats they had previously inflicted on the Government. When Disraeli defiantly proclaimed that he had no intention of 'changing my vote within 48 hours at the menace of a minister', he was greeted with great applause. Disraeli had arrived.

The inarticulate country gentlemen who peopled the backbenches had made a perplexing discovery. Disraeli's race, his manner, and his scandalous lifestyle as a young man, must have raised feelings of profound distaste and suspicion amongst these backbenchers but he alone seemed able to give voice to their feelings of anger and resentment towards Peel. Peel had appeared unassailable – the complete master of government business, speaking with the authority of a man who had spent three decades at the centre of public life. But he could not cope with Disraeli's cutting sarcasm. Whether reminding the House of Peel's questionable behaviour at the time of Catholic Emancipation, prophesying the Repeal of the Corn Laws or mocking Peel for his change of mind over Maynooth, Disraeli, again and again, made Peel squirm – a spectacle which delighted the Tory squires. Observers were stunned to see the great statesman reduced to 'nervous twitchings', and quite incapable of hiding his deep annoyance as his tormentor stirred the House to 'delirious laughter' at his expense.

Disraeli's campaign was to culminate in the bitter debates over the Repeal of the Corn Laws and the defeat of Peel's ministry. The style of his attacks made them all but unanswerable. It is worth noting that Peel's disciple, Gladstone, was out of the Commons for six months during the crucial debates.

Unable to intervene to save his leader, Gladstone never forgave Disraeli for the devastating attacks on Peel. Many commentators, however, have found the attacks lacking in substance. They have speculated that Disraeli was motivated by despair at his own prospects and a desire to revenge himself on the man who had blocked his career. In fact, there is a consistent and plausible theme of constitutional argument running through the speeches. Disraeli's claim was that Peel, by betraying the principles on which he was elected and ignoring the claims of party, was undermining the whole parliamentary system. Peel associated himself with a different tradition of government, asserting that it was the first duty of the Prime Minister and the Government to serve the sovereign, and through the sovereign, the interests of the nation as a whole, even if this meant riding roughshod over party interests and loyalties.

In Disraeli's eyes, probably the most damaging of Peel's deficiencies was his lack of vision, imagination and charisma. Instead of creating public opinion, Peel was following it: to be more precise, when he repealed the Corn Laws he was letting the arguments of the Anti-Corn Law League dictate the Government's economic policy. Peel had not merely betrayed his followers and tried to undermine the function of party: he had abdicated the greatest responsibility of leadership itself and had left the people to create their own leaders – or as Disraeli put it, to 'fashion their own divinities'.

Disraeli's attacks on Peel may well have been motivated by personal dislike. But it is wrong to dismiss them as *merely* personal. For it was Peel's defects of personality as much as the demerits of his policies, which made him, in Disraeli's eyes, unfit to lead the party or to govern the nation.

See pages 160–5 for debate over Repeal of the Corn Laws

KEY ISSUE

How did Disraeli's view of the duties of the Prime Minister differ from Peel's?

D *Conservative frustrations, 1846–65*

Although Disraeli had been the outstanding Protectionist speaker in the Repeal debates he lacked the authority and the personal reputation to emerge immediately as leader of the Protectionist backbenchers who now formed the backbone of the Conservative Party. This role fell to Lord Stanley, the only member of Peel's Cabinet to resign on the Repeal issue. In 1851, on his father's death he became Earl of Derby and, as Lord Derby, was Prime Minister in three minority Conservative governments.

Reunification with the Peelites was impossible until after 1850 because of the total division between them over the Repeal issue. The Peelites much preferred to keep the Whigs in power and so protect their

KEY ISSUE

Why, in the 1850s, did the Conservatives face a bleak future?

Free trade achievement than to flirt with the remaining protectionist Conservatives and put all that they had achieved in 1846 at risk.

After 1850 most Conservatives came to accept that Corn Law Repeal had not been the disaster that they had predicted it would be and that, in any event, repeal was now irreversible. At this point Disraeli himself became the main single obstacle to reunification of the two wings of Conservatism. His brilliant attacks in 1846 on Peel meant that the Peelites detested him. Peel's early death in 1850 strengthened Peelite revulsion. Disraeli's rise in Conservative ranks strengthened Peelite suspicions of his untrustworthiness and thrusting ambition and was compounded by a streak of anti-Semitism and moral outrage against the 'outsider'. Even Conservative backbenchers did not trust or warm to him and it took five years for him to emerge as party leader in the Commons. He overcame all the prejudices against him within his own party for the simple reason that the departure of the Peelites had left the Conservative front bench denuded of talent. The brilliance of Disraeli's attack on Peel had destroyed the unity of the party: it also ensured that he became indispensable as spokesman for that majority of Conservative MPs who had refused to follow Peel. In the 1850s he and his party leader Derby faced a bleak future.

ANALYSIS

The crisis of mid-Victorian Conservatism

● Between 1841 and 1874 the Conservative Party did not win one general election
● On three occasions – in 1852, 1858 and 1866 – they *did* take office. But these were minority governments entirely dependent for their power on internal Whig divisions. On each occasion the Whigs soon reunited to turn them out.
● When the Conservatives did get into power, they faced the contradictory tasks of legislating to please their own backbenchers and to prove to the electorate that they were a genuine national political party and not a mere agricultural pressure group.
● When Disraeli was made Chancellor of the Exchequer in 1852, he could not return to protectionism: such a move would immediately reunite the opposition groups in the Commons, and the Government would be defeated. But his attempts to find subtler means of keeping his backbenchers happy were denounced by Whigs and Peelites as unorthodox, and the Conservatives were defeated anyway. This was the time when Gladstone launched an overwhelming attack on Disraeli's budget, opening three decades of often bitter public rivalry between the two. By contrast, Gladstone's own budget, the following year, was a brilliant success.
● In 1859, Disraeli tried to improve the Tories' image with a modest proposal to extend the franchise. But his Cabinet col-

leagues diluted it even more, so as not to frighten the Tory backbenchers. The consequence was that Disraeli's Reform Bill ended up looking so half-hearted that neither Whigs nor Radicals (and the Tories' minority Government needed the support of some members of these groups in the House of Commons if it was to survive), nor the wider electorate, could summon any enthusiasm for it. Soon, the Tories were out again.

● Worse was to come. Palmerston's spell as Prime Minister from 1859 to 1865 was a disaster for the Tories. He curbed his Radical left-wing, thus preventing any unsettling domestic legislation, while his aggressive, headline-catching foreign policy guaranteed him massive popular support. The Tory Party seemed redundant. By this time Derby, Disraeli's 'chief', seemed to agree and was quite happy for Palmerston to remain in power.

See pages 320–7 for Palmerston's foreign policy

Disraeli's real breakthrough only came with Palmerston's death in 1865. The latter's replacement as Whig/Liberal leader was the aged Lord Russell – vain, unreliable and impulsive. Russell was anxious to cap his political career with a second instalment of parliamentary reform. This would disturb the more cautious Whigs. Even better for the Conservatives, Russell's obvious heir was not a Whig at all but Gladstone – intense, unpredictable, and showing Radical tendencies. It looked at last as though Conservative fortunes were going to pick up.

5 ⌐ 1867: THE SECOND REFORM ACT

A *Political turmoil, 1865–8*

It seemed inevitable that Palmerston's death would bring major changes to Westminster. But no one could have predicted all the extraordinary twists and turns of party politics that the next three years were to bring. That Russell and Gladstone would make a bid for parliamentary reform was expected. That in doing so they would run the risk of frightening off some of their more cautious supporters, split their party and lose office, was always possible. But that Derby and Disraeli would then bring a more radical Bill than Russell's and Gladstone's before Parliament, and in the course of its passage through the Commons, accept amendment after amendment until a total of over one million new electors were enfranchised, was inconceivable. But incredibly, the Conservatives, the natural party of reaction, were to do just this, and so revolutionise the Constitution. At the end of this tale, the emergence of the 'Jew Adventurer' Disraeli as Prime Minister and leader of England's landed, Anglican party, was ample confirmation that the world had been turned upside down.

B *The pressure for reform*

KEY ISSUE

Why did parliamentary reform become an important political issue after 1865?

By the mid 1860s, there was general agreement that a further, moderate instalment of parliamentary reform might be prudent.

- There were over five million adult males in England and Wales, but less than one million of them had the vote.
- Despite changes in the geographical distribution of population since the 1832 Reform Act, there had been no redistribution of seats and, of course the many anomalies left in 1832 still remained, a situation summed up in the remarkable statistic that one half of the borough constituency population of England and Wales was represented by a mere 34 MPs and the other half by 300 MPs.
- It was widely believed that the make-up and attitudes of many members of the working class had undergone a profound transformation since the days of Chartism. They deserved the vote, not of course as a right, but as a well-earned privilege. Of course, there was no question of making Britain into a democracy. But it would be safe to bring this labour aristocracy within the franchise. These were reckoned to be sober, upright and thrifty citizens.

Many Victorians thought it was vital to distinguish between the respectable working class and the feared and despised 'residuum' – the unskilled and semi-criminal proletarian under-class. The habits of the latter were drunken, violent and improvident. They took no interest in the life of the nation, and had they been foolishly given the vote too, would either have sold it for beer, or become prey to demagogues.

Quite how the franchise could be set to give the vote to the virtuous while still denying it to the rest was a thorny technical problem that was to trouble Gladstone and pro-reform Conservatives alike.

There was less agreement about what purposes enfranchisement should serve:

- The conservative argument, found amongst both Tories and Whigs, would have been familiar to Earl Grey in 1830. It was foolish to continue to exclude intelligent, responsible and property-owning elements of society from the parliamentary process: it was the surest way to turn them into revolutionaries.
- Liberals like Gladstone, and the more progressive Whigs, agreed with this, but added some more positive notes to the argument. Under Palmerston Parliament seemed to have grown sleepy and the executive passive. A widened electorate might re-energise politics.
- Radicals like Bright put this last point more aggressively. Two decades before, they had been convinced that the Repeal of the Corn Laws was bound to lead to the political dominance of the progressive middle class. In fact, the aristocratic constitution had proved exasperatingly resilient. Cabinets were no less aristocratic in their

make-up, the Commons remained dominated by landowners and/or relatives of peers in the Lords, and the distribution of seats still left the great industrial towns under-represented A wider franchise might be the first step towards other constitutional reforms.

The sort of enfranchisement the Radicals wanted was a good deal more far-reaching than anything Gladstone, let alone the Conservatives and many Whigs, would happily contemplate. Radical demands were designed to inaugurate a new era of far-reaching institutional reform that would show no mercy to the bastions of the old order such as the Anglican Church, the ancient Universities or the Army. These far-reaching ambitions made it all the more surprising that, in1867, Disraeli was to make so many concessions to the Radicals in the final weeks of his Reform Bill's passage through the Commons.

C *1866, Failure of the Liberal Reform Bill*

GLADSTONE'S PROPOSALS

When Gladstone began to prepare the Liberal Reform Bill in 1866, he hit a variety of problems. It proved very difficult to construct a measure that would siphon off the respectable working classes and leave 'the residuum' behind, because the level of rents or rates – the two most obvious measures by which to set the franchise – varied so much from region to region. To complicate the matter further, it was discovered that up to a quarter of the electorate were already from the working classes: mid-Victorian prosperity had already brought them within the £10 borough franchise of the 1832 Reform Act. Gladstone grew nervous. If the vote were to be given to those men who paid at least £6 annual rent, which was his first intention, he calculated that another 250 000 workers would be added to the electorate. This would make it possible for the working class to dominate many boroughs, a prospect which the Whigs would find intolerable. So, in his Bill, Gladstone settled on a £7 rental qualification, which would enfranchise 100 000 less than first intended. Reducing the county voting qualification from the 1832 rented property value of £50 to £14 would add about 170 000 to the county electorate, but this was less alarming as they were reckoned to be middle class, safe and, thankfully, generally Liberal.

WHIG REBELLION

Gladstone's caution was poorly rewarded. In June 1866, some 30 Whigs, encouraged by Disraeli, rebelled and defeated his Bill. Their motives were mixed. Their leading spokesman, Robert Lowe, feared that Gladstone had still gone too far, and that the rule of property and intelligence, which had been the glory of the Victorian parliament, would be swept away by a democratic torrent of corruption, demagogy and naked class-interest. Others Whigs, while sharing these anxieties, were especially concerned about the way in which Gladstone (whose personal arrogance they considered offensive in itself) seemed to be leading Palmerston's old party down unwelcome, unpredictable Radical paths. By rejecting his Reform Bill they would slap him down, and open up the possibility of reconstructing party allegiance and leadership along more conservative lines.

CONSERVATIVE RESPONSE

Derby and Disraeli were pleased to find the Liberals collapsing into division and confusion. But they had to be very careful about how they proceeded. Many Whigs now expected the creation of a coalition government of conservative-minded Liberals and liberal-minded Conservatives, who together could resist any radical demands. Such a 'fusion', however, had few attractions for either of the established Conservative leaders. Derby feared it would result in a dilution of the traditional Tory commitment to defend the privileges of the Church of England. Disraeli knew that it would end any possibility of his succeeding the ageing Derby as party leader. The negotiations with the Whig defectors came to nothing. The Conservatives' distinctive identity and Disraeli's ambitions were therefore preserved and a minority Conservative government took office in late June 1866.

> **KEY ISSUE**
>
> *Why were the Conservatives so determined to carry a parliamentary reform measure?*

D *The Conservative reform, 1867*

Perhaps surprisingly, it was the Conservative leader, Derby, based in the Lords, who won round the flamboyant Disraeli to the merits of a Conservative reform measure, if only to prevent Gladstone returning with even more radical proposals. It would of course be Disraeli's responsibility to carry the measure through the Commons. He would have to satisfy the Cabinet, Conservative backbenchers and at least some of the opposition MPs, who made up a majority of the Commons. It would be difficult for him to make a decision about who was to be given the vote in the boroughs, which would satisfy these various groups.

DISRAELI'S ORIGINAL PROPOSALS

Disraeli provided a deceptively simple answer: all male ratepayers in the boroughs would get the vote, a far more radical proposal than Gladstone had advanced. Under Disraeli's original proposals it was estimated that 400 000 new voters would be added to the approximately one million who already had the franchise. There would then be safeguards against the working class having too much electoral power, an issue that concerned many politicians, with a series of devices (so-called 'fancy franchises') giving the better educated and the wealthy more than one vote. In these original proposals the greatest safeguard against urban elections being swamped by working-class voters was, however, that only those who paid their rates directly, as opposed to paying them through their landlords as part of their rent, would be enfranchised. This device alone would deny the vote to a further 400 000 working-men, known as 'compound ratepayers'.

THE PASSAGE OF THE CONSERVATIVE REFORM

Four points should be noted. The Conservatives:

- had come to power with no thought-out reform plan in mind: Disraeli's proposals were hastily and inadequately improvised
- were, however, determined to deny Gladstone and the Liberals the political triumph of carrying a reform measure
- had, at an early stage, publicly proposed a ratepayer suffrage, after which the pressure of reform opinion, inside and outside Parliament, made it very difficult for them to abandon it and retain any political credibility
- were in a minority in the Commons so Disraeli's 'safeguards' would be very difficult to maintain.

The debates, the political intrigue and parliamentary manoeuvres that followed were very complex and are probably not worth mastering in detail. Hard-line Conservatives such as Cranborne (on his father's death he became Lord Salisbury and, in 1885, Prime Minister) had believed that all reform should be resisted and were deeply suspicious of Disraeli's proposals, which they thought to be a dangerous gamble. General Peel, Secretary for War and Sir Robert Peel's son, threatened to resign, Disraeli wavered and talked of a £5 qualification being substituted but Queen Victoria persuaded General Peel to stay and household suffrage was restored. Now Cranborne threatened to resign and Disraeli in response talked of a £6 franchise; other Conservatives felt that this was playing into Gladstone's hands and urged a return to the original proposals. Disraeli and Derby agreed and again prepared to defy their own diehards, at which point Cranborne and others finally did resign. The Government, however, persisted and the final details of a Reform Bill were cobbled together in one day of frantic meetings on their way to Cabinet approval and presentation to the Commons.

In the Commons, there was three months of heated debate and Disraeli was faced with a barrage of Liberal amendments, so he casually dropped the elaborate safeguards built into his original proposals. But still he was committed to carrying a Conservative reform measure and so thwarting Gladstone. He did this brilliantly.

All contemporaries agreed that Disraeli's performance in Parliament was dazzling. He managed to give the impression of being in calm control even when he was being rushed into improvisation and concession. He could conjure up statistics to befuddle critics or, in the turn of a phrase, make 'household suffrage' sound homely, solid and respectable, rather than forbidding, democratic and revolutionary. In stark contrast to Peel, he kept in close touch with his backbenchers, who the more happily accepted his authority. Disraeli warned them that defeat would mean the dissolution of Parliament and that that meant an election, which in turn, meant Gladstone. Instead, they could enjoy the spectacle of Gladstone reeling under the impact of their leader's jibes and sarcasms. To some Tories, seeing Gladstone outmanoeuvred and outwitted at every turn of the debate, was itself worth the price of reform. Furthermore, the exercise of power and the pleasure of being on the winning side were novel and intoxicating experiences for his party too. The Conservatives had achieved nothing for over 20 years. Now the party was, at last, showing that it *could* govern, and also deal decisively with a thorny problem that the Liberals had proved themselves incapable of solving. They could, at last, claim to be a national party again.

PICTURE 21

'The honest potboy', a cartoon from Punch

Q

1. *Who do you think are 'the inspectors' looking through the window?*
2. *Why do both Disraeli and Derby want a 'good measure' of reform in 1867?*

THE HONEST POTBOY.

DERBY (*aside*). " DON'T FROTH IT UP THIS TIME, BEN. GOOD MEASURE—THE INSPECTORS HAVE THEIR EYE ON US."

The terms of the Second Reform Act, 1867

The franchise:

- in parliamentary boroughs, all adult male owners and occupiers of houses could now vote; lodgers occupying lodgings worth £10 a year could vote; all had to prove 12 months residence
- in county constituencies, adult male owners and long (60 year) leaseholders of property worth £5 a year and occupiers of land worth £12 a year could vote.

Constituencies:

- 45 seats were taken from the smaller parliamentary boroughs (population under 10 000)
- 19 seats were given to larger boroughs including a third member for the four largest provincial cities
- 25 seats went to the largest counties
- London University was given one seat.

6 ⌐ WHY WAS THE SECOND REFORM ACT PASSED?

A *Because of fear of revolution?*

KEY ISSUE

How and why have historians differed in their views on why the Conservatives forced through such a radical Reform Act?

If Disraeli's manoeuvres in 1867 were intended to defuse the threat of revolution then this alone could justify what he did. He would have acted in the same tradition as those who had carried the Reform Act of 1832. Historians have disagreed over whether this was the case.

It is certainly true that in 1866–7 Bright and other Radicals built up a mass movement for reform. They aimed to exert popular pressure on Westminster and, through their 'monster demonstrations', coerce the MPs into conceding a substantial increase in the franchise. The activities of the contemporary pressure groups, the trade union based Reform League and the Bright's more middle-class Reform Union, were certainly on Derby's and Disraeli's minds. But it is very difficult to detect any sense in their letters or diaries that they were being forced to concede household suffrage by any perceived threat of revolution. One historian suggested that 'disturbance near the houses of the wealthier classes convinced conservative opinion that electoral reform could not be delayed'. This was a reference to the most violent incident of the whole radical campaign which occurred in Hyde Park, in July 1866, when the attempt to impose a ban on a pro-reform working class demonstration led to skirmishing with the police and the demolition of some park railings. This view later developed into the belief that Disraeli took the 'Hyde Park Railway' to reform and was influenced by the popular agitation to extend the provisions of his bill.

For details of events in
1831–2 see Chapter 3,
pages 46–50

Yet the events in Hyde Park hardly compare with the atmosphere of
crisis created by the riots of October 1831, and the conspiracies of the
Days of May in 1832 and more recent historians have tended to abandon this explanation.

The more recent view among historians, such as Maurice Cowling
and John Walton, is that pressures originating in the world of 'low (i.e.
popular) politics' and fear of revolution should not be given much
prominence at all in any explanation of the passing of the Second
Reform Act. They argue that the final Act, although superficially radical, is better understood as the outcome of a political struggle inside
Parliament: it was the price to be paid for the Conservatives holding
onto power, for Disraeli's victory over Gladstone, and, not least, for
Disraeli's emergence as Derby's certain successor as Conservative
leader. The debate is, however, not over, for Annette Mayer (see bibliography) argued in 1999 that the inability of the Government to prevent
the Hyde Park meeting was 'a serious humiliation' and that:

> The fact that significant concessions were made to the proposed
> reform bill shortly thereafter certainly suggests that external pres-
> sures were instrumental in affecting government opinion'

B *Because Disraeli had a master plan?*

Disraeli claimed that his intention in carrying a Conservative parliamentary reform rested on his belief that the working people of Britain
were naturally conservative. The Reform Act was an expression of 'Tory
Democracy', the Tories learning to trust the people. Later in 1867 Disraeli argued that promoting welfare legislation and an appeal to working class loyalty and imperial sentiment would consolidate their
support for his party. He was to return to this vision of 'Tory Democracy' both in opposition and as prime minister. Historians have since
debated how seriously he subscribed to it as a political programme.

For further discussion
of Tory democracy see
pages 194–5 of this
chapter

In his biography of Disraeli, Robert Blake considered that Disraeli's
1867 speech was simply to justify the many twists and turns involved in
carrying the conservative measure. In 1867 'Tory democracy' was as
devoid of substance as the earlier programme of social reform promoted by the Young England movement. Blake, and others subsequently,
have seen the Reform Act as the product of a particularly bitter inter-
party squabble in the Commons with Disraeli determined to carry a
Conservative reform and to beat Gladstone.

This may not be entirely fair to Disraeli who had, since the 1830s,
promoted his idea, of a working class affinity with Conservatism. His
vision of the 'Tory working man' made him more willing in 1867 to
enfranchise so many of them. It is true that Disraeli never had the systematic commitment to the ideal to work it into a programme of political action. When he achieved power in 1874 his Government's social
legislation was unplanned and piecemeal but in 1867 his vision of 'Tory
Democracy' made him more willing to accept the radical reform that

party and personal advantage made necessary. Arguably, Disraeli's belief in a Tory democracy helps to explain the confidence and self-assurance with which he embraced household suffrage.

C *Was it a radical reform?*

Certainly, with so many of Disraeli's original safeguards swept aside, the Reform Act was much more radical than almost any parliamentarian would have contemplated at the outset. By doubling the size of the electorate it went much further than the Liberal proposals of 1866. Its revolutionary impact was however limited in two ways:

- the extension of the franchise in county constituencies had been quite slight; the agricultural worker would have to wait for his vote until 1885
- the Act redistributed 45 parliamentary seats and helped the Conservatives because 25 of the seats went to the counties, where they usually did best.

7 ⌁ THE 1868 ELECTION

Disraeli became both party leader and Prime Minister in February 1868 when ill health forced Derby to retire. His breath-taking parliamentary triumph over reform had guaranteed his succession but the triumph was short-lived.

Gladstone's task, after the disaster of 1866–7, was to reunite the Liberal Party and to win the forthcoming general election. He could not have found a better 'cry' for either purpose than his proposal to **disestablish** the Irish 'branch' of the Church of England.

The injustice of imposing a 'foreign', Protestant institution on the overwhelmingly Catholic people of Ireland had become so blatant by 1868 that few Conservatives other than Disraeli could be found to defend it. The proposal to disestablish the Church of Ireland clearly had great appeal in Ireland itself, where in the election the Liberals enjoyed one of their best performances of the century. But it was also designed to appeal to, and reunite, the Liberal party on the mainland:

- to Nonconformists, it marked the first stage of a process that they hoped would climax in the disestablishment of the Church of England itself
- to the Whigs, it would remove an absurdity which caused unrest and which was a threat to law and order in Ireland
- to radicals it was a long-overdue attack on a grotesquely privileged institution.

All could join with Gladstone in a crusade for what was right. Gladstone himself had recognised, since the Maynooth crisis of 1845, that the only hope which might justify the existence of an Established

> **KEY ISSUE**
>
> *Why did the Liberals gain such an overwhelming victory in the 1868 Election?*

> **disestablishment** meant ending the links, which joined the Irish Church to the British state, and removing the privileges that these links had entailed

See pages 154–5 of Chapter 6 for Maynooth crisis

Church in Ireland – that it might begin to convert the Catholics to Protestantism – was forlorn. It was far better to rescue the Church of Ireland from its false position, both for the sake of Anglicanism and of the people of Ireland.

The general election produced an overwhelming Liberal majority in the Commons: 387 seats against the Conservatives' 271. The call for Irish disestablishment had been the greatest vote winner, but the promise of land reform in Ireland, educational reform in Britain, and cheaper and more efficient government in general (firmly associated with Gladstone's name) had also made their mark. But this was by no means an agreed party manifesto, and some observers were soon wondering how long the Liberal Party would hold together.

PICTURE 22
'Paddy's Bad Tooth, or Doctors Differ'. In the cartoon the bandage over the 'bad tooth' bears the label 'Protestant Church'. How do the doctors differ in their views of the treatment required? Is there a play on words in Dr Benjamin's proposed treatment?

PADDY'S BAD TOOTH, OR DOCTORS DIFFER.

Dr. Gladstone. "I SAY THAT IT OUGHT TO COME OUT AT ONCE!"
Dr. Benjamin. "I'M DECIDEDLY IN FAVOUR OF STOPPING!"

8 ⌒ BIBLIOGRAPHY

ARTICLES

T. A. Jenkins 'Parties, Politics and Society in Mid-Victorian Britain', *Modern History Review*, 1998.

K. Mann 'Whig/Liberal Dominance', *Modern History Review*, November 2000. A four page overview of the fluidity of British politics 1846–65.

J. Walton The Impact of the Second Reform Act, *History Review*, 1998.

BOOKS FOR AS/A LEVEL STUDENTS

A. Meyer *The Growth of Democracy in Britain*, Access to History series, Hodder & Stoughton, 1999, especially pages 44–50.

R. Pearce and R. Stearn *Government and Reform, 1815–1918*, 2nd edition, Access to History series, Hodder & Stoughton, 2000, pages 55–65, are excellent on the Second Reform Act

J. Walton *Disraeli*, Lancaster Pamphlet, Routledge, 1990.

D. Watts *Tories, Conservatives and Unionists 1815–1914*, Access to History series, Hodder & Stoughton, 2002, where Chapter 5 is particularly relevant to the material in this chapter.

D. Watts *Whigs, Radicals and Liberals, 1815–1914*, Access to History series, Hodder & Stoughton, 2002.

M. Winstanley *Gladstone and the Liberal Party*, Lancaster Pamphlet, Routledge, 1986.

FURTHER READING

Books

Note that the Chapter 8 bibliography also lists many other works on Disraeli and Gladstone which also cover this period.

M. Bentley *Politics without Democracy, 1815–1914*, 2nd edition, Fontana, 1996.

R. Blake *The Conservative Party from Peel to Major*, Fontana, 1996, Chapter 3.

R. Blake *Disraeli*, Methuen, 1966, and in several subsequent paperback editions. This is a vast and pre-eminent work that the ambitious A-level student should certainly dip into. Chapter 21 on the intrigues around the Second Reform Act is particularly rewarding.

B. Coleman *Conservatism and the Conservative Party in the Nineteenth Century*, Edward Arnold, 1987.

R Jenkins *Gladstone*, Macmillan, 1995, a very readable biography, Chapter 15 'The People's William' is particularly relevant to this chapter.

H. Matthew, *Gladstone 1809–74*, Oxford University Press, 1988, by the leading authority on Gladstone

P. Smith *Disraeli: A Brief Life*, Cambridge University Press, 1996.

J. Vincent *The Formation of the British Liberal Party 1857–68*, Penguin, 1966, is directly centred on the period covered in this chapter and is a masterly, if detailed, analysis of the various strands drawn together to form the Party.

Internet resources

There are numerous internet references to the statesmen referred to in this chapter but many are irrelevant and the rest are usually best seen as sources for introductory factual information, rather than worthwhile analysis suitable for developing the level of understanding needed for AS and A2 level work. Indeed, some of the views expressed need to be treated with a great deal of scepticism, which could provide useful practice in arriving at historical judgements. These sources are best explored at the beginning of studying a topic, where the Timelines can sometimes provide a useful perspective to the period. Feeding in the names of relevant statesmen into your favourite search engine will soon open up the opportunities and, alas, the limitations of the net at this level. Given these warnings, you could look up the 'Peel Web', which has a wider range of references than its title suggests, or call up the www.spartacus.schoolnet.co.uk website.

9 ⌐ STRUCTURED AND ESSAY QUESTIONS

Assessment of the topic areas in this chapter at AS level is usually through structured essays. Essays at A2 level are likely to be more open-ended and give candidates greater opportunities to select the historical evidence they choose to offer in support of their arguments and opinions. The A2 essays should encourage candidates to place the chosen topic in a wider historical context. Examples of both types of essays, for examination, study and revision use, are provided below.

A *Structured questions for AS Level*

This section provides issues to be discussed in class or a series of focus points for study and revision of the topic. It also gives an opportunity for AS students to practise planning and writing structured essays. Such practice, under timed conditions, will be very useful preparation for examination work. It should at least encourage careful reading of the intention of the questions: note, for example, the one word emphasised in Question 5 and reflect on what needs to be **omitted** from your answer.

1. Identify the main elements which, by the 1860s, had come together to create the Liberal Party. Consider which individuals played key roles in the process.
2. How can we explain the rise of Gladstone to pre-eminence in Parliament between 1846 and 1866?
3. What difficulties faced Derby and Disraeli as leaders of the Conservative party in the aftermath of Corn Law Repeal?
4. In what ways and to what extent was Gladstone as Chancellor of the Exchequer indebted to Peel?
5. What, in the period 1846 to 1866, were the main contributions to British **domestic** politics of Palmerston and Russell?

6. Why, in 1866, did Gladstone fail to carry a Parliamentary Reform Bill while Disraeli, in 1867, succeeded in doing so?

7. To what extent did the terms of the 1867 Reform Act change the arrangements for electing the House of Commons? In what ways had the Act been made more radical during its passage through the Commons?

B *Essay questions for A2*

1. 'After 1846 the Peelites were without power but they remained essential to stable government.' Discuss this opinion.

2. How far is it valid to describe the period from 1846 to 1868 as one of great fluidity in British parliamentary politics?

3. 'His becoming Prime Minister owed as much to his discarding long-held principles as it did to his expertise in matters financial.' Examine this verdict on Gladstone in the years to 1868.

4. How do you explain 'The Formation of the British Liberal Party', in the late 1850s and the 1860s?

5. What were the main achievements of Derby and Disraeli's Conservative Party in the period from 1846 to 1867?

10 ⌁ ADVICE AND ESSAY PLANNING

Some points to consider in planning answers to the A2 essays above:

● **Question 1** makes two distinct points. Taking each in turn seems obvious. Establish who and how many the Peelites were. You could then immediately agree that power on their own was impossible but then challenge the rest of the assertion, using Aberdeen's Coalition Government and Gladstone's later role as Palmerston's Chancellor to point up its limits. They were powerless alone but not when allied to the Whigs. There were different levels of co-operation possible. After 1846 Russell's Whig Government survived simply by the Peelites not voting it out because they distrusted the Conservatives' approach to Free Trade. On the other hand, even full Peelite participation in government, under the Peelite Aberdeen, was not enough to save his government when the disasters of the Crimean War overtook it. Palmerston was then able to govern for three years without them. It could be useful finally to consider the period after 1859. How far was Gladstone's role as Chancellor essential to the survival of Palmerston's and Russell's governments?

● **Question 2** needs a balanced answer. These can be quite difficult to construct without falling into the trap of contradicting yourself. One approach here would be to state, very briefly, that there is much(some) truth in the claim but it is not the full story. Then illustrate the fluidity by appropriate examples: presumably the short-lived Conservative governments have a place here. The movement of Palmerston out of Aberdeen's Government in 1855 and Gladstone refusing Derby in 1858 but accepting Palmerston in 1859 also illustrate how, with no automatic party majority in the Commons, individuals could add to the impression of fluidity. Then point out the limits of the claim, with Russell's 1846–52 and Palmerston's 1859–65 governments providing the counter-argument.

● **Question 3** could be opened by making the point that, before he could become Prime Minister, Gladstone had first to rise to parliamentary eminence in order to become Liberal leader. His reputation as a financier was arguably of central importance in this. Think about the issues here and then discuss how his financial reputation led to the Liberal leadership via his role as Chancellor in successive governments. The principles abandoned were religious and related to his 1830s claims that the Church of England alone should have state recognition and had the sole role of being the national conscience. Forgetting these conveniently allowed him to ally with the Nonconformists and, in 1868, to use Irish Catholic grievances as the centrepiece of his successful election campaign and to confirm support for the disestablishment of the Anglican Church in Ireland. Finally, try to offer a clear, even if qualified, verdict directly on the quotation.

● **Question 4** uses the title of John Vincent's book to pose the question. In an examination essay it might be most straightforward to suggest that there are two aspects to cover. One is the emergence of the party as an electoral force by the time of the 1868 election. The second is the emergence of a credible, even impressive, leadership in Parliament for the new party. You could then indicate the factors that you think led to each of these developments. In the first part you can range widely across social and economic changes but you will need to be selective and deal with each quite briefly. This part of the essay will swamp the ill-organised candidate. The second part of the essay can largely, and probably more briefly, be set around Gladstone's rising status within Parliament. An effective conclusion could explain how the nationwide and the parliamentary factors came together, where recognition of Bright's contribution would be both just and perhaps impressive.

● **Question 5**; first, briefly note the desperate circumstances in which the Conservative Party found itself after 1846. It could have become a small agrarian rump party but managed to avoid this, first by ditching any idea that it would re-introduce the Corn Laws. Disraeli's 1852 budget ended this fear. Note the three minority governments and the failed parliamentary reform bill effort of 1859 but save the bulk of your answer for the blocking of the Liberal reform proposal in 1866 and the passage of their own Reform Act in 1867, including the humiliation of Gladstone and the disarray created among the Liberal party. In these two years the Conservatives won the parliamentary battles. They lost the 1868 election but they had survived and, in a political world once again reduced to two main parties, they would continue to survive and, in 1874, to prosper.

Essay tip: never become so involved in your historical account that, at the end of your essay, you forget to offer a direct answer to the question set.

Gladstone and Disraeli, 1868–86

8

INTRODUCTION

Most of the period from 1868 to 1886 was characterised by government stability based on clear party majorities in the House of Commons. Disraeli's Conservative Government separated the two Liberal Governments led by Gladstone. The duel between the two party leaders, neither of whom thought highly of his opponent, represented the highpoint of Victorian party conflict.

Gladstone's First Ministry, following the Liberal triumph in the 1868 election, has been regarded as one of the greatest reforming ministries of the century. In assessing the Government's record you will need to consider a number of issues:

● how important was Gladstone's own role to the ministry's work?
● to what extent did the ministry put Liberal principles into practice?
● set against the problems the reforms were intended to resolve, what was their impact on society?
● why did the Government suffer such a loss of popularity and direction in its last years?
● what were the main features of Gladstone's conduct of foreign policy?

The Conservative election victory in 1874 made Disraeli prime minister for the second time and inaugurated another ministry marked by a series of important reforms. Much has been written about the nature and origins of Disraelian Conservatism and Disraeli himself has attracted attention from several leading biographers and historians.

The second Gladstone ministry (1880–5) had a less impressive legislative output than the first and was plagued by political difficulties ranging from the disruptive activities of Irish Nationalist MPs to a series of foreign policy embarrassments. The Government carried through the Third Reform Act but was then defeated when the Conservatives and Irish Nationalists combined to defeat the 1885 budget. Then, for six months, Lord Salisbury led a minority Conservative Government. The 1885 election gave the Liberals an 86 majority over the Conservatives and saw the election of exactly the same number, 86, of Irish Nationalist MPs.

It was in these fraught circumstances that Gladstone made public his momentous decision that Ireland should be granted Home Rule. This enabled him, with Irish support, to form his third ministry but this led in turn led to a split in the Liberal Party so that the Government survived for only a few months. In August 1886, Salisbury formed his

Years	Party	Prime Minister
1868–74	Lib	Gladstone
1874–80	Cons	Disraeli
1880–5	Lib	Gladstone
1885–6	Cons	Salisbury
1886	Lib	Gladstone

TABLE 10 *Governments and their leaders, 1868–86*

For Disraeli's career prior to 1868 see Chapter 7, from page 191. You will need to be clear on Disraeli's role within the Conservative Party both before and after 1868

second Government and heralded in six years of Conservative rule; stable party government had again been restored.

1 ᴔ GLADSTONE'S FIRST MINISTRY, 1868–74

See Chapter 7, page 208

PICTURE 23
William Gladstone, Prime Minister, 1868–74

The general election of 1868 produced an overwhelming Liberal majority: 387 seats against the Conservative 271. The greatest vote winner had been Gladstone's pledge to disestablish the Anglican Church in Ireland but the promise of land reform in Ireland, educational reform and cheaper and more efficient government in general (firmly associated with Gladstone's reputation as Chancellor) had also played a part.

Half of the Cabinet were Whigs. However, the radical John Bright, a leading Nonconformist and veteran Anti-Corn Law League campaigner, and the Peelite, Cardwell, were also members. Most of the strands that made up the Liberal Party were represented but the Whigs, like the Earl of Granville who was Foreign Secretary and Robert Lowe, who was the Chancellor of the Exchequer, were predominant.

Gladstone was to describe this Cabinet as 'one of the best instruments for government ever constructed'. His ministry certainly produced an exceptional volume of legislation and reforms, fearlessly taking on vested interests and deep-rooted problems. The Cabinet was united and even-handed in its approach, brushing aside the special pleading of friends and opponents alike, with surprisingly little thought for electoral consequences. In part, this reflected a confidence, bordering on arrogance, that the Liberals were the natural party of government. But they were also guided by a sense of duty, public service and self-sacrifice which might strike many modern politicians as quaint.

A *Gladstone and Ireland 1868–74*

The 1868 election result gave Gladstone a **mandate** to provide remedies for Irish grievances. With the mandate, he hoped to encourge most Irish people to accept the Union of Britain and Ireland, and also to browbeat possible opponents of his reforms in the Conservative-dominated House of Lords. He saw a recent and alarming upsurge in revolutionary Irish violence in mainland Britain as emphasising the urgency of the task, famously commenting 'My mission is to pacify Ireland'.

Gladstone introduced three important measures:

- **The Irish Church Disestablishment Act 1869**. This Act ended the official status of the Anglican Church as the national Church in Ireland. It also confiscated Irish Church wealth so that one third of the its annual revenue would be diverted to non-religious purposes such as workhouse and hospital improvements. This complicated and controversial measure was very much Gladstone's own work. His motives have been challenged and it has been argued that the attack

Tip: consult Chapter 9 for the important Irish dimension of this topic

on the Irish Church was a convenient cause, during and after the election, around which to unite the Liberal party.

- **The Land Act 1870**. This Act was as complicated as the Irish land question itself. The Act aimed to compensate the usually impoverished Irish tenants for any improvements they had made on their lands if they were evicted for any reason other than non-payment of rent. It outraged landowners, who saw it as an attack on property rights, yet failed to satisfy Irish tenant pressure groups who sought the 'Three Fs' – free sale, fair rent and fixity of tenure. Gladstone would have preferred a more radical measure but this was watered down to meet the concerns of his aristocratic Whig supporters who feared that extreme Irish legislation might encourage similar attacks on property rights elsewhere in Britain. The Land Act failed to pacify the Irish tenants and did nothing to promote Gladstone's dream of tenants and landlords in Ireland learning to work happily together as he believed they did on his own family's estates. Gladstone could gain no possible political advantage from tackling the Irish land question and yet he persisted. The 1870 Act failed to bring peace to Ireland and yet earned Gladstone the distrust of many Whigs for his 'extremism'.

- **Irish Universities Bill 1873**. This Bill aimed to re-structure the Irish university system, to go some way to meet the Catholic grievance that they lacked a suitable university. Gladstone never intended to give the Catholic Church leaders all that they wanted but he did wish to encourage the development of a Catholic professional class, not least to help bring stability to Irish society. The result was a complicated arrangement for a religiously neutral University to which existing Church colleges could attach themselves. The proposal had many opponents, particularly Whigs who thought it went too far and Irish Liberals who thought it too timid, and the Bill was defeated by three votes.

KEY ISSUE

Why did Gladstone's efforts to pacify Ireland have only limited success?

As with the Irish land question, Gladstone could gain no party advantage from his proposals for an Irish university. When defeated on this issue in 1873, he offered to resign. Disraeli declined to form a minority Conservative Government and so Gladstone's Government limped on. It had been badly damaged by this defeat and never recovered its reforming momentum. He had also been disappointed that his release in 1870 of Fenian prisoners gaoled for terrorist offences had failed to bring an end to rural violence in Ireland. This meant that coercion had to be introduced, with the power of magistrates to arrest and detain suspects increased. His other dream for Ireland, that the Prince of Wales would have an official residence in Dublin and become Viceroy of Ireland, failed to get past the opposition of Queen Victoria.

For more on Fenians, see page 273

Perhaps the best that can be said for Gladstone's Irish policies in these years is that he at least tried to introduce a series of initiatives to make Ireland more peaceful and more willing to accept rule from mainland Britain. His most successful measure, disestablishment, did mark a new, more positive, approach to Irish issues and brought the

British Liberal Party and the Irish Catholics into an unlikely alliance that was to have important long-term political consequences.

B *The domestic legislation of Gladstone's first ministry*

KEY ISSUE

How far is it true that Gladstone injected a strong element of conservatism into Gladstonian Liberalism?

GLADSTONE'S OWN ROLE

Gladstone was personally responsible for little of the domestic legislation of 1868–74. Although the nine or ten major Acts of Parliament which crowd these years can, taken together, be regarded as embodying many of the principles of Gladstonian Liberalism, it is important to recognise that Gladstonianism and Liberalism were not one and the same thing. In speeches Gladstone could appear radical, but in practice his most passionate commitments could be described as Peelite:

- he wished to modernise the nation's great institutions so as to preserve them. He was, for example, ready to reform the inefficient and outdated institutions of the judicial system as was evident in the 1873 Judicature Act, which dramatically streamlined the operations of the Upper Courts of Law
- he always sought to defend the public good against the selfishness of powerful minorities. In 1871, for example, he supported Robert Lowe, his Chancellor of the Exchequer, who increased the professionalism of the Civil Service by introducing recruitment by examination, as opposed to appointment by patronage, into most departments.

TIMELINE

Main Laws 1868–74

1870	Education Act
1871	University Tests Act
1871	Civil Service Reforms
1871	Trade Union Act
1871	Criminal Law Amendment Act
1872	Ballot Act
1872	Licensing Act
1873	Judicature Act

On the other hand, Gladstone lacked real enthusiasm for some of his ministry's most important reforms. Constitutionally speaking, the most important of the attacks on the old order was the Ballot Act (1872) which introduced secret voting. John Bright, the leading Radical, had long campaigned for this reform. Bright explained some of his reasons in his 1868 election address

What reasons are given, in this speech, for introducing the secret ballot? **Q**

Whether I look to the excessive cost of elections, or the tumult which so often attends them, or to the unjust and cruel pressure which is so frequently brought to bear upon the less independent class of voters, I am persuaded that the true interest of the public and of freedom will be served by the system of secret and free voting.

Gladstone, by contrast, admitted to a 'lingering reluctance' to abandon the old system of open voting. His instinctive conservatism is also evident in his defensive response to Radical and Nonconformist demands for the opening to non-Anglicans of all teaching posts at Oxford and Cambridge Universities. The cause of religious equality here conflicted with Gladstone's own commitment to protect the interests of the Church of England. He was only able to maintain some privileges for Anglicans in his University Test Act (1871) with the help of Conservative votes against his own backbenchers. In important ways, Gladstone was disappointing some of those Radicals and Nonconformists who had made him their hero.

THE EDUCATION ACT 1870

This pattern of voting across party lines noted above had first been seen during the passage of the Education Act (1870), which was perhaps the most important and controversial of all the domestic legislation of Gladstone's First Ministry. A string of Royal Commissions in the 1860s had pointed out that the British educational system was inadequate. Neither the Church of England-run National Schools nor the Nonconformists' British Schools had kept pace with the rapidly growing urban population. The implications of this were awful. How was Britain to retain its industrial lead with a largely ignorant, illiterate and innumerate workforce? Moral and spiritual peril seemed an even greater danger. To grow up in ignorance was to grow up incapable of self-improvement, and perhaps to be left languishing in godlessness, vice and criminality. The 'dangerous classes' had to be tamed. The 1867 Reform Act gave these fears greater urgency. Robert Lowe, one of the main opponents of Parliamentary Reform, had remarked pointedly that 'it will be absolutely necessary to compel our new masters to learn their letters'.

Although the problem was therefore recognised to be extremely pressing, it was equally obvious that any attempt to remedy it would involve grave political difficulties. Some all-embracing, national education scheme was widely called for. Yet this would entail a major extension of the role and power of the state in an age that deplored the idea of government intervention in society, and valued '**voluntaryism**' very highly. Any national scheme was also bound to be expensive.

> **voluntaryism** the ideal that the best way to meet social needs was through voluntary local initiatives

Above all, education was a religious battlefield in which Anglicans and Nonconformists vied for the upper hand. Church of England schools outnumbered their rivals by roughly 3:1. Anglicans, organising themselves into the National Education Union (1869), were determined that this lead be maintained, and with it the distinctive religious identity of their schools. The Radical/Nonconformist-influenced National Education League (1869), by contrast, pressed for the absorption of the Anglican schools within a new nationwide system in which education would be free, and free of religious bias. The fact that many Whigs supported the Education Union, while many Radicals, notably their future leader Joseph Chamberlain, were prominent in the Education League, shows how vulnerable to fragmentation the Liberal Party was on this issue. Nevertheless, the government took the problem on.

> **KEY ISSUE**
>
> *Why did religion in schools present the Liberal Government with such sharp political difficulties in 1870?*

The Education Act was mostly the work of W. E. Forster. He aimed to supplement the existing voluntary system rather than replace it, thereby saving money and continuing to draw on the energies of voluntaryism. The Education Department would find out which areas lacked adequate schools. There, elected School Boards were to be set up and empowered to raise money from local rates to build new ones. Forster believed that he could solve the religious difficulty by allowing each School Board to decide the nature of the religious instruction to be given in its area. This was coupled with a 'conscience clause' to allow, for example, Nonconformist parents to withdraw their children from lessons in which Anglican religious instruction was being given.

In fact, Forster had underestimated the religious divisions of Victorian Britain. There was widespread unease that a dangerous precedent was being set up for Irish primary education: the idea of possible future School Boards in Ireland providing Roman Catholic instruction with money raised in local taxes appalled many Liberals. But it was the Nonconformists who felt especially outraged by Forster's Bill. It proposed to increase the amount of state aid given to existing Anglican schools. Where schools did not as yet exist, if Anglicans were in a local majority, they would be fully entitled, under the Act's provisions, to levy a rate on Nonconformists through a 'School Board', forcing them to contribute to the building of a Church of England school to 'fill in the gap'. As far as the Nonconformists could see, far from dismantling the Anglican Church's network of elementary schools, Forster seemed set on extending it.

Compromise of a sort was finally reached in Parliament with the acceptance of an amendment put forward by a leading Whig MP, Cowper-Temple. His idea was that 'Board Schools' should base their religious lessons on a broad and simple bible-based Christianity. There was to be nothing distinctively Anglican or Nonconformist in style about the instruction offered.

Not all Liberals, however, could fully support the Act:

● Gladstone himself, in another sign of his conservatism, agreed only very reluctantly: he wrote that in accepting it, he had 'never made a more painful concession to the desire for [party] unity'. He feared that 'Cowper-Temple religion', as he dismissively called it, would dilute the eternal truths of the Anglican faith and prove too lukewarm to inspire zeal or fervent belief

● radicals regretted that attendance was to be neither compulsory nor free

● hard-line Nonconformists felt badly let down. The Government's education legislation had failed to advance the cause of Nonconformity. Instead, in vote after vote, Nonconformists had been left in a minority, outnumbered by a broad front of Anglican Liberals and Anglican Conservatives. They felt this humiliation deeply. Temporarily at least, there was a rupture between the party leader and his Nonconformist followers who had done so much to win the 1868 election.

Any judgement of the importance of the 1870 Education Act must be carefully balanced. It is typical of Gladstonian Liberalism in its scale, ambition and political courage. In the tradition of Peel himself (see Chapter 6) it met the responsibility of the Government to serve the national interest, however difficult the task. Although it was only a stage in the extension of educational provision in nineteenth-century

Britain (elementary education was not made compulsory until 1881, and was not free until 1891), it was a vital one, for with Forster's Act the state had come near to recognising a duty to provide some education for all.

Clearly this principle would have dramatic social consequences. It advanced the great Liberal aim of empowering individuals to make more of themselves and their talents. Gladstone, however, had little interest in the social aspects of education policy. His preoccupation was with its religious implications, and especially the need to uphold the teachings and influence of the Church of England in the nation's schools, which the increased state-grant for Anglican schools had helped to strengthen. The creation of 'equality of opportunity' was never one of his objectives. He remained too attached to the concept of a hierarchy of classes, headed by the aristocracy and with the lower orders deferring to their betters

ARMY REFORMS

Gladstone's belief in aristocracy did not prevent him from attacking privilege, especially where it posed a threat to the national good. His vigorous support of Cardwell, his Minister of War, is a striking example of this. Amateurism and incompetence were undermining the army's strength, as its poor performance in the Crimean War had shown. Cardwell, 'the greatest army reformer of the nineteenth-century', was a Peelite to his fingertips. He examined the problems dispassionately, and, by redesigning the whole pattern of regimental service, organisation and command, was able both to save money and leave the army a more efficient fighting force.

The most important army reform was the abolition of purchase, i.e. the practice by which wealthy young men, often with aristocratic connections, could buy themselves into the officer class, regardless of their fitness for command. This struck Cardwell and Gladstone as a gross abuse: potentially, the interests of the nation might be endangered by the selfishness and incompetence of the privileged few. But the few were well represented in the Lords and on the Tory backbenches in the Commons. They put up prolonged and impassioned resistance to Cardwell. Gladstone ultimately had to use a royal warrant to bypass the obstructive tactics in the Lords, a controversial move which infuriated the military-aristocratic elite.

The affair had significant consequences. It marks a turning point in Gladstone's relation with 'the classes' i.e. the upper ten thousand of Victorian society. Gladstone was appalled by the 'folly and selfishness' which 'the classes' displayed in the conflict over army purchase. From now on, Gladstone showed an increasing readiness to align himself with the people – or 'the masses' – against 'the classes'. Although he still believed in the ideal of aristocracy, there seemed to be fewer and fewer aristocrats ready to devote themselves to the service of the nation. Instead, he believed that the aristocracy, corrupted by wealth, was becoming obsessed with the defence of privilege and the pursuit of pleasure. The masses, by contrast, had the keenest moral sense and the

KEY ISSUE

Why did Gladstone's army reforms make him so many powerful enemies?

rhetoric impressive speaking for purposes of display

To read part of this speech, see the documentary exercise on page 262 of this chapter

picketing the practice of strikers stationing themselves outside places of work to persuade others not to enter

KEY ISSUE

What is the difference between Gladstone and Disraeli on Trade Union law?

truest appreciation of the needs of the nation. The Bible itself taught, so Gladstone believed, that the poor were 'better and wiser than the rich'.

This radical **rhetoric**, one of Gladstone's great themes of the 1870s and 1880s, reached its climax in a speech made in June 1886 to the electors of Liverpool. It helps to explain why Gladstone, despite his conservatism on many issues, seemed such an extremist to many of his contemporaries – at times like an agitator talking the language of class war. This doubtless added to his appeal as 'the People's William'. But it worried the Whigs, while 'the classes' in general began to regard him with fear and loathing.

TRADE UNION REFORMS

The fact that Gladstone came to value the political judgement of the masses more and more did not mean that he passed laws favouring the working class. This is clearest from the thrust of his Trade Union reforms. Despite the emergence, since the 1850s, of respectable New Model Unions of skilled workers many Victorians continued to regard trade unions with great suspicion. Some industrialists believed they were a menace to profits, while the Sheffield Outrages – where an over-enthusiastic trade union official had tried to encourage a non-member to join by blowing up his house with gunpowder – received great publicity. These problems had prompted Disraeli to appoint a Royal Commission of Inquiry. Its findings in 1867, largely sympathetic to the cause of responsible trade unionism, formed the basis for two laws passed by the Liberals:

● the 1871 Trade Union Act was designed to establish their legal rights beyond doubt
● the 1871 Criminal Law Amendment Act, however, especially as interpreted by Justices of the Peace, made **picketing** practically impossible, and consequently the organisation of effective strikes very difficult.

Gladstone can be seen here trying, not completely successfully, to balance the competing claim of employer and employee while above all defending the rights of the individual. Peaceful collective bargaining was sanctioned; but intimidation and violence were quite prohibited.

Gladstone had clearly resisted the temptation, which might have been strong after the Second Reform Act, to do organised labour any special favours. Gladstone believed that all groups in society – from the aristocracy to the working classes – liked to 'exaggerate their rights', as he put it. It had been one of the main functions of government since the days of Peel to challenge such pretensions. The speed with which Disraeli, in 1875, made his bid for working-class support with the Conspiracy and Protection of Property Act, repealing Gladstone's Criminal Law Amendment Act, reveals how far he operated on different political principles.

Why did the Liberals lose the 1874 election?

There were many reasons why the Liberals lost the 1874 election:

- the legislation of Gladstone's first ministry had annoyed a wide range of sectional interests with heroic impartiality. The trade union legislation doubtless cost working-class votes in the 1874 election
- some workers had already been annoyed by the Licensing Act of 1872. This restricted the opening hours of public houses and authorised magistrates to close some down in areas where there were too many. Drunkenness was a blight on Victorian society, but Conservatives exploited this supposed example of moralising government interference with the freedom of the working man to pursue his pleasures
- the Licensing Act also turned the large and influential Brewers' and Publicans' trades against the Liberals
- yet the United Kingdom Alliance, the important Nonconformist temperance pressure group, regarded the legislation as much too mild: they had wanted local councils to be given the power to enforce total prohibition
- Nonconformists, stirred up by Chamberlain, were still fuming about the Education Act.

By 1874, the commitment of Nonconformist and working-class activists to the Liberal cause was weaker than it had been for a decade.

Gladstone had given the Establishment a battering too:

- the privileged classes had been forced into retreat in the Civil Service and Army reforms
- die-hard Anglicans resented the fate of their Church in Ireland and also its loss of privileges in the universities of Oxford and Cambridge
- property-owners were anxious at the implications of the Irish Land Act in particular and the rise of Radicalism in general.

Disraeli claimed that the ministry had 'harassed every trade, worried every profession, and assailed or menaced every class, institution and species of property in the country' and he struck a chord. In 1874, even moderate Liberals wondered what Gladstone would do next. Some outrageous concession to Irish Catholics or British Nonconformists was unfairly, but widely, feared. Gladstone and his ministers had simply been too busy. Competence in government rather than constantly bringing in new laws was what the electorate expected. But, after a decade of Palmerstonian stagnation, such a programme was precisely what Gladstone believed the country had needed. He was convinced, in his own words, that the 'vital principle of the Liberal Party is action'. Legislative activity kept it together. But when the country tired of Liberal energies

> **KEY ISSUE**
>
> *Why, by 1874, did even Disraeli look a safer bet to many voters than Gladstone?*

and feared what the next moves would be, it was time to seek some peace and stability.

Gladstone's first ministry had marked a departure from Palmerston's style in foreign policy too. In place of the bluster and belligerence of Pam's 'gun-boat diplomacy', Gladstone sought compromise and conciliation.

Many observers, however, regarded this performance as spineless. Disraeli made great play of the Liberals' supposed inability to stand up for British interests in the world. The Conservatives, he claimed, were the truly patriotic party. The skill with which Disraeli draped himself and his party in the Union Jack was another important reason why Gladstone was defeated in 1874.

For more on foreign affairs see Chapter 11, pages 327–8

2 ～ DISRAELI'S SECOND MINISTRY, 1874–80

A *Disraeli in opposition 1868–74*

KEY ISSUE

Why were his two public speeches in 1872 so significant for both Disraeli and his party?

The triumph of carrying the 1867 Second Reform Act in the teeth of Liberal amendments led swiftly to disaster in the 1868 election. The scale of the Conservative defeat (271 seats to 387 Liberals) was shattering. There was little evidence that the newly enfranchised borough voters had voted Conservative and the Reform Act suddenly looked like a disastrous gamble. From 1868 to 1872 Disraeli's performance as party leader and as leader of the opposition to Gladstone's administration was lack-lustre and half-hearted. He was ill and seemed uninterested in fighting the successful Liberals. In 1872 a meeting of Party leaders almost decided he had to be removed: in that year, however, he made two celebrated speeches that transformed his fortunes. Against his recent dismal personal record, these speeches, at the Free Trade Hall, Manchester and at the Crystal Palace in London, take on extra significance. Through them he reasserted his authority within the party and silenced his critics. More importantly, he spelt out the issues on which the Liberals could be beaten, and developed his vision of what Conservatism meant. Together, they mark one of the turning points in Disraeli's career.

Disraeli's attack on Gladstonian Liberalism in 1872 was expertly judged. Disraeli identified the Government's weak spots, and scored hit after hit. Gladstone was presented as the (more or less) respectable front man for a party that, in its ultimate intentions, was in fact subversive of all that was best about England and her institutions. The Liberal radicals, Disraeli asserted, were conspiring to undermine the Church of England, the House of Lords, and the Monarchy itself. Disraeli also claimed that the Liberals were incapable of defending the interests and prestige of England abroad. In fact, with its obsession about cutting defence spending, which would weaken colonial ties, and its exaggerat-

PICTURE 24
Benjamin Disraeli, Prime Minister, 1874–80

ed regard for the rights of all peoples except the English, Liberal policy spelled the disintegration of Empire.

DISRAELI'S CONSERVATIVE APPEAL

Only the Conservatives, he argued, could be trusted as the guardians of England's destiny. It went without saying (although Disraeli repeated it) that they would uphold every branch of the ancient constitution. Disraeli argued that the era of constitutional reform was passing. The true interest of the working classes now lay in the pursuit not of more political power, but in improvements to their material well being, like better housing. Echoing the paternalistic themes of Young England, Disraeli claimed that the Conservatives had the welfare of the working classes closest to heart. Class harmony could be secured by reinvigorated social policy.

See page 194 on Young England

Binding the nation together was the great objective of Disraelian Conservatism. Disraeli realised that one of the most effective ways of achieving this was by a direct appeal to the spirit of national self-confidence that was nearing its peak in mid-Victorian England. In the absence of opinion polls, the historian cannot be sure, but rhetoric like this seems to have struck home:

> I express … my confident conviction that there never was a moment in our history when the power of England was so great and her resources so vast and inexhaustible. And yet, gentlemen, it is not merely our fleets and armies, our powerful artillery, our accumulated capital, and our unlimited credit on which I so much depend, as upon that unbroken spirit of her people, which I believe was never prouder of the Imperial country to which they belong.

Q

What is Disraeli appealing to here?

PICTURE 25 *A contemporary sketch of Disraeli. His two speeches in 1872 transformed both his own, and his Party's, fortunes*

Q

What impression of Disraeli does the artist convey?

Disraeli was putting his trust in the people, and dedicating the Conservative Party to their service.

Some historians, notably Lord Blake, have looked on these speeches with a degree of scepticism: their rhetoric might be suggestive, but they offered little in terms of concrete policy. It is quite true that Disraeli preferred to paint with a broad brush, and it would be difficult to trace the details of his later social or foreign policy to the impressionistic sketches offered in 1872. But such criticism misses the mark. In the nineteenth century the electorate did not expect detailed manifestos and elaborate policy studies but merely looked for a statement of general principles together with some indication of the direction which legislation might take. Disraeli's gestures were sufficient to do this.

It is equally mistaken to dismiss such speeches as *mere* rhetoric. Politicians then and now establish their own identity, and the identity of their parties, as much by what they say and how they say it, as by what they do. The experience of more than two decades in opposition had left Disraeli in no doubt about the effectiveness of the Liberals' image as the party of free trade, prosperity and competent Government. Disraeli somehow had to rival this unassailable reputation without seeming merely to imitate it. This he achieved in his speeches of 1872.

The distinctive Conservative identity, which Disraeli manufactured, contained the promise to:

- re-establish constitutional stability
- promote social harmony,
- defend and enhance Britain's status as a great power.

With these great themes, the Conservatives could at last claim to be a national party again, and a viable alternative government.

The Conservatives' greatest asset, however, was not Disraeli's skill as an image-maker: it was Gladstone. Since becoming the Liberals' leader, he had broken decisively with the Whig traditions. Whereas Palmerston had kept the Radicals on a tight rein, Gladstone at times seemed to identify himself with their cause and speak their language. Abroad, the difference was even more striking. Palmerston had known how to treat foreigners, especially the Greeks and the Chinese. He had conducted diplomacy in a style that reminded the world (and the electorate) that Britain was a mighty power. Gladstone deplored this dangerous and expensive mixture of bluff and belligerence. But his internationalism and readiness to seek compromise could be made to look weak in comparison.

KEY ISSUE

Why, by 1874, had Gladstone's reputation become an election winner for the Conservatives?

There were, perhaps, two faces to Disraelian Conservatism: the positive one of 'Tory Democracy' and the negative one of 'anti-Gladstonianism'. By the end of Gladstone's first ministry, Disraeli was emphasising the latter. The Liberals he argued, were incapable of upholding England's institutions or international standing: the previous five years would have been the better for 'a little more energy in our foreign policy and a little less in our domestic legislation'. The electorate seemed to agree and in 1874 returned Disraeli with a 110-seat majority.

B *Domestic affairs 1874–80: a Tory democracy?*

DISRAELI'S CABINET

The Cabinet that Disraeli was able to assemble in 1874 was a strong one:

● The 15th **Earl of Derby**, the son of the Conservative Party's leader between 1846 and 1868, was Foreign Secretary. He was seen by many as a potential Prime Minister but resigned in 1883 over foreign policy differences with Disraeli.

● **Sir Stafford Northcote**, who had mastered the rules of Peelite finance as Gladstone's Private Secretary in the 1840s, was Chancellor of the Exchequer Although his budgets were never inspired, his competence was undoubted.

● **Lord Salisbury**, who had begun to moderate his distaste for Disraeli and who was to succeed Derby as Foreign Secretary in 1878, was Head of the India Office His sheer intellectual power and reputation for the unwavering defence of true Conservative principles strengthened the Cabinet and also the cause of party unity.

● **R. A. Cross**, was Disraeli's only surprise appointment, as Home Secretary. As a Lancashire-based lawyer and banker, he was to bring invaluable knowledge of urban problems to a Cabinet that was otherwise dominated by the landed aristocracy. In his Departmental work, he combined the virtues of industry, efficiency and precision, and was responsible for most of the social legislation for which Disraeli's second ministry is celebrated. Cross was arguably the ministry's greatest success.

CONSERVATIVE SOCIAL POLICY AND ITS LIMITATIONS

Cross himself was rather less impressed by his Prime Minister. On taking office in 1874, he was surprised to discover that, despite Disraeli's famous pronouncements on social issues, he had no legislative schemes ready to put before the Commons. Characteristically, Disraeli was to rely on others to flesh out the rather vague promises made in 1872.

The achievements of 1875 were still considerable. Blake has described the Acts of that year as 'the biggest instalment of social reform passed by any one government in the nineteenth century'. However, on closer analysis, this impressive-looking list is revealed as rather less than a programme of full-blooded Tory paternalism. Instead, much of the legislation was a pragmatic response to practical problems that both parties recognised, and which might just as well have been passed by the Liberals. There was little that was far-reaching or innovatory about the legislation. Much of it was 'permissive', not compulsory, leaving it to the local authorities to decide whether a bill would be implemented. For example, the provisions of the Sale of Food and Drugs Act (1875) became operative only where a town council was ready to appoint trained analysts to report on incidents of adulteration. As a contemporary critic noted, the chances of cost-conscious councillors going to this expense were slight – not least as a fair number

> **KEY ISSUE**
>
> *How fully did Tory social reforms live up to the vision offered in Disraeli's 1872 speeches?*

TIMELINE

Main laws passed

1875	Artisans' Dwelling Act
1875	Public health Act
1875	Factory Act
1875	Sale of Food & Drugs Act
1875	Merchant Shipping Act
1875	Climbing Boys Act
1875	Conspiracy & Protection of Property Act
1875	Employers & Workmen Act
1876	Education Act

of them might be the very shopkeepers most likely to be hit by the analysts' findings!

Even greater practical deficiencies were apparent in one of Cross's most significant pieces of legislation – the Artisans' Dwelling Act (1875). The deplorable quality of much working-class housing had become – and was to remain – a major preoccupation of Victorian politicians. Slums were held to be the breeding grounds of vice and criminality. The well-being of society, even the future of the English race, was supposedly at stake.

This sense of urgency was ill-matched by the detail of Cross's actual legislation. Local authorities were given the power of compulsory purchase over property certified as unhealthy by a medical officer. But central government offered little help with the expense of slum clearance or the rebuilding that would follow, to make the proposition attractive. Councillors well knew that the ratepayers' likeliest response to the increases in local taxes would be to vote them out of office. Not surprisingly, only 10 out of 87 eligible authorities took up the powers offered to them by Cross. Here again, the promise of Disraelian social reform was not matched by the reality.

LIMITING FACTORS

KEY ISSUE

What factors limited the scope and the effectiveness of Disraeli's social reforms?

It is easy to list the deficiencies of the ministry's social legislation: but perhaps it is historically more valuable to understand the constraints and inhibitions under which Disraeli and Cross were operating.

Politically speaking, Disraeli knew that he had to tread carefully. Not one of the Acts passed in 1875 or 1876 was of the scale, or provoked anything like the controversy, of the 'big bills' that the Liberals specialised in. They were described by a sympathetic backbencher as 'suet-pudding legislation … flat, insipid, dull but … very wise and very wholesome'. Disraeli knew very well that the electorate had suffered more than enough legislative excitement at the hands of Gladstone. Further instalments of major reform would have been a poor reward for Conservative voters. There were also deeper, long-term reasons for avoiding major changes. From the 1830s, Disraeli had been quick to defend the independence of local government against the threat of central direction by Whitehall bureaucrats. He had not now become Prime Minister in order to undermine the power of ancient borough corporations and county magistrates. They constituted a part of the 'aristocratic settlement' which he was sworn to defend. Disraeli firmly believed that power should be left in the hands of those who, by tradition, legitimate influence and local knowledge, were best equipped to exercise it.

These old-fashioned Tory beliefs were reinforced by shifts in Tory thinking on economic policy. By the 1870s Tory and Liberal ideas on taxes, tariffs and state intervention were practically indistinguishable. Liberals and Conservatives alike believed in the ideal of a low-taxing, small-scale state. Underpinning this was a basic belief, that the dignity and the identity of human beings were inseparable from their freedom, as individuals, to make their own choices and assume responsibility for their own lives. Cross put the matter concisely in insisting that the very 'starting point' of the Conservative's social legislation was the principle that 'it is **not** the duty of the Government to provide any class of citizen with any of the necessities of life'. Clearly the Tory paternalism of Young England has here been seriously diluted. Equally obviously the origins of the twentieth-century Welfare State cannot be traced back to the social policy of Disraeli's second ministry.

On two occasions in 1876, however, the Government did intervene despite its belief in *laissez-faire* economics and for party political advantage.

THE MERCHANT SHIPPING ACT 1876

This was designed to make it difficult for unscrupulous ship owners to overload their ships and thereby put their crews' lives at risk. Disraeli had at first been reluctant to interfere with the owners' rights to make their own business decisions, reminding the Commons that 'the maintenance of freedom of contract is one of the necessary conditions of the commercial and manufacturing greatness of the country'. But Conservative MPs representing ports warned him that working-class feelings were running high, and a furious protest in the Commons by the Liberal MP Samuel Plimsoll, the leading campaigner for sailors' interests, focused much sympathetic public attention on the issue. Disraeli had to concede that government time and support would be found for Plimsoll's proposals to prevent the overloading of ships. However, the Lords still managed to weaken the bill: the final act did little to ensure the safety of merchant seamen.

THE EDUCATION ACT 1876

This Act was another example of apparently progressive social policy that was in reality motivated by narrow political calculations. It introduced compulsory education for children up to the age of ten: a marked increase of state power at the expense of parental freedom. The Conservatives were not inspired by any desire to encourage **social mobility**. What finally drove the Conservatives to legislate was a determination to reverse some unwelcome and unanticipated side effects of the 1870 Education Act. This had left the network of overwhelmingly Church of England 'Voluntary Schools' intact. But it had opened the possibility of setting up non-Anglican 'Board Schools' where existing voluntary establishments were failing to do the job. These new schools were to be run by popularly elected 'boards' – hence their name.

Board schools were widely hated in Conservative ranks. Their religious teaching was not specifically Anglican and Nonconformists often controlled them, through popular election. Worse still, the different way in which they were financed gave the Board Schools an advantage. Board Schools were paid for out of the rates. The Voluntary Schools were much more dependent on the small fees paid by their pupils. Low attendance and difficulty in collecting subscriptions meant that many of them were too poor to provide their catchment areas with the 'efficient' education required by the 1870 Act. There was therefore a danger

social mobility the movement of people between classes, e.g. a working-class person becoming middle class by education or training

KEY ISSUE

How far was the 1876 Education Act a political measure to help Conservatism rather than an Act to improve educational provision?

that the better-resourced Board Schools would increasingly take over the provision of education.

In these circumstances, making attendance at all schools compulsory was the easiest way of guaranteeing the Voluntary Schools an adequate income, through the parental fees, and so staving off the threat from the Board Schools. Preserving the Voluntary School system would also save ratepayers' money (Board School expenditure was hitting them hard), and offer 'a better security for moral and religious teaching'. The Voluntary Schools would remain, indirectly, a great source of strength to the Church of England, the local squire, and the Conservative interest in general.

The 1876 Education Act reveals traditional Conservatism at its most inventive: working with the grain of Liberal legislation to uphold the power of the local landowners and to preserve the political cohesion of the rural communities that remained the great stronghold of Conservatism.

C *Disraeli and Tory democracy*

KEY ISSUE

How sincere was Disraeli in seeking to bring about Tory Democracy? How successful was he in doing so?

The picture that has so far emerged of the social legislation of Disraeli's second ministry has led many historians to doubt the depth of his commitment to Tory democracy. There was indeed much that was piecemeal, ineffectual, reluctant or partisan about Conservative social policy between 1874 and 1876. But given the financial and intellectual constraints under which Disraeli had to work, it is perhaps surprising that anything significant was achieved at all. At least, Cross had made a sustained and wide-ranging effort to convert the vague pledges of 1872 into concrete legislation.

DISRAELI'S ROLE

Neither was Disraeli a mere passive observer of Cross's works. The strength of Disraeli's own commitment to the principles of Tory Democracy is most apparent in his decisive intervention in support of the 1875 Conspiracy and Protection of Property Act. This Act dramatically improved the rights of workers in industrial disputes. It prevented trade unions from being prosecuted for conspiracy when they organised strikes and it also legalised peaceful picketing. It thereby put right the deficiencies that working-class leaders had complained of in the Liberals' legislation of 1871. When considered with the 1875 Employers and Workman Act, which removed the threat of imprisonment from working men for breaking their contracts, Paul Smith (see Bibliography on page 261) has argued that they constitute 'easily the most important of the Government's social reforms'. Yet without Disraeli's support for Cross, in a hostile and sceptical Cabinet, the Conspiracy Bill would have been sunk before it even reached the Commons.

DISRAELI'S MOTIVES

Why was Disraeli so determined that the Conservatives should enact these pro-trade union laws? Undoubtedly pure political calculation played a large part. To have made concessions to the working classes which Gladstone had denied them was quite a coup. But Disraeli was not merely thinking of short-term tactical advantage. He wrote to two intimate friends that he expected the Act to:

> Gain and retain the Tories the lasting affection of the working classes...It is one of those measures that root and consolidate a party. We have settled the long and vexatious [annoying] contest between capital and labour.

There is something unrealistic and fanciful about this claim. It is more likely that, by removing a point of contention between the working classes and their Liberal allies, he unintentionally paved the way for their reconciliation, thus undermining the electoral calculations behind 'Tory Democracy'. Furthermore, Disraeli's dreams of having at last settled 'the contest between capital and labour' were soon to look ridiculous. Class tensions increased markedly from the late 1870s onwards, becoming one of the dominant issues in politics.

What did Disraeli intend? His sincerity is notoriously difficult to judge, but it is possible that Disraeli was at his most sincere precisely when he was at his most visionary and idiosyncratic. His obsession with Britain's prestige as an Asiatic, Imperial power was one example of this. His hopes of basing Conservatism on the affections of the working classes is another. The excitement Disraeli expressed at the passing of his trade union legislation, and the central role which he accorded it in securing the Conservatives' future successes can perhaps be explained if Disraeli is seen as fulfilling, in his own mind, the desire to make One Nation of England's Rich and Poor. These were ideas he had expressed 30 years earlier in his novel *Sybil* and which remained, for Disraeli, the great mission and opportunity of Conservatism.

See page 195

DISRAELI'S SUCCESS?

Yet even the immediate electoral impact of his social legislation is hard to trace. Instead of securing the working class vote, the Conservatives attracted more and more middle-class voters, in flight from Gladstonian Radicalism. By the end of the century, the Conservatives were to become the defenders of property interests and the party of resistance to working-class demands.

The rise of the New Unionism and a militant working class towards the end of the nineteenth century made the old Disraelian appeals to national solidarity and class harmony sound absurdly old-fashioned. By the turn of the century, the Conservative Party had become more the voice of high finance and big business than of the English counties, whose supposedly natural harmony was a model for Disraeli of what all social relations should be. Disraeli may well have believed in 'Tory Democracy', and the legislation of his second ministry did something to

For more information on trade union matters see Chapter 12

make a reality of the promise of his rhetoric: but in the evolution of Conservative Party social policy towards the working classes, it represents not a beginning but a dead end.

3 ⌐ DISRAELI'S FOREIGN POLICY

For more on Disraeli's foreign policy see Chapter 11, pages 327–32

Disraeli's hopes and achievements in the international arena are so central to his overall reputation that they need extended attention. The details of foreign policy can be found elsewhere in this book and the focus in this section is on the *domestic* impact of European and Imperial affairs.

A *Disraeli – the imperialist*

> **KEY ISSUE**
>
> *How did Disraeli's imperialism enhance the Conservatives' popular appeal?*

Disraeli believed in the greatness of Great Britain. He was determined that it should play a role in European and World Affairs that reflected its wealth and the extent of its Empire. He also had an acute sense of national self-interest, and was single-minded, even ruthless, in his defence of it. Unlike most of his contemporaries, he refused to let any idealism or considerations of a higher morality shape his foreign policy. He cared only for power and prestige. Symbolic of his dreams of imperial glory was his initiative in having the description 'Empress of India' added to the Queen's titles. This cost nothing, flattered Victoria and had the additional merit of making her furious at Liberal opposition to the proposal.

In his great speeches of 1872, Disraeli had declared his intention to defend Britain's imperial power and standing in the world. He also invited the working people of Great Britain to take pride in their country's imperial destiny. It seems likely that Disraeli struck a rich vein here for the Conservatives: the last quarter of the nineteenth century saw many displays of belligerent nationalism and popular imperialism, culminating in the Queen's Diamond Jubilee in 1897 and the 'Khaki' general election of 1900. Disraeli had successfully draped his party in the Union Jack and cast the Liberals in the role of un-English betrayers of the Empire.

In terms of increasing the Conservatives' popular appeal, this was a triumph of the first order and was perhaps also Disraeli's greatest long-term service to the Conservative Party. But what, exactly, were his attitudes to Empire? Undoubtedly it was the mystery and glory of India that seduced Disraeli's imagination. The preservation of British control there was the guiding theme of his foreign policy, and his European diplomacy should be seen from that perspective.

Disraeli was a passionate imperialist. But, unlike Joseph Chamberlain, later Colonial Secretary, he was not systematic or aggressively expansionist in his imperialism. There were no great plans for colonial development or closer colonial co-operation. As with social policy, he preferred to let others work out the practical implications of the visions he had sketched. It was one of Disraeli's misfortunes that he was not to find men of Cross's calibre to do his work in the outposts of Empire.

B *Disraeli and the Eastern Question*

In his handling of the Eastern Question, however, Disraeli was, at least at first, to show notable insensitivity to the feelings of many Victorians. The Eastern Question was arguably the most complex of all the problems faced by European diplomats in the nineteenth Century. The seemingly irreversible decay of the Ottoman (Turkish) Empire, and the Turks' oppression of the Christian races of the Balkans, encouraged these peoples' longing for freedom and nationhood. But it also encouraged the Russians to expand southwards at the expense of the Ottomans and to help fellow Slavs and Orthodox Christians. British involvement in the Question stemmed from the conviction that Russian expansion might ultimately threaten the Suez Canal, the lifeline to India. More generally, British prestige and influence in the Eastern Mediterranean and Central Asia were felt to be at stake.

KEY ISSUE

Why did the Eastern Question rouse such bitter feelings in Britain?

See Map 4 on page 325

DISRAELI AND THE BULGARIAN AGITATION

To Disraeli the issues were clear-cut. 'Constantinople,' he wrote 'is the key to India'. This assessment was dubious strategically but remained the central concern of British foreign policy under Disraeli. The consequence was that Britain was committed to uphold the integrity of the Ottoman Empire.

The stark simplicity of Disraeli's conclusion, and his conviction that the defence of Britain's great power status was his overriding duty, made it impossible for Disraeli to understand, let alone sympathise with, those who challenged his policy. His problems began in June 1876, when news reached London that the Turks had killed thousands of Christians, with appalling brutality, in repressing a rebellion in Bulgaria. As the details became public, a massive agitation galvanised the ranks of Radicals and Nonconformists. Disraeli, however, was casually dismissive of the stories of Turkish atrocities. Liberal newspapers, he implied, were merely trying to whip up political feeling against the Government and its pro-Turkish policies, and their reports were based on nothing more than 'coffee-house babble'. It was one of the worst judged responses of Disraeli's career: the phrase sounded callous and heartless, and provoked an intensification of the 'Bulgarian Agitation'. The blunder revealed one of Disraeli's weaknesses as a politician: insensitivity to the passionate moral feelings that inspired the political views of many Victorians.

All Disraeli could see in the opposition's campaign was a sickening exhibition of self-righteous moral indignation, all the more contemptible for being led by the hypocritical Gladstone. Worse, he believed that its scale convinced the Russians that Britain was too divided to take any effective action to restrain their ambitions. Indeed, it encouraged Russian designs on Constantinople and thus made the horrors and expense of war more likely. The two sides of the 'Agitation' faced each other in profound and mutual incomprehension, each believing they alone represented what was best in, and best for, Britain. Few popular political debates in Britain before or since have been con-

PICTURE 26
Political cartoon from Punch
showing Turkey in danger –
Disraeli's case

TURKEY IN DANGER.

Q

*How does this
cartoon help to explain
why, in the end, Disraeli
had the best of the
argument with
Gladstone over the
eastern Question?*

See pages 241–4 on
Gladstone and the
Bulgarian Agitation

ducted with the venom and spirit of loathing that marked the debate over the Eastern Question in 1876–8.

In the end, it was a debate Disraeli won. Although the agitation had a dramatic effect on the future of the Liberal Party, if anything it stiffened Disraeli's determination to stand firm against Russia. In fact, Gladstone struggled to maintain the momentum of 1876. His opening blast – the celebrated pamphlet on *The Bulgarian Horrors and the Question of the East* – had sold 200 000 copies in one month. But the follow-up, published in January 1877, sold only 7000. Gladstone had to curtail a planned Commons campaign against the Government because of lack of support and fear that his 'unpatriotic' line would damage his reputation and split the party. To some observers, the Liberal Party in 1877 seemed almost as divided as it had been in the disputes over parliamentary reform in 1866–7.

Public opinion, with a little prompting from Conservative activists, began to surge behind the Turks, whose rearguard action against the Russians was seen as heroic. In the absence of opinion polls, politicians looked to the outcome of by-elections – and even the popularity of music hall songs – as indicators of their changing levels of support. Both types of omen favoured the Conservatives. Indeed, the most popular song of the season has added a concept to the language of political analysis:

> We don't want to fight, but, *by Jingo* if we do,
>   We've got the ships, we've got the men, we've got the money too,
>   We've fought the [Russian] bear before, and, while Britons shall be true,
>   The Russians shall not have Constantinople.

The spirit of Jingoism, i.e. aggressive patriotism, which the international crisis had produced amongst sections of the working class, was ample confirmation of the belief Disraeli had expressed in 1872: that the nation took pride in its imperial greatness and would trust the Conservatives to defend it.

The changing national mood, and the renewal of the Russian advance towards Constantinople, brought about a decisive crisis in Cabinet. Here, the Government had been very badly divided. At one extreme was Disraeli, certain that there was only one way to check Russian expansionism: Russia had to be convinced that Britain would go to war if its vital interests in the eastern Mediterranean were threatened. To Disraeli, diplomatic warnings would not suffice. Men and ships had to be despatched to the potential war zone, ready to fight. At the other extreme was Derby, the Foreign Secretary. He was appalled by Disraeli's belligerence, arguing that such a provocative display was bound to be counter-productive.

Disraeli eventually won the Cabinet debate, just as the 'jingoes' had triumphed in the music hall. As the Russians advanced, Disraeli persuaded the Cabinet to call out the reserves and also move troops from India to Malta, as the first step to securing a strategic base deep in the eastern Mediterranean (six warships had already been sent to Constantinople to dissuade the Russians from seizing the city). Derby finally resigned.

His replacement was Lord Salisbury. This might seem surprising. For most of 1877, Salisbury had been an ally of Derby in the Cabinet debates and, in the past, he had been deeply suspicious of Disraeli, seeing him as an opportunist and adventurer. But Salisbury had gradually come to appreciate Disraeli's fundamentally Conservative instincts, as well his courage and keen sense of the national interest. Salisbury and Disraeli were to make a good team.

DISRAELI TRIUMPHANT: THE CONGRESS OF BERLIN 1878

Thus, Disraeli emerged victorious out of the political crisis in Cabinet. That he did so with a former bitter enemy at his shoulder shows that, even in old age, he could deploy impressive powers of persuasion and political manoeuvre. It marks one of the greatest – and least often recognised – triumphs of his career.

Disraeli was to cap these successes in Cabinet with a diplomatic triumph over the Russians. In the face of British resolution and Austrian opposition, they backed down. The Tsar agreed to renegotiate, under international supervision, the terms of his treaty with the Turks. Thus, at the Congress of Berlin, in the summer of 1878, Russia was forced to abandon many of her gains. The British were also allowed to take control of Cyprus, from where any future threat to her interests in the Eastern Mediterranean could be speedily countered. Salisbury had done much of the groundwork for the final settlement but Disraeli won the public acclaim for having achieved 'Peace with Honour'.

At the Congress of Berlin, called to resolve the crisis, Disraeli had emerged as a leading European statesman. The crisis also established Disraeli's credentials as a national leader as nothing previously had. If Disraeli had called a general election on his return from Berlin, there is every chance that the Conservatives would have won.

But reality broke in with a vengeance from November 1878 onwards. Disraeli was to enjoy a reputation for effortless and masterful statesmanship for less than six months.

C *Imperial disasters: Afghanistan and South Africa*

> **KEY ISSUE**
>
> *To what extent can Disraeli be held responsible for the imperial disasters in Afghanistan and South Africa?*

To Disraeli's surprise and considerable displeasure, in late 1878 and for most of 1879, Britain found itself involved in difficult and expensive colonial wars in Afghanistan and South Africa. In neither case does Disraeli bear much direct blame for the blunders and setbacks, which did much to discredit his government. His indirect responsibility is harder to assess but certainly existed.

● In **Afghanistan** which, in the eyes of many Britons seemed to provide a Russian invasion route to India, most of the problems were caused by Lord Lytton, the Viceroy of India. Without proper consultation with London, he sent an expeditionary force to the Afghan capital, Kabul, in order to impose a pro-British ruler there. The Afghans resisted and, in hostile terrain, the British troops became trapped. Disraeli had appointed Lytton in 1876, thinking that his ambition, imagination and theatricality would impress the Indian princes and reinforce the image of imperial rule projected by the Queen's new title, Empress of India. But Disraeli got more theatricality than he bargained for. Lytton lacked the judgement and tact needed to handle the complex and delicate situation developing in neighbouring Afghanistan. His aggressive policy led first to the humiliation, and then to the massacre, of the British forces.

● In **South Africa** misadventure and blunder also characterised Britain's imperial activities. The new governor, Sir Bartle Frere – like Lytton, acting contrary to his orders – wanted to 'teach the Zulus a lesson'. Instead, the incompetently-led British forces were themselves outmanoeuvred, outnumbered, outwitted – and defeated. Reinforcements and a new commander had to be despatched before British prestige was restored.

The bloody shambles into which imperial policy had collapsed in Afghanistan and South Africa put a severe drain on the Exchequer and dented both British self-confidence and Disraeli's reputation as a foreign-policy wizard. Gladstone exploited these reverses, as well as questioning the arrogant and racist prejudices that had led to them in the first place, in his brilliantly managed campaign at Midlothian in the winter of 1879–80. There is little doubt that his speeches and the publicity they received were a major factor in securing for the Liberals their victory in the 1880 general election.

For the Midlothian campaign see page 243 in this chapter

Gladstone's accusation that Disraeli was the evil architect of a reckless plan of imperial expansion was electorally powerful. But it was probably unfair. In one sense, it flattered Disraeli by exaggerating the coherence of his imperial vision. Gesture and improvisation – not cold and calculated blueprints for aggression – were at the heart of Disraeli's imperial style. Furthermore, on analysis, Disraeli is revealed to be the victim as much as the villain of the piece. Disraeli's wretched predicament was in large part the consequence of the misjudgement and incompetence of his subordinates. Both Lytton and Frere had acted rashly, and against orders. Given the distances involved, and the recognised need for imperial representatives to make their own decisions in emergencies, it was natural to allow Lytton and Frere a good deal of room for initiative. But they took too much.

Disraeli cannot be acquitted of all responsibility, however: it was characteristic of his style of cabinet government to devolve even important decision-making to his subordinates. He almost invariably left them to do the job of working out how his own vague aspirations and promises were to be put into practice. Furthermore, Disraeli's speeches of 1872 had implied that the Conservatives would seek to uphold the might and splendours of the Empire. The appointment of Lytton and Frere, both aggressive and self-reliant imperialists, was a natural result of this. Given their characters, the loose structure of government control from Britain and the high expectations Disraeli had created, the humiliations of 1878 and 1879 might be classed as accidents waiting to happen. They thus shed important light on the weaknesses of the Disraelian style of government.

4 ⌁ DISRAELIAN CONSERVATISM: AN ASSESSMENT

A full assessment of Disraeli's political contribution would need to take account of all the major episodes of his long and often complex political career. It would at least have to include:

● his responsibility for the split with Peel in 1846

- his work in helping the party to survive from then until the triumph of the 1874 election
- his motives and his achievement in enacting the 1867 Reform Act
- the achievements of, and his own role in, the 1874–80 ministry both at home and abroad.

Here, all that is attempted is a more general assessment of his contribution to the Conservative Party and Conservatism, as if seen at the point in 1880 when he retired from political life.

A *In defeat: the lessons of 1880*

KEY ISSUE

Why did the Conservatives lose the 1880 election?

In 1880 the prospects for Disraeli's party looked bleak and arguably he was largely responsible for this. The ministry's misadventures in Afghanistan and South Africa, so brilliantly exploited by Gladstone, were amongst the main reasons for the Conservatives' defeat in the 1880 general election. The fact that Britain was experiencing a sharp economic downturn added to their difficulties. Even so, the scale of the defeat surprised Disraeli: the Conservatives' total of 238 seats was their second worst performance of the whole Victorian era, only a handful better than that of 1847, when the party was still reeling from the split with the Peelites. In 1880, Tory Democracy, as a political philosophy, or as an electoral strategy, seemed to have been shown up as one of Disraeli's less happy inspirations. In the election, the Conservatives had only won 36 of the 159 largest boroughs which had been the great hope behind Tory Democracy. For all Disraeli's good spirits in the aftermath of defeat, there was an awful possibility that his Conservative ministry of 1874–80 would prove to be a mere interlude in a world made for, and largely populated by, Liberals.

The electoral campaign of 1880 had shown that no one in the ranks of the Conservative elite was capable of bridging the gap between the party at Westminster and the newly enlarged electorate. This was especially true of Disraeli, who had been created Lord Beaconsfield in 1876 so that constitutional convention made it impossible for him, as a member of the House of Lords, to go on tour, drumming up votes. In any event, the increasingly frail Prime Minister would have been unable to match Gladstone's performance at Midlothian and the election Manifesto he prepared for his party was eccentric and lacklustre. It was one of Disraeli's greatest political weaknesses, that for all his superlative performances in the Commons, he had never been able to conjure up the magical oratorical displays on the public platform that were Gladstone's speciality. Gladstone made himself the People's William. Disraeli was never the People's Benjamin.

In defeat, Disraeli seemed tired, old and increasingly infirm. Bronchitis, asthma, gout and insomnia had been taking their toll for some years and a chill he caught in 1881 proved fatal. The electoral prospects for Conservatism on his death were, at best, uncertain. The experiment in Tory Democracy seemed to have been suspended and the Liberals were expected to waste little time before introducing a Third Reform

Act, which would extend to the counties the household franchise established in the boroughs in 1867. Disraeli had been particularly concerned before his death by signs that the agricultural depression had opened divisions in the county community between landlord and tenant farmer. The Liberals would be well placed to benefit from any disintegration of the rural hierarchy; it was feared that the great rural stronghold of traditional Toryism was about to be undermined.

B *Better prospects after 1886?*

The Conservatives were not, however, in total despair. Many expected that tensions between the Whigs and the Radical wing of the Liberal Party were bound to worsen. Sooner or later the Whigs would have had enough, and realise that their future lay with the true friends of property and the constitution – the Tories. Gladstone himself might prove to be his enemies' trump card. He was ever more arrogant, frighteningly unpredictable and – many insiders seriously believed – half-mad. Who could put up with him for long? Anyway, his supposed lack of patriotism and liking for radical adventures would doubtless soon discredit him again with moderate Liberal voters.

By 1886, these predictions had been in many ways fulfilled. But the greatest damage that was inflicted on the Liberals in the 1880s came from a largely unexpected quarter: Ireland. The sustained scale and violence of the Land War that was to be waged there, and the ruthless determination with which a reinvigorated Home Rule Party set about achieving its objectives, staggered Conservatives, Whigs and Radicals alike. When Disraeli had complained that 'hard times' had wrecked the Conservative cause in Britain, he could hardly have guessed what agrarian depression and its social and political consequences would do to Liberalism in Ireland.

See Chapter 9, page 276

It was these, unforeseen, events that were to shape party politics after 1886 and it is therefore difficult to see what Disraelian Tory Democracy contributed to the better electoral prospects that the Conservative Party enjoyed after that, except of course in its continuing appeal to popular nationalist and imperialist sentiment.

opportunism grasping opportunities, often in an unprincipled way

C *Disraeli: opportunist or pragmatist?*

AN OPPORTUNIST?

On this issue Gladstone had no doubts. He loathed Disraeli, believing that his influence on public life had been wholly bad. He had corrupted his party, until it was no longer capable of speaking with the voice of authentic Conservatism, as its extraordinary performance in 1867 had shown. Disraeli had also tried to corrupt the public, exciting their baser, **chauvinistic** impulses and encouraging reckless imperialist adventures and gross extravagance. Gladstone believed that, whilst Disraeli had a mastery of the baser arts of politics, he was utterly deficient in the moral vision and intellectual integrity which the statesman needs to

pragmatism the matter-of-fact treatment of issues, judging policies simply by their practical consequences

chauvinistic excessively patriotic, often leading to contempt for foreigners

make good use of that power. Even in death, Gladstone could not extend charity to his foe. Disraeli's preference for a modest private funeral was judged by Gladstone to be contrived and drew from him the following comment: 'As he lived so he died – all display, without reality or genuineness'.

PRAGMATIST?

Modern views on what constitutes the proper business of government are very different from those held by Disraeli. Today, legislation is seen as the natural end of political activity: accordingly, the nineteenth-century Prime Ministers who tend to win our admiration and respect are Peel and Gladstone. Both of them demonstrated a supreme facility for working out practicable solutions (and sometimes impracticable ones!) to the most complex problems: at the height of their powers they achieved a remarkably clear overview of their ministries' whole legislative programmes.

Notoriously, Disraeli lacked these skills. But it is too easily forgotten that his objectives were different. In 1874, he reminded his Cabinet colleagues that: 'We came in on the principle of not harassing the country'. The country, he believed, had had enough of sweeping reforms and, once the largely practical measures of 1875 had been completed, the process of endlessly passing new laws dried up.

Of course, in terms of making historical judgements about the same event, one historian's 'mere opportunism' could be another's 'responsible pragmatism'. This is nowhere more the case than when assessing Disraeli. In 1848, Disraeli wrote to Derby, that the function of the leader of the Conservative Party was 'to uphold the aristocratic settlement of this country'. This was, he claimed, 'the only question at stake'.

Peel, of course, had also committed himself to the defence of the aristocratic settlement. But Disraeli, in 1867 and in his 1874–80 ministry, was merely to show more flexibility and inventiveness in working to achieve the same end. And it is not the least of his achievements that, unlike Peel, he held his party together in the process. The suggestion that, at his core, Disraeli was a 'conviction politician' might invite disbelief, but here even Lord Blake seems to agree:

> through all the twists and turns of his bewildering policy [the defence of the aristocratic settlement], remained to the end his guiding purpose.

It can be argued that the work of Disraeli's 1874–80 ministry was indeed tailored to this objective:

- the Education Act was designed to uphold the ascendancy of squire and parson in rural England
- the very deficiencies of the Artisans Dwelling Act, leaving the powers to implement policy (or not) with the local authorities, reflected

Note: when assessing Disraeli's record as Prime Minister, it is important not to judge him by early twenty-first century criteria

KEY ISSUE

How strongly can it be argued that the key principle behind the legislation of Disraeli's second ministry was defence of the aristocratic position in the state?

Disraeli's anxiety at the dangers which centralised, authoritarian, bureaucratic government spelled to the independence of the local communities
● the objective of Disraeli's trade union legislation was to ensure social harmony
● his foreign policy, with its stress on imperial greatness, invited all classes to identify with the nation and share its triumph.

Disraeli's message was the same throughout: Liberalism had a disintegrating effect; Conservatism an integrating one. And, for Disraeli, the landed interest, gentry and aristocracy together, stood at the apex of the national community, guaranteeing its stability; the very embodiment of its historical continuity.

D *Disraeli and the middle classes*

The integration of the increasingly conservative middle classes into the continuing rule of the aristocracy was probably the most important long-term political development that occurred during the period of Disraeli's leadership of the Conservative Party. But historians have begun to question whether Disraeli consciously set out to recruit middle-class support for the Conservative Party. Indeed, John Vincent has gone so far as to argue that 'Disraeli did not like the middle classes [and] he did not seek to encourage them'.

Such a claim might sound exaggerated. But contemporaries and insiders noted it too. In the 1870s Derby remarked that it was peculiar that 'the Premier [Disraeli] neither likes nor understands the middle class ... though [it is] the strength of our party'. None of Disraeli's legislation was designed to appeal to the middle class. Disraeli can take little credit for the fact that the apparent extremism of Gladstone's first ministry drove tens of thousands of middle-class voters from the ranks of the Liberals into the surprised but grateful arms of the Conservative Party. To secure the 1874 Conservative landslide, all Disraeli had to do was to promise to do nothing, except to reverse the processes of social and imperial disintegration upon which Gladstone had supposedly embarked.

If Disraeli had little regard for, or understanding of the middle classes, we should not be too surprised. Unlike Peel and Gladstone, he did not trace his roots to their ranks, and in contrast to Palmerston or Gladstone, he did not seek their support with regular tours of the northern industrial towns. Disraeli knew the world of Westminster and of fashionable society. At his country estate in Buckinghamshire, bought for him by rich Tories, he came to know the world of the gentleman squire: he took the responsibilities of being a leading figure in the county seriously, enjoying being a magistrate. The aristocratic settlement was a reality to him, and he was a part of it. But Disraeli was in many ways a foreigner to the new land into which industrialisation and urbanisation had been turning England. Again unlike Gladstone, he failed either to reach out to it or to capture its imagination.

> **KEY ISSUE**
>
> *How far did Disraeli consciously set out to recruit middle-class support for the Conservative Party?*

See Bibliography,
pages 260–1

HISTORIANS' DEBATE

Was Disraeli a failure?

In 1981, **John Vincent** published a brilliant and provocative essay, which dared to ask the question: *Was Disraeli a Failure?* He pointed out that, for all Disraeli's much advertised political genius, he lost five out of the six general elections he fought as a senior Tory. He also misjudged the public mood, forecasting victory in the general elections of 1857, and even of 1868, while being surprised by the victory of 1874, and the defeat of 1880.

Bruce Coleman

mounts a yet more severe attack in 'Conservatism and the Conservative Party in Nineteenth Century Britain'. He concludes that it is 'doubtful' whether 'anything which can properly be called Disraelian Conservatism' ever existed. For all his exotic personality and showy rhetoric, Disraeli left the party largely unchanged. In fact, according to Coleman, Disraeli should be a villain in the eyes of all thinking Conservatives. By destroying Peel, he destroyed the party's only chance of power in the 1850s. And simply by being Disraeli – the unscrupulous, unprincipled 'Jew Adventurer' – he was the single greatest obstacle to the long predicted but long-awaited absorption of the Whigs. Only under Salisbury would the Conservatives re-establish themselves as the party of property and resistance to change.

It is probable that Coleman underestimates Disraeli's case. Many Conservatives felt that, in 1846, Peel had got what was coming to him. Disraeli was only the political hit man: we should admire his professional skill rather than complain about his morals or motivation. Then, against all the odds, having achieved a position of prominence in his party, Disraeli managed to steer it away from the vote-losing policy of protectionism and, over the next two thankless decades, he not only kept the Party alive but also within sight of power.

He only had one real chance, with parliamentary reform in 1867, and he seized it with breathtaking skill. Thereafter, apart from remoulding the image of the party in his speeches of 1872, his greatest triumph was with the Eastern Question in 1878, when his brinkmanship, first in Cabinet, and then at Berlin, earned British diplomacy a triumph that, objectively, British arms did not merit.

These are significant achievements, but their long-term importance was limited. To identify Disraeli's more permanent contribution to Conservatism, we have to return to the difficult world of political images. John Walton, in his brief but penetrating survey of Disraeli's career, concludes that:

> there is much to be said for the view that Disraeli's contribution to the ... fortunes of the Conservative Party is much more to do with ideas, slogans, rhetoric and presentation than with specific policies and actual legislation.

This, perhaps, agrees with Disraeli's own assessment of his political role. For he had, in his own words, always 'recognised imagination in the Government of nations as a quality not less important than reason'. Disraeli was a compulsive mythmaker: about himself, about his party, and about the English nation. However shallow their roots in reality, the myths he wove have been extraordinarily powerful and enduring. This is what John Vincent means when he writes that of all the Victorian Tories ('a dull lot') 'Disraeli alone had the literary creativity which lies at the heart of politics'.

With his unique blend of constitutional, paternalistic and imperial themes, perhaps Disraeli's greatest achievement was that he made it possible for the Conservatives to project themselves as the National Party again, for them to be believed, and not least, for them to be elected. This scarcely amounts to failure.

5 ⌐ GLADSTONE AND THE LIBERALS IN OPPOSITION, 1874–80

A *Retirement and return to politics, 1874–6*

Gladstone was 65 years old when his first ministry came to its end in 1874. He wanted – at least he told himself he wanted – to retire. His religious ideals provided powerful personal reasons. A part of him longed to 'be out of the dust and heat and blast and strain, before I pass into the unseen world'. With more time for 'spiritual leisure', he would be able to 'cultivate the poor little garden of [his] soul'. Therefore, with thoughts of mortality, and hopes of salvation – and in the shadow of political failure – Gladstone resigned from the leadership of the party in December 1874.

More immediate political considerations also pushed him towards retirement. The election defeat by Disraeli had been a crushing personal reversal. Gladstone himself had determined the timing of the election, and he had devised the election 'cry' – a promise to abolish income tax. Tax-paying voters seem to have been sceptical about the promise – after all, it was not the first time Gladstone had made it – while to the hundreds of thousands of voters below the income tax threshold who had been enfranchised by Disraeli in 1867, it offered no benefits at all. Gladstone's 'gift' for discerning the moods and needs of the British people appeared to have quite deserted him. Neither could he see any way to restore the unity of his party. He was himself exasperated by the sniping and self-importance of many Radicals. The increasingly thankless and difficult job of party leader could, he felt, be done better by someone else.

See pages 327–32 on Disraeli and the Eastern Question

He was not to be given much time for spiritual leisure, however: God, it seemed, had other plans for him. Politics had always been a Christian vocation for Gladstone, and it was, he believed, a Call to rejoin His service in the world that brought him out of retirement. The political issue that offered Gladstone the platform for his return to politics was the agitation that many of his old political allies had raised against Disraeli's handling of the Eastern Question.

B *The Bulgarian Agitation, 1876–8*

Gladstone's friends were horrified at Disraeli's support for the Turks who had crushed Christian uprisings in their Balkan empire. Ghastly details of massacre and rape were soon filling the columns of British newspapers. Disraeli's reaction to these stories – initially dismissive and flippant, and never deviating from his insistence that Turkish power be upheld – scandalised his opponents and precipitated the 'Bulgarian Agitation'. Nonconformists joined with Anglicans, radicals and intellectuals in demonstrations and meetings all over England. They could not believe that the British state would support so cruel and anti-Christian a regime as that of the Ottoman Turks.

Gladstone was not at first at the forefront of the agitation, but he soon saw its potential. In August 1876, he wrote to Granville: 'good ends can rarely be attained in politics without passion: and there is now, the first time for a good many years, a virtuous passion'. In September, he published a pamphlet on *The Bulgarian Horrors and the Question of the East* which burned with righteous anger at the Turks' crimes and at Disraeli's complicity in them. Within a month it had sold over 200 000 copies, and made Gladstone the effective leader of the Agitation.

In practical terms, the Agitation was a failure. Disraeli dismissed Gladstone's pamphlet: 'Vindictive and ill-written – that of course. Indeed, in that respect, of all Bulgarian horrors, perhaps the greatest'. More to the point, the Government's policy was not altered and, by January 1878, public opinion actually appeared to be swinging behind the Turks. Disraeli's threat of armed intervention forced the Russians to back down, and the Congress of Berlin (June–July 1878) marked a clear check to Russia's ambitions. Disraeli returned from the Congress in triumph, claiming that he had secured 'Peace with Honour'.

But the Agitation did have a dramatic impact on the fortunes of Gladstone and the Liberal Party. Over its course, Gladstone had re-forged the links with militant Nonconformity and Radicalism, which had been eroded by the disappointments of his first ministry. The masses had, as in 1868, shown that they could be elevated in a great quest for justice, thus confirming in Gladstone's mind a pattern of politics-as-moral-crusade. Above all, the Agitation had served to bring Gladstone back to the forefront of politics. If Gladstone's opponents in the Liberal Party had hoped that Disraeli's apparent triumph in 1878 would force Gladstone into retirement again, they were to be disappointed. In fact, the practical failure of the Bulgarian Agitation made it

KEY ISSUE

Was Gladstone's campaign against the 'Bulgarian horrors' motivated mainly by moral outrage or by Party opportunism?

See pages 330–2 for details of the Congress of Berlin

essential, in Gladstone's own eyes, that he stand his ground until other means could be found of defeating the abominable Disraeli. He would not have long to wait.

C *The Midlothian campaigns, 1879–80*

The celebrated Midlothian Campaigns of 1879–80 (named after the Scottish constituency for which Gladstone stood in the 1880 general election) reinforced Gladstone's union with Nonconformity and Liberalism, and brought his battle with Disraeli to a climax. Gladstone deployed a striking range of approaches to capture the imagination of the voters within the constituency – and beyond.

KEY ISSUE

Why did the Liberals win the 1880 election?

There were cavalcades through the streets of Edinburgh, and whistle-stop tours of the countryside, with speech after speech to the thronging thousands. Then, nineteenth-century mass-communications took over. Every word would be recorded by the reporters on the campaign, telegraphed to London, type set in the massive steam presses of Fleet Street (and in the presses of the great provincial dailies too) and printed across acres of newspaper column for a nationwide readership the following morning. Never had British politics been so theatrically exciting and never had one man so impressed himself on a wider constituency. It is remarkable that Gladstone, who celebrated his 70th birthday in the middle of the campaign, was able to mobilise and give a sense of direction to the wide electorate created by the Second Reform Act. In all this, he outshone Disraeli.

The content of Gladstone's speeches was a sustained assault on Disraeli's foreign policy and style of government. Crucially, it was now possible to criticise the Government without appearing unpatriotic, for Disraeli could be held responsible for incurring defeats abroad. His representatives in Afghanistan and South Africa had independently promoted expensive, bloody and mostly unsuccessful military campaigns to extend British power in their corners of the Empire. Even if these had been more successful they would have made for an overextended Empire, increasingly difficult and expensive to maintain. But anyway, Disraeli's gambles had failed.

Gladstone portrayed Disraeli's foreign policy as misconceived in its objectives, incompetently delivered and, above all, morally bankrupt for Disraeli was ignoring the rights of other nations and peoples. The emotional peak of Gladstone's denunciations was reached in a celebrated speech to the women of Dalkeith, in Scotland, in November 1879. He described the actions of British troops burning down Afghan hill villages in reprisal raids, and contemplated the dreadful consequences.

Q

Why did the tone of Gladstone's speeches infuriate Disraeli?

The women and children were driven forth to perish in the snows of winter. Is not that a terrible supposition? Is not that a fact which … rouses in you a sentiment of horror and grief, to think that the name of England, under no political necessity, but for a war as frivolous as

> ever was waged in the history of man, should be associated with consequences as these? Remember the rights of the savage, as we call him. Remember that the happiness of his humble home, remember that sanctity of life in the hill villages of Afghanistan among the winter snows, is as inviolable in the eye of Almighty God as can be your own.

Gladstone's high moral rhetoric may well be as puzzling to some modern students as it seemed incomprehensible and hypocritical to Disraeli.

The onset of economic depression in 1879 allowed Gladstone one last but telling twist of the rhetorical knife. Unemployment was at levels unknown for 30 years. 'Beaconsfieldism', as he dubbed the Disraelian system, was to blame here too. (Disraeli had been created Earl of Beaconsfield in 1876.) His foreign policy had not merely been a moral disgrace – it had been extravagant and expensive as well. The taxpayer had had to foot the bill, creating, Gladstone claimed, a severe downturn in demand. Disraeli was not fit to manage the nation's finances.

In the Midlothian Campaigns, Gladstone made a combined appeal to the national interest and the consciences and pockets of the electorate that proved irresistible. In the light of the economic depression and the lack-lustre campaign fought by Disraeli, the Conservatives might have been heading for defeat anyway. But when the Liberals returned to power in 1880, with an 84-seat majority, most contemporaries saw it as Gladstone's triumph.

6 ⌐ GLADSTONE'S SECOND MINISTRY, 1880–5

To Queen Victoria's dismay, Gladstone became Prime Minister for the second time in April 1880. Although he had not fought the Midlothian campaign as party leader, its spectacular success led Hartington, who had succeeded him in the post in 1875, to concede that only Gladstone had the authority to lead the Party. But lead it where? For, in contrast to 1868, the Liberals had not fought the election on any positive legislative programme: instead, Gladstone had conducted a triumphant crusade against the evils of Beaconsfieldism. Indeed, he imagined that once the political system had been purged of Disraeli's crimes and its health restored, he could retire at last.

Gladstone's wishes were to be frustrated in two ways.

● First, the momentum of imperialism proved very hard to reverse. Britain's position in South Africa and Afghanistan only stabilised after tortuous manoeuvres and negotiations. Worse, Gladstone was to find himself, much against his will, ever more deeply embroiled in the tangled affairs of Egypt and the Sudan. The impossibility and expense of unravelling the imperial commitments left by Disraeli was one of the reasons for the Liberals' loss of office in 1885.

KEY ISSUE

Why was the reforming record of Gladstone's second ministry so much less impressive than that of his first?

● Second, and still more seriously, the Irish problem erupted with a violence and intensity that was unparalleled, and quite unexpected. Gladstone's Government arguably faced the United Kingdom's most threatening revolutionary mass movement ever – the Irish Land League.

Gladstone had no warning of the coming crisis as he assembled his cabinet. With one duke, one marquis and four earls, its centre of gravity

PICTURE 27

Gladstone, the 'Grand Old Man' (or GOM), as he became known to his followers

once again leaned towards the Whigs. This reflected both the predominantly landowning and cautious tone of the parliamentary party, as well as Gladstone's well-established preference for rule by aristocracy. The main controversy was the issue of representation for the party's Radical wing. In 1877, Joseph Chamberlain, the most prominent, ambitious and dynamic of the Radical leaders, had set up the National Liberal Federation. This was designed to co-ordinate the local constituency organisations, pressurise the party in Westminster into adopting more Radical policies, and propel Chamberlain, its President, into the Cabinet. In fact, many leading Radicals, suspicious of Chamberlain's style, refused to join the organisation. But this did not stop its President from claiming that the NLF's campaign had been instrumental in winning 60 seats at the general election.

Gladstone showed little respect for Chamberlain, and only reluctantly agreed to make him President of the Board of Trade. Over the course of the ministry Chamberlain was to feel increasingly underestimated by Gladstone – or the 'Grand Old Man', as his awe-struck colleagues now referred to him. Chamberlain's personal exasperation, as well as his political frustrations, go a long way to explain why he rejected his leader's proposal of Home Rule for Ireland in 1886.

A *The Government's record 1880–5*

The Third Reform Act of 1884 was the one major legislative achievement of Gladstone's second ministry, in distinct contrast to the abundance of his first. It increased the United Kingdom electorate from three to five millions. The main change was to end the different qualifications for voting in borough and county seats, with the 1867 head of household borough qualification applied to both types of constituency. The chief effect of the Act was to give the vote to many (male) rural householders. There was much concern, prior to the passage of the Act, as to its likely electoral consequences for the two main parties.

For details of the Redistribution Act, 1885 and its consequences see Chapter 10, pages 300–2

The Conservative leader, Lord Salisbury, was deeply suspicious of the likely effect of reform on his party's prospects in rural constituencies. As a peer he sat in the House of Lords where the Conservatives had a built-in majority. In return for not opposing the Reform Act in the Lords, he insisted on changes in constituency boundaries which, after 1886, were to prove remarkably advantageous to the Conservatives.

B *Early problems over Ireland*

See pages 276–7 on Parnell and the Land League

Irish issues are considered at length in Chapter 9. Here it is the impact of those issues on politics at Westminster that is examined. The creation of the Irish Land League in 1879 had given a fillip to Irish nationalism at Westminster. The fusion of an agrarian mass movement with revolutionary nationalism, coupled to Parliamentary agitation marked, as its leaders recognised, a new departure in the history of Irish Nationalism. Under the leadership of Parnell, this involved a more confrontational style, both more violent and more disciplined than under Isaac

Butt. The Home Rulers' behaviour in the Commons was designed to echo the violence and extremism of their Irish followers. Obstructing the business of the House became a standard tactic.

A difficulty for the Liberal Government was that their own ranks were divided on Irish matters. The Whigs wanted firm action to enforce law and order. Radicals, on the other hand, believed that social injustice was the root cause of Ireland's miseries. The Chief Secretary for Ireland, W. E. Forster, developed a two-edged policy, on the one hand a strong Coercion Act, on the other a far-reaching Second Land Act (1881) which finally conceded the three Fs so wanted by Irish peasants.

This interference with property rights greatly upset the Whigs. Then, in 1881, Forster persuaded Gladstone to imprison Parnell and other Land League leaders because he was convinced that the Land League was setting out to sabotage his policies. This mistaken decision gave renewed impetus to the Irish agitation, which forced the Government to release Parnell and negotiate the 'Kilmainham Treaty' with him. Gladstone had hoped that land reform and conciliation of the Catholic Church would create a situation in Ireland where the natural leaders of society would accept the British connection and Westminster rule. However, by 1882, these hopes were exposed as hollow and all his efforts since 1868 to 'pacify Ireland' had failed.

The three Fs

1. **Fixity of tenure** (security for tenants)
2. **Fair rents**
3. **Free sale** (of any improvements made by the tenant)

See page 277 for a fuller explanation

See page 277

C *Difficulties and defeat: the 1885 election*

If Gladstone expected some relief from his difficulties when he turned from Ireland to consider imperial affairs, he was to be disappointed. In the Midlothian Campaign, he had promised to reconstitute British foreign policy along Liberal lines. Peace was to be the ultimate objective. By working in close co-operation with the other leading European powers, respecting the rights of other nations and peoples, and keeping a careful eye on expenditure, the dangerous and extravagant adventurism, which had characterised Disraeli's foreign policy, could be avoided. The immediate priority was to roll back the frontiers of Beaconsfieldism and reduce British commitments in South Africa and Afghanistan. In the spring and summer of 1885, the Chancellor of the Exchequer revealed that the Government would have to find £10 million in extra taxes to pay for the imperial adventures embarked on earlier by Disraeli. This horrified and dismayed his Cabinet colleagues.

Party morale was low enough already. The Radicals lamented that events in Ireland, Egypt and the Sudan between them had squeezed out most of the reforms they had wanted. The Third Reform Act had left the Whigs worried as to the role they would have to play in the new electoral system. They rightly feared that Liberal constituency organisations would prefer to adopt Radical candidates rather than men of their own type to fight the new single-member constituencies. The Whigs were, finally, in retreat in the Liberal Party.

The situation in Ireland was deteriorating too. After two relatively quiet years, disorder was spreading at an alarming rate. The old Whig/Radical divisions opened up. The Lord Lieutenant of Ireland, Earl

See pages 333–5 for events in Egypt and Sudan

Spencer, argued for the necessity of coercion; Chamberlain insisted that this had to be counterbalanced by a more constructive approach, in particular by devolving to the Irish greater responsibilities for local government. The Cabinet could not agree and there was deadlock.

The Government was finally defeated on its Budget in June 1885 by a surprising – and short-lived – alliance of Conservatives and Irish Nationalists. The predominant feeling in Cabinet was one of relief. For the six months it would take to compile the new electoral registers required by the Third Reform Act, a minority Conservative Government under Lord Salisbury ruled Britain.

1885 was to bring one other disappointment for the Liberals in general, and the Radicals in particular. Chamberlain had hoped that the 1885 elections, which were finally held in November, would be a Radical triumph. In his 'Unauthorised Programme' and a series of speeches, he unveiled a package of proposals targeted at the newly enfranchised agricultural labourer. Elective county councils were to be created, with powers of compulsory purchase, to buy up parts of larger estates and sell the land off, on attractive terms, to create a new class of smallholders. Progressive taxation and 'Death Duties' were to be introduced, to pay for free education and better housing for the poor.

Chamberlain's campaign had a tremendous impact – but at least as much to the Conservatives' advantage as to the Liberals'. It is true that he seemed to catch the imagination of the farm workers: the Liberals made big gains in the counties. But Liberal losses in the middle-sized boroughs – their traditional strongholds – were greater. Salisbury had delighted in denouncing Chamberlain as a 'Sicilian Bandit'. Gladstone, trying to distance himself from the Radical assault, insisted that the Radicals' Programme had no official status. But middle-class, Anglican England was unconvinced. Instead, it was frightened for its property, and its Church. The Liberals lost over 25 seats to the Conservatives in November 1885, and Chamberlain was widely blamed for the setback. By the end of the year, having suffered the rejection of his local government scheme for Ireland and the failure of his 'Unauthorised' programme, Chamberlain had every appearance of being a coming man whose time had somehow gone.

KEY ISSUE

Why did Chamberlain's 'Unauthorised Programme' drive many Liberals into voting Conservative?

7 ~ GLADSTONE AND IRELAND: THE HOME RULE CRISIS, 1885–6

The most striking feature of the 1885 election was the return of 86 hard-line Nationalists – and not a single Liberal! – for Irish constituencies. Parnell could no longer be dismissed as an unrepresentative extremist: he spoke for the majority of the Irish people. What made Parnell's success particularly significant was that 86 was precisely the majority which the Liberals had over the Conservatives at Westminster. The Irish could make Gladstone Prime Minister again: or they could block him. That simple arithmetical fact lay behind the political drama of the next few months.

TIMELINE

A chronology of the Home Rule crisis

1885	**Nov**	General Election results – Liberals 335; Conservatives 249; Irish Nationalists 86
	17 Dec	Gladstone's supposed 'conversion' to Home Rule leaked to the press by his son.
1886	**26 Jan**	Liberals and Irish Nationalists voted together to end Salisbury's 'caretaker' administration. Gladstone formed his third ministry – but without Hartington, who disagreed with Home Rule.
	26 March	Chamberlain, finding Gladstone committed to Home Rule, left the Cabinet
	8 April	Gladstone introduced the Home Rule Bill into the Commons
	31 May	Chamberlain chaired the meeting of Radical Liberals who decided to vote against the Bill
	8 June	Home Rule Bill defeated by 30 votes, with 93 Liberals (led by Hartington and Chamberlain), voting against Gladstone. Gladstone called a general election.
	July	General elections results – Gladstonian Liberals 196, Tories 316, Liberal Unionists (i.e. anti-Home Rule Liberals) 74; Irish Nationalist 83

These were momentous events. The split in the Liberal Party became permanent and helped to ensure that the following two decades of British politics would be Tory-dominated. The 'Irish question', of course, is perhaps still unsolved today. It is hardly surprising, therefore, that historians continue to debate the merits of Gladstone's plans and the exact nature of his motivation, and the motives of his rivals – inside and outside the Liberal Party – over these crucial months.

A *What were Gladstone's motives for Home Rule?*

1 Gladstone's 'conversion' to Home Rule may have been purely partisan, intended to serve his own purposes by securing for his party the Irish support necessary for holding on to power. Arguably, by bringing the question of Home Rule to centre stage, Gladstone was inventing a reason for his own survival as party leader, for he, as no one else, had made Ireland into a mission. Hartington and Chamberlain, his potential rivals, would be left stranded.

2 However, the emphasis that this interpretation places on the rivalry between Gladstone and Chamberlain is misleading. The threat posed by Chamberlain has been exaggerated, for the Radicals were by no means as strong or as united as it suggested, and in any case Chamberlain's own star seemed to be waning in 1885. There was no need for Gladstone to use Home Rule to stave off a non-existent threat from the left.

3 He may have been guilty of opportunism, with Home Rule being the price Gladstone was prepared to pay for 86 Nationalist votes. Unfortunately, some of the vital evidence here is thoroughly

Class debate

Motion 'That Gladstone's public conversion to Home Rule for Ireland represented the triumph of statesmanship over Party advantage'

ambiguous. For example, Gladstone definitely hoped that the Home Rule question could be solved on non-party lines. In mid-December, he let it be known to Salisbury that the Liberals would support a Conservative Home Rule scheme, arguing that this would serve the national interest best, not least in securing a safer passage for the bill through both Houses of Parliament. Gladstone was prepared to sacrifice political power if he could thereby pass a law that he believed was vital for the well-being of the United Kingdom. Surely this marks the very opposite of political opportunism? On the other hand, as Salisbury realised, this could be a very clever way of letting the Conservative Party tear itself apart.

4   Equally, of course, Gladstone's conversion may have rested on a development of long-established principles based on his ideas of national identity. If this is the case, the charge of opportunism might be rebutted. One of the foundation stones of Gladstone's view of politics was indeed his belief in nationality. All peoples had a God-given right to freedom and independence and when, conscious of their nationhood, they rose up to claim that freedom, then it was a crime and a sin to oppress them or to aid their oppressors. Gladstone had followed this principle in the Balkans, in South Africa, in Afghanistan and in the Sudan. With Home Rule, Gladstone was merely applying the same principle to Ireland. The Irish people's sense of nationhood, inspired by Parnell, had grown dramatically over these years. They had spoken unequivocally in the 1885 election: the scale of the Home Rulers victory was to Gladstone 'a very great fact indeed'.

5   Gladstone's historical perceptions were changing too. The more Irish history he read, the more he became convinced that the Union had been a tragic mistake, and equally, the better he understood the Irish Nationalists' resentment of British misgovernment.

6   What appears finally to have crystallised these sentiments, and made Gladstone determined to act, whatever the odds, was the fear that gripped him towards the end of 1885 that Ireland was again on the brink of anarchy. His contacts repeatedly warned him that unless he took a bold initiative 'social dissolution' and 'revolution' in Ireland were inevitable. Home Rule alone could avoid the oncoming catastrophe.

It was indeed time for Britain to draw on the insight that had prompted Parnell's release in 1882, and recognise Home Rule itself as the only legitimate instrument by which social order could be upheld in Ireland, and the ultimate integrity of the Empire be maintained. Home Rule was now, as Gladstone put it, 'a source not of danger but of strength – the danger . . . lies in refusing it'.

B   *The 1886 Home Rule Bill*

Gladstone introduced the Home Rule Bill into the Commons on 8 April 1886. In its scale and ambition it was the greatest piece of legis-

" THE START."

(GREAT RACE BETWEEN THE G.O.M. AND " THE MARKISS.")

PICTURE 28 *A cartoon from* Punch *of Gladstone, the Grand Old Man (GOM), and the Marquess of Salisbury, the Tory leader, as they set out on the race to win political power*

KEY ISSUE

*Why was there such
strong feeling against
Home Rule for Ireland?*

lation he had ever devised. It was not a bill for Irish independence.
Gladstone's 'mission was still to pacify Ireland, not to liberate it'. But he
was convinced that the only way to pacify Ireland was to give Ireland its
own Parliament, so that the Irish could teach themselves the arts and
responsibilities of self-government. Accordingly, the Dublin Parliament
that Gladstone envisaged was to have considerable powers – for example, over law and order, and taxation. But defence, foreign affairs and
trade were to be left in the hands of the Imperial Parliament at Westminster. Ireland was to have no representatives there, although it would
be expected to contribute 1/15th of the total requirements of the Imperial exchequer.

The Home Rule Bill itself was lost by 30 votes in the House of Commons in early June, with Hartington, the leading Whig and Chamberlain, the leading Radical, at the head of the Liberal rebels.

Critics of the Bill had a strong case. They spotlighted a series of crucial flaws in the Bill that might well have made it unworkable.

● It seemed quite impossible to stabilise the constitutional status of Ireland at some halfway house between Union and Independence. No
 one could offer any meaningful guarantees that the Irish would not
 regard Home Rule as a mere staging post on the journey to full
 nationhood. The projected removal of all Irish MPs from Westminster in Gladstone's Bill was held to make ultimate separation more
 likely.
● The fate of Ulster, in the north of Ireland, posed a major problem
 too. Some predicted that Protestant Ulster would rebel rather than
 accept rule from Dublin. It was the wealthiest and most industrialised part of Ireland, whose commercial ties with the British mainland and the Empire beyond were far more important to it than any
 ties to the south. Would a Dublin parliament nurture or destroy its
 prosperity?
● More serious was Ulster's religious grievance. Parnell and Gladstone
 both mistook the genuine anxiety of the Protestant community for
 the **bigotry** of a few extremists. Many in Ulster believed that the
 Nationalists' ultimate aim was full independence, Home Rule was a
 profound threat to their prosperity and culture.

bigotry being intolerant
and narrow-minded

British prejudice and bigotry do also have their part to play in
explaining the strength of the reaction to Gladstone's proposals. Even
moderate Whigs, who prided themselves on tolerance, perceived
Catholic Ireland through spectacles warped by racial and religious contempt. Most Tories were a good deal worse: Salisbury was to sneer in
May 1886 that the Irish were no more capable of self-government than
savages in Africa. Imperialism was important for opponents of Home
Rule, both as an ideology and as world strategy. What business had the
backward, violent and superstitious Irish to turn their back on the civil-
ising influence of the richest and best-governed country in the world?
Not just Whigs and Conservatives but Radical Liberals like Chamberlain and Bright were appalled by the consequences for Britain's status as
a world power if she were seen to back down before a gang of 'ruffians'

and 'assassins'. And the prospect of separation raised the fearsome danger of an Irish alliance with some future continental enemy of Britain.

C *Who was to blame for the break up of the Liberal Party?*

All these complaints mentioned above, which were common to both Liberal Unionist and Tory alike, were voiced in the Parliamentary debates. The motives of the Whigs and those of Chamberlain and the Radicals were, however, not identical.

Chamberlain was motivated mainly be self-interest. He knew that if Gladstone were allowed to make Home Rule into the Liberals' new crusade, his own plans for domestic reforms, as outlined in the Radical Programme of 1885, would be sidelined indefinitely. Chamberlain was also convinced that Home Rule would be a vote loser, probably inside Parliament and certainly with the British electorate. It would be best if he distanced himself from the disaster that was closing in on Gladstone. The rejection of Home Rule would surely bring about Gladstone's retirement, when the party would turn to men with fresh ideas who were untainted by any Irish obsession – men like Chamberlain, perhaps?

Hartington, the Whig leader's motives are more difficult to interpret. Hartington wanted to be Prime Minister, and was the natural leader of any centre coalition – an outcome quite conceivable in early 1886. But it is not necessary to explain his opposition to Home Rule purely in terms of opportunism: he had long been committed to pursuing coercion first, and concession only second, as the way forward in Ireland. Even more than most Whigs, Hartington was exasperated by Gladstone's readiness to make concession after concession to the Irish Catholics. As far as Hartington could see, they were neither deserving nor grateful. But Gladstone's fund of generosity was as inexhaustible as the Irish problem itself appeared insoluble. That, Hartington concluded, was not a recipe for rational politics. As with Chamberlain, Hartington expected Home Rule to be rejected, Gladstone to retire and the Liberal Party to be restored to saner leadership – in this case, his own.

For **the Whigs** as a whole it has been argued that Home Rule was more the occasion than the cause of their break-away. They saw radical pressure rising in the Liberal Party and, with it, the challenge to the rights of property. In this analysis, 1886 becomes the moment when the class tensions within the Liberal Party were finally resolved, and the Whigs – wealthy, privileged and anxious – made their long-expected move towards the Conservative ranks.

This interpretation is attractive but not entirely convincing:

● the debate over the Second Land Act in 1881 had raised the threat to the rights of property owners far more directly than anything in the Home Rule Bill, but the party had survived that episode pretty much intact

KEY ISSUE

Why did the various Liberal Unionists leave the Liberal Party?

● the analysis is based on an exaggerated estimation of Chamberlain's prospects – not good early in 1886 – and the threat from Radicalism in general

● above all the Liberal break-up did not occur along the Whig-Radical fault-line. Many 'moderates' ended up staying with Gladstone, while 'Radical Joe' led 30 of his followers to vote alongside Hartington's Whigs and Salisbury's Tories.

What pressures could have forced the Radical, Chamberlain, and the Whig, Hartington, to move in the same direction? Both were anxious about the repercussions of Home Rule for British imperialism and national security. Neither wanted to sacrifice Ulster's Protestants to 'Rome Rule'. But most important of all, the events of 1885–6 had finally convinced them that Gladstone's style of leadership was simply intolerable.

Gladstone bears a heavy responsibility for the break up. Aged seventy-seven, he was increasingly a stubborn and self-deluding old man, deaf to warnings or criticisms even from close friends. His management of colleagues was distant and dictatorial. So obsessive and self-righteous was Gladstone's pursuit of justice for Ireland that he had hardly felt any obligation to consult with leading colleagues before his 'conversion' to Home Rule was made known. In particular, he had made no attempt to keep Hartington or Chamberlain in the picture. Gladstone staggered Harcourt, his Chancellor of the Exchequer, in late January 1886, when he revealed that he was ready to press on, if necessary, without support from either of them. In fact, he would, he mused later, have been 'prepared to go forward without anybody'.

Some Radical and Nonconformist activists might well be enraptured by such heroism, but to many Whigs it looked more like blind and destructive fanaticism. Gladstone's election speeches for Home Rule could only have confirmed Whig anxieties that he was ready to betray every principle of moderate, rational government that they held dear. Drunk on his own words, Gladstone had, in his opponents' eyes, become the slave of his own terrible sense of mission.

D *Defeat*

The chances of a majority for Home Rule slipped away between April and June 1886, despite a variety of concessions and promises from Gladstone. On 31 May, a vital meeting of disaffected Radicals led by Chamberlain took place and they agreed to vote against it. That meeting determined the outcome of the vote: a majority of 30 against the bill, including 93 dissident Liberals.

Gladstone threw himself into the following general election with awesome vigour for a man of 77 years, convinced that the people would respond to his call as they had done in 1868 and 1880. His optimism again suggests a slackening grasp on political reality. It is true that his own campaign produced echoes of the revivalist fervour of Midlothian. His hold over the party's radical activists had already been demonstrated by his remarkable capture in May of the National Liberal Federation

THE FINISH.

PICTURE 29   *'The Finish' from* Punch. *Salisbury beats Gladstone to the finishing line*

– Chamberlain's own power base – for Home Rule. But the commitment of Liberal enthusiasts did not compensate for the alienation of the electoral middle ground and the decisive desertion of the Liberal Unionists. With the latter, Gladstone fell victim to a masterstroke of opportunism by Salisbury who promised that Conservative constituency organisations would not put forward their own candidates against any defecting Liberal Unionists. This stiffened the latter's resolve in the last weeks of Westminster arm-twisting and helps to explain how 73 of them held on to their seats in the election. The Gladstonian Liberal party was reduced to 191 MPs, as against 316 Tories. The 83 Parnellites, now firmly locked to Gladstone, could not begin to bridge the gap. Home Rule, for now, was dead. The prospects for Gladstonian Liberalism were not any healthier.

8 ⌐ THE DECLINE OF GLADSTONIAN LIBERALISM

Gladstone treated the defeat of Home Rule as a temporary setback and resolved to fight on for justice for Ireland. Thoughts of retirement were abandoned. But Gladstone's position as Liberal leader was increasingly difficult: the break up of 1886 had purged the party of most of its Whigs, leaving it more consistently Radical in outlook than it had ever been before. Yet Gladstone had little interest in the Radical agenda. In 1891, at a meeting of the National Liberal Federation held in Newcastle, he only reluctantly gave his endorsement to the so-called Newcastle Programme of reforms – a ragbag including the introduction of death duties, free elementary education, parish councils, concessions to the powerful temperance lobby and disestablishment of the Anglican Church in Wales and Scotland – in return for the party committing itself to Home Rule as the number one priority.

> ## KEY ISSUE
>
> *How far can Gladstone personally be held responsible for the weak position the Liberal Party was in after 1886?*

What enthusiasm there ever had been for Home Rule in the party and amongst the electorate was now waning. In 1889, disaster struck the Irish Nationalist camp. For a decade, Parnell had had as his mistress the wife of Captain O'Shea, one of the Irish Home Rule MPs. This man now decided to divorce his wife and revelations in the courts ruined Parnell's reputation. Gladstone knew that his Nonconformist supporters would be appalled by the scandal, and strongly recommended that Parnell stand down as the leader of the Home Rulers. His refusal split the Home Rule party into Parnellites and anti-Parnellites, the latter with the full backing of the Irish Catholic hierarchy behind them. In an extraordinarily bitter campaign, the Parnellites were crushed. In October 1891, Parnell died, an exhausted, broken man.

This was the unhelpful background to Gladstone's last attempt, in 1893, to force a Home Rule Bill through Parliament. The Liberals had won the 1892 general election, but the big majority, which he had been expecting, failed to materialise. They had 273 seats, only four more than the Tories, and with 46 Liberal Unionists in the new Parliament, Gladstone would be completely dependent on the support of 82 Irish

Nationalist MPs. Although the Second Home Rule Bill passed through the Commons by a majority of 45, its rejection by the Lords was as overwhelming as it was predictable: 419 votes to 41.

For many reasons the final parting between Gladstone and his colleagues was near.

- Gladstone wanted to dissolve Parliament and fight one last election on the issue of justice for Ireland. His cabinet colleagues refused. They were convinced that Home Rule was a vote loser, and were exasperated by the way Gladstone's increasingly obsessive commitment to Ireland was blocking all other legislation.
- The tensions between the great powers were growing and the Admiralty was demanding a large increase in naval spending. Gladstone, reflecting that he had spent 60 years of his political life in 'a constant effort to do all I could for economy and for peace' could not accept such 'mad' proposals, despite the fact that they had won the support of the rest of the Cabinet. This was the issue on which, (with his hearing and eyesight increasingly failing) in March 1894, he chose to resign.
- He himself felt more and more like a 'survival' from another era. Not one of the principles of Gladstonian Liberalism appeared relevant to Britain's needs as the turn of the century approached.
- In the face of the rise of Labour, a new generation of Liberal thinkers was emerging, who were convinced that the state had the means and the duty to help the poor – and thus keep Socialism at bay. Gladstone, however, opposed any interference in the workings of the free market. For example, he had regarded pressure for a statutory eight-hour working day in the early 1890s as an ominous sign that even 'the working masses' had been warped by that spirit of self-interest which had long since corrupted 'the classes'.
- Gladstone seemed quite out of step with the political demands of the time. He seemed blind to the probability that the Liberals' survival as a major political party would depend on their success in retaining the support of the working class.

For more on the Labour Party see Chapter 12, pages 368–74

But even Gladstone could not freeze the process of social change in Britain. By the 1890s, it had become, predominantly, a horizontally divided class society. The remarkable alliance of different classes which had provided the social underpinning of Gladstonian Liberalism, had irreparably broken up. Whig aristocrats, moderate Anglican landowners, Nonconformist men of commerce and industry, radical artisans and progressive intellectuals no longer shared a common language or purpose. It had been the miracle of Gladstonian Liberalism to make them believe for so long that they had. But the lessons of the following two decades did not all serve to show the Grand Old Man up as a hopelessly out of date. The chaos and impotence into which the Liberal cabinet fell after his departure was a painful reminder of how far Gladstone's personal authority and political crusades had been necessary to keep the Liberal Party together and electorally successful. The Tories were to enjoy crushing victories in the 1895 and 1900 elections.

9 ∽ ASSESSING GLADSTONE

A *Political achievements*

Gladstone's political career spanned the period from 1832 to 1894. In that time he was out of Parliament for only six months, in 1846. This attempt to assess his career can provide only a very brief summary of the issues touched upon in Chapters 6–8. Gladstone's major achievements included the following:

- His financial measures, where his reputation rests first on his work in Peel's 1841–6 Government implementing free trade policies, and then as Chancellor of the Exchequer in the 1850s and 1860s striving to reduce government spending and to cut duties on trade still further. By the mid-1860s Britain was virtually a free trade country. His emphasis on low expenditure and low taxation set the dominant tone for Victorian public finance through to the end of the century and, in so doing, also set the limits on what was acceptable government activity.

- His reforms in the conduct of public life and administration, largely brought about in his great ministry of 1868 to 1874, swept away much of the inefficiency and corruption inherited from the eighteenth century.

- He came to symbolise and to lead, first at Westminster and then across the nation, the new British Liberal Party which emerged in the mid-century and which provided much of the energy of political life through almost to the century's end. Without his dominant leadership, it would have been a very different party but he was, at least in part, responsible for its loss of momentum and electoral difficulties after 1886.

- He introduced no great programme of social reforms. This would have undermined his central financial strategy and contradicted his belief in self-reliance and individual responsibility. In his last years this approach restricted the ability of his Liberal colleagues to meet the aspirations of the increasingly vocal working class.

- He offered a distinctive foreign policy, opposed to the assertive nationalism of both Palmerston and Disraeli, one based on moral judgement and conciliation, avoiding reckless international adventures and expensive overseas commitments. In practice, particularly in his 1880–5 ministry, he found these principles difficult to achieve.

- He was at his most radical in his Irish policies, with Church Disestablishment, the Land Acts and Home Rule. He had the courage and the imagination to promote solutions from which his opponents and many of his younger, allegedly more radical, colleagues shrank. In the end, of course, he failed and must in part be held responsible for that failure, which left Ireland unpacified.

B *The man*

As befits the greatest prime minister in his country's history, he was a very complex person, often a mystery to others and capable of great self-deception:

- his personal and his political life rested on his deep religious faith. His views on the role of religion in the state changed. He moved from support, in the 1830s, of the essential role of the Church of England to a more vague notion of the morality of the crowd as the basis of moral government and political action. He asserted the central role of a Christian morality as the basis for all political activity. He, no doubt, often deceived himself as to his own motives, in both personal life, as with his work in the 1850s, rescuing London's prostitutes, and in politics, with the convenient links forged with Nonconformists and Irish Catholics just as his views on the role of the Church of England became less rigorous
- in many matters he remained essentially a conservative. He favoured the aristocracy, continued to protect the privileged position of the Church of England and accepted the sharp inequalities in Victorian Society, including its poverty and the cruelties of the Poor Law, as part of the natural order of things
- he was most radical in his Irish and his foreign policies and arguably became more radical the older he became. In lesser matters he remained essentially conservative.

C *Style and reputation*

- Gladstone was a remarkably powerful parliamentary debater. In Parliament he made his reputation in the early 1850s with speeches lasting several hours, one savaging Palmerston's foreign policy over Don Pacifico, another destroying Disraeli's 1852 budget, a third presenting his own budget proposals in 1853. He retained this mastery of the Commons throughout his long political life.
- In the 1860s he reached out from the shelter of Parliament to reach mass audiences, often largely working men, in the industrial cities. He captivated them and they became a necessary stimulus to him, reaching its climax in the great Midlothian, and later moral, crusades over foreign policy. He transformed the style and practice of general elections, creating the national campaign, which was reported throughout the press and so united the parliamentary party with the people at large.
- In his last years his reputation bitterly divided opponents and supporters. For Liberal loyalists and his working-class audiences, he was simply the Grand Old Man. The Queen came to regard him as a pompous bore and for Disraeli he was always at heart a hypocrite. Divisions over Home Rule sharpened the tone of adverse opinions.

The arrangements for his state funeral outdid those for anyone not of royal blood, with the possible exceptions of the 1852 funeral of the Duke of Wellington and the 1965 funeral of Winston Churchill. The Prince of Wales was one of the distinguished pallbearers. The Queen, as was customary, did not attend the funeral of a commoner, nor was she lavish in her praise of her four times Prime Minister.

10 ⌐ BIBLIOGRAPHY

ARTICLES

M. Cole '1885: Democratic Watershed for Britain?' *Modern History Review*, February 1999.

G. D. Goodlad 'Gladstone and the People', *Modern History Review*, November 1999, which debates, in three pages, whether Gladstone was a radical or a reactionary.

D. Murphy 'Gladstone and Ireland' *Modern History Review*, November 1998, an ideal revision read.

J. Vincent 'Was Disraeli a Failure?', *History Today*, October 1981.

BOOKS FOR AS & A LEVEL STUDENTS
General

Paul Adelman *Gladstone, Disraeli and Later Victorian Politics*, Longman, 1983, which also includes interesting material on Salisbury.

A. Mayer *The Growth of Democracy in Britain*, Access to History series, Hodder & Stoughton, 1999, has a useful chapter on party politics from 1868 to 1906.

M. Pugh *The Making of Modern British Politics 1867–1939*, Basil Blackwell, 1982, which includes a brilliant chapter on Gladstone.

D. G. Wright *Democracy and Reform 1815–1885*, Longman, 1970.

Disraeli and the Conservatives

R. Blake *The Conservative Party from Peel to Major*, Fontana, 1996, Chapter 4.

J. Walton *Disraeli*, Lancaster Pamphlet, Routledge, 1990.

D. Watts *Tories, Conservatives and Unionists 1815–1914*, Hodder & Stoughton, 1994 is part of the Access to History series and has a useful chapter on Disraeli and the party.

Gladstone and the Liberals

D. Watts *Whigs, Radicals and Liberals 1815–1914*, Access to History series, Hodder & Stoughton, 2002, is packed with relevant information and exercises.

Michael Winstanley *Gladstone and the Liberal Party*, Lancaster Pamphlet, Routledge, 1990 – a superb synthesis, which, however, does not aim to cover the Irish dimension in much depth.

FURTHER READING

M. Bentley *Politics without Democracy 1815–1914*, Routledge, 1994, a challenging and exciting interpretation once the basics of the period have been mastered.

E. F. Biagini *Gladstone*, Macmillan, 2000, a brief and recent account (138 pages).

R. Blake *Disraeli*, Eyre and Spottiswode, 1966, is the classic study of the Conservative leader. It looks dauntingly bulky but is in fact very readable, has an excellent index, and its conclusion is only ten pages long.

B. Coleman *Conservatism and the Conservative Party in Nineteenth Century Britain*, Edward Arnold, 1988.

E. J. Feuchtwanger *Gladstone*, Macmillan, 1989, is a comprehensive and accessible biography.

R. Jenkins *Gladstone*, Macmillan, 1995 is a most readable personal and political biography.

T. A. Jenkins' *The Liberal Ascendancy*, 1830–1886, Macmillan, 1994, a brief and accessible survey.

I. Maskin *Disraeli*, Longman, Profiles in Power, 1995.

H. C. G. Matthew *Gladstone 1809–98*, Clarendon Press, 1997, perhaps *the* scholarly analysis by the man who edited most of Gladstone's Diaries. Use the index on a specific issue.

P. Smith *Disraeli: A Brief Life*, Cambridge University Press, 1996 sees his ideas and flamboyant image as more interesting than his political impact.

John Vincent's classic, *The Formation of the British Liberal Party 1857–68*, Harvester, 1976, is marvellous, if detailed, on the context and structure of Gladstonian Liberalism.

11 ⌐ STRUCTURED AND ESSAY QUESTIONS ON THE 1868–86 PERIOD

A *Structured questions for AS level*

1. (a) What problems was the 1870 Education Act intended to solve?
   (b) Why did the measure become so controversial?

2. (a) What were the main issues which contributed to the growing unpopularity of Gladstone' First Ministry?
   (b) How far should Gladstone be held personally responsible for this?

3. (a) What were the main themes of Disraeli's 1872 speeches in Manchester and at the Crystal Palace?
   (b) Why were they so important to him personally and to the Conservative Party?

4. (a) Identify the main international and imperial issues with which Disraeli was concerned in his 1874-80 ministry.
   (b) How far does he deserve his reputation as a great European statesman?

5. (a) Identify the main measures by which Gladstone, from 1868 to 1886, sought to pacify Ireland.
   (b) Why, by the end of his Third Ministry (1886), could he be considered to have failed in this task?

B *Essay questions for A2*

1. 'A great reforming ministry': how far do you agree with this verdict on Gladstone's Ministry of 1868–74?
2. 'A heroic failure': Is this a fair verdict on the Irish legislation of Gladstone's first ministry?
3. 'An unprincipled opportunist': discuss this verdict on Disraeli.
4. 'Disraeli did not win the 1874 general election; Gladstone lost it.' How far do you agree?
5. What do you consider were Disraeli's main services to the Conservative Party?
6. Why did Gladstone's Second Ministry achieve so much less than his first?
7. Why did Gladstone fail to solve the Irish Question?
8. 'An old, wild and incomprehensible man' (Queen Victoria 1892): why did so many of the Victorian upper class come to fear and loathe Gladstone?
9. 'A great national statesman but an indifferent leader of his party'. How far do you agree with this verdict on Gladstone?

12 ∽ DOCUMENTARY EXERCISE: GLADSTONE ON THE 'CLASSES' AND THE 'MASSES'

Read the following passage, an extract from a speech Gladstone made to a largely working-class audience at the conclusion of his 1886 election campaign. Then answer the questions that follow:

[The Liberals] are opposed throughout the country by a compact army, and that army is a combination of the classes against the masses. I am thankful to say that there are among the classes many happy exceptions still. I am thankful to say that there are men wearing coronets [small crowns] on their heads who are as good and as sound and as genuine Liberals as any workingman that hears me at this moment. But, as a general rule, it cannot be pretended that we are supported by the dukes, or by the squires, or by the Established clergy, or by the officers of the army, or by a number of other bodies of very respectable people. What I observe is this: wherever a profession is highly privileged, wherever a profession is publicly endowed, it is there that you will find that almost the whole of the class and the profession are against us ... in the main, gentlemen, this is a question, I am sorry to say, of class against mass, of classes against the nation; and the question for us is, Will the nation show enough unity and determination to overbear, constitutionally, at the polls, the resistance of the classes? ... We should consider which of them is likely to be right. Do not let us look at our forces alone; let us look at that without which force is worthless, mischievous, and contemptible. Are we likely to be right? Are the classes ever right when they differ from the nation? ('No.') Well, wait a moment. I draw this distinction. I am not about to assert that the masses of the people, who do not and cannot give their leisure to politics, are necessarily, on all subjects, better judges than the leisured men who have great advantages for forming political judgements that the others have not; but this I will venture to say, that upon one great class of subjects, the largest and the most weighty of them all, where the leading and determining considerations that ought to lead to a conclusion are truth, justice, and humanity, there, gentlemen, all the world over, I will back the masses against the classes.

Let me apply a little history to this question, and see whether the proposition I have just delivered is an idle dream and the invention of an enthusiastic brain, or whether it is the lesson taught us eminently and indisputably by the history of the last half-century. [Gladstone went on to list ten subjects, including the abolition of slavery, Parliamentary reform, the triumph of Free Trade, the disestablishment of the Irish Church and the destruction of Beaconsfieldism, which together had 'formed the staple employment, and food of our political life for the last 60 years'.] On every one of them, without exception, the masses have been right and the classes have been wrong. Nor will it do, gentlemen, to tell me that I am holding the language of agitation; I am speaking the plain dictates of fact, for nobody can deny that on all these ten subjects the masses were on one side and the classes were on the other, and nobody can deny that the side of the masses, and not the side of the classes, is the one which now the whole nation confesses to have been right.

Maximum marks

1. According to this extract:
   (a) what superficial advantages do the classes have over the masses in forming political judgements? (5)
   (b) why, on the most important questions, would Gladstone still 'back the masses against the classes'? (6)
   (c) How effectively might the language, style and content of Gladstone's address appeal to his mainly working-class audience? (4)
   (d) Making use of both this extract and your own knowledge, examine why, by 1886, Gladstone had become such a controversial political figure. (15)

   Total marks (30)

> **Examination tip**: in question (d) make sure you make use of the document extract **as well as** your own knowledge. There will probably be a minimum of marks for attention to each part.

13 ⌁ STUDENT ACTIVITIES

Examination modules on Gladstone and on Disraeli are offered at both AS and A2 levels. Though the assessment pattern varies from examination board to board, it is also probable that both essay and source-based questions will be set.

ESSAY PLANNING

Before the examination – it is important that you practise essay planning during your history course and certainly long before you enter the examination room. At this stage you can think through essay plans for a number of examination questions. Practice in such planning will also be invaluable if you have to write coursework essays to be assessed as part of your A-level performance. It can also serve as an excellent form of revision of your understanding of major historical topics.

ESSAY PLANNING IN THE EXAMINATION

The first priority is to identify a question you would like to answer and then decide on a line of argument. You will not have time to write out elaborate plans (and do not waste time writing out the question) and six or seven key words may give you all the paragraph structure you need. You should not, at this point, be jotting down information just in case you forget it later. The elaborate essay plans of your coursework have no place in the exam room but the practice you had with them will have prepared you well to structure your exam essays without such a detailed approach. Many history essays ask you, in one form or another, 'how far you agree' with an opinion. The most straightforward way to answer such essay questions is to take a view – you explain why you agree with the proposition and over several paragraphs give illustrations of why you do so. You are still entitled, in a final paragraph, to indicate that your agreement is not total, it has limits, and then briefly give the instances where you disagree with the proposition contained in the essay title.

Ireland from the Union to Partition, 1800–1921

9

See Map 3 on page 269

INTRODUCTION

In 1800 Ireland was still formally a separate country to Great Britain even though its administration was carried on under British control. The Act of Union of 1800 changed Ireland's constitutional status and made it a part of a new state, the United Kingdom of Great Britain and Ireland. This State survived until 1921, when Ireland was split, or partitioned, into two separate parts. The smaller, north-eastern part became known as Northern Ireland and remained within the United Kingdom. The larger part first became a 'Dominion' within the British Empire, known as 'The Irish Free State' and then, in 1949, became a republic with no constitutional ties to Great Britain at all.

From the very start of the Union in 1800 there was widespread opposition within Ireland to the arrangement. Irish opposition to the Union, however, was to become divided between two approaches. While some Irish Nationalists became determined to end the connection with Great Britain altogether, others saw this as either impossible to achieve or that it was against the best interests of Ireland. Nationalists following this second approach aimed simply to extract concessions which would give Ireland more independent control of Irish affairs whilst remaining within the Union. The years between 1800 and 1921 saw a gradual strengthening of those who wished for the radical option of an Irish Republic, completely separated from Great Britain. For the great bulk of the period the republicans remained a tiny minority in Ireland. Nevertheless it cannot be doubted that the events of the period 1800 to 1921 resulted in a great sense of bitterness which was widely and genuinely felt by Irish people against Great Britain. This chapter tells the story of Ireland in a period which was to shape and define the relationship between Great Britain and Ireland long after 1921 and lead to the troubles which afflicted Northern Ireland in the last 30 years of the twentieth century. Even as the twenty-first century unfolds it is a story which continues.

1 ⌐ THE ACT OF UNION, 1800

On 1 January 1801, the previously separate states of Great Britain and Ireland were united in a single state to be known as 'The United Kingdom of Great Britain and Ireland'. Under this Act of Union, the separate Irish Parliament was abolished. Instead, Irish voters would elect MPs to the British Parliament at Westminster. In this new parliament, Ireland was represented by 100 MPs (eventually increased to 105 under the terms of the 1832 Reform Act), in the House of Commons and by four bishops and 28 other Irish peers in the House of Lords. The Act of Union further provided that the Anglican Church of Ireland would be recognised as the official church of Ireland and that free trade between the two countries would be maintained.

The explanation for this major constitutional step is to be found in the immediate situation in which the British Government found itself in the late 1790s. Since 1793, Britain had been at war with France and, by 1800, the power of France appeared to be increasing. It seemed to threaten the security of Great Britain itself. Ireland, ruled by a British administration, was resentful of British domination and divided internally between Catholics and Protestants. Thus it was an obvious target for French subversion, or even invasion. A French military force had actually been sent to Ireland in 1796, but most of the ships were lost or forced to return home because of bad weather. When a rebellion broke out in Ireland in 1798, it came as no real surprise to the British Government.

The revolt was engineered by a group calling itself the 'United Irishmen'. It was led by a Dublin barrister named Wolfe Tone, who aimed to create a democratic and republican Ireland, free of both British control and religious divisions between Roman Catholics and Protestants. The movement, however, failed to secure much influence in Ireland as a whole. Its strength lay mainly in the north-eastern counties of Ulster and, when the rising began in May 1798, it was soon crushed. The revolt was supported by the French who sent two separate expeditions. One was defeated at sea, whilst the other landed, but was forced to surrender by the British Army. Tone, who had been in France organising the intervention at the time of the initial rising, was captured with the French forces and later committed suicide in prison. Although the rising was a total failure, the British Prime Minister, William Pitt, could not ignore the threat posed by a hostile Ireland. As the Irish historian, Professor J. C. Beckett observed, 'From the British point of view the union was little short of a military necessity'. Nevertheless, the Act of Union was intended not only to make Ireland easier to govern but also to try to create a more stable situation in which some of the traditional tensions and grievances of Ireland could be reduced or eliminated. This hostility, of the Irish towards the British, stemmed from the following issues:

- Ireland was a country in which the overwhelming majority of the population were Roman Catholics, whilst the majority of land was owned by English aristocrats
- many of these landowners did not even live on their Irish estates but employed agents, who were often ruthless with the tenants, to run the estates for them

KEY ISSUE

Why was the Act of Union passed?

- in most of Ireland (Ulster was the exception), tenants had virtually no legal rights and could be evicted at the will of the landlord even if they were meeting all the terms of their tenancy
- British administration had, since the seventeenth century, sought to identify Roman Catholics as political enemies of the constitution, and denied them political rights. Laws against Roman Catholicism at one time actually banned the religion itself.

During the eighteenth century most of the laws against Roman Catholics had been repealed. However, in 1801, when the Act of Union came into operation, the most obvious reminder of these 'Penal Laws' was still in existence. This was the parliamentary oath which MPs and peers had to swear upon admission to Parliament. This oath (which had also applied to the Irish Parliament) specifically required the swearer to renounce the central beliefs of Roman Catholicism and thus constituted an insuperable barrier to a political career for Roman Catholics. It was Pitt's intention to follow up the Act of Union with further legislation to amend the parliamentary oath and allow Catholics to be elected to Parliament. In this aim he was defeated by the opposition of King George III. Pitt felt that he had to resign and the new Government accepted the King's wishes. The failure to grant a revision of the oath, or 'Catholic Emancipation' as the issue became known, at this early stage, ruined any hope that the Union would be widely accepted in Ireland. The demand for Catholic Emancipation became a banner behind which to rally Irish opinion (and not only Roman Catholic opinion) in the three decades following the Union.

> **KEY ISSUE**
>
> *Why might many Irish people see the Act of Union as a betrayal?*

2 ⌐ FROM UNION TO FAMINE, 1801–45

A *Daniel O'Connell and Catholic Emancipation*

At first, the reaction in Ireland to the failure of the British Government to grant Catholic Emancipation was one of disappointment rather than angry rebelliousness. There was also an increasing realisation, on all sides, that the political momentum was running in favour of Catholic Emancipation. There was a strong body of opinion in the House of Commons in favour of the 'Catholic claims' and many of the leading politicians who emerged after 1801 also supported reform. In these circumstances it appeared reasonable to most middle-class Irish nationalists to await the natural progress of events which must, in the course of time, deliver Catholic Emancipation without the need for a militant campaign which might stir other, more democratic and therefore less acceptable, ambitions. This gradualist approach was totally disrupted by the arrival on the Irish political scene of a new figure who transformed the entire situation, Daniel O'Connell.

See pages 138–9 for an account from the Government's perspective

PROFILE

PICTURE 30
Daniel O'Connell

DANIEL O'CONNELL (THE 'LIBERATOR' 1775–1847)

Daniel O'Connell was a successful barrister and a Roman Catholic, who had already made a name for himself opposing the Act of Union. After its passing he continued the attack, urging its repeal. O'Connell came to realise that repeal was impossible without the presence of Roman Catholic MPs at Westminster and he diverted his efforts to emancipation, with the specific intention of using it as a springboard for a greater nationalist campaign. O'Connell was not only a nationalist – he was also a 'populist' – that is, he believed in direct appeals to mass emotions as a political weapon. It was immensely important to him that emancipation not only be won, but be won by a popular campaign which involved the mobilisation of the masses in Ireland. Such a victory would provide the momentum for the greater victory to come – the end of the Union and the restoration of an Irish Parliament. O'Connell was not a revolutionary and he did not intend that Ireland should be separated from Britain. What he wanted was equal status for Ireland with Britain.

As O'Connell's prestige grew, so the dilemma posed by Catholic Emancipation became more complicated. The Tory Governments which dominated British politics up to 1830 were divided on the issue and could only maintain their unity by making it an 'open question' and abstaining from any debate within the Cabinet. In Ireland there was suspicion of O'Connell's motives and methods. However, in 1823, O'Connell launched what turned out to be the decisive factor – the Catholic Association. Although containing some upper-class members, this was essentially a mass movement. It was organised at parish level and rested on the authority of the local Catholic priests and O'Connell himself. By devising the 'catholic rent', collected by the priests at a rate of a penny a month, O'Connell ensured an immense operating fund for the movement which he could deploy virtually as he saw fit. Against such a formidable organisation, the British Governments after 1823 could offer only a divided opposition using delaying tactics. When O'Connell personally challenged the continued exclusion of Roman Catholics from Parliament by standing as a candidate in the County Clare election in 1828, the whole edifice of die-hard resistance crumbled. Wellington and Peel, two of the most prominent opponents of reform in the past, were obliged to bring in Catholic Emancipation the following year.

At first sight the triumph of 1829 seemed to be complete. It was a personal victory for O'Connell whose prestige and oratory had given the movement its direction and it was a popular victory for the Catholic Association whose sheer size had helped to force the Government to give in. To this extent 1829 was all that O'Connell could have hoped for. And yet it was also a flawed victory – at least in terms of

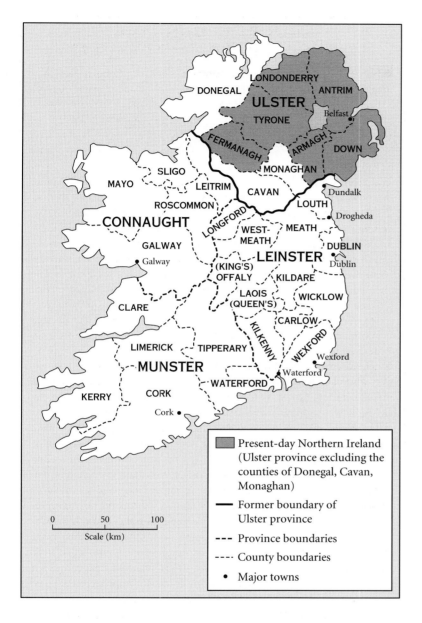

Present-day Northern Ireland (Ulster province excluding the counties of Donegal, Cavan, Monaghan)

━━ Former boundary of Ulster province

--- Province boundaries

---- County boundaries

• Major towns

MAP 3 *Ireland*

O'Connell's future aspirations. To begin with, the concession of Catholic Emancipation came with a sting in its tail. In order to limit the number of Roman Catholic MPs entering the House of Commons, Peel raised the Irish franchise qualification from 40s (or £2) freehold to £10. At a stroke this drastically reduced the size of the Irish electorate and the vast majority of those excluded were Roman Catholics. The Reform Act of 1832 increased the number of Irish seats to 105, in line with the increasing population but it maintained the £10 franchise and the post-1832 electorate remained smaller than that of 1829. Thus, O'Connell was deprived of the substantial number of supporters in the House of

KEY ISSUE

In what ways can the granting of Catholic Emancipation be seen as both a success and a failure for O'Connell?

Commons which he had counted upon to spearhead a new attack on the Union. Furthermore, he could no longer count upon the support of British politicians for his aims: many Tories and all the Whigs had supported emancipation, but none of them supported the repeal of the Union. British politics, once fatally divided, now spoke with one voice on the constitutional future of Ireland.

B *The decline of O'Connell*

The momentum for repeal of the Union, which O'Connell assumed would follow from Catholic Emancipation, simply failed to materialise. The reasons, however, were not entirely due to the unfavourable scene in British political circles. As the more perceptive members of the Wellington Government had foreseen, the admission of a limited number of Roman Catholic MPs, including O'Connell himself, had the effect of removing them from Ireland for substantial periods of the year when Parliament was sitting. Even O'Connell, whatever his talents, could not solve the problem of being in two places at once! As he adjusted to life in the House of Commons, he could not help but slacken his grip on affairs in Ireland. In the 1830s O'Connell waited in vain for constitutional reform of the Anglo-Irish connection to fall into his lap. He agreed to support the Whig Government in the so-called 'Lichfield House Compact' of 1835 in return for further reforms but the Whigs failed to deliver anything substantial. When the Conservatives, under Sir Robert Peel, came to power following the general election of 1841, O'Connell was forced to recognise that repeal of the Union was unlikely to be achieved purely by parliamentary pressure. Belatedly, he attempted to revive the 'monster' meetings of the old Catholic Association, in the hope that popular demonstrations would be as effective as they had been in the 1820s. This time, however, the situation was quite different. Peel headed a strong government which was determined to maintain the Union. The Whig opposition were themselves no supporters of repeal. Peel had his own agenda for Ireland (as exemplified by the Maynooth Grant and his Irish Universities policy), and his aim was to bind Ireland more securely to the Union rather than to slacken the ties. Moreover, O'Connell no longer enjoyed unquestioned support in Ireland itself. During the inactive period of the 1830s, younger Irish radicals had grown impatient with O'Connell and his gradualist approach. This movement, '**Young Ireland**', urged more extreme methods and a more complete separation of Ireland and Great Britain than O'Connell had ever intended.

In 1840, O'Connell had produced a plan for a restored Irish Parliament. To support this scheme, 1843 was designated by him as 'Repeal Year' with plans for a monster meeting at Clontarf near Dublin at the end of the year. The Government, fearing general disorder if the meeting went ahead, banned it, and O'Connell, who was always basically law-abiding at heart, accepted the ban. Despite this, O'Connell was arrested on a charge of sedition in 1844 and sentenced to a year in prison. His conviction was quashed by the House of Lords on appeal and he was released after serving only 14 weeks. The experience, however, was enough to break his spirit for continuing the struggle. He was

---

KEY ISSUE

Does Daniel O'Connell deserve the title 'The Great Liberator'?

See pages 153–5 for Peel's policy on Ireland

Young Ireland a movement of radical Irish nationalists. It was founded in 1841 in opposition to O'Connell's more moderate methods

nearly 70 and his health was failing; the attacks on him by 'Young Ireland' added to his disillusion. Bitter and broken he finally left Ireland in 1847 and died in Genoa in the same year. However, even before this, O'Connell's campaign, Peel's policies and the dreams of 'Young Ireland' had all been rendered largely irrelevant by the devastating catastrophe which struck Ireland between 1845 and 1851 – The Great Famine.

3 ⌐ FAMINE AND FENIANS

It is almost impossible to exaggerate the impact which the Great Famine has had upon Irish history. In the space of five years the population of Ireland was decimated by death and emigration. Before the Famine, the population was over eight millions, i.e. nearly a third of the total population of the United Kingdom as a whole. The Famine reduced this population to six and a half million and it continued to fall thereafter because of a sustained pattern of emigration. At the end of the nineteenth century, Ireland was the only part of Europe to have a lower population than it had in 1800. Even so it is important to remember that this crisis was only the *worst* of a series of food crises for the Irish peasant over the course of the nineteenth century. There had been famines before, notably 1817–18, and there were others after. Indeed the title 'Great Famine' originally was coined to mark its intensity and duration from the lesser examples. Food shortages for the poor were indeed an *annual* problem in Ireland. One British Government figure complained during the period 1845–9 that government relief measures were 'addressing the distress *normal* in Ireland at this time of year'!

The Great Famine changed more than just the population structure of Ireland. It bit deeply into the consciousness of the nation. Strictly speaking, there was no famine in Ireland during these years – only the potato crops were blighted and this was part of a Europe-wide disease pattern. In fact, vast quantities of food were being produced in, and

> **KEY ISSUE**
>
> *How did the 'Great Famine' change the nature of the Irish Question?*

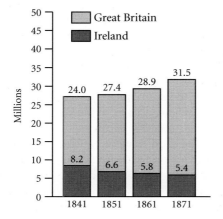

DIAGRAM 6
The population of Ireland and of Great Britain

even exported from, Ireland throughout the whole of this period. What led to mass starvation was:

- The Irish peasantry's dependence on potatoes for subsistence. Many Irish peasants especially in the south and west of Ireland ate virtually nothing else.
- The Irish peasant farmers barely used money. They grew cereals to pay their rent and lived off the potato, which was the only crop which could be grown in sufficient quantities on the small plots of land which they farmed for their own subsistence.
- There was intense pressure on the land because there had been a massive population explosion since the middle of the eighteenth century, ironically aided by the potato, which, when healthy, was an excellent and easily cultivated source of nutrition.

The loss of potato crops in successive blights from the summer of 1845 spelled disaster for the Irish peasant families unless some safety net could be put in place. The economic wisdom of the time was strongly against any use of large-scale government intervention, which was the only hope for many of the Irish people. Limited public works schemes were eventually set into motion and private charity did some good, but these efforts were on too small a scale to meet the need. The result was that up to a million Irish men, women and children perished from starvation and disease in the midst of plenty of food which they simply could not afford to buy. Perhaps as many as two million more fled from Ireland, some only to die on the hazardous voyage to North America. Many thousands made it only as far as the industrial towns of Britain where they lived in squalor, resented and despised by the local population.

In Ireland the political effects of the famine were immense. The repeal movement was crushed. Young Ireland was discredited and its members dispersed, some to remote areas of the globe. By 1847 O'Connell was dead and no leader of similar stature would emerge until the era of Parnell began in the late 1870s. In the immediate aftermath of the famine, the Irish were too exhausted to consider a political agenda. The collapse of Young Ireland, in particular, left a gap among the ranks of what would have been the rising generation of politicians. A complete fiasco of a 'revolt', in reality little more than a riot, in 1848, was Young Ireland's contribution to the nationalist cause. The leaders were arrested and imprisoned or else fled abroad to escape the authorities. Many joined a flow of emigration to the United States, where a huge Irish population was beginning to take shape. Emigration had been an increasing trend in Ireland even before the famine years and the effect of the famine was to so increase this trend that the Irish population in America quickly began to outstrip in size and wealth the population of the mother country. These Irish-Americans developed a tradition of violent hatred for Britain as the cause of Ireland's misfortunes.

Gradually, from the ashes of Young Ireland, a new movement for Irish national freedom began to take shape. In 1858, James Stephens, a former member of the Young Ireland movement, founded the Irish Republican Brotherhood. It became the inner element in a wider organisation, with branches not only in Ireland and Britain but also in Irish communities in the United States, which became known as the 'Fenians'. This term derives from the Old Irish word 'Fene' which means 'the people'. Stephens himself, and to some extent his movement too, existed for many years in a kind of fantasy world in which the establishment of a fully independent Irish Republic was held to be on the verge of becoming reality. The Fenian Oath confirmed this illusion:

> I, xxxx, in the presence of Almighty God, do solemnly swear allegiance to the Irish Republic, NOW VIRTUALLY ESTABLISHED…

The Fenians started their own newspaper, *The Irish People*, in 1863, and Stephens began calling himself, 'Chief Organiser of the Irish Republic'. In reality, the Fenians made little progress. Stephens travelled to the United States on regular missions to drum up support among the exiled Irish there and Fenian branches were also established in South Africa and Australia. Despite all this, however, the Fenians never became a truly national movement in Ireland itself. Stephens regularly promised a rising in Ireland, but year after year nothing actually happened.

When the Fenians finally rose in 1867 the result was a disaster which left the movement in ruins. The attempt was heavily promoted by Irish-Americans, some of whom (veterans of the American Civil War) actually travelled to Ireland to take part and more or less forced Stephens to act. There was some limited fighting, but the organisation and internal security of the movement was amateurish and chaotic. Stephens was arrested and sent to prison and although some of his American collaborators broke him out of prison and took him to the United States, his career was effectively over. However, the Fenians were saved from being a total failure by three factors.

KEY ISSUE

How successful was the Fenian Movement?

- The rising had an effect on the leading British politician, Gladstone. He had been concerned about the moral implications of the state of Ireland for some time. The Fenians did enough to ensure that he publicly declared his interest in the future of Ireland declaring in the 1868 General Election campaign that his 'mission' was 'to pacify Ireland'. He promised to disestablish the Anglican Church in Ireland which would end its official status and its right to levy tax on the population. He kept this promise in 1869 and even passed a Land Act in 1870 to try to give tenants some security.
- The aftermath of the rising created a set of martyrs for future generations to revere.
- In their failure, the Fenians managed to focus the attention of more moderate Irish politicians on ways to improve Ireland's situation by less extreme methods.

See pages 214–16 of Chapter 8 for full coverage of Gladstone's Irish policy 1868–74

The last two factors above hinged upon the fate of three Fenians who attempted to rescue some of their comrades from a police van taking them for trial in Manchester. They killed (probably accidentally) a police officer in the course of the rescue. The trial and execution of these 'Manchester Martyrs' for the murder of the policeman attracted the attention of mainstream Irish political opinion in a way the Fenians themselves had never been able to achieve. From this sprang a renewed interest in political solutions for Irish grievances and this led to the emergence of the concept which was to dominate Irish politics until the outbreak of the Great War in 1914 – Irish Home Rule.

4 ⌐ THE HOME RULE OPTION

The essence of the Home Rule solution for Ireland lay in the idea that, whilst it might be impracticable to aim for the complete separation of Ireland from Great Britain, it was reasonable and attainable to seek a compromise. Such a compromise would involve the granting of internal self-government to Ireland, whilst continuing the Union of the two countries. This would mean an Irish Parliament could control domestic issues like education, employment laws and policing. O'Connell had put forward similar proposals in the 1830s. The problem with this concept from the outset was that it seemed to some to offer too little, whilst to others it seemed to offer too much. For those who sought an independent Irish Republic, it was a cowardly betrayal of Ireland's true destiny. To those who placed the protection of the Union before all else, it was the thin end of a wedge which would ultimately be used to drive the two countries apart.

Nevertheless, the failure of the Fenian rising in 1867, left the way open for a more moderate movement to take the stage in Irish politics. The man who did most to develop the idea of Home Rule, (before it was eventually taken up by Gladstone), was Isaac Butt. He was effectively the founder of the Irish Home Rule Party which was to become the Irish National Party. Isaac Butt was an improbable leader of Irish Nationalism. Like O'Connell, he was a lawyer, but there the similarities ended. Butt was an Anglican (the son of a vicar in fact) and in his early political career he was looked on as a staunch Tory. As he grew older however, his views began to change. In 1848, he was impressed with the sincerity of the Young Ireland movement members, if not with their political ideals, and he represented some of them in court. After this he rather fell out of the political limelight, but the case of the 'Manchester Martyrs' brought him back to political prominence when he agreed to defend them at their trial. Subsequently he supported an unsuccessful appeal for an amnesty for the condemned prisoners. Butt was intelligent and sincere but ultimately he did not have the ruthlessness needed to lead a party with an aim which originally had virtually no support from either Liberals or Conservatives in Britain.

Butt's willingness to defend nationalists in court, gave him some degree of credibility amongst the extremists, although in reality he had almost nothing in common with them. This credibility, in addition to his genuine respectability, gave him a sufficiently broad political appeal to build an Irish National Party with a solid base in the House of Commons. In the 1874 general election, following general disappointment with Gladstone's Land Act of 1870, the Irish Home Rule Party won 60 out of the 105 Irish seats, almost double what Butt had expected. It was now a significant force in British politics. In close-run elections it might reasonably expect to hold the balance of power between the Liberals and the Conservatives.

5 ⌒ THE RISE OF PARNELL

It was at this point, with the Irish Party developing, but as yet unproven, as a political weapon, that a new, dynamic and aggressive Irish leader arrived upon the scene.

PROFILE

CHARLES STEWART PARNELL (1846–91)

Charles Stewart Parnell was the son of a Protestant landowner in County Wicklow. He was educated at a private school in England and went on to Cambridge University, where he refused to complete his degree after being temporarily suspended following a street brawl. He became an MP at a by-election in 1875, not it appears because of any great interest in politics, but because he was rather at a loss for any alternative career. All this would appear to make him even less likely to become a leader of Irish nationalism than Isaac Butt, but in this case the appearance is deceptive. Although they were Protestant gentry, Parnell's family traced their descent back to Sir John Parnell, who, at the time of the Act of Union, had bitterly opposed Pitt's policy, stressing instead the distinctive claim of Ireland to a separate identity. Not only that, but his mother was American and descended from a famous American Admiral, Charles Stewart, who had fought against Britain in the War of 1812–14. Both sides of his family tradition, therefore, gave to Parnell a decidedly anti-British attitude. This was reinforced by his own character and personality. He had deeply resented being sent to school in England, where he had felt both alienated and regarded as inferior. He had a violent and rebellious side to his nature which led him to disregard conventions and to take risks. He was also capable of great loyalty once his passions (which were often intense) were roused. Finally, he could display tremendous personal charm and had immense powers of persuasion. These made him, in turn, the object of great loyalty and passion amongst those who fell under his influence.

PICTURE 31
Charles Stewart Parnell

Once he had embarked on a political career, Parnell soon showed himself to be an adept and ruthless politician. He quickly became the leader of a small group of the more radical Irish MPs and organised them in disruptive tactics in the House of Commons. His debating and speech-making skills developed rapidly and he soon made himself a force to be reckoned with not only in the House but in Ireland at large. Even before Butt died in 1879, Parnell was universally recognised as the most dynamic force in Irish politics. After the general election of 1880, he succeeded to the leadership of what had by then become known as the Irish National Party and proceeded to mould it into a formidable parliamentary force. It has been said that, in the 1880s, no British Prime Minister could take office or decide policy without considering how Parnell might choose to use the position of power which he had built up.

> ## KEY ISSUE
>
> *How effective a leader of Irish Nationalism was Charles Stuart Parnell?*

A *Parnell and the Land League*

Parnell's rise to prominence in Parliament coincided with the return of bad conditions in Ireland, in the form of an agricultural depression. This led to a dramatic increase in the number of evictions of tenants for non-payment of rent. In 1879, a leading Irish nationalist, Michael Davitt, founded a Land League, which pledged itself to defend, with violence if necessary, the tenant-farmers from eviction. The League organised 'rent strikes' and even punished tenants who failed to stop paying their rent. The aim was to put financial pressure on the land-lords, who were themselves suffering from reduced incomes due to the depression. Davitt persuaded Parnell to become President of this Land League and the latter now drew close to the extremist fringes of Irish politics. He established contacts with the Fenians in the USA and, though he refused to go so far as to join the Irish Republican Brother-hood, he generally recast the Irish National Party in the mould of an anti-landowner, pro-tenant force with an ambiguous attitude to vio-lence. It was all very different from the image that Butt had originally intended. This populist approach, combined with his own powers of oratory and persuasion, raised Parnell to unparalleled heights of popu-larity, even of adoration, in Ireland, surpassing even O'Connell's posi-tion in its passion and intensity. By the early 1880s he was being openly referred to as the 'uncrowned King of Ireland'.

The revived land agitation inspired by the Land League forced Glad-stone, who had become Prime Minister again in 1880 to renew his interest in Ireland. The reforms during his first ministry – disestablish-ment of the Irish Church in 1869 and the 1870 Land Act – had been significant in British terms, but had little impact in Ireland. Gladstone had originally had no intention of producing any further reforms for Ireland. Indeed when Disraeli mentioned the dangerous state of Ireland during the 1880 election campaign, Gladstone accused him of trying to divert attention from the real issues, which he saw as foreign affairs and public finance. However the deteriorating situation in Ireland made it essential for Gladstone to take some action. In 1881, he produced a

See pages 214–16

more extensive Land Act which went much of the way to meeting the grievances of the Irish tenant-farmers:

- fixity of tenure was conceded – this ensured that, as long as tenants kept to the terms of their tenancy agreement, the landlord could not evict them
- freedom of sale of the tenancy by the tenant meant that tenants could gain the benefit of improvements they made to the land during the tenancy
- fair rents were ensured by the setting up of Land Tribunals which could impose a binding rent where landlord and tenant failed to agree.

These arrangements, conceding the so-called three 'Fs', meant that the crisis of the land which had dogged Ireland for generations was virtually solved. This, however, was not enough for the Land League leaders who basically wanted to get rid of the English landlords altogether. Gladstone faced resistance from his own party over the Second Land Act because of the extent to which it interfered with landlords' rights and because it seemed to be giving in to violence. He therefore accompanied it with a Coercion Act, allowing detention without trial, to curb the activities of the Land League.

B *The 'Kilmainham Treaty' 1882*

Parnell privately acknowledged the likely effectiveness of the new Land Act, but the Coercion Act gave him an excuse to go on condemning the British Government in inflammatory speeches. Gladstone responded by issuing a warrant for Parnell's arrest and imprisoning him in Dublin's Kilmainham Jail. This 'martyrdom' played into Parnell's hands. His popularity reached even greater heights and at the same time he was able to scale down his entanglement with the extremists without appearing to be weakening his nationalist zeal. Parnell was soon released from jail under the so-called 'Kilmainham Treaty'. This was an entirely unofficial and unwritten agreement between Parnell and Gladstone, negotiated indirectly by their representatives, under which:-

> For a full coverage of Gladstone's later Irish policy see pages 246–53 in Chapter 8

- Parnell undertook to use his influence to end the violence against landowners and to accept the Land Act as a final settlement of the land question.
- The British Government agreed to deal with the problem of unpaid rent (which had not been covered by the 1881 Land Act and could still lead to eviction), and to extend the fair rent clauses of the Act to include leaseholders, who had previously not been protected.

The Irish leader still faced a delicate political balancing act however. On the one hand, he recognised that some kind of collaboration with Gladstone and the Liberals was probably the only hope of securing Home Rule for Ireland; on the other hand, he could not afford to appear too conciliatory or he might start to compromise the goodwill of the political activists in Ireland who still hankered after an Irish

PICTURE 32
Punch *cartoon of 'Kilmainham Treaty'*

TREASON.

Q

1. *What overall message is this cartoon trying to convey about the Kilmainham Treaty?*
2. *In what ways might it be considered unreliable by historians?*

Republic. Publicly, Parnell appeared to support the Home Rule solution, but he frequently hedged this commitment with qualifications which gave the strong impression that he saw Home Rule as merely the first step to complete separation. His position was made more difficult by the Phoenix Park murders in 1882, which occurred shortly after his release from Kilmainham. The Irish Secretary, W. E. Forster, had resigned in protest at Parnell's release, and was replaced by Gladstone's nephew, Lord Frederick Cavendish. Shortly after arriving in Dublin, Cavendish, along with his assistant, an Irish Roman Catholic named Burke, were hacked to death, in Dublin's Phoenix Park, by a terrorist group wielding surgical knives. With Cavendish and Burke died any hope, in the short term, for any new initiatives on the Irish Question.

In 1883 and 1884, Parnell kept a fairly low profile politically. This was partly due to events in his personal life. For some years he had been involved in a love affair with a married woman. The fact that she had been about to give birth to his child (which died shortly after being born), had been one of the factors which had prompted Parnell to agree to the Kilmainham treaty in 1882. Another reason for his 'semi-retirement' was that the success of the Land Act had left him little room for manoeuvre, unless he adopted an extreme position. A final reason was that he was facing financial problems. Nevertheless, he returned to active politics in 1885, with a powerful speech, in which he demonstrated the ambiguity of his views on the long-term relationship between Ireland and Great Britain:

> It is given to none of us to forecast the future ... it is impossible for us to say in what way or by what means the national question may be settled ... We cannot under the British Constitution ask for more than the restitution of [an Irish] Parliament [i.e. Home Rule], but no man has the right to fix the boundary to the march of a nation. No man has the right to say to his country – 'Thus far shalt thou go and no further' ... while we struggle today for that which may seem possible for us ... we shall not do anything to hinder or prevent better men who may come after us from gaining better things.

Q
1. *What is the implication of Parnell's comments in this extract?*
2. *Why might English politicians suspect Parnell's good faith?*

6 ⌒ THE FAILURE OF HOME RULE

A *The First Home Rule Bill 1886*

Late in 1885 Gladstone finally reached the conclusion that only Home Rule could resolve the future of Ireland. The reasons for his conversion were varied.

● He was disappointed that his Irish policy had still not 'pacified' Ireland as he had pledged himself to do in 1868.
● It is clear that he was looking for a new 'moral' cause with which to stimulate the Liberal Party. He disliked both the radical wing led by Joseph Chamberlain and the 'Traditional Whigs' led by Lord Hartington.
● He was no doubt influenced by Parnell's decision, in the 1885 general election, to switch Irish National Party support to the Conservatives. Parnell did this in the mistaken belief that Conservative leaders were prepared to contemplate some kind of compromise on Home Rule.
● He also recognised that the Parliamentary Reform Act of 1884 had had the effect of increasing the number of seats in the House of Commons which the Irish National Party would normally win to over 80 and he was anxious to find a way to eliminate such a permanently disruptive force from the House.

Whatever Gladstone's reasoning, when his new position became public, Parnell immediately swung his party back behind the Liberals. When Gladstone introduced the Home Rule Bill early in 1886, Parnell gave it his support and even ventured to suggest that it represented the fullest expectation for Irish national identity that he could conceive.

The Home Rule Bill produced a split in the Liberal Party, which ensured its ultimate defeat in the House of Commons. It was, in any case, a seriously flawed bill. Gladstone was proposing that Ireland should have a Home Rule Parliament to deal with internal Irish affairs but no representation at Westminster. However, in matters of foreign affairs, defence and external trade, Ireland would still remain subject to the British Parliament. Parnell was disappointed by the loss of the bill, but reassured by the continued commitment of Gladstone to the principle of Home Rule. Whatever he said in public, it is clear that Parnell did not really believe that Home Rule would be the last word for Ireland. So long as the Liberal Party remained pledged to the idea, it seemed that sooner or later it must become a reality and, as such, a useful move towards Irish independence upon which to base further developments. Parnell was now content to bide his time until conditions should favour a further attempt. Although the House of Lords was bound to be implacably opposed to such a reform, the peers' opposition to constitutional changes could be overcome, as it had been in the 1832 Reform Bill Crisis, by the threat to create new peers. Gladstone was determined now to remain in politics until the cause was won.

See pages 248–53 on the defeat of Home Rule in Parliament

Parnell's waiting game strategy was upset in the late 1880s when his high-risk lifestyle finally began to catch up with him. In 1887 *The Times* published a series of letters, allegedly written by Parnell, which implied that he had, at least, approved of the Phoenix Park murders. Parnell denounced the letters as forgeries, but he did not sue *The Times* and doubts about his dubious political connections grew amongst the Liberals. Finally, in 1889, after repetitions of the allegations in *The Times*, Parnell did at last resort to legal action. He sued the newspaper for libel and in the ensuing court case a journalist named Piggott, under cross-examination by Parnell's lawyer, admitted to having forged the letters. Piggott later committed suicide. Parnell won the case and his political standing seemed unassailable, as even those who were generally critical of him joined in an ovation when he returned to the House of Commons. It was to be a short-lived triumph however. Parnell's earlier reluctance to sue *The Times* in 1887 had been partly due to his concern that his private life would not stand up to public scrutiny. His long-standing love-affair was with Mrs Katherine O'Shea, the wife of a fellow Irish Nationalist MP, Captain William O'Shea. Parnell had long since come to regard Mrs O'Shea as his wife in all but name and for many years her husband raised no objection to the relationship. Katherine was the heiress to a considerable fortune and both she and Parnell hoped that Captain O'Shea would agree to an uncontested divorce in return for a reasonable financial settlement. However, in 1890, O'Shea started divorce proceedings claiming adultery and named Parnell as the guilty party.

B *The downfall of Parnell, 1890–1*

Divorce hearings at that time were held before a judge and jury and evidence was heard in a manner similar to that of a criminal trial. The revelations about Parnell's relationship with Mrs O'Shea created a scandal of immense proportions. Almost overnight Parnell went from being the object of virtual adoration in nationalist Ireland to being the subject of bitter controversy. The priests of the Roman Catholic Church at once denounced him as an adulterer; families were split over whether to support him or not; the Irish National Party was also divided about its response. Gladstone, who was himself a devout churchman and also headed a party which relied to an extent on the support of the Nonconformist churches in Britain, stated that if Parnell were to continue as leader of the Irish Party, his own leadership of the Liberals would be rendered 'almost a nullity'.

Parnell himself never had the least doubt that he should continue as leader, but he was defeated by a majority of 54 to 32 when the issue was put to a vote of the Irish MPs. Neither Parnell nor the minority who supported him would accept this verdict and the party was therefore split into two bitterly hostile factions. Parnell tried to rally support for his diminished group by public speeches and by fighting by-elections. But his candidates were defeated and his speeches became more and more extreme. He began to appeal openly to the revolutionary and violent traditions of Irish national feeling. All the time he was struggling against the power of the priests who were denouncing him from the pulpits as the agent of the devil or even the devil himself. The strain began to tell on his health, which had always been fragile. He suffered from a long-term, incurable kidney complaint and finally, totally exhausted, he collapsed and died in October 1891.

The death of Parnell did not ease the divisions within the Irish Party. If anything, it actually worsened them in the short term as the Parnellites mourned their lost 'King' – hounded to his grave by, in their view, traitors and bigots. Soon, however, there was a hopeful distraction on the horizon. Gladstone returned to power in 1892, at the head of a minority government which depended for its majority on Irish Party support. Gladstone at once proceeded to introduce a new Home Rule Bill, and this time it achieved a safe passage through the House of Commons. There was never any doubt, however, as to what the verdict of the House of Lords would be. The peers threw out the Bill by the largest majority ever recorded in the House up to that time. Although Gladstone was in favour of taking on the Lords over the issue, he could not persuade the rest of his Cabinet to support him, and the second Home Rule Bill was thus consigned to the scrap-heap of history along with its predecessor.

> **KEY ISSUE**
>
> *How great had Parnell's political achievements been in the 1880s?*

C *Killing Home Rule with kindness*

Although there was natural disappointment with this outcome, the reaction in Ireland was generally less angry than might have been expected because:

- many people in Ireland had seen this result as inevitable anyway
- the second Land Act was benefiting the tenant farmers
- Ireland was too fatigued by internal division and too disillusioned by the tragedy of Parnell, to rouse from political apathy.

KEY ISSUE

Why did Gladstone's Irish policy enjoy so little success after 1880?

The relative calm with which the failure of the second Home Rule Bill was greeted was a reflection of a fundamental change slowly creeping over the country. Gladstone's 1881 Land Act had made provision for a policy of land-purchase, funded by government loans, aimed at enabling tenant farmers to buy out their landlords. The Conservative Government of Lord Salisbury approved of the concept, which they saw as calculated to cement Ireland more firmly into the Union, by removing one of the most fundamental popular grievances. The Conservatives, therefore, not only continued the policy; they greatly extended it and made funds available, both during the period 1886–92 and, subsequently, between 1895 and 1905. This policy created a class of peasant proprietors, naturally disinclined to revolutionary or even nationalist politics. This approach, known as 'killing Home Rule with kindness', worked in combination with the introduction of popularly-elected county councils in 1898, which signalled the end of the dominance of the old landlords in local government.

In these circumstances, it is not surprising that Ireland entered upon a relatively peaceful period between 1893 and the introduction of the third Home Rule Bill in 1912. Political apathy ruled the day. National pride and aspirations found their expression, increasingly, in a great cultural revival which emphasised the importance of restoring the status of the Irish language which had long been in decline; Irish sports began to flourish; Irish literature, dance and music recruited new enthusiasts. This movement was marked by the formation of organisations such as the Gaelic League, founded in 1893, and by the expansion of earlier groups such as the Gaelic Athletic Association (1884). Even so, despite the apolitical tone of the cultural revival, nationalism of this kind could not be wholly divorced from a political context. The fundamental message of the revival was anti-British. It condemned so-called 'West Britonism' and advocated a separate Irish consciousness. It required only a change in the political climate to harness this sense of a separate Irish identity to a new and specifically Irish political agenda.

7 ⌐ THE REVIVAL OF POLITICAL NATIONALISM

A *Irish Affairs at Westminster, 1895–1909*

The alliance of Conservatives and Liberal Unionists, which formed the Unionist Government of 1895–1905, hoped to bury the issue of Home Rule once and for all. Their Land Act of 1903 largely completed the transfer of land from landlords to tenants, which was the cornerstone of the Unionist strategy by which Ireland was, in Gladstonian terminology, to be 'pacified'. The Irish Home Rule Party was in two minds about this process. On the one hand, they could hardly condemn the end of the hated 'landlordism'; on the other, they recognised that with its passing they had lost one of their most potent political weapons. They consoled themselves with the thought that the Liberal Party remained pledged to the introduction of Home Rule and waited on events.

In 1906 this policy of patience appeared to have paid off when the Liberals won a great victory in the general election. The Liberals now had so great a parliamentary majority that they could, if necessary, contemplate a constitutional clash with the House of Lords if the peers proved obstructive to measures passed with massive support in the Commons. This was the situation which Gladstone had dreamed of, but never achieved, after his conversion to Home Rule. Unfortunately for the Irish Party, his successors lacked his commitment. From the outset the Liberal Government was determined not to allow Irish affairs to dominate their administration. Although the policy of Home Rule was not abandoned, it was no longer to be the Government's primary objective as Gladstone had desired. The Liberals, between 1906 and 1909, preferred to embark upon a general policy of social reform, before considering any fundamental constitutional change. This was an exact reversal of Gladstone's priorities. Nor was there much that the Irish Party could do to force the issue. The Government was not dependent on Irish support and was aware that Home Rule had never aroused much support or even interest among the English electorate, to whom social and economic issues were of far more importance.

B *The Emergence of the 'New Nationalists' in Ireland*

In the meantime, in Ireland itself, new nationalist forces were taking shape which would ultimately control Irish destinies and destroy the Irish National Party. A labour movement was growing, under the control of James Connolly, an ardent socialist and trade union organiser. Connolly was committed to the Marxist belief that socialism could only be achieved when a country was sufficiently industrialised for the industrial workers (or proletariat) to be strong enough to overthrow 'capitalist oppression'. He believed that Ireland had remained largely agricultural because it was subservient to the wider needs of the British economy. Therefore, to Connolly, Irish independence was essential if Ireland was to ever reach the stage at which a socialist state could be established. In aiming for a Socialist Workers' Republic, and in linking that idea with trade unionism, Connolly made a major breakthrough in the cause of Irish nationalism. He won over the urban working classes in Dublin to republicanism and therefore, by definition, to separatism. This provided a new and important political driving force for independence from Britain.

Connolly's movement, with its newspaper, the *Workers' Republic*, and its group of activists – the Citizen Army – was opposed by another

> **KEY ISSUE**
>
> *Was Irish Nationalism stronger by 1906 than it had been in the era of Parnell?*

Sinn Fein (which means 'Ourselves Alone') was founded by Arthur Griffith in 1905. It claimed, as the Fenians had, that Ireland was a free nation temporarily enslaved by the British. It aimed to create a *Dail* (or Parliament) to rule Ireland in the name of its people

new nationalist force, **Sinn Fein**. This movement, through its paper *The United Irishmen*, rejected socialism, violent revolution and the constitutional approach of the Irish National Party. Instead, its leader, Griffith, wanted a system of peaceful resistance in which a voluntary parliament would be formed to govern Ireland in defiance of the British Government. In effect this meant simply carrying on as if Ireland was already independent and ignoring British institutions, such as the courts and civil administration, as though they did not exist. In this way, the stranglehold of British power would be broken.

Apart from these two open organisations, there remained the underground groups dedicated to the Fenian tradition, such as the Irish Republican Brotherhood. Though republican, the IRB had no clearly defined political philosophy: it was not Marxist, and it therefore had little natural affinity with Connolly's movement, while its commitment to violence repelled Griffith. Thus there were serious areas of division between the various strands of Irish nationalism and, in these circumstances, the Irish National Party faced little in the way of a concerted challenge to its continued domination of Irish politics.

C *The Impact of the Constitutional Crisis, 1909–11*

See pages 413–20 for a full account of the constitutional crisis

In 1909 the British political scene began to change dramatically. The crisis over the 1909 budget resulted in some momentous developments for Ireland. The general election at the beginning of 1910 saw the Liberals lose their overall majority in the House of Commons. From now on they were to be a minority government, with the Irish Nationalist MPs holding the balance of power. This was followed by a constitutional crisis which ended with the passing of the Parliament Act of 1911, which deprived the House of Lords of its indefinite veto over legislation. These changes put Irish Home Rule right back at the top of the political agenda again.

KEY ISSUE

How did events in British politics affect the cause of Irish Nationalism?

During the crisis over the Parliament Act, John Redmond, the leader of the Irish National Party, based his support for the Government on the assurance that Irish Home Rule would be a priority once the curbing of the powers of the House of Lords had been achieved. In his negotiations with the Liberals he had made it clear that the Irish would act to disrupt Government policy if Home Rule remained on the shelf. Redmond's threat of disruption was in many ways a bluff since there was no prospect of an alternative government from which he might expect to obtain Home Rule. It was, however, a bluff which was not called. The Liberal commitment to Home Rule, though no longer Gladstonian in its intensity, was nevertheless genuine. This was not to say, however, that the Irish Party could simply present its demands and expect them to be met in full. Asquith, the Prime Minister, intended to introduce a modest measure that could not reasonably be represented as a staging-post to separatism. Other leading Liberals, like Lloyd George and Winston Churchill, believed that a separate deal for the largely Protestant counties of **Ulster** would have to be devised in the end. Asquith knew the Government would face fanatical opposition from Ulster itself, along with strong resistance from the Unionist Party in Britain. The Parliament Act, which was the key to overcoming opposition in the House of Lords, was in reality something of a mixed blessing. It ensured that a Home Rule Bill could be passed but the peers could reject the Bill twice before being constitutionally compelled to accept it on the third occasion. This meant that there would be a minimum period of two years, before it became law, during which passions would be whipped up to fever pitch.

> **Ulster** The counties of Ulster, in the north of Ireland, were mostly Protestant, unlike the rest of Ireland. For most of the Ulster Protestants, 'Home Rule meant Rome rule' (i.e. rule by a Catholic majority)

8 ⁓ THE ULSTER CRISIS, 1912–14

A *The Third Home Rule Bill 1912*

The Third Home Rule Bill was introduced into the House of Commons in April 1912. The terms were:

- an Irish Parliament consisting of an elected House of Commons and a nominated Senate with limited powers, especially restricted in financial affairs
- 42 Irish MPs still to sit at Westminster
- Ulster was to be included under the new Home Rule Parliament.

It was a moderate proposal which left considerable control of Irish affairs with the Westminster Parliament. To Redmond it was barely acceptable and could only be sold to the more extreme Irish National Party (INP) members as a starting-point for future progress. To the Unionists it was entirely unacceptable for the same reason and because of the inclusion of Ulster. At a huge Unionist rally in July 1912, Bonar Law, the Unionist leader, was provoked into saying that he could 'imagine no length of resistance to which Ulster can go in which I should not be prepared to support them'. Asquith responded by calling Bonar Law's speech 'reckless' and 'a complete grammar of anarchy'.

In this bitter atmosphere the Bill passed the Commons for the first time, eventually completing its stormy passage in January 1913. There was great disorder in the House during the debates and verbal abuse was common. The verdict of the Commons was immediately reversed in the Lords. The whole process then had to be repeated with totally predictable results. By August 1913 the Bill had been passed once more through the Commons, only to receive its routine rejection by the peers. A proposal for a constitutional conference in September 1913 was undermined by the extreme positions taken by the opposing forces. The most that the Ulster leader, Sir Edward Carson, would accept was Home Rule which excluded the whole of the nine counties of Ulster, including the largely Catholic counties of Cavan, Donegal and Monaghan (see map on page 269). These were impossible terms for Redmond and the most that Asquith would concede was a limited degree of independence for Ulster, within the Home Rule provisions. The scene was set for a new constitutional crisis.

B *The Unionist Resistance*

While attention had been focused on the fate of the Home Rule Bill at Westminster, events had been moving in Ireland itself. Ulster opinion had been hardening into die-hard resistance well before the introduction of the Bill and, in Sir Edward Carson, it had found an able and articulate leader. In September 1912 Carson drew up a 'Solemn League and Covenant' whose signatories pledged themselves to resist a Home Rule Parliament in Ireland should one ever be set up. Over 470 000 people signed this Covenant – some of the more passionate using their own blood as ink! In January 1913 the Ulster Volunteer Force was set up and soon numbered 100 000 men. This provoked the setting up of a nationalist counterpart organisation, the Irish National Volunteers, a body pledged to support Redmond, but which was quickly infiltrated by the Irish Republican Brotherhood. The creation of two para-military groups with totally opposed objectives meant that the long-feared risk of civil war began to emerge as a real possibility.

In December 1913, Asquith's Government resorted to a ban, by Royal Proclamation, on the import of arms and ammunition into Ireland. Neither of the two para-military forces were as yet properly armed, and the precaution seemed wise as well as justified. At the same time Asquith was also preparing to extract more concessions from the Irish National Party, in the hope that the opposition in Parliament to Home Rule could at least be reduced. He put pressure on Redmond to accept the exclusion of Ulster from Home Rule for a temporary period. This concession threatened the whole concept of Ireland as a single unit and can be seen as the first clear move towards the idea of partition. However, it was a risk Redmond felt he could take, because it seemed unlikely that Carson would ever accept any temporary exclusion. Carson duly obliged by rejecting the proposal as soon as Asquith put it forward.

In March 1914 the Government was rocked by the so-called 'Curragh Mutiny'. The Government had long been concerned that, in the event of a confrontation with the Ulster Unionists, the enforcement of Home Rule would depend on the Army. The Army units in Ireland (based at Curragh) were led largely by officers of Anglo-Irish Protestant background who were overwhelmingly Unionist in their sentiments. In an attempt to lessen the risk of widespread resignations from the army, the Secretary of State for War, Jack Seely, approved instructions to General Sir Arthur Paget, the Commander-in-Chief in Ireland, that officers whose homes were actually in Ulster could be allowed a temporary leave from duty. There were rumours that the Government was about to order the arrest of the Ulster leaders (they had been considering this for some time), and Paget, in briefing his officers, was deliberately pessimistic, suggesting that Ulster would be 'in a blaze by Saturday'.

As a result, 58 officers, including a Brigadier-General, resigned. Action against the defectors was impossible because sympathy for them was widespread throughout the army and even strong in the navy. The Government was forced to conciliate the rebels and Seely even went so

KEY ISSUE

Why and how did Ulster oppose Home Rule?

PICTURE 33

Sir Edward Carson, leader of the Ulster Unionists. A lawyer and an MP, he helped to organise the Ulster Volunteer Force and adopted the slogan 'Ulster will fight and Ulster will be right'

far as to suggest that force would not be used against the opponents of Home Rule. Although Seely was forced to resign, the Government appeared weak and indecisive. This encouraged the Ulster Volunteers to take action to arm themselves. In April a series of landings of armaments took place along the Ulster coast. There was no interference from the authorities and the Ulster Volunteers were thus transformed into a well-armed and formidable army. It was only a matter of time before the Irish National Volunteers responded. In June, guns for the Nationalists were landed near Dublin (this time in the face of official intervention which left three dead and nearly 40 injured), and, although it was by no means as successful an effort as the Ulster landings, it still left considerable quantities of arms in the hands of the nationalist force.

C *War Intervenes, 1914*

The Home Rule Bill was heading for the its final passage. Asquith, Bonar Law and Carson had agreed by June that an additional Amending Bill would be introduced to include some form of compromise. This in itself was of little use, however, since there was no agreement as to what these amendments should be. Furthermore, any amendments had either to be accepted by, or imposed on, Redmond and the Irish National Party. In late June the Government produced its first attempt at an amending bill. The main proposal was for the exclusion of the Ulster counties from the Home Rule Bill for a period of six years, with each county voting separately for its future. This idea had already been refused by Carson and the House of Lords amended the proposal to provide for the automatic exclusion of all nine Ulster counties on a permanent basis, a solution that the Government could not accept.

> **KEY ISSUE**
>
> *How close was Ireland to civil war in 1914?*

Encouraged by King George V, the politicians convened a constitutional conference at Buckingham Palace on 21 July 1914. The conference was intended to reach decisions in two stages: first to debate the area of Ulster to be excluded; secondly to debate whether the exclusion was to be temporary or permanent. In the event, the conference broke up in deadlock after three days and, barely a week later, Britain was at war with Germany.

The crisis of war overtook the Irish Question at a crucial point. All sides in the constitutional conference realised that some kind of compromise was inevitable. Carson, in particular, was far more moderate in private than he was prepared to be in public. If the parties had been forced to continue the negotiations, a constitutional settlement would almost certainly have been reached. In the event, the war enabled all sides to agree to shelve the issue in a way which virtually guaranteed the renewal of the crisis at some later date. The Home Rule Act was passed as an all-Ireland measure but was accompanied by a Suspensory Order which made it inoperable for the duration of the war. This was just about the worst outcome, short of actual civil war, which could possibly have been contrived for the Ulster Crisis.

9 ⌁ WAR, REBELLION AND PARTITION, 1914–21

Initially World War I seemed to have a positive effect upon Anglo-Irish relations. Support for the war was almost universal at the outset, with the fate of 'little Belgium' seeming to represent the interests of all small nations in their relations with those greater than themselves. In comparison to the threat of German militarism, even British rule seemed, or could be made to seem, comparatively benign. Ulster, already intoxicated with its Britishness and loyalism, rushed to the colours in a frenzy of patriotism. In the rest of Ireland the response was less passionate but, nevertheless, the men of Catholic Ireland also answered the call and marched to slaughter in France and Belgium. Probably never before in her history had Ireland seemed to be so much in harmony with Britain.

For John Redmond the war seemed the ideal opportunity for nationalist Ireland to demonstrate her loyalty to the Crown and secure, by her war effort, the future of Ireland under Home Rule. Even before the war he had, for political reasons, taken a strong grip over the running of the Irish National Volunteers organisation. Now he used his authority to bring them into the war. First, he declared that the Volunteers would defend Ireland against invasion, thus releasing the regular army to fight the Germans in the front line. He then went further and urged them to fight overseas. This move was intended to reassure opinion in England of Irish loyalty but to go so far was dangerous. Redmond was tolerated rather than respected by the leaders of the Volunteers and he was no Parnell in terms of his popular appeal.

> ### KEY ISSUE
>
> *In what ways did the outbreak of war in 1914 present both opportunities and dangers for the relationship between Great Britain and Ireland?*

A *The Easter Rising, 1916*

Support for the war split the National Volunteers. The majority, reflecting the overwhelming sentiment of public opinion, sided with Redmond and followed the path of loyalty to the British Empire. A minority, however, broke with Redmond, seeing the pro-war stance as collaboration with the British and a betrayal of Ireland's claim to nationhood. Their isolated, minority position drew them closer to Connolly's 'Citizen Army' (see bottom of page 283).

Herein lay the origin of the Easter Rising of 1916. To these extreme nationalists, the danger which Britain faced in Europe was an opportunity to strike for freedom and set up an Irish Republic. The rebellion was planned by a small group which included:

● Tom Clarke, a shopkeeper and former Fenian who had spent 15 years in prison for bombing offences
● Patrick Pearse, a lawyer, schoolteacher and bilingual poet, and
● James Connolly, the trade union leader and head of the Citizen Army.

Pearse, in particular, was deeply committed to the idea that Ireland's future could only be saved by a 'blood sacrifice'. In other words, even if the intended revolution failed, it would have purged the soul of Ireland which had been compromised by years of collaboration with the British oppressors.

The rebellion was ill-timed, ill-planned and chaotically executed. Many of these failings were not entirely the fault of the revolutionary leaders themselves. They were obliged to keep their plans secret, even from some of the key personnel involved, in order to maintain security. They counted on support from Germany in the form of an arms shipment, which in the event was intercepted. The Commanding Officer of the minority National Volunteers was not informed of the plans until the last possible moment and, when he learned that the arms shipment had been lost, he did everything he could to stop the rebellion. He cancelled the Volunteers' planned route-marches for Easter Sunday which were supposed to be the starting point for the Rising. The rebel leaders were forced to improvise by rescheduling the marches and the rising for Easter Monday.

Militarily, the Easter Rising was doomed to fail from the start. The number of rebels mobilised was far too few and they were inadequately armed. The declaration of Irish Independence and an Irish Republic was read by Patrick Pearse to a small, bewildered crowd, outside the General Post Office in Dublin, the headquarters of the rebellion. The rebels successfully took over several strategic points of access to the city, but had insufficient numbers to do more than wait for the reaction of the British Government. Even if the attempt had attracted immediate and widespread popular support, which it did not, the odds would have been against the rebels. In the event the Rising flew in the face of popular feeling and was almost universally condemned by the Irish people. Nevertheless, the rebels held the British Army at bay for the best part of a week and, although many saw no actual fighting at all before surrendering, some fought with great skill and courage against overwhelming odds before they were killed or captured. The centre of Dublin was reduced to rubble by British artillery fire. Fires raged out of control and the city took on the look of one of the war zones of the western front. This was glorious defeat when compared to the Fenian Rising of 1867, and its potential for exploitation by the extremists was immediately apparent to the Irish National Party, who urged leniency for the captured rebels upon the British Government.

These pleas fell on largely deaf ears. Admittedly, of over 70 death sentences initially passed, the great majority were commuted to terms of imprisonment, but any executions were likely to be controversial, given the nature of Irish history. In the end, 14 of the leaders, including Pearse and Connolly, were shot. As the executions progressed, so the mood in Ireland began to change and the fears of the Irish MPs grew.

> **KEY ISSUE**
>
> *Was the Easter Rising a miscalculation on the part of the Irish Republicans?*

B *The Aftermath of the Easter Rising, 1916–18*

The policy of executions brought about a most profound change in the atmosphere in Ireland. Few ordinary people knew much about the

PICTURE 34 *Members of James Connolly's Citizen Army at the time of the Easter Rising*

revolutionary leaders (apart, perhaps, from James Connolly) or their aims. The Rising became popularly known as the 'Sinn Fein' Rebellion although in fact Sinn Fein had no involvement in it. Gradually, however, the leaders and those they had led were transformed into heroic figures. Originally, when the captured groups of rebels had been marched to the Dublin docks to be shipped off to prison on the mainland, they had needed army protection from angry mobs of mothers, fathers, wives, sisters and even children of Irish soldiers fighting in France and Belgium, who had tried to attack them as cowards and traitors. Now these same people, for the most part, were demanding their release. The Government was, of course, in too difficult a position, at a crucial stage in the war, to adopt a lenient policy towards those who had committed treason. Nevertheless, it is impossible to escape the conclusion that, had the executions not been carried out, the subsequent course of Irish history might have been very different.

The rebellion and its aftermath hardened attitudes in Ireland beyond recall. To Protestant Unionist opinion, the rebels were traitors who had got what they deserved; to Catholic nationalist opinion, they had become heroes and martyrs. From this point onwards, the prospect of achieving an all-Ireland settlement by consensus was virtually extinguished. In 1917 Asquith, alarmed that the Irish Question might sour relations with the then still neutral United States, offered immediate Home Rule with a provision for the exclusion of the six north-eastern counties of Ulster which had a Protestant majority. The Government also sponsored a Convention to discuss the long-term future of the six counties. These initiatives had no chance of success. The Sinn Fein party, which was now an alliance of Griffith's original organisation and the remnants of the 1916 rebels, refused even to attend the Convention. At the end of 1917, the remainder of the rebels imprisoned on the mainland were released as a goodwill gesture. But, though welcomed in Ireland, this did little to improve the image of the British Government. Opinion in nationalist Ireland was now moving firmly in support of Sinn Fein.

The 1918 general election marked the end for the Irish National Party. It was ruined as a political force, winning only seven seats against the triumphant 73 won by Sinn Fein. Even allowing for some vote-rigging by Sinn Fein, there is little doubt that the result reflected a genuine demand in Ireland for a substantial degree of independence from Britain. The elected Sinn Fein candidates refused to take their places at Westminster, preferring instead to constitute themselves as Dail Eireann – the Assembly of Ireland – claiming to represent the only legitimate legislative authority for the country.

> ### KEY ISSUE
>
> *In what ways did the British Government mismanage its handling of the Easter Rising?*

C *The War of Irish Independence 1919–21*

The main organisers of the independent Dail were Griffiths, Eamon de Valera (a commander from the 1916 Rebellion, originally sentenced to death but reprieved mainly because of his American citizenship), and Michael Collins, a junior figure in the Rebellion, who had emerged as the leader of those imprisoned on the mainland. De Valera, who had been elected as President of Sinn Fein in October 1917, became the leader of the illegal government whilst Collins doubled as Finance Minister and organiser of the military arm of the nationalists – the Irish Republican Army (IRA). In the early months of 1919, as the victorious allied powers assembled at Versailles to discuss the peace settlement, the Irish leaders hoped that American goodwill and the principle of self-determination of nations, upon which the peace settlement was supposed to be based, would ensure that their claim to independence would be forced upon the British Government without the need to resort to military action. This was a forlorn hope. The American president, Woodrow Wilson, needed the co-operation of the British Prime Minister, Lloyd George, at the Paris Peace Conference and was not prepared to alienate him on behalf of Ireland.

In an atmosphere of disappointment, the situation quickly deteriorated. Local groups of IRA men soon began to take independent action to secure arms and explosives. Before long acts of terrorism became commonplace. The British Government responded in kind. Additional men were drafted into the Royal Irish Constabulary; they were known, due to the use of ex-army khaki to supplement the standard police uniform, as the 'Black and Tans'. The police, reinforced by the 'Tans', met terror with terror and, between 1919 and 1921, Ireland writhed in agony as these two groups of increasingly ruthless fighters battled for supremacy. To the IRA, it was a war of independence; to the British Government, it was an rebellion against the Crown. The Dublin Government of de Valera had scarcely any control over the IRA and Lloyd George's Government was hardly much better placed with the 'Black and Tans'. Pressure for a political resolution of the conflict began to mount from many quarters:

● the British Government, seeking a policy of international co-operation in the post-war world, was acutely aware that its policy in Ireland was the object of international contempt
● the press in Britain was increasingly critical of the actions of the 'Tans'
● there were demands from the Church of England and from King George V for peace
● the IRA were running out of both human and material resources to continue their war
● the Irish political leaders themselves were willing to negotiate a settlement.

D *The Partition of Ireland, 1921*

KEY ISSUE

Was there any alternative to the policy of Partition pursued by the British Government after the War?

The British Government, at the end of the War, was a Coalition of Unionists and Liberals headed by the Liberal, Lloyd George. The main base of support for the Coalition came, however, from Unionists and any solution the Government proposed had to be made acceptable to them. Lloyd George had already offered a legislative solution in the form of the Government of Ireland Act of 1920. This had proposed Home Rule for Northern and Southern Ireland separately, with a Council of Ireland drawn from the two parliaments to oversee an eventual reunification. The terms were broadly acceptable to the Ulster Unionists who, of course, had no intention of co-operating with the Council of Ireland idea. They realised that, once set up, the Northern Parliament would be in their control and they would be able to resist any future move to reunification.

Not surprisingly, the 1920 proposals were quite unacceptable to the nationalists and this led to the final irony in the Home Rule saga. Ulster, so long the rock upon which Home Rule had foundered, now prepared to embrace Home Rule for itself. In June 1921, the King, scorning threats of assassination, opened the first Northern Ireland Home Rule Parliament and used the occasion to deliver a plea for peace. De Valera immediately responded and an armistice was signed early in July. Months of negotiations then ensued and Griffith and Collins headed a delegation to London to complete the final agreement.

The 'final settlement' of the Irish Problem, if it can really be so termed, was arrived at in a manner typical of the confused and off-the-cuff approach which had always characterised British Government of Ireland. Lloyd George had become determined to end the crisis and he offered Dominion status (i.e effectively independent status within the British Empire, as enjoyed by Canada, for example) to southern Ireland along with an amazing offer to place Northern Ireland under the Dublin Government for a limited period. Collins and Griffith were as delighted as they were stunned, and accepted at once. The proposal was, however, vetoed by the Unionists in the Government and Lloyd George swiftly withdrew the idea of forcing Ulster into a temporary union with the South. Instead, he threatened to renew the war and crush the IRA, unless the offer of Dominion status, minus the North, was accepted at once. While the Irish negotiators attempted to grasp this sudden reversal, Lloyd George offered a final twist entirely of his own devising. A boundary commission would be set up to arrange a final settlement of the North-South border and, Lloyd George hinted, this commission would set a boundary so limiting to the North that it would ultimately be compelled to accept reunification.

Whether Lloyd George really believed that such a scheme could ever be carried out, or whether he simply threw it in to sweeten the pill knowing it would never happen, is impossible to determine. The offer had the desired effect. Collins and Griffith agreed to accept the formula despite their doubts as to how it would be received in Dublin. In doing so they condemned the new 'Irish Free State', as it was called, to a period of civil war. Collins was assassinated in 1922 by those who saw the 'Anglo-Irish Treaty' as a betrayal. The offer of Dominion status, though a major advance on anything previously offered, involved continued Irish membership of the British Empire and an oath of allegiance, by the Irish Free State Parliament and Government, to the British Crown. This was too much for some nationalists to bear. Although the Dail eventually ratified the Treaty by a narrow majority, opposition to the settlement in the Free State was bitter and ended only by ruthless action on the part of the new administration.

Many loose ends were left to cause problems for later generations. The Boundary Commission disappeared in 1925, leaving areas of South Armagh, South Down and Fermanagh, where there were Roman Catholic majorities, under Northern control. Thus a substantial and discontented Catholic minority was left inside the borders of Northern Ireland. The Council of Ireland was a dead duck from the start, since the Government of Northern Ireland refused to have anything to do with it. The IRA, which refused to accept the settlement, was ruthlessly hounded by the new Free State Government. Many of its members were imprisoned, some were executed and others fled to the USA. However, though the IRA was defeated, it was not eradicated and it survived, embittered, to continue its struggle through succeeding generations.

> **KEY ISSUE**
>
> *How satisfactory was Lloyd George's solution to the Irish problem in 1921?*

10 ⤳ BIBLIOGRAPHY

ARTICLES

The following articles from *Modern History Review* are particularly suitable for students who are following an Irish-centred approach.

Christopher Collins 'Britain and Ireland 1880–1921: Searching for a Scapegoat', April 1991.

Tim Chapman 'Ireland 1800–1850: John Bull's Other Island', September 1993.

Donald MacRadd 'Parnell and Home Rule', February 1993.

George Boyce 'The Origins of Northern Ireland 1914–22', November 1995.

BOOKS FOR AS/A LEVEL STUDENTS

Paul Adelman *Great Britain and the Irish Question, 1800–1922*, Access to History series, Hodder & Stoughton, 1996, excellently detailed and readable – particularly good for its assessments of the roles of individuals.

Joe Finn *Ireland and England, 1798–1992*, Hodder & Stoughton, 1995, provides sources with linking commentary.

Grenfell Morton *Home Rule and the Irish Question*, Longmans Seminar series, 1980. Part I contains a brief but effective coverage of the first half of the nineteenth century, while the bulk of the volume concentrates on Home Rule. There is a particularly useful selection of documents provided.

S. R. Gibbons *Ireland 1780–1914*, Blackie – Evidence in History series, 1978. This consists of an interesting selection of primary and secondary source extracts linked together with a commentary. It could be very useful for coursework material, especially if historiographical content is required, but it needs a good grasp of detail to be used effectively.

FURTHER READING

R. F. Foster *Modern Ireland, 1600–1972*, Penguin, 1988, would be useful for students wishing to take a longer-term view or doing coursework.

Patricia Jalland *The Ulster Question in British Politics to 1914*, Harvester Press, 1990, is good on the Ulster crisis over Home Rule.

11 ⤳ STRUCTURED AND ESSAY QUESTIONS

A *Structured questions for AS level*

1. (a) Why was the Act of Union passed in 1800?
    (b) What was the impact of the Act on Ireland between 1801 and 1829?

2. (a) What was Daniel O'Connell's role in the passing of Catholic Emancipation?

   (b) Does he deserve the title 'The Great Liberator'?

3. (a) Outline the steps which Gladstone took to 'pacify Ireland'.

   (b) How do you explain the failure of the first two Home Rule Bills of 1886 and 1893?

4. (a) By what methods did Parnell seek to advance the cause of Irish nationalism?

   (b) How successful was he in this cause?

5. (a) Outline the events, between 1914 and 1921, which led to the partition of Ireland.

   (b) Do you agree that 'the Easter Rising and its aftermath made a solution of the Irish problem virtually impossible'?

B *Essay questions for A2 level*

1. To what extent was the Great Famine 'the most significant event in Irish history in the period 1800–1921'?

2. Do you agree that British Government policy towards Ireland in the nineteenth century was a case of 'always too little and always too late'?

4. 'Parnell did more to damage the cause of Irish nationalism than he did to advance it'. Discuss this assessment.

5. Was the partition of Ireland always likely to be the eventual outcome of the Irish Question?

12 ⌁ DOCUMENTARY EXERCISES

(i) The significance of Parnell

... I have appealed to no [one] section of my country. My appeal has been to the whole Irish race, and if the young men are distinguished among my supporters it is because they know what I have promised them I will do. I have not promised to lead them against the armed might of England. I have told them that, so long as I can maintain an independent Irish party in the English Parliament, there is hope of our winning our legislative independence by constitutional means ... . So long as we keep our Irish party, pure and undefiled from any contact or fusion with any English parliamentary party, independent and upright, there is good reason for us to hope that we shall win ... . So long as such a party exists I will remain at its head. But when it appears to me that it is impossible to obtain Home Rule for Ireland by constitutional means, I have said this – and this is the extent and limit of my pledge ... the pledge which has been accepted by the young men of Ireland ... I will in a moment so declare it to the people of Ireland, and ... I will take counsel with you as to the next step.

SOURCE A
Parnell, speaking at a by-election in Kilkenny in 1890

SOURCE B

Michael Davitt, the organiser of the Land League, worked closely with Parnell in the 1880s but opposed him following the divorce case scandal of 1890. In the following source Davitt reflected on Parnell's career several years after the latter's death in 1891

Parnell's claim to greatness no Irish nationalist and few Irishmen will ever deny ... . Like all the world's historic characters, there were marked limitations to his greatness, not counting the final weakness which precipitated his fall ... . He was unlike all the leaders who had preceded him in his accomplishments, traits of character and personal idiosyncrasies ... In fact he was a paradox in Irish leadership ... an 'Englishman', moulded for an Irish purpose ... bearing no resemblance to those who handed down to his time the fight for Irish nationhood ... . What, then was the secret of his immense influence and popularity? He was above all ... a splendid fighter. He had attacked and beaten the enemies of Ireland in the citadel of their power – the British Parliament.

Q

1. *What light does the speech in Source A shed on Parnell's political tactics?*
2. *What is the significance of Parnell's reference to contact with 'any English parliamentary party'?*
3. *(a) What do you think Davitt means, in Source B, when he describes Parnell as 'an "Englishman" moulded for an Irish purpose'?*
(b) Do you agree with Davitt on this point?
4. *In what ways do these two sources contribute to an understanding of the importance of Parnell?*

(ii) Home Rule and Independence

SOURCE A

John Redmond, speaking in 1907, based his demand for the future self-government of Ireland on the concept of Home Rule

The national demand, in plain and popular language, is simply this, that the government of every purely Irish affair shall be controlled by the public opinion of Ireland and by that alone. We demand this self-government as a right. For us the Act of Union has no binding moral or legal force. We regard it as our fathers regarded it before us, as a great criminal act ... carried by violence and by fraud. ... We declare that ... no number of Land Acts ... no redress of financial grievances, no material improvement or industrial development, can ever satisfy Ireland until Irish laws are made and administered upon Irish soil by Irishmen ...

What is a free nation? A free nation is one which possesses absolute control over all its internal resources and powers.... Is that the case of Ireland? If the Home Rule Bill were in operation would that be the case of Ireland? To both questions the answer is: no, most emphatically, NO! A free nation must have complete control over its own harbours, to open or close them at will ... Does Ireland possess such control? No. Will the Home Rule Bill give such control ... it will not ... A free nation must have full power to nurse industries to health either by government encouragement or by government prohibition of the sale of goods of foreign rivals ... Ireland ... will have no such power under Home Rule ... A free nation must have full powers to alter, amend, or abolish or modify the laws under which the property of its citizens is held in obedience to the demand of its own citizens ... Every free nation has that power; Ireland does not have it, and is not allowed it by the Home Rule Bill ... all the things that are essential to a nation's freedom are denied to Ireland now, and are denied to her under the provisions of the Home Rule Bill, and Irish soldiers in the English Army are fighting in Flanders to win for Belgium, we are told, all those things which the British Empire, now as in the past, denies to Ireland.

SOURCE B
James Connolly, writing in the Workers Republic *in February 1916, explained why he rejected the concept of Home Rule as irrelevant to the needs of Ireland*

In the name of God and of the dead generations from which she receives her old tradition of nationhood, Ireland, through us, summons her children to her flag and strikes for her freedom ... supported by her exiled children in America and by gallant allies in Europe ... . We declare the right of the people of Ireland to the ownership of Ireland and to ... control of Irish destinies ... we hereby proclaim the Irish Republic as a Sovereign Independent State ... . The Republic guarantees religious and civil liberty, equal rights and equal opportunities to all its citizens ... cherishing all its children ... oblivious of the differences carefully fostered by an alien government, which have divided a minority from the majority in the past ... .

SOURCE C
Proclamation of Irish Independence – Easter 1916

I admit they were wrong ... but they fought a clean fight ... no act of savagery or act against the usual custom of war that I know of has been brought home to any leader ... the great bulk of the population were not favourable to the insurrection ... the insurgents [rebels] ... got no popular support whatever. What is happening is that thousands of people in Dublin, who ten days ago were bitterly opposed to ... the rebellion are now becoming infuriated against the Government on account of these executions and ... that feeling is spreading throughout the country ... . We who speak for the vast majority of the Irish people, we who have risked a great deal to win the people to your side in this great crisis [i.e. the Great War], we who have ... successfully endeavoured to secure that the Irish in America shall not go into an alliance with the Germans in that country – we, I think, were entitled to be consulted before this bloody course of executions was entered upon in Ireland.

SOURCE D
On 11 May 1916 John Dillon, a leading Irish Nationalist MP, warned the British Government of the dangers of executing the leaders of the Easter Rising

Q

1. *What is the basic difference between Redmond (Source A) and Connolly (Source B) in their views on the concept of Home Rule? (5)*

2. *Use sources A and B as well as your own knowledge to explain the differences between the views they express. (10)*

3. *What 'guarantees' did the proclamation (Source C) offer and why do you think these were included? (10)*

4. *(a) What do Dillon's comments reveal about the role of the Irish National Party in the Great War? (5)*

(b) What do you understand by Dillon's reference to having 'risked a great deal'? (5)

5. *Review and compare all the sources. How full an understanding do these sources provide of the nature of the Irish Question and the reasons why Ireland degenerated into violence in 1919–21? (25)*

Total marks 60

From Conservative Domination to Liberal Revival: 1886–1906

10

INTRODUCTION

There are two approaches to any analysis of why the Conservative Party dominated British politics in these 20 years. Great attention has traditionally been paid to the many weaknesses of the Liberal Party after 1886 and these are examined in Chapter 8.

It is, of course, essential to understand the problems created for the Liberals by Gladstone's adoption of Irish Home Rule in 1886 and by his inability to bring this to a successful conclusion. Home Rule split the Liberal Party and provided the Conservatives with valuable new recruits and new sources of funds: it also exposed the impotence of the elderly Gladstone as Liberal leader, increasingly stubborn and more and more isolated from his colleagues in Parliament. After a second attempt to carry Home Rule, in 1893, had failed, Gladstone retired from politics in 1894. The Liberal Government continued for a further year under Lord Rosebery before resigning. The party was severely mauled in the 1895 election and was then doomed to ten years of opposition to successive Conservative Governments. Concentration on Liberal weaknesses has tended to overlook the important part played by the Conservative leader, Salisbury, in reviving Conservative fortunes. The first half of this chapter, concentrating largely on Salisbury and the work of his governments, tries to redress the balance and to do justice to a great Conservative leader.

Towards the end of the century, with the British Empire at its height and its navy as strong as ever, a crisis of self-confidence crept into British life. It arose from perceptions that other nations were challenging Britain's economic pre-eminence and that, in terms of national and imperial defence, Britain might soon be more vulnerable than it had been for almost a century.

Increasingly questions were raised about the readiness of the nation to respond to these challenges. This new questioning mood, and some of the responses to which it gave rise, are examined in the central part of this chapter. Some time after 1900 Liberal fortunes began to revive as they found new causes around which to unite and the Conservative Government, led after 1902 by Salisbury's nephew, Arthur Balfour, lost some of its electoral appeal.

For more details on the weaknesses of the Liberal Party after 1886 see pages 256–7

1 ∽ ESTABLISHING THE BASIS OF CONSERVATIVE DOMINANCE

A *Lord Salisbury: a reactionary Conservative*

In 1881 Disraeli's successor as Conservative Party leader had been Lord Salisbury; they were a remarkably contrasting pair. Salisbury was essentially pessimistic. To him, human beings were mainly driven by greed – or fear. Mankind's lot could not be easily improved, least of all by governments, whose overriding domestic responsibility was to uphold law and order. As for Disraeli's 'Tory Democracy', Salisbury hated and feared the masses, and believed that industrial society was inevitably divided into antagonistic classes. In the long run, he could not see how the aristocracy could retain its power and wealth in the face of the democratic onslaught, but he was determined to fight a long and bitter rearguard action on its (and his own) behalf. Ultimate defeat could be postponed – perhaps for decades – if the Conservative Party would fulfil its function of organising and defending the interests of property against the attacks of Radicals and Socialists. It was to this task that Salisbury dedicated his political life. He was to surprise himself by the extent of his own success.

PROFILE

LORD SALISBURY (1830–1903)

Lord Salisbury came from one of England's oldest landed families whose fortunes had been founded in the sixteenth century. He had a reputation for unquestioned integrity and in later life was accepted as a figure with natural authority exuding reassuring charm. He sat in the Commons until 1869 under the courtesy title of Viscount Cranborne. He served in Disraeli's Cabinet from 1866 but opposed the 1867 Reform Act and resigned over it. In 1869 he succeeded his father as the Marquess of Salisbury and entered the House of Lords. He was Prime Minister in 1885–6, 1886–92 and 1895–1902.

PICTURE 35 *Lord Salisbury*

    Salisbury knew that the best means of strengthening the Conservatives was to recruit from the enemy those voters and parliamentarians in the Liberal ranks who were unwilling to follow Gladstone down his increasingly hazardous and unpredictable paths. The brinkmanship and far-sightedness that Salisbury displayed between 1884–6 were vital to the success of this strategy.

B *The Third Reform Act 1884–5*

Few commentators could have predicted that Salisbury would turn the Third Reform Act, a Liberal measure, into a Tory triumph: yet that is what he did. The prospect of further Parliamentary reform was full of menace for his party, not least because the logic of the Liberals' proposals was hard to resist. By 1884, Disraeli's Second Reform Act of 1867 had begun to seem like a job half done. He had generously conceded the vote to the ordinary householder in the boroughs. But on what grounds had the county householder – the agricultural labourer – been denied equal treatment? Most Liberals believed that it was high time that this anomaly was corrected. Equally, Disraeli's Act had failed to give a fair share of parliamentary seats to the rapidly expanding industrial centres of the North and the Midlands, or to London. When Gladstone finally took up the reform issue in 1884 he clearly intended to redress both these grievances.

KEY ISSUE

How did Salisbury turn Parliamentary Reform to the electoral advantage of the Conservatives?

The Conservatives had good reason to be worried. Perhaps 20 years earlier, giving the agricultural labourer the vote would have caused them little unease. But since then, the pro-Tory political loyalties of rural constituencies had been undermined in a variety of ways. The introduction of the secret ballot in 1872, and much stricter legislation outlawing bribery, in the Corrupt and Illegal Practices Act of 1883, had between them ruled out the more ruthless methods of winning votes. Worse, the combination of agricultural depression from the late 1870s onwards, and the growth of farm labourers' trades unionism, had diluted the landlord's influence. The county constituencies – for long the core of the Tory Party's parliamentary representation – seemed vulnerable to Liberal attack as they had never been before.

Prospects for Conservatism in the urban constituencies seemed even worse. Peel and Disraeli had tried, in their different ways, to swing urban votes towards the Conservatives. But hardly any of the big cities offered safe seats to Tory candidates. To many Conservatives, it must have seemed that the creation of more borough seats was as good as the creation of more Liberal MPs.

Pessimism came naturally to Salisbury, but for once he was probably not exaggerating when he prophesied that, if the Liberals were allowed to put their ideas for Parliamentary reform directly into practice, the Conservatives might find themselves excluded from political power for decades to come.

In fact, Salisbury was able to force the Liberals to accept vital changes to their plans. Risking a major constitutional crisis, he used the Tories' built-in majority in the Lords to block the advance of the Liberals' Reform Bill. Salisbury insisted that he be allowed a major say on the redistribution of constituencies as the price of allowing the bill to proceed. Anxious to bring the clash to an end, Gladstone reluctantly agreed.

When the ensuing cross-party negotiations had finished, it seemed at first as though Salisbury had got little out of them:

- the enfranchisement of the rural householder was to go ahead
- small boroughs with populations of less than 15 000 were to lose both their MPs
- boroughs with populations between 15 000 and 50 000 would lose one MP.

Salisbury was ready to let these traditional bastions of Conservatism disappear!

With 142 seats now available for redistribution, the major cities would at last receive something like their fair share of Parliamentary seats: the very rough rule of thumb was that every 50 000 of the population should be represented by one MP.

What did Salisbury get out of all this? Paradoxically, his master-stroke was his acceptance of the long-standing radical demand for single-member constituencies. This meant that the old electoral map, dominated by two-member constituencies, had to be torn up. It was agreed that the new constituency boundaries would be fixed so that, as far as possible, each new seat represented a distinct economic and social interest. Salisbury exploited this principle with insight and ruthlessness. He made sure that rural communities were cleansed of the 'corrupting', predominantly Liberal, influences of industry, which had often spilled over the old county boundaries. No less important, he saw to it that, in the big cities, middle-class suburbs were cordoned off from working-class areas. They would then be able to elect their own MPs. This was a vital breakthrough for urban Conservatism. Acute observers of the political scene had noted that there were islands of middle-class Conservatism waiting to be exploited in most of the big cities. But all too often this 'villa Toryism' was submerged at election time by the weight of popular Liberalism in the overlarge, two-seater urban constituencies. Salisbury was giving the 'villa Toryism' of the suburbs the chance to make itself heard loud and clear at election time.

The electoral consequences were striking. In formerly radical cities like Leeds and Sheffield, after 1885, the Conservatives regularly took two or three of the five seats. And in London, which had received almost 40 seats in the 1885 Redistribution Act, the Conservatives were to win, in 1895 and 1900, no fewer than 51 out of the total 59 seats. In 1859 and 1865, they had won none at all!

C *Home Rule, 1885–6*

KEY ISSUE

How was Salisbury able to exploit Liberal divisions over Home Rule?

Salisbury's handling of the Home Rule Crisis of 1885–6 was masterly. His objective was to maximise the damage that the Liberal Party seemed intent on inflicting on itself. Gladstone's apparent readiness to give in to Irish Catholic pressure in general and to Parnell in particular (no better than a terrorist in the eyes of many) seemed to prove what Conservative propagandists had been saying about the Liberals for years: they were the un-English party, the party of 'disintegration', incapable of upholding the rights of property owners, and unfit to be trusted as guardians of the British Empire.

Salisbury was ruthless in maximising the advantages he had been given. He made his intentions plain in December 1885. He brushed aside Gladstone's suggestion that, for the good of the nation (or so Gladstone claimed), he take up the cause of Home Rule himself. Salisbury had absolutely no intention of splitting the Conservatives, as Peel had done in 1846, and thereby giving the Liberals a hold on power for years to come.

When Gladstone's Home Rule Bill had been defeated in the Commons in June 1886, and a general election called, Salisbury did all he could to deepen the split in the Liberal ranks. He instructed local Conservative Party associations not to oppose defectors from the Liberals with their own candidates. This helped to secure the return of 79 Liberal Unionists. Gladstone's hopes that the Liberal opponents of Home Rule would either fade away or rejoin his ranks were to be disappointed. Indeed, most went on in 1895 to join up formally with the Conservative Party, together calling themselves the Unionist Party. But this happened on Salisbury's terms, not theirs.

In the meantime, the election of July 1886 was a total triumph for Salisbury. When the seats of the Liberal Unionists were added to those of the 316 Conservatives who were returned, he had an effective majority of about 120 over the combined forces of Gladstonian Liberals and Irish Home Rulers. Only six years earlier, after Disraeli's heavy defeat, many Conservatives had feared it would be decades before they might again enjoy such a majority. But this victory in 1886 was much more than any swing of the electoral pendulum: for Salisbury (with Gladstone's unwitting help) had smashed the Liberal Party – the dominant force in British politics for four decades. The Conservatives now entered two decades of political domination.

2 ～ SALISBURIAN CONSERVATISM IN POWER: 1886–92 AND 1895–1901

A *The virtues of doing nothing*

With such a large majority the Conservatives could have kept Parliament busy with a dynamic legislative programme. Nothing could have been further from Salisbury's intentions. He disliked legislation on principle. Salisbury's intellectual conviction that it was best to do as little as possible while in government was given added weight by party political considerations. He was highly sensitive to the fact that the endless barrage of Liberal legislation had repelled the upper and middle classes, who had increasingly become the natural supporters of the Conservative Party. 'All legislation', he wrote, 'is rather unwelcome to [these classes], as tending to disturb a state of things with which they are satisfied'. Salisbury concluded, therefore, that 'our Bills must be tentative and cautious, not sweeping and dramatic'. He was to prove as good as his word: his 13 years as Prime Minister produced only three significant items of legislation.

● The Local Government Act of 1888. This established elective County Councils, thereby ending centuries of control by the landed gentry in their capacity as Justices of the Peace (magistrates).
● The introduction of free elementary (primary) education in England.
● The Workmen's Compensation Act, 1897. It enabled workers to claim compensation from their employers, as of right, for injuries suffered at work.

Short as the list is, Salisbury would have preferred it to be shorter still. He approached the problems of local government and education with grudging pragmatism: if he didn't legislate, a future Liberal Government probably would, and Liberals would certainly show less tenderness to Tory interests than Salisbury. For example, by reforming local government on his own terms, Salisbury could do something to preserve the influence of the old authority figures in the counties – the Justices of the Peace – over the administration of justice, rather than risk them being completely swept away in some future Liberal reform. He could also ensure that the administration of the Poor Law, and the raising of local taxes to finance this primitive form of social security, remained in their hands and was not given to the newly created, popularly elected councils. Salisbury's thinking on education was similar. The predominantly Anglican-run voluntary schools were again, by 1891, struggling to match the quality of education offered by the rate-subsidised Board Schools. By abolishing all fees for elementary education, and increasing the funding from central government, Salisbury could put the Church of England schools on a much sounder financial footing. The Church of England had long been the Conservatives' friend, and Salisbury was determined to uphold its influence.

Of all the legislation for which his ministries were responsible, Salisbury was least enthusiastic about the Workmen's Compensation Act. This seemed to interfere in the contractual relationship between employer and workman in a way wholly advantageous to the latter. Under it, most workmen were now guaranteed compensation for any injury suffered at work, without having to prove that their employer had been negligent. The inspiration behind the Act was Joseph Chamberlain.

The ex-Radical had become Salisbury's Colonial Secretary in his 1895 ministry, when the Liberal Unionists had at last formally joined the Conservatives. Chamberlain hoped that this legislation would form a part of a much larger package of social reconstruction, including Old Age Pensions. He believed that if Salisbury's Government made imaginative concessions to the working classes, the latter could be kept out of the socialist camp. Salisbury disagreed. He believed that the more concessions the wealthy made to the workers, the more the workers would demand. Resistance, and the defence of the free market, was the best strategy for the Conservatives and their Liberal Unionist allies. The Workmen's Compensation Act was the only concession Salisbury was prepared to make to Chamberlain to keep him happy. It was just enough, for soon, the Boer War would be fully absorbing 'Radical Joe's' destructive energies.

KEY ISSUE

Why were so many people of different classes attracted to Salisbury's Conservative Party?

B *The social context of Salisbury's Conservatism*

Readers may have been puzzled by mention of Joseph Chamberlain as an influential Cabinet colleague of Salisbury. Salisbury himself had described the former leader of Liberal Radicalism as a 'Sicilian Bandit' as late as 1884. But Chamberlain's transition from the Conservative's 'enemy number one' to a central figure in the Unionist hierarchy illustrates a much broader shift of political allegiances which was crucial for the fortunes of Salisburian Conservatism.

The Liberals had flourished in the 1850s and 1860s, when economic growth was unprecedented, social harmony was unquestioned, and Gladstone's dreams of building a classless Christian society seemed eminently practicable. By the 1890s, this mood had largely disappeared. Britain's economic supremacy was under challenge from Germany and the United States. Furthermore, the rise of militant, unskilled trades unionism, sometimes inspired by outright socialism, began to give the flavour of 'class-war' to industrial relations. Salisbury's brand of Conservatism, with its emphasis on uncompromising resistance to radicals and socialists, increasingly seemed to make sense to many old Gladstonians. Such feelings help to explain how many businessmen, even those from Nonconformist backgrounds, came to vote Conservative in the 1890s and how some even found themselves sitting on the Conservative backbenches in the Commons.

But this long delayed achievement of Peel's dream – that the Conservative Party should become the natural home of all men of property, whether their wealth was landed, financial or industrial – cannot by itself explain the electoral popularity of Conservatism in the last two decades of the nineteenth century. The Party also succeeded in persuading a significant number of 'the masses' to vote Conservative. Why this happened has been much debated.

ANALYSIS

How did the Conservatives appeal to the masses?

Three main explanations have been offered: there is probably truth in all of them.

1   Social historians point to the growing size of the lower middle classes in later Victorian England. This group includes office workers, shopkeepers, insurance salesmen and elementary school teachers. It has been suggested that they were especially responsive to Salisbury's appeals for a union of all ranks of the educated and propertied against 'the mob'. Although they were often hardly better off than the working classes, they had a keen sense of their superior status. A Conservative vote was their way of asserting their own sense of identity with the wealthy – and it just as surely registered their anxiety at the danger of slipping backwards into the ranks of the poor.

2   It is probable that the Conservatives enjoyed a surprising amount of success in those quarters where Salisbury least expected it: the working classes. Election results from Lancashire and the East End of London suggested the existence of a 'slum Toryism' at least as vigorous as the 'villa Toryism' of the suburbs. Disraeli had been the first to appreciate how

For Gladstone and
Gordon see Chapter 11,
pages 334–5

chauvinism excessive
patriotism

much Conservatism could gain electorally from identifying itself with the glories of empire and the spirit of patriotism – especially as the Liberals made it so easy to have themselves smeared with accusations of spinelessness, defeatism and doing England down.

Salisbury's Conservative Party had no hesitation in continuing with Disraeli's strategy. The death of General Gordon at Khartoum in 1885, for which Gladstone was universally blamed, confirmed the negative stereotype of Liberalism's weaknesses. The Queen's Golden and Diamond Jubilees of 1887 and 1897, which coincided with Salisbury's premierships, were as much celebrations of the might and breadth of Britain's Empire as of Victoria's long reign. They helped to reinforce the association of Conservatism with imperial glory. By 1900, even Salisbury seemed to have appreciated the political capital to be extracted from popular **chauvinism**.

In 1900 he called an early general election – the so-called Khaki election – in the middle of the Boer War, at the height of a period of patriotic fervour. The Conservatives and their Liberal Unionist allies reaped splendid rewards. They won 402 seats, reducing the Liberals, who were bitterly divided over the war, to a wretched 183 MPs. Contrary to Salisbury's most fundamental beliefs, Toryism and democracy seemed distinctly compatible.

3 The creation and the popularity of the Primrose League, has been offered by the historian Martin Pugh (see Bibliography, page 317). Disraeli had founded the Primrose League in 1883 with the objective of promoting 'Tory principles – viz. the maintenance of religion, of the estates of the realm, and of the Imperial Ascendancy of Great Britain' through a 'true union of the classes'. Pugh is the first historian to draw out the full significance of the League's extraordinary popularity. By 1891, it boasted a membership of over one million. Through a stream of events and entertainments – dances, brass bands, visits to stately homes, 'magic lantern' shows, perhaps featuring pictures from distinct parts of the Empire – it engaged ordinary men – and women – in a Conservative political culture in a way that Salisbury himself could never dream of doing. He would have regarded the League's festivals and fairs with disbelief and distaste. But at election time, the League did crucial work in spreading propaganda and mobilising the Conservative vote. No less important, its more diluted political activities between elections were instrumental in building up a bedrock of popular attachment to Conservatism.

According to Pugh, the League 'formed the vital bridge between [the party's] parliamentary leaders and the [rapidly expanding] mass electorate'. It marked an essential development in the range and style of popular Conservatism, which Salisbury had done little to sponsor, but from which he was to derive much benefit.

3 ⌐ ASSESSING SALISBURY AS CONSERVATIVE LEADER

According to the historian Michael Bentley (see Bibliography, page 317) Salisbury was 'the most formidable politician the Conservative Party has ever produced'. Evidence for this is not hard to find: Salisbury's electoral record is the most impressive of any political leader in the Victorian era. The victories he scored in 1886, 1895 and 1900 were all by large margins, while the defeats of 1885 and 1892 were close enough to leave the Liberals deeply compromised in their reliance on the Irish Nationalists for working majorities.

But there is an element of exaggeration about Bentley's claim. Salisbury himself was reluctant to take too much personal credit for the Tories' electoral dominance. Instead, he argued – with much truth – that 'Mr Gladstone's existence was the greatest source of strength which the Conservative Party possessed'. Beyond this, it must not be forgotten that the social changes which characterised later Victorian Britain – especially the rise of the lower middle classes, and the perceived threat of an increasingly militant working class – were very helpful to the Conservative triumph. Of course, Salisbury showed much skill in exploiting the changing social climate – his warnings about 'disintegration' and class war were well judged to maximise the Conservatives' appeal to anxious property owners. But he was far from infallible. For example, his complete neglect of popular and working-class Conservatism could have proved very expensive.

KEY ISSUE

How much credit for Conservative dominance should be given to Salisbury personally?

SALISBURY AND PEEL

Comparison with Peel sheds some light on what Salisbury contributed to the success of nineteenth-century Conservatism. He shared with Peel a tough-minded authoritarianism and contempt for the masses. For both of them, the French Revolution and the guillotine were the monstrous shadows hanging over aristocratic politics: the great problem was to keep the masses in order. The best prospect for this, Salisbury and Peel would have agreed, was to unite all the forces of property under the Conservative banner.

But Salisbury rejected Peel's belief that a well-informed and bold government could master most problems to which it set its mind. To Salisbury the main function of government was to maintain law and order and uphold the workings of the free market and the rights of property, not to pass laws. Furthermore, he absolutely rejected Peel's notion – exemplified in the great crises of 1845 and 1846 – that the

For Peel as Conservative leader see Chapter 6, pages 165–70

Conservative executive might have to sacrifice the unity of the Conservative Party to the interests of the nation. To Salisbury, the true interest of the nation and the interests of the Conservative Party were indistinguishable. The Conservatives represented wealth, religion, intelligence, order – civilisation itself.

SALISBURY AND DISRAELI

For Disraeli's legacy to the Conservative Party see Chapter 8, pages 235–41

Comparison with Disraeli shows Salisbury rejecting important elements of the Disraelian legacy, too. He deplored Disraeli's opportunism and adventurism, which had reached their ruinous climax in the signally un-Conservative Second Reform Act of 1867. The notion of a 'Tory Democracy' struck Salisbury as a contradiction in terms. As to 'trusting the people', the only thing that Salisbury believed the people could be 'trusted' to do – if given half a chance – was to plunder the property of their betters. While Disraeli's dream was to make the two nations of Britain – 'the rich' and 'the poor' – into one, Salisbury was convinced that these two nations were necessarily divided and embattled. It was, Salisbury believed, the main responsibility of the Conservative Party to keep the poor from the throats and pockets of the rich. Salisbury's and Disraeli's visions of what British society could and should be like could hardly have been more different.

Yet in terms of practical politics the two leaders had important things in common:

- they shared an unashamed conviction that British interests had to be defended, by war if necessary, and that the electorate was more likely to be impressed by successful assertions of British power, than by higher principles
- both were determined not to 'harass the country' with too many laws as Gladstone had done.

Luckily for the Conservatives, even Salisbury's and Disraeli's differences proved oddly complementary. Disraeli had targeted the working classes as potential Tory voters: by contrast, he had neglected and even despised the middle classes, although their flight from Gladstonian Liberalism was the key to Tory success in the later nineteenth century. Salisbury's strategy was the reverse: oblivious to the potential of working-class Toryism, the linchpins of his strategy were 'resistance to socialism' and the cultivation of 'villa Toryism'. Nevertheless, to his great surprise, the phenomenon of working-class Conservatism not only persisted but grew. Disraeli's hopes that a Conservative political culture might capture the imagination of large sections of the lower classes was realised – a process in which the Primrose League, and imperialist rhetoric and celebrations, had a large role to play. Thus, Disraeli's and Salisbury's political blind spots were cancelled out: between them, in a way which neither of them as individuals would have thought possible, they were able to attract *both* working-class *and* middle-class voters to the Tory ranks. In that sense, the credit for Conservative political dominance in the last quarter of the nineteenth century should be jointly shared.

4 ⌐ A GREAT POWER IN DECLINE?

As the century drew to a close concern about Britain's future as a Great Power gathered momentum. It was based, broadly, on three considerations:

● first, there was the question of Britain's diplomatic 'isolation' and the increasing hostility with which she was regarded by other nations
● second, there was the question of Britain's economic performance and the extent to which other nations were catching up with, or even overtaking, Britain as the leading manufacturing and commercial power
● third, there was the question of the condition of the working classes in Britain and the extent to which this was undermining Britain both economically and socially.

Britain's 'isolation' is discussed in Chapter 11, page 340

A *The economy*

Concern about the performance of the British economy stemmed from the 1870s when, after nearly three decades of relatively consistent growth, the economy was suddenly afflicted by a series of slumps separated by temporary revivals. The last of these slumps ended in 1896 and was followed by a steady, if slow, period of economic expansion up to 1914. However, despite this 'recovery', the cycle of slumps over a 25-year period up to 1896 had been enough to undermine the confidence in British economic strength. Some economic historians used to refer to the last quarter of the nineteenth century as 'The Great Depression' but, more recently, economic writings have rejected this view, preferring to present the period as one involving a slowing down of the earlier, rapid expansion of the economy, until a lower, more sustainable pattern of growth was reached in the 1890s.

In retrospect it is easy to see that fears about the strength of the British economy in this period were exaggerated. In fact, the economy was performing in rather a mixed way. For example, the period after 1870 was precisely when Britain was emerging as the world's leading shipbuilding nation. Output of iron and steel continued to increase, despite competition from Germany and the USA, and even the inefficient coal industry continued to remain profitable in the years up to 1914. However, it is also true that Britain did not expand as rapidly as Germany and the USA in the newer industrial sectors, such as electrical engineering and chemical production.

The agricultural sector faced a more difficult problem: cheap imports of cereals from the 1870s put pressure on British farmers and forced them to reduce their corn production. Even livestock farmers faced some competition as steamships with refrigerators allowed the importation of cheap meat from abroad. In short, British farmers faced the kind of situation which the previous generation had feared would arise at the time of the repeal of the Corn Laws, but which had then failed to materialise. The case for a 'Great Depression' in the agricultur-

KEY ISSUE

Did Britain suffer from a 'Great Depression' in the last quarter of the nineteenth century?

DIAGRAM 7
Steel production in Britain continued to grow throughout this period but not nearly as fast as in the USA and Germany

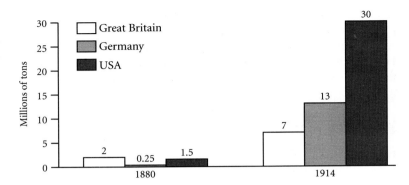

al sector is thus more convincing than that for industry, but even so the picture was not one of unrelieved gloom. Cheaper imports of cereals meant cheaper foodstuffs for livestock farmers and in some parts of the country, such as Lancashire, farm rents actually rose in this period as profits soared. Moreover, the availability of cheaper food meant that, across the nation as a whole, the value of real wages was consistently rising, despite the effects of the periodic slumps.

The most obvious, and most discussed aspect of economic performance, was the question of international trade. More specifically, there was the question of German imports and the size of the 'trade-gap', which began to increase after 1870: this meant that the value of imports into the country exceeded the value of exports in some years. Such gaps had existed even in the boom of the 1850s and were always covered by the value of so-called 'invisible' earnings from insurance and banking services, which brought increasingly vast profits into the British economy. London remained the commercial centre of the world and its dominance was unchallenged. Nevertheless, having noted that much of the concern about British economic performance was exaggerated, it is important to realise that what people at the time *believed* is often as important to understanding that period, as anything that history reveals to have actually been the case.

B *The condition of the working classes*

Concern about the condition of the working classes arose out of the publication of evidence resulting from more 'scientific' investigations of poverty that began to appear in the 1880s. Charles Booth, a shipping magnate, published details of his investigation into the London district of Tower Hamlets in 1887. He claimed that one-third of the population was living below the poverty line. Booth went on to conduct a series of investigations between 1891 and 1903. His work was paralleled by the study of poverty in York undertaken by Seebohm Rowntree and published in 1901. These investigations were intended to provide factual evidence about poverty and their chief value was to demonstrate that unemployment and poverty could not be viewed solely as the result of vice or laziness. The poor physical condition of many of the would-be

---

KEY ISSUE

Why did social problems attract such great interest in this period?

recruits for the Boer War of 1899–1902 then added fuel to the fires of publicity which scientific investigation had stoked.

See pages 339–40 on the Boer War

The idea that poverty was turning the British lower classes into some kind of sub-species had already provoked prophecies of doom about the decline of the British race. Booth had written that the 'lives of the poor lay hidden from view behind curtains on which were painted terrible pictures; starving children, suffering women, overworked men' … His (unrelated) namesake, William Booth, the founder of the Salvation Army, published a pamphlet in 1890 entitled '*In Darkest England and the Way Out*', in which he portrayed the working-class districts as more remote than darkest Africa from the experience of the upper and middle classes. This idea that the condition of the working classes posed some kind of threat to civilised society, or to the survival of the Empire, became a powerful force in promoting demands for government intervention in social matters

C *National efficiency and the reform of education*

It was perhaps inevitable that people concerned with both the apparent economic decline of Britain and the supposed 'physical deterioration' of the working classes should seek to establish some link between the two. The idea that national efficiency was being undermined and that something needed to be done about it was embraced by a wide range of writers, from socialists such as the Webbs, to imperialists such as Lord Rosebery. Social reform was an obvious objective for those who argued that poverty was the main cause of the social decline that was threatening national efficiency and the future of the British Empire. One particularly relevant social issue was that of popular education. The idea that Britain's education system was inferior to that of other countries had long been taking shape. In particular, British technical and scientific education was seen as inferior to that of Germany and France and thus undermining national economic performance.

THE 1902 EDUCATION ACT

The belief that national efficiency could be promoted or, to put it another way, that national decline could be halted by a reform of the education system was one of the reasons for the passing of a controversial Education Act by the **Unionist** Government in 1902.

The Duke of Devonshire, who was the Minister responsible for education, and Arthur Balfour, Salisbury's nephew and the Leader of the House of Commons, both favoured a fundamental reform of the education system. Both were impressed by the argument that an efficient and properly funded education system was essential for a modern state aiming to maintain its place in the world. In 1902, these two took charge of the drafting of an education bill designed to bring about a substantial measure of reform. Lord Salisbury was dubious about it but, since he intended to retire from the premiership in the near future,

Unionist the term increasingly used at this time to describe the Conservatives and their Liberal Unionist allies who, opposed to Home Rule for Ireland, stood firmly for the continued union of the United Kingdom

he did not oppose the idea. Joseph Chamberlain was also unenthusiastic, not because he undervalued education, but because, as a Nonconformist, he could anticipate the storm which would result from any attempt at government interference in the role played by the Churches in the provision of education, or from any attempt to fund Anglican schools from local rates. However, Chamberlain could not overrule Balfour who was the clear successor to Salisbury as Prime Minister.

The purpose of the 1902 Education Act was to provide a new structure for both elementary (primary) and secondary education under local authority control. The School Boards, which had been set up under the 1870 Act, had legal powers only in respect of elementary schooling. Over the years, many Boards had gone well beyond their authority by providing secondary education as well. This meant that they were using ratepayers' money without any legal basis. The situation came to a head in 1901, when a court case was brought against the London School Board for using local rates to provide secondary education courses. The judge ruled against the Board on the grounds that the 1870 Act implied that rates could only be spent on children taking basic subjects. This judgment led to severe restrictions on school board spending on technical, evening and adult classes, all of which had been expanding in recent years and all of which could be argued to be contributing to the formation of a better-educated population.

The Education Act of 1902 was passed, as Salisbury and Chamberlain had foreseen, amidst great controversy. The Act swept away the old school boards and created Local Education Authorities under the County and County Borough Councils. These 'LEAs' had responsibility for both elementary and secondary education and were also required to support the voluntary (Church) schools out of the rates. This latter provision caused the political uproar. Nonconformists were outraged by the idea of ratepayers' money being used to support the Anglican schools. The Liberals, conscious of their traditional political support among the Nonconformists, fought the proposal every inch of the way in the House of Commons and a great national campaign of opposition began, in which the Welsh radical and future prime minister, David Lloyd George, himself a Nonconformist, took a leading role. Attempts at compromise failed completely. Joseph Chamberlain suggested avoiding using the rates altogether by increasing government grants, but the cost of the Boer War ruled out that idea. Another possibility was a clause which would leave it to the local authorities to decide whether or not they wished to use the rates to support Church schools. Balfour was against this on the grounds that it would lead to endless arguments at local level as well as leaving some Anglican schools at the mercy of hostile local councils. A good many Tories sympathised with Balfour's position and the clause was removed.

The passing of the 1902 Education Act cost the Unionist Government dearly in political terms. The widespread dissatisfaction with the Act is illustrated by the 70 000 prosecutions for non-payment of rates in the following year. In Wales, where Nonconformity was strong, the

KEY ISSUE

Why did the 1902 Education Act arouse such fierce political controversy and prove so helpful to the Liberals?

opposition was particularly bitter. The Liberals reaped the benefit of a great revival in the political significance of Nonconformity, which had been markedly on the decline. It was also an issue that enabled Liberals to re-unite after the split which had occurred in their ranks over the Boer War. Within the Government itself, the Education Act had a divisive effect. One of the most important consequences of the Liberal Unionist – Conservative merger was that it brought together Anglican and Nonconformist opinion – the latter being most obviously represented by the prominent position of Chamberlain. The education controversy deeply embarrassed Chamberlain with his own Nonconformist supporters. He now had less of an obligation towards his Conservative partners not to rock the political boat with his own developing ideas.

JOSEPH CHAMBERLAIN (1836–1914)

A wealthy Birmingham manufacturer who, in the 1870s, as the city's Liberal Lord Mayor, became the most famous of the nineteenth-century municipal reformers. After the 1867 Reform Act, he organised the formidable Liberal election machine in the city and, in 1876, became one of its Liberal MPs, in which role he annoyed Gladstone by pressing for more state involvement in social reforms. In 1886, outraged by Gladstone's conversion to Irish Home Rule, he was the key figure in the secession of the Radicals from the Liberal Party, forming the Liberal Unionists. By the 1895 election he had linked up with the Conservative Party led by Salisbury and served as Colonial Secretary from 1895 to1903. In an age when imperialist sentiment was increasingly fashionable, he became perhaps its most famous and most formidable advocate, directing imperial policy in South Africa before and during the 1899–1902 Boer war. In 1903 he began to advocate the abandonment of free trade in favour of a policy of imperial preference with lower tariffs on goods traded within the British Empire. Extra tariffs levied on foreign imports could then be used to finance Britain's industrial regeneration or to pay for necessary social reforms. He failed to convince the Prime Minister, Balfour, and resigned from the Government to pursue 'his' cause outside the Government. This split seriously damaged the Conservative Government, contributing to its defeat in the 1906 general election, where dearer food because of possible import duties became a major issue. Chamberlain's political career was ended in1906 by a stroke, and he died in 1914.

PROFILE

PICTURE 36
Joseph Chamberlain, Colonial Secretary, 1895–1903

5 ⌐ TARIFF REFORM AND THE DECLINE OF THE UNIONISTS

In September 1902, Lord Salisbury retired from the premiership and was succeeded by his nephew, Arthur Balfour. There was no question of a struggle for the succession. The only possible alternative to Balfour was Chamberlain, who knew perfectly well that he was not acceptable, as leader, to most of the Conservatives. Chamberlain accepted this situation realistically and never made any attempt to intervene, despite some press efforts to stir up a campaign on his behalf. His acceptance of Balfour, however, did not mean that he was satisfied with the state of affairs within the Unionist Government.

Chamberlain's dissatisfaction stemmed from a variety of frustrations in his political life:

● he wanted to be Prime Minister but he knew that there was almost no prospect of this happening
● he increasingly felt that the Government's lack of achievements in social policy was undermining his credibility and playing into the hands of the socialists
● he was worried at the lack of progress, as he saw it, in ending British isolation in foreign policy
● he was, most of all, frustrated at the lack of progress which his plans for imperial integration and development were making.

KEY ISSUE

Why did Chamberlain's conversion to tariff reform cause such a political upheaval?

CHAMBERLAIN'S PROPOSALS

Since 1897 Chamberlain had made repeated efforts to advance the idea of an economic union made up of all the countries within the British Empire. So far, however, all his efforts to interest the Prime Ministers of the various Dominions and Colonies of the Empire, had failed. To Chamberlain this spelled disaster for the future of both the Empire and the United Kingdom. He firmly believed that the future lay with large countries with large populations and access to vast natural resources. For Britain to compete with the likes of the USA and Germany there was, according to Chamberlain's analysis, no alternative but the unification of the Empire or a decline to minor international status.

By 1902 Chamberlain was little short of desperate for a political initiative. The 'triumph' of the Boer War – 'Joe's War' as it was often called – had turned sour; the Education Bill was an acute embarrassment; Chamberlain became determined to embark upon a major scheme that would seize the public's imagination, rescue Unionism from the doldrums and, ultimately, capture opinion throughout the Empire for a great imperial cause. For many years he had been privately dubious about the wisdom of the United Kingdom continuing with a policy of free trade in a world that was increasingly turning to economic protection. It was not, it should be emphasised, that he was personally a protectionist in outlook. On the contrary, he hoped that international free trade could be restored. For the time being, however, he had come to

See pages 339–40 on the Boer War

the conclusion that British interests demanded the restoration of protection in order to give British industry a breathing space against cheap imports from government-subsidised producers abroad. The money raised from import tariffs, he believed, could be used to fund social reforms, as well as to assist the regeneration of Britain's industrial base.

POLITICAL DANGERS

Such a policy was politically dangerous. Taxing imports meant a certain rise in food prices; it would be difficult to sell the idea to the working classes; it would unite the Liberals in ferocious opposition; it risked dividing the Unionists. On the other hand, the scheme offered almost the last chance to inject some life into the concept of imperial unification: a protective tariff could be introduced, within a scheme of 'imperial preference' under which trade within the British Empire could be exempted from taxation or subjected to reduced rates. Whatever the risks, Chamberlain was not the man to shirk a challenge when such a prize was at stake. As early as May 1902, he hinted at the idea of an imperial trading system in a speech in his political stronghold, Birmingham. The Government had just been forced to introduce a small tariff on imported corn to help pay for the costs of the Boer War and had suffered criticism for doing so. In defending the tariff, Chamberlain hoped to undermine the out-of-date doctrine of free trade.

In early 1903, Chamberlain prepared himself for the launching of his great crusade. In May, once more in Birmingham, he made a momentous speech that unquestionably changed the course of politics in the years up to the First World War. He declared himself in favour of an **imperial preference** tariff system designed to bring about an economic integration of the Empire.

Chamberlain's speech initiated a debate that split the Unionists as a whole, with both Conservatives and Liberal Unionists divided over their response. Balfour attempted to preserve unity by adopting a fence-sitting strategy: he did not wish to break with Chamberlain and his supporters (who now, after all, included mainstream Conservatives) but, on the other hand, he was personally unconvinced of the case for 'tariff reform'. In any case, his main priority was party unity. While Balfour was using all his considerable political skills to keep the Unionists together, the opposing groups were formalising their positions: Chamberlain headed a Tariff Reform League; the free trade Unionists formed the Unionist Free Food League. Some Unionists, including the young Winston Churchill, decided to defect to the Liberals. The cartoon reflects the nature of the opposition to the idea of abandoning the principle of free trade.

BALFOUR RESIGNS, 1905

In September 1903, Chamberlain resigned from the Government in order to carry on a full-time protectionist campaign in the country at large. Leading free traders in the Cabinet also resigned, including the Duke of Devonshire. Balfour's weakened government limped on

> **KEY ISSUE**
>
> *Why would it be politically dangerous for the Conservatives to take up Chamberlain's policy of tariff reform?*

> **imperial preference** A system of tariffs in which goods imported from another part of the British Empire paid lower tariffs than goods imported from outside the Empire

Q

1. *In what ways does the cartoon present an unsympathetic view of the tariff reform campaign?*
2. *How would a supporter of tariff reform have countered the charges made in the cartoon?*
3. *How fully does the cartoon contribute to an understanding of the issues raised in the tariff reform campaign?*

PICTURE 37 *'Through the Birmingham Looking Glass',* Westminster Gazette, *6 October 1903*

For the 1906 election see Chapter 14, pages 403–5

unconvincingly until the end of 1905, when Balfour decided to resign without asking for a dissolution of parliament and therefore a general election. With the Unionists still deeply divided over tariff reform, he had the desperate hope that quarrels between the Liberal leaders, Rosebery and Campbell-Bannermann, would help his own party in a general election which had to be held by 1907 at the latest. Balfour had miscalculated, for Campbell-Bannermann had no difficulty in forming a Liberal Government and immediately called a general election for January 1906.

The outcome was a disaster for the Unionists and their long period dominating British politics was at an end.

6 ⌐ BIBLIOGRAPHY

ARTICLES

G. D. Goodlad 'Lord Salisbury and late Victorian Conservatism', *Modern History Review*, 1996.

T. A. Jenkins 'The Irish Question and the Victorians', *Modern History Review*, 1997.

D. Lowry 'When the World Loved the Boers', *History Today*, 1999 on the world-wide support that showed how isolated Britain was.

A. Roberts 'Salisbury: the Empire Builder who never was', *History Today*, 1999 the most recent biographer of Salisbury argues that he saw the Empire as a mixed blessing.

M. Rathbone 'The Liberal Party 1894–1906, *History Review*, September 2000.

J. Smith 'Joseph Chamberlain and the Campaign for Tariff Reform', *Modern History Review*, 2000.

BOOKS FOR AS/A-LEVEL STUDENTS

These books are all in the series Access to History, Hodder & Stoughton, aimed specifically at A-level students.

A. Mayer *The Growth of Democracy in Britain*, Chapter 4, 1999.

R. Pearce and R. Stearn *Government & Reform 1815–1918*, Chapter 4 (the last ten pages), 1994.

D. Watts *Tories, Conservative and Unionists 1815–1914*, Chapter 6, 2002.

D. Watts *Whigs Radicals and Liberals 1815–1914*, Chapter 5 (the second half), 2002.

FURTHER READING

Other books with useful chapters relevant to the years 1886–1906 include:

M. Bentley *Politics Without Democracy*, 2nd edition, Chapter 5, Fontana, 1996.

R. Blake *The Conservative Party from Peel to Major*, Chapter 5, Fontana, 1996.

B. Coleman *Conservatism and the Conservative Party in Nineteenth Century Britain*, Edward Arnold, 1988.

M. Pugh *The Making of Modern British Politics 1867–1939*, 2nd edition, Chapter 3, Basil Blackwell, 1993.

7 ↬ STRUCTURED AND ESSAY QUESTIONS

Most of the modules provided by the examination boards on this period of political history are at A2 level and student work is assessed through essay writing in examination conditions. Well ahead of the examination you will need to practise:

- your skills in quickly developing a line of argument relevant to the specific essay title in front of you
- briefly constructing an essay plan which will allow you to develop a relevant argument coherently and logically
- writing such essays in timed examination conditions and so forming a realistic idea of what is possible.

Such practice will also help you develop your historical understanding of the period. It will make you reflect on your understanding of the issues raised in this chapter and will develop your study skills as much as your examination skills.

A *Structured Questions for AS level*

1. In what ways did Gladstone's parliamentary reforms of 1884 and 1885 benefit the Conservative Party?
2. How was Lord Salisbury able to exploit the issue of Home Rule for Ireland to the advantage of the Conservatives?
3. On what grounds was there growing concern, towards the end of the nineteenth century, about Britain's future as a Great Power?
4. What factors, after 1902, helped to restore the political fortunes of the Liberal Party?
5. Why, in the period from 1886 to 1906, was Joseph Chamberlain so important a political figure?

B *Essay questions for A2*

1. 'A great leader of his party but a poor promoter of the interests of the nation.' How far do you agree with this verdict on Lord Salisbury in the period 1886 to 1902?
2. Why, in the years 1886–1902, did the Liberal party have so much difficulty in mounting an effective political challenge to the Conservatives?
3. 'Joseph Chamberlain's role in British politics, during the period 1895 to 1906, was essentially destructive.' Discuss.
4. Account for the domination of political life by the Conservatives in the period 1886 to 1902.
5. Why did the Unionists experience such a severe decline in the early twentieth century?

EXAMINATION TIPS

● **Questions 2 and 4** in the A2 essay questions cover the same territory but you will need to adapt to the different emphasis of the questions. Your time is limited so deal with Liberal weaknesses first in Question 2 and then go on, more briefly, to Conservative strengths. In Question 4 reverse your priorities.

● **Quotations**, as in Questions 1 and 3, often invite you to challenge what is written. Even if you largely agree with the opinions offered do think about whether they are entirely valid. Try to be critical.

Foreign and Imperial Policy, 1830–1914

11

INTRODUCTION

Two main objectives shaped British foreign policy throughout the period 1830–1914: the prevention of Britain from being dominated by another power or group of powers, and the protection of Britain's position as an imperial power with a range of overseas colonies and trading interests. International problems took various forms during these 85 years and individual foreign ministers differed in their approach to the conduct of foreign affairs, but, whatever the circumstances, these two objectives remained paramount. British foreign policy was determined by British interests.

As an island nation that depended on trade, Britain had for centuries been committed to safeguarding her trade routes and commercial rights. Her interest in Europe was primarily strategic and economic. She became involved with continental nations only when she became anxious about a possible invasion from Europe or a threat to her trade there. Although Pitt had claimed that Britain had gone to war with revolutionary and Napoleonic France in order to save Europe, the real reason had been that a French-dominated Europe would be an intolerable threat to Britain. Similarly, after 1815, Castlereagh and Canning had no wish to be involved in the internal affairs of Europe. They had supported the Congress System only for as long as they saw it as a convenient way of keeping France under control (see page 25).

Britain wanted peace and stability in Europe in order that she could go about her commercial business. If that stability could be maintained through diplomacy without recourse to war, so much the better; wars were expensive. It is a striking fact that in the 100 years between 1815 and 1914 Britain was engaged in a European military conflict on only one occasion, the Crimean War of 1854–6. This is a clear indication of the broad success of British policy in this period. The truth was that, as a trading nation, Britain looked overseas rather than to the continent. Her main concern was for India, 'the jewel in the Crown', the source of many commodities and a lucrative market for manufacturers. It was the need to defend her Indian connections that led Britain to take an abiding interest in the **Eastern Question**. She could not afford to be indifferent to the fate of Turkey, whose empire covered vitally important trade routes between Europe and India. That, indeed, was the primary reason for Britain's entering the Crimean War.

KEY ISSUE

What were the main objectives of British foreign policy in this period?

Q

Why was Britain worried about the Eastern Question?

> ## Eastern Question
>
> At its height in earlier centuries, the Turkish (Ottoman) Empire had been a great power. But by the nineteenth century it had become so enfeebled that it was referred to as 'the sick man of Europe', on the verge of collapse. What worried European states-men was the impact Turkey's disintegration would have on the balance of power in Europe. Britain's additional anxiety was that the decline of Turkey would encourage Tsarist Russia to expand into the regions that the Turkish Empire had previously pos-sessed. This would leave Russia in a position to threaten the route to India through the eastern Mediterranean and the Middle East.

1 ➤ FOREIGN POLICY UNDER PALMERSTON, 1830–65

1830–34	Foreign Secretary
1835–41	Foreign Secretary
1846–51	Foreign Secretary
1855–58	Prime Minister
1859–65	Prime Minister

TABLE 11
Palmerston's periods of office

Henry John Temple, third Viscount Palmerston, dominated British for-eign affairs for 35 years. Between 1830 and his death in 1865, there were only nine years in total when he did not direct foreign policy, either as Foreign Secretary or Prime Minister.

The principles which informed his policy and the style in which he conducted it are best studied by examining the major issues with which he was concerned during a critical period in international history.

THE BELGIAN ISSUE, 1830–9

In 1815, the Treaty makers at Vienna had incorporated the Austrian Netherlands (modern-day Belgium) into Holland in order to block French expansion along the coast of the English Channel. However, the Belgians resented this arrangement. Complaining that the Dutch treat-ed them as inferiors, they agitated for separation from Holland. Palmerston supported the Belgians and was instrumental in persuading the major powers to recognise Belgian independence in 1839. At the same time he was careful not to allow the French to reassert their con-trol over the region.

KEY ISSUE
In what ways did Palmerston seek to defend and advance British interests?

LIBERAL MOVEMENTS IN THE 1830s

Palmerston appeared to have a natural sympathy with radical move-ments on the continent. This contrasted markedly with his stern oppo-sition to such movements as Chartism in his own country. (It was said of him that he was 'a liberal abroad but a conservative at home'.) He worked to prevent the Austrians and the French from entering Italy to crush anti-government risings. He also gave valuable diplomatic sup-port to the progressive monarchs of Spain and Portugal who, having introduced liberal constitutions, were struggling to resist the reac-tionary forces they had overthrown. He was similarly sympathetic to the Polish nationalists in their struggle against Russian control although, in this case, he was not prepared to give direct military help to the Poles.

THE ANGLO-CHINESE WARS, 1839–42 AND 1856–60

Until the late eighteenth century, China had been able to preserve its ancient culture by remaining aloof from contact with other nations. But, by the early 1800s, the West's superior technology and military resources enabled a number of the European powers, including Britain, to impose themselves on China and force it to trade on unequal terms. Anti-foreigner bitterness among the Chinese reached breaking point in 1839 over the **opium trade**. The Chinese Emperor ordered the seizure of all British-owned opium and prohibited further Chinese trade with Britain. When the British merchants protested against this interference, Palmerston gave them his firm backing; on his orders, British warships shelled the Chinese city of Canton. The Chinese were too weak militarily to resist, and were obliged to sign the Treaty of Nanjing in 1842, in which they agreed to renew the opium trade and to hand over the port of Hong Kong to Britain.

The Chinese had to suppress their anger, which meant that it became even more intense. It needed only another incident for hostilities to be renewed. This duly arrived in the form of 'the Arrow' affair. In 1856, a Hong Kong vessel, 'the Arrow', sailing under the British flag, was seized by the Chinese after it had been caught in an act of piracy. The British Consul in Canton demanded both the release of the ship and an apology for the insult to the British flag. When the Chinese authorities were slow to respond, the Governor of Hong Kong ordered the shelling of Canton. The eventual outcome was that in 1860 the Chinese were forced to sign another humiliating peace treaty in which it accepted Britain's demands and gave over Kowloon harbour, in Hong Kong, to the British.

Palmerston, as Prime Minister, forced the doubters in his Cabinet into line by asserting that whatever the merits of the case, Britain's clear duty was to back her representatives in China. He appealed to the patriotism of the nation. Despite being outvoted in the Commons on the issue, Palmerston showed his unerring feel for public opinion by calling and convincingly winning a snap election in 1859.

THE 1848 REVOLUTIONS IN EUROPE

1848 was 'the year of revolutions' in Europe. Following the fall of King Louis-Philippe in France, many countries experienced serious risings against the existing political regime. Palmerston showed a broad sympathy for these liberal challenges to authority. He offered no help to Louis-Philippe and was quick to recognise the republic that replaced the French monarchy. This he did without consulting the Queen who for some time had complained that her Foreign Secretary disregarded constitutional conventions by choosing to ignore her when it suited him. Palmerston also gave his secret approval for weapons to be delivered to the nationalists in Italy to assist them in their rebellion against

Q

Why did Britain become involved in war with China?

opium trade Since the mid-eighteenth century, British merchants from India and Burma had been operating a large-scale opium trade with China. This produced high profits for the traders, but exhausted China's silver currency and increased drug addiction among the Chinese

KEY ISSUE

How did Palmerston react to the 1848 revolutions in Europe?

Austrian control. Similarly, he supported the liberals in Spain and Portugal. Palmerston calculated that if the risings were successful this would make it much more difficult for France and Austria to continue their domination of such areas.

Yet despite his delight in seeing the European powers embarrassed and preoccupied, Palmerston's did not wish to see the **balance of power** in Europe seriously disturbed. With the exception of those in Italy, he declined to support liberals movements within the Austrian Empire. This was because he wanted Austria to retain its strong position in central Europe so that it could continue to act as a barrier to westward expansion by Russia. Palmerston never allowed his sympathy for liberal movements on the continent to distract him from his central task of preserving the balance of power in Europe.

balance of power By the nineteenth century, it was an established notion that no one European nation or group of nations should be allowed to become so strong that it could be a threat to its neighbours. The keeping of the balance of power remained a consistent aim of British foreign policy throughout the nineteenth century

THE DON PACIFICO AFFAIR, 1850

Don Pacifico, who was a Portuguese Jew living in Greece, had his property damaged during an anti-Semitic riot in Athens in 1847. He claimed compensation from the Greeks and appealed to the British authorities to support him. His argument was that, since he had been born in the British colony of Gibraltar, he had a right to British citizenship. Pacifico had long been notorious as a shady character and he appeared to have greatly overvalued his losses. However, Palmerston's reaction to this quite minor incident offers a fascinating insight into his approach to foreign affairs. He chose to support Don Pacifico's claim fully. Rather than negotiate, Palmerston sent gun-boats to the port of Athens and ordered Greek ships to be seized. When the matter was debated in the House of Commons in 1850, he was sternly rebuked by some members for his 'reckless diplomacy'. Palmerston fought back in typical style. He delivered a lengthy speech in which he defended the whole of his foreign policy since 1830. He concluded by justifying his action over Don Pacifico in words that captured the public imagination and made him hugely popular in the country at large.

Q

What does the Don Pacifico episode reveal about Palmerston's attitude towards the protection of British interests?

Q

1. What aspects of Palmerston's policy and style are illustrated in this extract?
2. What type of people might have been
(a) impressed, and
(b) disturbed by Palmerston's speech?

As the Roman, in days of old, held himself free from indignity when he could say, "Civis Romanus sum" [I am a Roman citizen], so also a British subject, in whatever land he may be, shall feel confident that the watchful eye and the strong arm of England will protect him against injustice and wrong.

Lord Palmerston in the House of Commons, June 1850

THE CREATION OF THE SECOND FRENCH EMPIRE, 1851

In 1848, Louis-Napoleon Bonaparte had become President of the new French Republic. His aim was to restore the glories of his uncle Napoleon I. In 1851, he took power in a coup d'état, and a year later declared himself Emperor Napoleon III. At the time of the coup,

Palmerston, judging that Louis-Napoleon's imperial ambitions would be of little threat to Britain, formally congratulated him on his accession as Emperor. Yet again Palmerston failed to consult the Queen. With her patience finally exhausted, she insisted that Russell, the Prime Minister, dismiss him.

2 ◁ PALMERSTON AND THE CRIMEAN WAR, 1854–6

KEY ISSUE

Why did Britain become involved in the Crimean War?

Palmerston inherited from his predecessors, Castlereagh and Canning, a deep British distrust of Russia. This related to the Eastern Question, which essentially concerned the decline of Turkey and the growth of Russia. Palmerston was determined to prevent Russia sitting astride Britain's vital links with India. Wherever and whenever possible, therefore, he sought to restrict Russian expansion. One of his first successes as Foreign Secretary had been his outmanoeuvring of the Russians over the question of the Straits (see Map 4 on page 325).

In 1833, under the secret terms of the Treaty of Unkiar-Skelessi, Russia had persuaded Turkey to close the **Straits** to all foreign warships except those of Russia. When Palmerston learned this, he set in motion a subtle diplomacy that culminated in the major powers coming together in 1841 to force the Russians to sign the Straits Convention, which stated that the Straits were to be closed to all warships, and thus cancelled out Russia's original gain. Although this was a striking diplomatic success for Palmerston and Britain, the Eastern Question had not gone away. Russia, denied access to a vitally-needed warm-water port that did not freeze up in winter, was determined to undo the Straits Convention.

Given the underlying suspicions of Russia and Britain towards each other, and the weakness of the Turkish Empire, a Russo-British war was always likely to occur. Yet, when that war did come in the 1850s, it came over an issue that seemed of only marginal importance to Britain – the right to the **protectorship of the holy places in Palestine**.

The **Straits** were the waterways of the Dardanelles and the Bosphorus, which linked the Mediterranean and Black Seas (see Map 4 on page 325)

What did Palmerston hope to achieve by the Straits Convention of 1841?

Q

Protectorship of the holy places in Palestine

Palestine was part of the Turkish Empire. In the 1850s, the new French Emperor, Napoleon III, reasserted ancient French rights to guard the traditional Christian holy places in Jerusalem and Bethlehem. The Turkish Government agreed to recognise these rights. However, this angered the Tsar, who claimed that Russia had been given similar authority to protect the members of the Russian Orthodox Church in Palestine. The Tsar now extended that claim to the right to protect all Christians living within the Ottoman Empire. The Turks, knowing that this would give Russia unlimited power to interfere in their affairs, rejected Russia's claim.

In fact, the holy places issue was not the cause of war between Russia and Britain but simply the trigger for it. The truth was that, by the mid-1850s, Britain was eager for war with Russia. The long-standing British dislike of Russia and its autocratic Tsar Nicholas I (1825–55) had become deepened in the late 1840s by the revelations of Russian brutality in suppressing the attempted Hungarian revolutions of 1848–9. When France and Russia began rattling their sabres over the holy places, Britain naturally sided with the French.

A further push towards war was a report to Parliament by the British Ambassador in Russia of a conversation he had held with the Tsar. The most alarming passage in the Tsar's reported statement read:

Q

1. *What do you understand the Tsar to mean by the words: 'if the Turkish Empire falls, it falls to rise no more'?*
2. *Using your own knowledge, suggest reasons why there might have been a strong reaction in Britain to the Tsar's reference to his 'occupying Constantinople'.*

> Now Turkey has by degrees fallen into such a state of decreptitude [complete decay] that, eager as we are for the continued existence of the man [Turkey], he may suddenly die upon our hands; we cannot resuscitate what is dead; if the Turkish Empire falls, it falls to rise no more. It could happen that circumstances put me in a position of occupying Constantinople.

The Tsar's words as reported by Sir G. Hamilton Seymour to Lord John Russell, British Foreign Secretary, January 1853

Q

What was the impact in Britain of the revelation of the Tsar's attitude towards Turkey?

The Tsar's assertions were taken by some in Parliament as clear evidence that Russia had been plotting to bring about the collapse of Turkey. A vociferous pro-war group heightened the tension by emphasising the grave danger in which India now stood in the face of Russian expansionism. Strong demands were made that Britain immediately ally itself with France in an anti-Russian front. However, Lord Aberdeen and his ministers were not as certain of things as the hawks in Parliament. Aberdeen was certainly prepared to defend Constantinople should it be attacked, but he was unhappy about Britain making the first moves against Russia. Even when, in July 1853, the Russians occupied the Turkish Black Sea provinces of Moldavia and Wallachia, in an effort to increase the pressure on Turkey, Aberdeen's Government still held back.

It was the Turks who then forced the pace. They demanded that Russia withdraw her forces from Moldavia and Wallachia. When the demand was rejected they declared war. At first, Britain tried to remain neutral but, in November 1853, the Russians sank the Turkish fleet in the Black Sea. This led to intense public pressure in Britain for intervention. The Government felt compelled to act. In February 1854, Britain joined France in formally demanding the withdrawal of Russian troops from Moldavia and Wallachia. When they received no response to their ultimatum, the two countries made a treaty of alliance with Turkey and, in March, declared war on Russia. It was at that point that

MAP 4

Eastern Mediterranean and Black Sea showing the disputed areas at the time of the Crimean War

Russia began a belated withdrawal from Moldavia and Wallachia. Strictly speaking, therefore, Russia had met the terms of the ultimatum and there was now no longer a reason for war. But logic was not uppermost at this stage; having committed themselves this far, neither the French nor the British were willing to disengage before they had inflicted a military defeat on the Russians. So began a war which had lost its justification before the first shot had been fired.

Out of office since 1851, Palmerston had played no formal part in the diplomatic manoeuvres that resulted in war. He was, however, a whole-hearted supporter of the war. When Aberdeen resigned in 1855, following fierce parliamentary criticism of his poor handling of the war effort, there was really only one obvious choice of successor. Palmerston, as Prime Minister, brought to the running of the war a new energy and determination that contributed to Russia's eventual surrender in 1856. Yet it should be stressed that, important though Britain's military role was, the vital factors in the allied defeat of Russia were the scale of the French involvement (France put four times as many troops into the field as Britain) and Austria's threat, made early in 1856, to enter the war on the Franco-British side.

Palmerston was a powerful presence at the Paris peace talks in 1856. It was he who was responsible for the inclusion of Article XI in the

KEY ISSUE

What was Palmerston's role in the Crimean War?

Treaty of Paris, which prevented warships from entering the Black Sea. Since, in effect, the Article made Russia again accept the Straits Convention of 1841, it seemed to be a major British success. But it proved a hollow victory. Russia, as a great power, would not tolerate for long the limitations forced on it by the Treaty of Paris. Its determination to gain access to the Mediterranean and to reassert itself in the Balkans meant Russia was bound, in time, to re-assert itself in the area. As events were to show, the Eastern Question was far from settled.

Q

Using your own knowledge and the Source, explain why Article XI was likely to remain a cause of unrest in international relations.

The Black Sea is neutralised: its waters and its ports, thrown open to the mercantile marine of every nation, are formally and in perpetuity interdicted to the flag of war [closed to warships], either of the powers possessing its coasts, or of any other power.

Article XI of the Treaty of Paris, 30 March 1856

KEY ISSUE

How did the Crimean War affect the relations between the European powers?

The Crimean War had a far-reaching impact on relations between the European powers. The Austrians had failed to support the Russians in 1854 and even threatened to intervene against them late in the war. This ended the closeness which had endured between them since 1815. The Russians turned to the French as their best hope for diplomatic support in the future. This weakened Austria and opened the opportunity for Prussia under Bismarck to show its strength. Prussia swept aside the Danes and the Austrians in quick military victories in the 1860s; it then went on to overpower France in the Franco-Prussian war of 1870–1. The Treaty of Frankfurt, which ended the war, humiliated France by taking the key territories of Alsace-Lorraine from her and leaving the newly-created Germany dominant in Europe.

Significantly, these post-war developments took place without any reference to Britain. The 1860s and 1870s were not good decades for her diplomatically and she suffered a number of embarrassing setbacks. Palmerston had protested to the Russians over their ruthless suppression of the Polish rising in 1861 but had been pointedly ignored. When Prussia had threatened the Danes in 1863, Palmerston had been forthright in his support for Denmark. But none of this had impressed Bismarck; when war came between Prussia and Denmark in 1864, the Danes found themselves abandoned. This damaged British prestige and there was a strong reaction against Palmerston in Parliament. It was only by a narrow margin that he escaped being defeated in a no-confidence motion introduced by Disraeli.

> *Summary of Palmerston's foreign policy aims*
>
> ● To preserve the balance of power in Europe.
> ● To support stable constitutional states since they made good trading partners for Britain.
> ● To avoid direct engagement in European affairs unless British interests were involved.
> ● To support liberal movements against repressive regimes, if this involved no risk to Britain.

3 ⌐ GLADSTONE, DISRAELI AND THE EASTERN QUESTION

Palmerston died in October 1865 and was succeeded by Earl Russell, the most senior of his colleagues. But Russell, old and close to retirement, was himself soon replaced by Gladstone, who led the Liberals into government in 1868. As Prime Minister, Gladstone was determined to exercise a strong control over foreign policy. He had been a long-term critic of Palmerston's approach and was committed to the idea of raising the conduct of foreign policy to a higher moral level. He disapproved of interventionism and, instead, emphasised the rights of all nations to equality in international affairs. He was a firm believer in the **Concert of Europe**.

Gladstone's principles led him into conflict with Disraeli, who became leader of the Conservatives in 1868. Disraeli had been a great admirer of Palmerston. When the latter died, Disraeli was anxious to incorporate the Palmerstonian tradition into the image of the Conservative Party as the unflinching defender of the nation's interest before all other considerations. He made no attempt to disguise his contempt for what he regarded as Gladstone's lofty but unrealistic notions of a concert of Europe. The personal clash between Gladstone and Disraeli dominated a short but critical period of British politics between 1868 and 1881. It took its most dramatic form in their fierce disagreements over the Eastern Question.

A *The Bulgarian crisis and the Congress of Berlin*

The outbreak of the Franco-Prussian War in 1870 gave Russia the opportunity to achieve the main objective she had set herself since the end of the Crimean War – the reversal of Article XI of the Treaty of Paris, which denied her navy access to the Black Sea (see page 326). From the Russian point of view the Black Sea Clauses were a humiliation. This was a view with which Gladstone sympathised. He felt that Russia had been treated too harshly. He gave his approval, therefore, at an international conference held in London in 1871, to a proposal by Bismarck that Russia be freed from the Black Sea restrictions. He was

---

KEY ISSUE

In what ways did Gladstone and Disraeli differ in their conduct of foreign policy?

Concert of Europe In Gladstone's judgement the European nations should always attempt to avoid war by acting together to settle international issues when they arose. He regarded this 'concert' as being not so much a formal alliance system as an attitude of mind that regarded maintaining peace as an international priority

---

Q

What was Gladstone's attitude towards Russia?

Q *How did Disraeli differ from Gladstone on this issue?*

See Map 5 on page 330

immediately attacked over this by Disraeli, who asserted that, by accepting this concession, Gladstone had made it easier for Russia to renew her threat to Constantinople.

Disraeli's chance to reverse Gladstone's policy came when he returned to office as Conservative Prime Minister between 1874 and 1880. In July 1875, revolts occurred in the two Turkish provinces of Bosnia and Herzegovina. These two provinces were primarily inhabited by Serbs who wanted union with the province of Serbia. As Slavs, the Serbs looked to Russia, the great Slav nation, to support them. This was precisely the kind of situation Disraeli had feared. He was concerned that a weakened Turkey would open the door to further Russian expansion into the region, and so threaten Britain's position in the Eastern Mediterranean. This left him convinced that British interests demanded that Turkey maintain its territorial grip. However, when the revolts spread to Bulgaria and Montenegro, Disraeli found it increasingly difficult to keep to this line. From Bulgaria came appalling accounts of Turkish massacres of the Christians of the region. Public opinion in Britain was revolted, and a political storm erupted.

Disraeli's initial reaction to the first reports of the 'Bulgarian atrocities' in June 1876 was to dismiss them as exaggerations. In fact, the press estimates of deaths were considerably inflated (25 000 according to reports – nearer 12 000 in reality), but this counted for little in the face of the brutal treatment of defenceless women and children by the Turkish troops. There was a chorus of protest from the Liberals and public opinion turned against Turkey. The sense of moral outrage was powerfully expressed by Gladstone, who came out of retirement to write *The Bulgarian Horrors and the Question of the East*. His pamphlet, which appeared in the autumn of 1876, aroused an excited public response. The tone and force of Gladstone's language, which has been likened to the thunderings of an Old Testament prophet, can be judged from the following extract. He denounced the Turks for

> crimes and outrages so vast in scale as to exceed all modern example, and so utterly vile as well as fierce in character, that it passes the power of the heart to conceive, and of tongue and pen adequately to describe them. These are the Bulgarian horrors. An old servant of the Crown and State, I entreat my countrymen that our Government, which has been working in one direction, shall work in the other; and shall apply all its vigour to concur with the other States of Europe in obtaining the extinction of the Turkish executive power in Bulgaria.

Disraeli reacted by mocking the pamphlet as 'of all the Bulgarian horrors, perhaps the worst'. But the fact was that Gladstone had caught the public mood; majority opinion in Britain now wanted to see the Turks taught a lesson, even if that meant allowing the Russians to do it. Matters were made increasingly difficult for Disraeli by the refusal of the Turks to give way before diplomatic pressure from the European powers and lessen the severity of their suppression of the rebellious provinces.

Eventually Russia ran out of patience and declared war on Turkey in April 1877. Disraeli, at this stage, had little option but to declare Britain neutral and remind the Russians not to occupy Constantinople or interfere with any key British interests. In the event, the Turkish troops fought with great bravery and resource, holding out at the fortress of Plevna for nearly six months. They were eventually overrun and the Russian advance from then on was rapid. However, Russian plans for a quick war had been thwarted, and fickle public sympathy in Britain rapidly swung round to the Turkish side.

THE TREATY OF SAN STEFANO, 1878

By January 1878, Disraeli felt confident enough to warn the Russians not to attempt to alter the 1856 Peace of Paris without first gaining the general consent of the major powers. In February, the British fleet moved towards Constantinople to discourage any Russian advance on the capital. Realising that their diplomatic position was rapidly crumbling, the Russians hurriedly forced the Turks into a peace settlement – the Treaty of San Stefano – signed in March 1878. Under its terms, Serbia, Montenegro and Romania were to become independent with increased territory; Bosnia and Herzegovina were to be granted home rule, while Bulgaria was to become a self-governing principality, greatly enlarged and placed under Russia protection. The Turks signed the Treaty in the hope that Britain would be sufficiently disturbed by the Russian gains to wish to have it rapidly amended.

See Map 5 on page 330

Although the San Stefano agreement did not directly threaten British interests, since Constantinople remained untouched and the navigation of the straits was unaffected, the Treaty nevertheless represented a major extension of Russian power. Nor was Britain the only country to react. The Austrians were equally angered and joined Britain in calling for an international conference. For Disraeli, San Stefano was evidence of the dangers he had tried to warn the country against throughout the crisis. He spelled this out in a speech in the House of Lords in April 1878:

The Treaty of San Stefano completely abrogates [abolishes] what is known as Turkey-in-Europe ... it creates a large State which, under the name of Bulgaria, is inhabited by many races not Bulgarians. This Bulgaria goes to the shores of the Black Sea and seizes the ports of that sea; it extends to the coast of the Aegean ... The Treaty provides for the government of this new Bulgaria, under a prince who is to be selected by Russia; its administration is to be organised and supervised by a commissary [representative] of Russia; and this new State is to be garrisoned, I say for an indefinite period, but at all events for two years certain, by Russia ... The Sultan of Turkey is reduced to a state of absolute subjection to Russia.

1. *What significance do you attach to Disraeli's complaint that many non-Bulgarians were to be included in the new State?*
2. *In what ways, according to Disraeli, would Russia be able to influence Bulgaria?*

When Bismarck added his voice to the demand for an international conference and offered Berlin as a neutral venue, the Russians had little option but to agree. Realising that a coalition was forming against them, they knew they would have to make concessions. They tried to play for time by raising technicalities about the scope of the proposed discussion. Disraeli used the delay to good effect, calling up the army reserves and redeploying troops from India to the Mediterranean.

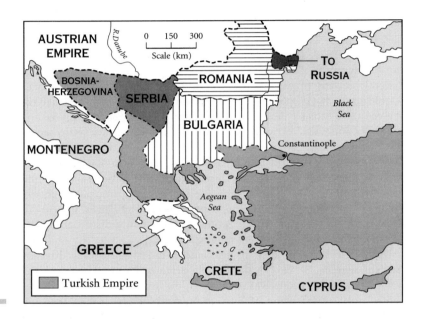

MAP 5

The Balkan Settlement under the terms of the San Stefano Treaty, March 1878

THE CONGRESS OF BERLIN, 1878

KEY ISSUE

What did Britain achieve at the Congress?

Disraeli was determined to go into the conference with the essentials already in place. At the end of May he secured agreement from the Russians that the 'big Bulgaria' concept would be abandoned. Early in June he concluded an agreement with the Turks under which Britain agreed to defend Turkey against Russia, in return for the purchase of Cyprus, which he planned to use as a military and naval base. It should be emphasised that although Disraeli set out the basic British aims in these matters, it was his Foreign Secretary, Lord Salisbury, who actually conducted the negotiations.

Disraeli attended the Congress in person and proved to be the outstanding statesman there. Bismarck acknowledged this by observing: 'Der alte Jude, *das* is der Man' (That old Jew, *that* is the man). Given the amount of preparation that had gone into it, it was hardly surprising that the Congress of Berlin ran smoothly. Its main terms were:

Q

In what ways do Maps 5 and 6 illustrate the extension of Russian influence under the Treaty of San Stefano and its restriction under the Treaty of Berlin?

MAP 6

The Balkan Settlement under the terms agreed at the Congress of Berlin, June 1878

- 'Big Bulgaria' was divided into three: an independent Bulgaria; a partly self-governing state to be known as Eastern Rumelia; and Macedonia which reverted to full Turkish control.
- Serbia, Montenegro and Romania became completely independent, but with only modest extensions to their territory.
- The Turks promised reforms and religious liberty for all their subjects.

The main gains for Britain were that the threat to Constantinople had been removed and that Turkey had been kept intact as a barrier to Russia. Disraeli returned to London claiming to have brought back 'peace with honour'. Few contemporaries disputed his claim at the time. Yet whatever Britain's success at Berlin may appeared to have been, later events were to show that the Treaty had not achieved a lasting settlement of the Eastern Question. The Treaty left countries of the Balkans feeling aggrieved and thus sowed the seeds of future conflict in that area. The main points of grievance were:

- Serbia and Montenegro resented the extension of Austrian influence and the curtailment of their own ambitions.
- Bulgaria, Greece and Romania had failed to achieve the territorial expansion they had expected.
- Russia and Austria had been left even more jealous and suspicious of each other than before.
- Russo-German relations had taken a turn for the worse. Although Bismarck subsequently attempted to placate Russia, relations between the two countries never really recovered.

There is a strong tendency in the early twenty-first century to sympathise with Gladstone's idealism in foreign policy. His notion of a

How realistic
were Gladstone's
policies?

concert of Europe and his wish to settle international disputes through negotiation chimes well with modern thinking. But there are grounds for suggesting that Gladstone was too far ahead of his time and that, therefore, he lacked realism. What made a genuine concert of European states unworkable was the strength of Germany. Created as a new nation under the leadership of Bismarck's Prussia in 1871, Germany had become the dominant power in Europe by the early 1880s. By making a set of key alliances with other major powers of central Europe, Germany effectively left France isolated. If the Concert of Europe had ever existed in the sense that Gladstone understood it, the rise of Germany had effectively destroyed it.

B *Lord Salisbury's foreign policy*

Foreign policy in late Victorian Britain was dominated by the Conservative leader, Lord Salisbury. He made foreign affairs his speciality and continued to hold the post of Foreign Secretary even when he was Prime Minister.

KEY ISSUE

How did Salisbury
approach foreign
affairs?

Salisbury's periods of office	
Foreign Secretary	1878–80, 1886–92, 1895–1900
Prime Minister	1885–6, 1886–92, 1895–1902

Salisbury approached foreign affairs with the belief that Gladstone had been wrong in thinking that Britain could become a leading member of a Concert of Nations. But he also calculated that Britain had declined as a major power and that consequently it was impossible to return to the aggressive foreign policies pursued by Palmerston and Disraeli. It followed, therefore, that the most prudent strategy was for Britain to wait on events rather than trying to direct them. This broad approach has been labelled 'splendid isolation', suggesting that Britain would avoid formal involvement with other powers unless it was unavoidable. Historians have long since pointed out that the term is not a wholly accurate description. There were important occasions when Salisbury's Government took the initiative in negotiating with other European countries. Interesting examples are the Mediterranean agreements Britain made with Spain, Austria and Italy in 1887, with the aim of limiting the influence of Russia and France in that region.

If the term splendid isolation is questionable when applied to Britain's relations with Europe, it is certainly inappropriate as a description of the **imperialism** that Britain developed in this period.

imperialism was an expansionist movement among the main European powers who competed for new overseas territories. Among their motives were economic and financial exploitation, religious missionary zeal, national rivalry, and the use of colonies as pawns in the game of European diplomacy

4 ∼ IMPERIAL EXPANSION, 1875–1914

In the late nineteenth and early twentieth centuries, Britain experienced an extraordinary extension of her empire. This took place in many parts of the world, but it is most clearly identified with Britain's involvement in what became known as **'the scramble for Africa'**.

A *Egypt and the Sudan*

EGYPT

An appropriate starting date for a study of imperial expansion is 1875. In that year Disraeli brought the recently-built Suez Canal under British control. The Canal, which linked the Mediterranean and the Red Sea and thus opened a shorter route to India, had been constructed for the Khedive (ruler) of Egypt by the French. However, in 1875 the Khedive, faced with bankruptcy, put up for sale in Paris over 175 million Canal shares. Disraeli, in a lightning move, borrowed £4 million from the bankers Rothschilds and, on behalf of the British Government, bought up the entire block. Gleefully he cabled the Queen, 'You have it, Madam; the French Government has been outgeneraled … and the entire interest is now yours'. Disraeli's dazzling stroke had profound implications. As the majority shareholder, Britain now controlled a strategically and commercially vital waterway. The need to protect the Canal became a constant British concern and made Egypt an area of particular significance.

In the late 1870s continued financial mismanagement in Egypt seemed to threaten the whole stability of the region. Since Egypt was a province of the Turkish empire, Britain joined France in demanding that the Sultan of Turkey depose the incompetent Khedive, and provide a more efficient administration. This he did, but resentment at what was seen as foreign interference led in 1881 to a revolt among the Egyptian army. The new Khedive appointed a new ministry to placate the rebels but, fearing for his long-term safety, he appealed to Britain and France for help.

True to his anti-imperialism, Gladstone, who had returned to office in 1880, was initially opposed to intervention. However, when riots broke out in Alexandria and Europeans were attacked, it was no longer possible for the British Government to stand aside. Gladstone persuaded France to co-operate in sending an Anglo-French fleet to Alexandria. Once there, however, it became apparent to the joint commanders that a military intervention on land would be required. At this point, the French drew back. They had been conducting separate negotiations with the rebels and feared that any major entanglement in Egypt would detract from their main obsession – the recovery of Alsace and Lorraine which they had lost to Germany in 1871. Therefore, Britain had to act alone or withdraw. Reluctantly, Gladstone chose the former course. Alexandria was bombarded and the Suez Canal was seized. In August 1882 a large British force landed near the Canal and proceeded to crush the Egyptian rebel forces.

'the scramble for Africa' Between the 1870s and World War I, the major European powers – principally France, Germany and Britain – rushed to establish colonies in the vast, undeveloped continent of Africa

KEY ISSUE

Why was there rapid and extensive increase in the size of Britain's empire in this period?

Q

Why did Gladstone authorise the British occupation of Egypt?

MAP 7
British Expansion in Egypt and the Sudan

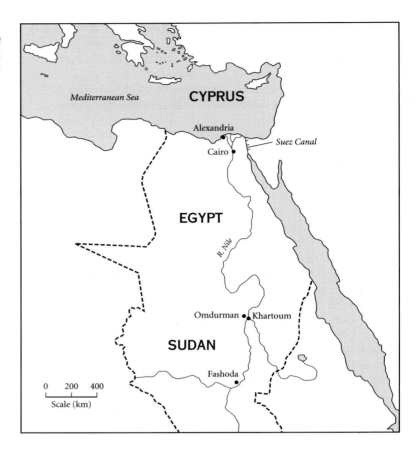

Gladstone had no wish to keep British forces in Egypt but he knew that the state of the country was so bad that a British withdrawal would result in anarchy. Sir Evelyn Baring (later Lord Cromer) was sent as Consul-general to take over the Khedive's administration. (The French were informed that they had forfeited their rights by previously backing out.) The official British line was that the occupation was only temporary. Gladstone began negotiations to set up an international board of control which eventually came into being in 1885; it contained representatives from Britain, France, Germany, Austria, Russia and Italy. The existence of the board, however, could not disguise the fact that Egypt was under British military control and that Britain had come to regard Egypt as an essential part of the Empire.

THE SUDAN

Soon after Britain took control, a serious complication arose. In 1883, the Sudan, which for 60 years had been occupied by Egyptian forces, rose in rebellion against the severity of the Egyptian repression. The Sudanese were led by the 'Mahdi', a former civil servant and slave trad-

KEY ISSUE

Why did Britain extend its control to the Sudan?

er, who proclaimed himself, the 'divinely guided one', sent to convert the world to Islam. In 1883 his forces defeated the British-led Egyptian army. Gladstone had no wish to become involved in the Sudan, but he could not allow British troops to be massacred. He was persuaded to send General Charles Gordon to oversee the British withdrawal from Khartoum, the Sudanese capital. Gordon, a strange mixture of stubbornness and mysticism, was a poor choice and the Government itself was not certain as to his exact role. Gladstone had been reluctant to send him at all. Gordon, whose military record had made him a public hero in Britain, had been governor of the Sudan (1877–80), and was known to favour resistance to the Mahdi.

It was not surprising, therefore, that having arrived in Khartoum, Gordon deliberately delayed the evacuation, calculating that public opinion would force the Government to send a large relief expedition. Gladstone had been prepared to leave him to his fate, but eventually, in February 1884, the Cabinet agreed in principle to send help. There then followed months of wrangling over the size of the force and whether a minister should accompany it. In the end, when the force under General Wolseley did reach Khartoum in January 1885 it was too late; Gordon had been killed two days earlier. Public opinion was outraged and Gladstone took the brunt of the anger. Previously he had enjoyed the affectionate nickname of the 'Grand Old Man' or 'GOM'. Now he became the 'MOG', the 'Murderer of Gordon'. Gladstone eventually decided to abandon the Sudan to the Mahdi in spite of demands for revenge for Gordon and the protests of the Egyptians. The Queen deliberately made public her view that 'Mr Gladstone and the Government have Gordon's innocent, noble, heroic blood on their consciences'.

The Mahdi died later in 1885 but clashes continued between the Egyptians and the Mahdi's successor, the Khalifa. In 1896 Salisbury decided to send a military force under General Kitchener to reconquer the Sudan. This change of policy was partly due to the increasing awareness of the Sudan's key position in controlling the waters of the Nile which were fundamental to Egypt's economy. Also, by now, other countries were showing some interest in Sudan, particularly France. Kitchener slowly secured Anglo-Egyptian control. After decisively defeating the Khalifa's forces at the Battle of Omdurman in September 1898, he went on to capture Khartoum and drive the Khalifa into exile. Thus, he secured British control of the Sudan.

THE FASHODA INCIDENT, 1898

Kitchener then became successfully involved in what became known as the Fashoda incident. Fashoda was a small outpost on the Upper Nile some 375 miles south of Khartoum. A French expeditionary force had occupied it in 1898. For a time it seemed that the French move might lead to war between France and Britain and there was great excitement in both countries. Kitchener received instructions from the Government to re-establish British authority in the area by obliging the French to withdraw:

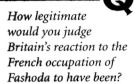

How legitimate
would you judge
Britain's reaction to the
French occupation of
Fashoda to have been?

It is possible that a French force may be found in occupation of some portion of the Nile Valley. Should this contingency arise Her Majesty's Government entertain full confidence in Sir Herbert Kitchener's judgement and discretion. They feel assured that he will endeavour to convince the Commander of any French force with which he may come into contact that the presence of the latter in the Nile Valley is an infringement of the rights of both Great Britain and of the Khedive.

Lord Salisbury to Lord Cromer, British Consul-General in Egypt, 2 August 1898

Kitchener carried out his instructions to the letter. At Fashoda he faced down the French, who withdrew without a fight. British supremacy over the whole of Egypt and the Sudan was secured.

B *Southern Africa*

See Map 8 on page 337

Britain had been closely involved in southern Africa since the late eighteenth century when she had seized Cape Colony from the Dutch. This takeover, which had been formally recognised at the Congress of Vienna in 1815, left a legacy of bitter relations between the British and Dutch (Boer) settlers. In a series of migrations in the 1820s and 1830s, the Boers left the Colony to escape British rule. Cape Colony was granted self-government in 1872. Natal, which had been largely Zulu territory, was annexed by Britain in 1843 and was also given self-government in 1872. The Convention of Bloemfontein in 1854 recognised the Transvaal and the Orange Free State as independent Boer republics. From the late 1860s, Britain proceeded to annexe further territory northwards, such as Basutoland in 1868. The aim was to prevent expansion of the Boer republics, but it left a dangerous situation. The British and the Boers regarded each other with hostility and both were resented by the native African peoples who had been forced off their land by the Europeans.

KEY ISSUE

Why was there rivalry between Britain and the Boers in South Africa?

When Disraeli returned to power in 1874, he was a committed imperialist who had made the expansion of empire a major part of his new brand of Conservatism. Clear examples of this were his buying of the Suez Canal shares for Britain in 1875 and his introduction of the **Royal Titles Bill** in 1876. His Colonial Secretary, Lord Carnarvon, was eager to extend Britain's imperial ambitions. He planned to annexe the Transvaal as a first step towards the creation of a British-dominated federation of South Africa. Sir Theophilus Shepstone, a former Lieutenant-Governor of Natal, was sent to the Transvaal to organise the annexation. Fortune favoured Shepstone. His visit coincided with an uprising of the Zulus in the Transvaal. The Boers subordinated their dislike of the British to the need for protection. Annexation followed in 1877, quickly followed in turn by a war against the Zulus which the new Governor of the Cape

Royal Titles Bill 1876
This measure conferred on the Queen the title of 'Empress of India', thus making her the personification of the imperial idea and declaring formally that Britain was an empire

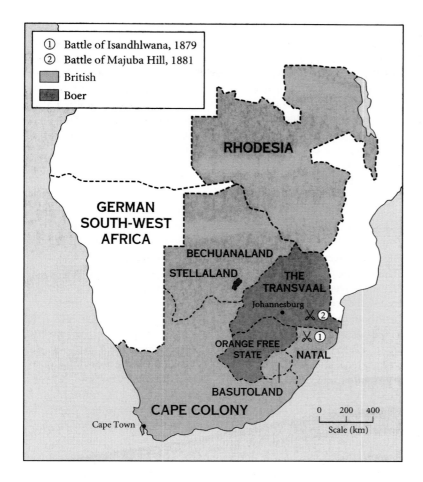

encouraged. The war was successful in the end but not before a British force had been massacred at **Isandhlwana** in 1879.

Once the Zulu threat had subsided the Boers were unwilling to remain under British control. Gladstone, who had roundly condemned Disraeli's policy in southern Africa, was prepared to support the Boer claim for independence when he returned as Prime Minister in 1880. But before he could move on this, the Boers had lost patience. They launched an attack on British forces in 1881, which culminated in a major Boer victory in the battle of Majuba Hill. Gladstone was embarrassed but stuck to his resolve by granting the Boers independence in the Pretoria Convention of 1881. When the Boers subsequently objected to a clause requiring them to recognise British 'suzerainty' (authority) it was removed in the Treaty of London of 1884, although the British kept control of the Transvaal's foreign policy.

CECIL RHODES AND THE GROWTH OF BRITISH AUTHORITY IN AFRICA

The extension of British influence into central Africa in the 1880s, owed much to the activities of one man, Cecil Rhodes. Born in Britain in

Isandhlwana was the scene of a disastrous defeat for the British when a column of 1200 troops were all but destroyed in a series of attacks by Zulu assegai warriors (spearmen)

1853, Rhodes, a fiercely self-driven man, had gone to southern Africa at the age of 17; he stayed to make a fortune in the diamond mines of Kimberley and the gold mines of Transvaal. He conceived a grand vision of a British empire in Africa which would extend the entire length of the continent from the Cape to Cairo. In 1885, Rhodes persuaded the British Government to take over Bechuanaland (now Botswana), arguing that it was under threat from the Germans. Believing that there were rich gold deposits to be found further north, Rhodes then set about securing concessions from the chiefs of the Ndebele and Shona tribes living in present-day Zimbabwe and Zambia. The expansion met considerable local opposition. The Ndebele, furious at what they saw as broken pledges, rose in 1893 and again in 1896. The Shona, who originally had collaborated with the British, joined in the second revolt.

In 1889 Rhodes secured a Royal Charter for his British South Africa Company (BSAC), which effectively gained control of these regions. There had been considerable opposition to the granting of a Charter in Britain, especially from religious groups who would have preferred the British Government to take direct responsibility. Rhodes, however, argued that control by the Company involved no expense to the taxpayer, only to the shareholders.

His view carried the day. The BSAC developed into a powerful organisation with what amounted to its own private army. It was backed by some of the richest organisations in the world including Rothschilds and De Beers. It not only controlled the land but also obtained mineral rights and the authority to impose taxes. Although, in theory, its powers were regulated by the British Government, in practice it had virtually sovereign rights. When Rhodes became Prime Minister of the Cape in 1890 his power and influence seemed limitless.

Nevertheless, there was one remaining barrier to Rhodes' vision of the future. The Boer states needed to be brought under full British control, especially the Transvaal with its great mineral wealth. These states were now completely encircled by British-controlled territory. Moreover, the means of bringing them to heel already existed. Many British miners and engineers had been drawn to the Transvaal by the prospect of the wealth to be obtained from mineral exploitation. The Boers had been obliged to allow in these 'Uitlanders' (Dutch for foreigners) because of the industrial expertise they brought to what was essentially an agricultural economy. The Boers, however, under the leadership of Paul Kruger, the Transvaal President, were determined to retain control. They subjected the Uitlanders to heavy taxation and denied them basic political and electoral rights. It was the resentment of the Uitlanders at this treatment that provided the potential for a revolt within the Transvaal, which the British then exploited.

THE JAMESON RAID, 1895

A major development in African affairs occurred with the appointment of Joseph Chamberlain as Colonial Secretary in 1895. Chamberlain was a fervent believer in the empire, whose expansion he regarded as vital to Britain's long-term prosperity. Spoiling for a fight with the Boers, he gave his full but secret support to a direct attack upon Boer authority. With the backing of Cecil Rhodes, Dr Starr Jameson, the chief administrator of the BSAC, led some five hundred armed men into the Transvaal in the hope of igniting a full-scale Uitlander rising against Kruger's Government. The raid was a fiasco. Jameson's force were easily overcome and he and the ringleaders were sent as prisoners for trial in London. Rhodes resigned as Prime Minister of the Cape. The Boers rightly suspected that Chamberlain had been in on the plot, though he managed to survive a parliamentary enquiry at Westminster.

The affair assumed a wider diplomatic significance when Germany decided to involve itself in the aftermath. The Kaiser, always anxious to cut an impressive figure internationally, sent an open telegram to Kruger congratulating him on his handling of the crisis. To the British, this implied that Germany considered herself free to intervene. This was diplomatically intolerable and Salisbury's Government demanded an explanation. The Kaiser then made some conciliatory noises, but there was no doubt Anglo-German relations had been damaged by the episode.

Despite the scandal of the Jameson Raid, Chamberlain was more than ever determined to force Kruger and the Boers into a position where they would have no option but to fight. To this end, in 1897, he appointed Alfred Milner as High Commissioner in the Cape. He judged that Milner's unpredictable character and fanatical belief in Britain's right to control southern Africa would hasten the collapse of negotiations with the Boers. Chamberlain's judgement proved an astute one. President Kruger found the Commissioner impossible to deal with; frustrated by the increasingly unreasonable demands put to him by Milner, Kruger abandoned any further talks. In October 1899, the Transvaal declared war on Britain.

THE ANGLO-BOER WAR, 1899–1902

The root cause of the war can be expressed in a simple direct question: who was to run South Africa? Was the area to be a British-dominated federal dominion or a Boer republic? It was a matter of sovereignty. As Kruger said to Milner during the final talks at Bloemfontein before war broke out, 'it is our country you want'.

The war lasted for three years. After much effort and many reverses, Britain's superiority in numbers and weaponry finally wore down the Boer guerrillas and forced their surrender. At home the conflict caused sharp division between 'anti-Boer' supporters of the war and 'pro-Boers', like the young David Lloyd George, who saw it as a piece of unnecessary bullying. One tragic aspect of the war which gained particular notoriety was the death from typhus and cholera of many Boer women and children who were imprisoned in British 'concentration' camps, where the insanitary conditions encouraged the spread of virulent disease.

The fighting was finally ended in May 1902 by the Peace of Vereeniging. Under its terms, the Boer Republics (Transvaal and the Orange Free State) were absorbed into the British Empire but with the promise

> **KEY ISSUE**
>
> *Why did the British go to war with the Boers in 1899, and what was the major outcome of the conflict?*

that they would eventually be granted independence. The commitment was honoured in 1907 when the two states became self-governing colonies. The Boers were sufficiently reconciled to the situation to enter the Union of South Africa in 1910.

In bringing about the Union, the British Government had to face the issue of the political rights of the native Africans. In the Cape Colony, Africans were entitled to the vote if they met certain qualifications. However, this entitlement did not apply in all areas of the Union. Although their rights were recognised in the Cape, the constitution of the Union excluded them from the franchise elsewhere. This issue split opinion in Britain. The Liberal Government in 1910 were in favour of granting the franchise to all qualified Africans throughout the Union, but this view found little support amongst whites in South Africa and, despite an appeal from the Prime Minister, Asquith, the Union Bill was not amended.

KEY ISSUE

How far did Britain abandon its policy of 'splendid isolation' at the beginning of the twentieth century?

The **Venezuela** Question, 1896 US President Cleveland intervened in a dispute between Britain and Venezuela over the boundary of British Guiana. His aim was to win patriotic support in his presidential election campaign by backing the Venezuelans against Britain. It was his way of restating the Monroe Doctrine (see page 28). When the case eventually went to court, all Britain's major claims were recognised

5 ⌐ RIVALRIES, ALLIANCES AND ENTENTES, 1890–1914

A *The end of splendid isolation*

As noted earlier (see page 332), the idea that Britain followed a policy of 'splendid isolation' in the late Victorian years needs careful qualification. The distinctive feature of British foreign policy in the 1890s was not so much that Britain was more isolated, but rather that she became alienated from so many other powers. The brush with the Germans over the 'Kruger telegram' and a serious border dispute with the USA over **Venezuela** were added to the long-standing strains in Britain's relations with France and Russia. The dispute with the Americans was bad enough to provoke threats of war from Washington. This widespread hostility towards Britain in the late 1890s prompted some contemporaries to suggest Britain's international isolation was dangerous rather than splendid.

A strong opponent of continued isolation was Joseph Chamberlain, the Colonial Secretary (1895–1903). He believed that Britain's future security required two things: the strengthening of the Empire and an alliance with Germany. Chamberlain considered that, for a wide variety of reasons, including economic links and racial and cultural similarities, Germany and Britain were 'natural' allies. On three occasions between 1898 and 1901, he proposed an alliance with Germany but nothing came of his initiatives. Neither Lord Salisbury nor Lord Lansdowne, who became Foreign Secretary in 1900, shared Chamberlain's confidence in the German option since they did not believe that the demand for an alliance was strong enough in either country. Nevertheless, they did recognise the need to increase Britain's popularity in the wider world.

Despite their dispute over Venezuela, both Britain and the USA wanted better mutual relations. The Americans were eager to proceed with their plan for constructing a canal at Panama which would link the Pacific and Atlantic. They were concerned to keep the venture under their sole control, but were worried that an Anglo-American treaty of 1850, which gave Britain equal rights in the undertaking, might obstruct this. Joint discussions aimed at amending the treaty began in 1899. They concluded in 1901 with Britain agreeing to cede to the USA full control of the Canal scheme in return for guarantees about freedom of access to the Canal for other powers. These negotiations had not been easy, but there was never any real doubt about their outcome. Lansdowne was anxious to develop Anglo-American friendship and was prepared to make any reasonable concession to secure it. A treaty was eventually signed, in November 1901, and with it Anglo-American relations were set on a new course for the new century.

BRITAIN AND THE FAR EAST

Britain had two related aims in the Far East: to expand her trade in the area and to maintain peace there. The threat to these aims came from Russia, which had undertaken a major extension of its railway system. Britain feared that this expansion would encourage Russian designs on Persia, Afghanistan, China, and India. The British were not alone in suspecting Russian intentions in the Far East. The Japanese had similar worries. Their particular concern was to strengthen their grip on Korea which they had forcibly taken from China in 1894. Japan had also gained extensive trading rights in northern China. This disturbed the Russians. They wished to dominate China themselves in order to secure their Pacific borders, but they now found they had a rival in Japan.

In 1895, the Russians persuaded France and Germany to join them in pressurising Japan to hand back its gains to the Chinese. However, the Japanese were still determined to keep Korea under their control, while the British were concerned to find a way to counter the growing Russian influence in the Far East. Thus the seeds of an Anglo-Japanese alliance were sown. The Japanese took the initiative. As they saw it, there were two possibilities. They could either reach an agreement with the Russians over Korea or they could link up with the British to counter Russian power. In the autumn of 1901 they began to explore both avenues. They approached the Russians via the French but made no progress. Britain, on the other hand, saw an opportunity and took it. Fearing that the Russians might move towards an agreement with the Japanese, the British entered into an alliance with Japan in 1902. The terms were:

- if either power was at war with a third party, the other would maintain strict neutrality
- if either power was at war with two other powers, the other would come to its aid
- both powers asserted their special interests in the region and Britain recognised Japan's claims in Korea.

This arrangement suited both parties well. Britain, like Japan, had tried in the past to reach an agreement with the Russians but without success. Neither country wanted war with Russia except as a last resort. On the contrary, both believed their the alliance made war with Russia less likely. Apart from the Russians themselves, the real losers were the French. They had been hoping for a Russo-Japanese deal since that would have increased the pressure on Britain to improve relations with France, something the French Government had long desired but had been unable to achieve.

THE ANGLO-FRENCH ENTENTE, 1904

KEY ISSUE

What led to the forming of the Anglo-French Entente?

entente is a French term meaning informal agreement. It was used to describe the warmer relations and better understanding between France and Britain

Although the Anglo-Japanese Treaty eased the pressure on Britain, she was still keen to improve relations with France. Initially, the French reaction to the Anglo-Japanese Alliance was hostile. But the French had to face realities. As there was little likelihood that they could bring Japan and Russia together or detach the Japanese from the British, they had to work for an understanding with the British. Thus events in the Far East made an Anglo-French **entente** increasingly likely, since both countries were ready to co-operate.

The biggest stumbling-block was likely to be French public opinion. Here the three-day visit of King Edward VII, in May 1903, proved to be of great value. The visit was a huge success. Parisians who turned out on the first day to boo and chant 'Long live the Boers' returned to wave Edward off on the final day, chanting 'Long live the King'. Anglo-French relations improved dramatically. In July 1903, the French President visited London and the British and French Foreign Secretaries began serious talks. There was one outstanding difficulty: the French knew that, to reach a genuine agreement with Britain, they would have to recognise the British position in Egypt – a major emotional obstacle for French opinion.

However, developments in the Far East helped hurry France towards the Entente, which was announced in April 1904. Earlier in that year, Japan, fearing a Russians invasion of Korea, launched a pre-emptive strike, and the Russo-Japanese war began. To the French, this now made agreement with Britain a necessity. The main terms were:

- Egypt and Morocco were recognised as British and French spheres of influence, respectively
- in the event of internal collapse in Morocco, France would establish a protectorate there
- various disputes in relation to Newfoundland, Madagasgar and Siam (Thailand today) were resolved.

THE ANGLO-RUSSIAN *ENTENTE* 1907

The alliance with Japan and the understandings reached with the USA and France transformed Britain's diplomatic position. The policy of rationalisation (making limited concessions in order to achieve objectives) and detente (reducing tension by eliminating areas of conflict) could now be applied to what seemed the most difficult area of all – Anglo-Russian relations. In the event, agreement proved less of a problem than it appeared. This was largely due to a changed attitude on the part of the Russians, brought about by the disastrous outcome of their war with Japan, which saw them heavily defeated on land and at sea. This humiliation and the news that the Anglo-Japanese Alliance had been extended in 1905 to include mutual support in the event of either party going to war with even a single power, made the Russians amenable to the idea of reconciliation with Britain.

The Anglo-Russian agreement which was reached in August 1907 resolved all the outstanding differences between Britain and Russia:

● Tibet was recognised as a neutral buffer-state and Russia abandoned contact with Afghanistan
● Persia (modern Iran) was the crux of the agreement: Russia was to have a sphere of influence in the north while Britain had a comparable arrangement in the south, with a neutral, central zone where both countries had equal rights of access. The Persians were not consulted about any of this.

This agreement which, with the inclusion of Russia, expanded Britain's 1904 *Entente* with France into a Triple *Entente*, seemed to have achieved everything Britain had hoped for on the diplomatic front. All the existing areas of tension seemed to have been diffused. Understandings had been reached with both Russia and France, without any formal commitment to come to their aid in the event of war. Although no agreement had been reached with Germany, this had been for the simple reason that there seemed to be no outstanding issues to resolve at this stage.

B *Anglo-German rivalry, 1900–14*

The growth of hostility between Britain and Germany came as a surprise to both countries. As was noted above, Germany in the 1890s came to be regarded by such figures as Chamberlain as a possible partner in a 'natural' alliance. Even sceptics like Salisbury and Lansdowne were prepared to see where negotiations might lead. At the turn of the century, Anglo-German relations seemed set to improve still further. The sharp commercial rivalry, which had marked the 1880s and 1890s, receded as trade improved; Britain experienced an economic upturn in which German custom was an important element. Even the increase in German naval power did not appear unduly alarming when viewed against the Anglo-Japanese alliance, which had reduced the demands on the British Navy in the Far East, and the Anglo-French Entente, which had eased the pressure in the Mediterranean. The Russian fleet had been eliminated by Japan and, over the period from 1898 to 1905, the balance of naval power moved decisively in Britain's favour.

At that point, Britain had massive naval superiority over France and Germany combined. Consequently, German naval expansion did not seem to matter greatly. However, even in 1904, there were some prominent persons who feared that the Anglo-French Entente might be seen as anti-German. Lloyd George recalled a conversation with Lord Rosebery (a former Liberal Prime Minister and Foreign Secretary):

Q

1. *Why should Rosebery, in the circumstances of 1904, have seen the Entente as meaning war with Germany?*
2. *Account for Lloyd George's view, at the time when he took office, that a war between Britain and Germany was unthinkable to anyone of sound mind?*

On the day when the Anglo-French Entente was announced, I arrived on a couple of days visit to the late Lord Rosebery. His first greeting to me was 'Well, I suppose you are just as pleased as the rest of them with this French agreement?' I assured him that I was delighted that our snarling and scratching relations with France had come to an end at last. He replied, 'You are all wrong. It means war with Germany in the end!' About a year after this prophetic utterance I became for the first time a Minister of the Crown. Had anyone then told me that before I ceased to hold office in the British Cabinet I should not only have witnessed a war between Britain and Germany, but have taken an active, and in fact leading part in its prosecution, I should have treated such a forecast as one of the many wild predictions of good or evil with which every public man is assailed by persons of unbalanced minds.

David Lloyd George, War Memoirs, *1920*

KEY ISSUE

Why did the question of naval strength become such a divisive issue between Germany and Britain?

The situation changed dramatically after 1905. In 1904, the British Government had ordered the building of a new battleship, the *Dreadnought*. When launched two years later, this vessel's firepower made all existing battleships obsolete. That was why its commissioning had been so controversial. There were those who felt that such an advanced warship would be seen as a threat by other powers and thus lead to an arms race. Lloyd George asserted in 1908 that Britain had not needed a new class of battleship and could easily have responded had another power built one. Against this, it was argued that another power might build its own vessel in secret and thus gain an initial and possibly decisive lead.

From the British point of view, there was no reason for Germany to engage in a naval race. Britain needed a navy to defend its widespread overseas empire; Germany, without such an empire, had no such need. Winston Churchill expressed typical British thinking of the time when he said that Britain's navy was a necessity, whereas Germany's was a luxury. This view, however, overlooked the German desire for a great navy which would match her status as a world power. As the years went by, the tensions between Britain and Germany over naval power proved intractable, not least because they were based on entirely different perspectives. The Germans believed that their possession of a great navy would make Britain respect them. However, the British reaction to German expansion was not respect but resentment at the mounting expense of an unnecessary naval race. Arthur Balfour, the Conservative leader, pointed out in an article written in 1912, 'Without a superior fleet, Britain would no longer count as a power. Without any fleet at all Germany would remain the greatest power in Europe.'

THE MOROCCAN CRISES OF 1905 AND 1911
For Britain, there was an obvious solution to the naval race – the Germans should reduce their building programme. But for Germany, the

development of a great navy was not simply a question of military strength; it was an expression of national pride. As early as 1908, the estrangement between the two countries had become clear. Nor was the tension solely due to the naval question. The 1904 entente had been a major blow to the German policy of isolating the French. Germany's displeasure at the Anglo-French Entente and, in particular, at the way that Germany had been ignored over Morocco, led to a crisis in 1905. The Kaiser, visiting Morocco in March 1905, assured the Sultan that Germany still recognised Moroccan independence. This was a deliberate challenge to the terms of the Anglo-French entente. Germany then demanded an international conference on Morocco, hoping to expose what she assumed to be Britain's lack of genuine commitment to France.

This was a misunderstanding of the British attitude. Sir Edward Grey, who was Liberal Foreign Secretary from 1905 to 1916, believed that it was vital for Britain to back the French so that they would be better able to resist falling under German domination. According to A. J. P. Taylor, the controversial modern historian, Grey was 'concerned about the European Balance (of power) in a way that no British Foreign Secretary had been since Palmerston'. Grey feared a 'continental league' of powers directed by Germany. He, therefore, constantly encouraged both the French and Russians to resist German pressure, this without actually making any British commitment to them. In supporting France against Germany during the Moroccan crisis, Grey adopted a new approach in British diplomacy. He authorised 'conversations' between the British and French military general staffs regarding how British forces could assist France in the event of war. This was all hypothetical, but it pointed to a conviction that Britain could not afford to let France be dominated by a greater power in Europe, any more than in the past she had been able to tolerate the domination of the rest of Europe by France. Now, in the early twentieth century, there was only one power capable of exercising such domination – Germany.

Thus, at the international conference at Algeçiras in 1906, which had been called by Germany in an attempt to weaken the French hold on Morocco, Britain supported France unswervingly. Similarly, in 1911, when Germany provoked a second Moroccan crisis by sending a gunboat to the port of Agadir with a view to intimidating France into withdrawing from Morocco, Britain urged the French to stand fast. In a celebrated speech in London, Lloyd George both appealed to the French not to give way and also gave a thinly-veiled warning to the Germans that Britain would not tolerate aggression on their part:

> I believe it is essential in the highest interests, not merely of this country, but of the world, that Britain should at all hazards maintain her place and prestige amongst the Great Powers. If a situation were to be forced on us, in which peace could only be preserved by allowing Britain to be treated as if she were of no account in the Cabinet of nations, then I say emphatically that peace at that price would be a humiliation intolerable for a great country like ours to endure.

KEY ISSUE

What was at issue in the Moroccan crises?

Q

1. *Explain in your own words what you understand Lloyd George to have meant by saying that 'Britain should at all hazards maintain her place and prestige amongst the Great Powers'.*
2. *Use your own knowledge to explain why Lloyd George was considered in this speech to be making a 'thinly-veiled' threat to Germany.*

The reaction of Britain to the Moroccan crises showed that she was ready to contemplate armed intervention against Germany. In 1911, the British fleet was prepared for action and, for the first time, was ordered to give priority to transporting an expeditionary force to northern France. Such remarkable developments indicated how seriously Anglo-German relations had deteriorated. This was ominous.

6 ∾ BRITAIN AND THE OUTBREAK OF WAR IN 1914

KEY ISSUE

Did Britain need to go to war with Germany in August 1914?

The event which is traditionally regarded as the immediate cause of the First World War is the assassination of the Austrian Archduke Franz-Ferdinand by a Bosnian Serb at Sarajevo on 28 June 1914. Yet, initially, the murder seemed scarcely to touch British interests at all. As late as 23 July, Lloyd George was telling the House of Commons that Anglo-German relations were better than they had been for many years. What pushed Britain towards war was the German attack on France. Britain already had an informal naval agreement with France, under which their fleets were positioned so that, in the event of war, France would defend

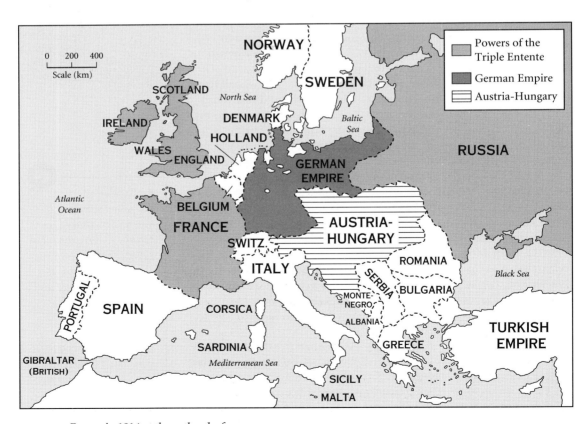

MAP 9 *Europe in 1914 at the outbreak of war*

the Mediterranean and Britain the Channel and North Sea. For a short time the fact that even the Cabinet knew little about the extent of Anglo-French preparations created uncertainty within the Government. However, the actual pretext for Britain's declaration of war was not the French issue but Germany's occupation of Belgium which was undertaken as a necessary prelude to the invasion of northern France. The German assault on independent Belgium persuaded the doubters in Britain that war with Germany was unavoidable.

TIMELINE
The countdown to war

June	28	Assassination of Austrian Archduke in Sarajevo
July	23	Austro-Hungarian ultimatum to Serbia.
	24	Russia considered **mobilisation** against Austria-Hungary. Grey proposed mediation.
	25	Austria-Hungary mobilised on Russian frontier
	26	France began military preparations
	27	Germany rejected the idea of an international conference
	28	Austria-Hungary declared war on Serbia
	29	Germany warned Russia against mobilisation; Grey warned Germany that Britain would not remain neutral in the event of a general European war
	30	Russia mobilised against Austria-Hungary and Germany
	31	Austria-Hungary ordered general mobilisation
Aug	1	Germany declared war on Russia
	2	Germany issued ultimatum to Belgium
	3	Germany declared war on France Belgium rejected German ultimatum; British army mobilised
	4	German forces invaded Belgium Britain issued ultimatum demanding German withdrawal On expiry of ultimatum, Britain declared war on Germany

mobilisation involves the preparation by a country of its armed services in readiness for war. It is not an act of war in itself and still leaves the country concerned the option of not going to war

The protection of Belgium was a long-standing British pledge which went back to Palmerston. In 1839, he had signed the London Treaty which guaranteed Belgian independence. Even Gladstone had been willing to contemplate war to defend this commitment. Belgium as a small power facing a mighty adversary evoked sympathy from the British public and gave a moral strength to Britain as a champion of the weak against the strong. Yet Britain had not been above ignoring the demands of principle. She had, for example, done nothing to assist the Danes in their war against Prussia in 1864. Although the Germans hoped that by some means the British might be kept out of the war they never counted on this in their planning. On the contrary, they had always assumed that they must prepare for the likelihood of Britain's

See page 326

assisting the French. But, since they also expected the war to be short, they attached little importance to the British threat. The Kaiser described the British army as 'contemptible', a reference to its size rather than its fighting skills or courage.

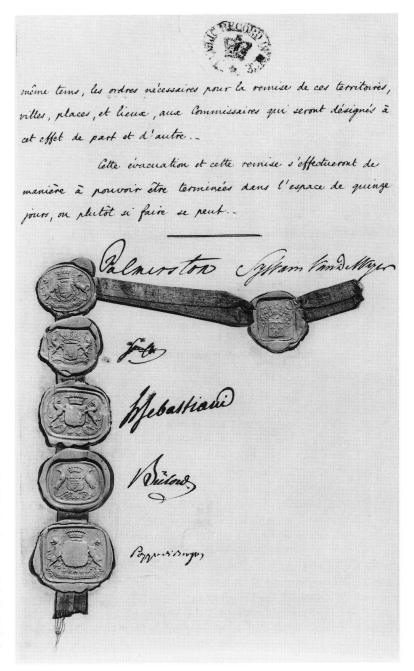

PICTURE 38

A British Government poster showing the signatures on the treaty of 1839, which guaranteed Belgian neutrality (Palmerston's signature is at the top). It was this treaty that the German Chancellor, Bethmann-Hollweg, referred to disparagingly to as 'the scrap of paper' when he learned that Britain was considering entering the war in accordance with its 1839 commitment

7 ⌖ DOCUMENTARY STUDY

What, according to Edward Grey, the British Foreign Secretary, were Britain's reasons for going to war in 1914?

After the war, Edward Grey was criticised for not having made the British position clear enough to the Germans in 1914. It was certainly true that foreign governments were known to complain that they could rarely be certain where Britain stood on international questions. Grey's position at the time of the gathering crisis in the summer of 1914 still appeared to be paradoxical: Germany was not to count on British neutrality, France and Russia were not to count on British support. His defenders, however, claim that the apparent paradox made sense in diplomatic terms. A war started by Germany and involving Russia alone might not require the intervention of Britain, but a war started by Germany and involving France certainly would.

In the event, the war with Germany that broke out in August 1914 involved both Russia and France and made the niceties of Grey's previous distinctions irrelevant. To stand aside was to risk allowing the complete domination of the continent of Europe by Germany. This was inconceivable on strategic and economic grounds, to say nothing of the question of British prestige. Neutrality in 1870 had been argued to be beneficial to the balance of power; neutrality in 1914 would have destroyed the balance of power and, with it, any chance of Britain playing an effective role in Europe. Grey justified his actions in a Commons' speech on 3 August 1914 shortly before Germany declared war on France. His main claims were that Germany's disturbance of the European power balance and her threat to Belgium had forced Britain to the brink of war.

I ask the House [of Commons] from the point of view of British interests, to consider what may be at stake. If France is beaten in a struggle of life and death, beaten to her knees, loses her position as a great Power, becomes subordinate to the will and power of one greater than herself, if that were to happen, and if Belgium fell under the same dominating influence, and then Holland, and then Denmark, then would not Mr Gladstone's words come true, that just opposite to us there would be a common interest against the unmeasured aggrandizement [forcible expansion] of any Power? It may be said, I suppose, that we might stand aside, husband our strength, and that, whatever happened in the course of this war, at the end of it intervene with effect to put things right, and to adjust them to our own point of view. If, in a crisis like this, we run away from those obligations of honour and interest as regards the Belgian Treaty, I doubt whether, whatever material force we might have at the end, it would be of very much value in face of the respect we should have lost. I do not believe for a moment, that we should be in a position to undo what had happened in the course of the war, to prevent the whole of the rest of Europe opposite to us — if that has been the result of the war — falling under the domination of a single Power.

Edward Grey, addressing the House of Commons, 3 Aug 1914

1. *According to Grey, how important is the role of Belgium?*
2. *Using your own knowledge, explain why Grey makes reference to Mr Gladstone.*
3. *How does this extract help you to understand Grey's approach to foreign policy and the reasons for the British declaration of war against Germany?*

The day after Britain had gone to war, Grey was even more forthright in stating the Government's reasons:

I have acted not from any obligation of Treaty or honour, for neither existed. There were three overwhelming British interests which I could not abandon:

1. That the German fleet should not occupy, under our neutrality, the North Sea and the English Channel.
2. That they should not seize and occupy the North-Western part of France opposite our shores.
3. That they should not violate the ultimate independence of Belgium and hereafter occupy Antwerp as a standing menace to us.

Edward Grey addressing the House of Commons, 5 Aug 1914

1. *What do you understand by Grey's statement that he had not acted 'from any obligation of Treaty or honour'?*
2. *How far does Grey's statement support the view that Britain entered the war purely for reasons of self-protection.*

Nobody knew in 1914 how long and destructive the war would prove to be. So many lives were lost and so great was the destruction in the four-year struggle that, after the war, the victors were anxious to prove the sacrifice had been justified by the nobility of their war aims. They claimed that they had fought in the cause of liberty against a power-hungry Germany. Grey, in his reflections, suggested that moral considerations had been uppermost in the Government's decision for war:

The real reason for going into the war was that, if we did not stand by France and stand up for Belgium against this aggression, we should be isolated, discredited, and hated; and there would be before us nothing but a miserable and ignoble future … We felt to stand aside would mean the domination of Germany; the subordination of France and Russia; the isolation of Britain and ultimately that Germany would wield the whole power of the Continent.

Edward Grey, Twenty-five Years 1892–1916, *1926*

Q

1. *According to Grey's account in this extract, what had been the main reasons for Britain's declaration of war in 1914?*
2. *What are the major differences in the reasons for war given here by Grey and those he listed in his Commons speech on 5 August 1914?*
3. *How would you explain these differences?*

Grey declared that Britain could not have allowed German domination of Europe. In logic, therefore, Britain' decision for war was not based on the Belgian issue since this was a only minor consideration in the larger European context. The image of a crusading Britain defending gallant little Belgium was a powerful one and was used effectively to convince the public of the justice of the British cause. But this was largely propaganda. As historians have since pointed out, it is inconceivable that Britain would have gone to war against France in 1914 had the French occupied Belgium in a pre-emptive move against Germany. Britain joined the struggle in August 1914 because she was not prepared to tolerate one nation upsetting the balance of power in Europe, thereby endangering her own security. It is difficult to see the issue of Belgian neutrality as anything other than a pretext for war.

> **KEY ISSUE**
>
> *How genuine was Britain's claim that she went to war to defend Belgium?*

Summary of reasons for Britain's entering the war in 1914

● the Anglo-German arms race
● Britain's fear that it was losing its naval supremacy
● Britain's membership of the Triple Entente (Britain, France and Russia)
● Britain's treaty obligations to Belgium
● Britain's sense of prestige and honour
● Britain's need to protect its economic interests
● British reluctance to contemplate a German-dominated Europe.

---

8 ↶ BIBLIOGRAPHY

ARTICLES

The following are especially written for A level students.

A. L. McFie 'The Eastern Question', *New Perspective*, September 1996.
Muriel Chamberlain 'Pax Britannica', *Modern History Review*, September 1996.
Kathryn Tidrick 'The British Idea of Empire', *Modern History Review*, March 1998.

Richard Wilkinson 'Lord Lansdowne and British Foreign Policy', *History Review*, March 2000.

Christopher Ray 'Britain and the First World War', *History Review*, March 1998.

BOOKS FOR AS/A LEVEL STUDENTS

Muriel Chamberlain *Lord Palmerston*, GPC Books, 1987, is a short but illuminating biography.

John Lowe *Rivalry and Accord: International Relations 1870–1914*, Hodder and Stoughton, 1988.

Robert Pearce *Britain and the European Powers 1865–1914*, Hodder & Stoughton, 1996. Both these books have substantial and informative sections on British foreign policy.

Michael Lynch *Gladstone and Disraeli*, Hodder & Stoughton, 1991, is a documentary study with linking commentary. It includes sections on the foreign and imperial policies of the two leaders.

M. C. Morgan *Foreign Affairs 1886–1914*, Collins, 1973, gives an excellent, detailed coverage of the diplomacy of the period. In particular, it contains a very useful chapter on the origins of World War I.

Richard Kelly and John Cantrell (Eds), *Modern British Statesmen 1867–1945*, Manchester UP, 1997, provides valuable and up-to-date assessments of foreign policy under all the prime ministers from Disraeli to Asquith.

Vyvyen Brendon *The Edwardian Age*, Hodder & Stoughton, 1996, has very helpful sections on the approach to the 1914-18 war, as does her *The First World War 1914–18*, Hodder & Stoughton, 2000.

FURTHER READING

Kenneth Bourne *The Foreign Policy of Victorian England, 1830–1902*, OUP, 1970, is an excellent treatment of all the themes in this chapter.

Muriel Chamberlain *Pax Britannica'? British Foreign Policy 1789–1914*, Longman, 1988, also deserves that description.

G. Clayton *Britain and the Eastern Question*, University of London Press, 1971, remains one of the best introductory texts on this tricky subject.

Judith Ward *British Foreign Policy 1870–1914*, Blackie, 1978, is very useful. It consists of extracts from primary and secondary sources, introduced and linked together by a short explanatory commentary.

A. J. P. Taylor, *The Struggle for Mastery in Europe 1848–1918*, OUP, 1954, is a classic which makes demanding, but rewarding reading. Its great value is that it allows the reader to place British policy in a broad context.

Andrew Roberts, *Salisbury: Victorian Titan*, Phoenix, 2000, is a provocative read and has stimulating chapters on its subject's foreign policy.

P. J. Marshall (Ed.) *The Cambridge Illustrated History of the British Empire*, CUP, 1996, is both informative and attractive to look at.

Peter Kain *British Imperialism Innovation and Expansion 1688–1914,* Longman, 1993 is difficult in places but is the most authoritative modern study of Britain's empire.

G. Martel *The Origins of the First World War*, Longman, 1988, is a brief but informative study.

Zara Steiner *Britain and the Origins of the First World War*, Macmillan, 1977, repays careful reading.

Keith Wilson (Ed.) *Decisions for War, 1914*, UCL Press, 1995, takes each of the major countries and explains why they went to war.

Niall Ferguson *The Pity of War*, Penguin, 1999, is long and detailed but its earlier chapters offer a striking interpretation of why Britain declared war in 1914.

9 ⌐ STRUCTURED AND ESSAY QUESTIONS

The following questions relate to the separate sections in this chapter. The questions are closely linked to the Key Issues and margin questions that are there to guide you through the material you are reading. So, in preparing your answers, do look back to the relevant Key Issues and Question boxes. They will point you to the information and ideas that you need. You will notice that some questions are straightforward in that they ask you to *describe*, while others are more demanding in that they ask you to *explain*. The number of marks allocated to each question reflects this difference. In the first case you have simply to use your *knowledge* to answer the question; in the second case you have to use your *judgement*. Put simply, it is the difference between being asked *what* happened and being asked *why* it happened.

No matter what type of question you are attempting, it is always worth your drawing up lists of key facts and points. If you find that the question is of the straightforward descriptive type, then a well-ordered and shaped list will provide the answer. If, however, you are being asked for an explanation or a judgement, then your list will provide the backing evidence that you then use in developing your argument.

A *Structured questions for AS level*
1. (a) Identify the basic objectives in the foreign policy of Lord Palmerston by reference to **three** of the major episodes in which he was involved. (30)
    (b) How far do you agree with the view that Palmerston's foreign policy was much more successful between 1830 and 1856 than it was between 1855 and 1865? (60)
2. (a) Trace the main steps by which Britain became involved in the Crimean War in 1854. (30)
    (b) Do you accept the view that 'Britain's involvement in the Crimean War served no genuine British interest'? Give reasons in support of your answer. (60)

3. (a) Identify the main differences between Disraeli and Gladstone in their approach to the Eastern Question. (30)
    (b) What did Disraeli mean by saying that he had brought back 'peace with honour' from the Congress of Berlin in 1878? How justified do you think he was in making that claim? (60)

4. (a) Outline the steps by which Britain occupied and consolidated its authority over Egypt and the Sudan in the period, 1882–99. (30)
    (b) Who was more to blame for the outbreak of the war between them in 1899 – the British or the Boers? Explain your verdict. (60)

5. (a) Describe the main alliances and agreements that Britain entered into with other foreign powers in the period 1902–7. (30)
    (b) Why was it that, in the first decade of the twentieth century, Britain entered into agreements with France and Russia, but not with Germany? (60)

6. (a) Trace the main steps which led to Britain's declaration of war on Germany in 1914. (30)
    (b) Lloyd George said that in 1914 'the nations slithered over the brink into the boiling cauldron of war'. How true was this in Britain's case? (60)

B *Essay questions for A2*

1. 'The striking feature of Palmerston's conduct of foreign affairs was his readiness to adapt his policies to fit the circumstances.' How acceptable do you find this description?

2. How accurate was Lord Salisbury in his assertion that 'Britain had backed the wrong horse' in regard to the Eastern Question in the nineteenth century?

3. How far do you agree with the view that 'Gladstone's foreign policy was governed by principle, Disraeli's by expediency'?

4. Examine the motives that inspired Britain's expansion of empire between 1875 and 1902.

5. How important a factor was the German invasion of Belgium in explaining why Britain went to war in 1914?

6. Examine the view that Britain's entry in to the war in 1914 was the logical outcome of its foreign policy after 1902.

Trade Unions and the Rise of Labour, 1850–1906

INTRODUCTION

In 1850, trade unions were legally permitted but their position was very uncertain. When they called strikes or took other industrial action, they invariably found that the law was against them. The courts tended to side with the employers in any dispute between them and their workers. During the next half century, the trade union movement underwent a major transformation. It gained greater control over its funds, formed a Trade Unions Council (TUC) as a central body to represent itself nationally, and made important legal gains from new laws passed by Parliament. Most important of all, trade unionism changed in character. New unions came into being which were drawn from the mass labour force of skilled and semi-skilled workers. They differed markedly from the old craft unions, which had been exclusive bodies with membership open only to skilled workers. Between 1882 and 1906, trade-union membership rose from 400 000 to over two-and-a-half million.

The growing confidence which these developments produced among trade unionists worried the employers, who responded by forming organisations to protect their own powers and rights. Fierce industrial conflicts occurred in the last decades of the century. The suspicion among trade unionists that the law was still against them seemed to be borne out by a series of legal decisions which left the unions largely unable to defend themselves. In a critical ruling in 1901, the unions were declared to be responsible for paying any damages or losses that the employers might suffer as a result of a strike.

It was this Taff Vale decision, delivered by the House of Lords, that re-doubled the determination of those increasing numbers of trade unionists who believed that, unless and until the workers were directly represented by a party in Parliament, the law would always be against them. What was needed, they argued, was a political party, quite separate from the Liberals and Conservatives. The success of this argument came in 1900 with the formation of the Labour Representation Committee (LRC). This new party committed itself to defend the interests of the workers and to use its influence in the House of Commons to bring about pro-union changes in the law. After the election of 1906, the LRC, which had seen 29 of its candidates returned as MPs, renamed itself the Labour Party.

KEY ISSUE

In what ways did the 'model' unions differ from previous trade unions?

friendly societies were self-help organisations which were officially registered and protected by law. Their members paid subscriptions into a fund from which they could then draw in times of need, such as unemployment or illness. By 1870 some 4 million people (predominantly working class) belonged to friendly societies

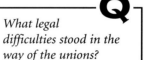

What legal difficulties stood in the way of the unions?

1 ⁓ THE MODEL UNIONS, 1850–75

The third-quarter of the century was notable for the development of what became known as the 'model' unions. Although they were new in attitude and organisation, the 'model' unions were a logical extension of the amalgamated societies of workers that had developed during the first half of the century. For example, three quarters of the membership of the Amalgamated Society of Engineers (ASE), formed in 1851, came from the Society of Journeymen Steam Engine Makers, first established in 1826. The amalgamated societies had stressed the role of the trade unions as providers of sickness and unemployment benefit for members and their families. This was possible because many of the unions had formed themselves into '**friendly societies**', which entitled them legally to act as a form of insurance company. Their high subscription rates enabled them to build up reliable funds. Between 1875 and 1879 the ASE paid out £350 000 in unemployment benefit.

What was different about the 'model' unions was their emphasis upon efficient organisation and their willingness to negotiate with employers. They appointed full-time officials to administer the unions' affairs and to pay particular attention to the raising and protecting of their funds. Whenever possible, the unions preferred to settle their disagreements with their employers through discussion rather than by strikes. As Robert Applegarth, General Secretary of the Amalgamated Society of Carpenters and Joiners (ASCJ), which was set up in 1860, advised his members, 'Never surrender the right to strike but be careful how you use a double-edged weapon'. Strikes did not disappear in this period but they ceased to be a union's first weapon. The centralised organisation of the new unions reinforced the movement towards moderation, since the decision to strike could be officially taken only at district or national level, not locally.

The unions that came to prominence in the middle decades of the century made the achievement of legal status their prime target. Since the repeal of the Combination Act in 1824, it had no longer been an offence to belong to an association acting 'in restraint of trade'. Nevertheless, the unions felt that, in practice, the law was still against them. Employees could still be prosecuted for breach of contract when undertaking strike action. In addition, under an amendment to the repeal of the Combination Act in 1825, 'molestation' [picketing] of other workers had been made a crime. By the middle of the century, it was clear that unions did not yet have the right peacefully to persuade workers to join a strike or a union. Worse still, the unions discovered that their funds were not legally protected. It had been widely assumed that, since most unions were registered as friendly societies, their funds were safeguarded by the Friendly Societies Act of 1855. But when, in 1867, in the case of *Hornby* v. *Close*, the Boilermakers attempted to sue a dishonest official for the return of union funds which he had stolen, the judgement went against them. Evidently, the unions were still not regarded in law as genuine friendly societies, and their funds were unprotected.

The push for full legal status was led by the London Trades Council, formed in 1860. This group, later known as the '**junta**', attended the first Trades Union Congress (TUC), which was held in Manchester in 1868, with 34 delegates representing 118 367 members. The TUC, which resolved to meet annually, mounted a campaign to amend the labour laws.

Despite its conciliatory approach, the 'junta' encountered the traditional resistance to the unions. Opponents condemned the unions' efforts to promote the collective rights of the workers as an attack on the freedom of the individual. Public concern was aroused in 1866 by the 'Sheffield Outrages', a series of assaults by saw-grinders on fellow workers who refused to join their union. The troubles led to the appointment, in 1867, of a Royal Commission to investigate the whole issue of trade unions. Much of the evidence that was presented to the Commission was gathered by the 'junta', who stressed the advantages to society of a co-operative and legally protected trade union movement.

They were helped in this by the presence on the Commission of two middle-class supporters of new unionism: Frederick Harrison, a radical lawyer, and Thomas Hughes, an author and MP. The unions presented themselves as responsible and law-abiding bodies, not as the violent, strike-prone organisations which their critics described them as being. The Royal Commission was impressed, and supported the unions' request to be given the same protection for their funds as the friendly societies enjoyed. Although the Commission did not recommend the full legal status that unionists wanted, its generally fair-minded report helped to lessen hostility to the unions. In the 1870s, Gladstone's Liberal Government and Disraeli's Conservative Government passed a number of Acts which granted the unions the status they had claimed.

the '**junta**' consisted of the leaders of five new model unions; William Allen of the ASE, Applegarth of the ASCJ, Daniel Guile of the Ironfounders, Edwin Coulson of the Bricklayers and George Odger of the shoemakers

KEY ISSUES

In what ways were the laws relating to the trade unions changed in the 1870s?

TIMELINE

1871   **Trade Union Act** (Liberal) – registered trade unions were given full legal status and granted the same legal protection for funds as enjoyed by friendly societies

1871   **Criminal Law Amendment Act** (Liberal) – restricted the right of picketing; the unions organised extensively in opposition to this act arguing that the Liberals had given with one hand only to take away with the other by their two pieces of legislation in 1871

1875   **Conspiracy and Protection of Property Act** (Conservative) – conceded the right to peaceful picketing, repealing the Criminal Law Amendment Act

1875   **Employers and Workmens Act** (Conservative) – breach of contract was no longer a criminal offence.

By 1875 the unions had gained full legal recognition of their right to exist as associations of workers and to act on behalf of their members. This did not mean, however, that the unions were now approved of by all classes. Employers continued to describe the unions as threats to the freedom of the individual. The following statement presented to the

Royal Commission was a typical example of the case made by the employers against the unions:

Statement of Messrs W. B. and N. Smith of Birmingham to the Royal Commission, 1867

> The object and rules of the policy of the council of such trades unions as have come under our observations has been with respect to wages, to raise them artificially; with respect to the hours of labour to limit them; with respect to apprenticeship, to keep down the number; with respect to piecework, to prevent it altogether; with respect to overtime, to prevent it as far as possible by increasing the cost; with respect to non-union men to prevent their employment.

1. *What is meant by the suggestion that trade unions were raising wages 'artificially'?*
2. *What other criticisms of the unions are made in this passage?*

Nevertheless, the new model unions, by their responsible behaviour, had shown themselves to Parliament and the wider public as the acceptable face of trade unionism. What aided them was that, at many points, the unions appeared to accept the prevailing values of respectable mid-Victorian society These points can be listed as follows.

- *Thrift* – the unions stressed their Friendly Society role in providing benefits for their members, which encouraged them to save regularly and spend wisely.
- *Self-reliance* – the unions argued that their members, who were entitled to draw benefits from subscriptions paid into the union, would never have to depend on public or private charity.
- *Sobriety* – many of the union leaders were prominent in the temperance movement, which campaigned against the drinking of alcohol. The new unions dropped the custom of holding their meetings in public houses.
- *Moral behaviour* – Allen declared to the Royal Commission in 1867: 'We have a controlling power over them [the members]; if men misconduct themselves through drinking or anything of that kind, we have the opportunity of dealing with them, and we do our best to keep them up to the mark so far as regards their position'.
- *Domestic harmony* – the unions argued that adequate wages for male workers would enable their wives to remain at home and look after the family. The TUC stated in 1877, 'Wives should be in their proper sphere at home, instead of being dragged into competition for livelihood against the great and strong men of the world'.

KEY ISSUE

What benefits for the unions and for society generally followed from the legalising of the trade unions?

After 1850, the characteristic working-class activist was not the orator of the Chartist movement but the official of a large union, working through negotiation to improve conditions for his workers.

The granting of legal status to the unions held out the promise of better industrial relations and, therefore, greater social stability. If trade unions were recognised by the law, they would be disinclined to break the law. Moreover, if their funds were protected, the unions would feel increasingly secure and be less inclined to take strike action. This hope appeared to be borne out by an 1867 report by the Royal Commission on Trade Unions, which recorded that the ASE, with total funds of £459 000, had paid out only £26 000 in strike relief over a ten-year period whilst the Ironfounders with total funds of £210 000 had spent a mere £5300 supporting strikes.

However, the harmony on the labour front in the mid-Victorian period should not be overstated. The legalising of the unions did not mean their end as a radical movement. Their underlying aim was still to achieve the advancement of the workers in a society in which they felt disadvantaged. *The Times* newspaper (which tended to be anti-union) stated in what was meant as a warning to the country at large: 'Trade Unions will continue to exist, and to number half a million members, whether they are protected by Act of Parliament or not'.

2 ⌐ TRADE UNIONISM AND THE LATE VICTORIAN RECESSION

The Times' warning took on particular significance when the British economy ran into difficulties during the last quarter of the nineteenth century. During this period Britain began to lose its economic lead as Germany, France and the USA emerged as industrial powers in their own right. British industry was slow to respond to this challenge, and as a result many firms began to suffer a fall in their profits. This has led to the period being labelled as the **'late Victorian recession'**.

The belief that Britain was in recession had a disruptive influence on worker-employer relations in Britain. Companies and firms struggled to maintain their profits by lowering wages; the workers retaliated by making determined efforts to prevent the cuts. The industrial calm, which had led to the trade unions being made legal in the 1870s, gave way to renewed conflict that recalled the dark days of Chartism. Two major developments followed. First, there was an unprecedented growth of unionism. In 1880, only 5 per cent of the total workforce had belonged to unions, but by 1914 the figure had grown to 25 per cent. The most dramatic outcome of this was a set of major strikes in the years 1888–93. The period also witnessed the birth of a new political party in 1900, dedicated to the representation of working-class interests. These developments are described in the following sections of the chapter.

The harmful aspects of the rapid industrialisation and urbanisation that had occurred in Britain had become very evident in the last decades of the nineteenth century. Poverty, malnutrition and ill-health were the lot of large numbers of workers and their families. People became increasingly aware of the great gap between the rich and poor in society. Historians now agree that it was this awareness that turned the working class into a considerable political force in the late nine-

KEY ISSUE

What is meant by the term the 'late Victorian Recession' in Britain?

The **'late Victorian recession'** refers to the industrial decline that occurred between the early 1870s and the turn of the century. However, many historians regard the use of the word 'recession' to be misleading. The truth was that Britain continued to grow economically during this time, but at a slower rate than in previous decades and more slowly than its main competitors. In other words, the British economy was only in relative decline. Nevertheless, to industrialists at the time, this was very disturbing and there were widespread fears among them that the economy was in crisis

real wages Refers to the purchasing power of earnings when set against prices. If prices are high, money buys less; if prices are low, the same amount of money will buy more. For example, weekly earnings of £2 in one year might buy more than £3 would in a time of higher prices in another year. Therefore, although the £2 is obviously lower nominally than the £3, in *real* terms it can buy more. If, as happened in the late Victorian period, wages go up at a faster pace than prices, there will be a rise in real wages

---

KEY ISSUE

What was new about 'new unionism'?

---

teenth century. This is what historians have in mind when they refer to the period as being one of 'class politics'.

Yet, oddly for a period described as a recession, **real wages** were actually increasing. One reason for this was that workers benefited from cheaper foodstuffs now available from overseas as a result of the development of refrigerated transport.

The rise in real wages might have led to a widespread improvement in living standards but for the fact that there were many more people looking for work. The employable population grew by at least 10 per cent each decade between 1870 and 1910. Since this coincided with a slowing down of economic growth, it resulted in intense competition for jobs. Significantly, the word 'unemployed' appeared in the Oxford English Dictionary for the first time in 1882. This entry was extended, for the 1888 edition, to include the term 'unemployment' which had, by then, been recognised as one of the major social problems of the day. It was against this background of social and economic distress that trade unionism grew in strength and that eventually a new political party emerged.

3 ⌐ NEW UNIONISM, 1888–93

In the three years from 1889 to 1891, the total membership of trade unions doubled. This remarkable growth was partly the result of the emergence of a number of new unions with a characteristically different approach to industrial relations. As we noted earlier in the chapter, the mid-Victorian 'model' unions, typified by the Amalgamated Society of Engineers, were exclusive bodies of skilled workers. Their high subscription rates restricted membership to the 'labour aristocracy'. Furthermore, since they represented only a small proportion of the workforce, they were more acceptable to the employers.

The new unions of the 1880s were different in three important respects.

- They aimed at recruiting members among the less skilled sector of the workforce, many of whom had not previously been in unions. The new unions were, therefore, less exclusive than the 'model' unions of the mid-Victorian period. An important example of this was the lower subscriptions they charged their members, usually a penny a week.
- They were more militant than their craft-based counterparts. In part this was because they tended to be led by active socialists. But an equally important factor was that the members of the new unions were the less skilled workers, whom employers regarded as easier to lay off than skilled craftsmen. Employers were, therefore, unwilling to negotiate with them. The consequence was that industrial action by the less skilled was likely to be aggressive and troublesome.
- Many of the leaders of the new unions were members of the **socialist** clubs and associations that had grown in the 1880s.

The year 1884 saw the creation of three socialist organisations in Britain.

- The Social Democratic Federation (SDF) – this was a Marxist organisation led by H. M. Hyndman, known as the 'gentleman reformer' because of his comfortable background. It advocated a policy of 'class warfare' leading to revolution and the construction of a fair and equal society.
- The Socialist League – this began as a breakaway group from the SDF. It drew a number of significant recruits into its ranks. Among them was the poet and artist William Morris who, like Hyndman, came from a middle-class background and saw socialism as a way of creating an equal society. Morris argued that industrialisation had separated the worker from the joy of creative work: in his words, 'useful work' had become 'useless toil'. Morris believed that society could be reconstructed as a 'Commonwealth', based on equality and a simple lifestyle.
- The Fabian Society – this included in its ranks George Bernard Shaw, the Irish playwright, and Sydney and Beatrice Webb, the husband and wife team who founded the London School of Economics. The Fabians took their name from Fabius Maximus, the Roman general who believed that victories were best achieved by patience and siege warfare rather than frontal assault. Unlike the SDF and the Socialist League, they argued for 'gradualism', the notion that the necessary economic and social reforms could be achieved not by overthrowing existing institutions but by making them truly efficient, so that that they genuinely served the public good. The Fabians did not aim to arouse the workers to revolution, but to persuade those already in authority to introduce progressive reform.

While acknowledging that the ideas of these socialist groups were provocative and interesting, we should not exaggerate their importance as organisations. Their membership was small and drawn overwhelmingly from middle-class intellectuals, sometimes referred to dismissively by their critics as 'drawing-room' socialists. The SDF, for example, had only 1000 members in 1885; when it put up two candidates in London in the election of that year, they polled a mere 59 votes between them.

But both the SDF and the League could claim some success in organising a London-based protest movement at this time. The SDF, in particular, concentrated its efforts on the growing number of unemployed in the capital. In 1886, during a notably harsh winter, an SDF open-air meeting turned into a riot, which *The Times* described as the greatest threat to private property since 1832. This was followed by two days of clashes between demonstrators and police, greeted hopefully by Morris as 'the first skirmish of the Revolution'. In 1887, groups of the unemployed, organised by the SDF under the slogan 'Work not Charity', squatted in Trafalgar Square. On 13 November 1887, known afterwards as 'Bloody Sunday', the Square was cleared by a police baton-charge, which left 200 demonstrators injured.

socialist Socialism has shades of meaning. It can refer to Communism, the movement associated with Karl Marx, the German revolutionary, that advocated revolutionary class conflict. But socialism, usually spelt with a small 's', can also refer to the radical but non-revolutionary movement which held that the State should use its power to correct the economic injustices and inequalities existing in society. It was this latter form of socialism that the early Labour Party followed

KEY ISSUE

How influential were these new socialist organisations?

Such disturbances suggest that the socialist movement had been successful in raising the political consciousness of trade unionists and in adding to the atmosphere of tension which produced a number of industrial disputes in this period. The most serious and important of these were the Match Girls' Strike of 1888 and the Great Dock Strike a year later.

A *The Match Girls' Strike, 1888*

A clear sign that trade unionism was no longer a solely male activity came in July 1888, when the women workers at Bryant and May's match factory in the East End of London came out on strike against the appalling conditions in which they worked. They were encouraged in their action by Annie Besant, an influential middle-class socialist, who was a member of both the SDF and the Fabians. Besant was already well known as a campaigner for birth control and was editor of a socialist paper called *The Link*. In June 1888, in an article entitled 'White Slavery in London', she drew attention to one of the worst-paid sectors of the workforce. Bryant and May's women workers received an average of 5 shillings (25p) for a 70-hour week in extremely unhealthy conditions, which produced such diseases as 'phossy jaw', a distortion of the bones of the face, often accompanied by a disfiguring skin complaint. The disease took its name from the poisonous phosphorus which the workers used in making the match heads. Nearly 1400 women stayed out for a fortnight in a strike that was partially successful in that it persuaded the company to increase the women's pay rates. However, little was done to improve their working conditions. Nevertheless, the strike was followed by the formation of a union of some 800 women workers at the factory. Annie Besant became its first Secretary.

B *The Great Dock Strike, 1889*

The summer of 1889 saw two more victories for groups of workers organising themselves virtually for the first time. In March, the Gas Workers and General Labourers Union was formed in London by Will Thorne, a worker at the East Ham Gasworks. Thorne, an ex-navvy from Birmingham, was a member of the SDF and had been taught to read and write by Karl Marx's daughter, Eleanor. Within four months, his union had gained 20 000 members. In August, Thorne demanded an eight-hour day and called his members out on strike. He was helped in organising the strike by two other prominent members of the SDF, Tom Mann and John Burns, who were engineering workers. These three men epitomised the fervour and zeal of new unionism. Tom Mann had established the Eight Hours League in 1886 to agitate for a reduction of hours for all industrial workers. This was a particular feature of new unionism, the attempt to establish aims common to all industries. At the same time, trade unionists began talking of a 'living wage' for all workers.

PICTURE 39
Will Thorne, the late-nineteenth century union leader

The emphasis was upon the interest of the whole workforce, rather than the sectional interests of individual unions. In 1889, the veteran Chartist leader, George Julian Harney, enthused: 'Not since the high and palmy days of Chartism have I witnessed a movement corresponding in importance and interest.' The comparison with Chartism helps us to understand the character of new unionism whose aim was to attract mass support among the workers.

Will Thorne's union was successful in its strike, which spurred on other groups of workers. Attention now turned to London's docks. A pay dispute had broken out at the South West India Dock. The men were led by Ben Tillett, an ex-sailor who was now a tea porter. The dispute swiftly spread. The dockers were employed on a casual basis; each morning they waited at the dock gates hoping to be selected for work. When they were taken on, the work was exhausting and the pay was low. Tillett, assisted by Burns, Mann and Thorne, now set about drawing all the dockers into the dispute. A demand was drafted for a minimum wage of 6d (2$^1/_2$ pence) an hour, the 'docker's tanner'. The Stevedores' Union, which represented the skilled crane drivers, agreed to come out in support.

Despite the vulnerability of the dockers, who, as casual workers, could easily be replaced, the strike was solid. With 150 000 men on strike, for a month almost nothing was shipped through the Port of London, the heart of the nation's trade. Each day, Burns led a huge

KEY ISSUE

How did the Great Dock Strike stimulate trade union membership?

procession through the City. The orderly conduct of the demonstrators won the widespread support of large numbers of the public, who had initially feared a repeat of the riots of 1887. The distribution of strike pay put a great strain on union funds, but the dockers were supported financially by workers at home and abroad. Australian trade unionists contributed £30 000. The British public seemed to rally to the dockworkers as an oppressed group who were conducting themselves with dignity. Even the Stock Exchange made a contribution to strike funds. Eventually, Henry Manning, the Catholic Cardinal, agreed to act as arbitrator between employers and workers. His role was acceptable to the dockers since many of them were Irish Catholics. In an almost carnival atmosphere, the strike ended in victory for the dockers.

Following the strike, the Tea Operatives' Union that Tillett had formed in 1886 was re-modelled as the Dock, Wharf, Riverside and General Labourers' Union. Tom Mann became its first President; by 1890 it had 56 000 members. The age of mass general unionism had arrived. This was undoubtedly the most lasting effect of the dock strike. Tillett's union was to remain in existence until 1920, when it was reformed as the Transport and General Workers' Union. The Seamen's Union, established in 1889, had acquired a membership of 65 000 only two years later. The General Railway Workers' Union, also formed in 1889, began to enrol the unskilled workers whose lack of qualifications had previously excluded them from the Amalgamated Society of Railway Servants.

The 'new unions' attended the Trades Union Congress (TUC) for the first time in 1890. Their influence was soon evident in the agreement of Congress to back the demand for an eight-hour day, and to give its formal support to the first May Day celebrations to be held in Britain. What was especially significant was that the new unions were beginning to carry the established craft unions with them. Relations between these skilled unions and the employers had begun to deteriorate by the 1880s. In the strained conditions produced by the late Victorian recession, employers found it difficult to maintain wage **differentials** in line with what the skilled workers had come to expect.

differentials The term refers to the system of paying different rates of pay to the workers in accordance with their skills and qualifications

A temporary improvement in trade in the late 1880s created a demand for workers. Many unions took advantage of this to expand membership and to re-organise. The mineworkers, for example, had established local associations in most areas in the 1860s. These formally came together in 1889 as the Miners' Federation of Great Britain. One of the Federation's first moves was to call for an eight-hour day. The last two decades of the nineteenth century also saw a remarkable increase in the membership of many of the model unions. By 1900 they accounted for over two thirds of all trade unionists. What explained their growth was the decision of the model unions to open their ranks to lower-grades workers. One example of this was the Amalgamated Society of Railway Servants, which, having been denied official recognition by the railway companies, agreed to accept the less skilled railway workers into its ranks. An equally interesting development was the decision of the Lancashire textile unions to allow women workers to join their ranks.

4 ⌐ THE EMPLOYERS' RESPONSE TO NEW UNIONISM

KEY ISSUE

How did the employers attempt to meet the challenge of the new unions?

Faced with the strengthening of trade unionism in the 1880s, and the growth of foreign competition, the employers drew together to defend their common interests. They did this by forming associations for mutual support and by using the law to their advantage. The employers invariably won their legal battles with the unions in the 1890s. But this left a legacy of bitterness that was to prove long-lasting. It also confirmed the belief among many trade unionists in the necessity of creating a separate political party that would represent the unions in Parliament and, thus, be in a position to change the unfair laws against them.

The Shipping Federation, which was formed in 1890, represented the owners of 85 per cent of British merchant vessels. It immediately set out to break the hold of the dockers' unions in the ports. Its first move was to withdraw its recognition of the settlement that had ended the Dock strike in the previous year. Then, in an attempt to destroy the influence of Tillett's union in the London docks, it began employing non-union workers. The dock unions reacted by calling a series of strikes against the Shipping Federation. However, the struggle was effectively over by 1893 when the unions were defeated in a dispute in the Hull docks which saw troops and naval gunboats brought in to protect the strike-breakers. The employers' victory led to a sharp decline of dock-union membership. Tillett's union which had had 56 000 members in 1890, had shrunk to 23 000 by the end of 1892, and to 14 000 by 1900.

Q

What tactics did the employers use to outmanoeuvre the unions?

In Lancashire, the mill owners, having formed the Federation of Master Cotton Spinners in 1891, felt strong enough to cut wages by five per cent in the following year. Workers who refused to co-operate were locked out. This produced a bitter struggle which was not resolved until 1893 with the Brooklands Agreement. This established an accepted system of collective bargaining in the textile industry: in future, a joint committee of employers and union representatives would adjust wage levels in relation to the price of cotton.

A similar development occurred in the mining industry. A fall in the price of coal led the owners in the Yorkshire, Lancashire and Nottingham coalfields to demand a 25 per cent reduction in wages. The newly formed Miners' Federation resisted, but was faced with unprecedented determination on the part of the owners. In July 1893, lock-outs were enforced in every pit where the workers had rejected the new terms. The dispute lasted until November, involving 300 000 miners; clashes took place between troops and strikers which left two miners dead. The situation was so serious that the Government decided to step in. Gladstone, the Liberal Prime Minister, used his influence to bring the two sides together for talks. These resulted in the establishment of a Conciliation Board, but the miners' demand for a minimum wage was not granted.

KEY ISSUE

Why did the Government become involved in the miners' dispute?

This was the first strike to be settled through direct government involvement. It set a precedent. Strikes and lock-outs were too damaging to the nation economy to be tolerated. The Conciliation Act of 1896 laid down procedures for settling disputes by referring them to a

neutral third party. However, it did not go so far as to make such negotiation compulsory. It relied on the goodwill of the two sides involved.
A great engineering lock-out in the following year suggested that this
trust was misplaced.

The tensions in the engineering industry, caused by the introduction
of new methods of work, snapped in 1897. The Engineering Employers'
Federation had been formed in 1896 with the declared intention of
crushing the Amalgamated Society of Engineers. When the ASE
demanded an eight-hour day in July 1897, the employers imposed a
nationwide lock-out. The dispute lasted until January 1898, and ended
in a humiliating defeat for the union. The ASE was forced to accept a
settlement in which it promised never again to 'interfere' in 'the management of business'. So it was that in the major industries, the employers' associations overcame the militancy of the new unions. This was
consolidated in 1898 by the establishment of the Parliamentary Committee of the Employers' Federation whose purpose was to lobby Parliament in the same way as the TUC's Parliamentary Committee.

Some historians have argued that the employers' organisations were
clearly bent on the destruction of the trade unions. Other writers have
found this too simple a view. They suggest that it was not really in the
employers' interest to destroy the trade unions. After all, it had been
demonstrated earlier in the century that compliant unions, who were prepared to control their members, were useful to employers. Strong centralised unions were a force for peace in the workplace. It is notable that the
defeat of a union in an industrial dispute was invariably followed, not by
the destruction of the union, but by the introduction of collective bargaining procedures into the industry concerned. In this way, the employers'
counter attack played on divisions within the unions between militant officials, who wanted confrontation, and those who believed in negotiation.

5 ⌐ TRADE UNIONS AND THE LAW – THE TAFF VALE CASE, 1900–1

KEY ISSUE

*Why was the Taff Vale
case so significant in
labour relations?*

The main weapon of militant trade unionists remained the strike, reinforced by well-organised picketing. Such activity had been made legal
by the legislation of the 1870s. In the 1890s, however, employers began
to challenge union rights in a series of court actions. In three test cases
in the 1890s, the employers successfully restricted the right of unions to
engage in picketing during an industrial dispute. These victories were
consolidated in 1901 by the final decision in the Taff Vale case.

Following a strike, in August 1900, by members of the Amalgamated
Society of Railway Servants (ASRS) against the Taff Vale Railway Company in South Wales, the Company sued the union for damages caused
to their business. The court upheld the Company's case, and although
this was quashed on appeal, the House of Lords in 1901 upheld the
original decision. The ASRS was ordered to pay damages amounting to
£23 000. The Lords' ruling had profound implications for all trade
unions. It meant that, in law, they were regarded as corporate bodies

who could be sued for actions taken on their behalf by their officials. In the case of *Quinn* v. *Leathem*, heard by the Lords two weeks after their decision on Taff Vale, it was held that the threat of industrial action could be considered a conspiracy.

After Taff Vale, a union could be sued for damages for organising a strike; after *Quinn* v. *Leathem*, it could be sued simply for threatening a strike. It appeared that all the legal gains made by the unions in 1860s and the 1870s had been reversed. The unions had been returned to the position they were in after the repeal of the Combination Acts in 1824: they were legal bodies but when they acted they were likely to break the law.

There were a few cautious union leaders who hoped that, by discouraging strikes, the Taff Vale decision would help them discipline their militant 'rank and file'. However, most trade unionists were alarmed at the implications of the decision. It demonstrated the legal weakness of the unions and the need for legislation to restore their right to take industrial action on behalf of their members. Neither the Liberals nor the Conservatives were ready to introduce such a measure. Both parties tended to side with the employers when it came to industrial disputes. Since the late 1880s, socialist groups had been arguing that working people needed their own parliamentary party. Previously, not all the trade unions had been convinced that this was necessary. Taff Vale removed their doubts. The unions now saw the necessity of independent labour representation in Parliament. Their conversion was a decisive factor in the emergence of the Labour Party.

> **Q** *What impact did the Taff Vale decision have on trade union attitudes?*

> **Q** *What disadvantages suffered by the labouring classes are depicted in the poster?*

PICTURE 40
'Whips for Labour's back' – a Labour Poster at the time of Taff Vale drawing attention to worker grievances.

6 ∽ THE EMERGENCE OF THE LABOUR PARTY

A *The demand for a separate party to represent Labour interests*

KEY ISSUE

Why did it take so long for a parliamentary labour party to emerge?

With hindsight, the question is not why did the Labour Party come into being in 1906, but why had it taken so long. The working classes had been involved in British politics, in one form or another, since 1815. The 1867 and 1884 Reform Acts had extended the vote to large numbers of working men. Yet, by the end of the nineteenth century, the working class was still grossly under-represented in Parliament. Working-class voters had tended to look mainly to the Liberal Party to defend their interests. However, working-class Conservatism was strong in Lancashire, often as a form of opposition to Liberal employers.

Q

What was the attitude of the Liberals and the Conservatives towards working-class representation in parliament?

Both Liberals and Conservatives recognised the need to win over working-class voters, but neither party was prepared to extend real political power to them. The Liberal Party accepted working men as Parliamentary candidates in some areas. But there were a mere eight 'Lib-Lab' MPs in 1889, and this had increased to only 11 by 1900. Around half of these were from coal mining areas where a well-developed trade union tradition made it relatively easy to raise the funds to support working men in the unpaid role of MP. The idea of Lib-Lab representatives had seemed promising in the 1870s, but the result was a sparse and geographically very patchy representation of the working community. Even when the Lib-Lab MP, Henry Broadhurst, the Secretary of the TUC, had been made Under-Secretary at the Home Office in Gladstone's Government of 1886, it seemed merely a gesture.

Indeed, many activists had begun to question whether there could ever be a genuine alliance between the workers and the Liberal Party. The new trade unionism of the 1880s and the 1890s re-opened the debate over the redistribution of wealth that had been pushed into the background since the decline of Chartism. The Liberals were still committed to a free-trade market system which allowed only a minimum of government interference to correct the imbalances in the economy and the injustices in society. This made it difficult for the unions to believe that the Liberal Party was equipped to understand, let alone promote, the hopes of the working classes.

B *Keir Hardie and the 'Labour Alliance'*

KEY ISSUE

What obstacles stood in the way of an effective working-class alliance?

The process by which the working class shifted its support away from the Liberal Party to an independent labour party is well illustrated by the career of **James Keir Hardie**.

JAMES KEIR HARDIE (1856–1915)

Keir Hardie was the illegitimate son of a servant-girl in Scotland. He became a skilled miner and a leading trade unionist in the Ayrshire coalfields. He was a Nonconformist, a teetotaller and a Liberal. After the miners gained the vote in 1884, he tried to persuade them to vote Liberal. But two events led him to lose faith in the Liberal Party – the violent breaking by police and soldiers of a strike by Lanarkshire miners in 1887, and the failure of the Liberal opposition in Parliament to support the Scottish miners' call for an eight-hour day. He became convinced that it was essential for the workers to be represented politically by an independent labour party.

PROFILE

PICTURE 41
James Keir Hardie

Keir Hardie was nominated as an independent candidate, sponsored by the miners, in the Mid-Lanarkshire by-election of 1888. This was the first time an independent labour candidate had stood against the two main parties. Although defeated, he took heart from the 614 votes he received; two weeks after the by-election, he established the Scottish Labour Party. This was the first time the term 'Labour Party' had been used in British politics. The party was small, but it managed to field five candidates in the general election of 1892. London socialists, including Will Thorne, persuaded Keir Hardie to stand as an independent Labour candidate for West Ham South in the general election of 1892. He was elected, along with two other labour candidates: John Burns, and Joseph Havelock Wilson, the leader of the Seamen's Union.

The movement for independent working-class representation was also gaining ground in the north of England. In 1891, the Manchester Labour Party was formed, on the lines of Keir Hardie's Scottish model. By 1893, Labour Unions had been formed in a number of the northern textile towns. In the words of the Bradford Labour Union, the aim of these associations was to 'further the cause of direct Labour representation on local bodies and in Parliament.' In 1893, Keir Hardie was asked to chair a conference in Bradford to bring these labour organisations together and link them with those in other areas. It was at this meeting that the Independent Labour Party (ILP) came into being.

Among the 120 delegates who met in Bradford there were few from those areas already represented by Lib-Lab MPs, such as the mining areas of Northumberland and Durham, and the Midlands. The Fabians and the SDF sent delegates, but the London socialist groups thought little could come of the move. More than a third of the delegates came from Yorkshire, and most of them from O'Connor's old stronghold, the West Riding. This area, and particularly Bradford, had by this time become the focus of the demand for Labour representation. On the face of it, this was an unlikely location. It was dominated politically by families of large Liberal Nonconformist employers, supported by working men's Liberal Associations.

In Bradford, as in so many other places, it was the experience of industrial conflict that had created the demand for change. The attempt by the owners of Manningham Mills, a large local woollen firm, to lower their employees' wages by 15–30 per cent in 1890 led to a long and violent strike, involving the Weavers' Association and thousands of workers. Although the owners, backed by the other textile employers in the area, were able to break the strike in 1891, employer–employee relations had been embittered in the process.

C *The Independent Labour Party*

KEY ISSUE

What traditions did the ILP represent?

The ILP was a national organisation with a socialist programme. Its aim was to 'secure the collective ownership of the means of production, distribution and exchange.' In its vision of the future, 'the people', rather than individuals, would run the economy. This version of socialism drew on three traditions – liberalism, trade unionism, and Nonconformity – and it was these that made it very different from the more revolutionary socialism of Europe. Hardie specifically rejected the 'class war' strategies of the SDF.

THE LIBERAL TRADITION

Many of the ILP's leaders in its early years were recent converts from the Liberal Party. James Ramsay MacDonald, a warehouse clerk turned journalist, spent four years as private secretary to a radical Liberal MP. In 1894, disillusioned by the unwillingness of the Liberals to accept working men as parliamentary candidates, he joined the ILP. Thirty years later he was to become the first Labour Prime Minister. His route from Liberal to Labour was typical of many who came to support independent labour representation. Ramsay MacDonald believed that the parliamentary, not the revolutionary, path was the correct one to take. Progress would be achieved by persuasion and would come gradually by the reform of existing institutions rather than their overthrow. Historians sometimes refer to this as a policy of 'reformism'.

THE NONCONFORMIST TRADITION

Religious Nonconformity was a powerful influence on British socialism. It was often said that labour leaders were more familiar with the Bible than with Marx. As Hardie was fond of explaining, 'the final goal of Socialism, is a form of Social Economy very closely akin to the principles set forth in the Sermon on the Mount.' One historian, examining those areas of the North and Scotland where the ILP expanded rapidly, referred to the 'religion of socialism'. Certainly, in terms of the energy and zeal shown by Party members, the growth of the ILP was very close in character to a religious revival. By 1895 the Party had 35 000 paid-up members.

THE TRADE UNION TRADITION

As well as having an association with the Liberal Party, many of the ILP's supporters were also trade unionists. This was evident in their practical approach to things. The ILP was always more comfortable with specific aims, such as the introduction of Old Age Pensions and the eight-hour day, than with developing theories of class struggle. John Burns referred to the theory of socialism as 'the chattering of Continental magpies'. Keir Hardie also considered that the ILP should be primarily concerned with achieving realistic social and economic reforms. This was far more likely to win supporters than discussing revolution. He felt that if the Party wanted to attract trade unionists away from the Liberal Party, it needed to stress its moderation. He even insisted that the term 'socialist' should *not* appear in the name of the party, arguing 'labour' was of broader appeal.

Despite this enthusiasm, the ILP met a good deal of working-class opposition, particularly from the older trade unions who were worried that the new party would begin to dominate the TUC. In a move designed to prevent this, the TUC's Parliamentary Committee introduced the 'block vote' in 1895. Previously, all delegates' votes had

KEY ISSUE

Why did the ILP meet with resistance from within the working class?

A BIT OF A BREEZE.

C.-B. (*Organ Grinder, to* Independent Labour Party). "AIN'T YOU A-GOIN' TO JOIN IN WITH YOUR FRIEND, MISS ?" I. L. P. "NOT ME! SHE AIN'T MY CLASS!"

Q

How accurately does the cartoon portray the divisions within the labour movement?

PICTURE 42

'A Bit of a Breeze' – a Punch *cartoon of May 1906, depicting the aloof ILP refusing to co-operate with the supporters of Lib-Lab pact.*

counted equally; now they were to be counted in proportion to the size of the union which a delegate represented. This strengthened the hand of the larger unions, who wanted co-operation with the existing political parties to continue. As one Lib-Lab union leader put it, 'We saw that Congress was losing whatever influence it had, and we were determined to pull it back again into the old paths.' The TUC also voted to exclude delegates from the Trades Councils which had, in many areas, been taken over by ILP supporters.

A further setback was suffered by the ILP when all 28 of its candidates in the general election of 1895 were defeated, including Keir Hardie. The party also found itself isolated with the outbreak of the Anglo-Boer War in 1899. It took an anti-war stance. In the eyes of the public this was tantamount to being unpatriotic and 'pro-Boer', and the ILP became the object of much hostility. Such developments convinced Keir Hardie that gaining popular support for the Party was a difficult and unpredictable process. He reluctantly recognised that most workers were not socialist in outlook and that, therefore, the best hope for the ILP was to play down its socialism and work with other working-class groups in a broad 'Labour alliance'.

See pages 339–40 on the Boer War

THE FORMATION OF THE LABOUR ALLIANCE

The opportunity to form such an alliance came at the TUC conference of 1899. The ASRS introduced a resolution calling on the Parliamentary Committee to convene a conference of all organisations committed to 'securing a better representation of the interests of labour in the House of Commons.' The resolution was passed by 546 000 votes to 434 000. The bulk of the no votes were cast by the coal and textile unions. But their opposition was now a minority one. In the circumstances of the day the majority of trade unionists could see no other way of protecting themselves against the powerful employer organisations than by forming their own parliamentary party.

7 ↬ FROM THE LRC TO THE LABOUR PARTY

The 129 delegates who met in February 1900, in response to the TUC's resolution, came from the socialist societies (the SDF, Fabians and the ILP) and 67 trade unions representing about a quarter of total trade union membership at the time. The conference was a notable success for the ILP. It was able to steer the delegates between the 'class war', advocated by the SDF, and the desire of some of the trade unionists to limit the Parliamentary actions of working-class MPs to particular issues. Keir Hardie formally proposed the creation of an organisation which would support a 'distinct Labour group in Parliament who shall have their own whips and agree upon their own policy'. This was accepted. He had originally wanted this to be called the 'United Labour Party' but the conference opted for the title Labour Representation Committee (LRC) as being less controversial.

Aware that the LRC depended on trade union backing, Keir Hardie accepted that compromises had to be made. Interestingly, a new word had entered the political debate around this time, 'socialistic', meaning sympathetic to the broad aims of socialism but without a firm commitment to state ownership. The LRC was 'socialistic' and Keir Hardie was prepared to accept this compromise as the price of union support. This was too much for the SDF, who rapidly left the LRC. The LRC was open to any political group that was prepared to work for the election of Parliamentary candidates. Thus, the LRC was drawn from groups with varying objectives, but who were prepared to sink their differences to achieve a common goal. This could not hide the fact, however, that from its beginning the LRC was subject to severe strains between its socialist members and its moderate trade unionists.

Nevertheless, the new organisation got off to a good start when two of its candidates, Keir Hardie and Richard Bell, were elected for Merthyr and Derby respectively in the general election of 1900. Bell, who was the Secretary of the Amalgamated Society of Railway Servants, was not a socialist. But the ASRS, having been consistently refused recognition by the railway companies, saw Parliamentary action as the only way to secure a legal status for all unions. This view was shown to be realistic by the Taff Vale ruling in 1901. The Lords' judgement on the case finally converted the doubting unions to the cause of independent Labour representation, and it was this that gave political force to the LRC.

Since neither the Liberal nor Conservative Parties were prepared to introduce legislation to protect the unions after the Taff Vale case, the LRC was the obvious political alternative to which the unions could now turn. In the wake of the Lords' ruling, 127 unions joined the LRC, including the Engineers and the Textile Workers. This raised the total membership from 353 000 in 1901 to 847 000 by 1903. Trade union affiliations to the LRC continued over the next few years, providing it with vital financial support. Keir Hardie's main aim had been achieved; a vital link had been forged between the parliamentary representation of working people and their trade unions. In a speech to the TUC in 1904, Ramsay MacDonald accurately observed, 'The Labour Representation Committee is neither sister nor brother to the Congress, but its child'.

In most constituencies where the Labour Representation Committee hoped to be successful, their main rivals for the workers' vote were the Liberals. Having been defeated in the general elections of 1895 and 1900, the Liberal Party was well aware that the LRC could split the working-class vote in many constituencies. Soon after its creation, the LRC won two by-elections, in 1902 and 1903. In neither of these were the successful LRC candidates opposed by Liberals, and this emphasised the likely advantages for Labour from an electoral agreement between the two parties not to contest key seats. In 1903 an LRC candidate, Arthur Henderson of the Ironworkers, who had once worked as a Liberal election agent, beat both Conservatives and Liberals to win a by-election.

- Two ILP members
- Two SDF members
- One Fabian
- Seven trade unionists

TABLE 12
Composition of the first Labour Representation Committee in 1900

KEY ISSUE

In what ways did the Taff Vale ruling prove helpful to the LRC?

KEY ISSUE

Why were the Liberals and the LRC willing to enter into the Lib-Lab Pact of 1903?

This pushed many Liberals to the conclusion that they could best avoid such embarrassing defeats in the future by making an electoral arrangement with the LRC. In Parliament, the five LRC members already liaised closely with the Lib-Labs, and a working agreement between the parties to defeat the Conservatives was a logical extension of this, despite its unpopularity with the socialist rank and file of the ILP. In 1903, Ramsay MacDonald negotiated an electoral agreement with the Liberal Chief Whip, Herbert Gladstone (the youngest son of W. E. Gladstone). Under this 'Lib-Lab Pact', the Liberals agreed not to contest a number of seats at the next general election. In return, the successful LRC members of Parliament would support an elected Liberal Government.

Knowing that the pact with the Liberals would cause divisions in the labour movement, Keir Hardie and Ramsay MacDonald decided to keep the arrangement a secret from the rest of the LRC, even to the extent of denying its existence. (This was one of many instances in Labour Party history when principle had to give way to expediency.) In the event, the LRC gained greatly from the pact, and 29 of its candidates including Keir Hardie, Philip Snowden and Ramsay Macdonald, were successful in the general election of 1906. On taking their seats in the House of Commons, these MPs renamed themselves the Labour Party.

8 ∾ BIBLIOGRAPHY

ARTICLES

Joyce Howson 'The Dock Strike of 1889', *Modern History Review*, 1995.

BOOKS FOR AS/A LEVEL STUDENTS

Vyvyen Brendon *The Edwardian Age*, Hodder & Stoughton, 1996, is a short book, in the 'History at Source' series, and has an excellent section on the trade unions.

Harry Browne *The Rise of British Trade Unions 1825–1914*, Longman, Seminar series, 1979, is also a very helpful short study.

Paul Adelman *The Rise of the Labour Party 1880–1945*, Longman, Seminar series, 1996, provides a very clear coverage of Labour's early years.

FURTHER READING

J. Belchem *Class, Party and the Political System in Britain 1867–1914*, Blackwell, 1990, is not always an easy read, but it covers the developments of the period and the historical debate over them.

K. D. Brown (Ed.) *The First Labour Party 1906–1914*, Croom Helm, 1985, is a collection of useful essays on a range of important issues; particularly helpful is Pat Thane's essay on the early Labour Party's approach to social reform.

Eric Hobsbawm *Labouring Men*, Weidenfeld and Nicolson, 1964, offers a left-wing view of the new unions and the rise of labour. The author updated this work in his collection of essays, *Worlds of Labour*, Weidenfeld and Nicolson, 1984.

Keith Laybourn *The Rise of Socialism in Britain*, Stroud, Sutton, 1997, presents an informed study of the relations between the trade unions and the various socialist groups in late Victorian and Edwardian Britain.

Keith Laybourn *A Century of Labour: A History of the Labour Party 1900–2000*, Sutton Publishing, 2000, is a very readable and up-to-date account.

K. Laybourn and J. Reynolds (Eds) *Liberalism and the Rise of Labour 1890–1918*, Croom Helm, 1984, is collection of essays which explore the relationship between the two parties in a particular locality, West Yorkshire.

R. Miliband *Parliamentary Socialism. A Study in the Politics of Labour*, Allen and Unwin, 1961, is a committed but lively left-wing analysis which is entertainingly critical of the pragmatism of the early party.

Kenneth O. Morgan *Keir Hardie Radical and Socialist*, Weidenfeld and Nicolson, 1975, has become an established work. It is particularly strong on labour's early relationship with the Liberals.

G. Phillips *The Rise of the Labour Party 1893–1931*, Routledge, 1992, is a well-written general history of the party.

D. Tanner *Political Change and the Labour Party 1900–1924*, Cambridge University Press, 1990, is a difficult book for the first-time reader but provides many interesting insights.

9 ⌒ STRUCTURED AND ESSAY QUESTIONS

The following questions relate to the separate sections in this chapter. The questions are closely linked to the Key Issues and margin questions that are there to guide you through the material you are reading. So in preparing your answers do look back to the relevant Key Issues and Q boxes. They will point you to the information and ideas that you need. You will notice that in each case the (a) questions are more straightforward in that they ask you to *describe*, whereas the (b) questions are more demanding in that they ask you to *explain*. The number of marks allocated to each question reflects this difference. In the first case you have simply to use your *knowledge* to answer the question; in the second case you have to use your *judgement*. Put simply, it is the difference between being asked *what* happened and being asked *why* it happened.

A *Structured questions for AS level*

1. (a) In what ways did the 'model' unions differ from previous trade unions? (30)
   (b) What were the chief aims of the model unions and how far did they achieve these aims? (60)
2. (a) What is meant by the term 'the late Victorian Recession'? (30)
   (b) Describe and explain the ways in which the recession affected relations between employers and workers? (60)

3. (a) Outline the story of **either** the Match Girls' Strike of 1888 **or** the Great Dock Strike of 1889. (30)
   (b) Why were there so many serious industrial disputes in the period, 1888–93? (60)
4. (a) What methods did the employers adopt to counteract the influence of new unionism? (30)
   (b) How successful were the employers in their efforts to meet the challenge of the new unions? (60)
5. (a) Outline the main developments in the Taff Vale dispute from the beginning of the strike of Amalgamated Society of Railway Servants in 1900 to the House of Lords judgement in 1901. (30)
   (b) Examine the impact of the Taff Vale case on the attitude of the trade unions towards industrial relations. (60)
6. (a) Trace the main stages that led to the formation of the Labour Representation Committee in 1900. (30)
   (b) How significant was Keir Hardie's contribution to labour unity? (60)
7. (a) Which party gained more from the Lib-Lab Pact of 1903, the Liberals or the LRC? (60)
   (b) How far was the creation of the LRC in 1900 and of the Labour Party in 1906 a triumph for socialism? (60)

B *Essay questions for A2*
1. How accurate is it to describe the Great Dock Strike of 1889 as 'the revolt of unskilled labour'?
2. In what sense could the Taff Vale ruling in 1901 be said to be a turning point in the development of the trade union movement?
3. To what extent was the development of the labour movement in Britain in the last quarter of the nineteenth century influenced by socialist ideas?
4. 'Between 1882 and 1906, trade-union membership rose from 400 000 to two and a half million'. How would you explain this growth?
5. 'The real question is not why a Labour Party was formed in 1906, but why it had taken so long to happen.' Examine this statement and say how far you agree with it.

10 ⤻ DOCUMENTARY EXERCISE ON THE TRADE UNIONS AND LABOUR, 1850–1906

The sun shone down brilliantly from a cloudless August sky that morning on a vast congregation of upturned faces, stretching from the East India Dock gates across the roadway to the pavement beyond. Thousands of men were there – seedy dockers and sturdy stevedores, sailors and firemen, in the fresh enthusiasm of their new trade union, weather-stained lightermen, and coalies cleaned up for Sunday — all branches, in short, of riverside labour; and on the outskirts of the crowd stood not a few engineers and other skilled artisans ready to show their sympathy with the revolt of unskilled labour.

SOURCE A
*H. Llewellyn Smith
and Vaughan Nash
The Story of the Dockers'
Strike, 1889*

In conclusion, we repeat that the real difference between the 'new' and the 'old' is, that those who belong to the latter, and delight in being distinct from the policy endorsed by the 'new', do so because they do not recognise, as we do, that it is the work of *the trade unionist to stamp out poverty from the land*. They do not contend, as we contend, that existing unions should exert themselves to extend organisations where they as yet do not exist. They know the enormous difficulties under which hundreds of thousands labour, and how difficult it is for them to take the initial steps in genuine trades unionism and how valuable a little 'coaching' would be from those who have had experience in such matters; but they have not done what they might to supply this — we shall. A new enthusiasm is required, a fervent zeal that will result in the sending forth of trade union organisers as missionaries through the length and breadth of the country.

SOURCE B
*Tom Mann and Ben Tillet
The 'New' Trade Unionism,
1890*

That this Congress, having regard to its decisions in former years, and with a view to securing a better representation of the interests of labour in the House of Commons, hereby instructs the Parliamentary Committee to invite the co-operation of all the co-operative, socialistic, trade union, and other working organisations to jointly co-operate on lines mutually agreed upon, in convening a special congress of representatives from such of the above-named organisations as may be willing to take part to devise ways and means for securing the return of an increased number of labour members to the next parliament.

SOURCE C
*Resolution of the Amalgamated
Society of Railway Servants,
Trades Union Congress, 1899*

Has the legislature authorised the creation of numerous bodies of men, capable of owning great wealth and of acting by agents, with absolutely no responsibility for the wrong they may do to other persons by the use of that wealth and the employment of those agents? In my opinion Parliament has done nothing of the kind. I can find nothing in the acts of 1871 and 1875 to warrant such a notion.

SOURCE D
*Lord Macnaughten, ruling on
the Taff Vale case, House of
Lords, July 1901*

Q

1. *Study Source A*
   From this source and your own knowledge, explain the description of the Great Dock Strike as 'the revolt of unskilled labour' **(10)**
2. *Study Source B*
   Assess the value of this source as evidence of the tension between the traditional and the 'new unions'. **(25)**
3. *Study Source C*
   Using Source C and your own knowledge, explain why the Resolution of the ASRS was such a significant moment in trade union history. **(25)**
4. *Study all the sources*
   *Using **all** these Sources **and** your own knowledge, examine the view that the period 1889–1901 saw a revolution in British industrial relations.* **(60)**

ADVICE FOR STUDENTS: POINTS TO CONSIDER IN ANSWERING THE QUESTIONS.

A general point to make, which applies to all source-based questions, is that, before you attempt to answer, you must make sure you have understood what you have read. That may mean re-reading the documents a number of times. If so, it is time well spent. The chances are that, if you tackle the questions without having grasped what is in the sources, you will make a poor showing. Another broad point is that, unless specifically told otherwise, you must attempt all parts of the questions. Never leave gaps or blanks. You are throwing marks away, and you can see just how many by looking at the numbers in brackets.

- **Question 1**: notice that you are being asked to use both the source and your own knowledge. You do not have a choice; you must include the two aspects in your answer.
- **Question 2**: this is asking for an assessment based on what is in the source. Your task is to analyse the document and its provenance (or origins).
- **Question 3**: as in Question 1, you have to call on your own knowledge as well your understanding of the source. Be careful not to slip into writing a full essay. Keep to the point of the question.
- **Question 4**: here you have to use all the sources. Therefore, make sure that, at some stage in your answer, you refer individually to A, B, C and D. It would be a good idea to define what you understand by 'a revolution' in this context. That would make it easier for you to examine the proposition in the question.

Votes for
Women

INTRODUCTION

In 1918, for the first time in history, women over the age of 30 voted in a British Parliamentary election. It had taken almost 60 years of campaigning, a lot of violence and World War I to achieve even this partial franchise (right to vote). It is difficult to trace the origins of the women's suffrage movement because, like most political crusades, it had somewhat confused and erratic beginnings. It began slowly with several people in different towns thinking and agitating about the right to vote.

The members of the first women's suffrage organisations, (their members were called **suffragists**) favoured peaceful protest. Then, in 1903, a new organisation, the Women's Social and Political Union (WSPU) was founded by Emmeline Pankhurst. This organisation, whose members were called **suffragettes**, broke the mould of women's politics. For the first two years of its existence the WSPU was virtually identical to all the other suffrage organisations working for votes for women. It used the conventional forms of protest: holding public meetings, leafleting, petitioning Parliament and writing letters. In 1905 this changed as a radically different strategy began to emerge: militant action. As time went on, militancy took on an increasingly aggressive and physically destructive form with members breaking windows, destroying works of art and blowing up houses. This chapter will consider whether the militancy of the WSPU helped or hindered the campaign for women's suffrage.

Of course, only Parliament could pass laws to give women the vote. Even though the suffrage eventually became headline news, not one of the political parties was prepared to adopt women's suffrage before 1918. As a result, all the suffrage bills in Parliament were put forward by sympathetic MPs as private members' bills, which meant that they had little chance of success because they did not have majority party backing. Between 1860 and 1914 no bill for women's suffrage ever got beyond its second reading. (Each bill has to go through three readings in Parliament before it becomes law.) Eventually, in 1910, in an attempt to break the party deadlock, a group of MPs from all sides of the House of Commons formed a Conciliation Committee, which consisted of 25 Liberals, 17 Conservative, six Labour and six Irish Nationalists, to marshal support across party lines.

The outbreak of war in August 1914 put an end to suffrage activity. The two main organisations, the National Union of Women's Suffrage Societies, the suffragists, and the WSPU, the suffragettes, abandoned

suffragists and suffragettes the two groups shared the same goal, female suffrage, and, at times, co-operated with each other. However, the suffragettes of the WSPU tended to adopt the more militant tactics

their campaign for the vote in order to work for the war effort. This chapter will assess the extent to which women were granted the vote as a result of their contribution to the war or whether votes for women would have been granted anyway.

1 ~ ORIGINS OF WOMEN'S SUFFRAGE

In 1860, there were no women's suffrage societies campaigning for votes for women whatsoever, but by 1914 there were approximately 56 groups with a combined membership of 300 000. Some historians date the movement from 1832, when the first women's suffrage petition was presented to Parliament. Others date the origins of the suffrage movement much later and suggest that it really took off in 1866 when some of the most notable feminist campaigners of the nineteenth century drafted a petition to Parliament demanding the enfranchisement of all householders regardless of sex. Emily Davies and Elizabeth Garrett carried the petition, signed by almost 1500 women, to the House of Commons where two of the handful of sympathetic MPs, John Stuart Mill and Henry Fawcett, presented it. In 1866 too, the Manchester National Society for Women's Suffrage was formed, followed shortly after by similar organisations in Birmingham, Bristol, Edinburgh and Ireland. Each of these groups was independent but in 1868 they amalgamated to become the National Society for Women's Suffrage (NSWS). However the ideal of unity, symbolised by the NSWS and its capacity for organised national action, was not to last – the early women's suffrage movement was characterised by internal rifts and divisions. Like other political associations with just one goal, and often without any real power, the suffragists and later the suffragettes, differed over the best way to achieve their objective.

TIMELINE

Main steps towards Votes for Women

1897	National Union of Women's Suffrage Societies (NUWSS) formed
1903	Women's Social and Political Union (WSPU) founded by Emmeline Pankhurst
1906	Liberals win a landslide victory; WSPU moves to London
1908	Women chain themselves to railings for first time; first window smashing
1909	Suffragettes banned from Liberal meetings; first hunger strikes and forcible feeding
1910	Failure of first Conciliation Bill promising votes to propertied women
1911	Failure of second Conciliation Bill; WSPU violence resumes
1913	'Cat and Mouse' Act
1914	Suffragettes suspend militancy and support the war effort
1918	Women over 30 gain the vote

A *The emergence of the NUWSS*

At the end of 1888 another major split occurred, precipitated by two major disagreements over political strategy. Firstly a number of – mostly younger and radical – suffragists wanted to affiliate to the women's section of the Liberal Association because the Liberal Party was perceived to be sympathetic to votes for women. Others – mostly the older members – disagreed because they wanted to keep the suffrage organisation independent of party politics. Secondly, younger members wanted to link suffrage with other female reforms (in particular the campaign for greater property rights), while the older members preferred to keep suffrage distinct. Once again the suffrage movement split into two, rather confusingly named, groups: the National Central Society for Women's Suffrage and the Central Committee National Society for Women's Suffrage. This particular split – which lasted until 1897 – coincided with a lull in suffrage activity. Nevertheless, all the numerous splits and divisions which occurred in the suffrage movement of the nineteenth century paved the way for the new organisational directions of the twentieth. In 1897 the National Union of Women's Suffrage Societies (NUWSS) brought together all the various suffrage organisations into one organisation. By the end of the nineteenth century the women's suffrage movement appeared to be united and strong, with NUWSS branches all over Britain. In 1910 the membership had grown to 21 571. Just before the outbreak of war in 1914 there were approximately 400 societies in England, Scotland and Wales. However, the suffragists were to face new challenges in the early twentieth century when a new organisation, the Women's Social and Political Union (WSPU), erupted onto the political scene.

> **KEY ISSUE**
>
> *Why did the supporters of votes for women disagree so strongly over tactics?*

Arguments for and against Women's Suffrage

ANALYSIS

There were many different arguments in support of votes for women. Those who opposed women's suffrage marshalled equally numerous arguments *against* votes for women.

Why women should have the vote	*Why women should not have the vote*
● no race, class or sex can have its interests properly safeguarded in the laws of a country unless it is represented by direct suffrage ● while men, who are voters, can get their economic grievances listened to, non-voters are disregarded	● all government rests ultimately on force, to which women, for physical, moral and social reasons, are not capable of contributing ● past legislation in parliament shows that the interests of women are perfectly safe in the hands of men

- politics and economics go hand in hand – as long as women have no political status they will be the 'bottom dogs' as wage-earners
- the current set of laws discriminate against women : these laws will not be altered until women get the vote
- all the more important and lucrative positions are barred to women, and opportunities in public service are denied them
- wherever women have become voters, reform has proceeded more rapidly than before.

(These arguments were put forward in a leaflet produced by the National Union of Women's Suffrage Societies in 1907)

- there is little doubt that the vast majority of women have no desire for the vote
- the acquisition of the vote would logically involve admission to Parliament itself, and to all Government offices. It is scarcely possible to imagine a woman being Minister for War, and yet the principles of the Suffragettes involve that and many similar absurdities
- women have, at present, a vast, indirect influence through their menfolk, on the politics of this country
- the physical nature of women does not fit them for direct competition with men
- women's suffrage is based on the idea of equality of the sexes, and tends to establish those competitive relations which will destroy chivalrous consideration.

(These arguments came from a pamphlet by Grace Saxon Mills in the early 20th century entitled *Against Woman Suffrage.*)

Both sides advanced powerful arguments, but it is fair to say that, at first, those who opposed women's suffrage (the 'Antis' as they came to be labelled by their opponents) seemed to be winning the debate. Early campaigners for the vote had to be particularly careful in their speeches and their leaflets to advance a rational defence, whereas the Antis had to do little more than laugh at them to gain support. By 1914, however, many of the ideas of the Antis appeared ludicrously old-fashioned and it was evident that the argument for votes for women had, more or less, been won. Both sides, however, considered that their own particular assertions were correct and that it was therefore clear that the debate could not be decided intellectually. Instead, political pressure would play a decisive role in the outcome.

B *Similarities in the arguments on both sides*

There were some surprising similarities in the arguments used by those who supported and those who opposed women's suffrage. Most of those involved in the suffrage debate seemed to believe that votes for women was the means to an end. The law-abiding suffragists, the militant suffragettes and the Antis all believed that the vote would bring about a social revolution. However, whereas the former welcomed such change it struck fear into the Antis. Suffragists and suffragettes looked forward to the day when women would be able to end the exploitation of their sex by changing the laws and increasing educational and employment opportunities. For them, the vote would herald a new dawn of equality. In contrast, the Antis feared the reforming zeal of enfranchised women because it would undermine the authority of the male.

In addition, the suffragists, the suffragettes and their opponents all recognised women's contribution to local government. Those who supported women's suffrage used this to convince people of women's ability to engage in national politics, whereas the Antis used the same argument to demonstrate that women had already fulfilled their political potential. In fact, some Antis considered local government to be women's proper sphere because it concerned education, health and housing.

Suffragists and suffragettes developed numerous justifications for women's franchise but what is remarkable is the consistency of those arguments over time. Indeed there were no specifically 'suffragist' and 'suffragette' justifications. Both groups claimed the right for women to vote on the same terms as men in Parliamentary elections although, as the nineteenth century progressed, the meaning of this demand changed. The first women's suffrage bill in 1870 was decidedly elitist, as only a very few rich women would have been enfranchised, whereas by 1914, as the property qualification for men was lowered, more and more women would be eligible to vote. What *did* change was the confidence with which the case was argued; whereas early suffragists very tentatively argued their point, the Edwardian suffragettes, more secure in the justice of their cause, produced the most startling propaganda in support. Similarly, both the suffragists and the suffragettes saw the vote as a symbol of citizenship in a democratic country and argued for women to be represented. The literature produced by both groups suggests that they wanted the vote to end the economic, social and moral exploitation of women.

2 ⌐ THE NUWSS AND THE WSPU

By the outbreak of World War I it seemed as if the suffrage movement was divided into two major camps: the suffragists and the suffragettes. However, such an analysis is misleading. Certainly, at leadership level there were distinct differences between the two groups but this was not the case among the general membership. Many suffrage supporters joined both a militant and a constitutionalist society,

> ### KEY ISSUE
>
> *What were the similarities and differences between the NUWSS and the WSPU?*

paid two membership fees, attended two sets of meetings and campaigned for both groups. Such women may not have seen the suffrage movement as made up of antagonistic groups vying for members but as one movement with a common aim. The two organisations were certainly distinct in the ways they were led and managed and there is no doubt that the National Union of Women's Suffrage Societies (NUWSS) was more democratic than the Women's Social and Political Union (WSPU). However, before judgements are made, we should consider the implications of the notion of democracy in the heady atmosphere of Edwardian politics. Democracy is time-consuming: leaders have to be elected; votes have to be canvassed; and policies have to be discussed. It could be argued that the emphasis by the NUWSS on democratic principles hindered direct action. In stark contrast, Emmeline Pankhurst's WSPU spent little time discussing policy: in the immortal words of its leader, 'Deeds not Words' were paramount.

PROFILE

PICTURE 43
Emmeline Pankhurst

EMMELINE PANKHURST (1858–1928)

Emmeline Pankhurst is one of the most fascinating, and indeed one of the most controversial, female figures in modern British history. There is a statue of her outside the House of Commons, a portrait of her in the National Portrait Gallery and a Pankhurst Centre built from one of her former homes in Manchester.

Throughout her adult life she had involved herself in political activity: she was a Poor Law Guardian, a member of the Manchester School Board, a founding member of the Manchester Independent Labour Party and was active in four different suffrage societies at the turn of the century. In 1903, frustrated that women were no nearer to being given the vote, she founded the Women's Social and Political Union (WSPU) and promoted a very different, confrontational style of politics. By 1914, the WSPU was notorious for its militant actions: breaking windows, destroying golf-courses and blowing up buildings.

Although Emmeline Pankhurst did not initiate window smashing nor the other forms of illegal activities perpetrated by the suffragettes, she proclaimed 'I have advised, I have incited, I have conspired … I accept the responsibility for it'. Not surprisingly, the Government constantly summonsed, arrested, tried and imprisoned her.

LIFE IN PRISON

For someone as fastidious as Emmeline Pankhurst, prison was especially shocking. She complained that the cells were damp, verminous and smelt of sewage. By 1912 she was given the status of political prisoner. The prison authorities claimed that she was well treated in this period. Certainly she was well-fed and it is reported that, every day, she drank a half bottle of the great Bordeaux wine, Chateau Lafitte, a gift sent in by a wealthy suffragette friend. Even so Emmeline Pankhurst was not an ideal prisoner. In July 1913 she refused to be medically examined, refused to sit down or to lie down on the prison bed. In July 1914 she was brought in front of the Visiting Committee of Holloway and charged with being abusive, of using offensive language and of striking an officer.

Then she refused to eat, drink or sleep. In-mid July 1914 she 'lost almost a stone in weight. She suffered greatly from nausea and gastric disturbances and was released in a toxic condition with a high temperature and a very intermittent pulse'. By this time she was in such a weak and exhausted condition, and was experiencing a great deal of cardiac discomfort and poor digestion, that she had to be transported everywhere by ambulance. The Government, fearful of public criticism, never force-fed Emmeline Pankhurst but released her from prison when her health was critical and she had the 'odour of malnutrition' about her.

With the outbreak of World War I, Emmeline Pankhurst ceased campaigning for the vote and instead worked closely with her former enemy, Lloyd George, to recruit women munition workers, prevent strikes and promote the war effort in Russia, Canada and America. After the war, when a partial vote was won, she went to Canada and became a national figure in Canadian politics leading a campaign to prevent venereal diseases. When she eventually returned to England in 1926 she was adopted as Conservative candidate for the working-class district of Whitechapel.

A *Who were the suffragists and suffragettes?*

The stereotypical image of the female suffragist is of a middle-class spinster. Socialist historians have shown that a significant number of working-class women, particularly in the north of England, participated in the suffrage movement. These findings certainly make the suffrage movement look more inclusive and balanced in its membership, but, overall, there is still far too little known about the composition of the suffrage movement at grass roots level: it will be impossible to gauge the extent of working-class support until historians have built up a national picture based upon local research. Certainly at leadership level, the middle classes dominated. Suffrage leaders were usually married to wealthy men or belonged to wealthy families and were undeniably middle or upper-middle class. In a political movement which relied upon the unpaid work of women only those who were economically independent or married to men who were financially secure could afford to engage in political action. For example, the nineteenth-century suffragist Lydia Becker was able to devote her life to the suffrage cause because she was not expected to engage in paid work. Similarly, Barbara Bodichon, the daughter of a wealthy radical MP, enjoyed a large independent income. In the twentieth century, Lady Constance Lytton and Emmeline Pethick Lawrence were wealthy enough not only to support themselves but also to donate large sums of money to the WSPU.

B *Strategies, methods and tactics*

At first the methods used by all the suffrage groups were peaceful and legal but, as time went on, more violent – and illegal – methods were favoured, particularly by the WSPU. As a consequence the suffragists of the NUWSS are deemed to be constitutional, whereas the suffragettes of the WSPU are regarded as militant. But we should bear in mind that suffragists were considered militant in 1860 when they dared to speak at meetings whereas, by 1914, public speaking was seen to be quite acceptable female behaviour.

It is assumed, wrongly, that because of the differences over political tactics there was hostility between the various women's suffrage organisations. The NUWSS were said to be antagonistic towards the WSPU because its members used violent methods, whereas the latter were said to condemn the NUWSS's lack of imagination. This interpretation too needs to be reassessed, as the NUWSS initially condoned the militancy of the WSPU and held banquets in honour of those who had been imprisoned. The Criterion Restaurant in Piccadilly, London, was even hired to host welcoming parties for women who had just been released from gaol. This support was not to last. The increasingly violent tactics of the WSPU gradually alienated the NUWSS and, by 1909, it was voicing public disapproval of the WSPU's tactics. Nevertheless, the divisions between the two groups were not always constant. For example, when the WSPU called a temporary halt to militancy (which, apart from a brief lapse in November 1910, lasted from January 1910 to November 1911) the old spirit of unity reappeared and the suffrage groups organised joint meetings and demonstrations.

Legal	Illegal
Meetings	Tax evasion
Demonstrations	Census resistance
Pilgrimages	Smashing windows
Propaganda techniques	Arson attacks
Distributing leaflets	Vandalising private and public property
Canvassing politicians	Hunger strikes
	Various bouts of civil disobedience

TABLE 13
Legal and illegal methods used to promote the cause of women's suffrage

3 ◟ THE WSPU'S MILITANT APPROACH

Of course, the popular image of the militant is of a woman chained to railings outside government offices shouting 'Votes for Women'. In fact, the first illegal methods used by the suffragists and suffragettes were little more than mild forms of civil disobedience. At first, women tried to undermine the Liberal Government by interrupting their meetings but, from 1908, the WSPU intensified the political pressure and promoted new and confrontational methods to force MPs to give women the vote.

The reason for this turn to violence is open to debate. Some unsympathetic observers saw militancy as a reflection of the instability of women in general, and of their fanatical and hysterical dispositions in particular. To them it was proof that women should not be allowed to vote. However, the suffragettes themselves argued that violence emerged, and escalated, for a number of strategic reasons:

KEY ISSUE

Why did the WSPU turn to militancy?

- militancy was adopted in response to the failure of years of peaceful campaigning to which politicians were seen to have turned a deaf ear
- militancy was a reaction to the 1906 Liberal Government which, by excluding women from public meetings and refusing to meet suffrage deputations, had denied suffragettes the main forms of agitation open to the disenfranchised;
- violence was the only realistic option left open to suffragettes as they were forbidden access to peaceful protest.
- militancy was seen as a retaliatory measure against a government which imprisoned and force-fed those who participated in direct action – if the government chose to treat women roughly, then it too would be intimidated.

In addition, suffragettes believed themselves to be continuing a long and respected tradition of protest as previous extensions to the franchise, for instance in 1832 and 1867, had been preceded by great disturbances. The WSPU was not slow to draw on historical examples of the unlawful exercise of physical force to justify its tactics – it explicitly identified the suffragettes with past revolutionary and resistance heroes. Emmeline Pankhurst told her audiences that, just before middle-class men were enfranchised in the 1832 Reform Act, half the city of Bristol was burned down in a single night of protest; the 1867 Reform Act, which enfranchised working men, was preceded by rioting and unrest; and the last male franchise reform in 1884, which enfranchised the agricultural labourer, was marked by threats of civil disorder.

The suffragettes were undoubtedly convinced that the government would not grant women the vote until they were forced to do so. Comparisons were drawn between the suffragettes and other pressure groups who advocated violent methods. Christabel Pankhurst, for instance, noted that miners had succeeded in gaining improved pay and conditions in 1911 because they made themselves a nuisance. Similarly, the tactics of the Ulster Unionists, even when they involved the loss of human life, were successful in stopping the move towards Irish Home Rule. The suffragettes believed that the achievements of these groups demonstrated that the vote would only be obtained through violent action.

It is often assumed that this kind of behaviour was orchestrated by the WSPU leadership who marshalled their obedient members to commit crimes. Militancy, however, often began at a local level with a few ardent activists and was only adopted as WSPU policy when it received extensive support from the membership. As Sandra Holton has pointed out, window smashing, arson, letter burning and hunger striking were

See Bibliography on page 398

all initiated by rank and file members. Indeed, there is evidence to suggest that, rather than encourage threatening behaviour, the WSPU leadership tried to restrain the enthusiasms of its rank and file for increasingly violent tactics. Every time Emmeline Pankhurst was imprisoned, members of the WSPU created various forms of social havoc and mayhem. Her conviction in April 1913 was followed, according to the WSPU, by the biggest revolutionary outbreak that the country had seen since the struggle for the Reform Bill in 1832. Suffragettes burnt down country houses in Chorley Wood and Norwich, set fire to several houses, a Free Church in Hampstead Garden Suburb and a house in Potters Bar; destroyed a grandstand at Ayr race-course and tried to burn down Cardiff and Kelso race stands; exploded a bomb at Oxted station; set off an explosion near Dudley Castle; damaged a portion of a goods train; set fire to a number of public buildings; cut telephone wires; ruined flower beds; broke the glass of thirteen famous paintings in Manchester Art Gallery; damaged several pieces of art elsewhere and destroyed letters and other materials in post boxes.

PICTURE 44
*Emmeline Pankhurst being
arrested during a suffragette
demonstration*

A *To what extent were WSPU methods effective?*

The destructive methods of the WSPU have been the subject of much historical research. Until 1900, only peaceful methods were used, whereas by 1914, suffragette violence was at its height. And it is this turn towards violence that has tended to dominate the history texts. However, the WSPU did not break with the suffragist past but built upon it; violent measures did not replace constitutional ones so much as supplement them. Throughout this whole period both the suffragists and suffragettes continued to use the traditional forms of protest such as petitioning Parliament, lobbying MPs and demonstrating. Furthermore, both the suffragists and the suffragettes often tried to end the impasse between themselves and the Liberal Government by supporting the three **Conciliation Bills** put forward in the House of Commons to enfranchise women. On these occasions, all the suffrage organisations co-operated with each Conciliation Committee which proposed the Bill. They lobbied MPs, sent speakers to various organisations and directed local constituency groups to pressurise MPs to vote for each Bill. And while negotiations continued, the WSPU called a truce. All the Conciliation Bills, as we know, failed to become law. The defeat of each disillusioned the suffrage groups and many NUWSS women resigned from the Liberal Party. The WSPU reverted to violence.

> **Conciliation Bill** a Bill to give women the vote which was presented by the Conciliation Committee in Parliament

There is no doubt that the NUWSS leaders, although working towards the same goal, grew irritated by the increasingly destructive tactics of the WSPU. Over the years, they had tried to prove that they (and, by association, women in general) were calm, sensible and rational beings and so they put forward measured arguments and used democratic methods to get their message across. It was feared that the use of violence discredited the suffrage movement and undermined suffragist efforts to be seen as mature adults who could be trusted with the vote. However, the NUWSS leaders were reluctant to criticise the WSPU openly and publicly in case it further hardened the Government's obstinate opposition.

It is sometimes argued that the violence of the suffragettes lost the WSPU the sympathy and support of the country at large and provided the Liberal Government with an ideal excuse to deny women the vote. Not surprisingly, the WSPU leaders denied the accusation that violence was counter-productive. On the contrary, to believe that militancy damaged the suffrage cause was to be ignorant of all the lessons taught by history. To their minds, persuasive approaches were ineffective since the peaceful methods of the suffragists had brought the vote no further forward in 1905 (when militancy is said to have begun) than it had 50 years before. And so the WSPU, their patience exhausted, hoped to force the Government into conceding votes for women by using violent tactics. Nevertheless, suffragette violence was still circumscribed by their ideological beliefs. Although they were prepared to sacrifice their own lives in the pursuit of votes for women, the suffragettes generally confined themselves to attacks on property rather than people. Certainly, until 1914, when the WSPU ceased its campaigning, Cabinet Ministers and others were rarely in any personal danger because the WSPU stated that they held a scrupulous respect for human life. However, it is tempting to speculate whether this belief in the sacredness of human life would have continued if war had not broken out. For the suffragettes had already begun to throw slates and other missiles at government ministers.

4 ⮒ THE POLITICAL PARTIES AND WOMEN'S SUFFRAGE, 1906–14

It has been argued that Conservatives disliked any extension of democracy, whereas the Liberals, fearful of the property-based qualification for the vote, were convinced that propertied women would support the Conservatives. Labour, of course, much preferred universal franchise to what was perceived to be a middle-class female vote. However, such a clear-cut party interpretation underestimates the variety of opinions which existed within the parties concerned. It is safe to say that while the Conservative leaders endorsed votes for women and the rank and file opposed it, the reverse was true of the Liberals. Most of the Liberal party membership agreed with women's suffrage, so when the Liberals won a landslide victory in 1906, after 20 years of Conservative rule, the women's suffrage movement was optimistic that votes for women would soon be won.

This was not to be the case. In 1908 Asquith became Prime Minister and obstructed any advance towards votes for women and persistently refused to see women's suffrage deputations. Nonetheless, despite setbacks, by 1914 suffrage had certainly become the foremost political question for women and was firmly on the national agenda of male politics. The painstaking work of the suffragists in the nineteenth century had made women's suffrage respectable and, by the beginning of the twentieth century, many politicians were convinced of the inevitability of votes for women.

Nonetheless, the Liberal Government, beset by problems in Ireland, in the House of Lords and with trade unionists, was reluctant to give in to female violence. When the Women's Social and Political Union (WSPU) began its illegal activities, the Liberal Government reacted by denying them democratic forms of protest. In an attempt to stop potential disruption, women were forbidden to attend Liberal meetings unless they held a signed ticket. The Government refused to meet deputations or accept petitions, banned meetings in public places and censored the press in an attempt to silence the WSPU. The Commissioner of Police, directed by the Home Office, refused to allow suffragettes to hold meetings in any London parks and persuaded the management at the Albert Hall not to let it out to suffragettes. When the WSPU managed to hire a different venue, the owner of the hall was threatened with the withdrawal of his licence. The Government also prosecuted the printer of *The Suffragette*, periodically raided the offices and homes of

> ## KEY ISSUE
>
> *How did the Liberal Government respond to the actions of the suffragettes?*

the WSPU members and eventually forced Christabel Pankhurst to flee to Paris, where she directed the movement from exile.

On numerous occasions the Government acted even more harshly towards the suffragettes. As Home Secretary in charge of civil order, Winston Churchill was held responsible for the notorious police violence towards women on Friday November 18th 1910, later termed 'Black Friday' by the suffragettes. On this day, approximately three hundred suffragettes marched to the House of Commons in protest at the failure of the first Conciliation Bill. When they tried to enter Parliament the police behaved with unexpected brutality. Instructed not to arrest the suffragettes, they forced the women back, kicked them, twisted their breasts, punched their noses and thrust knees between their legs.

Suffragettes who broke the law were imprisoned. Once they had been sentenced, suffragettes were allocated to one of three prison categories: the First Division, the Second Division or the Third Division. First division prisoners were granted the status of political prisoners because they had been convicted of a political, rather than a criminal, offence; second division prisoners were deemed to be respectable people from decent families; and third division prisoners were defined as hardened criminals long-past redemption. Each prisoner was treated according to her divisional category. First division prisoners were permitted to wear their own clothes, provide their own food and receive as many visitors, books and letters as they wished. Second and third division prisoners were less fortunate: they were served only prison food and had their correspondence, reading material and visitors severely restricted. At first suffragettes were given first division status but this right was soon taken away and they were removed to the second and third divisions.

A *Conditions in prison*

Conditions were atrocious for second and third division prisoners. On their arrival, prisoners were undressed and searched, forced to relinquish all their personal belongings and made to take a bath. They were given a prison uniform branded with a broad arrow in several places. Second division prisoners wore green serge dresses whereas those in the third division wore brown. All were forced to wear white caps, blue and white check aprons and were given one big, blue and white check handkerchief a week. Underwear was coarse, ill-fitting and stained; thick, shapeless black stockings with red stripes had to be worn without garters or suspenders. The shoes, which were heavy and clumsy, did not always come in a pair. Each prisoner was made to wear a large badge, made of yellow cloth, bearing the number of the cell and the letter and number of the prison block. To make sure that personal identity was completely eroded, prisoners were only ever called by their number, not their name.

When they were dressed, prisoners were given sheets for their bed, a toothbrush and a Bible. They were then taken to a cell which contained a wooden bed, a mattress and a pillow filled with grass, two narrow blankets and a woollen quilt. In the corner of the cell was a shelf upon which, in strict and unchanging order, was a pint pot for the prisoner's food, a wooden spoon, a wooden saltcellar, a piece of soap and a case containing the prison rules. Opposite the cell door a basin, a slop pail which was used as a lavatory, a small water can, a plate and a dustpan, all made of tin, a bath brick, cleaning rags and two sweeping brushes were to be found. At 6 am each morning prisoners emptied their 'slop' bucket. Later they were given a bucket of water and a scrubbing brush with which to scrub the cell floor, the tins, the bed, the stool, the shelves and the cell floor. Breakfast, generally consisting of a pint of oatmeal gruel and 6 oz (170 g) of brown bread, was brought round to each cell. At about 8.30 am the prisoners went to chapel: first division prisoners sat behind a screen at the side of the altar; second division prisoners sat near the front of the chapel and the rest of the chapel was occupied by the third division. Lunch, served between eleven and mid-day, consisted of potatoes, beans and some meat for second division prisoners but oatmeal porridge and bread for those in the third division. Supper, consisting of more gruel and bread, was at five.

After chapel prisoners were expected to work: second division prisoners were given sewing or knitting to do but those in the third division were given the most menial tasks such as cleaning the corridors and other parts of the prison. Second division prisoners were allowed to exercise every day but those allocated to the third division were only allowed to exercise three times a week. Exercise consisted of marching slowly in single file, several yards apart, around a paved yard. No one was allowed to speak. Suffragette prisoners were kept separately from the other prisoners and had a different exercise time.

B *The hunger strikes*

The suffragettes considered themselves to be political prisoners and they objected to this treatment. The first hunger striker, Miss Wallace Dunlop, had been arrested in July 1909 for writing extracts from the Bill of Rights on to the walls of the House of Commons and was sentenced to one month's imprisonment in the second division. Considering herself to be a political prisoner, Wallace Dunlop refused to be treated as a common criminal and went on hunger strike to secure full rights as political prisoners for herself and others. Succeeding prisoners followed her example. From this time on, large numbers of suffragettes went on hunger strike, both as a protest against the prison regulations and because they were treated as common criminals rather than political prisoners. Eventually, in March 1910, Winston Churchill, after much public pressure, agreed that suffragettes be allowed to wear their own clothing, not be compelled to have their hair cut nor required to take a bath on reception. They were relieved from cell cleaning and, for a small sum, could pay for someone else to clean and arrange their furniture and utensils. In addition, they were employed on the lighter forms of labour, were able to exercise more regularly, were permitted to have books sent in, receive a letter every fortnight and visitors every month;

KEY ISSUE

How did the Government re-act to hunger strikes?

each prisoner was allowed to receive a parcel of foods from their friends once a week. But women still continued to hunger strike.

At first, hunger strikers were released from prison but soon the Government introduced force-feeding for women who consistently refused to eat. Sylvia Pankhurst, Emmeline Pankhurst's daughter, who was force-fed a number of times, said

the doctors came stealing in behind. Someone seized me by the head and thrust a sheet under my chin ... I felt his fingers trying to press my lips apart – getting inside – and I felt them and a steel gag running round my gums ... two of them were wrenching at my gums ... Then I felt a steel instrument pressing against my gums, cutting into the flesh. and forcing its way in ... I was struggling madly and trying to tighten the muscles and keep my mouth closed up... Often I vomited during the struggle ... Sometimes I felt the tube go right down into the stomach. It was a sickening sensation, especially when it passed midway between the throat and the stomach ...

Q

What conclusions do you draw from the extract?

Q

Far more Conservatives voted against women's suffrage than Liberals did. Yet the poster calls on electors to vote against the Liberal Government. How would you explain this?

THE GOVERNMENT'S METHODS OF BARBARISM.

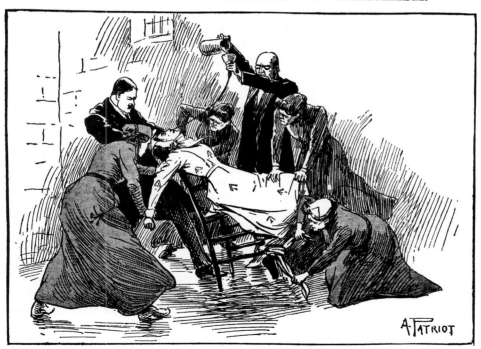

FORCIBLE FEEDING IN PRISON.

In some cases, instead of nasal feeding as in the picture, the still more dangerous practice of feeding through the mouth, by a tube, down the throat, is adopted. This was done in the case of Jane Warton.

PICTURE 45
A poster showing a suffragette being force fed, 1910

On April 25th 1913, as a result of adverse publicity, the Prisoners' Temporary Discharge for Ill-Health Act became law. This temporarily released persistent hunger strikers from prison giving them time to recover before re-arresting them. This new piece of legislation may have been an ingenious device by the Government to put an end to hunger striking but it was soon dubbed, mockingly, the 'Cat and Mouse Act' by the suffragettes.

5 ⌒ SOCIETY'S RESPONSE TO THE SUFFRAGETTES

KEY ISSUE

How do you explain the variety of responses to the Suffragettes?

The suffrage movement failed to win over the majority of British men. The evidence that is available – from famous individuals, from popular music hall songs, from the banning of women from certain venues, and from the increasing level of violence in the crowds that gathered around women's demonstrations – all points to a generally hostile response. However, it is difficult, if not impossible, to measure the extent to which these particular groups were representative of male opinion as a whole.

The citadels of high culture certainly appeared unsympathetic to women's suffrage. Fear of militancy closed many of the country's art galleries and museums to the public completely or sometimes to women only. The rule of 'No muffs, wrist bags or sticks' was widespread: the Royal Academy and the Tate Gallery were closed to women and the British Museum announced that it was open to all men but only open to women if accompanied by men who were willing to vouch for their good behaviour. They said that unaccompanied women 'were only allowed in on presentation of a letter of introduction from a responsible person vouching for the bearer's good behaviour and accepting responsibility for her acts'. This response may be evidence of justifiable anxiety about the prospect of suffragette violence rather than of an unfriendly attitude.

Recent research indicates that many suffragettes were violently and indecently assaulted when they participated in demonstrations. Antagonistic men often sexually harassed women on demonstrations, ripping their clothes and whispering obscenities in their ears. Gangs of 'roughs' often lay in wait for suffragettes who tried to get into the House of Commons. In Glasgow in March 1912, 200 men broke up the WSPU shop by throwing iron bolts and weights through the windows. At the Eisteddfod in Wales that year suffragettes who dared to heckle the local hero Lloyd George were seriously assaulted, had their hair pulled and their clothing ripped – one woman was stripped to the waist, two women's shirts were cut up and the pieces given to the crowd. Time and time again the suffragettes were subjected to this kind of brutal and sexual harassment so that it became impossible for the WSPU to hold outdoor meetings because they feared violence by the crowd.

Suffragists and suffragettes may have received an antagonistic response from some men but they drew support from unexpected quarters. Many leading department stores, both in London and the provinces, displayed the WSPU colours of green, purple and white in their windows. In 1908 in Lewisham, one large department store employed a WSPU speaker to address one of their sports day events while Sainsburys' featured green, purple and white clothes in their shopfront. Many other retail stores stocked clothes and other items in the suffragette colours. In 1910 the Votes for Women slogan was even printed on the wrappers of Allison's bread. This, of course, may have been just good business sense – the suffragettes were seen to be wealthy customers – but the displaying of suffragette colours may have antagonised more people than it attracted.

6 ～ THE IMPACT OF WORLD WAR I

World War I had a profound effect on suffrage politics. In August 1914, as Britain was going to war against Germany, the WSPU declared peace with the Liberals – the sex war was swamped by the Great War, as Martin Pugh has pointed out (see Bibliography, page 399). In one of her characteristic aphorisms, Emmeline Pankhurst remarked that there was no point in continuing to fight for the vote when there might be no country to vote in. The rest of the major suffrage societies agreed with her, discontinued their suffrage campaign and shifted their energies to the war effort.

It has been argued that the greatest effect of the war on women's suffrage was that women were granted the vote towards the end of it. On 6 February 1918, eight million women, out of an electorate of 21 million, were given the opportunity to vote. Until fairly recently, historians generally agreed that women were awarded the vote as a token of gratitude for their war work. It has been said that the highly skilled and dangerous work done by women during the war in the munitions factories and in the nursing service at the Front was probably the greatest factor in women being granted the vote. However, the evidence for this interpretation is inconclusive and several historians have questioned the direct correlation between women's war work and women's suffrage. They argue that the emphasis placed on women's economic contribution to the war underestimates the groundwork put in by the pre-war suffrage campaign. To complicate matters, a few historians have even suggested that the war, far from facilitating votes for women, actually postponed its implementation. Women's suffrage, they suggest, was on the verge of being granted just before the war broke out.

Thus it would be naive to believe that women received the vote solely for services rendered in World War I. It must be remembered that only women over thirty were given the vote and they were not the ones who had made the most substantial contribution to the war effort. Indeed the very women who had done most to help – the young women of the munitions factories in particular – were actually denied the vote. The vote, as with the Second Reform Act, was conferred only on those considered to be respectable and responsible.

KEY ISSUE

Did women gain the vote because of their work in the war?

A *Trade Unionists' reaction to women's war work*

The significance of women's war work in the achievement of the vote is therefore perhaps not as great as first assumed. In reality, women were greatly resented in both agriculture and industry because, even though they received more money than perhaps they had ever earned before, they still undercut male wages. There was a great fear that low paid and unskilled women workers would peg wages below acceptable levels. Male trade unionists were far from enthusiastic about women joining a union to increase their rates of pay. It is true that a few unions encouraged women to join but many, like the Amalgamated Society of Engineers, excluded or ignored them. Thus five-sixths of women workers remained outside the unions during war time. Even on an individual level, there was hostility from male workers. Engineering workers, such as those at Vickers, objected to setting up machines for women working in the factory. Men 'froze out' women workers, gave them no assistance, incorrect instructions and even sabotaged their work. In one incident a woman had her desk drawer nailed up while, another time, oil was poured over the contents. Farmers, too, disliked women workers and preferred to employ young boys or old age pensioners, arguing that women lacked the strength for the more strenuous work on the farm.

But women's jobs in these industries were not, and were never meant to be, permanent. As men returned from fighting in the trenches they wanted their jobs back in the factories, in transport and in offices. In 1918, a trade union conference called for women to be banned from 'unsuitable' trades, for their hours to be regulated and for the exclusion of married women from work. In 1920 unemployed ex-servicemen in Bristol smashed the windows of tram cars and attacked female conductresses in protest at women working. And when women resisted the return to domestic service, they found their unemployment benefit withdrawn and were criticised in the press as 'slackers with state pay'. Not surprisingly, by 1921, most women had relinquished their war-time jobs.

B *The war and the timing of the franchise*

Undoubtedly, the pre-war suffrage movement prepared the ground for votes for women. French women, for example, were not enfranchised despite their participation in the war effort, largely because there had been no women's suffrage movement in the period leading up to the outbreak of war. Furthermore, it seemed likely that the women's suffrage movement would recommence once the war had ended with perhaps a renewal of the militancy which had plagued previous governments. Indeed, Emmeline Pankhurst insisted that 'we're like a dog that has buried a bone. They think we have forgotten all about it but we've got the place marked'. One can only assume that, because the political climate was very different in 1918 than it had been in 1914, it would be inconceivable for the Government to imprison those self-same women who had so publicly participated in the war effort.

In many ways, the war may have delayed the franchise. Just before the outbreak of war there were conciliatory gestures by key MPs: Asquith received deputations from the NUWSS, Sir John Simon emerged as a cabinet supporter, and Lloyd George offered a place on his platform to suffrage speakers. There was also evidence to suggest that the Liberal Party was pressurising prospective MPs to support women's suffrage and replacing those unsympathetic to the suffrage cause with those who agreed with it. In addition, the Liberal leadership seemed ready to make women's suffrage part of its party programme. This, of course, is mere speculation. Negotiations between the Government and women's suffragists had taken place many times before but had never provided votes for women. There was no guarantee that they would have done so this time.

Nevertheless, the war may have acted as a catalyst for women's suffrage. First, there was a need for franchise reform because large numbers of the armed forces were ineligible to vote because of current voting regulations. Women's suffrage could easily be accommodated in any future franchise Bill. Secondly, there were a number of key changes in Parliament which altered the balance between those who opposed and those who were in favour of votes for women. In particular, Lloyd George, who was (more or less) sympathetic to women's suffrage, replaced Asquith as Prime Minister in December 1916. Thirdly, in May 1915, the Liberal Government evolved into a Coalition Government which meant that women's suffrage supporters were no longer fragmented between three political parties. The old fears that one party might benefit from women's suffrage was at last laid to rest.

Of course, neither the view that women achieved the vote because of their pre-war campaigns nor the view that women achieved the vote because of the war is ultimately sustainable. As with most historical judgements, there are a number of reasons for such a significant event and historians much prefer a synthesis of causes to crude over-simplification. It must also be remembered that the vote was still not entirely won, as full adult universal suffrage was not achieved until 1928.

7 ↩ WOMEN'S SUFFRAGE: THE ACHIEVEMENT

So was it all worth it? Did the vote bring about the changes that the suffragists and suffragettes yearned for? Many certainly thought so. From this vantage point, historians of the suffrage movement can assess whether the franchise accomplished what those who energetically campaigned for it desired, or whether the vote marked the end of women's achievements. Controversy, however, is at the heart of history and so, not surprisingly, historians differ on the effect that the vote had on women's lives, especially since the consequences of votes for women, are in many ways, still working themselves out.

At first suffragists, elated at the prospect of voting, insisted that the vote had a tremendous significance for women's rights. To their minds,

KEY ISSUE

What was achieved by women's suffrage?

the enfranchisement of women would revolutionise government thinking as the voting power of the new electorate could not be ignored. Historians share this optimism and claim that, because of their newly acquired voting power, women made considerable gains. For example, there were 21 pieces of legislation between 1918 and 1929 which concerned women. However, a significant group of historians maintain that women did not benefit from the vote – politically, economically or socially. They hold that any advances made by women in this period were due to post-war feminist campaigning and to the continuation of Edwardian Liberalism, which was sympathetic to social reform, rather than to the franchise and its consequences.

Nevertheless, in 1918, for the first time in legal and political history, women had the opportunity to participate in the democratic process. Britain could now claim that she had a representative government as electoral democracy was no longer the preserve of men. After many years of struggle, Britain allegedly had a just and balanced government as the majority of the population was now enfranchised. The 1918 Representation Act may well have been the last great reform act, but these views must be approached with some caution as women aged between 21 and 30 were still denied the vote. Not until 1928 did all women over the age of 21 receive the vote, thus properly marking the beginning of modern democracy in Britain.

8 ⌐ BIBLIOGRAPHY

ARTICLES

Paula Bartley 'Suffragettes, class and pit-brow women', *History Review*, December 1999, focuses particularly on the involvement of working-class women in the WSPU.

Brian Harrison 'Anti-Suffragists', *Modern History Review*, September 1990.

Martin Pugh 'The Gentle Touch' *BBC History Magazine*, April 2000.

Martin Pugh 'Votes for Women', *Modern History Review*, September 1990.

BOOKS FOR AS/A LEVEL STUDENTS

Diane Atkinson *Votes for Women*, Cambridge University Press, 1998, is a useful introduction for students who have never studied this topic.

Paula Bartley *Votes for Women*, Hodder & Stoughton, 1998.

Martin Pugh *Women's Suffrage in Britain 1867–1928*, Historical Association, 1986.

Harold Smith *The British Women's Suffrage Campaign, 1866–1928*, Longman 1998. The last three books were written for further and higher education students so are invaluable texts for this subject.

FURTHER READING

Sandra Stanley Holton *Feminism and Democracy: Women's Suffrage and Reform Politics in Britain, 1897–1918*, Cambridge University Press, 1986.

This book examines the ethos of the suffrage movement and assesses the impact of the nineteenth-century women's suffrage campaign.

Sandra Stanley Holton *Suffrage Days*, Routledge, 1996. Based on the activities of several less well-known suffrage activists, this book places their lives within a wider historical context.

Martin Pugh *The March of the Women*, Oxford University Press, 2000. This book, as with Holton's, argues that the nineteenth-century women's suffrage campaigns were more effective than is usually presumed.

June Purvis and Sandra Stanley Holton (Eds) *Votes for Women*, Routledge, 1999, reviews the historiography and charts the history of the movement in Britain. The introductory chapter is extremely useful as are chapters on the WSPU.

9 ∼ STRUCTURED AND ESSAY QUESTIONS

A *Structured questions for AS level*
1. (a) What were the main similarities and differences between the suffragists of the NUWSS and the suffragettes of the WSPU?
   (b) To what extent did their differences weaken the campaign for women's suffrage?
2. (a) What forms of militant action did the WSPU adopt in their campaign for women's suffrage?
   (b) In what ways, and with what results, did the Liberal Government respond?

B *Essay questions for A2*
1. Why, and with what success, did the suffragettes adopt a militant approach to their campaign in the years leading up to the outbreak of World War I?
2. Why did women fail to achieve the vote before World War I but succeed in achieving it immediately afterwards?

10 ∼ DOCUMENTARY EXERCISE ON WOMEN'S SUFFRAGE

I have always contended that if once we opened the door and enfranchised ever so small a number of females, we could not possibly close it, and that it ultimately means adult suffrage. The government would then be handing over to a majority who would not be men, but women. Women are creatures of impulse and emotion and do not decide questions on the ground of reason as men do.

SOURCE A
William Cremer, MP for Shoreditch, speaking in Parliament, 1906

SOURCE B (PICTURE 46) *From the cover of* The Suffragette, *1913*

SOURCE C
Emmeline Pankhurst, 1914

The struggle for the full enfranchisement of women has not been abandoned; it has simply, for the moment, been placed in abeyance [is suspended]. When the clash of arms ceases, when normal, peaceful, rational society resumes its functions, the demand will again be made. If it is not quickly granted, then once more the women will take up the arms they today generously lay down.

Our movement has received great accessions [increases] of strength during recent months, former opponents now declaring themselves on our side, or at any rate withdrawing their opposition. The change of tone in the press has been most marked ... . The view has been widely expressed in a great variety of organs of public opinion that the continued exclusion of women from representation will ... be an impossibility after the war.

SOURCE D
Millicent Fawcett writing to Prime Minister Asquith, May 1916

Some years ago I ventured to use an expression 'Let the women work out their own salvation'. Well, Sir, they have ... . How could we have carried on the war without them? ... The questions which will arise with regard to women's labour and women's functions are questions in which I find it impossible to withhold from women, the power and the right of making their voices heard. And let me add that, since the war began, now nearly three years ago, we have had no recurrence of that detestable campaign which disfigured the annals of political agitation in this country, and no one can now contend that we are yielding to violence what we refused to concede to argument.

SOURCE E
Asquith speaking in Parliament, March 1917

1. *Study Source B. What image of the Suffragettes does it portray? (3)*
2. *Study sources A and B. How do you explain these two different views of the women who campaigned for the suffrage? (7)*
3. *Study sources C and D. Assess the value of these two sources to an historian studying the history of the women's suffrage campaign. (8)*
4. *Study sources C, D and E and use your own knowledge. To what extent do you agree with the view that 'it was the war that won the vote for women'. (12)*

(Total marks 30)

14 Britain in a New Century: Labour, Liberals and Unionists 1906–14

INTRODUCTION

The period 1906–18 was one of the most turbulent periods of British political history. During that time both of the main political parties, the Liberals and the Conservatives, suffered fluctuating fortunes and underwent traumatic changes. In 1906 the Liberal Party won a General Election victory on such a scale that its political position seemed assured for the future. In the same election a new political force, the Labour Party, secured a foothold in the House of Commons. The issue of female suffrage was transformed from an obscure issue into a national crusade which challenged the political system and defied the rule of law. The House of Lords, which had regarded itself for so long as the guardian of the Constitution, was reduced to a shadow of its former power and prestige. Welfare legislation raised government intervention to new and unprecedented heights. Irish affairs plunged political life into turmoil and even seemed to threaten a civil war within the British Isles. Disputes between employers and trade unions, often with the government sandwiched uncomfortably between them, brought class conflicts to the surface.

Before the 1906 General Election, the political world had been dominated by an alliance between the Conservative Party and those Liberal Unionists who had split from Gladstone over the issue of Irish Home Rule in 1886. So strong did this theme of 'Unionism' become that, for a time, the term 'Conservative Party' almost fell out of use.

Liberalism, too, underwent a dramatic change. The Liberal Party which won the General Election in 1906 was a very different one from that which had been led by Gladstone. Many active Liberal supporters had defected to the Unionist side, including, in particular, many from the world of industry and commerce who abandoned their traditional liberalism for the apparent safety of the Conservatives or Liberal Unionists. Their defections were partly the result of increasing signs of radicalism within the Liberal Party; an increasing number of its members were now demanding that the Government intervene more in order to deal with social problems. This 'New Liberalism', seemed far removed from the largely non-interventionist and individualist traditions of Gladstonian Liberalism. The huge scale of the Liberal Party's victory in the 1906 general election, guaranteed many new faces among the ranks of Liberal MPs. The 'New Liberal' element among them ensured that traditional Liberal emphasis on the importance of individual liberties and 'self-help' would increasingly give way to demands for social welfare.

This chapter outlines and discusses the major political issues in the years leading up to World War I and ends with a brief examination of the impact of the war on Britain.

1 ⌁ THE GENERAL ELECTION OF 1906

On 4 December 1905, Arthur Balfour resigned as Prime Minister and brought to an end the Coalition Government of Conservatives and Liberal Unionists which had held power since 1895. Balfour did not, however, advise the King to dissolve Parliament and hold a General Election. Constitutionally, this meant that the King had to send for the Liberal leader, Sir Henry Campbell-Bannerman, and invite him to form a new government. This was part of Balfour's strategy. He hoped to provoke a crisis in the Liberal Party which would weaken it and allow him, eventually, to win another General Election for the Unionists. Why did Balfour resort to such a complicated strategy?

Campbell-Bannerman and another leading Liberal, the former Prime Minister, Lord Rosebery had clashed in November 1905 over the issue of Irish Home Rule. Rosebery wanted to abandon it as a Liberal policy – Campbell-Bannerman intended to retain it.

It was well known that Campbell-Bannerman's position as leader was insecure. Asquith and Sir Edward Grey were possible alternatives as was Lord Rosebery. There was doubt, therefore, as to whether Campbell-Bannerman would actually be able to form a government. If the Liberals failed in the attempt, the Unionist position would be massively strengthened.

The Unionists had been, according to all the political commentators of the day, heading for a serious defeat at the next election, which would have to be held, at the latest by the middle of 1907. They had however done better than expected in two by-elections in November 1905. This encouraged Balfour to think that perhaps the tide had turned and a bold strike to undermine the Liberals' credibility might swing electoral opinion back towards the Unionists.

Balfour's strategy was too subtle for its own good. The Liberals were by no means as divided as they had appeared. Campbell-Bannerman had no real problems forming a government. Neither Asquith nor Grey was prepared to put at risk the chance of holding high office, especially when 'C-B' was 70 years old and not in good health. (He died in 1908.) Asquith became Chancellor of the Exchequer and Grey became Foreign Secretary. Lord Rosebery had little or no personal support in the Liberal Party and his eventual refusal to serve in the Liberal Government was

KEY ISSUE

How did the Liberal Party achieve its landslide victory of 1906?

no surprise. Once his Government was formed, Campbell-Bannerman immediately asked the King to dissolve Parliament so that a General Election could be held in January 1906. The result was a landslide victory for the Liberals. The Unionist dominance was totally over-turned as shown in Table 14.

TABLE 14

Seats in the House of Commons after the 1900 and 1906 elections

	1900	1906
Unionists	402	157
Liberals	186	400
LRC/Labour	2	52*
Irish National Party	82	83

*Comprised of 29 LRC MPs who were joined by 21 Miners' Union MPs and two Independent Labour MPs after the Election to form the Labour Party.

A *Why did the Unionists suffer such a humiliating defeat?*

There is no single factor which alone explains the catastrophe which befell the Unionists in 1906. It was rather that a number of factors developed and worked together to undermine the Unionists both inter-nally and in the way they were seen by the electorate.

See page 339

See pages 366–7 in Chapter 12 for the Taff Vale case

- The Unionists had come to be seen as the party of imperialism; after the scandal of the Boer War 'concentration camps', this was a liability rather than an asset.
- The Unionists were seriously divided over economic policy. Some supported the continuance of Free Trade, while others increasingly wanted to adopt a system of protective tariffs as advocated by Joseph Chamberlain (see page 313). Many historians see this as a critical factor because abandoning Free Trade meant taxing food imports which would put up food prices.
- The Education Act of 1902 (see page 311) had reunited many non-conformist voters behind the Liberals.
- Trade Unionists were particularly active and well organised – some in support of the Liberals and some in support of the Labour Representation Committee (LRC) – because of the 1901 Taff Vale Case.
- The Unionists had failed (despite much discussion) to produce social reform legislation in key areas, such as child welfare, unem-ployment and sickness benefits and old age pensions.
- Balfour, despite being a superb analyst with considerable intellectual and administrative skills, was a poor leader. He had little feel for mass issues and could be very indecisive – for example, over the issue of protective tariffs, in which he failed to give a clear lead.
- In 1903 the Liberals agreed on a secret 'Electoral Pact' with the LRC. Under its terms the Liberals agreed not to put up candidates in some seats where the LRC had the better chance of winning. The LRC agreed to reciprocate in other seats where the Liberals were stronger.

The arrangements centred on those constituencies where the Unionists might possibly win the seat in the event of a split vote between the Liberals and the LRC. It was not a binding commitment and it worked through an informal, personal agreement reached by Herbert Gladstone, for the Liberals, and Ramsay MacDonald, for the LRC. Even so, this arrangement enabled the LRC to achieve its breakthrough electorally and also secured a number of otherwise marginal seats for the Liberals.

- Finally, a scandal erupted in South Africa over the terrible working conditions being endured by Chinese contract workers in the South African mines. The scandal, described as 'Chinese Slavery' by the press, reinforced the image of the Unionists as the hardfaced, uncaring, party of worker exploitation, even though, in reality, they had no responsibility for, or ability to change, the conditions of the Chinese workers.

The result of these factors, taken together, was catastrophic for the Unionists. Balfour himself lost his seat at the election and was forced into fighting a by-election later in the year before he could return to the House of Commons. Two-thirds of the remaining Unionist MPs were Chamberlain supporters who wanted to abandon Free Trade, while the other third were pledged to retain it. The Liberals, likely to be supported in most things by both the Irish Nationalists and the Labour Party, were now capable of amassing immense majorities (over 350) in the House of Commons. In the Commons at least, the Unionists were now almost an irrelevance.

2 ∽ THE LIBERAL GOVERNMENT AND SOCIAL REFORM, 1906–14

The Liberals took office in 1905 with a general commitment to the principle of social reform, but with few specific proposals. In part this was due to the suddenness of the general election, but it also stemmed from the divisions which they had endured in recent years and the potentially controversial nature of new social reform legislation. Advocates of 'New Liberalism', such as David Lloyd George, wished to see governments intervening much more directly to assist in improving life for the lower classes with national schemes for unemployment and sickness benefits and even child allowances. More traditional Liberals still clung to the notion of individual effort and enterprise as the means to self-improvement. Although the leading Liberals mostly leaned towards intervention, they were only too aware of the need to move cautiously in the interests of maintaining unity within the parliamentary party.

> **KEY ISSUE**
>
> *How radical were the reforms introduced by the Liberal Governments?*

PROFILE

PICTURE 47
David Lloyd George

DAVID LLOYD GEORGE (1863–1945)

David Lloyd George was born in Manchester in 1863, the son of a school headmaster who died very soon after his son's birth. Lloyd George's mother, left with no other means of support, returned to her home village in North Wales to live with her brother, a shoemaker. Lloyd George was therefore brought up in a Welsh-speaking environment in which English was very much a second language. It was also a Nonconformist environment, hostile to both the Anglicanism and social predominance of the local, anglicised gentry families. Lloyd George's background was financially limited but culturally rich. His uncle, effectively his adopted father, was a man of intellect and strong religious faith. He taught himself French in order to be able to enhance his nephew's education, and saw Lloyd George safely through legal studies and into a career as a solicitor.

At 26, after making a name for himself as a rising nationalist figure on local political issues, Lloyd George was elected as Liberal MP for Carnarvon in the face of determined opposition from the Conservatives who had previously held the seat. He continued to represent the constituency for the next 55 years. In 1902–3 he took a leading role in the Nonconformist opposition to the Balfour Education Act. In 1906, following the Liberals' election triumph, he became President of the Board of Trade. He at once showed his administrative potential and, in 1908, when Asquith became Prime Minister, Lloyd George replaced him as Chancellor of the Exchequer. In this post he oversaw the completion of the Old Age Pensions legislation initiated by Asquith and developed the Budget of 1909 (see below). During the conflict with the House of Lords which followed, Lloyd George became a leading critic of the peers' resistance, first to the Budget and then to the Parliament Bill. In 1911 he oversaw the first National Insurance legislation. During World War I he was successively Minister of Munitions, Secretary for War and Prime Minister. His appointment to the latter post caused a clash with Asquith which had disastrous consequences for the future of the Liberal Party. After the War he continued to lead a coalition Government with the Conservatives until their backbenchers withdrew their support in October 1922 forcing him to resign. He never held office again.

His private life was controversial, especially his relationships with women, and he became the first Prime Minister to live openly with his mistress (who was 25 years his junior). Remarkably, although his lifestyle was well-known, no public scandal resulted during his lifetime. In 1944, with his health in serious decline, and knowing he could not possibly fight another election campaign after the war, he reluctantly accepted a peerage in the hope of being able to contribute to the post-war debates on the peace settlement. However, he died in February 1945 with the war still unfinished, having never taken up his place in the Lords.

The debate about the condition of the working classes revolved around three basic issues:

- the condition of children
- the condition of the elderly
- the problems associated with poverty resulting from sickness and unemployment.

A *Children's Welfare Reforms 1906–8*

The least controversial of these, by far, was the question of the condition of working-class children. This group was not only the most directly vulnerable in society, it was also the only group which could not be held in any way accountable for its problems. Sickness could be characterised as malingering; unemployment as the result of sheer idleness; even the elderly could be seen as poverty-stricken in old-age because of a lack of thrift during their working lives; none of these accusations could be levelled at children. Even so, some Liberals still instinctively felt that children were solely the responsibility of their parents and that any supportive intervention on their behalf would undermine the basic parental role. Despite such views, however, there was a general feeling (in which many Unionists joined) that the pitiful condition of the poorest working-class children was nothing short of a national disgrace.

The first direct move to alleviate the plight of deprived children came in 1906 with the passing of the Education (Provision of Meals) Act. The issue of malnourished children had increasingly surfaced since the extension of rate aid to all schools and the creation of Local Education Authorities (LEAs) in 1902, so that the problem of children too hungry and physically weak to benefit from education was well-documented by 1906. The result was a Private Member's Bill introduced by a Labour MP, which the Liberal Government (which approved of the idea anyway) took over and adopted as Government policy. The Act enabled LEAs to provide school meals for needy children by levying an additional rate of a halfpenny in the pound, but it was not compulsory and many LEAs did not rush to take up this new power which they now enjoyed. By 1911, less than a third of them were using rates to support school meals provision and so the Board of Education decided to take additional powers to make such provision compulsory.

In 1907, a second Education Act made medical inspections for children compulsory. Under this Act, the Board of Education was able to specify that at least three inspections must take place during a child's school years and that these were to be conducted on school premises and during school hours, with the first inspection coming as soon as possible after the child had started school. The more compulsory nature of this legislation was the result of two factors:

- compulsory elements in legislation on public health issues had been used since the first Public Health Act of 1848 so compulsion was not controversial.

● the sense of urgency, produced by the recruitment of volunteers for the Boer War, which had revealed the appalling health suffered by large numbers of the working-class population.

In 1908, the Children's Act introduced a variety of measures to deal with child neglect and abuse. Juvenile courts and remand homes were set up to remove child offenders from the adult courts and prisons. Severe penalties were introduced for the ill-treatment of children, and also for selling them tobacco, and alcohol in unsealed containers. Finally, in the Budget of 1909, Lloyd George introduced direct financial assistance for child support in the form of child allowances at a rate of £10 per year per child for poorer families.

The measures to improve the welfare of children constituted the principal achievements of the Liberals' social legislation during their first two years in office. The Liberals failed in their attempt to introduce an eight-hour day for the mining industry and, although Workmen's Compensation was extended to cover some six million workers, overall, it did not seem a very impressive record. Some of the more radical Liberals, such as Lloyd George, were less than satisfied. In April 1908,

PICTURE 48
Winston Churchill, who was President of the Board of Trade from 1908. He and Lloyd George were the driving force behind the passing of many of the Liberal social reforms

Campbell-Bannerman was forced to resign through ill-health. Asquith was his natural successor and, in the Cabinet reshuffle which followed, Lloyd George, who had built a formidable reputation at the Board of Trade, was promoted to the Exchequer. In turn, Lloyd George was succeeded at the Board of Trade by Winston Churchill, a former Conservative who had rebelled against tariff reform in 1903 and had since established himself as a radical reformer. Lloyd George and Churchill were determined to use their new seniority to push for a much more ambitious programme of social reform. Not only did they genuinely want more radical reforms, they also believed that it was a political necessity for the Liberals to show themselves capable of developing a dynamic policy.

B *Old Age Pensions 1909*

During the last phase of his time as Chancellor of the Exchequer, Asquith had been working on proposals to introduce Old Age Pensions. The budget proposals for 1908 contained provision for financing the introduction of a scheme and it was Lloyd George's good fortune to inherit the responsibility for finalising and presenting the budget details. He then piloted the Old Age Pensions Bill through the Commons. The provision which this legislation made for the poorest of the elderly was limited, especially when set against the length of time it had taken to get any form of assistance provided, outside of the hated Poor Law. The first payments were made on 6th January 1909. The terms of the Act were:

● pensions of 5 shillings (25p) per week would be paid to those aged 70 or over (37.5p to married couples) who had annual incomes of £21 or less
● for those with annual incomes over £21 a sliding scale of descending, graduated payments would be made up to a ceiling of a £31 annual income, at which point the payments ceased
● there were a number of exclusions: those who had claimed poor relief in the previous year or had been in prison in the previous ten years had no entitlement. Also excluded were those who had failed to work regularly. In practice these barriers did not result in a great reduction in the number of claimants. The qualifying period for ex-convicts was subsequently reduced to two years. By 1914, there were 970 000 claimants, costing the Exchequer £12 million a year.

Though often criticised for the relatively high starting age (70 was a tougher milestone to achieve then than it has subsequently become), the system had a marked impact on the lives of the beneficiaries. The 'Lloyd George money', as it became known, released many from the threat of the workhouse or dependence on often hard-pressed relatives. A pensions system had been under discussion since the 1880s at least. The Liberals made it a reality.

KEY ISSUE

How great an achievement was the introduction of Old Age Pensions?

	Shillings	Pence
Rent	2	3
Paraffin (pint)		$1\frac{1}{2}$
Coal		$2\frac{1}{2}$
Tea		1
Sugar		$1\frac{1}{2}$
Potatoes		1
Mutton	1	0
Flour	1	
Porter (a type of beer)		$1\frac{3}{4}$
Pepper, salt and vinegar		$1\frac{1}{2}$
Loaf of bread		$2\frac{1}{2}$
Total:	5	$4\frac{1}{4}$ (22p)

TABLE 15
Typical weekly spending of an elderly person in 1908 (from a radical magazine The Woman Worker*)*

Q

What is the value of this kind of evidence to a historian studying the introduction of Old Age Pensions in 1909?

C *Insurance against sickness and unemployment, 1911*

Once the issue of Old Age Pensions had at last been addressed, Lloyd George was determined to confront the problem of hardship caused by loss of earnings due to unemployment and sickness. By the middle of 1908, this was a pressing issue because the general economic situation was becoming difficult for the lower-income groups. Unemployment was rising and wages were static or falling. At the same time, inflation was reducing the real value of wages. At the Board of Trade, Churchill introduced an Act setting up labour exchanges in 1909. The aim was to make it easier for the unemployed to get in touch with potential employers. Meanwhile, in 1908, Lloyd George went to Germany to study the German system of social insurance at first hand. By the autumn of 1908, civil servants were working on the principles of a scheme to introduce unemployment and sickness insurance.

Although work on the schemes was well advanced by 1909, their eventual implementation was delayed until the National Insurance Act of 1911, while the first payments were not made until the summer of 1912 (for unemployment) and the beginning of 1913 (for health). The delay was primarily because Lloyd George and Churchill, who were the politicians in charge of the details, wanted to deal with both sickness

Mr. LLOYD GEORGE'S National Health Insurance Bill provides for the insurance of the Worker in case of Sickness.

PICTURE 49
The Dawn of Hope, a Government poster

Support the Liberal Government
in their policy of
SOCIAL REFORM.

and unemployment at the same time. Unemployment insurance was relatively uncontroversial and, standing alone, could probably have been introduced without difficulty in 1909. Sickness benefits, however, were an entirely different matter. There were some powerful vested interests already operating in this field. The Friendly Societies, industrial insurance companies and doctors would all be affected by the intrusion of the state into this kind of benefit provision. The insurance companies and friendly societies collected millions of pounds a year in premiums from working-class families and it took months of difficult negotiations for Lloyd George to work out and agree suitable safeguards and compromises with the various companies, who were often as suspicious of each other as they were of the Government. Opposition from the doctors' organisation, the British Medical Association, came mainly at the instigation of the wealthier medical practitioners who feared that the status of their profession might be compromised. However the adoption of the panel system, which allowed insured patients to choose their own doctor from a panel of practitioners under the control of a local health committee, proved popular with the less well-off doctors, especially those in the inner cities, who quickly saw that their incomes must rise from this new source of patients.

The National Insurance Act was in two distinct parts. Part I dealt with Health Insurance and was the responsibility of the Treasury. Part II dealt with Unemployment Insurance and was the responsibility of the Board of Trade. The Insurance system worked as described below.

The National Insurance Act 1911

Health Insurance

- All workers earning less than £160 per year and aged between 16 and 60 were included – around 15 million in all.
- Weekly contributions were taken from the worker (4d), the employer (3d) and the Government (2d). This encouraged Lloyd George to coin the slogan '9d, for 4d', in his attempts to popularise the concept.
- The resulting entitlement was: sickness benefit of 10s (50p) per week for 13 weeks (7s 6d for women); 5s (25p) per week for a further 13 weeks thereafter; a 30s maternity grant; 5s a week disability benefit; and free medical treatment under a panel doctor.
- Wives and children were not covered by the scheme, nor was hospital treatment, except for admission to a sanatorium which was intended to benefit tuberculosis sufferers.
- Later, the reduced benefit for the second 13-week period was abolished in favour of full benefit throughout the term of 26 weeks.

Unemployment Insurance

This was a less ambitious scheme. The main features were:

- It covered far fewer workers: a total of some 2.25 million, mainly in construction and engineering trades which were susceptible to fluctuating employment levels. The idea was to tide workers over a short period of unemployment. It was not meant to tackle the problem of long-term unemployment.
- weekly contributions were $2^1/_2$d each from workers, employers and the Government, which entitled the insured workers to a payment of 7s per week benefit for up to a maximum of 15 weeks.

The overall impact of these schemes of insurance, plus the provision of labour exchanges, old age pensions and child welfare provision, meant a significant increase in government intervention. The State had now assumed an unprecedented degree of responsibility for individuals in the lower classes of society. A great expansion in the Civil Service was required to oversee the administration of the new machinery. The sums expended on benefits exceeded all estimates. This welfare legislation entirely by-passed the operations of the Poor Law and, to a considerable degree, appeared to make the question of its reform irrelevant. The Unionist Government had set up a Royal Commission to examine the Poor Laws in 1905. By the time it reported in 1909, there was little political interest in any party in a major overhauling of the system.

Numerous other reforms were also undertaken by the Liberal Governments and can be summarised as follows:

See page 421 for more on the Trades Disputes Act

- **'Trades Disputes Act'** in 1906 protected trades unions on strike from being sued by employers
- **'Workmen's Compensation Act'** in 1906 ensured all categories of worker were covered by compensation for accidents at work and extended protection to cover injury to health
- **'Merchant Shipping Act'** in 1906 brought in by Lloyd George provided tight controls on standards of food and accommodation on British Merchant Ships
- **'Coal Mines Act'** in 1908 introduced a maximum 8 hour day for miners
- **'Trade Boards Act'** in 1909 set up Boards to impose minimum wages in the so-called 'sweated trades' where low pay and long hours had long prevailed. Tailoring, box-making, chain-making and lace-making were initially covered. The act was widened to include more trades in 1913
- **'Shops Act'** in 1911 entitled shop assistants to one-half day off each week.

The overall impact of the Liberals' social reforms has often been criticised as 'too little, too late'. Left-wing historians tend to dismiss them as limited concessions aimed at propping up the capitalist system. The reality for people at the time was that by 1912, when the National Insurance provisions began to take effect, a very considerable boost had been given to the incomes of the poorest families. The combined effect of child welfare support, old age pensions, employment legislation, child allowances and National Insurance meant that a significant safety net had been established against poverty. Few poor families could fail to benefit from at least some aspect of this legislation. In particular, the relief to working-class budgets in supporting elderly relatives brought about by the introduction of Old Age Pensions should not be underestimated. It is not clear how the Liberals could have done much more at the time, given the prevailing constraints on taxation, and the fact that their philosophy was not socialism and did still recognise a role for individual enterprise and personal responsibility.

3 ⌐ THE CONSTITUTIONAL CRISIS, 1909–11

A *The Liberal Government and the House of Lords*

The origins of the constitutional crisis, which was triggered by Lloyd George's budget proposals of 1909, did not lie in reactionary opposition to 'New Liberalism'; for example, to the Government's welfare reforms. On the contrary, the Unionist leadership generally welcomed the welfare reforms and even promised to improve upon them if returned to office. The real roots of the crisis lay in the political powerlessness which the Unionists felt in the House of Commons after the 1906 general election. With only 157 MPs, the Unionists were almost irrelevant in the Lower House and it was not surprising that they considered how they might use their continued predominance in the Lords to try to redress this imbalance. The Unionist leader Balfour made a rather unwise comment in the heat of the electoral campaign, saying that 'the great Unionist Party should still control, whether in power or opposition, the destinies of this great Empire'. This was not intended as a commitment to blanket opposition to a future Liberal Government. In fact, it was aimed at the specific issue of Irish Home Rule. Balfour was only too aware that the power of the Lords needed to be used selectively and with caution, if it was to be effective. From 1906 to 1909, therefore, the targets chosen for obstruction by the Unionist peers were identified carefully, in the hope of extracting the maximum embarrassment for the Liberals whilst steering away from issues where the Government might secure popular support.

The first confrontation came in 1906 over the Government's proposed Education Bill. This Bill amounted to a political pay-off to the Nonconformists for their support following the Education Act of 1902 (see page 311). The Government felt indebted to its Nonconformist supporters and was committed to addressing their grievances, despite the fact that some members of the Cabinet privately accepted the value of the 1902 Act. The 1906 Education Bill proposed that all church schools should be taken over by the local authorities, who would appoint teachers without applying religious tests.

The provisions of this Education Bill angered the Anglicans as much as the 1902 Act had enraged the Nonconformists. Balfour had planned that controversial legislation should be opposed initially in the Commons and then amended to reach a compromise in the Lords. In this first test, however, the strategy failed since it proved impossible to hammer out a compromise which both sides could accept. Consequently, the Government was forced to withdraw the Bill, which they had seen as forming the centrepiece of their programme for the session. Two other major bills were rejected by the Lords in the period 1906 to 1908:

KEY ISSUE

Why did relations between the Liberal Government and the House of Lords become strained after 1906?

- a bill to end plural voting (i.e. the right to vote in more than one constituency) and
- a licensing bill aimed at further restrictions on the sale and consumption of alcohol.

This hardly amounted to a wholesale wrecking of the Government's legislative programme. On the contrary, the targets were carefully selected. Significantly, trade union reform in 1906 was allowed to pass, as were the social reforms detailed in the previous section.

The intention of the Unionists was to try to confuse and demoralise the Liberals and they were, to some extent, successful. By 1907, the Government was trying to decide whether or not to confront the peers. One major problem was the lack of a really popular cause with which to appeal to the electorate. The Education Bill was important to certain sections of the Liberal Party, but it was not a matter of great importance to the public at large. In 1907, therefore, Campbell-Bannerman did no more than introduce 'resolutions' into the Commons calling for limitations on the power of the Lords to delay, amend or veto legislation. These resolutions were naturally passed by the huge Liberal majority since they were supported not only by Liberals but also by Labour and the Irish Nationalists. They remained, however, no more than a warning shot at the Upper House. When the 1908 session of Parliament opened, reform of the House of Lords remained conspicuously absent from the Government's proposals.

It was not surprising that the Government failed to address the issue of the powers of the Lords in 1908, since the Cabinet was entirely undecided as what exactly to do. Some, like Campbell-Bannerman, simply wished to curb the power of the peers over legislation. However others, including Sir Edward Grey, preferred to change the composition of the Lords. Some moderate Unionist peers themselves were in favour of the latter course and there had even been a proposal from them to end automatic hereditary entry to the Lords during 1907. This proposition had been opposed by both the Government and the more right-wing Unionist peers, although for differing reasons. The right-wing peers opposed *any* interference with the Lords' powers or composition. The Government feared that reform of the composition of the Lords would make it harder, in the end, to justify limiting their legislative powers.

The political climate in 1907 and 1908 was hardly encouraging for the Liberals. Overall, the trend in by-election results was against them and most commentators expected a considerable Unionist revival when the next general election came. Despite the introduction of Old Age Pensions and child welfare reform, there was little improvement in the political fortunes of the Liberals by the beginning of 1909. The problem was that, however much children and the elderly deserved the Government's attention, neither group actually amounted to much in electoral terms. The Government, therefore, urgently needed something compelling with which to regain the political initiative. Fortunately for them, there was a very obvious issue upon which to make a stand.

B *The Budget of 1909*

The budget for 1909 was going to have to be a major reforming piece of legislation. There was no alternative to this because increasing expenditure on defence, along with increased spending on social welfare, meant that taxation had to be increased. Politically, the Government could not afford to cut back in either sector but nor could it fund both from the existing taxation arrangements. As Lloyd George became increasingly aware of the extent of the future budget deficits, so he and Asquith exerted increasing pressure on the rest of the Cabinet to agree to an extensive reform of taxation. It was an accepted constitutional practice that the House of Lords could not amend or reject financial legislation but, as rumours grew that the 1909 budget would contain radical proposals, so speculation mounted that the Lords might consider breaking with tradition on the grounds that the budget went beyond normal financial provisions. In the event, some of Asquith and Lloyd George's colleagues were less than enthusiastic about some of the proposals and there was a row within the Cabinet (which became public) over naval spending, which Lloyd George wanted to limit as far as possible. It was hardly the best background against which to launch a revival of the Government's fortunes and there is little doubt that, far from aiming to provoke confrontation, the budget was intended to strike enough of a balance to pass without causing a crisis with the Lords. This, however, proved to be a forlorn hope.

> ### KEY ISSUE
>
> *Why did the 1909 Budget lead to a Constitutional Crisis?*

The 1909 Budget

Lloyd George proposed to:

- **raise income tax** on incomes over £3000 per annum to 1s 2d (6p) from the standard rate of 9d (4p) while additionally bringing in an additional tax of 6d ($2^{1}/_{2}$p) in the £ on incomes over £5000 pa.
- **increase duties on spirits**, tobacco, liquor licenses and stamp duties
- **increase death duties** on estates valued between £5000 and £1 million
- **introduce land taxes** on (a) the increased value of land when it changed hands, (b) the annual value of land ($1^{1}/_{2}$d in £) and (c) the annual value of land leased to mining companies (1s in £)
- **set up a Road Fund** by putting taxes on petrol and introducing licenses for motor vehicles
- **introduce Child Allowances** at a rate of £10 a year for every child under the age of 16. This was payable to families with an annual income of less than £500.

RICH FARE.

The Giant Lloyd-Gorgibuster: "FEE, FI, FO, FAT,
I SMELL THE BLOOD OF A PLUTOCRAT;
BE HE ALIVE OR BE HE DEAD,
I'LL GRIND HIS BONES TO MAKE MY BREAD."

PICTURE 50
Cartoon depicting Lloyd George as a giant threatening the rich

Q

How reliable is this cartoon for an understanding of the 1909 budget? A 'Plutocrat' is a person who is powerful because of great wealth.

Concern about the budget and even opposition to it was more widespread than is generally appreciated in the traditional 'Peers versus the People' version of the constitutional crisis:

● many Liberals (including some in the Cabinet) had their doubts
● the Irish Nationalist MPs opposed the duty on spirits fearing it would damage the whisky export trade, which was vital to employment in Dublin especially
● the brewers and distillers were obviously outraged

- the motorists (not as large a lobby then, of course, as they would later become) were similarly unimpressed
- most of all, the landowners felt that they were being subjected to unfair treatment and they were particularly incensed by Lloyd George's intention to set up a Development Commission, one of whose tasks would be to carry out a comprehensive land valuation survey to provide the basis for calculating the new taxation on land. This seemed to be the thin end of a socialist wedge, which in future years could be used to attack wealth and force a redistribution of property on a significant scale.

Initially, Balfour and Lord Lansdowne (the Unionist leader in the House of Lords) did not intend that the Lords should go so far as to actually reject the budget. They thought in terms of extracting concessions which would undermine the budget and keep up the mounting pressure on the Government. This, however, was a miscalculation. Neither Balfour nor Lansdowne appreciated at first the limited room for manoeuvre which each side had. Lansdowne, in particular, underestimated the emotions which had been raised amongst the rank-and-file Unionist peers. A major reason for this was the fact that the Unionist leaders did not view the budget in quite the same way as their supporters. To the latter, the budget proposals were an outright attack on the rights of property; the former were much more concerned about the future political implications which the proposals raised for Unionist policies.

The crux of the problem was that, by 1909, Unionism had effectively been won over to **tariff reform**. One of the key arguments of the tariff reformers was that large-scale social reform could only be funded effectively through the money which would be raised through taxing imports. The Liberals' budget, by proposing a method of funding social reform whilst preserving free trade, therefore cut right to the heart of any popular appeal tariff reform might have. The Government knew this only too well and saw that this was a golden opportunity to underpin free trade once and for all and make the Unionists seem even more irrelevant. Thus the budget crisis of 1909 was in essence an extension of the Free Trade versus Protection debate and both sides believed that their political fortunes were at stake in its outcome. It was the Unionists who were in the more difficult position. Their case was difficult to put in a popular campaign since it involved some fairly complex arguments about the relationship between tariff reform, taxation and spending, on both social welfare and defence. The Government had the much easier task of presenting the issue as simply one of the selfishness of a privileged class. By-elections in the summer of 1909 showed a swing to the Liberals and underlined the fact that the Government was winning the argument in the country. Balfour and Lansdowne were increasingly driven into a corner. Surrender would split the party because of the expectations of resistance which had been raised. Resistance could only lead to a constitutional crisis. In the event the matter was taken out of their hands since Lansdowne effectively lost control of the Unionist peers. In

tariff reform was the policy of protecting home-produced food and industrial goods by imposing duties on imports from abroad. For further explanation, see pages 314–15 in Chapter 10

November 1909, the Lords rejected the budget and Asquith immediately asked for a dissolution of Parliament.

The general election of January 1910 produced results which were unsatisfactory for almost everybody. The Liberals won 275 seats, the Unionists 273 and Labour won 40; only the Irish could take much encouragement since, with 82 seats, they now held the balance of power. The Liberals could continue in office but only as a minority government. Their immediate problem with the Budget was solved because there was still a majority for it in the Commons. The Irish were prepared to support it in spite of their concerns about whisky duty. Their support, however, came at a price. They wanted Home Rule for Ireland. However, since a Home Rule Bill stood no chance of passing an unreformed House of Lords, they wanted a Parliament Bill to limit the Lords' powers to be passed first. In the circumstances, the Liberal Government had little option but to agree to this. Ordinary Liberal MPs were demanding as much anyway. In view of the result of the election, the Lords had no choice but to pass the budget, but the battle had now moved on to the question of their powers and most peers were set on a confrontation.

C *The Reform of the House of Lords, 1911*

KEY ISSUE

Should the outcome of the Constitutional Crisis be seen as a success or a failure for the Liberal Government?

The Parliament Bill which the Government introduced in 1910 contained no surprises. It stated that:

- the Lords could not reject or amend financial legislation
- there would be a limit of two rejections or amendments on other legislation in successive sessions within the life of a Parliament
- the maximum duration of a parliament (i.e. the length of time between general elections) would be reduced from seven to five years. This was actually a concession to the Lords since it reduced the time a government with a majority had to pass laws before facing a new election.

In essence, this meant that the Lords could expect to delay legislation for a minimum period of two years, assuming that the proposals were immediately passed again by the Commons after each rejection, and as long as there was no general election in the interim. The Lords resisted this to the bitter end, but to no avail. The death of King Edward VII in May 1910 gave them a temporary respite since Asquith was anxious not to appear to be pressing the new King, George V, too soon on the question of creating new peers. However, the delay was brief and, by the end of 1910, Asquith was ready to call a second election, this time armed with the mandate to create as many new peers as might be necessary to see the Parliament Bill through.

The result of the general election of December 1910 produced no real change in the political balance. The Irish and Labour both advanced marginally to 84 and 42 seats respectively; The Liberals and Unionists tied on 272 seats each. This left the Government in a position to force through the bill. In August 1911, after Asquith had publicly threatened a mass creation of peers, the Parliament Bill was finally passed. Even then, some of the moderate (or more responsible) Unionist peers had to be drafted in to vote for the Government in order to ensure that the bill was not voted down by the 'last-ditchers', some of whom by now had so lost their grip on reality that they preferred to bring the Lords to a 'glorious death' rather than relent.

The constitutional crisis was a classic case of political miscalculations which led to political passions running out of control. This was most obviously the case on the Unionist side, but the Government had also miscalculated the impact which the budget would have. Asquith was eventually forced into threatening a mass-creation of peers which was very much against his inclination. Lloyd George raised passions to fever pitch during the summer of 1909 with highly provocative speeches designed to whip up support for the budget and put pressure on the Lords. However, despite his revolutionary utterances, Lloyd George was not intent on destroying the wealthy classes. On the contrary, he was employing his considerable abilities to the task of becoming wealthy himself! During 1910 the political leaders on both sides had tried, behind the scenes, to get a grip on the situation and restore some order to the political chaos. Between June and November 1910, a series of meetings was held between the Liberal and Unionist leaders aimed at finding a compromise. This process, known as the 'Constitutional Conference', failed in the end to find a solution but it was a sign that both sides had realised that things were getting out of hand. In August, Lloyd George proposed a coalition government be set up, with an agenda covering all the major issues of the day – economic, social and constitutional – so as to seek consensus solutions for them all. Balfour was much attracted to this idea in theory but doubted whether it was practical given the political climate. Asquith was also interested, but both leaders found a hostile response within their parties and the scheme came to nothing.

The outcome of the constitutional crisis was scarcely revolutionary.

- Its most immediate effect was to make the Liberal Government more dependent on the Irish Nationalists.
- It did not result in a flood of legislation needing to be forced through the Lords since the Government's reforms since 1906 had already been extensive.
- Its chief victim was Balfour, who paid the penalty for a failed campaign which he had never wanted in the first place! Late in 1911, faced with mounting criticism of his leadership, he decided upon a dignified stepping down rather than awaiting the inevitable and distasteful coup. He was succeeded by the relatively unknown Andrew Bonar Law, who had only entered Parliament in 1900, and whose chief qualification at that point was that he was a compromise candidate when other leading contenders might have split the party.
- The crisis cost the Liberals their overall majority and exposed them to the demands of the Irish Nationalists. The reputations of their leaders, particularly Asquith and Lloyd George, were enhanced, but

the necessity for dealing with the question of Irish Home Rule meant that the Government was bound to face a new constitutional crisis almost immediately.

It should be remembered, however, that Home Rule was not a new policy for the Liberals. In that sense it had not been forced on them by the Irish Nationalists – it had been an official party commitment for over 20 years.

See pages 285–7 on the Home Rule crisis

4 ↩ THE LABOUR PARTY, 1906–14

The title the 'Labour Party', was formally adopted in 1906. Following the General Election (see pages 403–4) the MPs elected as LRC candidates, Miners Union candidates and Independents (in effect, all those sitting specifically to represent working-class interests), informally agreed to act as a single parliamentary party. Even so, the Miners did not officially merge with the Labour Party until 1908 and, when they did so, it was seen as marking a clear change in the political weight of the party as the cartoon (Picture 51) on page 422 suggests.

The role, and the extent of the influence, of the Labour Party in the Parliament of 1906–10 is controversial:

- mainstream 'Labour' historians tend to emphasise the importance of the Labour Party by suggesting that it encouraged, or even forced, the Liberals to adopt policies directly favourable to the working class
- more 'Marxist' historians see the Party as abandoning socialist principles and collaborating with the capitalist employers
- other historians argue that the Party was not strong enough to have any decisive influence on the decisions taken by the Liberal Government.

KEY ISSUE

How important was the Labour Party during this period?

It is clear that the Liberal Government was committed to a policy of extensive reforms when it came to power. It is equally clear that the official policy of the Labour Party differed little in essence from that of the Liberal Party. The Electoral Pact arrangement of 1903, even though it was a secret and informal agreement, meant that both parties' manifestos for the 1906 General Election had been designed to ensure reasonable acceptability to a range of potential voters who, in some vital constituencies, were expected to offer their support to a candidate who would, in effect, be representing both parties. The subsequent role of the Labour Party has therefore been discussed primarily (and logically) in relation to those reforms which most directly affected the interests of the working class. The problem with this is that *so much* of the Liberals' legislation was centred on the welfare of vulnerable and disadvantaged groups that it is difficult to establish whether the Labour Party MPs had any decisive effect on the legislation involved. The fact that they supported it, encouraged it or even took a part in its formulation is not in itself evidence that such reforms would not have taken place without them. The following key examples illustrate the point.

See pages 373–4 in Chapter 12 for the Lib-Lab Pact of 1903

● **The Trades Disputes Act 1906.** This Act is often seen as direct evidence for the influence of the Labour Party since it changed the law to protect Trade Unions involved in strike action from being sued for damages by employers. Thus, it reversed the Taff Vale verdict of 1901 in which the Railway Union had been successfully sued by the Taff Vale Railway Company for damages (i.e. loss of trade) caused by its members during a strike. However, the need for a change in the law had been accepted by both the Liberal and Unionist parties in the years after 1901. The Balfour Government initially rejected calls for a change in the law but then had a rethink and set up a Royal Commission to look into the issue. The only doubt thereafter was whether the law should be reformed to allow *full* or only *partial* protection for union funds. The Liberal Prime Minister, Campbell-Bannerman, favoured full protection. However, due to the concerns of other cabinet ministers, the Liberal Government originally proposed a bill offering partial immunity for unions. The Labour Party countered this with its own bill offering full immunity. Campbell-Bannerman, entirely on his own initiative, then committed the Government to accepting the Labour version, which totally accorded with his own view and indeed the views of many Liberal backbenchers, who had actually championed such an option during the General Election campaign.

● **The Education (Provision of Meals) Act 1906.** Again, the pressure for such a direct aid for malnourished schoolchildren was much greater before 1906 than is generally acknowledged. The Balfour Government, responding to pressure inside and outside parliament, had issued an order for 'destitute' schoolchildren to be fed through the Poor Law, but this proved difficult to administer. In any case the term 'destitute' strictly only covered those children who were totally without means of support. The Liberals favoured direct legislation to address the problem more widely than that, but had not devised a specific proposal at the time of the General Election. When a newly-elected Labour MP brought forward a Private Member's Bill authorising Local Education Authorities to feed 'needy' children using rate-money, the Liberal Government seized on the proposal and made it Government policy. A Labour initiative most certainly, but hardly imposed on the Government.

See page 407 on the Education Act of 1906

The picture that therefore emerges tends to support the view that while the Labour Party did put pressure on the Liberal Government between 1906 and 1910, the Government's responses were dictated by its own agenda. This picture is reinforced by the fact that the Labour Party itself was a broadly-based organisation with no clear commitment to a full programme of socialism. In 1908, Ben Tillett, a member of the Independent Labour Party, which still maintained a distinct identity within the Party as a whole, published a pamphlet entitled '*Is the Parliamentary Labour Party a Failure?*' which criticised the moderate line the Party was adopting. This was followed up in 1910 by an even more critical, alternative election manifesto, '*Let us Reform the*

KEY ISSUE

Why did the Labour Party make only modest progress in the years to 1914?

PICTURE 51
*'Forced Fellowship', a Punch
cartoon of 1909 commenting on
relations between Liberals and
Labour*

Q

*What message is
this cartoon projecting?
How accurate is its
representation of the
relationship between
Liberalism and Labour?*

FORCED FELLOWSHIP.

SUSPICIOUS-LOOKING PARTY. "ANY OBJECTION TO MY COMPANY, GUV'NOR? I'M AGOIN' YOUR WAY"—(*aside*) "AND FURTHER."

PICTURE 52
Cartoon 'Cause and Effect'

Q

*To what extent
do you agree with Keir
Hardie, the Labour
leader?*

Keir Hardie: 'Look at that list, Mr Bull — not one of them would have been passed if it hadn't been for our Labour Party!'

Labour Party. This was again the work of the ILP, which called for a shared platform with the overtly Marxist Social Democratic Federation. Divisions in the Labour Party ran deep. Issues such as the female suffrage created significant problems. The idea of women voting was not popular amongst many trade unionists. Working-class men were generally among the least sympathetic to the idea. Hostility towards the militant suffragettes was probably greater amongst these groups than any other. However, the more committed socialists (especially Keir Hardie of the ILP) were passionately committed to the cause of Women's suffrage. In the General Election of 1906, serious disputes arose in some constituencies over whether LRC candidates should accept help from suffragette activists in their election campaigns.

A *Was there a decline in Labour Party influence after 1910?*

From 1910 the situation at Westminster changed dramatically and it did not favour the position of the Labour Party. In the General Election of 1910, the Labour Party fielded only 70 candidates. This was partly the result of fears about financial problems resulting from the Osborne Judgement of 1909, which had made Trade Union contributions to political parties illegal. This was reversed in 1913 by the Trade Union Act but, in the meantime, the Labour Party faced a cash-flow crisis. The result of the election was that 40 Labour MPs were elected – all from constituencies where no Liberal candidate had stood. This rose by two in the second General Election that year, but Labour had still fallen back in overall strength from 1906. Thereafter, between 1910 and 1914, Labour candidates failed to hold seats in a series of by-elections so that, by 1914, the Party had only 36 MPs.

Perhaps even more serious, in some ways, for the Labour Party, was the ending of the Liberal Party's overall majority. Before 1910, the Liberal Government had enjoyed more or less complete freedom of action in terms of developing its policies. The emergence of 'New Liberalism' made many in the Liberal Party sympathetic to those they regarded as natural allies. However, from 1910, the Irish National Party held the balance of power in the House of Commons. Twice the size of the Labour Party in terms of MPs, it could now exercise a more decisive pressure on the Liberal Government than the Labour Party had ever done. The new focus on Liberal-INP relations, House of Lords reform and Irish Home Rule, moved the political agenda away from the natural territory of the Labour Party. The extent of the Liberal reforms up to 1911 had in any case removed (or at least reduced the urgency of) many of the issues which had united Liberals and Labour in 1906. On the eve of World War I, the Labour Party was making encouraging progress in *local elections* and securing control of some local authorities but, on the national level, the future of the Labour Party seemed far less assured.

Q

Why did the Labour Party have less influence on the Government agenda after 1910?

5 ⌐ INDUSTRIAL UNREST, 1910–14

The years between 1910 and the outbreak of World War I in 1914 saw a huge increase in trade union membership from 2.5 million to 4 million. This was a trend which would continue strongly during the war and into the post-war period. The period from 1910 to 1914 was also marked by a wave of strikes. The increased militancy can be attributed to the following factors:

- from around 1900 the value of real wages was gradually falling due to increases in the cost of living
- from 1910 there was a fall in the levels of unemployment which reduced the 'fear factor' amongst many workers and they became more willing to confront the employers
- prices rose particularly steeply in 1911–12
- as living standards either remained static or worsened for manual workers, the middle and upper classes were actually improving their position, leading to increased class hostility.

The first major, violent confrontation came in the South Wales coal-field in the autumn of 1910. A dispute arose over payments for miners working difficult seams of coal. Militancy had been on the increase in South Wales for a number of years and the general mood of bitterness soon resulted in a rash of strikes. It was not long before confrontations between strikers and the authorities produced violence. During rioting in Tonypandy in 1911, a man died from injuries he had sustained in a fight with local police officers and many others suffered less serious injuries. The Home Secretary, Winston Churchill, felt that the seriousness of the situation required that army units be drafted in to support the local police. This decision elevated the Tonypandy Riots to mythological status in working-class history. The wave of strikes went on for ten months before ending in defeat for the miners. This, however, was only the start of the unrest.

KEY ISSUE

How do you explain the extent of industrial unrest?

In June 1911, the Seamen's Union went on strike. Dock workers and railwaymen came out on strike in sympathy. In August 1911, two strikers were shot dead by troops in Liverpool after a general riot had broken out. In the same week, troops shot dead two men who were part of a crowd attacking a train at Llanelli in South Wales. In 1912 the first ever national pit strike began, lasting from February until April with the miners demanding a national minimum wage. The Government responded to this with a compromise, passing the Minimum Wage Act for the mining industry. This set up local boards in mining districts to fix minimum wages for miners working on difficult seams. In the same year, there were also strikes in the London docks and amongst transport workers. In 1913, there were strikes in the metal-working industries of the Midlands and a major strike of transport workers in Dublin. The sheer numbers of people involved in these industrial disputes was unprecedented. Since the late 1890s, more and more unskilled workers had been drawn into trade unionism. By 1910, around 17% of workers were in trade unions and the unrest did not act as a deterrent;

quite the contrary, by 1914 the figure had risen to 25%. The rise in female membership of unions was one of the most remarkable features of the period. In 1904, there were 126 000 women trade union members, the result of a very rapid rise over the past 15 years. However, by 1913, there were 431 000, making up 10% of all trade unionists.

6 ～ BRITISH POLITICS ON THE EVE OF WORLD WAR I

A *Confrontation and consensus*

Much of this chapter has been concerned with confrontation. Some of the issues which led to confrontations are discussed in other chapters (e.g. Ireland in Chapter 9 and the campaign for Women's Suffrage in Chapter 13). In particular, however, the relationship between Liberalism and Unionism seems to have been one of unremitting hostility over a period of years. The raising of the issue of tariff reform by Joseph Chamberlain and its eventual adoption by the Unionist Party, seemed to polarise party principles into the opposite corners of free trade and protection. The constitutional crisis confirmed that division and led into the bitter period of confrontation surrounding the Ulster crisis of 1912–14. On the eve of World War I, therefore, it would seem, at first sight, that the two main political parties had never been further apart in their policies and rarely more hostile in their attitude to each other.

> **Q**
>
> *How far apart were the Conservatives and Liberals in this period?*

The bitter climate of party politics was real enough. It worried many contemporaries who saw in it the seeds of the disintegration of the political system. Few could have predicted, in the middle of 1914, that a war would soon engulf Europe and, temporarily at least, make the issues over which these divisions had emerged irrelevant. Lloyd George's proposal for a coalition government, dismissed as impractical in 1910, became a reality in 1915 under the pressure of war. Coalitions were to rule the country for 21 out of the next 30 years. Of course, the circumstances which brought these coalitions about and then kept them together were exceptional, but the ease with which politicians of all parties accepted them reveals something deeper about the nature of politics in the period before World War I.

The reality was that, underneath the apparent hostility, there was a greater degree of consensus than the confrontational atmosphere would suggest. This was particularly true of the leaders of the parties. Their public clashes seemed to be the essence of the highly-charged political atmosphere. Yet all the time, behind the scenes, these very leaders were to be found seeking compromises and conciliations which were often wrecked, not by their own divisions or hostilities, but by the nature of the problems they were seeking to resolve. For example, during the constitutional crisis, the failure to reach a compromise was largely due to the fact that neither side could afford, politically, to be seen to be giving in rather than to the existence of a genuinely unbridgeable gulf. During the Ulster crisis, it was the entrenched posi-

See pages 285–87 on the Irish Home Rule crisis

tions of the Irish Nationalist and Ulster Unionist leaders, rather than those of Asquith and Bonar Law, which made progress in the 1914 negotiations impossible.

On a broad range of issues there was a remarkable degree of consensus amongst the major politicians on both sides:

- The Unionists were more willing to consider social reform than is often supposed and, after 1903, free traders and tariff reformers within the Unionist Party sought to outbid each other with promises of social reform.
- Once the economy went into a slump between 1907 and 1910 the Unionists, by now committed to some kind of new deal on tariffs, linked their policy to social reform and tried to outbid the Liberals on the issue.
- The desire to preserve *laissez-faire* values in social policy was, if anything, stronger amongst the more traditional Liberals than it was amongst the Unionists.
- The demand for female suffrage found both supporters and opponents amongst the Liberals and Unionists and both sides were ultimately more concerned about the practical political problems that the issue posed than they were about the moral principle.

Even the division between Liberalism and Unionism over protection and free trade was not so clear-cut as it appeared. The support of the Liberal leadership for free trade was a political necessity. Privately, leaders such as Asquith and Lloyd George knew that there was a case to be made for the reform of fiscal policy: specifically, of the methods by which government revenue was obtained. The budget of 1909 was barely sufficient to meet the projected spending requirements of immediate policies. Even with Lloyd George's 'unprecedented' tax increases, the Government still required a £3 million transfer from the Sinking Fund (the money set aside for paying off the National Debt) in order to balance the books. It was perfectly obvious that some other method of raising revenue would be needed in the longer term if further social reform was to be contemplated. The Unionist answer was tariff reform. The socialist solution was never an option for the Liberals (even the Labour Party leaders could not bring themselves to face that fully!), therefore they had to be prepared to think about that which was officially 'unthinkable'. Lloyd George once remarked to a close colleague that he did not regard free trade as 'sacred' and his inclusion of the question of tariffs as part of his agenda for a coalition government in 1910 was a recognition of this reality.

The picture that emerges of political life in the period before World War I is one in which the two main parties were both as divided internally as they were from each other. This is especially true of the relationships between the party leaders and their respective followers. Both Liberal and Unionist leaders had to face the problem of trying to reconcile conflicting attitudes within their parliamentary parties and in the constituencies at large. Frequently, it was not simply a case of trying to accommodate differing opinions, but also of trying to force party members to abandon their prejudices and face up to political realities.

It is hardly surprising, in these circumstances, that the party leaders frequently found it easier to deal with each other, than to satisfy the demands of their own supporters.

B *The condition of the Liberal Party in 1914*

Was the Liberal Party doomed to decline in 1914?

1. **G. R. Dangerfield:** *The Strange Death of Liberal England.* In 1936, at a point where the fortunes of the Liberal Party had sunk low and its future existence was a matter of some doubt, Dangerfield, in this famous book, put forward an explanation for the decline of the once great party. According to Dangerfield, the crucial period in the Liberal decline was 1911–14, following the constitutional crisis, during which basic inadequacies and limitations of liberalism had made the Government incapable of governing effectively. This view was far from gaining universal acceptance in the years that followed; indeed many historians regarded Dangerfield as entertaining but little more. The general trend of studies of the Liberal Party was usually to look for alternative explanations for the party's decline; in particular the view emerged that decline had set in much *earlier* than Dangerfield supposed. The idea that it might *not* have been in decline before 1914 was not seriously considered.

2. **Trevor Wilson:** *The Downfall of the Liberal Party.* The topic became controversial, however, with the appearance, in 1966, of Wilson's book which argued that the decline of the Liberal Party was the result of the damaging split that developed during World War I between Asquith and Lloyd George (see the following section). According to this view, the Liberal Party remained an effective political force in 1914 and could have gone on indefinitely as a major party competing with the Conservatives for power. Until the publication of Wilson's book, the decline of the Liberal Party had received little attention from Labour historians since it had been assumed that the fall of the party could be satisfactorily explained by the Dangerfield thesis or the various alternatives and, more importantly, as the natural result of the rise of the Labour Party. The impact of World War I had been regarded as simply the accelerator of a natural process of political evolution, or natural selection, in which the Labour Party, as the fittest instrument for advancing social reform and representing working-class aspirations, had inherited the role of opposition to the forces of conservatism.

Following the publication of the 'Wilson thesis', a number of other historians began to develop the argument that the Liberal Party still had a bright future in British politics on the eve of the War. These historians, for the most part, concentrated on the impact of 'New Liberalism' in order to argue that the party had freed itself of the limitations which had been imposed on it by Gladstonian principles, and had become a party with a relevant message and electoral appeal in an increasingly democratic and class-based political climate. The clear implication of this view was that the Labour Party was destined either to remain a minor third force on the political fringe or to be absorbed into the Liberal Party. Such a concept naturally incensed those Labour historians for whom the destiny of the Labour Party was an unquestionable inevitability.

3. **Ross McKibbin**: *The Evolution of the Labour Party 1910–1924*. A series of studies, intended to counter Wilson's 'heresy', culminated, in 1974, in the publication of McKibbin's book which emphasised the extent to which the Labour Party was a competitor, rather than a collaborator, with the Liberals and to insist that Labour was making genuine inroads into Liberal support. This argument rests upon analyses of Labour progress in local elections during the period 1911 to 1914 and on studies of local constituency level politics which show that rivalry between the Liberals and Labour at local level was often intense.

Throughout the debate over the condition of the Liberal Party in 1914, the less ideologically committed historians have also contributed to the debate about the long-term survival of the Liberal Party by questioning the strength of enthusiasm for the principles of New Liberalism amongst traditional Liberal supporters and party activists. Supporters of the future viability of the Liberal Party have tried, in their turn, to counter the attacks on the Wilson thesis by arguing that, but for the outbreak of war in 1914, the Liberals would have sustained or even increased their electoral appeal. Certainly there is nothing in the attitudes of the Liberal Party itself to suggest that it was lacking in confidence or living in fear of the Labour Party. After all, in 1913, the Liberal Government passed a Trade Union Act permitting Trade Unions to subscribe funds for political purposes, a reversal of the Osborne Judgement of 1909, which had done so much to damage Labour Party funds. This was hardly the action of a government faced with a dangerous rival.

There is no doubt that the Liberal Government intended to embark upon a major political offensive in the period before World War I. It was Lloyd George who supplied the strategy. In 1912 he began to revive the idea of land reform. The intention was to offer a comprehensive package of reforms, including a guaranteed minimum wage for agricultural workers with rent tribunals to ensure fair rents and, possibly, even arrange for deductions to be made directly from rental income to fund the minimum wage. Lloyd George also intended to include urban land in the reforms, though he had no specific ideas for this more complex area. Initially, he merely indicated that he hoped that rural land reform would help to halt the flow of migrants from the land to the towns and thus help to raise urban wages. Lloyd George intended the land campaign to be the centrepiece of the Liberal revival which would carry them through the next general election, due by the end of 1915 at the latest. He set up a Land Enquiry Committee to provide detailed information and proposals. The committee, however, was not an independent group. It was a political body appointed and directed by Lloyd George and financed privately by some of his wealthy political associates.

The land campaign was specifically intended to damage the Unionists electorally. It aimed to firm up Liberal support in the rural constituencies as well as play on the sympathies of the urban working class. It was also intended to increase divisions amongst the Unionists, who found it difficult to respond with land reform initiatives of their own, without risking upsetting at least some of their supporters. However, the need for some kind of initiative of this kind was urgent. By 1912 it was apparent that land taxation as envisaged in the 1909 budget was never going to raise the amount of revenue needed to fund even the existing provision of social welfare, let alone any extension of it. The National Insurance scheme was far from popular with many sections of the working classes, especially the lower paid such as agricultural labourers, who saw the contributions as a burden. Liberalism desperately needed a new electoral appeal and, by 1914, the evidence of by-elections seemed to suggest that the land campaign was having the desired effect. Moreover, the Unionists were openly divided between those supporting the Unionist Social Reform Committee, who wished to respond to Lloyd George's campaign with their own radical proposals, and members of the reactionary 'Land Union' who were still hoping to commit the party to the repeal of the 1909 land taxes.

Ultimately, the question of the electoral strength and future viability of the Liberal Party in 1914, remains a matter of historical judgement upon which historians are bound to disagree. Because of World War I, the effect of the land campaign must remain a matter of speculation. Its impact in a general election was never put to the test. Similarly, it cannot be certain that the progress made by the Labour Party before 1914, at local level, provides a genuine guide to its likely fortunes in a general election. All that is certain is that success in local elections is not a sure indicator that similar success would be sustained in a general election. After all the Labour Party lost a series of parliamentary by-elections between 1910 and 1914 which reduced their seats to 36 by the eve of World War I. On balance there would appear to be no conclusive evidence to suggest that the Liberals were already in irreversible decline in 1914. Even leading members of the Labour Party, such as Ramsay MacDonald, did not rule out an ultimate alliance with the Liberals at that stage. Similarly, the land campaign clearly shows that the Liberals were capable of developing a significant new initiative in matters of social and economic policy.

7 ~ THE IMPACT OF WORLD WAR I, 1914–18

A *The political consequences*

The question of Britain's entry into the War in August 1914 was divisive for the two main British parties, the Liberals and the Unionists. It was most divisive of all for the Labour Party.

KEY ISSUE

Why did World War I have such a crucial effect on the Liberal and Labour Parties?

- The **Liberal Party** contained significant numbers of people with pacifist instincts who opposed the idea of war on moral grounds. These people had to decide whether to sacrifice their views for the national interest or stick to their principles. Two cabinet ministers resigned on these grounds. There were also some Liberals who had long admired Germany as a modern state with an advanced system of social welfare. For them, the declaration of war was a blow. Most Liberals, however, were suspicious of German militarism and disliked the German constitution, which gave a lot of direct power to the Emperor and his Chancellor. On the whole, Liberals were able to support the war, but the eventual methods of fighting it, 'Total War' as it became known, with conscription into the armed forces and extensive intervention in economic affairs, became very difficult for Liberals to accept.

- The **Conservative Party** was the most united in its support for the war, but it still contained a significant minority, including some at a high level, who felt that war against Germany was a mistake. These Conservatives saw Germany, with its strongly authoritarian system of government in which the Kaiser held real power, as a bastion against revolution. Equally, the impact on economic and financial affairs, given that Germany was Britain's biggest trade partner, was a source of concern.

- The **Labour Party** was the most bitterly divided of all. Pacifism was strong within the party and many others felt that the war was essentially a capitalist conflict in which the working classes had little or nothing to gain. This view stemmed from the Marxist idea that war and imperialism were simply devices of the ruling classes to prop up declining capitalism. Despite the influence of pacifism and Marxism, however, there was also a strong patriotic response, particularly prevalent among some of the Trade Union leaders, which argued that ideology must take second place to national danger.

Initially the Liberal Government aimed to continue in office to conduct the war along traditional lines, which meant raising volunteer armies and relying on the free market to purchase the war supplies needed for the armed forces. The Conservatives agreed to support the Government as a 'loyal opposition' for the duration of the conflict. Direct opposition came only from a minority of the more outspoken Irish Nationalist MPs and a small group of dissident Labour MPs – even this opposition was fairly low-key. Since the press also decided to suspend political hostilities, the political *status quo* seemed set to be maintained. However, it quickly became apparent that the Government could not meet the demands of the war simply by relying on the existing system. By early 1915, there was an acute shortage of munitions of all kinds and especially artillery shells. The 'shell scandal' led to the press threatening to withdraw its support and publicly expose the shortages. The Conservatives said that if this happened they would have no alternative but to also condemn the Government. The result was that, in May 1915, Asquith and the senior Liberals agreed to form a coalition government in which the leading Conservatives took cabinet posts along with one member of the Labour Party.

This arrangement, in turn, might well have served to protect the status quo so long as the war lasted. However, in December 1916, the coalition foundered. Asquith had for months been prey to depression and excessive alcohol consumption. Shattered by the death of his son on the western front, he became a pathetic shadow of the once brilliant politician he had been. His inability to provide adequate leadership led to a move within the coalition, not to oust him from the premiership as such, but to hand over the day-to-day running of the war to a new small committee headed by Lloyd George. Lloyd George had been given the job of Minister of Munitions in the 1915 coalition and had made such a success of it that he was now seen on all sides as the most dynamic and effective war politician the nation possessed. Asquith refused to accept the figurehead role allotted to him in this proposal and this forced a crisis in which Lloyd George and several other cabinet ministers threatened to resign. In the end, Asquith himself resigned and Lloyd George became Prime Minister. Asquith went into opposition supported by roughly two-thirds of the Liberal Party. It was a conflict which was to destroy the Liberal Party's position in the British political system and allow the Labour Party to emerge as the natural party of opposition to the Conservatives.

B *Women and the war*

One political issue which was effectively resolved by the war was the question of the female suffrage. In July 1915, the Women's Social and Political Union (WSPU) organised a great rally to demonstrate women's support for the war effort. Following the rally, Mrs. Pankhurst met Lloyd George, who was by then Minister of Munitions, to demand a fuller role for women in the war. As a result the following agreements were reached:

- the WSPU would suspend their demand for female suffrage for the time being
- women would be allowed into virtually all forms of employment, including munitions production
- fair minimum wage rates would be set
- on certain types of work where pay was determined by output, women would get equal pay with men.

The vital role played by women in the war effort in the years that followed transformed many perceptions of women and their fitness for the parliamentary vote. Women engaged in many new forms of employment which had hitherto been considered only suitable for men. In the munitions industry, the dangers of the work resulted in many casualties. In

PICTURE 53
Women delivering coal during the war

one incident in a munitions factory in 1916, over 50 people were killed, most of them women. In such circumstances, resistance to the idea of the female suffrage crumbled away. For example, Asquith, one of the bitterest opponents of the idea before the war, announced his conversion to the idea of women's political rights in 1917. Though some historians have recently questioned the importance of the war in bringing forward the parliamentary vote for women, the evidence to support the case remains compelling. It is true that some moves for conciliatory discussions between the Government and supporters of the women's suffrage were in prospect just before the war, but evidence that the Liberals were prepared to put the female suffrage on their official agenda is highly speculative. The war was critical in overcoming the objections of those who felt that allowing any significant female suffrage was giving in to violence. In any case, women's votes were not the only issue. The war also overcame the last remaining objections to full voting rights for men. In 1918 an Act for substantially extending the right to vote was passed.

See pages 395–7 for a fuller discussion of Women and the War

- All men over the age of 21 became entitled to vote.
- Men over the age of 19 who had seen active service in the war got the vote for the next general election.
- Women over 30 became entitled to vote – the later age justified mainly so as to overcome any lingering prejudice and ensure that there was minimal opposition to the passage of the bill. Any such extensive proposal for the female suffrage – pre-war – would have been unthinkable.

Although women had not achieved political equality with men, this was not long delayed. In 1928, the Conservative Government introduced legislation to give women the vote at 21.

C *The Social and Economic Impact*

As seen above, the war had a significant effect on the political perception of women. This was, in effect, a social change as well. Women worked with men on more equal terms than ever before and became more financially and personally independent than ever before. With men away at the front, wives and mothers became the decision-makers in the home – even if they had not been so previously! Class distinctions began to blur. The upper classes had to 'rough it' comparatively as they were deprived of the vast retinues of servants to which they were accustomed. Girls went into war work rather than domestic service – not only was the pay better, but it was a national duty. At the front, men from different social classes shared a common experience of horror and hardship. The disastrous mismanagement of the war by the military elite led to despair and anger in equal proportions. Unquestioning acceptance by the lower classes of deference to their social superiors was at an end – it might be accepted, but it would be questioned. It would be absurd to suggest that class harmony in adversity ran deep or that deeply-rooted social prejudices were overturned. It is fair to say that, after the war, many social barriers and conventions were readopted or at least reimposed. However, nothing could wholly eradicate the social effects of over four years of total war. As A. J. P. Taylor observed:

KEY ISSUE

In what areas did war have the most dramatic impact?

'The First World War cut deep into the consciousness of modern man'. After it, nothing could ever really be the same.

What was true in the social sense was even truer when it came to the sphere of finance and the economy. If social change was hesitant and variable, the economic impact was bold and thorough. It quickly became apparent in 1914 that a modern war could not be fought using the *laissez-faire* assumptions which had dominated the nineteenth century. Initially the Government passed a Defence of the Realm Act which gave it control of the armaments factories but little was done to actually take control of output. The resulting shell shortages led to a drastic rethink which enabled Lloyd George to rapidly build munitions production. Government intervention went much further, however, than just munitions. To fight a 'total war' the whole population and the entire economic resources of the nation had to be mobilised. Vast sums of money had to be raised and deployed. Labour had to be directed and controlled. Output had to be specified and delivered on time. To achieve victory the financial and economic life of the nation had to be planned. To be effective, planning had to be supported and carried through by state power. In 1915 a new Defence of the Realm Act gave the Government virtually total control of the labour force and the economic resources of the country. Also in 1915, the trades unions, in return for guarantees on wages and conditions, reached an accommodation with Lloyd George, called the 'Treasury Agreements', in which they agreed to a no-strikes arrangement so long as the war lasted. They also agreed to override the usual restrictive working practices, which protected workers' jobs, in the interests of efficiency while the war lasted. Vast amounts of government money were pumped into every aspect of war production. From being a largely food-importing nation in 1914, Britain became 80% self-sufficient in food by 1918. Mining was effectively nationalised during the war. Controls were imposed on wages, employment conditions, profits and prices. Such a massive transformation of the economy could not be wholly reversed at the end of the war. Even though there was initially an attempt to restore pre-war conditions, post-war governments found themselves increasingly compelled to intervene in economic matters.

8 ↪ BIBLIOGRAPHY

ARTICLES

Trevor Fisher 'The Strange Death of Liberal England: Whatever happened to the Liberal Party', *Modern History Review*, November 1999, provides a useful summary of the historiographical debate.

E. H. H. Green 'The People's Budget of 1909', *Modern History Review*, February 1999. This gives a good, detailed analysis of the issues surrounding this key development.

BOOKS FOR AS/A LEVEL STUDENTS

Robert Pearce and Roger Stearn *Government and Reform 1815–1918*, Access to History series, Hodder & Stoughton, 2000, Chapter 7, on the period 1906 to 1914, gives detailed and very readable coverage of the constitutional crisis.

Duncan Watts *Whigs, Radicals and Liberals 1815–1914*, Access to History series, Hodder & Stoughton, 2002. Chapter 6 on 'Liberalism 1894–1914', has useful sections on New Liberalism and the Social Reforms. Chapter 7 is a summary of the whole period from 1815, finishing with some very worthwhile discussion on the state of the Liberal Party by 1914 and the challenge represented by the Labour Party.

Michael Lynch *Lloyd George and the Liberal Dilemma*, Personalities and Powers series, Hodder & Stoughton, 1993. Chapters 5 and 6 are particularly useful but give Chapter 1 a try – this has an interesting presentation of the wider political context. Of course, this book goes well beyond the period and focuses on Lloyd George's personal role.

FURTHER READING

J. Feuchtwanger *Democracy and Empire: Britain 1865–1914*, Edward Arnold, 1985. The last three chapters relate to this period and are stimulating and challenging reading. More able students with a strong interest in the subject can expect a rich reward for their efforts.

Robert Blake *The Conservative Party from Peel to Major*, Fontana Press, 1996. Chapters 5 and 6 provide excellent coverage of the Unionist years from the 1890s to 1914. Anyone proposing any kind of coursework essay on this topic will find these chapters very useful.

Judith Loades (Ed.) *The Life and Times of David Lloyd George*, Headstart History, 1990. A collection of short studies published to coincide with the centenary of Lloyd George's first election to the House of Commons. Ian Packer's contribution on the period 1912–14 is particularly valuable in assessing how actively the Liberals, and especially Lloyd George, were considering and preparing reform measures for the future.

John Grigg *Lloyd George – The People's Champion 1902–12*, Methuen, 1978. The second volume provides not only a detailed biographical study but a useful analysis of the political context in which Lloyd George operated. This is terrifically readable stuff for the enthusiastic student who simply must know more about it all.

David Powell *The Edwardian Crisis – Britain, 1901–1914*, Macmillan, Perspectives in History Series. Demanding reading but stimulating for the able student and especially good for supporting an ambitious coursework study.

9 ⌁ STRUCTURED AND ESSAY QUESTIONS

A *Structured questions for AS level*

1. Why did the Unionists suffer such a devastating defeat in the general election of 1906?

2. What policies expressed the principles of 'New Liberalism' between 1906 and 1911?

3. Describe the policies adopted by the Liberal Government to help the most vulnerable groups in society in the period 1906–1909.
4. Explain the stages of the constitutional crisis of 1909–11 and show what problems it created for the Government.
5. Why did the Labour Party fail to achieve a more decisive breakthrough in parliamentary politics before World War I?

ANSWERING AS EXAMINATION QUESTIONS

At AS level, candidates are generally asked to **describe** developments or **explain why** things happened. Take question 3 above:

Describe the policies adopted by the Liberal Governments to help the most vulnerable groups in society during the period 1906–1909

Analysis of the marking schemes used by examination boards shows that to secure good marks for your answer to this type of question you must do more than simply list the policies you consider to be relevant. You need to write in continuous prose and avoid the use of bullet points and numbered lists, etc. If you do not do this you will lose marks for the structure and written expression of your answer. Equally, you need to show that you are thinking through your answer and not merely throwing in every policy you can remember. In this particular question, for instance, it would be useful to begin by showing how you would define the expression 'most vulnerable groups'. How widely are you going to interpret this? Obviously children and elderly people HAVE to be included, but, given the time constraints of an examination, how much wider can you afford to go, if at all? The dates impose their own limits. Legislation on National Insurance to help the sick or unemployed fall outside the period prescribed. Also, you should aim to show what, precisely, the policies were intended to address, e.g in describing what the School Meals legislation involved, make the point that it was aimed at solving a particular set of inter-related problems affecting working-class children. In the course of your answer you should also attempt to prioritise the importance of the material, i.e. identify any particularly important Acts or parts of Acts.

B *Essay questions for A2*
1. How fully did the reforms of the Liberal Governments 1906–11 tackle the problems facing the working classes?
2. Was the period of crisis between 1909 and 1911 a triumph or a disaster for the Liberals?
3. To what extent was the Labour Party 'merely a radical wing of the Liberal Party' during the period 1906–14?
4. Was the Liberal Pary in decline on the eve of the First World War?

ANSWERING ESSAY QUESTIONS AT A2 LEVEL

At A2 level you will be expected to be much more analytical in your answer and the style of question will reflect this. Take Question 1 above:

How fully did the reforms of the Liberal Governments 1906–11 tackle the problems facing the working classes?

To answer this question at a high level, you must address the **evaluative** element of the question expressed in the wording 'How fully'. To do this effectively, you need some kind of overview fairly early in your answer to establish the scope and severity of the problems facing the working classes. You may go further and differentiate between different types of workers, recognising, for example, that some classes of worker already enjoyed some social benefits either through their Trade Unions or by their own independent provision. You must select a reasonable range of Acts and assess them in terms of their merits and limitations. You should try to identify those problems which received a more extensive remedy and those which only secured minimal redress. For example, you could, in this particular question, show the distinction between the approach to unemployment and the approach to sickness in the 1911 National Insurance Legislation.

10 ⌐ AS LEVEL DOCUMENTARY EXERCISE ON THE PEOPLE'S BUDGET 1909

The money thus raised is to be expended, first of all, in insuring the inviolability [safety] of our shores. It has also been raised in order not merely to relieve but to prevent unmerited distress within those shores. It is essential that we should make every necessary provision for the defence of our country. But surely it is equally imperative that we should make it a country even better worth defending for all and by all ... I am told that no Chancellor of the Exchequer has ever been called on to impose such heavy taxes in a time of peace. This is a War Budget. It is for raising money to wage implacable warfare against poverty and squalidness. I cannot help hoping and believing that, before this generation has passed away, we shall have advanced a great step towards that good time when poverty and wretchedness and human degradation ... will be as remote to the people of this country as the wolves which once infested its forests.

SOURCE A
Closing comments from Lloyd George's Budget Speech 1909

These taxes (on land) are justifiable if you believe that land is national property, and that it should be the business of Parliament to nationalize the land of the United Kingdom. That is the view of the Chancellor of the Exchequer, for he has avowed [declared] that nationalization of land must come by easy stages. Here is the first stage he presents to us ...

The character of the Government's proposals, destroying as they will do, the balance between direct and indirect taxation*, is injurious alike to the Capitalist and the Wage Earner and threatens the position of the money market [i.e. The Stock Exchange]; the motive which inspires the proposals is not a single-minded pursuit of the national welfare, but is tainted by a desire to strike at those whose existence is a bar to the dominion of the demagogue [political leader who appeals to the prejudices of the masses].

SOURCE B

Comments by leading peers in the House of Lords during debates on the Budget, 1909 (*Direct taxes are those imposed on actual income or possessions. Indirect taxes are those imposed on things consumed such as fuel or food, etc.)

SOURCE C (PICTURE 54)
An election poster, from the January 1910 General Election, attacking Lloyd George's Budget of 1909, which at that time had still not been passed in the House of Lords

'Is there anything wrong ... in the methods by which the taxes have been raised? .... There are some which are levied on capital, there is a super tax on income. It is said they press too heavily upon wealthy men .... The only alternative is to tax poverty. If these taxes are not to be imposed upon income, if death duties are not to be imposed, taxation must fall upon the necessaries of life. That is a policy to which we in this government are wholly opposed.'

SOURCE D

From a Speech by the Lord Chancellor, a senior Cabinet Minister, made in the House of Lords 1909

Q

1. Study Source D. Using your own knowledge, and giving examples, explain what is meant by the reference to 'the necessaries of life'. *(4)*
2. Study Sources A and D. What justifications are offered in these sources for the taxation proposals in the Budget? *(6)*
3. Study Sources A and B. In what ways and for what reasons do these sources differ in their attitude to the Budget? *(10)*
4. Study Sources C and D. How useful are these sources to a historian studying the issues raised by the 1909 Budget? *(10)*
5. Study all the Sources and use your own knowledge. How far would you agree that the explanation for the budget crisis lies purely in the financial self-interest of the upper classes? *(20)*

Total 50 marks

15

Britain 1815–1914: A Century of Change

Britain, in 1815, still had much in common, socially, economically, politically and in terms of the appearance of the country and the everyday lives of its inhabitants, with Britain around 1700. By 1914, the outstanding impression is of the scale and the pace of change over the previous 100 years in almost every aspect of personal and national life. Studying change for its own sake can be both useful and dangerous for the historian. It provides useful criteria for judging what is important but it can also distort what actually happened at the time. Selected themes can easily be studied out of context and even given undue importance. History can become a game of selecting winners and losers, good guys and bad guys: the good being those who apparently promoted progress towards the future, the bad those who allegedly retarded such progress. In the nineteenth century such historical interpretation, known as Whig history, was very common.

The examination boards require that, in some part of the A2 (but not of the AS) examination, students' knowledge and understanding of *change over time* should be assessed with the minimum time to be studied for this purpose defined as one hundred years. The purpose of this chapter is, first, to alert you to this requirement and, then, to give examples of how you could use your study of nineteenth-century British history to answer examination questions of this type.

It is possible to construct a long list of changes across this crowded century:

- in people's private lives; jobs, housing, family life, living standards
- in the economy; industrial growth, transport change, agriculture
- in the growth of empire, switches in foreign policy, techniques of warfare
- in population growth and distribution, emigration and immigration.

And many more. In almost every area of life, vast changes can be identified. Having drawn up such a list, a useful historical exercise would be to take each area in turn and try to list the continuities, the areas where, even in 1914 and after a century of change, the patterns and practices of 1815 were still discernible. It is important that your study of change should also embrace the significant continuities in British life.

CHANGE AND CONTINUITY

There are too many examples of change and continuity to study them all in worthwhile depth. This book has been primarily concerned with political history Therefore two themes of 'change over time' are considered below:

- the reforms to the political system
- the changing role of the state in regard to social provision for its weaker inhabitants.

Remember, however, that changes in these areas must be seen against the pattern of change in all the other aspects of nineteenth century life: for example, growth in medical knowledge and engineering expertise helped to transform what was possible in terms of social reform while the development of a railway system played a part in parliamentary reform. You will also need to refer to the earlier chapters of this book where the themes, which are only briefly referred to here, are dealt with in greater depth.

> **Examination tip**: when answering questions on change over time, do not lecture the examiner about the defects of Whig history, get on with answering the question set.

1 ⌁ PROGRESS TOWARDS DEMOCRACY: PARLIAMENTARY REFORM

A *The early nineteenth century*

The constitution, based on the balance between King and Parliament, had evolved since the Middle Ages. In eighteenth-century Parliaments, both the Commons and the Lords represented the propertied interests in the state. The power of the Lords was entirely inherited. That of the Commons rested on the long-established right of each county and each borough with a royal charter to send two members of parliament to Westminster.

> **Note**: be aware of the idea of the state as made up of interest groups which were represented in Parliament.

The Commons were seen to represent the various 'interests' in the state. This is a difficult concept for us to grasp but it is important. The two MPs for each borough represented the interests of that community, including its economic interests; for example, the MPs for ports were regarded as representing not just their own town but also, collectively, the maritime interests of the nation. Similarly, for example, the MPs for a woollen town like Stroud in Gloucestershire were expected to represent the interests of the woollen industry. County MPs were obviously part of the landed interest and even the MPs for some pocket boroughs were seen as representing the important West Indian sugar or trading interests. The reforms in the franchise across the nineteenth century only gradually undermined this ill-defined, but important, pattern. The deliberate creation of artificial, single-member constituencies in 1885 marked its end for practical purposes but it was not until 1919 that it was replaced by, what is to us, the familiar principle of one person one vote.

Population growth and industrialisation in the early nineteenth century made the long-standing arrangements for representing the nation's 'interests' increasingly unsatisfactory. The new wealth and the new classes produced by economic change were under-represented in the

House of Commons. In terms of geography, the North of England and the Midlands, along with London, were seriously under-represented, while the smaller rural counties of the South and the smaller boroughs, also often in the South, had too many MPs. Many of the small boroughs had declined in importance over the centuries and still they elected MPs while many new large industrial towns had no MPs separate from the surrounding county. In the former, small electorates and open voting associated with corruption (rotten boroughs) or total domination by neighbouring great landlords (pocket boroughs). Tentative steps to introduce reforms in the late eighteenth century were blocked, and then overtaken, by the ideas and the violent events of the French Revolution. These spurred some radicals to press for reform but also persuaded many in power that any political change could lead to revolutionary violence.

After 1815, pressure for reform of the electoral system increased, sometimes leading to violent demonstrations, but the Governments of Lord Liverpool and his Liberal Tory successors in the late 1820s, stood firmly against making concessions that would, in their view, lead to anarchy.

In 1828 and 1829, there were important breaches made in this Tory defence of the status quo when, first, Nonconformists and then, in order to avoid conflict in Ireland, Catholics were granted the right to sit in the Commons. These two were arguably the first steps on the long road of parliamentary reform.

> Note that Catholic Emancipation in 1829 was a major constitutional reform.

B *1832, The Great Reform Act*

Catholic Emancipation in 1829 split the Tories and led to a Whig victory in the 1830 election. Grey's Government then introduced a Reform Bill. At the time, opponents saw the Whig proposals as quite extreme but their intentions were far from revolutionary. Grey sought a reform that would satisfy enough of the new interests in the state so that calls for further political change would be ended.

In essence, the Reform Act left intact the power of the landed class in the county seats but, for the first time, created a standard qualification for voting in borough constituencies (the £10 householder) which, broadly, gave the vote to middle-class male householders and denied it to the vast majority of their working-class fellows. In addition, the worst, but by no means all, of the anomalies in terms of the size of constituencies were addressed. The Reform Act increased the electorate from over 400 000 to over 600 000 out of a total population, in the 1831 census, of around 16 million. Before the next reform measure, in 1867, population growth and improved living standards meant that a further 400 000 men had qualified to vote. The parliamentary fight for reform had, however, aroused great excitement in the country and, for the working class, the final outcome of the 1832 Act was a major disappointment.

In the process of political change, the 1832 Act is often seen as a crucial turning point. This is perhaps true, but it was the precedent it

> For more detail on the 1832 Reform Act, see Chapter 3

> **KEY ISSUE**
>
> *Does the 1832 Reform Act deserve to be called 'Great' and, if so, why?*

created, the first change in how MPs were elected and thus in the centuries-old constitution, rather than in its revolutionary consequences for Parliament and political life, that made it so. You will need to be able to argue both the significance of the Act as a first step and a precedent but also be able to point up the quite severe limitations of the Act, for example:

Examination tip: when facing questions on an event being a 'turning-point', try to assess both its impact and also its limitations. Continuity is often as important as change.

- very few of the working-class gained the vote
- there was no secret ballot and so elections remained open to corrupt pressures
- many of the middle class gained the vote and a few even entered the Commons but parliament remained dominated for decades by the old aristocratic families
- rural, southern, England still had a disproportionate number of MPs and urban, industrial England too few.

C *Political developments after 1832*

The 1832 Act required voters to be on an electoral register and this encouraged the development of political party organisation, committed to ensuring that sympathetic voters were on the register and to challenging the registration of opponents. The 1830s and 1840s saw the emergence, in the constituencies, of a more tightly organised Conservative Party with central links to the newly founded Carlton Club. The Reform Club, founded at the same time, eventually served the Liberals in a similar capacity, though the key period of its development came in the late 1850s and the 1860s.

Working-class disappointment with the Great Reform Act led to the emergence of Chartism (see Chapter 5) which flourished between 1838 and 1848 but which failed to persuade Parliament to bring in any measure of further political reform. Chartism's ambitious political programme indicates the limits of the 1832 legislation. The Chartist failure to put effective pressure on those in parliament illustrates the political impotence of the working class.

THE SECOND REFORM ACT, 1867

The next changes in the electoral system came from within Parliament. In the 1860s, the Conservative and the Liberal Parties were both anxious to ensure that they, and not their opponents, gained the credit for any further extension of the franchise. Although politicians remained deeply suspicions of the great mass of the less reputable working class, the growth of a respectable working class, headed by the new model trade unions of skilled workers, was increasingly recognised. It would be wise to secure their support for the constitution, as had been done with the middle class in 1832, and also secure their grateful votes for the right party. The Second Reform Act, 1867, was a product of this party rivalry rather than a result of mass agitation in the country at large. This conclusion has, however, been debated by historians and you should remind yourself of the course of that debate.

For the Second Reform Act see Chapter 7, pages 199–207

The final outcome of the complex parliamentary tussles of 1866 and 1867 gave the vote, in borough constituencies, to the male heads of most working-class households. Alterations to the franchise in county constituencies, where a £12 occupation qualification was introduced, had a less dramatic effect. The Act added some 950 000 voters to the existing 1 050 000, making an electorate of two million males from a total United Kingdom population of 29 million. The Act followed the precedent set in 1832 by re-allocating 45 Commons seats, taken from the smaller boroughs, to the larger counties and towns, new boroughs and large cities. Symbolically, it ensured that working-class voters were in the majority in almost all urban constituencies. It was to be some decades before this numerical advantage led to any serious changes, either in the social and political composition of the Commons or brought about legislation clearly intended to meet working-class needs.

THE SECRET BALLOT, 1872

The extension of the franchise by legislation was only one aspect of change in the British political system. Changes in electoral practice were equally important. In 1872, during Gladstone's first ministry, the use of the secret ballot was introduced. It was a natural consequence of the 1867 Reform Act which, for the first time, granted the vote to large numbers of workingmen. It removed the bribes, pressures and threats on voting intentions to which voters had always previously been subject. It was reinforced, in 1883, by a second piece of Gladstonian legislation, the Corrupt Practices Act, which limited the amount of expenses which could be incurred in fighting an election. These two measures did much to make British elections both more free and more fair. It is surprising that their impact has received so little notice from historians.

THE THIRD REFORM ACT, 1884

In 1884, Gladstone's Government also passed the Third Reform Act, after elaborate negotiations with the Conservative leader, Salisbury. Its main thrust was to make the county franchise more democratic by bringing it into line with the borough franchise; now the male heads of households had the vote in both types of constituency. The measure created some two million new male voters, raising the number of United Kingdom voters to five million out of a total population, in 1881, of 35 million. Its main importance was that, allied to the secret ballot, it helped to break the monopoly of political power in the counties which had been enjoyed by the landed class. The latter, however, continued to enjoy much influence in the political parties and here too the change, however important for the personal dignity of the new voters, was scarcely revolutionary.

The Act was followed, in 1885, by an important Redistribution Act, pressed on Gladstone by Salisbury, which redrew constituency boundaries and largely ended the pattern of two MPs representing most constituencies and replaced this by the now familiar pattern of single-member constituencies. These were based, admittedly very imperfectly, on the principle that constituencies should have comparable numbers of

KEY ISSUE

Why has the 1885 re-distribution of constituencies been seen as marking a fundamental change in the relationship between the Commons and the nation?

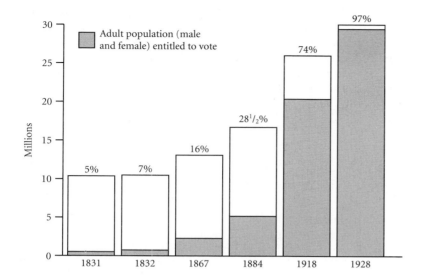

DIAGRAM 8
Percentage of adult population (male and female) who were entitled to vote

voters. To achieve this, many of the old constituencies were swept away and replaced by ones based on artificial boundaries drawn across maps. In creating the new system, little or no attention was paid to the existence of the historic communities that had been the core of the pre-1832 parliamentary system.

D *Politics without democracy*

It is all too easy to see the process of political change in nineteenth-century Britain as an inevitable progress towards a twentieth-century democracy. Some early textbooks give the impression that, after the legislation of 1884 and 1885, and with the lamentable exception that women still did not have the vote, Britain was virtually a democratic society. This was far from the truth.

Undemocratic elements of the constitution at the end of the century included:

● women did not have the vote
● only three out of five adult males had the vote
● the House of Lords still had a veto on legislation.

Only the last of these was to be addressed prior to 1914.

THE PARLIAMENT ACT, 1911
This Act ended the Lords veto on legislation and replaced it with a power to delay the enactment of any law for up to two years. The change was provoked by the partisan use of the veto power by the huge Conservative majority in the House of Lords. Much of the legislation of Gladstone's last ministry (1892–4), for example, was blocked by the Lords, who had been content to allow the legislation of the preceding

TIMELINE

Major parliamentary reforms

1832 The Great Reform Act (Ch 3)
1867 The Second Reform Act (Ch 7)
1872 Secret Ballot introduced
1883 Corrupt Practices Act
1884 The Third Reform Act (Ch 10)
1885 Redistribution Act (Ch 10)
1911 Parliament Act (Ch 14)
1918 Representation of the People Act (below)

KEY ISSUE

To what extent did the Parliament Act of 1911 affect the relative importance of the Commons and the Lords?

The details of this complex topic are examined in Chapter 14, pages 413–20

Conservative Government an uninterrupted passage. The large Liberal majority in the Commons after 1906 meant that a resumption of hostilities between the Houses was inevitable. Ending the status of the House of Lords as the equal partner to the Commons can be seen as a remarkably radical constitutional change but the following should also be remembered.

● The balance between the Houses of Parliament had been tilting in favour of the Commons since the seventeenth century. Until the final crisis provoked by the Liberal budget of 1909 it had, for example, been generally accepted that the Lords would not interfere with Bills raising money for government expenditure. The Lords had also been reminded, when they appeared to be about to block the 1832 Reform Act that, if the king supported the majority view in the Commons, he could always create so many Peers that that view would prevail in any vote in the Lords. In any crisis after 1832 the majority in the Lords acted under that potential constraint.

● Even after 1911, the House of Lords still had formidable reserve powers. A promise, during the 1910–11 crisis, to reform the membership of the unelected house came to nothing and it marched on, largely unreformed, until the very end of the twentieth century. The 1911 Parliament Act had, moreover, tried to balance the reduction in the Lords powers with a parallel reduction in those of the Commons. From 1911, MPs had to face the voters in a general election at least every five years rather than every seven years, arguably an important step towards democratic accountability. The shorter duration of Parliament also greatly increased the value of the Lords delaying power. Their power to obstruct measures that they did not like was still formidable. They had, of course, to accept that it would be unwise to appear to defy the will of the people as expressed in a general election and it is true that in 1948 their power to delay was reduced to one year.

VOTES FOR WOMEN

The question of granting at least some women the vote in parliamentary elections had first been seriously raised in the 1860s and is best viewed as one important aspect of the changing status of women in the late nineteenth and early twentieth centuries. This topic is the central theme of Chapter 13. Early efforts to secure women the vote had concentrated on the case for enfranchising women who owned property. The campaign had been legal and respectable and had achieved nothing. Tactics changed at the end of the century with the arrival of the Pankhursts and the suffragettes who deliberately publicised their cause by increasingly outrageous, illegal and eventually violent, means. They showed much courage, achieved great personal publicity and attracted great animosity. Sadly, by 1914, they were no nearer their goal and, indeed, some of the impetus had gone from their campaign.

At the outbreak of World War I, half the adult population of the United Kingdom still could not vote in parliamentary elections simply because of gender. The opposition to the suffragettes and to the issue they raised came from many, but not all, leading politicians. This indicates how far the country still had to go before a participating democracy was achieved. Continuity and conservatism remained important elements in society even in this century of dramatic political change; this point is worth underlining by noting the lukewarm support given to the women's cause by the allegedly radical Liberal and Labour Parties and, perhaps even more tellingly, by the opposition of many women to their being given the vote. Women's lives had changed greatly since the early nineteenth century but significant continuities, of attitude and status, remained largely unchanged.

E *Epilogue, post-1914*

THE PARLIAMENTARY REFORM ACT, 1918

This Act went through Parliament before the war was won and was carried, in the historian A. J. P. Taylor's phrase, 'almost without fuss'. As Taylor also noted, it 'added more voters to the electoral register than all its predecessors put together', an invaluable comment on the limits of the earlier, nineteenth century, legislation. By giving the vote to women over thirty it ended that increasingly untenable gender disqualification. Even Asquith, a notable earlier opponent of votes for women, acknowledged, patronisingly but in an interesting illustration of contemporary attitudes, that, by their work during the war, women had earned the vote. Perhaps equally important, in the midst of war against Germany, few politicians can have welcomed the prospect of a resumption of hostilities with the suffragettes. The Act also virtually established the principle of 'one person one vote' for now only university graduates and the owners of some business premises retained a second vote.

In 1928 the vote was extended to women on the same terms as men (i.e. from 21), virtually without debate either in or outside Parliament.

In 1948 the University seats and second votes for graduates were abolished and the delaying power of the Lords was reduced to one year.

2 ⌐ THE ORIGINS OF THE WELFARE STATE?

A *1800–50: the obstacles to be overcome*

From the sixteenth to the eighteenth century the state had been active in regulating trade, the economy and, indeed, traditional working practices. Only after 1750 did this come to be questioned in any systematic way, first with regard to trade, then in respect of other economic matters. In the economic sphere, the work of Adam Smith was central to the new spirit advocating free competition, unregulated by government, as the best route to economic expansion. But the notion of the desirability of minimum government interference spread to the social sphere. Here the work of

KEY ISSUE

Why, in the early nineteenth century, was it so difficult to remedy great social evils?

See page 63 for the views of Adam Smith

Census	Population (millions)	% living in towns with population over 2500	No. of towns with population over 100 000
1801	11	33	1
1831	16	43	7
1851	21	54	10
1871	26	65	17
1901	37	78	33

Thomas Malthus was the key. His pessimistic view that population growth would always press on limited resources, and so drag those at the bottom of society down into poverty and destitution, effectively discouraged large-scale reforms to alleviate the condition of the weakest in society. The rapid growth of population in the early nineteenth century seemed to vindicate Malthus' view and the sheer scale of the problems prevalent in the new industrial towns made any hope of improvement unlikely.

In order to explain the slow pace of change, it is worth listing and being able to comment on some of the obstacles facing social reformers in the early nineteenth century:

- the daunting size of many of the problems
- lack of money to take effective action on any scale
- lack of knowledge, e.g. medical or engineering knowledge, on what steps to take
- prevailing views that the role of government should be tightly restricted to maintaining law and order at home and the protection of national interests abroad. In other spheres, governments should pursue a policy of *laissez-faire*, leaving well alone lest greater evils are promoted
- the desire for low taxation, especially in view of the cost of financing the National Debt
- the absence of any agencies to implement reforms
- apathy among the better-off, often based on their ignorance of the situation
- the view of many religious people that everyone had a moral duty to strive to save their immortal souls and that self-help and hard work were important steps on the way to this. Nothing should be done to undermine the self-reliance of even the poorest in society.

The obstacles were all the more formidable because they seemed to make a complete package. Ideas of *laissez-faire*, minimal government and low taxation all complemented each other and were sustained in turn by the moral imperative of self-reliance and the difficulty of deciding what *could* be done. Nineteenth century reformers in many spheres would have to chip away at the climate of opinion thus created. The case for each and every reform would have to be fought.

B *The motives behind reform*

Different problems produced different inspirations for reform.

- Humanitarian reformers, usually with a religious inspiration to motivate them, dominated the demand for abolition of slavery in the British Empire. They were also largely responsible for the early attempts to regulate child labour conditions and to provide elementary education. The key figures were Wilberforce (slavery) and Shaftesbury (child labour and education).

See Chapter 4, pages 64–6

- Utilitarian reformers, followers of the philosopher Jeremy Bentham, were crucial to the reform of the Poor Law and to Public Health reform. The key figure was Edwin Chadwick. These reformers sought administrative efficiency in the arrangements to meet problems. Surveys, reports and statistics were central to their efforts.
- The administrators who emerged soon became a source of further reforms as the gaps and inefficiencies in the early legislation became apparent. As time progressed, they became important in all fields of reform.
- Socialists influenced the changing emphasis for reform, in the late nineteenth century, from simply regulating abuses to calls for the state to provide 'essential' services in education, housing and in providing remedies for poverty. The Labour party was created to promote such ideas but non-socialists, like the social commentators Booth and Rowntree, were also influential and, by 1900, had created a climate of opinion that favoured more positive state action to solve social problems.

C *The main areas of reform*

It will be valuable, in answering questions on change over time, to be able to offer specific illustrations to back up general comments. The most useful topic areas for this purpose may well be:

KEY ISSUE

Why were some social problems easier to tackle than others?

- The **abolition of slavery**, by 1833, in the Empire. This was not a typical reform. It was dominated by the religious convictions of committed humanitarians who had already half-opened the door in 1807 by securing a ban on the slave trade in British ships. It cost Britain £20 million to compensate the slave-owners, about half the annual budget for running the country. This showed that money could be found for reforms when the reformers were able to whip up public support, but this was never to be so easily achieved in other fields, probably because the slavery payment was a one-off, whereas other problems would need repeated doses of finance.
- **Factory Law**, concentrated at first on child labour in the textile industry. Groundbreaking legislation in 1833 included the provision of inspectors to enforce the regulations. The 1842 Mines Act extended protection to underground working. Do not exaggerate the effect of the early Acts: there were many loopholes and vast numbers of

children worked in unregulated industries until at least the 1870s. Most adults remained unprotected until after the end of the century.

● **Education**, where again the impetus for reform had largely religious motives based on anxiety that the population at large should one day be able to read the Bible. The Churches were the first mass providers of elementary (primary) education: the first annual government grant to aid them was given in 1833. A key date was 1870 when the Education Act required elementary schools to be established, paid for out of the local rates, where no Church schools existed. In 1902, state regulation reached out further to make the first national arrangements to provide and regulate publicly-funded secondary schools. Both elementary and secondary schools became the responsibility of county councils created in 1891, an important indicator of the fact that social reforms relied for their implementation on the emergence of appropriate administrative bodies. By this time, national efficiency in the face of foreign competitors was an important motive for reforms in education.

● The **Poor Law,** where the main legislation was the 1834 Poor Law Amendment Act, which was arguably the most significant social reform of the century. It imposed central regulation and standards in an area that, since the sixteenth century, had been the province of largely unregulated, local authorities. Poor relief still relied on locally-raised finance via property rates and was to be based on provision for the destitute (paupers) via workhouses. The Act was not intended to solve the problem of poverty but to rationalise the provision of poor relief, discourage dependence on relief and restrict expenditure. It was an administrative, not a humanitarian, measure and gave rise to the charge that the Victorians were treating poverty as a crime. In minor ways the harshness of the system was ameliorated as the century progressed but the system itself was rarely the subject of political controversy or general public outrage. The Poor Law's general acceptance, and its unfortunate consequences for hundreds of thousands of the poor, mark out the Liberal social reforms from 1906 as a major turning point in welfare provision, in principle if not in immediate impact.

● **Public Health** problems were most acute in the poorer districts of rapidly growing industrial towns, well hidden from the view of the powerful and better off. Fortunately, in 1835, a national pattern for borough government had been established by the Municipal Reform Act which created town councils, elected by ratepayers, to replace the previous chaos of unelected, self-perpetuating town corporations. Again, administration was central to successful reform. This Act, a Whig political measure intended to break Tory control of the earlier town corporations, gave councils minimal sanitary powers and did nothing for the many new towns which had not previously been made boroughs by royal charter. It was not until the 1840s that urban sanitary conditions began to arouse sustained public concern. Edwin Chadwick, the secretary of the Poor Law Commission, which had been set up to run the new poor law, researched the causes of pauperism and argued that sickness was one major factor; if sickness could be reduced, then so could the burden of the poor law rates. This message was powerfully reinforced by successive outbreaks of cholera, their cause as mysterious as the symptoms were awful. In 1844–5, a Royal Commission reported to Parliament on the state of health of the inhabitants of large towns. The pressure gradually built up until, in 1848, the first effective Public Health legislation was enacted. It was, in essence, another administrative measure giving local authorities powers to spend money on eradicating sanitary dangers. Once the network of local bodies was set up and properly supervised, they were available to take on more and more new sanitary duties. Arguably, the 1848 Public Health Act provided a basis for the creation of civilised life in urban Britain.

The Chronology of Reform

It is possible to construct a simplified chronology of reform across the nineteenth century. It should be used with care for you may well feel that the pattern of reform varied from one problem to another.

- 1800–50: the key period for arousing influential public opinion to the existence of a serious social problem and for creating a climate of opinion that something had to be done. The first, often tentative and inadequate, legislation came in a variety of fields in this period.
- 1850s–1880s: a period of consolidation and elaboration of the earlier measures. It is difficult to get excited about this period but this is when most of the reforms started to have an impact on people's lives. Schools were built, drains, sewers and water pipes laid, streets were paved. At this time, towns started systematically to tackle many different problems and **municipal socialism** was born.
- 1880–1900: a period when pressure for more radical reforms built up, particularly in the provision of education, housing and in steps to tackle poverty. The pressure was often linked to the growth of socialist ideas and to concerns about the nation's fitness to respond to foreign rivals.
- 1906–14: The Liberal Government's reforms – Old Age Pensions, Health and Unemployment Insurance – were a response, however inadequate, to the new pressures. They also mark the beginning of the disintegration of the Victorian system of social provision. This last period of reform accelerated greatly during and after World War I (1914–18) and led later to the fundamental reforms of the post-1945 Labour Government that finally established what became known as the Welfare State.

municipal socialism
Local government, especially in towns and cities, taking responsibility for essential social services like health, education and relief of the poor

D *1850–80, Consolidating the reforms*

> It was the practical application of reforms that started to improve people's lives and not just the passing of laws.

The legislation of these years lacked the drama of the struggles to achieve the first steps of the earlier period. It was, however, at this time that the lives of the masses started to be affected by the reforms already enacted. There were two aspects to this consolidation.

● **Enacting further legislation to plug gaps in the early Acts.** Numerous sanitary laws and regulations expanding existing laws were introduced in the aftermath of the 1848 Public Health Act. The early powers of the Local Boards of Health, set up under the Act, were largely limited to improving drainage and sewage disposal and regulating such problems as overflowing cemeteries and filthy streets. By the 1870s, however, so many sanitary and linked regulations had been issued that it was necessary, in the 1875 Public Health Act, to codify and rationalise them. The sanitary code issued in 1875 served as the basis of sanitary law until the 1920s. A significant extension of public health policy also came in1875 with the Artisans Dwellings Act, which gave local authorities the power to buy up and clear slum property. Like all legislation in this field, the benefits came only slowly. It is unwise to assume that making laws meant the early end of an abuse. Progress under this Act was particularly slow because the Act *permitted* action rather than *requiring* it and because of the costs to local bodies of buying up property even in slum areas. It was, however, a very significant first step in housing policy. The 1870 Education Act was another landmark in consolidation. Since 1833, the state had given grants to Church elementary schools but many urban areas were not provided for. This Act required that those gaps be filled by schools financed from local rates and over 5000 new schools were created. It was followed by legislation making elementary schooling compulsory (1880) and then free (1891). Only at this stage did working-class urban children as a whole begin to benefit.

● **The practical application of the growing body of laws by an ever-expanding army of local government inspectors, doctors and engineers.** The growth in the profession of elementary school teacher and the practice of regular school inspections gave life to the schools created by the 1870 Act. The work of the engineers provided the sewers and the drains that made civilised life in the towns possible. Joseph Bazalgette, for example, transformed the prospects of life in London by building the complex arrangement of underground waterways that still forms the basis of the capital's drainage system. Large towns, in particular, started to use money from rates and loans to provide a vast range of facilities for their inhabitants. Arguably nothing was more important than their work in street paving and draining but many reached far beyond this: Manchester laid water pipes over one hundred miles to its newly constructed reservoirs in the Lake District. Birmingham and Liverpool did the same in Wales. Libraries, evening-institutes, public baths, even public gas-works gave rise, in this age of capitalist expansion, to municipal socialism on a vast scale. The Government could only provide the legislation to allow it to be done; local initiative had to do the rest.

PICTURE 55
Sewers being built, 1862. It required engineering expertise, as well as medical knowledge, to improve sanitation and sewerage in Victorian cities

E *1880–1900, new pressures*

Amidst all this dramatic change, Poor Law provision remained set in the mould of 1834. There seemed to be no affordable solution to the problem of poverty: only a harsh lifeline to the truly desperate could be provided. The new mass trade unions and tiny left-wing political groups that emerged in the 1880s and 1890s began to produce a more radical social agenda. Their influence was slight but changing national circumstances favoured their programme.

The challenge to Britain's economic supremacy from continental Europe was succeeded by sharper anxieties caused by failures in the Boer War, including the failure of so many volunteer soldiers to reach the low minimum health requirements, and by the military might of a recently united Germany. An excited debate about national efficiency followed and, in both major political parties, proposals for more extensive social reform were heard. Most of nineteenth-century legislation had involved issuing regulations or empowering local bodies to make social provision. The principle that government expenditure, and therefore government activity, should be kept to a minimum could, therefore, continue to be observed. From around 1900, this principle was increasingly breached, with profound consequences for levels of expenditure and taxation, which would make the twentieth-century State,

> **KEY ISSUE**
>
> *How valid is it to argue that the Liberal social reforms from 1906 to 1914 marked the beginning of a new era in welfare provision?*

See pages 311–14 on the debate about national efficiency

and its relations with individual citizens, profoundly different from the *laissez-faire* state of the nineteenth century.

F *New legislation, 1900–14*

These can only be introduced here. They would only bear fruit over the first half of the twentieth century. The 1902 Education Act was introduced because the Conservative Prime Minister, Balfour, was obsessed with the notion of national efficiency. The Act made local authorities responsible for the provision of both elementary and secondary education, abolishing the school boards set up in 1870. The councils were required to finance this provision from money raised by local rates. The historian, Ensor, in his masterly *England 1870–1914*, described this measure as 'among the two or three greatest constructive measures of the twentieth century': it created a national framework of elementary and secondary educational provision. Writing in 1936, Ensor considered that the Act had 'worked admirably'. It did, however, involve local councils in vast new areas of responsibility and expense so that they soon had to turn to the government for grants of extra finance. This led to their becoming financially dependent on central government so that the great era of Victorian, independent, municipal socialism came to an end, as indeed did the era of low taxation. Change over time indeed.

The social reforms introduced by the Liberal Government from 1906 to 1914 are generally regarded as the major step from Victorian self-help to the **welfare state** of the mid-twentieth century. The most important features were the introduction, in 1908, of non-contributory old age pensions for people aged over 70 and the 1911 Health and Unemployment Insurance schemes. The former insurance scheme covered most of the working population, the latter a very restricted range of employment. Both insurance schemes were based on compulsory contributions from workers and employers which were then topped-up by the state. They were a further blow to the belief that low taxation should be the first principle of sound government, although they were soon overtaken in this respect by the vast increase in the National Debt (from around £800 million to £8000 million) resulting from World War I.

> For the Liberal reforms after 1906, see Chapter 14

> **welfare state** A state which takes full responsibility for the essential social, health and educational needs of all its people

3 ⌁ BIBLIOGRAPHY

A2 LEVEL

Your first line of attack on questions related to change over time in the nineteenth century, which examination boards are required to set at A2 level, could sensibly be based on the relevant chapters of this book, making use of the index as well as the contents page. There are three books which will be of immediate use in your research on the two major themes of change considered in this chapter. They are in the specifically-designed, A-level series 'Access to History', published by Hodder and Stoughton.

A. Mayer *The Growth of Democracy in Britain*, 1999.
P. Murray *Poverty and Welfare 1830–1914*, 1999.
R. Pearce and R. Stearn *Government and Reform 1815–1918*, 1994.

FURTHER READING

P. Bartley *The Changing Role of Women 1815–1914*, Hodder & Stoughton, 1996, sets an important aspect of social and political change in a wider context.
M. Bentley *Politics without Democracy 1815–1914*, 2nd edition, Fontana, 1996, which is valuable in stressing the limits to political change prior to 1914.
E. Evans *The Complete A–Z: 19th & 20th Century British History*, Hodder & Stoughton, 1998, which is a useful reference and revision source.
D. G. Wright *Democracy and Reform 1815–85*, Longman, 1970.

4 ↝ STUDENT ADVICE: ANSWERING QUESTIONS ON CHANGE OVER TIME

Assessment modules at A2 Level, which are intended to test your ability to interpret issues of change over time, are likely to use structured essay or standard essay questions for this purpose.

A *Structured essay questions on political change*
1. Read the document and then answer the questions below.

> Lord John Russell began his speech (introducing the Reform bill) at six o'clock. Never shall I forget the astonishment of my neighbours as he developed his plan. Indeed all the House seemed perfectly astounded; and when he read the long list of the boroughs to be either wholly or partially disfranchised there was a sort of wild ironical laughter … . When Lord John sat down we of the Mountain cheered long and loud; although there was hardly one of us that believed such a scheme could, by any possibility, become the law of the land … Burdett and I agreed that there was very little chance of the measure being carried, and that a revolution would be the consequence.

SOURCE A:
Recollections of John Hobhouse, a Radical MP, entry for 1 March 1831

(a) How do you explain the reaction of MPs, as described above, to Russell's reform proposals? (5)
(b) Why were the many opponents of parliamentary reform unable to prevent Lord John Russell's Reform bill becoming law? (5)
(c) Why, in the period from 1832 to 1914, did pressure to extend the franchise repeatedly attract strong opposition? (15)

Total marks 25

> **Examination tip**: In answering any document sub-questions you must adapt the length of your answer, and the time you spend on it, to the maximum number of marks on offer.

2. (a) Examine the view that the terms of the 1832 Reform Act did little to correct the defects of the pre-1832 parliamentary system. (**10**)

(b) 'Politics without democracy': how valid is this view of the British constitution in the late nineteenth century? (**15**)

Total 25 marks

B *Essay questions on the changing role of the state in social policy*

1. (a) What do you consider to have been the most serious obstacles to **either** sanitary **or** elementary education reform in the nineteenth century? (**10**)

(b) How far do you agree that, between 1815 and 1914, the United Kingdom had moved from being a *laissez-faire* state to being a welfare state? (**15**)

Total 25 marks

2. (a) In what ways, in the course of the nineteenth century, did promoters of social reforms rouse public opinion to support their concerns? (**10**)

(b) Why, across the period 1815 to 1914, did reliance on self-help come to be seen as an unsatisfactory solution to the problems of poverty? (**15**)

Total 25 marks

3. To what extent, by 1914, had the everyday lives of the British working class been improved by laws passed in the previous 100 years? (**25**)

Glossary

Index